TEACHER'S EDITION • Unit 2

Houghton Mifflin Harcourt

CALIFORNIA JOURNEYS

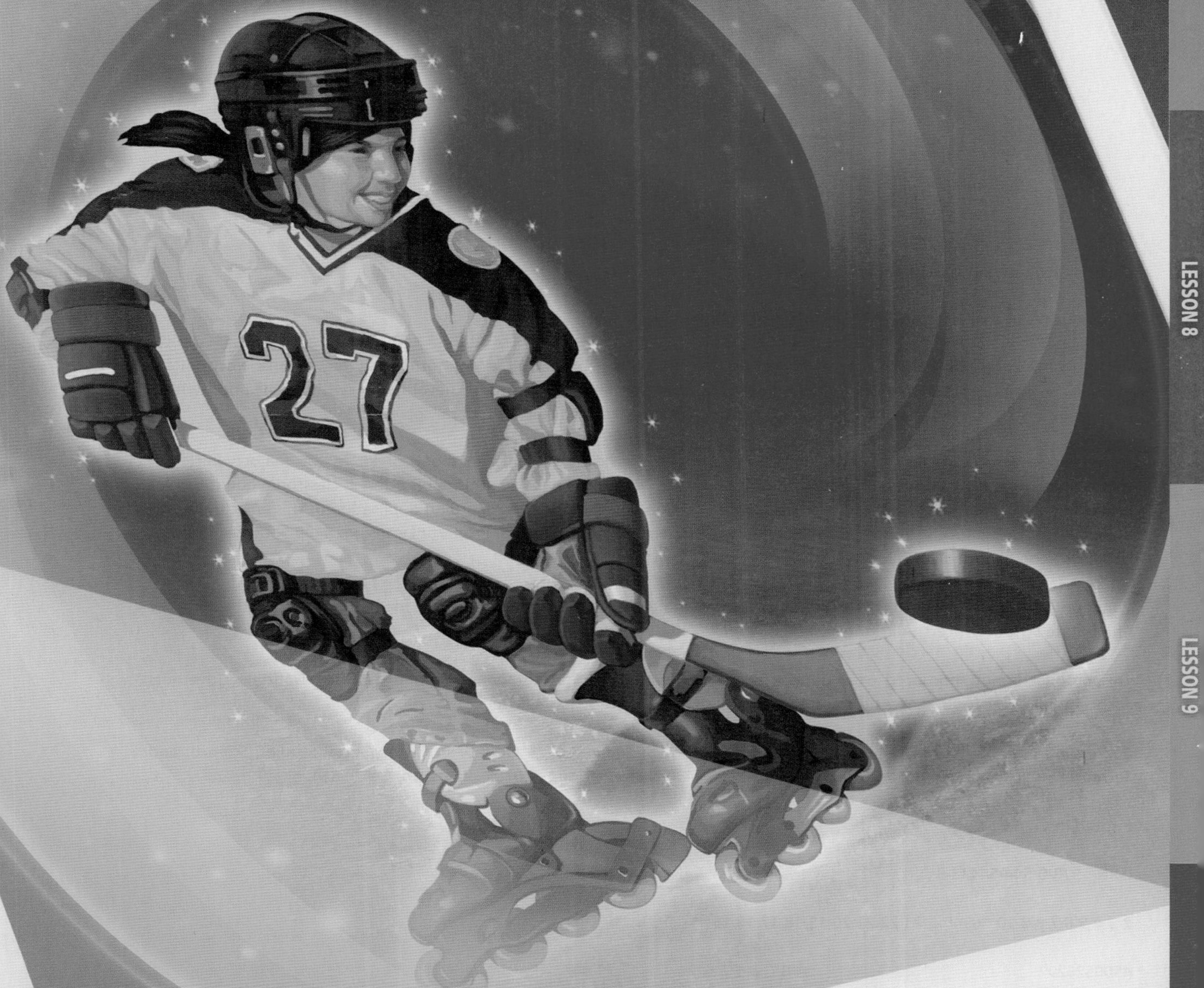

5

Printed in China

ISBN 978-0-544-54438-3

2 3 4 5 6 7 8 9 10   0940   23 22 21 20 19 18 17 16 15

4500526292   A B C D E F G

Houghton
Mifflin
Harcourt

CALIFORNIA JOURNEYS

Program Consultants

Shervaughnna Anderson · Marty Hougen

Carol Jago · Erik Palmer · Shane Templeton

Sheila Valencia · MaryEllen Vogt

Consulting Author · Irene Fountas

5

Program Consultants

Teach with confidence. Journeys *is a research-based, comprehensive English Language Arts program developed by literacy experts and backed by proven results.*

Shervaughnna Anderson Director of the California Reading and Literature Project at UCLA. Ms. Anderson brings an extensive knowledge of coaching and has experience in establishing and nurturing professional learning communities. She is a former teacher, coach, and site- and district-level administrator. In addition, she has served on state committees addressing English Language Arts instruction, English Learners, and instructional practices for African American students.

Martha Hougen National consultant, presenter, researcher, and author. Areas of expertise include differentiating instruction for students with learning difficulties, including those with learning disabilities and dyslexia. Recently her focus has been on working with teacher educators to enhance teacher and leader preparation to better meet the needs of all students.

Carol Jago Teacher of English for 32 years and director of the California Reading and Literature Project at UCLA. Past president of the National Council of Teachers of English, Ms. Jago edits the journal of the California Association of Teachers of English, *California English*. Ms. Jago has served on the planning committee for the 2009 NAEP Reading Framework and the 2011 NAEP Writing Framework.

Erik Palmer Veteran teacher and education consultant based in Denver, Colorado. Dr. Palmer's areas of focus include improving oral communication, promoting technology in classroom presentations, and updating instruction through the use of digital tools. He has worked with school districts in the United States and Mexico in the area of teaching speaking skills to 21st century learners. He has also worked with private and public schools as a consultant on two topics: teaching oral communication and showing non-tech-savvy teachers practical ways to use technology in the classroom. He is a frequent presenter and keynote speaker at state, regional, and national conferences of education professionals.

Shane Templeton Foundation Professor Emeritus of Literacy Studies at the University of Nevada, Reno. A former classroom teacher at the primary and secondary levels, Dr. Templeton's research has focused on developmental word knowledge in elementary, middle, and high school students. He is co-author of *Words Their Way; Vocabulary Their Way: Word Study for Middle and Secondary Students; Words Their Way with Struggling Readers, Grades 4–12;* and *Words Their Way with English Learners.* His other books include *Teaching the Integrated Language Arts* and *Children's Literacy: Contexts for Meaningful Learning.*

MaryEllen Vogt Distinguished Professor Emerita of Education at California State University, Long Beach. Dr. Vogt has been a classroom teacher, reading specialist, special education specialist, curriculum coordinator, and university teacher educator, and served as president of the International Reading Association. Her research interests include improving comprehension in the content areas, teacher change and development, and content literacy and language acquisition for English learners. Dr. Vogt was inducted into the California Reading Hall of Fame and received her university's Distinguished Faculty Teaching Award.

Sheila Valencia Professor of Language, Literacy, and Culture at the University of Washington, where she teaches and conducts research in the areas of literacy assessment, instruction, policy, and teacher development. Dr. Valencia began her career as a 6th grade teacher in an urban district in New York City, followed by several years as a teacher in a rural district, and then as director of a reading clinic for students with reading difficulties. She went back into public education for six years before returning to academia as a teacher educator and researcher. In 2008, Dr. Valencia was inducted into the International Reading Association Reading Hall of Fame.

SPECIAL CONSULTANT

Irene Fountas Former classroom teacher, language arts specialist, and consultant in school districts across the nation and abroad. Ms. Fountas works extensively in the literacy education field and directs the Literacy Collaborative in the School of Education at Lesley University. She spends her time providing training to literacy coaches and key administrators who play roles in teacher development and school improvement. Along with her co-author, Gay Su Pinnell, she has developed the country's most widely used standard for leveling text for small group instruction. Dr. Fountas is the recipient of the Greater Boston Council and the International Reading Association's Celebrate Literacy Awards.

Unit 2

Wild Encounters

Student Book Table of Contents

Hound Dog True
REALISTIC FICTION
by Linda Urban

Lesson Topic
By reading multiple texts about the same lesson topic, students build content knowledge from different perspectives and apply it to their writing, research, and discussion activities.

Wild Encounters

Cognate Wall/Pared de Cognados

All Proficiencies Begin an English-Spanish cognate wall for this unit, focusing on general academic vocabulary and domain-specific vocabulary. Start with words useful for the activities on this page. Add simple sketches or pictures to help students remember the words. Guide them to use the words in their everyday speech and writing. **ELD** ELD.PI.5.12a

English	Spanish
animal	animal
crocodile	cocodrilo
lion	león
observe	observar

Use Visuals Use online Picture Cards as a discussion aid and to help students think of words about the topic of having wild encounters. Suggested images: *alligator, eagle, grizzly bear, lizard, octopus,* and *panther*

Motivate and Engage

Have students open to **Student Book p. 169** and read aloud the unit title, Wild Encounters. Play the Stream to Start media to spark curiosity about the unit topic and discuss it. Ask questions such as these: **ELA** SL.5.1a **ELD** ELD.PI.5.1, ELD.PI.5.6a

- *What are some situations during which you might experience a wild encounter?*

- *What might you learn from a wild encounter?*

Access Prior Knowledge

Write *Wild Encounters* in the center of a web on the board and read it aloud. Then ask students when someone might encounter wild creatures. Have students recall information from the video or from their own experience as you add their ideas to the web. Throughout the unit, add new information to the web when students mention something new they have learned about wild encounters.
ELA SL.5.1c, SL.5.1d **ELD** ELD.PI.5.1, ELD.PI.5.12a

```
        observing
        nature in a forest
viewing
zoo animals        Wild
                  Encounters
    deep-              working to
    sea diving         save endangered
                       species
```

ENGLISH LANGUAGE SUPPORT Encourage students to express their knowledge about the idea of encountering wild animals in their first language or by using gestures or acting out words. Say the English phrase as you add each to the web, use it in a sentence, and have the group repeat. **ELD** ELD.PI.5.1, ELD.PI.5.12a

Analyze an Image

Ask students to look at the photograph on **Student Book p. 169** and to imagine that they are in the scene, observing sea creatures while swimming underwater.

Think Allow some time for students to think about the image. Ask them what this person is doing and how she is having a wild encounter.

Pair Have partners describe the scene and discuss these questions:

- Where is this person, and what is she doing? How can you tell?

- What might this person be learning during this wild encounter? What evidence in the photo helps you know?

Share Have pairs share their responses and evidence from the photograph that supports their insights. Discuss similarities and differences in students' ideas. Guide them to follow discussion rules, such as taking turns speaking and staying on topic.
ELA SL.5.1b, SL.5.1c **ELD** ELD.PI.5.1, ELD.PI.5.3, ELD.PI.5.5, ELD.PI.5.6a

ENGLISH LANGUAGE SUPPORT Write these frames on the board and help students use them to respond: *This woman is ____. She is having a wild encounter by ____. I know because I see ____ in the photo.* **ELA** SL.5.1b, SL.5.1c **ELD** ELD.PI.5.1, ELD.PI.5.3

UNIT 2

Wild Encounters

Stream to Start

> 66 One touch of nature makes the whole world kin. 99
>
> — William Shakespeare

Performance Task Preview

At the end of the unit, you will think about the texts you have read. Then you will write an informational essay about how people have worked to protect animals in the wild.

hmhfyi.com

Channel One News®

169

Discuss the Quotation

Read aloud to students the quotation on **Student Book p. 169** and then reread it with them. Discuss how the quotation and the photograph are connected. Have students describe ways they have felt touched by nature and how this might have affected how they feel about all of creation. **ELA** SL.5.1 **ELD** ELD.PI.5.1

ENGLISH LANGUAGE SUPPORT Tell students that things that are kin are closely related, like members of a family. However, in the quotation, the living creatures that make up the whole world are not necessarily closely related, but a person who has come to care for nature will feel as if they are all one family. Use this example to illustrate the concept: *Whales are kin to dolphins.*

Preview Unit Texts

Have students page through the unit texts to identify titles, authors, and images that they find interesting and tell why. Discuss how the selections might include examples of wild encounters. **ELA** SL.5.1c **ELD** ELD.PI.5.1

Performance Task Preview

Read the information on **Student Book p. 169** with students. Explain that at the end of the unit, they will use what they have read to help them write an informational essay about how people have worked to protect animals. The unit texts and lessons below will prepare students for this culminating task.

Lesson	Grammar	Writing
6	Verbs	Procedural Composition
7	Direct and Indirect Objects	Compare-Contrast Essay
8	Conjunctions	Cause-and-Effect Essay
9	Complex Sentences	Prewritten Research Report
10	Direct Quotations and Interjections	Revise Research Report

Digital Resources

Encourage students to research the unit topic on their own.

hmhfyi.com

Channel One News®

ESSENTIAL QUESTION	Lesson 6 Why is it important to research and protect endangered animals?	Lesson 7 How can dangerous situations bring people closer together?	Lesson 8 What reasons do people have for protecting the environment?
Whole Group			
Oral Language • Listening Comprehension	**Teacher Read Aloud** "America's Eagle"	**Teacher Read Aloud** "Annie's Pride"	**Teacher Read Aloud** "Attack of the Alien Species"
Vocabulary	Target Vocabulary Synonyms and Antonyms	Target Vocabulary Adages and Proverbs	Target Vocabulary Prefixes *en-, re-, pre-, pro-*
Text-Based Comprehension • Skills and Strategies • Craft and Structure	**Target Skill** Cause and Effect **Target Strategy** Question **Analyze the Text** Quotes and Description, Domain-Specific Vocabulary **Anchor Text** "Quest for the Tree Kangaroo" **Connect to the Topic** "Why Koala Has No Tail"	**Target Skill** Understanding Characters **Target Strategy** Visualize **Analyze the Text** Author's Word Choice, Dialect **Anchor Text** "Old Yeller" **Connect to the Topic** "What Makes It Good?"	**Target Skill** Author's Purpose **Target Strategy** Analyze/Evaluate **Analyze the Text** Explain Scientific Ideas, Domain-Specific Vocabulary **Anchor Text** "Everglades Forever" **Connect to the Topic** "National Parks of the West"
Research and Media Literacy **Speaking/Listening**	Research and Media Literacy: Investigate Different Aspects of a Topic	Speaking and Listening: Report on a Text	Speaking and Listening: Explain an Author's Argument
Foundational Skills • Fluency • Decoding	**Fluency** Expression **Decoding** Common Beginning Syllables	**Fluency** Intonation **Decoding** Vowel + /r/ Sounds	**Fluency** Adjust Rate to Purpose **Decoding** Homophones
Whole Group Language Arts			
Spelling **Grammar** **Writing**	**Spelling** Vowel + /r/ Sounds **Grammar** Verbs **Writing** Procedural Composition	**Spelling** More Vowel + /r/ Sounds **Grammar** Direct and Indirect Objects **Writing** Compare-Contrast Essay	**Spelling** Homophones **Grammar** Conjunctions **Writing** Cause-and-Effect Essay
Small Group			
Vocabulary Reader	Differentiate *The Lost World of Papua New Guinea*	Differentiate *Black Bears*	Differentiate *Mangrove Swamp*
Leveled Readers	● *Kangaroos* ▲ *On the Trail of Rain Forest Wildlife* ■ *Mad for Marsupials!* ◆ *Animals in the Rain Forest*	● *Young Eagle and His Horse* ▲ *On the Long Drive* ■ *Riding with the Camel Corps* ◆ *The Long Cattle Drive*	● *Guardian of the Everglades* ▲ *America's Urban Parks* ■ *The Salton Sea* ◆ *America's City Parks*
Differentiate Instruction	Differentiate Comprehension and Vocabulary Strategies	Differentiate Comprehension and Vocabulary Strategies	Differentiate Comprehension and Vocabulary Strategies

Key   ● Struggling Readers   ▲ On-Level Readers   ■ Advanced Readers   ◆ English Learners

Persuasive Posters

Students will create a persuasive poster focusing on protecting endangered animals and then present the poster to the class.

Checkpoints

☐ Gather ideas for content and visuals.
☐ Design and write text for the poster, conducting research as needed.

☐ Revise drafts of the poster to make it logical and clear.
☐ Present the poster and answer questions about it.

Lesson 9

How can an act of courage reveal a person's true nature?

Teacher Read Aloud
"A Watery Grave"

Target Vocabulary
Greek and Latin Roots

Target Skill Conclusions and Generalizations
Target Strategy Infer/Predict
Analyze the Text Point of View, Characterization
Anchor Text "Storm Warriors"
Connect to the Topic "Pea Island's Forgotten Heroes"

Speaking and Listening: Hold a Literature Discussion

Fluency Phrasing: Punctuation
Decoding Compound Words

Spelling Compound Words
Grammar Complex Sentences
Writing Prewrite: Research Report

Differentiate *Saved from the Sea*

● *Sugaring Weather*
▲ *The River Kept Rising*
■ *Night of the Killer Waves*
◆ *The Rising River*

Differentiate Comprehension and Vocabulary Strategies

Lesson 10

What can a scientist learn by observing the behaviors of a particular animal?

Teacher Read Aloud
"Who Tamed the Cat?"

Target Vocabulary
Shades of Meaning

Target Skill Main Ideas and Details
Target Strategy Monitor/Clarify
Analyze the Text Explain Scientific Ideas, Domain-Specific Vocabulary
Anchor Text "Cougars"
Connect to the Topic "Purr-fection"

Research and Media Literacy: Integrate Information from Multiple Texts

Fluency Stress
Decoding Recognizing Schwa + /r/ Sounds

Spelling Final Schwa + /r/ Sounds
Grammar Direct Quotations and Interjections
Writing Draft, Revise, Edit, Publish: Research Report

Differentiate *Big Cats*

● *Sharks*
▲ *The Return of the Yellowstone Grizzly*
■ *Saving the Mexican Wolves*
◆ *Grizzly Bears Return to Yellowstone*

Differentiate Comprehension and Vocabulary Strategies

Performance Tasks
• Write About Reading
• Write a Story

EXTENDED READING

The last two weeks of this unit are dedicated to the Extended Reading Trade Book lesson for *Hound Dog True* by **Linda Urban**. Use the instructional plan on pp. T383–T428 to guide a **close reading and analysis** of this **realistic fiction text**. The trade book lesson also features:

• Teacher Read Aloud

• Build Background with Media

• Content-Area Vocabulary

• Integrated Language Arts: Grammar, Spelling, and Writing

• Collaborative Project

For daily **Intervention** lessons, see the tab at the back of this *Teacher's Edition*.

	Lesson 6 *Quest for the Tree Kangaroo*	**Lesson 7** *Old Yeller* 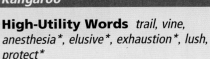	**Lesson 8** *Everglades Forever*
Begin with High-Utility Words **Tier 1 Words** * = Spanish cognates	**High-Utility Words** *trail, vine, anesthesia*, elusive*, exhaustion*, lush, protect** • Language Support Card 6 • Oral Language Chant, Blackline Master ELL6.2 • Online Picture Card Bank	**High-Utility Words** *bear, cub, angry, charged, grabbed, scared, scream* • Language Support Card 7 • Oral Language Dialogue, Blackline Master ELL7.2 • Online Picture Card Bank	**High-Utility Words** *plants, trees, water, balance, natural*, preserve*, restoration*, wetland* • Language Support Card 8 • Oral Language Chant, Blackline Master ELL8.2 • Online Picture Card Bank
Develop Foundational Literacy Skills • Fluency • Decoding • Linguistic Transfer	**Fluency & Decoding** • Expression • Common Beginning Syllables **Vocabulary Strategies** • Synonyms and Antonyms	**Fluency & Decoding** • Intonation • Vowel + /r/ Sounds **Vocabulary Strategies** • Adages and Proverbs	**Fluency & Decoding** • Adjust Rate to Purpose • Homophones **Vocabulary Strategies** • Prefixes *en-, re-, pre-, pro-*
Develop Academic Language **Tier 2 & 3 Words** * = Spanish cognates	**Target Vocabulary** *beaming, calculate*, dwarfed, enthusiastic*, outfitted, perch*, presence*, procedure*, snug, transferred** • Vocabulary in Context Cards **Reading/Language Arts Terms** *cause and effect*, informational text*, syllables*, question*, expression*, synonym*, antonym*, infer*, myth*, verb*, procedural composition*, transition words** **Understanding How Language Works** • Language Support Card 6 • Text X-Ray • Language Detective	**Target Vocabulary** *bounding, checking, frantic*, lunging, picturing, romp, shouldered, strained, stride, wheeled* • Vocabulary in Context Cards **Reading/Language Arts Terms** *character, character traits, historical fiction*, vowel*, visualize*, intonation*, adage*, proverb*, persuasive text*, direct object*, verb*, compare*, contrast** **Understanding How Language Works** • Language Support Card 7 • Text X-Ray • Language Detective	**Target Vocabulary** *adapted*, attracted*, conserving*, endangered, guardians*, regulate*, responsibility*, restore*, unique*, vegetation** • Vocabulary in Context Cards **Reading/Language Arts Terms** *author's purpose*, persuade*, reasons*, narrative nonfiction*, homophone*, context*, analyze*, evaluate*, persuasive*, rate, prefix*, base word*, word root, informational text*, graph*, conjunction*, cause and effect* **Understanding How Language Works** • Language Support Card 8 • Text X-Ray • Language Detective
Scaffold Comprehension	**Build Background** • Language Support Card 6 • Unit 2 Stream to Start Video • Selection Blackline Master, ELL6.3 **Comprehension** • Anchor Text Support • Paired Selection Support **Cause and Effect** • Language Support	**Build Background** • Language Support Card 7 • Unit 2 Stream to Start Video • Selection Blackline Master, ELL7.3 **Comprehension** • Anchor Text Support • Paired Selection Support **Understanding Characters** • Language Support	**Build Background** • Language Support Card 8 • Unit 2 Stream to Start Video • Selection Blackline Master, ELL8.3 **Comprehension** • Anchor Text Support • Paired Selection Support **Author's Purpose** • Language Support
Scaffold Language Production	**Informative Writing** Procedural Composition • Common Core Writing Handbook, Procedural Composition **Grammar:** Verbs • Linguistic Transfer: Verb Tense • Language Support Card 6: Conditional with *Would*; Gerund Subjects **Collaborative Conversation**	**Informative Writing** Compare-Contrast Essay • Common Core Writing Handbook, Compare-Contrast Essay **Grammar:** Direct and Indirect Objects • Linguistic Transfer: Word Order • Language Support Card 7: Introductory Phrases; Quotations **Collaborative Conversation**	**Informative Writing** Cause-and-Effect Essay • Common Core Writing Handbook, Cause-and-Effect Essay **Grammar:** Conjunctions • Language Support Card 8: Auxiliary Verbs *Should, Could*; Action Verbs **Collaborative Conversation**

Lesson 9
Storm Warriors

High-Utility Words *ship, shore, ocean, fisherman, injured, rescue, shipwreck, swim*
- Language Support Card 9
- Oral Language Dialogue, Blackline Master ELL9.2
- Online Picture Card Bank

Fluency & Decoding
- Phrasing: Punctuation
- Compound Words

Vocabulary Strategies
- Greek and Latin Roots

Target Vocabulary *annoyance, bundle, clammy, commotion*, critical*, demolished*, elite*, realization, secured, squalling*
- Vocabulary in Context Cards

Reading/Language Arts Terms *conclusion*, generalization*, historical fiction*, compound word, infer*, predict*, phrasing, root, informational text*, complex sentence, subordinating conjunction*, comma*, research report, source, outline*

Understanding How Language Works
- Language Support Card 9
- Text X-Ray
- Language Detective

Build Background
- Language Support Card 9
- Unit 2 Stream to Start Video
- Selection Blackline Master, ELL9.3

Comprehension
- Anchor Text Support
- Paired Selection Support

Conclusions and Generalizations
- Language Support

Informative Writing
Prewrite a Research Report
- Common Core Writing Handbook, Research Report

Grammar: Complex Sentences
- Linguistic Transfer: Subordinating Conjunctions
- Language Support Card 9: Future Tense with *Will*; *Work As* + Occupations

Collaborative Conversation

Lesson 10
Cougars

High-Utility Words *cougar, fur, camouflage*, hidden, hunt, predator*, prey**
- Language Support Card 10
- Oral Language Chant, Blackline Master ELL10.2
- Online Picture Card Bank

Fluency & Decoding
- Stress
- Recognizing Schwa + /r/ Sounds

Vocabulary Strategies
- Shades of Meaning

Target Vocabulary *available, contentment*, detecting*, ferocious*, keen, mature*, particular*, resemble, unobserved, vary**
- Vocabulary in Context Cards

Reading/Language Arts Terms *main idea, details*, informational text*, schwa, monitor, clarify*, stress, synonym*, thesaurus*, infer*, poetry*, poem*, imagery*, direct quotation, interjection*, quotation marks, research report, topic sentence, conclusion**

Understanding How Language Works
- Language Support Card 10
- Text X-Ray
- Language Detective

Build Background
- Language Support Card 10
- Unit 2 Stream to Start Video
- Selection Blackline Master, ELL10.3

Comprehension
- Anchor Text Support
- Paired Selection Support

Main Ideas and Details
- Language Support

Informative Writing
Write a Research Report
- Common Core Writing Handbook, Research Report

Grammar: Direct Quotations and Interjections
- Linguistic Transfer: Quotations and Punctuation
- Language Support Card 10: Sentence Structure: Subject + *Is/Are* + Noun Phrase; Subject + *Can* + Action Verb

Collaborative Conversation

LANGUAGE WORKSHOP

Language Workshop lessons provide skill and strategy instruction targeted to individual proficiency levels.

Lesson 6
Language Skills and Strategies

Collaborate: Gain and Hold the Floor

Interpret: Distinguish Among Different Words' Effects

Produce: Use Modal Expressions

How English Works: Connect Ideas

Vocabulary Network

Lesson 7
Language Skills and Strategies

Collaborate: Negotiate with Others in Conversations

Interpret: Describe Ideas and Text Elements

Produce: Write Informational Texts

How English Works: Understand Text Cohesion

Vocabulary Network

Lesson 8
Language Skills and Strategies

Collaborate: Provide Counterarguments

Interpret: Ask and Answer Questions

Produce: Use Technology Where Appropriate

How English Works: Expand Noun Phrases

Vocabulary Network

Lesson 9
Language Skills and Strategies

Collaborate: Persuade Others in Conversation

Interpret: Determine the Meanings of Unknown Words

Produce: Write Literary Texts

How English Works: Use Verbs and Verb Phrases

Vocabulary Network

Lesson 10
Language Skills and Strategies

Collaborate: Adapt Language Choices

Interpret: Evaluate an Author's Language Choices

Produce: Plan and Deliver Oral Presentations

How English Works: Expand Sentences to Add Detail

Vocabulary Network

Persuasive Posters

Selections in this unit deal with human/animal interaction and with persuading a community to take action. Students will create a poster and an oral presentation promoting the protection of an endangered animal by identifying the issues, explaining the animal's ecosystems, and persuading an audience to address the problem.

Materials
- trifold or regular posterboard
- markers, scissors, glue
- magazines, encyclopedias, and other print and digital research materials

▶ SHARE OBJECTIVES
- Consult several print and digital sources to locate and integrate information.
- Write persuasive text that includes sound reasoning and is based on research. LANGUAGE
- Include a visual display in an oral presentation to enhance development of main ideas.

DEVELOP BACKGROUND
- Discuss how changes to an environment affect the plants and animals living there. Ask students to identify animals that have become endangered because of environmental changes caused by humans. Discuss possible solutions to the animals' predicament.
- Point out that people often rely on visuals to convey information. Explain that students will need to make careful choices about what to include because of space limitations.

ENGLISH LANGUAGE SUPPORT

Linguistic Transfer

All Proficiencies Tell students that the word *human* has a Spanish cognate: *humano/a*. Remind students to look for cognates as they read to help them figure out the meanings of key words.

Step 1   ELD ELD.PI.5.1

Plan and Gather Student pairs plan the purpose and criteria for the project. They gather ideas and materials.

a Students brainstorm the major points they want to make about protecting endangered animals.

b Students brainstorm possible visuals to include and ways to organize those visuals to enhance their message.

c Students discuss possible print and digital resources for both information and visuals.

Research Skills

Step 2   ELA RI.5.7, W.5.7   ELD ELD.PI.5.1, ELD.PI.5.2

Organize Students research, design, create, and organize information for the project.

a Working with partners, students decide on the focus of the poster and the information they will need to present to support their argument.

b Partners conduct necessary research and create diagrams and illustrations. They locate existing visuals they want to use and draft copy for their posters.

c Students revise their persuasive points so that they are clear, logical, and well supported. Remind students to use the language skills they are learning in the unit.

Step 3   ELA SL.5.5, SL.5.6   ELD ELD.PI.5.7, ELD.PI.5.9

Complete and Present Remind students that they will give an oral presentation based on their research and poster. Allow time to rehearse.

a Student pairs complete their posters.

b Pairs decide how they will present information about their chosen animal and the solution they propose for protecting it.

c Pairs display their posters, deliver their presentations, and answer questions about their proposed solution.

ENGLISH LANGUAGE SUPPORT Guide students to compare and contrast their proposed solutions with those of other pairs. Use these sentence frames: *Your proposal is similar to ours because _____. Your position is different from our because _____.*

For instruction in the following applicable study skills, see the lessons in the **Resources** section, pp. R2–R33.

Unit 2 Research Skills

p. R2	• Research Appropriate Reference Sources
p. R3	• Use Magazines; Library Research
p. R4	• How to Read a Diagram
p. R6	• Persuasion; Poster
p. R7	• Internet Strategies
pp. R28–R33	• Keyboarding

PROJECT ASSESSMENT

Assess students' work on the project by reviewing multiple factors:

☑ **Reading Informational Text:** Do students adequately draw on and integrate information from several sources?

☑ **Speaking and Listening:** Do students present their arguments clearly and refer to their visual displays?

☑ **Writing:** Do students organize their poster content in a clear, logical manner? Do the included visuals make the posters more persuasive?

 Have students record progress of their **Research and Media Performance Task** in *my*WriteSmart.

ENGLISH LANGUAGE SUPPORT   ELD ELD.PI.5.12a

Expand Language Production

Emerging Guide students to discuss the main argument and the details they will use to support it.

Expanding Have partners outline key points and supporting details. Help them choose the most important points and details.

Bridging Have partners write a paragraph describing their project, including its key points, visuals, and reference sources.

Teacher Notes

Correlations

California Common Core State Standards for English Language Arts

Standard	Standard Language	Key Citations	Additional Practice and Application
LITERATURE			
Key Ideas and Details			
RL.5.1	Quote accurately from a text when explaining what the text says explicitly and when drawing inferences from the text.	**5-1:** T32–T33 **5-2:** T112–T113, T247, T252, T253, T260–T261, T269, T411 **5-3:** T34 **5-4:** T258, T259, T336, T337 **5-5:** T36–T37	**5-1:** T32, T33, T34, T39, T64, T65, T94, T100, T108, T109, T110, T111, T146, T147, T148, T149, T150, T151, T154, T172, T173, T178, T180, T182, T184, T190, T191, T192, T193, T197, T222, T223, T224, T225, T226, T227, T271, T294, T295, T326, T328, T330, T332, T338, T339, T340, T341, T374, T375, S7, S15, S19, S27, S29, S35, S37, S39, S45, S47, S49 **5-2:** T45, T100, T104, T106, T107, T114, T116, T146, T147, T148, T149, T246, T248, T253, T254, T256, T257, T258, T261, T262, T263, T264, T265, T296, T297, T298, T299, T302, T395, T398, T399, T401, T402, T403, T404, T405, T413, T414, T417, T425, S15, S25, S29, S31, S35, S37, S39 **5-3:** T18, T20, T26, T30, T33, T35, T36, T37, T68, T69, T70, T71, T72, T73, S11 **5-4:** T20, T21, T24, T26, T28, T29, T31, T32, T33, T34, T35, T39, T64, T65, T66, T67, T68, T72, T94, T96, T102, T104, T106, T110, T111, T112, T113, T142, T143, T144, T145, T146, T150, T222, T240, T242, T244, T246, T248, T254, T255, T257, T258, T259, T260, T261, T290, T291, T292, T293, T294, T298, T326, T328, T336, T337, T338, T339, T374, T375, T376, T380, S11, S21, S41, S44 **5-5:** T22, T26, T28, T36, T37, T38, T39, T70, T71, T72, T73, T74, T78, T100, T102, T104, T106, T108, T112, T113, T114, T146, T147, T148, T152, T226, T260, T261, T262, T294, T295, T296, T297, S14, S30, S41 **5-6:** T64, T82, T158, T160, T161, T163, T166, T174, T204, T216, S15, S17, S19, S31, S35, S41
RL.5.2	Determine a theme of a story, drama, or poem from details in the text, including how characters in a story or drama respond to challenges or how the speaker in a poem reflects upon a topic; summarize the text.	**5-1:** T17, T90, T105, T106–T107, T121, T333, T336–T337, T345 **5-3:** T351 **5-4:** T241, T244, T248, T333, T334–T335	**5-1:** T26, T32, T64, T65, T87, T109, T110, T111, T113, T116, T120, T146, T147, T148, T149, T150, T151, T154, T180, T186, T190, T197, T270, T319, T322, T332, T338, T339, T341, T344, T374, T375, T376, T377, T378, T379, T382, S5, S9, S11, S17, S19, S21, S27, S44, S47, S51 **5-2:** T44, T104, T113, T254, T273, T342, T417, T418, S17, S19, S27, S29, S31, S37, S39, S41 **5-3:** T196, T346, T351 **5-4:** T20, T22, T24, T26, T28, T29, T33, T98, T110, T136, T188, T189, T241, T244, T246, T248, T250, T252, T257, T313, T333, T334, T335, T343, T360, T364, T365, S31, S35 **5-5:** T24, T98, T109, T111, T113, T119, T144, T145, T146, T147, T148, T152, T165, T192, T193, T255, T340, S14 **5-6:** T61, T62, T65, T69, T74, T94, T120, T168, T215, S11, S14, S17, S19
RL.5.3	Compare and contrast two or more characters, settings, or events in a story or drama, drawing on specific details in the text (e.g., how characters interact).	**5-1:** T99, T106–T107, T181, T188–T189, T338–T339 **5-2:** T107, T110–T111 **5-4:** T253 **5-5:** T36– T37	**5-1:** T94, T96, T98, T100, T102, T104, T113, T114, T116, T121, T169, T172, T174, T178, T180, T182, T190, T191, T193, T222, T223, T224, T225, T226, T227, T230, T326, T329, T341, T368, S9, S19, S21, S24, S25, S27, S29, S49, S51 **5-2:** T41, T96, T98, T102, T108, T144, T145, T146, T147, T148, T149, T256, T258, T401, T424, S15, S17, S19, S39 **5-3:** T20, T24, T35 **5-4:** T117, T172, T250, T252, T257, T336, T364 **5-5:** T13, T20, T28, T30, T39, T96, T102, T250, T254, T263 **5-6:** T13, T68, T74, T76, T166, T215, S19, S51

Correlations

Standard	Standard Language	Key Citations	Additional Practice and Application
Craft and Structure			
RL.5.4	Determine the meaning of words and phrases as they are used in a text, including figurative language such as metaphors and similes. **(See grade 5 Language standards 4–6 for additional expectations.) CA**	**5-1:** T114, T330 **5-2:** T252, T254 **5-3:** T20, T24, T124–T125 **5-4:** T20, T324, T345 **5-5:** T29, T34–T35, T251, T258–T259	**5-1:** T24, T28, T40–T41, T94, T98, T113, T118, T176, T177, T189, T344 **5-2:** T41, T42, T100, T104, T250, T252, T254, T395, S35, S37 **5-3:** T20, T24, T68, T69, T196, S3, S13, S23, S43 **5-4:** T20, T22, T97, T109, T134, T174, T244, T246, T248, T254, T320, T322, T324, T328, T329, T332, T334, T335, S3, S13, S23, S33, S43 **5-5:** T34, T35, T62, T100, T192, T248, T251, T252, T254, T256, T284, S3, S13, S23, S33, S43 **5-6:** T27, T64, T74, T120, T200, T214
RL.5.5	Explain how a series of chapters, scenes, or stanzas fits together to provide the overall structure of a particular story, drama, or poem.	**5-1:** T27, T30–T31, T101, T106–T107 **5-2:** T394, T399, T410 **5-3:** T351 **5-4:** T103, T108–T109, T112, T316–T317, T338	**5-1:** T13, T16, T18, T25, T34, T64, T65, T66, T67, T68, T69, T72, T96, T100, T102, T105, T108–T109, T110, T296, T297, T304, T334, T368, S4. S7, S11, S17, S19, S27, S31, S37, S47 **5-2:** T42, T106, T250, T258, T342, T391, T403, T413, T415, T417, T418, T419, T422, S41 **5-3:** T28, T76, T194, T196, T346, T351 **5-4:** T20, T24, T87, T92, T106, T109, T134, T144, T145, T146, T150, T178, T179, T186, T188, T313, T318, T323, T330, T335, T360, T372, T373, S14 **5-5:** T13, T16, T18, T23, T26, T28, T37, T72, T73, T74, T78, T90, T104, T192, T244, T250, T259, T292, T293, T300, T340 **5-6:** T26, T75, T156, T158, T166, T168, T214
RL.5.6	Describe how a narrator's or speaker's point of view influences how events are described.	**5-1:** T25, T30–T31 **5-3:** T351 **5-4:** T101, T108–T109 **5-5:** T253, T258–T259	**5-1:** T33, T270, T332, T344, S4, S5, S7, S9, S11 **5-2:** T102, T194, T255, T261, T263, T342, T413, S16, S17 **5-3:** T23, T24, T26, T33, T196, T346, S40 **5-4:** T20, T21, T24, T26, T96, T101, T109, T111, T134, T170, T172, T178, T179, T188, T320, T322, T324, T327, T335 **5-5:** T106, T114, T192, T246, T253, T254, T259, T284, T340 **5-6:** T26, T64, T121, T166
Integration of Knowledge and Ideas			
RL.5.7	Analyze how visual and multimedia elements contribute to the meaning, tone, or beauty of a text (e.g., graphic novel, multimedia presentation of fiction, folktale, myth, poem).	**5-1:** T125 **5-3:** T25, T32–T33 **5-4:** T27, T30–T31 **5-5:** T105, T110–T111	**5-1:** T20, T22, T98, T100, T108, T112, T114, T116, T118, T331, T334, T344, S19 **5-2:** T41, T44, T104, T254, T258, T393, S37, S39 **5-3:** T22, T25, T28, T33, T60, S17 **5-4:** T22, T24, T26, T27, T31, T32, T56, T100, T252, T320, T326, S7 **5-5:** T22, T32, T105, T111, T136, T256, T261 **5-6:** T64, T205, S4, R2
RL.5.8	(Not applicable to literature)		
RL.5.9	Compare and contrast stories in the same genre (e.g., mysteries and adventure stories) on their approaches to similar themes and topics.	**5-1:** T121, T345 **5-4:** T343 **5-5:** T45, T119	**5-2:** T424 **5-6:** T26, T27, T75, T94, T121, T166, T167, T215
Range of Reading and Level of Text Complexity			
RL.5.10	By the end of the year, read and comprehend literature, including stories, dramas, and poetry, at the high end of the grades 4–5 text complexity band independently and proficiently.	**5-2:** T98–T111, T383–T422 **5-3:** T18–T33 **5-4:** T18–T31, T242–T257, T318–T335 **5-5:** T98–T111	**5-1:** T18, T34, T110, T112, T174, T175, T192, T224, T225, T226, T227, T268, T323, T324, T330, T335, T340, S5, S7, S9, S11, S15, S17, S19, S25, S27, S29, S31, S35, S37, S39, S45, S47, S49, S51 **5-2:** T40, T114, T194, T248, T264, T322, S15, S17, S19, S25, S27, S29, S31, S35, S37, S39, S41 **5-3:** T18, T36, T112, T113, T171, T192, T193, T197, T263, T264, T265, T266, T267, T270, T340, T341, T342, T343, S3, S4, S7, S11, S13, S14, S17, S21, S23, S24, S27, S31, S33, S34, S37, S41, S43, S44, S47, S51 **5-4:** T18, T30, T34, T38, T92, T112, T116, T181, T182, T183, T184, T185, T187, T242, T260, T264, T318, T338, S3, S4, S5, S7, S11, S13, S14, S17, S21, S23, S24, S27, S31, S33, S35, S37, S43, S44, S45, S51 **5-5:** T18, T38, T42, T44, T98, T114, T118, T186, T187, T188, T190, T246, T262, T267, T334, T335, T336, T337, S5, S7, S15, S21, S23, S35, S40, S42, S43, S47, S51 **5-6:** T24, T62, T110, T156, T164, T165, T168, T205, S3, S5, S7, S9, S11, S13, S15, S17, S19, S21, S23, S25, S27, S29, S31, S33, S35, S37, S41, S43, S51

Standard	Standard Language	Key Citations	Additional Practice and Application

INFORMATIONAL TEXT

Key Ideas and Details

Standard	Standard Language	Key Citations	Additional Practice and Application
RI.5.1	Quote accurately from a text when explaining what the text says explicitly and when drawing inferences from the text.	**5-2:** T269, T324 **5-3:** T98, T110–T111, T179, T188-T189 **5-5:** T186–T187	**5-1:** T38, T39, T196, T197, T251, T254, T255, T256, T257, T258, T264, T265, T266, T267, T271 **5-2:** T20, T22, T24, T26, T28, T29, T32, T36, T37, T38, T39, T45, T118, T170, T172, T174, T187, T188, T189, T190, T191, T220, T221, T222, T223, T224, T225, T228, T320, T330, T336, T337, T338, T339, T380, T388, T406, T425, S9, S49 **5-3:** T47, T109, T113, T140, T148, T149, T150, T151, T152, T156, T190, T191, T214, T222, T224, T225, T226, T230, T245, T263, T264, T265, T270, T288, T296, T297, T298, T299, T300, T304, T376, T377, T378, T379, T380, T384, S11, S21, S51 **5-4:** T13, T16, T38, T116, T168, T214, T215, T216, T217, T218, T237, T264, T269, T342, T388, T391, T394, T398, T400, T406, T408, T410, T411, S11, S21 **5-5:** T40, T42, T44, T167, T185, T187, T220, T221, T222, T266, T267, T315, T372, T373, T374, T378, S27, S31, S47, S49 **5-6:** T72, T112, T162, T164, T165, T169, T202, T205, T208, T216, T234, T360, T361, T364, T368, T372, T376, T377, T380
RI.5.2	Determine two or more main ideas of a text and explain how they are supported by key details; summarize the text.	**5-3:** T248–T249, T254, T258, T261, T262–T263 **5-4:** T175, T180–T181 **5-5:** T171, T174, T177, T184–T185, T331, T332–T333	**5-1:** T256, T260, T271, S14, S29, S49 **5-2:** T20, T24, T28, T36, T78, T118, T178, T180, T183, T184, T194, T220, T221, T222, T223, T224, T225, T228, T268, T292, T293, T320, T324, T325, T330, T331, T332, T335, T337, T372, T373, T374, T375, T376, T377, T380, T388, S5, S7, S9, S44, S47, S49 **5-3:** T13, T40, T43, T110, T111, T113, T116, T189, T190, T191, T245, T264, T288, T340, T341, S30 **5-4:** T206, T388, T394, T395, T400, T408, S35 **5-5:** T40, T42, T44, T137, T171, T180, T186, T189, T266, T334, T335, T370, T371, T372, T373, T374, T378, S44 **5-6:** xxi, T20, T27, T59, T68, T71, T75, T114, T118, T136, T138, T198, T208, T209, T211, T217, T358, T354, T364, T368, T372, T380, T382, S6, S7, S11, S44
RI.5.3	Explain the relationships or interactions between two or more individuals, events, ideas, or concepts in a historical, scientific, or technical text based on specific information in the text.	**5-2:** T23, T34–T35, T176, T180, T183, T186–T187 **5-3:** T255, T262–T263, T347 **5-5:** T40, T42, T44, T325, T332–T333	**5-1:** T196, T199, T221, T245, T248, T255, T263, T298, T300, T301 **5-2:** T16, T22, T26, T28, T32, T37, T70, T71, T72, T73, T74, T75, T152, T171, T174, T178, T182, T184, T194, T268, T320, T324, T325, T326, T328, T330, T331, T332, T335, T365, S5, S7, S9, S11, S44, S49, S51 **5-3:** T111, T150, T151, T152, T156, T189, T190, T224, T225, T226, T248, T250, T252, T254, T258, T259, T261, T265, T296, T297, T298, T299, T300, T304, T322, T324, T325, T326, T330, T334, T336, T339, T340, T341, T347, T376, T377, T378, T379, T380, T384, S39, S49 **5-4:** T216, T217, T218 **5-5:** T40, T42, T218, T219, T318, T320, T328, T334, T335 **5-6:** T17, T23, T72, T114, T208, T364, T365, T369, T376

Craft and Structure

Standard	Standard Language	Key Citations	Additional Practice and Application
RI.5.4	Determine the meaning of general academic and domain-specific words and phrases in a text relevant to a grade 5 topic or subject area. (See grade 5 Language standards 4–6 for additional expectations.) CA	**5-2:** T27, T28, T34–T35, T177, T186–T187 **5-3:** T183, T184, T188–T189, T330 **5-5:** T322	**5-1:** T220, T221, T298, T300, T301, T372, T373 **5-2:** T37, T68, T69, T72, T73, T74, T75, T176, T218, T219, T268, T327, T335, T337, T407, S2, S3, S5, S11, S43, S45, S50 **5-3:** T40, T42, T109, T114, T116, T120, T140, T191, T214, T270, S3, S9, S13, S23, S33, S43 **5-4:** T38 **5-5:** T42, T118, T137, T187, T266, S3 **5-6:** T108, T110, T112, T116, T222, T226, S4, S5
RI.5.5	Compare and contrast the overall structure (e.g., chronology, comparison, cause/effect, problem/solution) of events, ideas, concepts, or information in two or more texts.	**5-2:** T195, T343 **5-3:** T271, T347	**5-3:** T288 **5-4:** T402, T416, T417 **5-5:** T358 **5-6:** T75, T372
RI.5.6	Analyze multiple accounts of the same event or topic, noting important similarities and differences in the point of view they represent.	**5-3:** T114, T118, T122, T123 **5-5:** T267	**5-2:** T424 **5-4:** T402, T416, T417 **5-6:** T120, T372, T386

Correlations

Standard	Standard Language	Key Citations	Additional Practice and Application
Integration of Knowledge and Ideas			
RI.5.7	Draw on information from multiple print or digital sources, demonstrating the ability to locate an answer to a question quickly or to solve a problem efficiently.	**5-1:** T39, T43 **5-2:** T45 **5-3:** T47, T275 **5-5:** T123, T345	**5-1:** T197, T201, T275, R2, R4, R5 **5-2:** xiii, T195, T269, T347, T406, T424, T425, R2, R5, R7 **5-3:** S3, S5, S7, S13, S15, S19, S23, S25, S33, S35, S37, S39, S45 **5-4:** T121, T390, T398, T402, T406, T416, S3, S5, S9, S13, S15, S17, S19, S23, S25, S27, S29, S35, S43, S49 **5-5:** S5, S7, S9, S13, S17, S19, S23, S29, S33, S35, S39, S43, S47, S48 **5-6:** T22, T23, T112, T361, S23, S25, S29, S35, S37, S39, S47
RI.5.8	Explain how an author uses reasons and evidence to support particular points in a text, identifying which reasons and evidence support which point(s).	**5-2:** T176, T185, T186–T187, T189, T199 **5-4:** T265	**5-2:** T24, T30, T118, T119, T170, T172, T178, T180, T182, T184, T188, T220, T222, T223, T224, T225, T324, T325, T404, S5, S7, S9 **5-4:** T237, T262, T264, T340, T342, T394, T395, T400, T402, T411, T417 **5-5:** xii, T188, T315, T335 **5-6:** T108, T113, T116, T117, T152, T209, T212
RI.5.9	Integrate information from several texts on the same topic in order to write or speak about the subject knowledgeably.	**5-1:** T43 **5-2:** T49, T347 **5-3:** T197 **5-5:** T267, T345	**5-1:** T275 **5-2:** T45, T269, T343, T392, T400, T404, T406, T424, T425 **5-3:** T47, **5-4:** T269, T402, T416 **5-5:** T358 **5-6:** T27, T72, T75, T121, T167, T386
Range of Reading and Level of Text Complexity			
RI.5.10	By the end of the year, read and comprehend informational texts, including history/social studies, science, and technical texts, at the high end of the grades 4–5 text complexity band independently and proficiently.	**5-2:** T18–T35, T172–T187 **5-3:** T96–T109, T324–T339 **5-4:** T394–T395, T398, T400, T406, T408, T410–T411 **5-5:** T172–T185, T320–T333 **5-6:** T349–T384	**5-1:** T194, T196, T250, T266, T342 **5-2:** T38, T116, T190, T192, T266, T326, T338, T340, T405, T406, S5, S7, S9, S11, S45, S47, S49 **5-3:** T40, T112, T114, T127, T176, T192, T250, T266, T268, T342, S17, S27, S31, S37, S41, S51 **5-4:** T36, T114, T184, T185, T262, T340, T402, S21, S41 **5-5:** T40, T116, T188, T264, T336, T338, S3, S25, S27, S31, S45 **5-6:** T11, T14, T16, T18, T20, T28, T68, T72, T109, T112, T114, T116, T118, T122, T163, T164, T165, T204, T208, T224, T372, S4, S5, S6, S7, S9, S19, S45, S47
FOUNDATIONAL SKILLS			
Phonics and Word Recognition			
RF.5.3a	Know and apply grade-level phonics and word analysis skills in decoding words. Use combined knowledge of all letter-sound correspondences, syllabication patterns, and morphology (e.g., roots and affixes) to read accurately unfamiliar multisyllabic words in context and out of context.	**5-1:** T127, T203 **5-2:** T201 **5-3:** T277, T353 **5-4:** T45, T123 **5-5:** T273	**5-1:** T66, T67, T68, T69, T70, T71, T73, T126, T154, T155, T231, T277, T302, T303, T304, T305, T351, T382, T383, S4, S8, S10, S14, S18, S20, S24, S28, S30, S34, S35, S38, S40, S44, S48, S50 **5-2:** T51, T79, T125, T153, T228, T229, T275, T303, T349, T381, S4, S8, S10, S14, S18, S20, S24, S25, S28, S30, S34, S38, S40, S44, S48, S50 **5-3:** T49, T61, T77, T129, T141, T157, T203, T215, T231, T277, T289, T305, T365, T385, S4, S6, S8, S10, S14, S18, S20, S24, S28, S30, S34, S38, S40, S44, S47, S48, S50 **5-4:** T57, T73, T123, T135, T151, T195, T207, T223, T271, T283, T299, T349, T361, T381, T388, S4, S8, S10, S14, S18, S20, S24, S28, S30, S34, S38, S40, S44, S48, S50 **5-5:** T51, T63, T79, T125, T137, T153, T199, T211, T227, T273, T285, T301, T347, T359, T379, S4, S8, S10, S14, S18, S20, S24, S25, S28, S34, S38, S40, S44, S46 **5-6:** T37, T38, T47, T85, T95, T225, T226, T235, S4, S6, S8, S10, S14, S18, S20, S24, S28, S30, S34, S38, S40, S44, S48, S50

Standard	Standard Language	Key Citations	Additional Practice and Application
Fluency			
RF.5.4a	Read with sufficient accuracy and fluency to support comprehension. Read on-level text with purpose and understanding.	**5-1:** T126, T175, T202 **5-2:** T19, T323 **5-3:** T97, T177 **5-4:** T44, T194, T270 **5-5:** T116, T173, T321	**5-1:** T12, T34, T37, T41, T44, T45, T67, T72, T86, T93, T110, T112, T113, T117, T148, T149, T150, T151, T154, T168, T192, T195, T196, T220, T221, T224, T225, T226, T227, T228, T229, T230, T244, T251, T269, T276, T298, T300, T301, T318, T325, T330, T335, T340, T343, T350, T372, T373, T376, T377, T378, T379, S5, S6, S7, S9, S11, S15, S19, S25, S27, S29, S31, S35, S36, S37, S39, S41, S45, S47, S49, S51 **5-2:** T12, T22, T32, T38, T50, T68, T69, T70, T71, T72, T73, T74, T75, T79, T99, T115, T116, T124, T144, T145, T152, T166, T173, T192, T200, T220, T249, T264, T274, T294, T295, T296, T297, T298, T299, T302, T303, T316, T329, T338, T341, T348, T374, T375, T376, T377, T394, T406, T409, S5, S7, S11, S15, S16, S17, S19, S25, S27, S29, S31, S35, S37, S39, S41, S45, S46, S49 **5-3:** T12, T36, T40, T42, T48, T70, T71, T72, T73, T90, T114, T128, T150, T151, T152, T170, T192, T195, T202, T224, T225, T226, T251, T266, T276, T298, T299, T300, T325, T342, T352, T378, T379, T380, S6, S16, S25, S26, S36, S45, S47 **5-4:** T12, T30, T34, T37, T66, T67, T68, T86, T112, T115, T122, T164, T184, T187, T194, T216, T217, T218, T236, T260, T263, T292, T293, T294, T312, T338, T348, T374, T375, T376, S6, S16, S23, S25, S26, S27, S36 **5-5:** T38, T40, T50, T72, T73, T74, T92, T114, T117, T124, T146, T147, T148, T166, T188, T191, T198, T220, T221, T222, T240, T262, T264, T272, T294, T295, T296, T297, T314, T336, T339, T346, T372, T373, T374, S6, S15, S16, S26, S35, S37, S38, S42 **5-6:** T15, T46, T63, T106, T109, T110, T111, T112, T114, T119, T120, T122, T157, T158, T160, T163, T168, T186, T203, T354, T372, T387, S2, S3, S5, S6, S7, S8, S9, S11, S15, S17, S19, S21, S23
RF.5.4b	Read with sufficient accuracy and fluency to support comprehension. Read on-level prose and poetry orally with accuracy, appropriate rate, and expression on successive readings.	**5-1:** T44, T126 **5-2:** T43, T50, T193, T200 **5-3:** T41, T48, T115, T128, T276 **5-4:** T37, T44, T341, T348 **5-5:** T191, T198	**5-1:** T12, T23, T45, T66, T67, T68, T69, T86, T95, T117, T168, T185, T202, T253, T276, T327, T350, T383, S6, S16, S26, S46 **5-2:** T12, T21, T103, T117, T124, T166, T179, T242, T251, T274, S16, S26, S36 **5-3:** T12, T112, T150, T151, T152, T224, T225, T226, T298, T299, T300, T318, T352, T378, T379, T380, S3, S5, S6, S7, S13, S15, S16, S17, S23, S25, S26, S27, S33, S35, S36, S37, S43, S46 **5-4:** T43, T66, T67, T68, T70, T71, T72, T73, T86, T122, T144, T145, T146, T216, T217, T218, T292, T293, T294, T342, T374, T375, T376, T402, S3, S5, S6, S7, S13, S15, S16, S17, S23, S25, S33, S35, S37, S43, S45, S47 **5-5:** T72, T73, T74, T92, T93, T117, T124, T146, T147, T148, T166, T167, T191, T198, T220, T221, T222, T240, T265, T272, T294, T295, T296, T297, T372, T373, T374, S3, S5, S6, S7, S13, S15, S16, S17, S23, S25, S26, S27, S33, S35, S36, S37, S43, S45, S46, S47 **5-6:** T10, T19, T25, T27, T36, T58, T67, T73, T75, T84, T106, T115, T119, T120, T130, T131, T152, T159, T165, T167, T176, T177, T207, T213, T215, T222, T224, T354, S6, S11, S15, S16, S21, S23, S25, S26, S27, S33, S35, S36, S37, S43, S45, S46, S47
RF.5.4c	Read with sufficient accuracy and fluency to support comprehension. Use context to confirm or self-correct word recognition and understanding, rereading as necessary.	**5-1:** T40–T41, T126, T198–T199 **5-3:** T48 **5-5:** T265, T272	**5-1:** T70, T71, T72, T220, T221, T228, T229, T230, T372, T373, S3, S5, S23, S25, S33, S37, S43, S46, S47 **5-2:** T228, T295, T302, T378, T379, T388, T394, T406, S2, S3, S7, S10, S13, S17, S23, S25, S35, S43, S45 **5-3:** T12, T21, S6, S16, S35 **5-4:** T43 **5-5:** T249, S35, S36 **5-6:** T12, T32, T33, T34, T154, T224, S2, S3, S4, S5, S6, S7, S10, S13, S15, S17, S19

Correlations

Standard	Standard Language	Key Citations	Additional Practice and Application
WRITING			
Text Types and Purposes			
W.5.1a	Write opinion pieces on topics or texts, supporting a point of view with reasons and information. Introduce a topic or text clearly, state an opinion, and create an organizational structure in which ideas are logically grouped to support the writer's purpose.	**5-3:** T58, T138, T212, T360 **5-5:** T60, T132–T134, T206–T208, T354	**5-1:** T33, T191, T339 **5-2:** T152, T189, T337, T374, T375, T376, T377 **5-3:** T77, T111, T231, T341, T368, T369, T385 **5-4:** T33, T111, T183, T259, T391, T393, T413, T414, T417 **5-5:** T59, T261, T362, T363, T364, S9 **5-6:** xiii, T125, T375, T379
W.5.1b	Write opinion pieces on topics or texts, supporting a point of view with reasons and information. Provide logically ordered reasons that are supported by facts and details.	**5-2:** T49 **5-3:** T58, T138, T212, T360–T361 **5-5:** T58–T60, T132–T134, T206–T208, T354	**5-1:** T33, T191, T339, S19, S29, S39, S49 **5-2:** T189, T337, S9, S39, S49 **5-3:** T111, T341, T368, T369, S19, S29, S39 **5-4:** T33, T111, T183, T259, T391, T393, T413, T414, T417, S40 **5-5:** T261, T362, T363, T364 **5-6:** xiii, T125, T375, T379, S19, S29, S39, S49
W.5.1c	Write opinion pieces on topics or texts, supporting a point of view with reasons and information. Link opinion and reasons using words, phrases, and clauses (e.g., *consequently, specifically*).	**5-3:** T58, T138, T212, T360–T361 **5-5:** T58–T60, T206–T208, T354	**5-1:** T33 **5-3:** T369, S42, S46, S48, S49 **5-4:** T33, T391, T393, T413, T414, T417 **5-5:** T261, T134, T363, T364 **5-6:** T375, T379
W.5.1d	Write opinion pieces on topics or texts, supporting a point of view with reasons and information. Provide a concluding statement or section related to the opinion presented.	**5-3:** T58, T138, T212, T360–T361 **5-5:** T58–T60, T134, T208, T354	**5-1:** T191 **5-2:** T337 **5-3:** T369 **5-4:** T183, T391, T413, T414, T417 **5-5:** T363, T364 **5-6:** T125, T375, T379
W.5.2a	Write informative/explanatory texts to examine a topic and convey ideas and information clearly. Introduce a topic clearly, provide a general observation and focus, and group related information logically; include formatting (e.g., headings), illustrations, and multimedia when useful to aiding comprehension.	**5-2:** T58–T60, T134, T210, T356, T358	**5-1:** T109 **5-2:** T37, T229, T303, T365, T366, T381, T401, T405, T412, T425 **5-3:** T35 **5-4:** T337, T365, T366, T397, T405, T408 **5-5:** xiii, T113, T187 **5-6:** T44, T79, T91, T92, T136, T137, T138, T183, T184, T222, T371, T378, T382, T387
W.5.2b	Write informative/explanatory texts to examine a topic and convey ideas and information clearly. Develop the topic with facts, definitions, concrete details, quotations, or other information and examples related to the topic.	**5-2:** T60, T132–T134, T208–T210, T356–T358	**5-1:** T265, S40, S50 **5-2:** T37, T365, T366, T391, T392, T405, T412, T425, S30, S50 **5-3:** xiii, T35, S10 **5-4:** T337, T365, T366, T397, T400, T405 **5-5:** xiii, T113, T187, T335 5-6: T43, T44, T90, T91, T92, T124, T136, T138, T183, T184, T371, T378, T382, T387
W.5.2c	Write informative/explanatory texts to examine a topic and convey ideas and information clearly. Link ideas within and across categories of information using words, phrases, and clauses (e.g., *in contrast, especially*).	**5-2:** T58–T60, T134, T210, T356–T358	**5-1:** S10 **5-2:** T37, T303, T365, T366, T392, T401, T405, T412, T425 **5-3:** S42, S46, S48 **5-4:** T365, T366 **5-6:** T136, T138, T232, T371, T378, T382, T387
W.5.2d	Write informative/explanatory texts to examine a topic and convey ideas and information clearly. Use precise language and domain-specific vocabulary to inform about or explain the topic.	**5-2:** T37, T132–T134, T358 **5-5:** T187	**5-1:** T125, S13, S20, S23, S30, S33, S40, S43, S50 **5-2:** T60, T153, T189, T210, T365, T366, T392, T401, T405, T412, T425, S3, S10, S13, S20, S30, S40 **5-4:** T365, T366, T397 **5-5:** T335 **5-6:** T91, T92, T136, T138, T232, T371, T378, T382, T387, S8, S10, S20
W.5.2e	Write informative/explanatory texts to examine a topic and convey ideas and information clearly. Provide a concluding statement or section related to the information or explanation presented.	**5-2:** T60, T134, T210, T358	**5-1:** T265 **5-2:** T358, T365, T366, T392, T401, T405, T412, T425, S50 **5-4:** T365, T366 **5-6:** T44, T92, T371, T378, T382, T387

Standard	Standard Language	Key Citations	Additional Practice and Application
W.5.3a	Write narratives to develop real or imagined experiences or events using effective technique, descriptive details, and clear event sequences. Orient the reader by establishing a situation and introducing a narrator and/or characters; organize an event sequence that unfolds naturally.	**5-1:** T54, T358–T360 **5-4:** T132, T203–T204, T357–T358	**5-1:** T39, T73, T155, T212, T231, T305, T367, T368, T393 **5-2:** T393, T397, T409, T413, T421, T422 **5-5:** T341 **5-6:** T31, T359, T363, T367, T384
W.5.3b	Write narratives to develop real or imagined experiences or events using effective technique, descriptive details, and clear event sequences. Use narrative techniques, such as dialogue, description, and pacing, to develop experiences and events or show the responses of characters to situations.	**5-1:** T53–T54, T135–T136, T211, T358–T360 **5-4:** T132, T203–T204, T357–T358	**5-1:** T125, T211, T212, T367, T368 **5-2:** T393, T397, T409, T413, T421 **5-3:** S20, S30, S40, S50 **5-4:** S10, S50 **5-5:** T341, S10, S20, S30, S40, S50 **5-6:** T31, T76, T359, T363, T367, T384, S30, S40, S50
W.5.3c	Write narratives to develop real or imagined experiences or events using effective technique, descriptive details, and clear event sequences. Use a variety of transitional words, phrases, and clauses to manage the sequence of events.	**5-1:** T360 **5-4:** T204, T356–T358	**5-1:** S31, T367, T368 **5-2:** T393, T397, T409, T413, T421 **5-3:** T356, T357, S42, S46, S48 **5-4:** T200 **5-5:** S4 **5-6:** T171, T359, T363, T367, T384
W.5.3d	Write narratives to develop real or imagined experiences or events using effective technique, descriptive details, and clear event sequences. Use concrete words and phrases and sensory details to convey experiences and events precisely.	**5-1:** T53–T54, T135–T136, T211, T358–T359 **5-4:** T131–T132, T203–T204, T357–T358	**5-1:** T212, T305, T367, T368 **5-2:** T393, T397, T409, T413, T421 **5-4:** S50, S51 **5-5:** T341 **5-6:** T31, T77, T78, T90, T91, T92, T171, T359, T363, T367, T384, S10, S20
W.5.3e	Write narratives to develop real or imagined experiences or events using effective technique, descriptive details, and clear event sequences. Provide a conclusion that follows from the narrated experiences or events.	**5-1:** T54, T360 **5-4:** T132, T204, T356–T358	**5-1:** T73, T367, T368 **5-2:** T393, T397, T409, T413, T421, T422 **5-4:** T343 **5-6:** T31, T44, T231, T359, T363, T367, T384

Production and Distribution of Writing

Standard	Standard Language	Key Citations	Additional Practice and Application
W.5.4	Produce clear and coherent writing (**including multiple-paragraph texts**) in which the development and organization are appropriate to task, purpose, and audience. (Grade-specific expectations for writing types are defined in standards 1–3 above.) **CA**	**5-1:** T358–T360 **5-3:** T56–T58 **5-4:** T52–T54, T204, T358 **5-5:** T59–T60, T134, T208, T355	**5-1:** T54, T64, T73, T136, T155, T221, T231, T300, T305, T367, T368, T379, T383 **5-2:** T59, T60, T79, T134, T153, T195, T209, T210, T229, T296, T297, T298, T299, T365, T366, T374, T375, T376, T377, T381, T391, T393, T397, T401, T405, T409, T412, T413, T417, T421, T425, S40 **5-3:** xiii, T35, T57, T60, T77, T138, T157, T212, T231, T360, T362, T368, T370, S19, S29, S39, S49 **5-4:** T73, T132, T151, T223, T299, T365, T366, T381, T393, T397, T400, T405, T407, T408, T409, S9, S19, S29, S39, S49 **5-5:** T79, T153, T227, T363, T364, T379, S9, S19, S29, S39 **5-6:** T31, T39, T43, T44, T63, T78, T79, T87, T124, T133, T138, T157, T171, T179, T184, T226, T227, T230, T232, T359, T363, T367, T371, T375, T378, T379, T382, T384, T387, S10, S29, S39, S49
W.5.5	With guidance and support from peers and adults, develop and strengthen writing as needed by planning, revising, editing, rewriting, or trying a new approach. (Editing for conventions should demonstrate command of Language standards 1–3 up to and including grade 5.)	**5-1:** T284–T286, T360 **5-2:** T283–T284, T358 **5-3:** T284–T286, T362 **5-4:** T279–T280, T358 **5-5:** T281–T282, T356	**5-1:** T53, T54, T135, T136, T154, T211, T212, T366, T368 **5-2:** T59, T60, T133, T134, T209, T210, T357, T365, T393, T397, T401, T405, T409, T412, T413, T417, T421, T425 **5-3:** xiii, T57, T58, T137, T138, T211, T212, T368 **5-4:** T53, T54, T131, T132, T203, T204, T365, T366, T393, T407 **5-5:** T60, T133, T134, T208, T362, T363, T364 **5-6:** xiii, T44, T91, T92, T138, T171, T179, T183, T184, T230, T231, T232, T359, T363, T367, T371, T375, T378, T379, T387
W.5.6	With some guidance and support from adults, use technology, including the Internet, to produce and publish writing as well as to interact and collaborate with others; demonstrate sufficient command of keyboarding skills to type a minimum of two pages in a single sitting.	**5-1:** T360 **5-2:** T358 **5-3:** T362 **5-4:** T358 **5-5:** T356	**5-2:** T347, T412, T413 **5-3:** T47 **5-4:** T407 **5-5:** T345, T364, S13 **5-6:** T371, T378

Correlations

Standard	Standard Language	Key Citations	Additional Practice and Application
Research to Build and Present Knowledge			
W.5.7	Conduct short research projects that use several sources to build knowledge through investigation of different aspects of a topic.	**5-1:** T43, T275 **5-2:** T49 **5-3:** T47 **5-4:** T121	**5-1:** xxxvii **5-2:** xiii, T45, T269, T284, T392, T400, T412 **5-3:** T127, T275 **5-4:** T269, T401, T416 **5-5:** xii, T49, T123, T345 **5-6:** T175, T222, T370, T378
W.5.8	Recall relevant information from experiences or gather relevant information from print and digital sources; summarize or paraphrase information in notes and finished work, and provide a list of sources.	**5-2:** T357 **5-3:** T47, T127, T275 **5-4:** T53–T54, T121, T203, T269, T357 **5-5:** T49	**5-1:** T43, T275 **5-2:** T49, T283, T284, T365, T392, T401, T404, T405, T412, T425 **5-3:** T286 **5-4:** T279–T280, T401, T416 **5-5:** T197, T345 **5-6:** T43, T44, T370
W.5.9a	Draw evidence from literary or informational texts to support analysis, reflection, and research. Apply *grade 5 Reading standards* to literature (e.g., "Compare and contrast two or more characters, settings, or events in a story or a drama, drawing on specific details in the text [e.g., how characters interact]").	**5-1:** T33, T109, T191 **5-2:** T113 **5-4:** T33	**5-1:** T33, T43, T339, S20 **5-2:** T263, T347, T365, T401, T417, T422 **5-3:** T35 **5-4:** T111, T259, T337, T365, T366 **5-5:** T37, T345, T363, T364
W.5.9b	Draw evidence from literary or informational texts to support analysis, reflection, and research. Apply *grade 5 Reading standards* to informational texts (e.g., "Explain how an author uses reasons and evidence to support particular points in a text, identifying which reasons and evidence support which point[s]").	**5-2:** T37, T49, T189, T337, T347 **5-3:** T111, T265, T341 **5-4:** T121, T269	**5-1:** T275 **5-2:** T347, T409 **5-3:** T47, T275 **5-4:** T183, T393, T401, T404, T416 **5-5:** T187
Range of Writing			
W.5.10	Write routinely over extended time frames (time for research, reflection, and revision) and shorter time frames (a single sitting or a day or two) for a range of discipline-specific tasks, purposes, and audiences.	**5-1:** T136, T191, T358–T361 **5-2:** T113, T358 **5-3:** T58 **5-4:** T203–T204 **5-5:** T134	**5-1:** xxxix, T33, T39, T64, T73, T92, T109, T135, T211, T212, T230, T265, T271, T300, T305, T339, T345, T366, T379, T383 **5-2:** T37, T57, T59, T60, T119, T133, T134, T171, T189, T195, T209, T229, T263, T269, T337, T357, T365, T391, T393, T397, T401, T405, T409, T412, T413, T417, T421, T425 **5-3:** T35, T58, T111, T137, T191, T211, T265, T341, T368, S3, S5, S7, S9, S11, S13, S15, S17, S19, S21, S23, S25, S27, S29, S31, S33, S35, S37, S39, S41, S43, S45, S47, S49, S51 **5-4:** T33, T54, T111, T132, T169, T183, T259, T317, T337, T365, T366, T392, T393, T397, T400, T401, T418, S3, S5, S7, S9, S11, S13, S15, S17, S19, S20, S21, S23, S25, S27, S29, S30, S31, S34, S35, S37, S39, S41, S43, S45, S49, S51 **5-5:** T37, T59, T60, T77, T113, T187, T261, T335, T345, T354, T355, T356, T362, T363, T364, S3, S5, S7, S9, S11, S13, S15, S17, S19, S21, S23, S25, S27, S29, S30, S31, S33, S35, S37, S39, S41, S43, S45, S47, S48, S49, S50, S51 **5-6:** T31, T39, T44, T79, T87, T92, T125, T133, T157, T171, T179, T222, T227, T232, T357, T359, T363, T367, T371, T375, T379, T382, T384, T386, T387, S23, S24, S25, S27, S29, S31, S33, S35, S37, S39, S41, S43, S45, S47, S49

Standard	Standard Language	Key Citations	Additional Practice and Application

SPEAKING AND LISTENING

Comprehension and Collaboration

Standard	Standard Language	Key Citations	Additional Practice and Application
SL.5.1a	Engage effectively in a range of collaborative discussions (one-on-one, in groups, and teacher-led) with diverse partners on *grade 5 topics and texts,* building on others' ideas and expressing their own clearly. Come to discussions prepared, having read or studied required material; explicitly draw on that preparation and other information known about the topic to explore ideas under discussion.	**5-1:** T349 **5-2:** T273 **5-3:** T34 **5-4:** T347	**5-1:** xxxii, xxxiii, T32, T108, T148, T149, T150, T151, T190, T201, T264, T265, T298, T199, T300, T301, T302, T303, T304, T338, T345, T376, T377, T378, T379 **5-2:** vi, xxii, T36, T72, T73, T74, T75, T112, T113, T146, T147, T148, T149, T188, T199, T220, T228, T262, T278, T294, T295, T296, T297, T298, T299, T302, T336, T374, T375, T376, T377, T378, T379, T398, T390, T391, T396, T400, T404, T408, T416, T420, T422, T426 **5-3:** vi, xxii, T42, T43, T46, T47, T90, T91, T110, T170, T171, T190, T191, T196, T197, T264, T270, T271, T340, T346, T347, T350, T351 **5-4:** vi, xxii, T12, T13, T17, T32, T91, T110, T169, T182, T188, T189, T241, T258, T259, T317, T390, T392, T396, T399, T401, T404, T407, T414 **5-5:** vi, vii, xxii, xxiii, T17, T36, T97, T112, T171, T186, T260, T266, T267, T270, T271, T314, T315, T319, T334, T336, T337, S23 **5-6:** T27, T75, T121, T123, T125, T167, T168, T215, T354, T356, T357, T358, T361, T362, T365, T366, T369, T370, T372, T374, T377, T378, T381, T382, T383, T384, T388
SL.5.1b	Engage effectively in a range of collaborative discussions (one-on-one, in groups, and teacher-led) with diverse partners on *grade 5 topics and texts,* building on others' ideas and expressing their own clearly. Follow agreed-upon rules for discussions and carry out assigned roles.	**5-1:** T349 **5-2:** T273 **5-3:** T351 **5-4:** T347	**5-1:** xxxii, xxxiii, S5, S9, S15, S17, S19, S27, S29, S39, S45, S47, S49 **5-2:** vi, xxii, T188, T199, T396, T400, T404, T408, T416, T420, T426, S9, S29, S37, S39, S49 **5-3:** vi, xxii, T46, T47 **5-4:** vi, vii, xxii, T182, T390, T392, T396, T399, T401, T404, T407, T414 **5-5:** vi, xxii, T270, T271 **5-6:** T108, T354, T356, T357, T358, T361, T362, T365, T366, T369, T370, T372, T374, T377, T378, T381, T382, T383, T384, T388, S15, S19, S32
SL.5.1c	Engage effectively in a range of collaborative discussions (one-on-one, in groups, and teacher-led) with diverse partners on *grade 5 topics and texts,* building on others' ideas and expressing their own clearly. Pose and respond to specific questions by making comments that contribute to the discussion and elaborate on the remarks of others.	**5-1:** T349 **5-2:** T273 **5-3:** T17, T110, T323 **5-4:** T317, T347 **5-5:** T319	**5-1:** xxiii, xxxii, xxxiii, T32, T34, T108, T110, T190, T192, T201, T246, T264, T266, T338, T340 **5-2:** vi, vii, xxii, T14, T17, T36, T38, T97, T112, T113, T114, T171, T188, T190, T199, T247, T262, T264, T273, T321, T336, T390, T391, T392, T396, T400, T404, T408, T416, T420, T426 **5-3:** vi, xxii, T17, T34, T36, T37, T46, T47, T95, T170, T171, T175, T190, T191, T192, T193, T196, T197, T249, T264, T266, T270, T271, T320, T323, T340, T342, S2, S5, S7, S9, S11, S12, S15, S17, S19, S21, S22, S25, S27, S29, S32, S35, S37, S39, S41, S42, S45, S47, S49 **5-4:** vi, xxii, T17, T32, T91, T169, T110, T112, T182, T184, T241, T258, T259, T260, T268, T269, T388, T390, T392, T395, T396, T399, T401, T404, T408, T414, T418, S2, S5, S7, S9, S11, S12, S15, S17, S19, S22, S25, S27, S29, S32, S35, S37, S39, S41, S42, S45, S49, S51 **5-5:** vi, xxii, T17, T36, T38, T97, T112, T114, T118, T119, T168, T171, T186, T188, T245, T260, T262, T270, T271, T334, S2, S5, S7, S9, S11, S12, S15, S17, S19, S22, S25, S27, S29, S30, S32, S35, S37, S39, S41, S42, S45, S47, S48, S49, S50, S51 **5-6:** xiii, T27, T75, T121, T125, T161, T167, T215, T222, T354, T356, T357, T358, T361, T362, T365, T366, T369, T370, T372, T374, T377, T378, T381, T382, T383, T384, T388, S22, S25, S27, S29, S31, S32, S35, S37, S39, S41, S42, S45, S47, S49
SL.5.1d	Engage effectively in a range of collaborative discussions (one-on-one, in groups, and teacher-led) with diverse partners on *grade 5 topics and texts,* building on others' ideas and expressing their own clearly. Review the key ideas expressed and draw conclusions in light of information and knowledge gained from the discussions.	**5-1:** T349 **5-2:** T273 **5-4:** T193, T347	**5-1:** xxxii, xxxiii, xxxix, T108, T190, S9, S15, S17, S19, S27, S29, S39, S45, S47, S49 **5-2:** vi, xxii, T95, T262, T336, T390, T391, T392, T396, T398, T400, T404, T408, T416, T420, T422, T426, S9, S29, S37, S39, S49 **5-3:** vi, xii, xxii, T95, T190, T264, T340, S2, S27, S37, S47 **5-4:** vi, xii, xxii, T86, T87, T110, T182, T388, T390, T396, T399, T401, T404, T414, T418 **5-5:** vi, xxii, T112, T186, T260, T270, T271 **5-6:** xiii, T10, T123, T354, T356, T357, T358, T361, T362, T365, T366, T369, T370, T372, T374, T377, T378, T381, T382, T383, T384, T388, S15, S19, S32
SL.5.2	Summarize a written text read aloud or information presented in diverse media and formats, including visually, quantitatively, and orally.	**5-3:** T127, T275 **5-4:** T43 **5-5:** T49, T197	**5-1:** T13, T87, T125, T169, T245, T319 **5-2:** T13, T93, T167, T199, T243, T317, T388, T416 **5-3:** T12, T13, T170, T171, T318, T319 **5-4:** T86, T87, T164, T165, T236, T237, T312, T313 **5-5:** T92, T166, T167, T240, T241, T362 **5-6:** T59, T76, T152, T168, T175, T198, T354, T356, T381
SL.5.3	Summarize the points a speaker **or media source** makes and explain how each claim is supported by reasons and evidence, **and identify and analyze any logical fallacies. CA**	**5-1:** T197, T201 **5-2:** T199 **5-5:** T49, T197	**5-1:** T125, T169 **5-3:** T127 **5-4:** T43, T269, T347, T388, T401, T404, T405 **5-6:** T83, T125, T198, T381

Correlations

Standard	Standard Language	Key Citations	Additional Practice and Application
Presentation of Knowledge and Ideas			
SL.5.4a	Report on a topic or text or present an opinion, sequencing ideas logically and using appropriate facts and relevant, descriptive details to support main ideas or themes; speak clearly at an understandable pace. **Plan and deliver an opinion speech that: states an opinion, logically sequences evidence to support the speaker's position, uses transition words to effectively link opinions and evidence (e.g., consequently and therefore), and provides a concluding statement related to the speaker's position. CA**	**5-1:** T201 **5-3:** T341 **5-4:** T269	**5-1:** T43, T125, T197 **5-2:** T14, T49, T347, T416 **5-3:** xiii, T126, T127, T274, T275 **5-4:** T121, T400, T407, T413, T417 **5-5:** xiii, T197 **5-6:** T381, T383
SL.5.4b	Report on a topic or text or present an opinion, sequencing ideas logically and using appropriate facts and relevant, descriptive details to support main ideas or themes; speak clearly at an understandable pace. **Memorize and recite a poem or section of a speech or historical document using rate, expression, and gestures appropriate to the selection. CA**	**5-2:** T341 **5-3:** T127, T345 **5-5:** T191	**5-1:** T43, T125, T197 **5-2:** T49, T123, T347 **5-3:** T126, T274, T275 **5-5:** T193,
SL.5.5	Include multimedia components (e.g., graphics, sound) and visual displays in presentations when appropriate to enhance the development of main ideas or themes.	**5-3:** T201 **5-4:** T121, T193 **5-5:** T123	**5-1:** T43, T125 **5-2:** xiii, T400, T412, T416 **5-4:** T407 **5-5:** xiii **5-6:** T76, T222, T383, T381
SL.5.6	Adapt speech to a variety of contexts and tasks, using formal English when appropriate to task and situation. (See grade 5 Language standards 1 and 3 for specific expectations.)	**5-1:** T201 **5-2:** T123 **5-3:** T201, T275 **5-4:** T121, T193, T269 **5-5:** T123, T197	**5-1:** T148, T149, T150, T151, T197, T206 **5-2:** xiii, T49, T146, T147, T148, T149, T222, T223, T224, T225, T347, T416 **5-3:** xiii, T126, T127, T274, T275 **5-4:** T393, T404, T405 **5-5:** T196, T197, T340, T341 **5-6:** T381, T383
LANGUAGE			
Conventions of Standard English			
L.5.1a	Demonstrate command of the conventions of standard English grammar and usage when writing or speaking. Explain the function of conjunctions, prepositions, and interjections in general and their function in particular sentences.	**5-2:** T204–T207, T278–T281, T353–T355 **5-3:** T208 **5-4:** T198–T201, T354	**5-1:** T282, S28 **5-2:** T229, T381, T413, T421, S22, S28, S32, S38, S46 **5-3:** T54, T134 **5-4:** T207, T223, S22, S26, S28 **5-5:** T56, T204
L.5.1b	Demonstrate command of the conventions of standard English grammar and usage when writing or speaking. Form and use the perfect (e.g., *I had walked; I have walked; I will have walked*) verb tenses.	**5-5:** T128, T129, T130, T352	**5-2:** S48 **5-3:** S18, S22, S28, S47 **5-5:** T153, S6, S8, S12, S16, S18 **5-6:** T89, T95
L.5.1c	Demonstrate command of the conventions of standard English grammar and usage when writing or speaking. Use verb tense to convey various times, sequences, states, and conditions.	**5-2:** T54–T56, T57, T59–T60, T354	**5-1:** T282 **5-2:** T153, T405 **5-3:** T207, T215 **5-5:** T14, T79, T128, T129, T153
L.5.1d	Demonstrate command of the conventions of standard English grammar and usage when writing or speaking. Recognize and correct inappropriate shifts in verb tense.*	**5-3:** T132–T135, T282 **5-4:** T128	**5-3:** T141, T157, T370 **5-6:** T228
L.5.1e	Demonstrate command of the conventions of standard English grammar and usage when writing or speaking. Use correlative conjunctions (e.g., *either/or, neither/nor*).	**5-2:** T278–T281 **5-3:** T54, T134	**5-2:** T303

Standard	Standard Language	Key Citations	Additional Practice and Application
L.5.2a	Demonstrate command of the conventions of standard English capitalization, punctuation, and spelling when writing. Use punctuation to separate items in a series.*	**5-3:** T280, T282–T283 **5-4:** T201, T276 **5-5:** T130	**5-1:** T282 **5-2:** T205, S26 **5-3:** T305, S36, S38 **5-5:** S46 **5-6:** T181
L.5.2b	Demonstrate command of the conventions of standard English capitalization, punctuation, and spelling when writing. Use a comma to separate an introductory element from the rest of the sentence.	**5-3:** T281–T283 **5-4:** T276 **5-5:** T130	**5-2:** T79 **5-3:** T289, S38 **5-6:** T134, T135, T141, T180, T181, T187, S22, S28
L.5.2c	Demonstrate command of the conventions of standard English capitalization, punctuation, and spelling when writing. Use a comma to set off the words yes and no (e.g., Yes, thank you), to set off a tag question from the rest of the sentence (e.g., It's true, isn't it?), and to indicate direct address (e.g., Is that you, Steve?).	**5-3:** T281–T283 **5-4:** T276 **5-5:** T130	**5-1:** T282 **5-3:** T289 **5-6:** T134, T135, T141, T187
L.5.2d	Demonstrate command of the conventions of standard English capitalization, punctuation, and spelling when writing. Use underlining, quotation marks, or italics to indicate titles of works.	**5-4:** T352, T353, T354,T355 **5-5:** T278	**5-4:** T361, T381 **5-5:** S42, S48 **5-6:** T89, T95, T229
L.5.2e	Demonstrate command of the conventions of standard English capitalization, punctuation, and spelling when writing. Spell grade-appropriate words correctly, consulting references as needed.	**5-1:** T278–T279 **5-2:** T202–T203 **5-3:** T204–T205, T278–T279 **5-4:** T196–T197, T350–T351	**5-1:** T47, T129, T205, T353 **5-2:** T53, T127, T277, T351, T397, T405, T409, T413, T417, T421 **5-3:** T51, T131, T355, T368 **5-4:** T47, T125, T273, T364, T393 **5-5:** T53, T127, T201, T275, T349 **5-6:** T38, T39, T86, T87, T132, T133, T178, T179, T226, T227

Knowledge of Language

Standard	Standard Language	Key Citations	Additional Practice and Application
L.5.3a	Use knowledge of language and its conventions when writing, speaking, reading, or listening. Expand, combine, and reduce sentences for meaning, reader/listener interest, and style.	**5-2:** T130–T131, T206, T280 **5-4:** T200, T201, T358 **5-5:** T37	**5-1:** T170, S28 **5-2:** T145, T207, T263, T280, T303, S32, S38 **5-3:** T53, T92, T361, S38 **5-5:** T94 **5-6:** T41, T135, T141, T181
L.5.3b	Use knowledge of language and its conventions when writing, speaking, reading, or listening. Compare and contrast the varieties of English (e.g., dialects, registers) used in stories, dramas, or poems.	**5-1:** T183, T188–T189 **5-2:** T101, T110–T111 **5-4:** T253, T256–T257 **5-5:** T271	**5-1:** T121, T178, T193 **5-4:** T282 **5-5:** T271

Vocabulary Acquisitions and Use

Standard	Standard Language	Key Citations	Additional Practice and Application
L.5.4a	Determine or clarify the meaning of unknown and multiple-meaning words and phrases based on *grade 5 reading and content*, choosing flexibly from a range of strategies. Use context (e.g., cause/effect relationships and comparisons in text) as a clue to the meaning of a word or phrase.	**5-1:** T40–T41, T198–T199 **5-5:** T46–T47, T268–T269	**5-1:** T14, T70, T71, T72, T88, T144, T145, T152, T153, T170, T220, T221, T228, T229, T230, T246, T294, T295, T320, T372, T373, T378, T379, T380, T381, T382, S3, S5, S13, S15, S23, S33, S37, S43, S45, S46 **5-2:** T14, T27, T37, T68, T69, T76, T77, T78, T94, T152, T168, T197, T226, T227, T228, T229, T244, T292, T293, T295, T300, T301, T302, T318, T334–T335, T337, T370, T371, T380, T381, T407, T413, S3, S7, S10, S13, S15, S23, S27, S33, S35, S43 **5-3:** T14, T92, T146, T147, T172, T220, T221, T246, T320, T374, T375, S3, S5, S13, S15, S17, S23, S25, S32, S33, S43 **5-4:** T62, T63, T88, T140, T141, T212, T213, T288, T289, T314, T370, T371, T403, S3, S13, S23, S25, S33, S43, S45 **5-5:** T14, T62, T68, T69, T76, T77, T94, T142, T143, T168, T216, T217, T242, T284, T290, T291, T298, T299, T300, T316, T368, T369, S3, S13, S15, S23, S25, S33, S35, S43, S45 **5-6:** T32, T33, T34, T46, T64, T81, T108, T154, T234, S2, S3, S4, S5, S6, S7, S10, S13, S15, S17, S19, S23, S25, S33, S35, S43, S44, S45

Correlations

Standard	Standard Language	Key Citations	Additional Practice and Application
L.5.4b	Determine or clarify the meaning of unknown and multiple-meaning words and phrases based on *grade 5 reading and content*, choosing flexibly from a range of strategies. Use common, grade-appropriate Greek and Latin affixes and roots as clues to the meaning of a word (e.g., *photograph, photosynthesis*).	**5-1:** T122–T123, T272–T273 **5-2:** T196–T197, T270–T271 **5-3:** T272–T273, T348–T349 **5-4:** T266–T267	**5-1:** T302, T303, T304, T346–T347, T380, T381, T382, S17 **5-2:** T28, T226, T227, T300, T301, T302 **5-3:** T302, T303, T304, T382, T383, S32 **5-4:** T41, T70, T71, T72, T296, T297, T298, T403 **5-5:** T267 **5-6:** T131, T132, T173, T177, T141, T186, T187, T226, T234
L.5.4c	Determine or clarify the meaning of unknown and multiple-meaning words and phrases based on *grade 5 reading and content*, choosing flexibly from a range of strategies. Consult reference materials (e.g., dictionaries, glossaries, thesauruses), both print and digital, to find the pronunciation and determine or clarify the precise meaning of key words and phrases **and to identify alternate word choices in all content areas. CA**	**5-2:** T344–T345 **5-3:** T44–T45, T198–T199 **5-4:** T118–T119 **5-5:** T120–T121	**5-1:** T14, T41, T62, T63, T70, T71, T72, T123, T152, T153, T220, T221, T228, T229, T230, T273, T304, T320, T347, T380, T381, T382 **5-2:** T37, T47, T78, T120–T121, T142, T143, T150, T151, T197, T218, T219, T226, T227, T300, T301, T302, T337, T366, T378, T379 **5-3:** T14, T45, T74, T75, T76, T92, T146, T147, T228, T229, T230, T246, T266–T267, T273, T274, T294, T295, T348, T374, T375 **5-4:** T41, T88, T119, T148, T149, T150, T267, T314, T403 **5-5:** T150, T151, T152, T168, T194–T195, T242, T269, T316 **5-6:** T33, T81, T94, T173, T221, T242
L.5.5a	Demonstrate understanding of figurative language, word relationships, and nuances in word meanings. Interpret figurative language, including similes and metaphors, in context.	**5-1:** T114 **5-2:** T254 **5-3:** T108–T109, T124–T125 **5-4:** T101, T344–T345 **5-5:** T29, T34–T35, T251, T258–T259	**5-1:** T176, T252, T254, T260, T344 **5-2:** T395 **5-3:** T154, T155, T156, T191 **5-4:** T166, T378, T379, T380 **5-5:** T267 **5-6:** T29, T127
L.5.5b	Demonstrate understanding of figurative language, word relationships, and nuances in word meanings. Recognize and explain the meaning of common idioms, adages, and proverbs.	**5-1:** T28 **5-2:** T120–T121 **5-3:** T104, T124–T125 **5-4:** T344–T345 **5-5:** T183, T184–T185, T194–T195	**5-1:** T177, T182, T189, T258 **5-2:** T150, T151 **5-3:** T140, T154, T155, T156 **5-4:** T360, T380 **5-5:** T137, T224, T225, T226 **5-6:** T77, T126–127, T140
L.5.5c	Demonstrate understanding of figurative language, word relationships, and nuances in word meanings. Use the relationship between particular words (e.g., synonyms, antonyms, homographs) to better understand each of the words.	**5-2:** T46–T47, T344–T345 **5-4:** T190–T191 **5-5:** T46–T47, T342–T343	**5-1:** S3, S13, S15, S33, S43 **5-2:** T76, T77, T78, T152, T229, T318, T337, T378, T379, T381, S3, S7, S10, S13, S15 **5-3:** T29, T33, S32 **5-4:** T220, T221, T222 **5-5:** T78, T376, T377, T378 **5-6:** T122
L.5.6	Acquire and use accurately grade-appropriate general academic and domain-specific words and phrases, including those that signal contrast, addition, and other logical relationships (e.g., *however, although, nevertheless, similarly, moreover, in addition*).	**5-1:** T267 **5-2:** T27, T34–T35, T36–T37, T177, T186–T187, T191, T198, T327, T334–T335 **5-3:** T113, T183, T188–T189, T193, T356–T358 **5-4:** T200 **5-5:** T337	**5-1:** T14, T35, T42, T88, T111, T124, T154, T170, T193, T200, T220, T221, T246, T274, T298, T300, T301, T302, T303, T320, T341, T348, T380, T381, S3, S5, S10, S13, S15, S18, S20, S23, S30, S33, S37, S38, S40, S43, S45, S46, S47, S48, S50 **5-2:** T14, T28, T39, T48, T68, T69, T76, T77, T93, T94, T95, T115, T122, T152, T168, T176, T198, T228, T244, T265, T272, T295, T302, T318, T337, T339, T346, T364, T366, T378, T379, T380, S3, S7, S10, S13, S15, S17, S23, S25, S27, S30, S33, S43, S45, S47 **5-3:** T14, T37, T46, T92, T109, T113, T126, T146, T147, T162, T193, T201, T220, T221, T246, T267, T274, T294, T295, T338, T343, T350, T364, T365, T374, T375, T384, T385, S3, S6, S10, S13, S20, S23, S30, S33, S40, S43, S50 **5-4:** T35, T42, T88, T113, T120, T166, T185, T192, T238, T261, T268, T314, T339, T346, T360, T393, T403, S3, S10, S13, S20, S23, S30, S33, S40, S43, S50 **5-5:** T14, T39, T48, T62, T94, T115, T122, T136, T168, T189, T196, T210, T242, T263, T270, T271, T284, T316, T337, T344, T358, T362, S3, S10, S13, S20, S23, S30, S33, S40, S43, S50 **5-6:** T12, T32, T33, T34, T40, T46, T47, T82, T60, T94, T122, T124, T126, T127, T140, T154, T174, T222, T373, S2, S3, S4, S5, S6, S7, S8, S9, S10, S13, S15, S17, S19, S20, S23, S30, S33, S36, S37, S40, S43, S50

California English Language Development Standards

Standard	Standard Language	Key Citations

PART I: INTERACTING IN MEANINGFUL WAYS

A. COLLABORATIVE

1. Exchanging information and ideas

Standard	Standard Language	Key Citations
ELD.PI.5.1	**Emerging** Contribute to conversations and express ideas by asking and answering *yes-no* and *wh-* questions and responding using short phrases. **Expanding** Contribute to class, group, and partner discussions, including sustained dialogue, by following turn-taking rules, asking relevant questions, affirming others, and adding relevant information. **Bridging** Contribute to class, group, and partner discussions, including sustained dialogue, by following turn-taking rules, asking relevant questions, affirming others, adding relevant information, building on responses, and providing useful feedback.	**5-1:** xxxii, T14, T15, T17, T20, T28, T30, T32, T34, T35, T36, T39, T62, T63, T65, T66, T67, T68, T69, T70, T71, T72, T86, T88, T89, T91, T96, T104, T106, T108, T110, T111, T112, T113, T120, T122, T144, T145, T146, T147, T148, T149, T150, T151, T152, T153, T154, T168, T170, T173, T186, T188, T190, T192, T193, T194, T196, T197, T222, T223, T224, T225, T226, T227, T244, T246, T249, T260, T262, T264, T265, T266, T267, T271, T284, T294, T295, T296, T297, T298, T300, T301, T302, T303, T304, T318, T320, T322, T323, T332, T334, T336, T338, T340, T341, T345, T346, T349, T358, T366, T372, T373, T374, T375, T376, T377, T378, T379, T380, T381, T382, S2, S4, S5, S6, S8, S9, S12, S16, S18, S19, S24, S25, S26, S27, S29, S32, S34, S36, S42, S45, S46, S47, S48, S49 **5-2:** xxii, xxiii, T12, T14, T17, T32, T34, T36, T45, T58, T68, T69, T70, T71, T72, T73, T74, T75, T76, T77, T78, T79, T92, T96, T97, T114, T115, T118, T119, T120, T121, T132, T142, T143, T144, T145, T146, T147, T148, T149, T150, T151, T152, T153, T166, T168, T171, T184, T186, T188, T190, T191, T192, T194, T195, T196, T199, T218, T219, T220, T221, T222, T223, T224, T225, T226, T227, T228, T242, T244, T246, T247, T258, T260, T262, T264, T265, T268, T269, T270, T273, T282, T292, T293, T294, T295, T296, T297, T298, T299, T300, T301, T302, T316, T318, T320, T321, T336, T338, T339, T342, T343, T356, T364, T370, T371, T372, T373, T374, T375, T376, T377, T378, T379, T380, T388, T394, T399, T403, T408, T411, T415, T426, S4, S9, S12, S16, S18, S28, S29, S30, S34, S36, S37, S38, S39, S42, S46, S49 **5-3:** xxii, xxiii, T12, T17, T34, T35, T36, T37, T40, T42, T43, T44, T46, T66, T67, T68, T69, T70, T71, T72, T73, T74, T75, T76, T77, T90, T94, T95, T110, T112, T113, T116, T123, T124, T136, T146, T147, T148, T149, T150, T151, T152, T153, T154, T155, T156, T157, T170, T175, T190, T192, T193, T196, T197, T210, T220, T221, T222, T223, T224, T225, T226, T227, T228, T229, T230, T244, T266, T267, T270, T271, T284, T294, T295, T296, T297, T298, T299, T300, T301, T302, T303, T304, T305, T320, T321, T322, T323, T340, T342, T343, T347, T348, T360, T368, T374, T375, T376, T377, T378, T379, T380, T381, T382, T383, T384, T385, S2, S5, S7, S9, S11, S12, S14, S17, S18, S19, S24, S25, S27, S28, S29, S32, S36, S39, S41, S42, S48, S49, S50 **5-4:** xxii, xxiii, T12, T14, T16, T17, T28, T30–T31, T32, T34, T35, T36, T38, T39, T52, T62, T63, T64, T65, T66, T67, T68, T69, T70, T71, T72, T73, T86, T91, T106, T108–T109, T110, T111, T112, T113, T116, T117, T125, T140, T141, T142, T143, T144, T145, T146, T147, T148, T149, T150, T151, T164, T169, T178, T180–T181, T182, T184, T185, T186, T188, T189, T212, T213, T214, T215, T216, T217, T218, T219, T220, T221, T222, T223, T236, T238, T241, T244, T254, T258, T259, T260, T261, T265, T266, T278, T288, T289, T290, T291, T292, T293, T294, T295, T296, T297, T298, T299, T312, T314, T317, T332, T336, T337, T338, T339, T343, T344, T347, T356, T364, T365, T366, T370, T371, T372, T373, T374, T375, T376, T377, T378, T379, T380, T381, T390, T393, T395, T396, T397, T398, T400, T401, T405, T408, S2, S4, S5, S6, S7, S8, S9, S11, S12, S14, S15, S17, S18, S19, S22, S25, S26, S27, S28, S29, S32, S34, S35, S36, S37, S38, S39, S41, S42, S45, S46, S47, S48, S49, S50, S51 **5-5:** xxii, xxiii, T12, T16, T17, T38, T39, T45, T46, T68, T69, T70, T71, T72, T73, T74, T75, T76, T77, T78, T79, T92, T96, T97, T108, T114, T115, T116, T119, T120, T121, T142, T143, T144, T145, T146, T147, T148, T149, T150, T151, T152, T153, T166, T168, T170, T171, T188, T189, T193, T194, T206, T216, T217, T218, T219, T220, T221, T222, T223, T224, T225, T226, T227, T231, T240, T244, T249, T262, T263, T264, T267, T280, T290, T291, T292, T293, T294, T295, T296, T297, T298, T299, T300, T301, T314, T318, T319, T336, T337, T341, T343, T362, T363, T364, T368, T369, T370, T371, T372, T373, T374, T375, T376, T377, T378, T379, S2, S5, S6, S7, S8, S9, S11, S12, S13, S15, S16, S17, S18, S19, S20, S22, S25, S26, S27, S28, S29, S32, S34, S35, S36, S37, S38, S39, S42, S44, S45, S47, S48, S49, S50, S51 **5-6:** T10, T12, T16, T18, T20, T24, T27, T28, T30, T60, T61, T64, T65, T68, T75, T76, T78, T106, T108, T109, T118, T121, T122, T123, T124, T125, T129, T154, T155, T158, T167, T168, T170, T171, T200, T214, T215, T216, T218, T219, T354, T356, T358, T359, T361, T362, T363, T364, T365, T366, T367, T369, T371, T374, T375, T377, T378, T379, T380, T382, T383, T386, T387, T388, S2, S4, S6, S7, S8, S9, S12, S14, S15, S16, S17, S18, S19, S22, S24, S25, S26, S27, S29, S31, S32, S34, S35, S36, S37, S38, S39, S41, S42, S44, S45, S46, S47, S48, S49, S50

Correlations

Standard	Standard Language	Key Citations
2. Interacting via written English		
ELD.PI.5.2	**Emerging** Collaborate with peers on joint writing projects of short informational and literary texts, using technology where appropriate for publishing, graphics, etc. **Expanding** Collaborate with peers on joint writing projects of longer informational and literary texts, using technology where appropriate for publishing, graphics, etc. **Bridging** Collaborate with peers on joint writing projects of a variety of longer informational and literary texts, using technology where appropriate for publishing, graphics, etc.	**5-1:** T15, T39, T89, T120, T208, T210, T211, T231, T247, T271, T282, T321, T357, S46 **5-2:** T15, T38, T39, T45, T57, T95, T110, T169, T171, T188, T189, T245, T263, T319, T337, T345, T392, S16, S26, S46, S48 **5-3:** T15, T93, T112, T113, T173, T191, T247, T265, T271, T283, T321, T343, T368, S6, S16, S34 **5-4:** T14, T33, T89, T111, T167, T239, T259, T299, T315, T390, T392, T393, T408, S6, S14, S16, S26, S36, S46 **5-5:** T15, T45, T95, T119, T169, T193, T243, T317, T335, S6, S16, S26 **5-6:** T356, T358, T359, T361, T363, T367, T370, T371, T375, T377, T379, T386, T387, S20, S36, S46
3. Offering opinions		
ELD.PI.5.3	**Emerging** Negotiate with or persuade others in conversations using basic learned phrases (e.g., *I think . . .*), as well as open responses, in order to gain and/or hold the floor. **Expanding** Negotiate with or persuade others in conversations using an expanded set of learned phrases (e.g., *I agree with X, but...*), as well as open responses, in order to gain and/or hold the floor, provide counter-arguments, etc. **Bridging** Negotiate with or persuade others in conversations using a variety of learned phrases (e.g., *That's an interesting idea. However . . .*), as well as open responses, in order to gain and/or hold the floor, provide counter-arguments, elaborate on an idea, etc.	**5-1:** xxxii, T12, T17, T28, T33, T38, T91, T104, T121, T131, T149, T173, T186, T197, T260, T334, T344, S4, S8 **5-2:** xxii, T41, T195, T219, T247, T343, T396, T400, T408, T412, T416, S24, S26, S48 **5-3:** xxii, T94, T190, T264, T270, T323, T340, S21, S28 **5-4:** xxii, T12, T17, T38, T91, T188, T264, T342, T401, T407, S8, S12, S28, S40, S46, S48 **5-5:** xxii, T17, T97, T171, T192, T266, T280, T319, T340, T354, T362, S24, S39 **5-6:** T27, T75, T106, T121, T124, T125, T167, T170, T215, T365, T375, T378, T386, T388, S6, S9, S15, S16, S17, S24, S38, S50
4. Adapting language choices		
ELD.PI.5.4	**Emerging** Adjust language choices according to social setting (e.g., playground, classroom) and audience (e.g., peers, teacher) with substantial support. **Expanding** Adjust language choices according to purpose (e.g., persuading, entertaining), task (e.g., telling a story versus explaining a science experiment), and audience with moderate support. **Bridging** Adjust language choices according to purpose, task (e.g., facilitating a science experiment), and audience with light support.	**5-1:** T15, T32, T33, T35, T62, T63, T65, T89, T108, T111, T125, T148, T149, T150, T151, T190, T193, T197, T247, T267, T321, T338, T341 **5-2:** T15, T32, T36, T39, T41, T95, T112, T113, T115, T119, T169, T171, T184, T188, T191, T194, T195, T245, T258, T262, T264, T265, T319, T332, T336, T339, T365 **5-3:** T15, T37, T93, T110, T113, T123, T190, T193, T264, T267, T340, T343 **5-4:** T28, T32, T35, T39, T106, T178, T182, T185, T254, T258, T261, T265, T332, T336, T339, T364, T365, T366 **5-5:** T108, T362, T363, T364, S42 **5-6:** T87, T171, T219, T359
B. INTERPRETIVE		
5. Listening actively		
ELD.PI.5.5	**Emerging** Demonstrate active listening of read-alouds and oral presentations by asking and answering basic questions with prompting and substantial support. **Expanding** Demonstrate active listening of read-alouds and oral presentations by asking and answering detailed questions with occasional prompting and moderate support. **Bridging** Demonstrate active listening of read-alouds and oral presentations by asking and answering detailed questions with minimal prompting and light support.	**5-1:** xxxii, T12, T66, T67, T68, T69, T72, T86, T120, T121, T146, T147, T148, T149, T150, T151, T168, T222, T223, T224, T225, T226, T227, T244, T268, T269, T270, T304, T318, T343, T344, T374, T375 **5-2:** xxii, T12, T43, T70, T71, T78, T92, T132, T144, T145, T146, T147, T148, T149, T166, T193, T222, T223, T224, T225, T228, T242, T296, T297, T298, T299, T316, T341, T343, T372, T373, T374, T375, T376, T377, T380, T388, T400, T420, S32 **5-3:** xxii, T12, T41, T66, T67, T90, T120, T146, T147, T170, T195, T220, T221, T244, T269, T318, T374, T375, S44, S46 **5-4:** xxii, T12, T62, T63, T86, T115, T140, T141, T164, T187, T212, T213, T236, T289, T312, T393, T404, T411, T412, S24 **5-5:** xxii, T12, T43, T92, T117, T142, T143, T166, T191, T193, T216, T217, T240, T265, T294, T295, T314, S4 **5-6:** T10, T26, T58, T106, T125, T152, T170, T198, T223, T383

Standard	Standard Language	Key Citations

6. Reading/viewing closely

Standard	Standard Language	Key Citations
ELD.PI.5.6a	**Emerging** Explain ideas, phenomena, processes, and text relationships (e.g., compare/contrast, cause/effect, problem/solution) based on close reading of a variety of grade-level texts and viewing of multimedia with substantial support. **Expanding** Explain ideas, phenomena, processes, and text relationships (e.g., compare/contrast, cause/effect, problem/solution) based on close reading of a variety of grade-level texts and viewing of multimedia with moderate support. **Bridging** Explain ideas, phenomena, processes, and text relationships (e.g., compare/contrast, cause/effect, problem/solution) based on close reading of a variety of grade-level texts and viewing of multimedia with light support.	**5-1:** xxxii, T14, T16, T20, T22, T24, T25, T26, T27, T31, T32, T64, T65, T66, T67, T68, T69, T72, T73, T74, T75, T90, T92, T94, T96, T97, T98, T99, T100, T101, T102, T104, T105, T107, T108, T109, T113, T114, T116, T118, T120, T121, T146, T147, T172, T173, T176, T177, T178, T179, T180, T181, T182, T183, T184, T186, T188, T189, T190, T191, T196, T248, T250, T252, T254, T255, T256, T257, T260, T263, T265, T268, T270, T296, T324, T325, T326, T327, T328, T329, T330, T332, T335, T337, T338, T339, T382, S4, S6, S8, S11, S14, S15, S17, S19, S21, S24, S25, S26, S27, S29, S34, S36, S37, S38, S46, S48, S49, S51 **5-2:** xxii, T16, T18, T20, T23, T24, T28, T29, T30, T31, T32, T35, T42, T44, T78, T96, T98, T101, T102, T104, T105, T106, T111, T112, T113, T116, T144, T145, T146, T147, T148, T149, T152, T170, T174, T176, T178, T180, T182, T183, T184, T185, T187, T188, T189, T194, T220, T221, T222, T223, T224, T225, T228, T246, T247, T253, T254, T255, T256, T257, T258, T261, T262, T263, T269, T296, T297, T298, T299, T302, T320, T322, T330, T331, T332, T333, T334, T335, T336, T337, T342, T372, T373, T401, T424, T425, S7, S9, S11, S14, S15, S16, S17, S19, S24, S26, S27, S28, S29, S31, S38, S39, S44, S51 **5-3:** xxii, T16, T18, T33, T34, T35, T43, T68, T69, T70, T71, T72, T73, T76, T94, T109, T110, T111, T114, T118, T120, T122, T123, T150, T151, T152, T153, T156, T174, T189, T190, T191, T194, T196, T221, T224, T225, T226, T227, T230, T248, T263, T264, T265, T268, T270, T298, T299, T300, T301, T322, T323, T339, T340, T376, T377, T378, T379, T380, T381, T384, S8, S9, S14, S16, S18, S19, S26, S28, S29, S34, S36, S39, S40, S42, S48, S49 **5-4:** xxii, T16, T20, T21, T22, T26, T28, T29, T32, T33, T64, T65, T66, T67, T68, T79, T72, T90, T96, T100, T101, T103, T110, T111, T116, T144, T145, T146, T147, T150, T168, T172, T175, T177, T178, T179, T182, T216, T217, T218, T219, T222, T240, T250, T251, T252, T253, T255, T258, T259, T290, T291, T292, T293, T294, T295, T298, T316, T323, T337, T364, T365, T366, T374, T375, T376, T377, T380, T392, T393, T395, T402, T403, T406, T409, T411, T413, S6, S8, S18, S24, S26, S28, S36, S39, S45, S47, S48 **5-5:** xxii, T16, T23, T70, T71, T72, T73, T74, T75, T78, T96, T144, T145, T146, T147, T148, T149, T152, T170, T175, T218, T219, T220, T221, T222, T223, T226, T244, T292, T293, T294, T295, T296, T297, T300, T318, T362, T363, T364, T370, T371, T372, T373, T374, T375, T378, S4, S6, S8, S14, S16, S18, S19, S24, S25, S26, S28, S29, S34, S36, S38, S41, S44, S47, S48, S49 **5-6:** T13, T22, T23, T24, T26, T27, T28, T61, T64, T65, T66, T68, T70, T71, T72, T74, T75, T76, T109, T112, T114, T118, T120, T121, T154, T155, T159, T160, T162, T164, T166, T167, T168, T169, T201, T204, T205, T206, T211, T212, T214, T215, T216, T217, T360, T361, T365, T369, T372, T377, S8, S9, S11, S14, S18, S19, S29, S34, S38, S44, S49
ELD.PI.5.6b	**Emerging** Use knowledge of frequently-used affixes (e.g., *un-, mis-*), linguistic context, reference materials, and visual cues to determine the meaning of unknown words on familiar topics. **Expanding** Use knowledge of morphology (e.g., affixes, roots, and base words), linguistic context, and reference materials to determine the meaning of unknown words on familiar and new topics. **Bridging** Use knowledge of morphology (e.g., affixes, roots, and base words), linguistic context, and reference materials to determine the meaning of unknown words on familiar and new topics.	**5-1:** T40, T41, T70, T71, T72, T78, T88, T122, T123, T152, T153, T154, T170, T198, T199, T220, T221, T228, T229, T230, T272, T273, T294, T295, T302, T303, T304, T320, T330, T346, T347, T372, T373, S2, S17, S18, S28, S46 **5-2:** T28, T31, T35, T47, T68, T69, T76, T77, T142, T143, T152, T176, T177, T187, T189, T196, T197, T218, T219, T226, T227, T228, T250, T252, T254, T270, T271, T292, T293, T294, T295, T300, T301, T302, T327, T335, T370, T371, T378, T379, T380, T382, T410, T419, S5, S7, S8, S10, S32, S42, S48 **5-3:** T44, T45, T272, T273, T339, T348, T349, **5-4:** T40, T41, T46, T70, T71, T72, T118, T119, T148, T149, T150, T178, T266, T267, T296, T297, T298, T324, T375, T394, T397, T400, T406, T413, S28 **5-5:** T120, T121, T152, T175, T178, T268, T269, T274, T298, T299, T300, T348, S44 **5-6:** T32, T33, T38, T39, T64, T80, T81, T86, T87, T108, T127, T133, T165, T168, T172, T173, T178, T179, T220, T221, T361, T365, S10, S16, S42

Standard	Standard Language	Key Citations
7. Evaluating language choices		
ELD.PI.5.7	**Emerging** Describe the specific language writers or speakers use to present or support an idea (e.g., the specific vocabulary or phrasing used to provide evidence) with prompting and substantial support. **Expanding** Explain how well writers and speakers use language resources to support an opinion or present an idea (e.g., whether the vocabulary used to provide evidence is strong enough, or if the phrasing used to signal a shift in meaning does this well) with moderate support. **Bridging** Explain how well writers and speakers use specific language resources to support an opinion or present an idea (e.g., the clarity or appealing nature of language used to provide evidence or describe characters, or if the phrasing used to introduce a topic is appropriate) with light support.	**5-1:** T345 **5-2:** T41, T111, T119, T133, T208, T220, T254, T327 **5-3:** T122, T189, T347, T375, T385 **5-4:** T177, T178, T189, T253, T265, T410, S41 **5-5:** T266, T267, T364, S6 **5-6:** T26, T64, T70, T74, T76, T116, T117, T118, T120, T168, T204, T210, T214, T223
8. Analyzing language choices		
ELD.PI.5.8	**Emerging** Distinguish how different words with similar meanings produce different effects on the audience (e.g., describing a character as *angry* versus *furious*). **Expanding** Distinguish how different words with similar meanings (e.g., describing an event as *sad* versus *tragic*) and figurative language (e.g., *she ran like a cheetah*) produce shades of meaning and different effects on the audience. **Bridging** Distinguish how different words with related meanings (e.g., *fun* versus *thrilling*, *possibly* versus *certainly*) and figurative language (e.g., *the stream slithered through the parched land*) produce shades of meaning and different effects on the audience.	**5-1:** T28, T31, T43, T94, T98, T114, T118, T184, T189, T254, T258, T260, T271, T342, T345 **5-2:** T27, T40, T44, T46, T47, T78, T100, T101, T104, T105, T120, T121, T318, T340, T343, T344, T345, T378, T379, T397, T398, T421 **5-3:** T33, T40, T109, T191, T196, T370 **5-4:** T20, T23, T97, T124, T125, T174, T190, T191, T193, T198, T199, T246, T328, T331, T344, T345 **5-5:** T29, T40, T46, T47, T76, T77, T78, T190, T193, T194, T195, T267, T271, T342, T343 **5-6:** T28, T29, T120, T122, T126, T127
C. PRODUCTIVE		
9. Presenting		
ELD.PI.5.9	**Emerging** Plan and deliver brief oral presentations on a variety of topics and content areas (e.g., providing a report on a current event, reciting a poem, recounting an experience, explaining a science process) with moderate support, such as graphic organizers. **Expanding** Plan and deliver longer oral presentations on a variety of topics and content areas (e.g., providing an opinion speech on a current event, reciting a poem, recounting an experience, explaining a science process) with moderate support. **Bridging** Plan and deliver oral presentations on a variety of topics in a variety of content areas (e.g., providing an opinion speech on a current event, reciting a poem, recounting an experience, explaining a science process) with light support.	**5-1:** T43, T125, T197, T201, T368 **5-2:** T49, T123, T269, T347, T366, T392, T404, T408 **5-3:** T127, T201, T370 **5-4:** T38, T43, T121, T193, T269, T341, T343, T364, T366, T409, S21 **5-5:** T43, T49, T123, T197, T265, T339, T341, T363, T364, S18 **5-6:** T74, T76, T83, T129, T175, T223, T370, T381, S4, S17, S19
10. Writing		
ELD.PI.5.10a	**Emerging** Write short literary and informational texts (e.g., a description of a camel) collaboratively (e.g., joint construction of texts with an adult or with peers) and sometimes independently. **Expanding** Write longer literary and informational texts (e.g., an informative report on different kinds of camels) collaboratively (e.g., joint construction of texts with an adult or with peers) and with increasing independence using appropriate text organization. **Bridging** Write longer and more detailed literary and informational texts (e.g., an explanation of how camels survive without water for a long time) collaboratively (e.g., joint construction of texts with an adult or with peers) and independently using appropriate text organization and growing understanding of register.	**5-1:** T33, T73, T109, T121, T155, T231, T339, T366, T368, T383 **5-2:** T45, T170, T189, T207, T221, T229, T263, T303, T305, T365, T366, T391, T392, T397, T404, T425 **5-3:** T35, T111, T153, T197, T341, T347, T368, T370, T381, S18, S21, S26, S40, S50 **5-4:** T111, T117, T130, T183, T259, T337, T364, T365, T366, S20, S30 **5-5:** T191, T193, T245, T341, T353, T363, T364, S10, S30, S40 **5-6:** T28, T30, T31, T39, T77, T78, T79, T87, T111, T125, T133, T157, T170, T179, T203, T216, T219, T227, T359, T363, T367, T371, T379, T384, T387, S30, S40, S50
ELD.PI.5.10b	**Emerging** Write brief summaries of texts and experiences using complete sentences and key words (e.g., from notes or graphic organizers). **Expanding** Write increasingly concise summaries of texts and experiences using complete sentences and key words (e.g., from notes or graphic organizers). **Bridging** Write clear and coherent summaries of texts and experiences using complete and concise sentences and key words (e.g., from notes or graphic organizers).	**5-1:** T14, T64, T65, T191, T265, T271, T320, S20, S30, S34, S46 **5-2:** T113, T115, T355, T390, T422, S6, S16, S26, S40, S44, S46 **5-3:** T43, T122, T127, T191, T244, T275, T318, T359, S6, S10, S11, S30, S31, S34, S36, S41, S51 **5-4:** T43, T265, T342, T418, S6, S14, S16, S26, S31, S34, S35, S36, S41, S46, S50 **5-5:** T116, T218, T219, T264, T338, T364, S6, S11, S20, S21, S26, S31, S41, S46, S50, S51 **5-6:** T24, T26, T34, T58, T72, T118, T122, T152, T164, T166, T168, T171, T175, T198, T212, T359, T382, S6, S10, S16, S31, S36, S41, S44

Standard	Standard Language	Key Citations
11. Supporting opinions		
ELD.PI.5.11a	**Emerging** Support opinions by expressing appropriate/accurate reasons using textual evidence (e.g., referring to text) or relevant background knowledge about content with substantial support. **Expanding** Support opinions or persuade others by expressing appropriate/accurate reasons using some textual evidence (e.g., paraphrasing facts from a text) or relevant background knowledge about content. **Bridging** Support opinions or persuade others by expressing appropriate/accurate reasons using detailed textual evidence (e.g., quoting the text directly or specific events from text) or relevant background knowledge about content.	**5-1:** T12, T38, T201, T264, T270, T338, T339, S4, S5, S7, S9, S38, S46, S48, S49 **5-2:** T36, T39, T45, T112, T119, T188, T189, T195, T262, T336, T337, T374, T375, T376, T377, T395, T408, T418, S26, S28, S31, S34, S46, S48 **5-3:** T34, T35, T56, T110, T190, T191, T197, T264, T284, T340, T360, S4, S7, S8, S15, S17, S27, S28, S37, S44, S46, S47 **5-4:** T111, T117, T183, T259, T337, T343, T405, T413, T414, T416, S24, S26, S28, S38, S40, S43, S48 **5-5:** T42, T45, T58, T118, T119, T132, T193, T206, T267, T341, T363, T364, S6, S9, S14, S19, S24, S27, S39, S47, S48 **5-6:** T34, T72, T83, T124, T125, T129, T375, T379, S15, S26, S31
ELD.PI.5.11b	**Emerging** Express ideas and opinions or temper statements using basic modal expressions (e.g., *can, has to, maybe*). **Expanding** Express attitude and opinions or temper statements with familiar modal expressions (e.g., *maybe/probably, can/must*). **Bridging** Express attitude and opinions or temper statements with nuanced modal expressions (e.g., *probably/certainly, should/would*) and phrasing (e.g., *In my opinion...*).	**5-3:** S28 **5-4:** T414, T416 **5-6:** T124, T375
12. Selecting language resources		
ELD.PI.5.12a	**Emerging** Use a select number of general academic and domain-specific words to create precision while speaking and writing. **Expanding** Use a growing number of general academic and domain-specific words, synonyms, and antonyms to create precision and shades of meaning while speaking and writing. **Bridging** Use a wide variety of general academic and domain-specific words, synonyms, antonyms, and figurative language to create precision and shades of meaning while speaking and writing.	**5-1:** xxxii, T14, T15, T35, T42, T43, T63, T88, T89, T111, T118, T124, T170, T193, T194, T200, T246, T267, T274, T320, T341, T348, S2, S38, S40, S50 **5-2:** xxii, T14, T15, T37, T39, T48, T76, T77, T94, T95, T115, T122, T152, T168, T169, T189, T191, T198, T244, T245, T266, T272, T318, T319, T337, T346, T364, T365, T366, T391, T397, T407, T425 **5-3:** T14, T37, T42, T56, T113, T120, T126, T136, T172, T173, T191, T193, T200, T210, T221, T246, T247, T267, T274, T284, T320, T321, T342, T343, T360, T368, S13, S24, S42, S43, S48 **5-4:** xxii, T14, T15, T35, T88, T89, T113, T120, T166, T167, T185, T192, T238, T239, T261, T268, T339, T346, T364, T365, T366, S10, S44 **5-5:** xxii, T14, T45, T46, T47, T48, T58, T94, T115, T122, T168, T189, T190, T196, T206, T242, T270, T280, T263, T314, T315, T316, T337, T344, T354, T362, S3, S14, S16, S22, S32, S36, S44 **5-6:** T10, T12, T16, T20, T28, T29, T31, T60, T61, T64, T77, T78, T79, T108, T123, T154, T158, T162, T170, T200, T204, T205, T209, T218, T219, T360, T373, S2, S8, S22, S32, S42
ELD.PI.5.12b	**Emerging** Select a few frequently used affixes for accuracy and precision (e.g., She walk*s*, I'm *un*happy.). **Expanding** Select a growing number of frequently used affixes for accuracy and precision (e.g., She walk*ed*. He like*s*..., I'm *un*happy.). **Bridging** Select a variety of appropriate affixes for accuracy and precision (e.g., She's walk*ing*. I'm *un*comfortable. They left reluctant*ly*.).	**5-1:** T122, T123, T272, T273, T346, T347, S38 **5-2:** T196, T197, T342, S42 **5-3:** S26 **5-4:** T266, T267
PART II: LEARNING ABOUT HOW ENGLISH WORKS		
A. STRUCTURING COHESIVE TEXTS		
1. Understanding text structure		
ELD.PII.5.1	**Emerging** Apply basic understanding of how different text types are organized to express ideas (e.g., how a narrative is organized sequentially with predictable stages versus how opinions/arguments are organized around ideas) to comprehending texts and writing basic texts. **Expanding** Apply growing understanding of how different text types are organized to express ideas (e.g., how a narrative is organized sequentially with predictable stages versus how opinions/arguments are structured logically around reasons and evidence) to comprehending texts and writing texts with increasing cohesion. **Bridging** Apply increasing understanding of how different text types are organized to express ideas (e.g., how a historical account is organized chronologically versus how opinions/arguments are structured logically around reasons and evidence) to comprehending texts and writing cohesive texts.	**5-1:** T24, T31, T52, T53, T62, T63, T64, T65, T72, T107, T109, T189, T248, T262, T263, T298, T300, T301, T304, T337, T358, S4, S27, S31, S34, S36 **5-2:** T58, T70, T71, T72, T73, T74, T75, T152, T192, T220, T267, T282, T342, T356, T364, T365, T396, T406, T425, S41 **5-3:** T35, T136, T189, T190, T194, T196, T211, T263, T265, T339, T341, T346, T368, T369 **5-4:** T86, T90, T142, T143, T144, T145, T146, T147, T150, T186, T202, T278, T316, T324, T357, T336, T337, T364, T365, T366, T372, T373, T374, T375, T376, T377, T380, S11, S14, S44 **5-5:** T40, T72, T73, T74, T75, T78, T114, T116, T132, T252, T281, T338, T354, T362, T363, T364, S20, S44 **5-6:** T13, T17, T24, T31, T62, T74, T110, T115, T156, T166, T171, T202, T209, T219, T368, S24, S46

Correlations

Standard	Standard Language	Key Citations
2. Understanding cohesion		
ELD.PII.5.2a	**Emerging** Apply basic understanding of language resources for referring the reader back or forward in text (e.g., how pronouns refer back to nouns in text) to comprehending texts and writing basic texts. **Expanding** Apply growing understanding of language resources for referring the reader back or forward in text (e.g., how pronouns or synonyms refer back to nouns in text) to comprehending texts and writing texts with increasing cohesion. **Bridging** Apply increasing understanding of language resources for referring the reader back or forward in text (e.g., how pronouns, synonyms, or nominalizations refer back to nouns in text) to comprehending texts and writing cohesive texts.	**5-1:** T134, S39 **5-2:** T111, T153, T189, T209, **5-3:** T34, T35, T53, T54, T55, T92, T296, T297, T304 **5-4:** T50, T173, T182, T183, T203, T274, T275, T276, T277, S38 **5-5:** T354 **5-6:** T361, S32
ELD.PII.5.2b	**Emerging** Apply basic understanding of how ideas, events, or reasons are linked throughout a text using a select set of everyday connecting words or phrases (e.g., *first/next, at the beginning*) to comprehending texts and writing basic texts. **Expanding** Apply growing understanding of how ideas, events, or reasons are linked throughout a text using a variety of connecting words or phrases (e.g., *for example, in the first place, as a result*) to comprehending texts and writing texts with increasing cohesion. **Bridging** Apply increasing understanding of how ideas, events, or reasons are linked throughout a text using an increasing variety of academic connecting and transitional words or phrases (e.g., *consequently, specifically, however*) to comprehending texts and writing cohesive texts.	**5-1:** T33, T51, T261, T298, T199, T300, T301, T304, T337, T366, S10, S14, S24, S25, S30, S31 **5-2:** T207, T263, T281, T364, T365, T403, T405, T418, T425, S36, S46, S50 **5-3:** T57, T109, T356, T357, T358, T359, T368, T369, S2, S8, S36, S38, S42, S44, S46, S48 **5-4:** T33, T176, T200, T364, T365, T366, S51 **5-5:** T59, T219, T362, T364, S4, S18, S34, S36 **5-6:** T18, T21, T69, T74, T171, T208, T326, T368, S6, S28, S34, S45
B. EXPANDING & ENRICHING IDEAS		
3. Using verbs and verb phrases		
ELD.PII.5.3	**Emerging** Use frequently used verbs (e.g., take, like, eat) and various verb types (e.g., doing, saying, being/having, thinking/feeling) and tenses appropriate for the text type and discipline (e.g., simple past for recounting an experience) on familiar topics. **Expanding** Use various verb types (e.g., doing, saying, being/having, thinking/feeling) and tenses appropriate for the task, text type, and discipline (e.g., simple past for recounting an experience, timeless present for a science description) on an increasing variety of topics. **Bridging** Use various verb types (e.g., doing, saying, being/having, thinking/feeling) and tenses appropriate for the task and text type (e.g., timeless present for science description, mixture of past and present for narrative or history explanation) on a variety of topics.	**5-1:** T52, T132, T179, T189, T259, T264, T285, T338, T355, T367, S15 **5-2:** T54, T55, T56, T57, T94, T153, T194, T208, T258, T261, T324, T336, T337, T354, T357, S2 **5-3:** T14, T40, T132, T133, T134, T135, T157, T206, T207, T208, T209, T231, T282, T284, T340, T341, T358, T361, S13, S18, S22, S26, S28 **5-4:** T49, T105, T126, T127, T130, T28, S32 **5-5:** T14, T54, T55, T56, T79, T92, T128, T129, T130, T153, T202, T203, T204, T206, T227, T277, T350, T351, T352, S2, S8, S12, S15, S18, S20, S22 **5-6:** T86, T160
4. Using nouns and noun phrases		
ELD.PII.5.4	**Emerging** Expand noun phrases in simple ways (e.g., adding an adjective to a noun) in order to enrich the meaning of sentences and add details about ideas, people, things, etc. **Expanding** Expand noun phrases in a variety of ways (e.g., adding comparative/ superlative adjectives to noun phrases or simple clause embedding) in order to enrich the meaning of sentences and add details about ideas, people, things, etc. **Bridging** Expand noun phrases in an increasing variety of ways (e.g., adding comparative/superlative and general academic adjectives to noun phrases or more complex clause embedding) in order to enrich the meaning of sentences and add details about ideas, people, things, etc.	**5-1:** T21, T31, T50, T190, T210, T211, T280, T281, T282, T283, T305, T354, T355, T356, T357, T383 **5-2:** T262, T263, T280, T283, T350, T366 **5-3:** T56, T246 **5-4:** T48, T49, T50, T52, T73, T201, T250, T258, T259, T277, T279, T299, T356, S16, S32 **5-5:** T106, T133, T166, T204, T278, T279, T316, S32 **5-6:** T122, T161, T206, S2, S8
5. Modifying to add details		
ELD.PII.5.5	**Emerging** Expand and enrich sentences with adverbials (e.g., adverbs, adverb phrases, prepositional phrases) to provide details (e.g., time, manner, place, cause, etc.) about a familiar activity or process. **Expanding** Expand and enrich sentences with adverbials (e.g., adverbs, adverb phrases, prepositional phrases) to provide details (e.g., time, manner, place, cause, etc.) about a familiar or new activity or process. **Bridging** Expand and enrich sentences with adverbials (e.g., adverbs, adverb phrases, prepositional phrases) to provide details (e.g., time, manner, place, cause, etc.) about a variety of familiar and new activities and processes.	**5-1:** T32, T98, T108, T134, T135, T170, T248, T284, T318, T359, S6 **5-2:** T112, T132, T181, T187 **5-3:** T92, T360 **5-4:** T51, T98, T110, T111, T126, T127, T130, T131, T151, T198, T200, T202, T223, T238, T249, T312, T356, S16, S18, S22, S26, S28 **5-5:** T94, T200, T201, T240, T277, T314, S28, S40 **5-6:** T31, T170, T218, T219, S20

Standard	Standard Language	Key Citations

C. CONNECTING & CONDENSING IDEAS

6. Connecting ideas

Standard	Standard Language	Key Citations
ELD.PII.5.6	**Emerging** Combine clauses in a few basic ways to make connections between and join ideas (e.g., You must X because X.) or to provide evidence to support ideas or opinions (e.g., creating compound sentences using *and, but, so*). **Expanding** Combine clauses in an increasing variety of ways (e.g., creating compound and complex sentences) to make connections between and join ideas, for example, to express cause/effect (e.g., *The deer ran because the mountain lion came.*), to make a concession (e.g., *She studied all night even though she wasn't feeling well.*), or to provide reasons to support ideas (e.g., X is an *extremely good book because* X.). **Bridging** Combine clauses in a wide variety of ways (e.g., creating compound and complex sentences) to make connections between and join ideas, for example, to express cause/effect (e.g., *The deer ran because the mountain lion approached them.*), to make a concession (e.g., *She studied all night even though she wasn't feeling well.*), to link two ideas that happen at the same time (e.g., *The cubs played while their mother hunted.*), or to provide reasons to support ideas (e.g., *The author persuades the reader by* X.).	**5-1:** T65, T207, T210, T211, T263, T282 **5-2:** T24, T36, T37, T59, T204, T205, T206, T207, T278, T279, T280, T281, T303, T340, T364, T401, T403, T413, S4, S8, S12, S22, S28, S32, S38, S46 **5-3:** T110, T134, T136, T137, T148, T149, T358, T360, T369, S4, S24, S46 **5-4:** T199, T200, T236, T337, T365, T366 **5-5:** T22, T58, T362, T363, T364 **5-6:** S36, S38

7. Condensing ideas

Standard	Standard Language	Key Citations
ELD.PII.5.7	**Emerging** Condense clauses in simple ways (e.g., through simple embedded clauses as in, *The book is on the desk. The book is mine. ---> The book that is on the desk is mine.*) to create precise and detailed sentences. **Expanding** Condense clauses in an increasing variety of ways (e.g., through a growing number of types of embedded clauses and other condensing as in, *The book is mine. The book is on the desk. The book is about science. ---> The science book that's on the desk is mine.*) to create precise and detailed sentences. **Bridging** Condense clauses in a variety of ways (e.g., through various types of embedded clauses and some nominalizations as in, *They were a very strong army. They had a lot of enemies. They crushed their enemies because they were strong. ---> Their strength helped them crush their numerous enemies.*) to create precise and detailed sentences.	**5-1:** T65, T207, T210, T211, T263, T282, **5-2:** T24, T36, T37, T59, T204, T205, T206, T207, T278, T279, T280, T281, T303, T340, T364, T401, T403, T413, S4, S8, S12, S22, S28, S32, S38, S46 **5-3:** T110, T134, T136, T137, T148, T149, T358, T360, T369, S4, S24, S46 **5-4:** T199, T200, T236, T337, T365, T366 **5-5:** T31, T58, T178, T362, T363, T364 **5-6:** S36, S38

Part III: USING FOUNDATIONAL LITERACY SKILLS

Foundational Literacy Skills (See Appendix A-Grade 5):

Standard	Standard Language	Key Citations
ELD.PIII.5	Literacy in an Alphabetic Writing System • Print concepts • Phonological awareness • Phonics & word recognition • Fluency	**5-1:** T44, T45, T46, T126, T127, T128, T202, T203, T204, T276, T277, T278, T350, T351, T352, S4, S5, S6, S7, S8, S9, S10, S11, S14, S15, S16, S18, S19, S20, S23, S24, S25, S26, S27, S28, S29, S30, S31, S33, S34, S35, S36, S37, S38, S39, S40, S41, S42, S43, S44, S45, S46, S47, S49, S50, S51 **5-2:** T50, T51, T52, T124, T125, T126, T200, T201, T202, T274, T275, T276, T348, T349, T350, S2, S3, S4, S5, S7, S8, S9, S10, S11, S13, S14, S15, S16, S17, S18, S19, S20, S23, S24, S25, S26, S27, S28, S29, S31, S34, S35, S36, S37, S38, S39, S40, S41, S42, S43, S44, S45, S46, S47, S48, S49, S50, S51 **5-3:** T41, T48, T49, T50, T115, T128, T129, T130, T195, T202, T203, T204, T276, T277, T278, T345, T352, T353, T354, S3, S4, S6, S7, S8, S10, S13, S14, S15, S16, S17, S18, S20, S23, S24, S25, S26, S27, S28, S30, S33, S34, S35, S36, S37, S38, S40, S43, S44, S45, S46, S47, S48, S50 **5-4:** T44, T45, T46, T122, T123, T124, T194, T195, T196, T263, T270, T271, T272, T341, T348, T349, T350, S3, S4, S5, S6, S7, S8, S10, S13, S14, S15, S16, S17, S18, S20, S23, S24, S25, S26, S27, S28, S30, S33, S34, S35, S36, S37, S38, S40, S43, S44, S45, S46, S47, S48, S50 **5-5:** T43, T50, T51, T52, T124, T125, T126, T198, T199, T200, T265, T272, T273, T274, T346, T347, T348, S3, S4, S5, S6, S7, S8, S10, S13, S14, S15, S16, S17, S18, S20, S23, S24, S25, S26, S27, S28, S33, S34, S35, S36, S37, S38, S40, S42, S43, S44, S45, S46, S47 **5-6:** T19, T25, T27, T36, T37, T38, T67, T73, T75, T84, T85, T86, T115, T119, T121, T130, T131, T132, T159, T165, T167, T176, T177, T178, T207, T213, T215, T224, T225, T226, S3, S4, S5, S6, S7, S8, S9, S11, S13, S14, S15, S16, S17, S18, S19, S21, S23, S25, S26, S27, S28, S30, S33, S34, S35, S36, S37, S38, S43, S45, S46, S47, S48, S50

Teacher Notes

 **JOURNEYS**

 **Anchor Text**

 **Paired Selection**

DIGITAL RESOURCES

Teacher Dashboard

Log onto the Teacher Dashboard and *my*SmartPlanner. Use these searchable tools to customize lessons that achieve your instructional goals.

Interactive Whiteboard Lessons

- Grammar: Verbs
- Vocabulary Strategies: Synonyms and Antonyms

- Write About Reading
- Informative Writing: Procedural Composition

Interactive Lessons

▶ Participating in Collaborative Discussions
▶ Writing to Sources
▶ Informative Writing

✓ **Assess It Online!**

- Weekly Tests
- Assessment-driven instruction with prescriptive feedback

Student eBook

✎ **Annotate it!** Strategies for Annotation

Guide students to use digital tools for close reading.

Students may also use the interactive features in their Student eBooks to respond to prompts in a variety of ways, including:

- short-answer response
- spoken response
- fill-in-the-blank
- drag-and-drop
- multiple choice

fyi
hmhfyi.com

High-Interest Informational Texts and Multimedia

Have students explore the FYI website for additional information about topics of study.

ENGLISH LANGUAGE SUPPORT

Culturally Responsive Teaching

Endangered Animals of the World Tell students that this week, they will be reading and thinking about endangered animals.

- Create a classroom display about endangered animals of the world. Invite students to add labeled drawings and images of endangered animals in different parts of the world to the display.

- Invite English learners to teach the class the names for different endangered animals in their home languages, and add the information to the display.

- During the week, encourage students to find and share information about an endangered animal, and explain if its situation is improving or if its situation is worsening.

- Have students create a "How You Can Help" action exhibit, and post ways people can support efforts to help or protect endangered animals.

Activate Background Knowledge To prepare for and support discussing concepts about wildlife and world regions, find out what your English learners already know. Use visuals to present different wildlife species, and the regions in which they live. Guide students to identify and describe what they know about the images or the region.

Language Support Card

Use the Lesson 6 Language Support Card to activate prior knowledge, frontload vocabulary, and teach academic English.

 TEXT X-RAY

Use the Text X-Ray on page T9 to review the language demands of "Quest for the Tree Kangaroo" with the needs of English learners in mind.

Language Workshop for Designated ELD

- Connection to Essential Question
- Vocabulary Network
- Focus on Interacting in Meaningful Ways
- Discussion Frames
- How English Works
- Word Learning Strategies

You may wish to use the following suggestions to modify instruction for some students, according to their needs.

Classroom Routines and Access

For students who do well with a predictable structure, continue to provide a classroom schedule in writing, as well as visually and orally. You may want to use some or all of these strategies to improve access:

- Meet with each student who has special needs to determine which parts of the day are most rewarding and most challenging, and make adjustments.
- Consider allowing some students to skip a particular responsibility to gain more time for another activity or for transitioning.
- Allow more breaks as needed to avoid discomfort.
- For a student who uses large-print materials, provide a large reading surface.
- For a student who uses a wheelchair, ensure clear access to his or her seating area.
- A student who uses American Sign Language may benefit from an interpreter to help him or her fully access instruction and discussion.
- Assess whether seating arrangements and routines are successfully minimizing distractions.

Flexible Learning Environment

Use the following modifications as needed.

- **Provide Extra Time** for completing seatwork or for transitioning, for example, by having some students begin to clear work areas before others.
- **Break Down Directions and Tasks** into smaller chunks. Provide visuals when possible. Ask students to restate directions in their own words to ensure they understand what they are to do.
- **Use Alternative Methods for Student Response** to prepare them to complete their assignments. For example, have students share their ideas orally or by drawing a picture as preparation for writing.

Student eBook

- **Audio** can be activated to support fluency, decoding, and comprehension.
- **Alternative Text** provides spoken information that can be used in place of the information provided in the book's images.
- **Vocabulary Pop-Ups** contain point-of-use definitions for selection vocabulary.

Theatre

Collaborate to Dramatize Scenes Have small groups work collaboratively to dramatize and present scenes from "Quest for the Tree Kangaroo."

- Choose sections from "Quest for the Tree Kangaroo" that students can dramatize for informal performances.
- Help students organize themselves into groups, and assign a scene to each group.
- Have group members choose roles, such as director or co-directors, actors, and technical director. While the directors work together to discuss the best ways to dramatize the scene, actors can work together to read and rehearse their lines.
- Provide time for groups to collaborate and rehearse, try different methods, and then have them present their dramatized scenes for the class.
- Invite groups to debrief and share what they learned from the collaboration, such as challenges the group encountered, and effective ideas and solutions they came up with.
- To extend the activity, encourage groups to create a video recording of their dramatized scenes.

DOMAIN: **Life Science**

LESSON TOPIC: **Wild Animals**

LESSON **6**

Our Focus Wall

ANCHOR TEXT

Quest for the Tree Kangaroo
Informational Text

Why Koala Has No Tail
Myth

ESSENTIAL QUESTION

Why is it important to research and protect endangered animals?

WRITING

Writing

Informative Writing:
Procedural Composition

Focus Trait: Organization

READING LITERATURE & INFORMATIONAL TEXT

Comprehension Skills and Strategies

☑ **TARGET SKILL**
- Cause and Effect
- Quotes and Description
- Domain-Specific Vocabulary

☑ **TARGET STRATEGY**
- Question

FOUNDATIONAL SKILLS

Fluency

Expression

Decoding

Common Beginning Syllables

LANGUAGE

☑ Target Vocabulary

dwarfed	calculate
presence	snug
procedure	perch
outfitted	enthusiastic
transferred	beaming

Spelling

Vowel + /r/ Sounds

glory	barely
aware	torch
carton	barge
adore	soar
aboard	beware
dairy	absorb
ordeal	armor
pardon	stairway
warn	perform
vary	former

Grammar

Verbs

Vocabulary Strategies

Synonyms and Antonyms

Whole Group Resources

Quest for the Tree Kangaroo
GENRE: Informational Text

TEXT X-RAY

Prepare for Complex Texts For a comprehensive overview and analysis of key ideas and academic language features of this lesson's Anchor Text, see pages T8–T9.

Why Koala Has No Tail
GENRE: Myth
21st Century Theme: Environmental Literacy

Digital Resources

▶ **eBook: Annotate It!**

▶ **Interactive Whiteboard Lessons**
• Vocabulary Strategies: Synonyms and Antonyms
• Grammar: Verbs

▶ **Multimedia Grammar Glossary**

▶ *my*SmartPlanner

▶ **Parent Resource**

Additional Resources
• Vocabulary in Context Cards 51–60
• Reader's Notebook, pp. 61–72
• Lesson 6 Blackline Masters
• Literacy and Language Guide

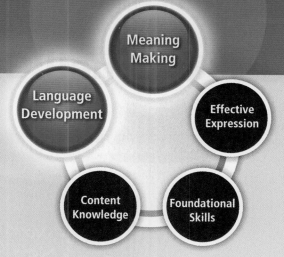

LINGUISTICALLY DIVERSE LEARNERS

∨ Integrated English Language Support

● Interacting in Meaningful Ways

Classroom Conversations
- Talk About It, p. T17
- Collaborative Conversation, pp. T12, T32, T36

Interactive and Collaborative Writing
- Question, p. T32
- Write About Reading, p. T37
- Procedural Composition, p. T58

Self-Selected Reading, p. T38

Sentence Frames for Writing, pp. T49, T58

● Learning About How English Works

Scaffold the Texts
- Text X-Ray: Focus on Academic Language, p. T9
- Connecting Ideas, pp. T24, T36, T59

Language Detective
- Target Vocabulary, p. T14
- The Language of Science Texts, p. T31

Communicative Modes
- Write About Reading, p. T37
- Procedural Composition, p. T58

● Using Foundational Literacy Skills

Fluency: Expression, p. T50
Decoding: Common Beginning Syllables, p. T51

Apply Language Skills
- Verbs, p. T54

Support Linguistic Transfer
- Synonyms and Antonyms, p. T46
- Vowel + /r/ Sounds, p. T52
- Verbs, p. T54

∨ Standard English Learners

- Pronunciation: Voicing /l/, p. T23
- Verbs, p. T56

ASSESSMENT

● Formative Assessment
- Target Vocabulary, p. T15
- Target Strategy: Question, pp. T22, T30
- Target Skill: Story Structure, p. T35
- Vocabulary Strategies: Synonyms and Antonyms, p. T46
- Decoding: Common Beginning Syllables, p. T51
- Using Data to Adjust Instruction, p. T63

● ✓ Assess It Online!
- Weekly Tests

Performance Tasks
- Write About Reading, p. T37
- Write an Explanatory Essay, p. T364

Vocabulary Reader

The Lost World of Papua New Guinea
by David Martin

HOUGHTON MIFFLIN HARCOURT

Vocabulary Reader
for all levels

Provide strategic scaffolding to support all students in reading on-level text and in acquiring general academic and domain-specific vocabulary. Use the instructional supports on pp. T68–T69 or the Leveled Reader Teacher's Guide.

Guided Reading Level: R

Lexile: 1010L

DRA: 40

Leveled Reader Teacher's Guide

Weekly Leveled Readers

Guide students to read and comprehend additional texts about the lesson topic. Use the instructional supports on pp. T72–T75 or the Leveled Reader Teacher's Guides.

Struggling Readers

Guided Reading Level: S

Lexile: 850L

DRA: 790L

Leveled Reader Teacher's Guide

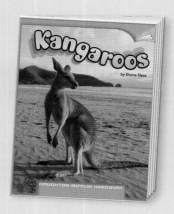

Kangaroos
by Elaine Ness

HOUGHTON MIFFLIN HARCOURT

On Level

Guided Reading Level: T

Lexile: 1230L

DRA: 44

Leveled Reader Teacher's Guide

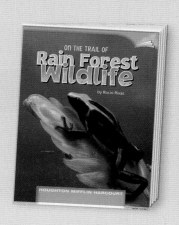

ON THE TRAIL OF
Rain Forest Wildlife
by Rocio Rivas

HOUGHTON MIFFLIN HARCOURT

Advanced

Guided Reading Level: U

Lexile: 1040L

DRA: 50

Leveled Reader Teacher's Guide

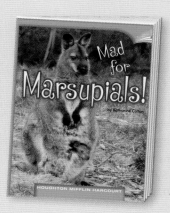

Mad for Marsupials!
by Katharine Cotton

HOUGHTON MIFFLIN HARCOURT

English Language Learners

Guided Reading Level: T

Lexile: 960L

DRA: 44

Leveled Reader Teacher's Guide

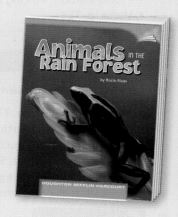

Animals in the Rain Forest
by Rocio Rivas

HOUGHTON MIFFLIN HARCOURT

Language Workshop for Designated ELD

- Provides reteaching and practice in the key foundational skills for reading: print concepts, phonological/phonemic awareness, phonics and word recognition, and fluency.

- Explicit, sequential, and systematic instruction designed to bring students up to grade level.

- Screening and Diagnostic Assessments (within Intervention Assessments) place individual students within the system.

Lesson 6 Focus

Collaborate: Gain and Hold the Floor

Interpret: Distinguish Among Different Words' Effects

Produce: Use Modal Expressions To Express Ideas

How English Works: Connect Ideas

Vocabulary Network

Intervention

 Strategic Intervention Tier II

Write-In Reader: *Will the American Chestnut Survive?*

- Interactive worktext with selection that connects to the lesson topic
- Reinforces the lesson's vocabulary and comprehension
- Build skills for reading increasingly complex texts
- Online version with dual-speed audio and follow-text

Daily Lessons See this week's daily Strategic Intervention Lesson on pp. S2–S11.

- Preteach and Reteach daily instruction
- Oral Grammar
- Decoding
- Comprehension
- Fluency
- Grammar
- Written Response
- Unpack Meaning
- Return to Anchor Text

 Decoding Power: Intensive Intervention

- Provides reteaching and practice in the key foundational skills for reading: print concepts, phonological/phonemic awareness, phonics and word recognition, and fluency.

- Explicit, sequential, and systematic instruction designed to bring students up to grade level.

- Screening and Diagnostic Assessments (within Intervention Assessments) place individual students within the system.

✓ Assess It Online!

▶ **Screening and Diagnostic Assessments** (within Intervention Assessments) place individual students within the system.

▶ **Progress-Monitoring Assessments** (within Intervention Assessments) ensure students are making satisfactory progress and provide a measure of student readiness to exit the system.

What My Other Students Are Doing

Digital Resources

▶ **Literacy Centers:** Word Study, Think and Write, Comprehension and Fluency

▶ **Interactive Lessons:** Writing to Sources, Writing Informative Texts: Introduction, Participating in Collaborative Discussions

⦿ Additional Resources

- Vocabulary in Context Cards 51–60
- Reader's Notebook, pp. 61–72
- Independent Reading
- Lesson 6 Blackline Masters

LESSON 6

Literacy Centers

Managing Independent Activities

Comprehension and Fluency

Materials
- Student Book
- self-stick notes
- computer with Internet access
- Reading Log
- pencil or pen

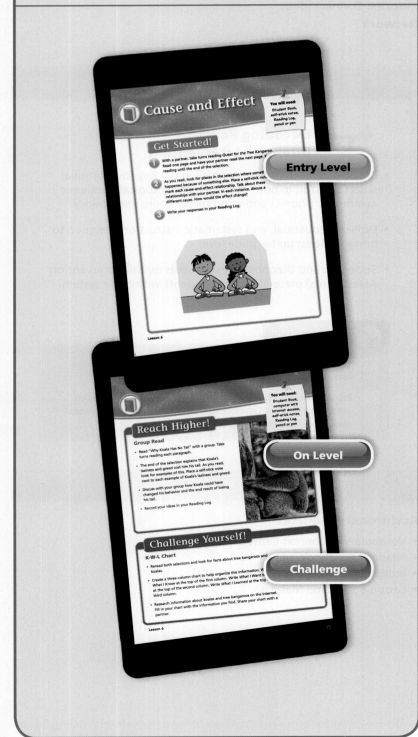

Word Study

Materials
- Student Book
- index cards
- thesaurus
- paper
- pencil or pen

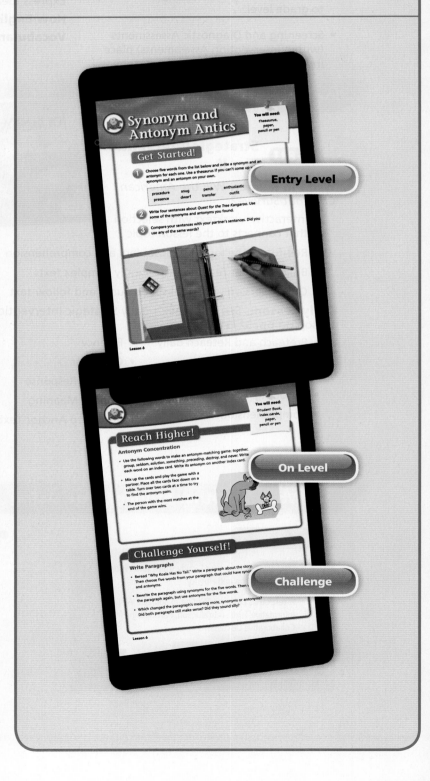

Assign Literacy Center activities during small group time. Each center contains three activities. Students who experience success with the entry-level activity move on to the on-level and challenge activities, as time permits.

Meaning Making

Effective Expression

Language Development

Content Knowledge

Foundational Skills

Think and Write

Materials
- computer with Internet access
- paper, index cards, poster board
- pencil, pen, colored markers
- old magazines

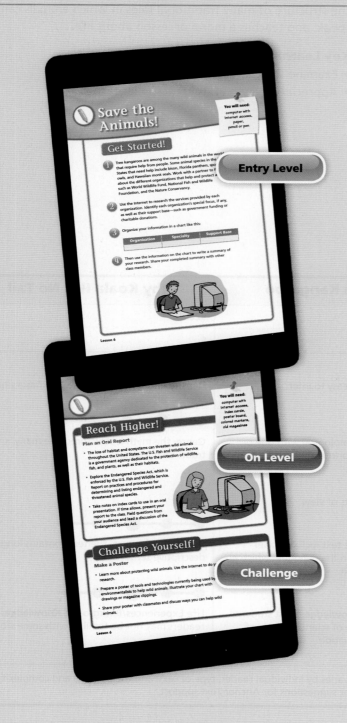

Entry Level

On Level

Challenge

Independent Reading

Book Selection Strategies Help students develop strategies to select books based on difficulty, content, and interest. Introduce these strategies separately:

- **Five-Finger Method** Students read from one to a few pages of the book, depending on the number of words per page. They count their miscues on their fingers. If they miss five or more words, the book is probably too hard for independent reading. If they miss three words, the book is probably at their independent level. If they miss no words or one word, the book may be too easy.

- **Book Walk** Students browse through the book. They look at the amount of text, the ratio of pictures to text, and the length and complexity of the captions. Students determine if they are interested enough to read the entire book.

See p. T38 for additional independent reading support.

See p. T38 for additional independent reading support.

ELA RL.5.10, RI.5.10

Prepare for Complex Texts

Quest for the Tree Kangaroo
by Sy Montgomery

GENRE: Informational Text

Why This Text?

Students regularly encounter informational text in reading textbooks, periodicals, and their own independent reading. This text relates the work of a team of scientists who are trying to study the elusive Matschie's tree kangaroo in Papua New Guinea. It gives insight into the scientific field through a familiar narrative structure.

Key Learning Objectives
• Explore the relationship between cause and effect.
• Examine the use of quotations and descriptions in a text.
• Identify and learn domain-specific vocabulary.

"Why Koala Has No Tail"
by Vivian Fernandez

GENRE: Myth

Why This Text?

Students encounter myths in textbooks, literature anthologies, and magazines. This myth explains physical traits of the koala. The text follows the structure of many traditional tales in which animals can speak, and teaches a moral or lesson about life.

Key Learning Objectives
• Examine the characteristics of myths.
• Appreciate a myth and the lesson it teaches.

⚠ TEXT COMPLEXITY RUBRIC

		Quest for the Tree Kangaroo	Why Koala Has No Tail
Quantitative Measures	Lexile	1010L	920L
	Guided Reading Level	V	S
Qualitative Measures	Meaning and Purpose	**Purpose:** the purpose is implied but easy to infer.	**Density and Complexity:** the text has a single level of simple meaning.
	Text Structure	**Organization:** the text is mostly chronological with one or two flashbacks and descriptions of concurrent events. **Narration:** the text has shifting points of view.	**Genre:** the myth is structured like many traditional folktales.
	Language Features	**Standard English and Variations:** the text includes brief examples of a creole language within the dialogue, which are explained in footnotes and in context.	**Sentence Structure:** the text contains longer, descriptive sentences.
Knowledge Demands		**Subject Matter Knowledge/Prior Knowledge:** most students will possess at least basic knowledge of scientific study of wildlife through tracking and observation.	**Life Experiences/Background Knowledge:** readers may not be familiar with some story concepts
Reader/Task Considerations		Determine using the professional judgment of the teacher. This varies by individual reader, type of text, and the purpose and complexity of particular tasks. See **Reader and Task Considerations** on p. T19 for suggestions for Anchor Text support.	

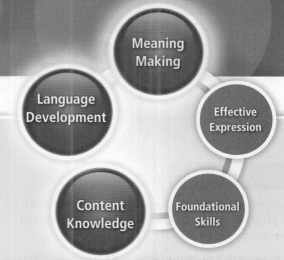

 ENGLISH LANGUAGE SUPPORT Use the Text X-Ray below to prepare for teaching the Anchor Text. Use it to plan, support, and scaffold instruction in order to help students understand the text's **key ideas** and **academic language features**.

Zoom In on Key Ideas
Students should understand these **key ideas** after reading *Quest for the Tree Kangaroo*.

Key Idea | pp. 176–179
The author and photographer have joined a team of scientists in Papua New Guinea who want to study a hard-to-find animal known as the Matschie's tree kangaroo. Once located and trapped, the animals will be fitted with radio collars and returned to the wild so the scientists can learn more about and help to protect the species..

Key Idea | pp. 179–183
The trackers use sticks and brush to build a low fence around the tree. Three trackers get ahold of an adult male and an adult female tree kangaroo. The animals are carried back to camp, where each animal is put to sleep with anesthesia in order to insert tracking devices and identification chips.

Key Idea | pp. 183–189
The radio tracking collars will be put in place. These will transmit signals to the scientists, recording their location twice a day. The information is downloaded to the chips.

The scientists work very quickly on the female. They give the animal a vitamin injection, check teeth, and put the it back in the sack, just as it starts to regain consciousness. It takes four men to hold the male down until the anesthesia kicks in. In just ten minutes, their work on the male is over.

Key Idea | p. 189
The team has built a two-room enclosure to shelter the tree kangaroos for a short time before releasing them to the wild. The collars are tested and working well. Everyone is pleased with their success. They even made history by being the first to collar a male Matschie's tree kangaroo.

Zoom In on Academic Language
Guide students at different proficiencies and skill levels to understand the structure and language of this text.

Focus: Text Level | pp. 176–189
Students may have some difficulty following the narrative. Point out that the first section of the narrative is in the present tense. The second section on p. 179 is a **flashback** to earlier that morning and explains how the animals were first spotted.

Focus: Word Level | p. 177
Support English learners and others in understanding the term *tree 'roo* in the second line on p. 177. If they have difficulty, remind them that the title of the selection and the introduction on p. 176 refer to the *tree kangaroo,* then elicit from or remind students that an **apostrophe** can be used to indicate that part of a word is missing.

Focus: Sentence Level | p. 177–189
On p. 177, point out the following sentences: "Lisa is washing her clothes *when* we get the news," and "It takes us *nearly an hour* to reach the site." Ask students which event happens first? Next? Have students note other indicators of time and sequence.

Focus: Word Level | pp. 183, 185
Domain-specific vocabulary is a common feature of informational texts. You may preview words and phrases, such as *degrees Fahrenheit,* (most non-Americans will be more familiar with *degrees Celsius* and the *centigrade* system), *humidity, anesthesia, respiration,* and *stethoscope.*

Content and Language Instruction Make note of additional **content knowledge** and **language features** students may find challenging in this text.

Weekly Planner

my SmartPlanner

Auto-populates the suggested five-day lesson plan and offers flexibility to create and save customized plans from year to year.

See **Standards Correlations** on p. C1. In your eBook, click the Standards button in the left panel to view descriptions of the standards on the page.

	DAY 1	DAY 2
	Materials • ELL Blackline Masters 6.2, 6.3 • Graphic Organizer 13 • Lesson 6 Language Support Card • Literacy and Language Guide p. 66 • Projectables 6.1, 6.4, 6.7 • Reader's Notebook pp. 64, 67 • Strategy Projectables S1–S8 • Student Book pp. 170–189 • Vocabulary in Context Cards 51–60	**Materials** • Graphic Organizer 13 • Interactive Lessons: Listening and Responding, Writing to Sources • Literacy and Language Guide p. 66 • Projectables 6.2, 6.5 • Reader's Notebook pp. 65, 68, 72 • Student Book pp. 174–193

Whole Group

Oral Language
Listening
Comprehension

Teacher Read Aloud
"America's Eagle," T12–T13

Turn and Talk, T36

Vocabulary
Text-Based Comprehension
• Skills and Strategies
• Craft and Structure

Research and Media Literacy

☑ **Introduce Vocabulary**
Vocabulary in Context, T14–T15
☑ **Read and Comprehend,** T16–T17
FIRST READ **Think Through the Text**
Read the Anchor Text:
"Quest for the Tree Kangaroo," T18–T33
Research/Media Literacy, T49

SECOND READ
☑ **Dig Deeper: How to Analyze the Text,** T34–T35
• Cause and Effect
• Quotes and Description
• Domain-Specific Vocabulary
• The Language of Science Texts
Analyze the Text
Reread the Anchor Text: "Quest for the Tree Kangaroo," T23, T27, T29
☑ **Your Turn,** T36–T37
Research/Media Literacy, T49

Foundational Skills
• Fluency
• Decoding

☑ **Fluency**
Model Expression, T12

☑ **Fluency**
Teach Expression, T50
Practice Expression, T21

Whole Group Language Arts

Spelling
Grammar
Writing

☑ **Spelling**
Vowel + /r/ Sounds: Pretest, T52
☑ **Grammar**
Daily Proofreading Practice, T54
Teach Verbs, T54
☑ **Informative Writing: Procedural Composition**
Analyze the Model, T58

☑ **Spelling**
Vowel + /r/ Sounds: Word Sort, T52
☑ **Grammar**
Daily Proofreading Practice, T55
Teach Main and Helping Verbs, T55
☑ **Informative Writing: Procedural Composition**
Focus Trait: Organization, T59

Small Group

 Suggestions for Small Groups (See pp. T66–T67.)

DAY 3

Materials
- Instructional Routine 6
- Literacy and Language Guide pp. 67, 126–127
- Projectables 6.6, 6.8
- Reading Log Blackline Master
- Reader's Notebook pp. 61–62, 69
- Student Book pp. 174–189

Classroom Collaboration, T39

Independent Reading, T38
- Reader's Guide: "Quest for the Tree Kangaroo"
- Self-Selected Reading

Apply Vocabulary Knowledge, T39
Research/Media Literacy, T49

☑ **Decoding**
Common Beginning Syllables, T51
☑ **Fluency**
Practice Expression, T21

☑ **Spelling**
Vowel + /r/ Sounds: Word Families, T53
☑ **Grammar**
Daily Proofreading Practice, T55
Teach Verb Tenses, T55
☑ **Informative Writing: Procedural Composition**
Prewrite, T59

DAY 4

Materials
- Interactive Whiteboard Lesson: Synonyms and Antonyms
- Literacy and Language Guide pp. 126–127
- Projectable 6.3
- Reader's Notebook pp. 63, 66, 70
- Student Book pp. 194–199

Classroom Conversation, T40

Connect to the Topic
- Read Myth: "Why Koala Has No Tail," T40
- Think Through the Text, T41, T42, T44
☑ **Compare Texts,** T45
☑ **Vocabulary Strategies**
Synonyms and Antonyms, T46–T47
Research/Media Literacy, T49

☑ **Fluency**
Practice Expression, T43

☑ **Spelling**
Vowel + /r/ Sounds: Connect to Writing, T53
☑ **Grammar**
Daily Proofreading Practice, T56
Review Verbs, T56
☑ **Informative Writing: Procedural Composition**
Draft, T60

DAY 5

Materials
- Cold Reads
- Graphic Organizer 6
- Interactive Lessons: Participate in Collaborative Conversations, Writing Informative Texts: Introduction
- Interactive Whiteboard Lesson: Verbs
- Projectable 6.9
- Proofreading Checklist Blackline Master
- Reader's Notebook p. 71
- Student Book pp. 200–203
- Writing Rubric Blackline Master

Speaking and Listening, T49

Extend the Topic: Wild Animals
- Domain-Specific Vocabulary, T48
- Research/Media Literacy, T49
- Optional Second Read: "Why Koala Has No Tail," T40

☑ **Fluency**
Progress Monitoring, T63

☑ **Spelling**
Vowel + /r/ Sounds: Assess, T53
☑ **Grammar**
Daily Proofreading Practice, T56
Connect Grammar to Writing, T56–T57
☑ **Informative Writing: Procedural Composition**
Revise for Organization, T60

Tier II Intervention provides thirty minutes of additional daily practice with key parts of the core instruction. See pp. S2–S11.

Teacher Read Aloud

- Listen to fluent reading.
- Identify details to comprehend a text.
- Summarize a text that is read aloud by condensing ideas. LANGUAGE

ENGLISH LANGUAGE SUPPORT
Use Visuals

All Proficiencies To assist students with accessing the content and topic of the Teacher Read Aloud, discuss the High-Utility Words on the Lesson 6 Language Support Card ⬆.

✓ PREVIEW
Target Vocabulary

presence current existence

outfitted equipped

procedure method

dwarfed made smaller by comparison

snug close fitting

perch a spot above ground for resting or sitting

transferred passed from one place to another

calculate to figure; to compute

enthusiastic showing a high or excited interest

beaming smiling radiantly

Model Fluency

Expression Explain that good readers read with expression by changing the tone and volume of their voices and stressing certain words and phrases to convey meaning in a text.

- Display Projectable 6.1 ⬆. Read a few sentences without expression. Then reread the same sentences with expression to demonstrate the difference.

- Explain that punctuation and the context of the selection provide clues about the expression a reader should use when reading aloud.

- Reread the sentences aloud with students, modeling appropriate expression. **ELA** RF.5.4a, RF.5.4b

Listening Comprehension

Read aloud the selection. Pause at the numbered stopping points to ask students the questions below. Discuss the meanings of the highlighted words, as needed, to support the discussion.

1 *Why does the author consider the sighting of a bald eagle's nest a sign of hope? It could mean that in the past, eagles were threatened in some way. The nest is a sign that eagles are present and breeding, so it is hopeful.* **MAKE INFERENCES**

2 *What details support the idea that bald eagles make excellent parents? They are good nest builders, they take turns warming the eggs, they watch out for predators, and they feed their young small bits of food at a time.* **SUPPORTING DETAILS**

3 *What caused bald eagle populations to decline and then to recover? Eagle numbers dropped due to hunting, loss of habitat, and use of pesticides that harmed the eagles by entering their food supply. Eagles recovered once waterways were cleaned, harmful pesticides were banned, and nesting sites were protected.* **CAUSE AND EFFECT**
ELA SL.5.2a

💬 Classroom Collaboration

Ask students to describe the information found in *America's Eagle*, condensing their ideas into a brief summary. *The bald eagle is a bird of prey whose nesting sites include the area of the upper Mississippi River. Its characteristics include impressive nest building, good parenting, and excellent hunting skills. Its once very large population dropped after the arrival of European settlers. Recently numbers have grown, and the eagle is thriving.*
ELA SL.5.2 **ELD** ELD.PI.5.1, ELD.PI.5.5, ELD.PII.5.7

ENGLISH LANGUAGE SUPPORT

Read Aloud—Second Read Project the Target Vocabulary Preview. Introduce each word to students. Use visuals, gestures, or yes/no questions to help them understand the meaning of each word. Have students listen to the Read Aloud again and signal when they hear a Target Vocabulary Word. **ELD** ELD.PI.5.5

America's Eagle

1 Along the upper Mississippi River is an increasingly familiar sight. In the high branches of a winter-bare tree sits a giant-sized bird's nest. The **presence** of such a large nest near the water is a sign of hope. Bald eagles may be nesting there.

Although the feathers on their bodies are brown, bald eagles have white feathers on their tails and heads. The wingspan of the larger adult female can reach 8 feet (2.5 meters). The male's wingspan reaches about 6.5 feet (2 meters).

Eagles are expert nest-builders—they have to be. Their nests must be **outfitted** to withstand harsh winter weather, including high winds, icy rain, and wet snow. Using twigs, grass, and other natural materials, the birds construct nests that average 5 feet (1.5 meters) across and 3 feet (about 1 meter) deep. Nest building is an ongoing **procedure** for the eagle. During nesting season, the birds create new nests or repair and enlarge old nests. Even these large birds of prey are **dwarfed** by the size of their own nests.

Once settled in their quarters, bald eagles make excellent parents. Females lay from one to three eggs during the nesting season. The mother and father birds take turns sitting on the eggs to keep them warm. They carefully fit the eggs under their warm bodies until **snug**. When a parent isn't hunting or egg sitting, it may guard the nest from a **perch** nearby. Raccoons or crows would love to help themselves to an eagle's egg.

2 Once the eaglets hatch, they must be fed. Eagles are very skilled hunters. The parents hunt for fish and small animals such as rodents, rabbits, turtles, and smaller birds. The eagles fly the food up to the nest and tear off small bits of meat before it is **transferred** to the open beaks of their young.

3 Experts **calculate** that when settlers first arrived in North America, perhaps half a million bald eagles may have lived on the continent. Over time, hunting, loss of habitat, and pesticide contamination of the eagle's food supply led to steep declines in eagle populations. Luckily, Americans felt **enthusiastic** about helping the eagle to recover. Cleaner waterways, protection of nesting sites, banning of dangerous pesticides, and other measures have helped the eagle to thrive.

If this fierce and magnificent bird could smile, it would almost be **beaming.** In 2007, the bald eagle was removed from the federal list of threatened and endangered species. The North American bald eagle continues to be studied and is expected to flourish.

Introduce Vocabulary

▶ **SHARE OBJECTIVE**
- Acquire and use vocabulary.
- Use knowledge of linguistic context to determine the meaning of unknown words. LANGUAGE

Teach

Display and discuss the <u>Vocabulary in Context Cards</u> ⬀, using the routine below. Direct students to use **Student Book pp. 170–171.**

1 **Read and pronounce the word.** Read the word once alone and then together.

2 **Explain the word.** Read aloud the explanation under *What Does It Mean?*

ENGLISH LANGUAGE SUPPORT Review these cognates with Spanish-speaking students.

- *calcular (calculate)*
- *entusiasta (enthusiastic)*
- *presencia (presence)*
- *procediamento (procedure)*

3 **Discuss vocabulary in context.** Together, read aloud the sentence on the front of the card. Help students explain and use the word in new sentences.

4 **Engage with the word.** Ask and discuss the *Think About It* question with students. **ELA** L.5.6

Apply

Give partners or small groups one or two **Vocabulary in Context Cards.**

- Help students complete the *Talk It Over* activity on the back of each card.
- Have students complete the activities for all cards during the week.

🔍 **Language Detective** Have partners take turns using the Vocabulary words to ask and answer questions about each photo. Provide sentence frames like this one to help students use the words.

An ant would be <u>dwarfed</u> by a grasshopper, a much larger insect. **ELA** SL.5.1c, L.5.4a, L.5.6 **ELD** ELD.PI.5.1, ELD.PI.5.12a

T14 • Unit 2 Lesson 6 (SB p. 170)

Lesson 6

Vocabulary in Context

🔍 **LANGUAGE DETECTIVE**

Talk About the Writer's Words
Work with a partner. Take turns asking and answering questions about the photos. Use the blue Vocabulary words in your questions and answers.

myNotebook
Add new words to **myWordList**. Use them in your speaking and writing.

170
ELA SL.5.1c, L.5.4a, L.5.6
ELD ELD.PI.5.1

1 dwarfed
This baby kangaroo is dwarfed by the larger mother kangaroo.

2 presence
Wildlife photographers have to be careful that their presence doesn't scare away animals.

3 procedure
The veterinarian explained the procedure and said the cat would be fine.

4 outfitted
This woman is outfitted, or equipped, with a glove to protect her from the owl's talons.

ENGLISH LANGUAGE SUPPORT

Use Visuals

Emerging Use pictures and gestures to show the meanings of *snug, perch,* and *beaming.* Have students point to the pictures as you say the words again. For further practice, show a picture of a person smiling. Then, provide sentence frames like this one: *These people are <u>beaming,</u> so they must be happy.*
ELD ELD.PI.5.12a

Expanding Use pictures to show the meaning of *perch.* Ask, *How does a person or animal perch?* Tell students to use a complete sentence.
ELD ELD.PI.5.12a

Bridging Ask students questions to confirm their understanding. For example, *How can you tell that a shirt is snug? If a shirt is snug, it will be a little too small.*
ELD ELD.PI.5.1, ELD.PI.5.12a

▶ Study each Context Card.

▶ Use a dictionary or a glossary to clarify the part of speech of each Vocabulary word.

5 transferred

This baby alligator will be transferred, or moved, to another area when it grows larger.

6 calculate

To calculate a cheetah's speed, measure the time it takes to cover a certain distance.

7 snug

It is important for an animal's collar to be snug, but not so tight that it is uncomfortable.

8 perch

Eagles and many other birds roost high on a perch to see prey or to avoid predators.

9 enthusiastic

This dog is quite enthusiastic about chasing and catching flying discs.

10 beaming

This girl is beaming over the news that her family is going to adopt the puppy.

171

Are students able to understand and use Target Vocabulary words?

IF...	THEN...
students **struggle**,	▶ use **Vocabulary in Context Cards** and differentiate the **Vocabulary Reader,** *The Lost World of Papua New Guinea,* for Struggling Readers, p. T68
students are **on target**,	▶ use **Vocabulary in Context Cards** and differentiate the **Vocabulary Reader,** *The Lost World of Papua New Guinea,* for On-Level Readers, p. T68.
students **excel**,	▶ use **Vocabulary in Context Cards** and differentiate the **Vocabulary Reader,** *The Lost World of Papua New Guinea,* for Advanced Readers, p. T69.

SMALL GROUP Options **Vocabulary Reader,** pp. T68–T69 *Scaffold instruction to the English Learner's proficiency level.*

ENGLISH LANGUAGE SUPPORT

Read and Write Together

Emerging/Expanding

Read Together Display ELL6.2 in Grab-and-Go™ Resources 🔗. Read aloud the title and have students repeat. Have students look at the images on the page. Then, have them predict what they think the text will be about.

• As you read the text aloud, display Vocabulary in Context Cards for *procedure*, *presence*, *outfitted*, and *enthusiastic*. Then, have students read the text chorally with you.

• Have students draw a picture of a volunteer helping an animal. Brainstorm words or phrases that name things a person can do to

help protect a wild animal. Have students include language from **ELL.6.2**. Write and display the words and phrases.

Write Together Display sentence frames, such as the following, and have partners use them to write complete sentences.

1. Many volunteers are *enthusiastic* to help wild animals.

2. The tree kangaroo may *perch* for a long time in a tree. **ELD** ELD.PI.5.2, ELD.PI.5.4, ELD.PI.5.12a

Read and Comprehend

Read and Comprehend

▶ SHARE OBJECTIVES

- Identify cause-and-effect relationships in informational text.
- Explain relationships between individuals, events, ideas, and concepts within a text.
- Engage effectively in collaborative discussion. LANGUAGE

☑ TARGET SKILL

Cause and Effect

- Read the top section of **Student Book p. 172** with students.
- Tell students that a cause makes something else happen, and that an effect is something caused by an earlier event.
- Point out that cause-and-effect relationships exist between individuals, events, ideas, and concepts described in informational texts.
- Refer to the graphic organizer on **Student Book p. 172.** Tell students that as they read, they can use a graphic organizer like this one to record causes and effects within the text.
- Explain that students should use the first box in the graphic organizer to note the cause of an event; in the next box they should note the direct effect. Point out that a cause may have more than one effect, and that an effect may be the result of more than one cause. **ELA** RI.5.3 **ELD** ELD.PI.5.6a

ENGLISH LANGUAGE SUPPORT Scaffold Anchor Text Before reading the selection, distribute <u>ELL6.3 in Grab-and-Go™ Resources</u> ⌐.

Review Cause and Effect Reread aloud the text. Write *cause* and *effect*. Say the words aloud.

- Explain that to cause something is to make it happen. An effect is what happens.

Guided Practice Display a cause-and-effect diagram. During reading, complete it with students.

- Help students identify causes and effects.
- Display a completed cause-and-effect diagram as a reference throughout the week. **ELD** ELD.PI.5.6a

---

Read and Comprehend

☑ TARGET SKILL

Cause and Effect As you read "Quest for the Tree Kangaroo," look for causes and their effects. A **cause** is an event that makes something else happen. An **effect** is something that happens because of an earlier event. Use text evidence and a graphic organizer like this one to help you identify the cause-and-effect relationships in the selection.

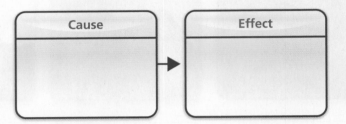

☑ TARGET STRATEGY

Question As you read "Quest for the Tree Kangaroo," pause frequently to ask yourself what events lead to others and what events are caused by earlier ones. Asking and answering **questions** as you read can help you identify cause-and-effect relationships.

172   **ELA** RI.5.3, SL.5.1c   **ELD** ELD.PI.5.1, ELD.PI.5.6a

ENGLISH LANGUAGE SUPPORT

Comprehensible Input

Emerging Write on the board: *Tree kangaroos are difficult to study because they live in trees.* Point out the cause, the effect, and the signal word *because.* Ask volunteers to create similar sentences.	**Expanding** Have students read the photo caption on **Student Book p. 177.** Ask them to identify the cause and effect described. Have volunteers create similar sentences. **ELD** ELD.PI.5.6a	**Bridging** Have students identify cause-and-effect relationships in the Preview the Topic passage on **Student Book p. 173.** **ELD** ELD.PI.5.6a

PREVIEW THE TOPIC

Wild Animals

Wild animals are those that have not been domesticated, or tamed, by humans. They include the squirrels and pigeons you see every day and the exotic animals that live in faraway jungles and deep ocean waters. Many wild animals are endangered—their numbers are so low that they might disappear completely. Climate change, loss of habitat, and overhunting all contribute to the decline in animal populations.

The Matschie's tree kangaroo is an endangered species. It lives in the rain forests of Papua New Guinea. Because tree kangaroos spend most of their time in trees, scientists must work hard to locate and study them. When you read "Quest for the Tree Kangaroo," you will go along on one of these scientific adventures.

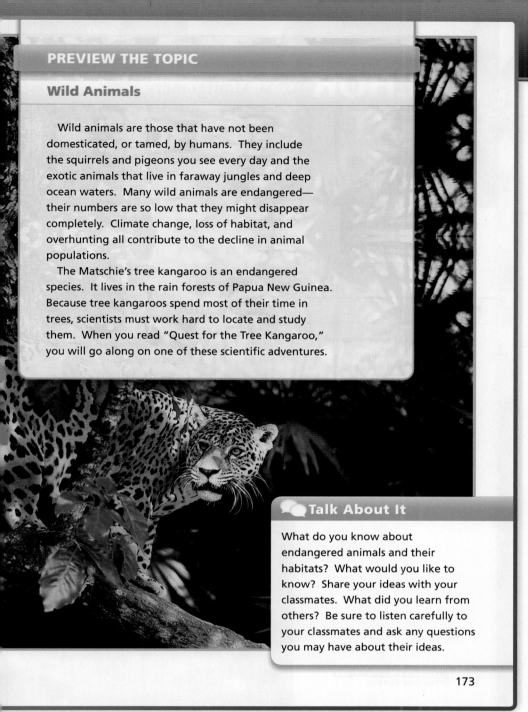

💬 Talk About It

What do you know about endangered animals and their habitats? What would you like to know? Share your ideas with your classmates. What did you learn from others? Be sure to listen carefully to your classmates and ask any questions you may have about their ideas.

173

COMPREHENSION STRATEGIES

Use the following strategies flexibly as you read with students by modeling how they can be used to improve comprehension. See scaffolded support for the strategy shown in boldface during this week's reading.

- **Monitor/Clarify**
- **Summarize**
- **Infer/Predict**
- **Visualize**
- **Analyze/Evaluate**
- **Question**

Use the Strategy Projectables S1-S8 🔗, for additional support.

✅ TARGET STRATEGY

Question

- Read the bottom section of **Student Book p. 172.** Tell students to ask themselves questions as they read "*Quest for the Tree Kangaroo*" to identify the causes of events and conditions. Point out that **questioning** is a good strategy for finding cause-and-effect relationships in informational texts.

- Point out that when students read about an event in the text, they should pause and ask themselves why it happened. They may have to go back or read ahead to identify the cause of the event.

- Next, explain that you will demonstrate how to use this strategy when you read "Quest for the Tree Kangaroo" together.

PREVIEW THE TOPIC

Wild Animals

- Tell students that today they will begin reading "Quest for the Tree Kangaroo."

- Read the information at the top of **Student Book p. 173** with students.

- Explain to students that endangered animals struggle to adapt and survive both as individuals (for example, through access to food, water, and habitat) and as a species through access to factors that affect their ability to produce offspring.

Talk About It

- Have individual students use the questions to think about what they already know about the topic. Give partners time to discuss how their knowledge is similar and different.

- Guide students to ask questions about any new information they learned from other students. Encourage students to make comments that contribute to the discussion and link to the remarks of others. **ELA** SL.5.1c **ELD** ELD.PI.5.1

ENGLISH LANGUAGE SUPPORT **Access Prior Knowledge: All Proficiencies** Use the image on Lesson 6 Language Support Card 🔗 to review the selection topic with students. Show the completed chart again, and help students summarize its content.

FIRST READ

Read the Anchor Text

✓ **GENRE**

Informational Text

- Read the information on **Student Book p. 174** with students.

- Preview the selection with students and model identifying characteristics of informational text.

Think Aloud *The selection has photographs with captions and includes facts and details about tree kangaroos. I think this is informational text.*

- As you preview, have students point out other features, such as the inclusion of domain-specific words, that describe informational texts.

ENGLISH LANGUAGE SUPPORT
Access Prior Knowledge: All Proficiencies Write the following statements on the board.

1. Informational texts are only read in school.
2. Informational texts are always easy to understand.
3. It is important to study animals in the wild.
4. All scientists do their work in a lab.

Have pairs take turns reading a statement to each other and sharing their opinions. Provide these frames for support: *The statement says _____. I agree/disagree because _____. What do you think?* Have students record their opinions to refer to later. During reading, have students check their opinions and note whether they have changed.

ELA RI.5.10 **ELD** ELD.PI.5.6a

Lesson 6

ANCHOR TEXT

QUEST FOR THE TREE KANGAROO
AN EXPEDITION TO THE CLOUD FOREST OF NEW GUINEA

✓ **GENRE**

Informational text gives facts and examples about a topic. As you read, look for:
▶ text structure, or the way ideas and information are organized
▶ facts and details about a specific topic

MEET THE AUTHOR

Sy Montgomery

Award-winning author Sy Montgomery travels the world to study animals. Sometimes she faces the unexpected. "Once, in Borneo, an orangutan ate my interview tapes," she says, describing one of many memorable incidents. Her adventures can require her "to hike for days and swim for miles." She calls her trip to the cloud forest of New Guinea her most physically difficult one so far.

MEET THE PHOTOGRAPHER

Nic Bishop

Nic Bishop is a nature photographer and author of many books. Some of his animal photographs are taken in a studio, while others are taken in far-off places, in animals' natural habitats. After traveling a great distance for a project, there is a lot of pressure to capture great photographs. "I simply cannot afford to be tired, or get ill, since there is never going to be a chance to repeat anything," he says.

174   **ELA** R1.5.3, R1.5.10, RF.5.4a, RF.5.4b, L.5.6
ELD ELD.PI.5.6a, ELD.PI.5.12a

Scaffold Close Reading

Strategies for Annotation	Think Through the Text	Analyze the Text	Independent Reading
	FIRST READ	**SECOND READ**	
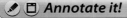 **Annotate it!** As you read the selection with students, look for ✎ 🗂 *Annotate it!* . It indicates opportunities for students to annotate the text independently.	Develop comprehension through - Guided Questioning - Target Strategy: Question - Vocabulary in Context	Support analyzing short sections of text: - Cause and Effect - Quotes and Description - Domain-Specific Vocabulary - The Language of Science Texts Use directed note taking by working with students to complete a graphic organizer during reading. Distribute copies of Graphic Organizer 13 🗂.	- Students analyze the text independently, using the Reader's Guide on pp. 61–62 of the Reader's Notebook 🗂. (See p. T38 for instructional support.) - Students read independently in a self-selected trade book.

QUEST FOR THE TREE KANGAROO

by Sy Montgomery
photographs by Nic Bishop

ESSENTIAL QUESTION

Why is it important to
research and protect
endangered animals?

175

READER AND TASK CONSIDERATIONS

Determine the level of additional support that students will need to read and
comprehend "Quest for the Tree Kangaroo" successfully.

READERS

- **Motivate** Ask students to share what they
hope to learn from reading the selection.

- **Talk It Over** Use Lesson 6 Language
Support Card ⬀ for a discussion about
animal conservation.

- **Access Knowledge and Experiences**
Remind students of the information on
Student Book p. 173. Ask partners to
share one other thing they know about tree
kangaroos or other endangered animals.

TASKS

- **Increase Scaffolding** Guide students to
use the Summarize strategy as they read the
text. Have them apply the strategy after
reading sections of the text.

- **Foster Independence** Have small groups
of motivated readers read the text together.
Tell them to think through the text by
pausing to ask questions of themselves and
each other to understand the text, its
structure, and challenging vocabulary.

Read aloud the **Essential Question** on **Student
Book p. 175**: *Why is it important to research
and protect endangered animals?* Then tell
students to think about this question as they
read "Quest for the Tree Kangaroo."

Predictive Writing

- Explain to students that they will write a
paragraph to explain what they expect "Quest
for the Tree Kangaroo" to be about. Ask them to
think about how the Essential Question relates to
what they noticed while previewing the selection
or what they already know from their own
experiences or past readings.

- Guide students to think about the genre of the
selection to help them write.

Set Purpose

- Tell students that good readers set a purpose for
reading, based on their preview of the selection,
what they know about the genre, and what they
hope to learn from the selection.

- Model setting a reading purpose.

> **Think Aloud** *Informational text provides facts
> and details about a topic. The title names an
> animal called the tree kangaroo. One purpose for
> reading could be to learn facts and details about
> the tree kangaroo.*

- Have students set their own purpose for reading.
Then ask several students to share their reading
purposes. **ELA** RF.5.4a

**ENGLISH LANGUAGE SUPPORT Preteach
Academic English: Emerging/Expanding** Guide
students to complete the Academic English
activities on Language Support Card 6.

FIRST READ

Think Through the Text

Cite Text Evidence

1 *What is a tree 'roo? A tree 'roo is a Matschie's tree kangaroo. Why do you think the author uses this term? It may be how many people in Papua New Guinea refer to the tree kangaroo.*

2 *Think about what you have read so far. Summarize the purpose of the expedition. The team wants to locate tree kangaroos and fit them with radio collars so that they can be tracked and studied.* **ELA** RI.5.2 **ELD** ELD.PI.5.6a

3 *What does the tree kangaroo look like? Use clues from the photo and quotes from the text to form your description. Sample answer: The author describes the animal as "gorgeous," having red and gold coloring, including a long golden tail it uses to hang on to trees. The photo shows it has pointed ears, small dark eyes, and a pink snout.* **ELA** RI.5.1

ENGLISH LANGUAGE SUPPORT Provide these sentence frames to support participation.
I would describe the tree kangaroo as _____. In the photo, I can see _____. The text tells me that _____.

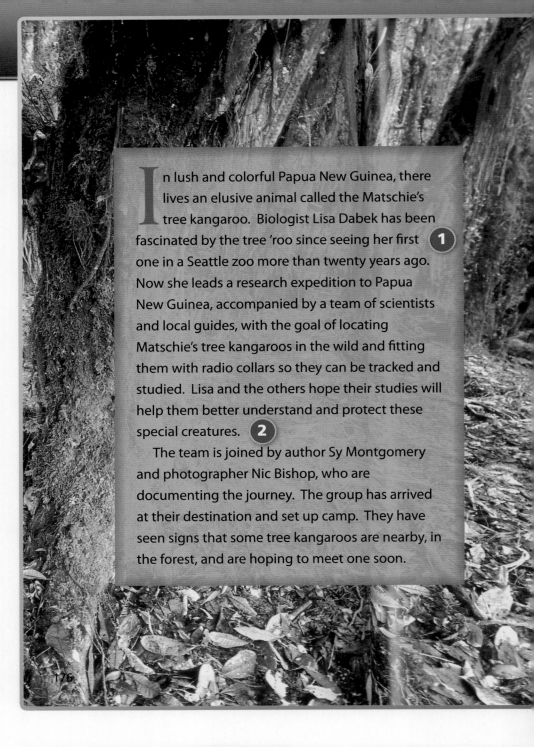

I n lush and colorful Papua New Guinea, there lives an elusive animal called the Matschie's tree kangaroo. Biologist Lisa Dabek has been fascinated by the tree 'roo since seeing her first **1** one in a Seattle zoo more than twenty years ago. Now she leads a research expedition to Papua New Guinea, accompanied by a team of scientists and local guides, with the goal of locating Matschie's tree kangaroos in the wild and fitting them with radio collars so they can be tracked and studied. Lisa and the others hope their studies will help them better understand and protect these special creatures. **2**

The team is joined by author Sy Montgomery and photographer Nic Bishop, who are documenting the journey. The group has arrived at their destination and set up camp. They have seen signs that some tree kangaroos are nearby, in the forest, and are hoping to meet one soon.

176

ENGLISH LANGUAGE SUPPORT

Expand Language Production

Emerging	Expanding	Bridging
For each question, accept one-word responses and expand them. For example, if the student's response to question 1 is "kangaroo," expand it by saying, *Yes, a* tree 'roo *is a Matschie's tree kangaroo.*	Provide a sentence frame in response to each question, and have students complete it. Then have students repeat the complete response.	Encourage students to respond to the questions in complete sentences. Provide corrective feedback as needed.

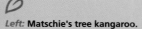
Left: **Matschie's tree kangaroo.**

Opposite page: **Cool winds have dwarfed some parts of the forest so it is only about twenty feet high.**

LISA IS WASHING HER CLOTHES IN THE RIVER WHEN WE GET THE NEWS: "TREE 'ROOS," CALLS HOLLY. *"TWO* OF them!"

One of the trackers has run back to camp to tell us. The two tree kangaroos are "klostu"[1] us—and still up a tree. While Holly and Christine ready the medical equipment, the rest of us race after the tracker to see.

We run past the tree kangaroo house, past the kunai,[2] down a trail—and then into the trackless bush. Will the tree kangaroos still be there when we get there?

It takes us nearly an hour to reach the site. We see the long golden tail hanging down from the branches of a Saurauia[3]—and then the animal to whom it belongs: a gorgeous red and gold tree kangaroo sitting eighty feet above us, looking down with ears pricked forward. **3**

"I can't believe it!" Lisa says.

And then, in the tree right next to this tree kangaroo, we see another tail—leading to another tree kangaroo.

"Bigpela pikinini!" one of the trackers exclaims. "Pikinini" is Tok Pisin for child or baby. And "bigpela"? You guessed it: If this is her baby, it's a big one.

---

[1] klostu: "close to" in Tok Pisin—a popular language spoken in Papua New Guinea
[2] kunai: the area where Lisa and her team have set up camp, named for the kind of grass it has
[3] Saurauia: tree kangaroos love to eat the shoots of this flowering tree

177

Practice Fluency

Expression Read aloud the text on **Student Book p. 177** while students follow along. Model reading with expression to convey the team's excitement over their discovery.

- Point out to students that this particular informational text contains a lot of action and is narrated by someone who is participating in the tree kangaroo study expedition. Explain that some parts of the text should be read in an excited way, while others should be read with more careful interest.

- Tell students that reading an informational text with expression helps make the facts and details more memorable and easy to understand.

- Have students echo read each sentence after you read it.

- When the dialogue begins, read with expression that reflects a conversational tone. Have students explain how your expression changed once the dialogue began.

- The Fluency lesson on p. T50 provides further opportunities for modeling and practice with expression. **ELA** RF.5.4b

LESSON TOPIC: Wild Animals

Cross-Curricular Connection Point out that Matschie's tree kangaroos have developed certain adaptations to survive in the rain forests, such as long tails, to help balance their weight as they move through tall trees. Discuss the impact the loss of rain-forest habitat would have on the animals. *Without rain forests, the tree kangaroo would probably have a hard time surviving.* **Guide** students to understand that the loss of rain forests would affect other animals, plants, and people, too.

Think Through the Text

Cite Text Evidence

4 *What does biologist Lisa Dabek mean when she talks about the "miracle" of working in Papua New Guinea? Use quotes from the text to explain.* Finding the tree kangaroos, despite all the difficulties involved, is the miracle. The animals are "so elusive" but then "you finally find them." **ELA** RI.5.1

☑ **TARGET STRATEGY**

Question

Read aloud the second paragraph on **Student Book p. 179**. Then, model the strategy:

> **Think Aloud** *I am looking for cause-and-effect relationships. The text says that the trackers have left camp feeling lucky. I ask the question, "What causes the trackers to locate the kangaroo?" If I read ahead in the text, I see that the weather is warm and sunny, which tree kangaroos like, and that the men have been working to drive any nearby tree kangaroos closer to the camp.*

Tell students to practice using the Question strategy as they continue reading.

5 *Why does the tracker bark like a dog when he sees the kangaroo tail?* He wants to keep the animal in the tree and alert Lisa and her team.
ELD RI.5.3

ANALYZE THE TEXT

Cause and Effect When the tracker climbs a nearby tree, what effect does it have on the tree kangaroos?

 Matschie's tree kangaroo is one of the world's rarest and most elusive mammals.

178

FORMATIVE ASSESSMENT 3 2 1 **RtI**

Question

IF students have difficulty applying the Question strategy as they read… **THEN**, use this model:

> **Think Aloud** *In the sixth paragraph, the trackers decide to build a low fence around the tree. I ask myself, "What effect will this fence have?" I continue to read carefully and see that the fence is meant to slow the kangaroo down as it tries to hop away.*

Guide students to understand that the trackers are looking for ways to capture the tree kangaroo.

"This is the miracle of doing work here," Lisa says. "They are so elusive. And then you finally find them. The whole field season is riding on these moments."

The men had left camp that morning feeling lucky. "It was sunny and warm," Gabriel recalled. "A good day for the tree 'roos to come out and warm themselves." They changed their strategy: "For the first three days, we were traveling more than one kilometer each day to find tree 'roos. I had wanted our presence to drive them closer to camp. So we decided today to try closer—and it worked."

The men spread out. One tracker decided he would look for a plant that the tree kangaroos love to eat. It grows high on tree branches and is easy to spot. The underside is brown and the top green. He found one in a tree— but no tree kangaroo. He scanned the next tree over—the Saurauia—and there was the tail!

"Immediately," the tracker explained through Gabriel, "I barked like a dog because that would keep her up in the tree. Everyone else heard the barking and knew what happened. Everyone ran and admired the 'roo. We all stood looking for about two minutes. And then someone noticed there was another tail." **5**

We photograph and videotape and watch the two tree kangaroos for ten minutes. Now to get the animals down …

The trackers have been thinking about this puzzle. Shortly after they spotted the animals, they began to cut sticks and brush to build a low fence they call an "im" around the tree. If the tree kangaroo leaps down and starts to hop away, the im will slow him down.

One of the trackers takes off his tall rubber boots. Barefoot, he begins to climb a smaller tree next to the *Saurauia*. Within two minutes, he's as high as the tree kangaroo.

"Joel, do you see where she is?" asks Lisa. Joel has the 'roo in his binoculars. "She's still there," he assures.

But the tree kangaroo isn't happy to see a human approaching. She climbs another 30 feet up to get away. If she jumps, it's a 110-foot drop.

179

FOR STANDARD ENGLISH LEARNERS Pronunciation Some students may need help mastering Standard English pronunciations when reading aloud or speaking in a more formal register. Students may have trouble voicing /l/ in words, such as *people, myself,* and *help.* They may omit the /l/ sound and voice the words as "peopuh," "myse'f," and "he'p." Write this sentence on the board: *The trackers had been thinking about this puzzle.* Read the sentence aloud, emphasizing the /l/ sound in *puzzle.* Have students echo your reading several times.

Cause and Effect

- Read the Analyze the Text box on **Student Book p. 178** with students. Then distribute Graphic Organizer 13 .

- Explain that the structure of an informational text may be based on a chain of cause-and-effect relationships. Remind students that an event, the cause, leads to another event, the effect.

- Display Projectable 6.2 , and tell students that you will work together to analyze the text on **Student Book p. 179** to accurately identify cause-and-effect relationships.

- Show the first item in the Cause box on Projectable 6.2 : *Trackers look for a tree the kangaroo likes to eat.* Ask students what happens next. *The trackers find the kangaroo in that tree.* Have students look in the text to find the effect of the tracker climbing the tree. *The tree kangaroo climbs higher to try to escape.*

ENGLISH LANGUAGE SUPPORT Tell students that authors sometimes use cause and effect signal words, such as *because, due to,* and *as a result,* to show relationships between events. Explain that at other times, these relationships are implied by the order in which they're included in a text. Point out that there is no signal word to link the events in the example above, and the cause and effect must be inferred. Tell students that one way to check this kind of inference is by rephrasing the text, using a cause and effect signal word. Write on the board: *The tree kangaroo climbs higher to try to escape because it has been found by the trackers.* Work with students to infer another cause and effect relationship in the text, and check it by rephrasing with a cause and effect signal word.

- Continue to analyze the text, guiding students to recognize the cause-and-effect relationships between events. **ELA** RI.5.3 **ELD** ELD.PI.5.6a

🖉 🗐 *Annotate it!* Have students underline important events in the selection and highlight their causes and effects.

Think Through the Text

Cite Text Evidence

6 *What evidence does the author use to show that the tree kangaroo can move "like an acrobat"? The author writes, "he catches a vine with his front paws, turns himself around, and lands on the ground with his feet."*
ELA RI.5.1, RI.5.8 **ELD** ELD.PI.5.6a

ENGLISH LANGUAGE SUPPORT Tell students that an acrobat is a person who performs tumbling or gymnastic tricks. Acrobats might be found in a circus show, walking on tightropes or flying on a trapeze. Point out that by comparing the tree kangaroo to an acrobat, the author paints a clear picture of how skillfully the animal moves.

7 *What details does the author use to support the idea that the captured tree kangaroos are mates? Sample answer: They find the kangaroos together. One kangaroo is a female; the author refers to her as "she." The second kangaroo was thought to be her baby, but the crew finds out it is a "fully grown adult male" on a "tree kangaroo date."* **ELA** RI.5.1

8 *How does the author support the ideas that this is a scientific expedition and that it has the goal of collecting precise data? The crew sets up an exam table with medical supplies, measuring tools, and data sheets. The author writes, "every detail is important" and describes how the animals are carefully weighed. These details demonstrate that the crew is gathering evidence and making testable observations.* **ELA** RI.5.2, RI.5.8 **ELD** ELD.PI.5.6a

---

Suddenly, she leaps, her forearms outstretched. She drops 30 feet. She grabs a smaller tree on the way down. And now she begins to back down the tree.

She's almost to the ground when one of the trackers grabs her by the tail and puts her in the burlap bag.

"Pikinini! Pikinini!" the men call. The other tree kangaroo is 65 feet up in a *Decaspermum* tree, and they don't want him to get away. The tree kangaroo lets go of the branch. Like an acrobat, he catches a vine with his front paws, turns himself around, and lands on the ground on his feet. One tracker holds the chest, another holds the back legs, and another man holds the front. **6**

It's only now that we realize that the "baby" is a fully grown adult male. "Man na meri" the trackers say—this pair is no mother and baby, but a grown-up male and female on a tree kangaroo date. By 10:10 A.M., both tree kangaroos are in burlap bags, heading back to camp. **7**

Twenty-five minutes later, we're all back in camp, where Holly and Christine have set up the exam table—a picnic table built from saplings lashed with vines. They've laid out medical supplies and sample vials, measuring tools and data sheets. Each tree kangaroo will be given medicine to make it sleep while the team puts on the radio collar and conducts a health exam.

We want to find out as much as we can. Because so little is known about tree kangaroos, every detail is important.

First, while the animals are in their burlap bags, they are weighed. The female weighs 6.4 kilograms (about 24 pounds) with the bag. The scientists will make sure to subtract the weight of the bag alone later. The male, with bag, weighs 8 kilograms. **8**

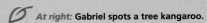 **At right:** Gabriel spots a tree kangaroo.

ENGLISH LANGUAGE SUPPORT

How English Works: Interpretive

Connecting Ideas As students read this selection, have them look for places where the author uses connecting words to build sentences. Explain to students that authors use special words to connect, or put together, ideas. Tell students that "and" and "because" are examples of connecting words. Read aloud *They've laid out medical supplies and sample vials, measuring tools and data sheets* while students follow along in the text.

- Help students identify the connecting words and explain their functions. *Sample answers: the word* and *is used twice to connect a list of items and combine them into a single sentence.*
- Tell students to identify other places in the text where the author uses connecting words.
- Have partners practice using connecting words to build sentences.
- Collect samples from volunteers and write them on the board. **ELD** ELD. PII.5.6

181

DOMAIN: Life Science

LESSON TOPIC: Wild Animals

Cross-Curricular Connection Explain to students that the Matschie's tree kangaroo is much smaller than the more familiar red kangaroos of Australia. The ground-dwelling red kangaroos have relatively short front legs and longer, stronger hind legs they use for hopping. Discuss why the tree kangaroo's front and back limbs are about the same length. *Tree kangaroos don't need longer hindquarters. Their limbs are adapted for tree climbing.* Guide students to understand that differences between related species have to do with adaptations.

Think Through the Text

Cite
Text Evidence

9 *How do the scientists prepare to collect information about the kangaroos after the animals are released?* The scientists fit the tree kangaroos with a radio collar and insert a chip that will give them more information.

ENGLISH LANGUAGE SUPPORT Provide this sentence frame to support participation. *The scientists prepare to collect information about the kangaroos by _____.*

10 *What is the importance of the radio collar's weight?* The collar should weigh as little as possible so that it does not cause discomfort for the kangaroo. **ELA** RI.5.3

182

Sentence Frames

Emerging Guide students to answer the questions by using sentence frames requiring single word responses. For example: *They fit the kangaroo with a radio _____. collar*

Expanding Have students complete sentence frames using phrases. For example: *They fit the kangaroo _____. with a radio collar*

Bridging Have partners answer the questions in complete sentences. If they have difficulty phrasing a response, provide a sentence frame as a guide.

Joel notes the temperature and humidity, too: It's 56.2 degrees Fahrenheit, 81 percent humidity.

"Let's measure the male's neck, to make sure the radio collar will fit on him," says Lisa. "But let's do the female first."

"With the female, we'll have the same priorities," Holly tells the group. "We'll measure the neck, put on the radio collar, insert the ID chip, pluck fur for more testing, check the pouch—see if she has a baby."

We hope to find out as much as we can while the animal is asleep. But anesthesia can be dangerous. That's why we'll be carefully watching how often she breathes in and out and how fast her heart is beating during the procedure. We'll have to work fast. Everyone will help.

"Christine will call out pulse and respiration every five minutes," says Holly. "Is everybody ready?"

"Do you have the radio collar?" Lisa asks Gabriel.

Gabriel is holding a leather collar much like one a dog might wear. Instead of metal tags, though, it has a little box of waterproof plastic. This contains a transmitter powered by a square battery and outfitted with an internal antenna. Each radio collar also has a computer chip. Without knowing it, the tree kangaroos will be sending their position not only to the scientists tracking them on the ground, but also to satellites circling thousands of miles above Earth. At six A.M. and six P.M.—times the 'roos are likely to be in the trees and the weather is likely to be less cloudy—the satellites read the animals' exact position on the earth's surface. They download this information to the chips in the collars, and this data can be transferred to a computer when the collar automatically falls off, after five months. The whole thing weighs less than half a pound. **10**

9

Above: **A Matschie's looks down from eighty feet in the canopy.**

> **ANALYZE THE TEXT**
>
> **Domain-Specific Vocabulary**
> What science terminology does the author use on this page while describing the purpose of the radio collar being fitted on the tree kangaroo? How does it affect your understanding?

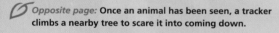*Opposite page:* **Once an animal has been seen, a tracker climbs a nearby tree to scare it into coming down.**

183

DOMAIN: Life Science

LESSON TOPIC: Wild Animals

Cross-Curricular Connection Explain that using anesthesia on wild animals poses a greater risk than using it on pets, such as cats or dogs. Because wild animals are not used to being handled by humans, they are under increased stress when the drug is given. Also, since it is difficult to examine wild animals, we know less about how they react to certain drugs. How do these factors add to the challenges of studying wild animals? *The stress of being handled by humans and the lack of opportunities for testing make wild animals' responses to exams and medicines unpredictable.* Guide students to understand the differences between studying wild and domestic animals.

Domain-Specific Vocabulary

Analyze the Text

- Read the Analyze the Text box on **Student Book p. 183** with students.

- Discuss domain-specific words with students. Remind them that a subject area can have its own special vocabulary.

- Point out that scientific words express ideas and concepts related to scientific activities, such as taking measurements and gathering data.

- Explain that some of the domain-specific words in the text are related to the scientific practice of medicine.

- Have students read **Student Book p. 183** silently. Then ask: *What are some of the scientific terms used in the first section?* The author mentions temperature, humidity, degrees Fahrenheit, radio collar, ID chip, *and* anesthesia.

- Guide students to use context to determine the meanings of unfamiliar domain-specific words within a text. Ask: *How can we determine the meaning of the word* anesthesia *by reading the sentences before and after it? The first sentence of the fourth paragraph says that the animal "is asleep." The sentences after that mention a procedure. Anesthesia must be something that helps the animal to sleep through a medical procedure.* **ELA** RI.5.4, L.5.4a, L.5.6 **ELD** ELD.PI.5.6b

✏ 🖹 Annotate it! As they read, have students highlight domain-specific words in the text and note the context clues that clarify the words' meanings.

Think Through the Text

Cite Text Evidence

11 *What has happened to cause the tree kangaroo to relax? A mask has been placed over its nose to deliver anesthesia before the exam.* **ELA** RI.5.3

12 *What context clues can you use to determine the meaning of respiration? The author explains that the kangaroo is "breathing thirty-two times a minute." Respiration, therefore, has to do with the act of breathing.* **ELA** RI.5.1, RI.5.4, L.5.4a, L.5.6 **ELD** ELD.PI.5.6b

13 *What main idea does the author convey on this page? The crew must work quickly to gather information about the kangaroo's health. What text details support the main idea? Even before the kangaroo is asleep, Lisa asks if the screwdriver is ready for putting on the radio collar. The team quickly moves through taking the animal's vital signs—temperature, respiration, and heart rate—before putting on the collar.* **ELA** RI.5.2 **ELD** ELD.PI.5.6a

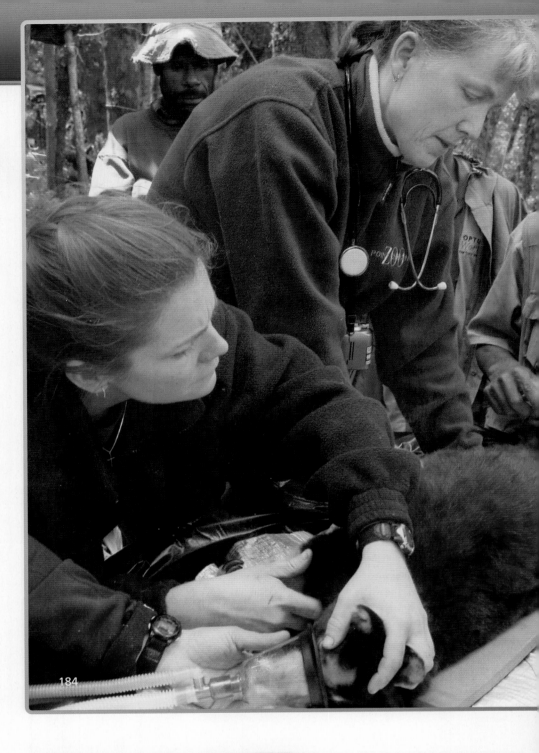

184

ENGLISH LANGUAGE SUPPORT

Comprehensible Input

Emerging Use gestures and mimic the act of falling asleep to support understanding of how anesthesia renders the kangaroo unconscious.

Expanding Paraphrase "the anesthesia's working." *The drug is beginning to make the kangaroo relax.*

Bridging Have students identify clues that help them understand the meaning of "the anesthesia's working."

"Do you have the screwdriver to put the collar on?" asks Lisa.

"Yes, yes," says Gabriel, holding the squirming bag on his lap. "We're ready!"

But the tree kangaroo isn't. Gabriel talks to the animal in the bag. "Wait, wait, come here," he says gently. And then, to two trackers: "Hold 'im!" Soon a pink nose pokes out through a hole in the bag.

It's 10:55 A.M. and Holly places the mask on the nose. A paw comes out through the hole. But within forty-five seconds, the tree kangaroo relaxes. The anesthesia's working. She's asleep. **(11)**

Out comes the kangaroo. "Thermometer?" Holly requests.

The kangaroo's body temperature is similar to a person's: 97.1 degrees.

(12) "Respiration is thirty-two," says Christine. That means she's breathing thirty-two times a minute. That's healthy.

Holly leans forward to listen to the heart through her stethoscope. For five seconds, she counts the beats. She wants to calculate the beats per minute. "Heart rate is sixteen times twelve. You do the math," she tells Joel, who is recording everything on a data sheet.

Meanwhile, Gabriel is putting on the collar. "Make sure the collar is comfortable but snug," says Lisa. (Yesterday Christine discovered that Ombum[4] had taken his off and left it on the floor of his cage.) **(13)**

---

[4] Ombum: a tree kangaroo that was examined earlier and is being treated for an injured leg

🖉 Opposite page: **Christine and Holly get to work.**

ANALYZE THE TEXT

Quotes and Description Why do you think the author includes quotes from the research team and detailed descriptions of their work?

185

FOR STUDENTS WITH DISABILITIES Have students work in small, mixed ability groups to read "Quest for the Tree Kangaroo." Have group members take turns reading each section of the text aloud and discussing it before moving on to the next. Have group members summarize each section, and then summarize the entire text.

Quotes and Description

Analyze the Text

- Read the Analyze the Text box on **Student Book p. 185** with students.

- Explain to students that authors of informational texts often include descriptions and direct quotations to help bring their subject to life for readers.

- Point out that the use of quotes and descriptions helps readers imagine that they are part of the action. Explain that an engaged reader is likely to understand and remember facts and details from the text.

ENGLISH LANGUAGE SUPPORT Tell students that dialogue such as that in the passage on p. 185 may contain a lot of pronouns. Explain that readers need to pay close attention to what these pronouns refer to in order to get a clear understanding of what's happening. Point out these sentences in paragraph 7: *"Respiration is thirty-two," says Christine. That means she's breathing thirty-two times a minute. That's healthy."* Ask students to identify the pronouns. That *refers to the kangaroo's respiration rate;* she *refers to the kangaroo.*

- Have students read **Student Book p. 185** silently. Then ask: *What do you think Gabriel is feeling when he is holding the squirming kangaroo on his lap? Sample answer: He seems to be excited. He's worried about the animal getting loose.* Ask: *How does the author show you what Gabriel is feeling? She uses Gabriel's exact words.*

- Point out that the author describes the examination in detail. Like quotes, details help place the reader in the scene. Read aloud the third paragraph on the page. Ask: *what details does the author include to help you imagine the scene? Gabriel "talks to" the kangaroo "gently"; "a pink nose pokes through a hole in the bag."* Then ask: *why do you think the author includes these details? By Gabriel's tone we can understand that he cares about the kangaroo and wants to calm it. By mentioning the pink nose and the bag, we can imagine what the animal is experiencing and doing.* **ELA** RI.5.1 **ELD** ELD.PI.5.6a

🖉 🖻 *Annotate it!* Have students highlight details in the text that help them feel like they're part of the action.

FIRST READ

Think Through the Text

Cite Text Evidence

☑ **TARGET STRATEGY**

Question

Tell students to practice the Question strategy as they read **Student Book pp. 186–187**. Ask volunteers to point out where the strategy helped them identify cause-and-effect relationships.

14 *Why do you think Holly does a "pouch check"? She wants to see if the kangaroo carries a baby.*

15 *What is the author's purpose in marking the exact time? It helps readers know how long each exam takes and what is happening throughout the day.*

16 *What evidence does the author offer to support the point that the scientists' work is accurate and valid? The author uses measurements of heart rate, respiration, and neck diameter to show that the scientists carefully record data from each kangaroo.* **ELA** RI.5.8 **ELD** ELD.PI.5.6a

14 Holly puts in the microchip and Joel records its number: 029-274-864.

"I'm going to do a pouch check," says Holly. Meanwhile, the other scientists measure everything they can as fast as they can.

"Pouch is empty," says Holly. "Now for the vitamin-mineral shot."

"This is it," says Lisa. She calls an end to the exam. Because he was injured, Ombum's exam took much longer; but we don't want to subject this tree kangaroo to the anesthesia any longer than necessary, for safety's sake.

Holly removes the face mask and quickly checks the teeth. She's coming to. It's 11:06 A.M. **15**

"Put her in the bag," says Lisa. "Tail first, so she can sit." They name her Tess, in honor of my dog, a Border collie who died last year at age sixteen. The new Tess rests in her bag on a tracker's lap while we prepare for the male.

11:20 A.M.: "Anesthetic machine? Gas ready? Radio collar?" Holly asks. "And is the other 'roo OK?"

"OK," answers the team. "We're ready!"

The team works fast while the tree kangaroo is anesthetized.

186

FORMATIVE ASSESSMENT △ **RtI** (3 2 1)

Question

IF students have difficulty applying the Question strategy... **THEN**, use the following model:

Think Aloud

When Gabriel unties the kangaroo's bag, I notice that something happens. Since this event might signal a cause-and-effect relationship, I pause and apply the Question strategy. I ask, "What was the effect of Gabriel untying the bag?" I then read, "immediately the burlap boils with movement." So, untying the bag caused an effect: the kangaroo became agitated.

Guide students to understand that when humans interact with animals, cause-and-effect events are likely to occur.

Each collar allows scientists to track a tree kangaroo for several months.

Gabriel unties the top of the male's bag, and immediately the burlap boils with movement.

"He's doing somersaults in the bag," Gabriel reports. It's all he and Joshua can do to hold the 'roo.

Through the bag, the male grabs one man's glove and pulls it off. He bites another tracker on the finger. Now four men are struggling, "I've got his head here," says Gabriel, "but I can't get it out—but the nose is right here!"

Through the burlap, Holly delivers the anesthetic. "Oh, but he's tough!" says Gabriel.

Finally the bag stops wiggling. At 11:30 A.M. the male is lifted out of the bag and laid out on the table. The team goes to work.

"Seventeen times twelve is the heart rate," Holly tells Joel.

"Twenty-two point seven, circumference of neck," says Toby. "Here's the collar. Let's put it on."

"Respiration is twenty," says Holly. "Now we'll take his temperature. Next the chip. And after that we'll go for the hair." **16**

187

Q Language Detective

The Language of Science Texts

- Tell students that as they read science-related texts, they can expect to see some common language features, such as quotations, procedure steps, and detailed explanations of events. Point out that some of these features might contain language that is unfamiliar, or technical wording that might be confusing to readers.

- Explain to students that slowing their reading rate will help them understand these text features. Tell students that it also might help to reread, to use context, or to restate sections of the text in their own words.

- Read aloud **Student Book p. 187** and have students follow along. Then model the thinking.

> **Think Aloud** *On this page, the team has used anesthetic to put the 'roo to sleep. The text talks about checking and measuring the animal: "Twenty-two point seven, circumference of neck," says Toby. "Here's the collar. Let's put it on." I'm not sure what the word circumference means. When I slow down and reread for context, I see that the team says it's a measurement, and then talks about fitting the collar on. Circumference must be the distance around the tree kangaroo's neck.*

- Now have partners or small groups choose a three-page section of the text and reread it together, looking for unfamiliar words, detailed explanations, and quotations from Lisa's team. Have students slow their reading rate, reread, use context, or rephrase challenging parts of the text in order to understand it. **ELA** RI.5.3, RI.5.4, L.5.6 **ELD** ELD.PI.5.6a, ELD.PI.5.6b

🖉 🗒 ***Annotate it!*** Have students highlight other examples of science-related language in the text.

▶ DOMAIN: Life Science

LESSON TOPIC: Wild Animals

Cross-Curricular Connection Point out that the Matschie's tree kangaroo has been classified as an endangered species. Discuss how logging and mineral mining threaten the tree kangaroo's rain-forest habitat. Say: *Any time an animal's habitat is disturbed, whether by the cutting of trees, road building, mining, or other human activities, the animals may be forced from the area or may become too stressed to reproduce.* Explain that local hunters also threaten the species, and that efforts to help the tree kangaroo include a program to establish a reserve in which the kangaroos can live safely.

FIRST READ

Think Through the Text

Cite Text Evidence

17 *How does the photo relate to what you have read about in the text so far?* The biologist is taking samples from the kangaroo's hair for DNA testing, one of several ways in which the scientists gather information about the kangaroos. **ELA RI.5.3**

18 *What details support the idea that the team members are delighted with the way their work is progressing?* The radio collars "work fine." One tracker is so happy that he would like to "hunt for more tree kangaroos this very afternoon." Lisa says, "But the hotel is full!" She means that all the research cages are full of kangaroos. **ELA RI.5.1**

ENGLISH LANGUAGE SUPPORT Ask this question in a different way. *How is the team feeling about the way their work is going so far? What details from the text tell you this?*

19 *The selection ends with Gabriel's exclamation, "History!" What do you think he means?* Placing a radio collar on a male kangaroo for the first time is a significant moment. He means that they have "made history by doing something that hasn't been done before." **ELD ELD.PI.5.6a**

Classroom Conversation

Have students discuss "Quest for the Tree Kangaroo," either as a whole class or in small groups. Have them focus on this prompt: *Is it important for authors to write about the kind of work Lisa does in this selection? Explain.* Tell students to use text evidence to support their thinking. Remind students to follow discussion rules and to ask and respond to questions. Remind them also to give everyone a chance to speak, and to state their opinions clearly and in complete sentences. **ELA SL.5.1a, SL.5.1b, SL.5.1c**
ELD ELD.PI.5.1, ELD.PI.5.4

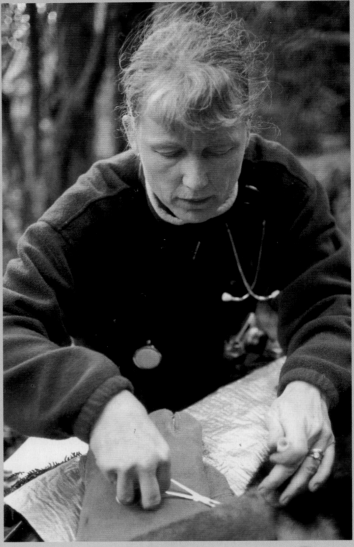

Holly takes a hair sample for DNA analysis. **17**

188

ENGLISH LANGUAGE SUPPORT

Collaborate: Question

Teach/Model Remind students that to *question* is to ask questions about a text before, during, and after reading it. Use a Think Aloud to model asking questions about "Quest for the Tree Kangaroo."

(Think Aloud) *Why would scientists need to capture a wild tree kangaroo in order to learn about it? How does capturing the animal help scientists study it?*

Guided Practice Write the questions and have the class repeat them after you. Remind students to think of these questions as they reread "Quest for the Tree Kangaroo."

• Review **Teach Academic Language** on Lesson 6 Language Support Card ☐.

• Remind students to use the conditional with *would* and gerund subjects to ask questions.

Everything is going like clockwork. Then Christine warns, "Respiration slowing …"

"That's it. Let's pull the mask off," says Lisa.

It's 11:37 A.M. "His ears are twitching. Let's get him back in the bag," says Holly.

It's all over in just ten minutes. "Great work," says Lisa.

Noon. We're at the tree kangaroo house.[5] The men have cut fern fronds and lined the two apartments inside with this soft, moist carpet. They've used ferns to screen the wall between the new pair and Ombum, so the animals won't upset each other. Ombum looks calm. Though his leg is no better, he is now taking banana leaves from Christine's hands.

We all sit quietly while one of the trackers opens the cage door. Tess climbs out of the bag and scurries up a perch. She regards us with interest, but no fear. Lisa has named the male Christopher—in honor of my pig, who grew to 750 pounds and lived to age fourteen. The kangaroo Christopher rushes out of his bag and climbs to the highest perch.

Joel and Gabriel want to make sure the collars are working, so they have brought their radio receivers along to check. Each animal has its own frequency, almost like a phone number. If Joel wants to tune in to Tess, he dials up channel 151.080. Christopher's channel is 150.050. Both collars work fine.

We're all delighted. One tracker is so enthusiastic, he wants to go out and hunt for more tree kangaroos this very afternoon. "But the hotel is full!" says Lisa. Since Christopher and Tess are healthy enough to return to the wild, they will be released tomorrow. For now, though, the cage has all the tree kangaroos it can hold.

We all shake hands, hug, and smile. Everyone is beaming with a mixture of excitement, exhaustion—and relief.

"The first collared male Matschie's tree kangaroo," says Gabriel. "History!" **19**

---

[5] tree kangaroo house: a fourteen-foot by eight-foot enclosure the team has built using sticks, vines, and mosses to keep the kangaroos comfortable

189

Scaffolded Practice and Application

Emerging Have partners copy the questions and then circle words that will help them answer the questions.

Expanding Have partners write answers to the questions. Have volunteers share their sentences with the class.

Bridging Have partners brainstorm cause and effect questions about the anchor text and write their answers.

Dig Deeper *Use Clues to Analyze the Text*

▶ SHARE OBJECTIVES

- Identify cause-and-effect relationships in informational text.
- Notice the effect of quotations and descriptions in informational text.
- Understand the importance of domain-specific vocabulary and determine meaning in context.
- Understand the use common language features in science texts. LANGUAGE

ENGLISH LANGUAGE SUPPORT

Comprehensible Input

Emerging Ask students to give the meaning of the following quote from **Student Book p. 187**: *"Oh, but he's tough!" says Gabriel.* Accept one-word responses and expand them. For example, if the student's response is "hard," expand it by saying, *"Yes, the kangaroo is hard to control.*

Expanding Have students use phrases to give the meaning of the quote.

Bridging Ask students to use complete sentences to explain the meaning of the quote. **ELD** ELD.PI.5.1

Text-Based Comprehension

1 Teach/Model

Terms About Informational Text

cause-and-effect relationship related events in which one event causes another to occur, sometimes setting off a chain of events

quotation the exact words spoken by someone

descriptions impressions of people, places, or events

domain-specific words vocabulary commonly used within a given subject area

---

- Remind students that they have just read an informational text about the Matschie's tree kangaroo of Papua New Guinea.

- Read **Student Book p. 190** with students. Point out that many events presented in informational texts have a **cause-and-effect relationship**. Tell students it is possible for one event to create multiple effects. Then, explain that an event can be both a cause and an effect. Tell students that identifying causes and effects in a scientific text can help them explain the relationships between events. Discuss cause and effect using the following model:

> **Think Aloud** *In "Quest for the Tree Kangaroo," trackers spot two tree kangaroos. As a result, a tracker runs back to camp to alert the others. The announcement causes the rest of the team to race after the trackers. The effect, therefore, is that the team sees the kangaroos. This is a chain of cause-and-effect events.*

Next, read **Student Book p. 191** with students.

- Explain that authors use **quotations** and **descriptions** to present facts and details in an informational text. In "Quest for the Tree Kangaroo," quotations let readers see how team members interact with each another while conducting research, and details give readers a clearer picture of events as they unfold.

- Remain students that authors use **domain-specific words** to deliver information specific about a subject area—in this case, life science and wild animals. Point out that as students determine the meanings of domain-specific words and phrases in context as they read, they will develop a deeper understanding of the text's subject.

- **Q Language Detective: The Language of Science Texts** Explain that informational texts that focus on science topics contain common features, such as procedures, quotes from experts, and detailed explanations. Tell students that these features can make reading science texts challenging, but slowing down to read carefully, breaking the text into sections, and rephrasing difficult parts of the text can help readers understand an author's key ideas.

🔍 BE A READING DETECTIVE

Dig Deeper

Use Clues to Analyze the Text

Use these pages to learn about Cause and Effect, Quotes and Description, and Domain-Specific Vocabulary. Then read "Quest for the Tree Kangaroo" again to apply what you learned.

Cause and Effect

In the informational text "Quest for the Tree Kangaroo," many of the events have **cause-and-effect** relationships. One event, called the cause, leads to a later event, called the effect. This effect can then become the cause for another effect, creating a chain of events that are related.

Look back at page 189 of "Quest for the Tree Kangaroo." After the male tree kangaroo has been under anesthesia for several minutes, his respiration begins to slow. What decision does Lisa make as a result? What effect does her decision have?

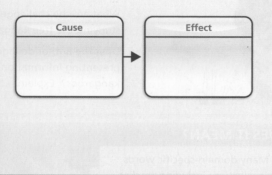

Cause		Effect
	→	

Quotes and Descriptions

To share information with readers in an engaging way, the author of "Quest for the Tree Kangaroo" includes **quotations**, or the exact words spoken by the team members. She also writes detailed **descriptions** of what the scientists see and do. Look back at pages 186–189. The conversation and the explanation of the scientists' actions help readers imagine they are right there as the tree kangaroos are examined.

Domain-Specific Vocabulary

Many subject areas have their own special set of vocabulary. These terms, known as **domain-specific words**, express precise ideas and concepts related to the subject. By using domain-specific terms in their writing, authors can communicate accurate information to their readers. For example, the scientists in this selection don't just give the tree kangaroos "some medicine"— they administer *anesthesia*, a medicine that makes the animals unconscious for a short time.

Habitat

190   **ELA** RI.5.3, RI.5.4, RI.5.10, RF.5.4a, RF.5.4b   **ELD** ELD.PI.5.6a, ELD.PI.5.12a

191

---

2 Guided Practice/Apply

Analyze the Text

Begin a second read of "Quest for the Tree Kangaroo" with students. Use the stopping points and instructional support to guide students to analyze the text:

• Cause and Effect, p. T23   **ELA** RI.5.3 **ELD** ELD.PI.5.6a

• Domain-Specific Vocabulary, p. T27   **ELA** RI.5.4, L.5.6 **ELD** ELD.PI.5.6a

• Quotes and Description, p. T29   **ELD** ELD.PI.5.6a, ELD.PII.5.7

• The Language of Science Texts, p. T31   **ELA** L.5.4a **ELD** ELD.PI.5.6a, ELD.PI.5.6b

Directed Note-Taking The graphic organizer will be completed with students during the second read on p. T23.

FORMATIVE ASSESSMENT   RtI

Are students able to identify cause-and-effect relationships in a text?

IF...	THEN...
students struggle,	**Differentiate Comprehension** for Struggling Readers, p. T70.
students are on track,	**Differentiate Comprehension** for On-Level Readers, p. T70.
students excel,	**Differentiate Comprehension** for Advanced Readers, p. T71.

SMALL GROUP Options | **Differentiate Comprehension, pp. T70–T71**
Scaffold instruction to the English Learner's proficiency level. |

SECOND READ

Your Turn

Cite Text Evidence

▶ **SHARE OBJECTIVES**

• Contribute to a discussion on a topic.

• Use context and reference materials to determine the meanings of domain-specific words.

• Write a response paragraph using text evidence as support. **LANGUAGE**

RETURN TO THE ESSENTIAL QUESTION

As partners discuss the Essential Question, tell them to accurately quote text evidence to support their thinking. Remind them to prepare for the discussion by reviewing the text.

ELA RI.5.1, RI.5.2, SL.5.1a **ELD** ELD.PI.5.1

Classroom Conversation

Have students continue the discussion of "Quest for the Tree Kangaroo" by explaining their answers to the three questions. Remind students to make comments that contribute to the discussion and to elaborate on the remarks of others. See Digital Lesson: Listening and Responding .

ELA RI.1.1, RI.1.2, SL.5.1a, SL.5.1c **ELD** ELD.PI.5.1, ELD.PI.5.6a

ENGLISH LANGUAGE SUPPORT Use sentence frames such as the following to support discussion.

• *I think the team members feel _____. I think this because _____.*

• *Some of the challenges of studying the tree kangaroo are _____.*

• *The author (does)/(does not) do a good job of presenting information about tree kangaroos. I think this because ____.*

As students share their ideas, tell them to use text evidence to support their responses.

ELD ELD.PI.5.1, ELD.PI.5.4, ELD.PI.5.11a

Your Turn

RETURN TO THE ESSENTIAL QUESTION

 Turn and Talk Review the selection to prepare to discuss this question: *Why is it important to research and protect endangered animals?* With a partner, list reasons drawn from text evidence and your prior knowledge. Share them with the class.

 Classroom Conversation

Continue your discussion of "Quest for the Tree Kangaroo" by using text evidence to answer these questions:

1 How do the team members feel about the work they are doing? How do you know?

2 What are the challenges of studying the tree kangaroo?

3 Does the author do a good job of presenting information about tree kangaroos? Explain.

WHAT DOES IT MEAN?

Look It Up Many domain-specific words are used in this selection, including *tracker, humidity, anesthesia, respiration, stethoscope, transmitter, antenna, microscope,* and *frequency.* Use a print or digital dictionary to look up the definitions of these words or others that you find in the text. Then write a new sentence using each word. Share your sentences with a partner.

192   **ELA** RI.5.3, W.5.2d, W.5.9b, SL.5.1a, L.5.4c, L.5.6 **ELD** ELD.PI.5.1, ELD.PI.5.6a, ELD.PI.5.10a, ELD.PI.5.12a

---

ENGLISH LANGUAGE SUPPORT

How English Works

Connecting Ideas Before students begin their discussion, have them plan to use connecting words in their responses. Tell students that speakers use special words to connect, or put together, ideas in sentences. Give the following examples: *because, even though.* Provide a model sentence such as, *The boy wore a sweater because it was cold outside.* Help different proficiency levels build word banks of connecting words to use during their discussions. **ELD** ELD.PII.5.6

Performance Task

WRITE ABOUT READING

 **WriteSmart**

Response Think about all the effort that Lisa and her team put into studying the Matschie's tree kangaroo. What do they hope to learn? Why? Write a paragraph in which you explain how the information that Lisa and her team collect will help protect the species. Use specific facts and details from the text to develop your explanation.

Writing Tip

As you write your draft, use precise language and domain-specific vocabulary. Include transitions to show the connections between your ideas.

193

ENGLISH LANGUAGE SUPPORT

Collaborative Writing

Step 1 Guide students to complete a web to discover ideas and support them with reasons based in text evidence.

Step 2 Explain that you will work together as a class to write a response to reading by using the completed graphic organizer. Point out to students that they will say ideas and sentences, and you will write them down for the group to see and read.

Step 3 Have students develop the response by referring to the graphic organizer and answering questions such as these:

- What words will help begin this response?
- What information should we include? How do we say that in a sentence?
- What is the first reason that we should write?
- What text evidence will we use?

Step 4 Read the unfinished response aloud to students. Repeat, and have students read aloud with you. Ask students if they see or hear anything they would like to change.

Extra Scaffold Without purposely making mistakes, revise in the moment by using Think Alouds. **ELD** ELD.PI.5.2

WHAT DOES IT MEAN?

Tell students to locate each listed word in the selection, and use context to predict the word's meaning. Then, provide print dictionaries or access to online dictionaries. Ask students to confirm their thinking by looking up the words' true definitions. Once students understand the correct meanings, ask them to write a sentence for each word.

ELA RI.5.4, L.5.4a, L.5.4c, L.5.6 **ELD** ELD.PI.5.12a

WRITE ABOUT READING

 Performance Task

Have students think about the purpose of the expedition and what its members hope to achieve. Guide students to understand the cause-and-effect relationship. Point out that the efforts of the team may result in better protection for the tree kangaroo. Remind students to quote text evidence accurately as they develop their paragraphs.

ELA RI.5.1, RI.5.3, W.5.2a, W.5.2b, W.5.9b, W.5.10 **ELD** ELD.PI.5.6a, ELD.PI.5.10a

ENGLISH LANGUAGE SUPPORT Tell students to state their main idea in the opening sentence. Provide this frame:

> *I think Lisa and her team's research (will)/ (will not) help protect the tree kangaroo.*

Suggest that they explain why the team studied the tree kangaroo using these frames:

> *I think this because _____.*
> *In addition, the text says _____.*

Remind students to use connecting words in their paragraph. See Digital Lesson: Writing to Sources. **ELD** ELD.PII.5.6

Writing Tip Make sure students read the Writing Tip before beginning their paragraphs. Guide them to pause as they write to look for places where domain-specific words could clarify their points. Have them review their drafts for the purpose of adding transition words and phrases, such as *for example, then, after,* and *next* between ideas.

ELA W.5.2c, W.5.2d, L.5.6 **ELD** ELD.PI.5.12a, ELD.PII.5.6

WriteSmart Have students complete the Write About Reading activity through *my*WriteSmart. Students will read the prompt within *my*WriteSmart and have access to multiple writing resources, including the Student eBook, Writing Rubrics, and Graphic Organizers.

Independent Reading

▶ SHARE OBJECTIVES

- Read and comprehend informational text.
- Quote accurately from a text to support analysis and inferences.
- Read independently from a "just right" book.
- Ask and answer questions about key details.
LANGUAGE

ENGLISH LANGUAGE SUPPORT

"Just Right" Books for English Learners

All Proficiencies Sometimes an English learner's "just right" book will be one in his or her first language. Reading a first-language book builds confidence for both Emerging and Bridging English learners as they get an opportunity to practice biliteracy skills. Encourage students to share their first-language books with English-speaking partners.

Reader's Guide

Use Text Evidence Tell students that they will read "Quest for the Tree Kangaroo" on their own to analyze important ideas in the text.

Have students use the Reader's Guide pages in their Reader's Notebook, pp. 61–62 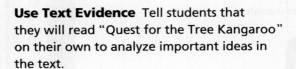. Explain that they should support their responses to the prompts with text evidence.

Model Questioning Demonstrate generating a complex question about a section of "Quest for the Tree Kangaroo." For example, write this question on the board: *What do the trackers do to show that they are good problem solvers?* Reread **Student Book p. 179** with students, working together to respond to the question.

Generate Questions Have students work independently or collaboratively to generate questions about "Quest for the Tree Kangaroo." Ask students to share their questions. Begin a class discussion of questions that students have in common or that are most significant to their understanding of the text. **ELA** RL.5.1, RL.5.10, RF.5.4a, SL.5.1c **ELD** ELD.PI.5.1

Self-Selected Reading

Topics of Interest Have students make a list of topics that interest them and choose their favorite. Review how to find books by topic in a library using a card catalog. Then tell students to select a book on their chosen topic for independent reading. Ask students to use their Reading Logs in Grab-and-Go™ to record their progress and thinking about the book.

FOR STUDENTS WITH DISABILITIES Students may have particular difficulty comprehending informational text. Remind them to reread to find important details and to stop after a page or a section to summarize the information in their own words.

Fluency

Partner Read Have students read aloud with expression to a partner, using their self-selected reading books. Then have them give each other feedback and reread to apply it. **ELA** RF.5.4b

Apply Vocabulary Knowledge

✅ Review Target Vocabulary

Classroom Collaboration Read aloud each of the following questions. Have students discuss their answers. Allow several students to respond to each question to provide a variety of possible responses for discussion.

ELA L.5.6 **ELD** ELD.PI.5.12a

1. How do most wild animals react to the **presence** of humans?

2. To be properly **outfitted** for a camping trip, what would you buy or take?

3. What is the **procedure** for exiting the school during a fire drill?

4. How do you **calculate** the amount of time you need to study for a test?

5. What hobby or pastime are you most **enthusiastic** about?

6. Why might some plants and trees be **dwarfed** by other vegetation nearby?

7. Why do squirrels, birds, and other animals choose a high **perch** for their resting places?

8. How could you help a classmate who just **transferred** to your school from a different one?

9. If someone is walking down the hall **beaming**, what might you infer?

10. Why is it important that a dog's collar be **snug**?

Quick Write Display the following prompt: *Explain how you view tree kangaroos after reading this selection. Use the vocabulary words you have learned in your writing.*

Tell students to support their opinions with important facts and other text evidence from the selection. Remind them to quote accurately. When they have finished writing, tell students to exchange papers with a partner and discuss whether they used the words correctly in their paragraphs.

ELA RL.5.1, L.5.6 **ELD** ELD.PI.5.1, ELD.PI.5.4

▶ **SHARE OBJECTIVES**

- Acquire and use vocabulary in speaking and writing. LANGUAGE
- Collaboratively respond to questions about familiar vocabulary. LANGUAGE

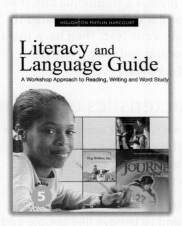

HOUGHTON MIFFLIN HARCOURT

Literacy and Language Guide
A Workshop Approach to Reading, Writing and Word Study

GRADE 5

For additional practice with the lesson's Target Vocabulary, use the activities on pages 126–127 of the **Literacy and Language Guide.**

- "Because" Sentences
- Suffix -ic
- Eponyms
- Four-Square Map

ENGLISH LANGUAGE SUPPORT

Use Sentence Frames

All Proficiencies Have students complete sentence frames such as these to help them support their opinions in their writing.

After reading the text, I think that tree kangaroos _____.
I think this because _____.

Guide students to support their opinions with specific references in the text.

ELD ELD.PI.5.4, ELD.PI.5.11a

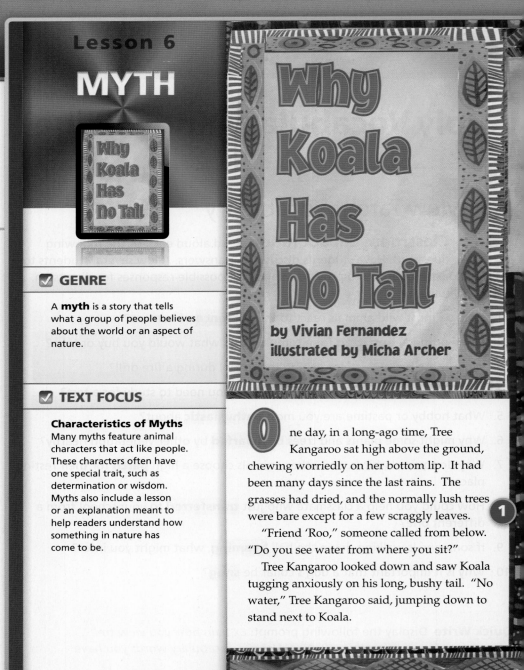

DOMAIN: **Life Science**
LESSON TOPIC: WILD ANIMALS

CONNECT TO THE TOPIC
Myth

Preview The Myth

- Tell students that a myth is a traditional tale that reflects the beliefs of the culture that created it. Ask students to preview the text. Then have them set a purpose for reading and read the myth independently. **ELA** RL.5.10, RF.5.4a

Discuss Characteristics of Myths

- A myth is a traditional tale that explains a part of the natural world. This can include people, animals, and geographic features such as mountains and rivers.

- Myths may have animals as main characters. Animal characters tend to behave like people and have human traits, such as laziness. Sometimes they can talk or have other special abilities.

- Myths usually have a moral, or lesson, that teaches people about the best ways to behave. The moral may be stated directly, or it may be up to the reader or listener to figure it out.

- Ask students to look for the following features of myths as they read.

moral	lesson that teaches people how they should behave
myth	tale in which animals are often the main characters
animal characters	animals that have human traits and characteristics

Lesson 6
MYTH

✓ **GENRE**

A **myth** is a story that tells what a group of people believes about the world or an aspect of nature.

✓ **TEXT FOCUS**

Characteristics of Myths
Many myths feature animal characters that act like people. These characters often have one special trait, such as determination or wisdom. Myths also include a lesson or an explanation meant to help readers understand how something in nature has come to be.

194 **ELA** RL.5.10, RF.5.4a, RF.5.4b **ELD** ELD.PI.5.6a

Why Koala Has No Tail
by Vivian Fernandez
illustrated by Micha Archer

One day, in a long-ago time, Tree Kangaroo sat high above the ground, chewing worriedly on her bottom lip. It had been many days since the last rains. The grasses had dried, and the normally lush trees were bare except for a few scraggly leaves.

"Friend 'Roo," someone called from below. "Do you see water from where you sit?"

Tree Kangaroo looked down and saw Koala tugging anxiously on his long, bushy tail. "No water," Tree Kangaroo said, jumping down to stand next to Koala.

1

ENGLISH LANGUAGE SUPPORT

Idiomatic Language

Emerging Explain the meanings of the common expressions *looked around* and *hard work* on p. 196. Point out the different uses for *around* and *hard* with the examples *look around the door* and *hard chair*. **ELD** ELD.PI.5.8

Expanding Explain the meanings of the expressions *catch her breath* (to rest) and *sliced clean off* (to cut) from p. 197. Have students restate the following sentences using the expressions. *The runner stopped to rest. The branch was cut.* **ELD** ELD.PI.5.8

Bridging Have students find the common expressions *thought it over* and *easy enough* on p. 195. Have them create their own sentences using these expressions. **ELD** ELD.PI.5.8

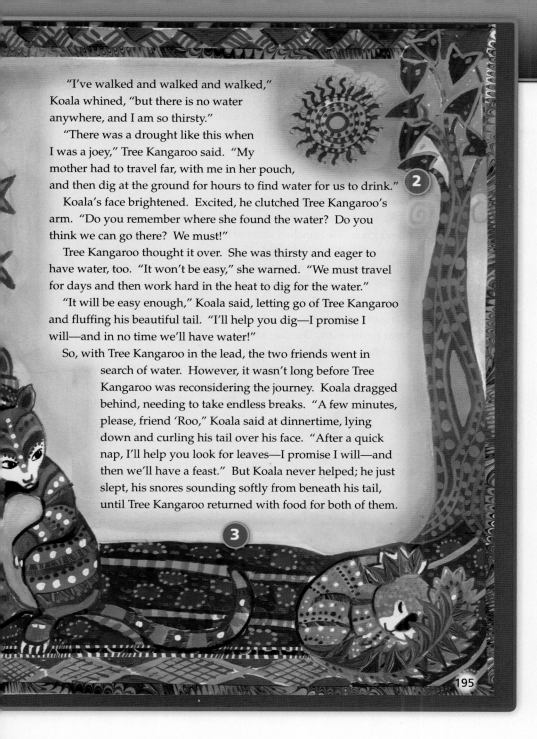

"I've walked and walked and walked," Koala whined, "but there is no water anywhere, and I am so thirsty."

"There was a drought like this when I was a joey," Tree Kangaroo said. "My mother had to travel far, with me in her pouch, and then dig at the ground for hours to find water for us to drink."

Koala's face brightened. Excited, he clutched Tree Kangaroo's arm. "Do you remember where she found the water? Do you think we can go there? We must!"

Tree Kangaroo thought it over. She was thirsty and eager to have water, too. "It won't be easy," she warned. "We must travel for days and then work hard in the heat to dig for the water."

"It will be easy enough," Koala said, letting go of Tree Kangaroo and fluffing his beautiful tail. "I'll help you dig—I promise I will—and in no time we'll have water!"

So, with Tree Kangaroo in the lead, the two friends went in search of water. However, it wasn't long before Tree Kangaroo was reconsidering the journey. Koala dragged behind, needing to take endless breaks. "A few minutes, please, friend 'Roo," Koala said at dinnertime, lying down and curling his tail over his face. "After a quick nap, I'll help you look for leaves—I promise I will—and then we'll have a feast." But Koala never helped; he just slept, his snores sounding softly from beneath his tail, until Tree Kangaroo returned with food for both of them.

195

Think Through the Text

Cite Text Evidence

Pause at the stopping points to ask students the following questions.

1 *What word in this sentence means the opposite of lush?* bare ELA RL.5.4

ENGLISH LANGUAGE SUPPORT Explain to students that trees that are *lush* are very healthy looking and are growing fast. ELD ELD.PI.5.12a

2 *How is the way Koala speaks different from the way Tree Kangaroo speaks? Koala "whines" about not finding water, while Tree Kangaroo tells a story about overcoming a problem.* ELA RL.5.3

3 *How does this illustration help show the relationship between the two characters? Koala is sleeping, and Tree Kangaroo is not happy because Koala doesn't help with the work.* ELA RL.5.3, RL.5.7

💬 Classroom Collaboration

In the myth, Koala is lazy, and Tree Kangaroo is hard-working. Why did the author choose these two animals? As a class, have students create their own list of animals they feel are lazy and animals they feel are hard-working. Encourage them to explain why they would put each animal on the list. ELA SL.5.6 ELD ELD.PI.5.3

DOMAIN: Life Science

LESSON TOPIC: Wild Animals

Cross-Curricular Connection Tell students that before scientific methods were developed, people observed wild animals and tried to explain their appearance and actions. Discuss other myths that students know. Work with them to think of other animals with a unique appearance (such as a giraffe) and what a myth might explain about each animal (e.g., how the giraffe got a long neck). Ask students how scientists might explain the same things.

Think Through the Text

Cite Text Evidence

Pause at the stopping points to ask students the following questions.

4 *What pattern in Koala's behavior is repeated in different scenes?* He says he will help but then just takes a nap. **ELA** RL.5.5

5 *How would you paraphrase what Koala means when he says, "Be right there"?* "I'll do it in a minute" or "Wait just a minute." **ELA** RL.5.4

ENGLISH LANGUAGE SUPPORT Use these sentence frames to help students point out Koala's pattern of behavior:

On the journey to the riverbed, Koala does not help Tree Kangaroo. Instead, he _____. takes a nap

When it was time to dig for water, Koala does not help Tree Kangaroo. Instead, he _____. takes a nap **ELD** ELD.PI.5.6a, ELD.PI.5.8

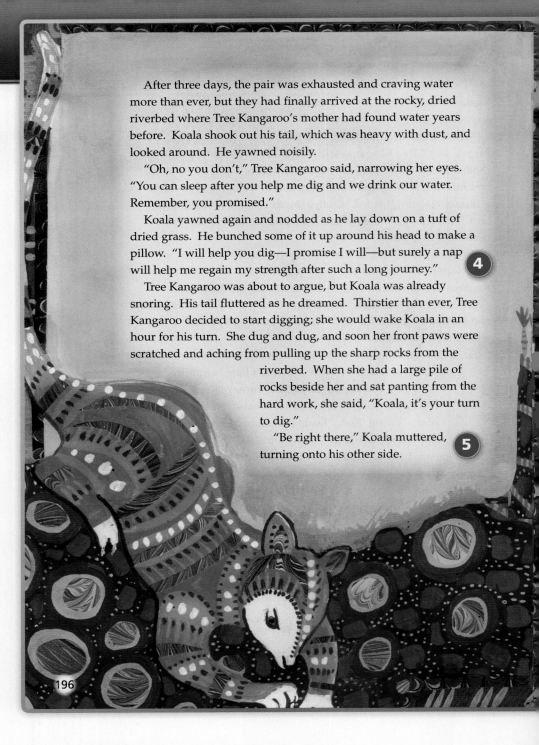

After three days, the pair was exhausted and craving water more than ever, but they had finally arrived at the rocky, dried riverbed where Tree Kangaroo's mother had found water years before. Koala shook out his tail, which was heavy with dust, and looked around. He yawned noisily.

"Oh, no you don't," Tree Kangaroo said, narrowing her eyes. "You can sleep after you help me dig and we drink our water. Remember, you promised."

Koala yawned again and nodded as he lay down on a tuft of dried grass. He bunched some of it up around his head to make a pillow. "I will help you dig—I promise I will—but surely a nap will help me regain my strength after such a long journey."

Tree Kangaroo was about to argue, but Koala was already snoring. His tail fluttered as he dreamed. Thirstier than ever, Tree Kangaroo decided to start digging; she would wake Koala in an hour for his turn. She dug and dug, and soon her front paws were scratched and aching from pulling up the sharp rocks from the riverbed. When she had a large pile of rocks beside her and sat panting from the hard work, she said, "Koala, it's your turn to dig."

"Be right there," Koala muttered, turning onto his other side.

196

ENGLISH LANGUAGE SUPPORT

Use Sentence Frames

Emerging Ask students to complete these sentence frames: *Tree Kangaroo works very hard, but Koala is _____ and sleeps a lot. Koala often _____ to do things he doesn't do.* **ELD** ELD.PI.5.6a

Expanding Ask students to complete each of these sentences with a phrase: *Tree Kangaroo works very hard, but Koala _____. Koala often promises _____.* **ELD** ELD.PI.5.6a

Bridging Ask students to compare Tree Kangaroo and Koala using complete sentences. For example, ask them to compare how much they work and how well they keep their promises. **ELD** ELD.PI.5.6a

Tree Kangaroo took another minute to catch her breath, using her paws to shield her eyes from the bright, hot sun. She was exasperated, but still thirsty, so she continued to dig. Koala slept on. Eventually, Tree Kangaroo began to see a shimmer of moisture on the rocks she was digging out, and her tender paws touched wet soil, and then—"Water!" she cried, overjoyed.

"Finally!" Koala said, instantly awake. He ran to where Tree Kangaroo was bent over the hole, tasting the delicious water at last. As he pushed Tree Kangaroo out of his way and took a long, greedy drink, his twitchy tail cut across the edge of one exceptionally sharp rock in Tree Kangaroo's pile. "My tail!" he cried when he saw it had been sliced clean off. Not even a small fluffy nub remained. Forgetting the water, he ran away, wailing, never to return to the area again.

197

Practice Fluency

Expression Have students listen as you read aloud the second and third paragraphs on **Student Book p. 196**, starting with Tree Kangaroo saying, "Oh, no you don't." **ELD** ELD.PI.5.5

- Remind students that good readers use the expression in their voices to add interest and to convey meaning as they read.

- Have students do repeated readings of the paragraphs with a partner. Remind them to use their voices to express the emotions of the characters in the text. **ELA** RF.5.4b

Think Through the Text

Cite Text Evidence

Pause at the stopping points to ask students the following questions.

6 *Think about the lesson that Koala learns in this myth. How would you state the theme of the story, or the message that readers are supposed to understand? Sample answer: It is better to work hard and to share than to be lazy and greedy.* **ELA** RL.5.2 **ELD** ELD.PI.5.6a

7 *How does this illustration help you understand the ending of the myth? It shows that Koala lost his tail and that he is very upset about it.* **ELA** RL.5.7

Koala's laziness and greed had cost him his beautiful bushy tail, and since that day, all koalas have been born tailless as a reminder to work hard and to share. **6**

7

198

ENGLISH LANGUAGE SUPPORT

Idiomatic Language

Emerging Help students understand the meaning of *cost* in "Koala's laziness and greed had cost him his beautiful bushy tail." Discuss what it means to "pay the cost" for an action or behavior. **ELD** ELD.PI.5.8

Expanding Ask students to explain the meaning of *cost* in "Koala's laziness and greed had cost him his beautiful bushy tail." Have them give examples of "paying the cost" for bad behavior. **ELD** ELD.PI.5.8

Bridging Ask students to restate "Koala's laziness and greed had cost him his beautiful bushy tail" in their own words. *Sample answer: Because Koala was lazy and greedy, he lost his tail.* **ELD** ELD.PI.5.8

Compare Texts

TEXT TO TEXT

Compare Genres Review "Quest for the Tree Kangaroo" and "Why Koala Has No Tail." With a partner, complete a T-Map, recording details from each selection that describe the tree kangaroo. Compare and contrast the details and images of the tree kangaroo that each selection conveys. Then discuss how the genre of each text—an informational text versus a myth—influences how the tree kangaroo is portrayed.

TEXT TO SELF

Write a Letter What do you find most interesting or admirable about the work that Lisa and her team are doing? Write a letter to a member of the expedition, sharing your feelings about the scientists' activities. Support your opinions with text evidence and quotes.

TEXT TO WORLD

Make a Poster With a partner, do further research on the tree kangaroo or another endangered animal. Use reliable print or electronic sources to find out more about the animal, why it is endangered, and what is being done to help protect it. Make an awareness poster, presenting the key points of your research. Share your poster with the class.

ELA RI.5.1, RI.5.7, RI.5.9, W.5.7 **ELD** ELD.PI.5.1, ELD.PI.5.6a, ELD.PI.5.10a

199

Compare Texts

TEXT TO TEXT

Before students begin their charts, remind them of the roles that animal characters play in myths. Then discuss the methods of scientific observation used in *Quest for the Tree Kangaroo*. Help students identify the purpose of each selection as they make comparisons.
ELA RL.5.1, RI.5.1, RI.5.9 **ELD** ELD.PI.5.1

TEXT TO SELF

Display these sentence frames to help students organize information for their letters.

Lisa's team is _____.

This is interesting to me because _____.

This is important because _____.

Review the correct form for writing a personal letter, and remind students to proofread their work before making a final copy.
ELA RL.5.1 **ELD** ELD.PI.5.10a, ELD.PI.5.11a

TEXT TO WORLD

Have students organize ideas in a chart with these headings: *Endangered Species; Why They Are Endangered; Efforts to Protect Them*. Review guidelines for identifying reliable print and digital sources. **ELA** RI.5.7, W.5.7 **ELD** ELD.PI.5.2

ENGLISH LANGUAGE SUPPORT

Compare Texts

Organize Concepts Help students complete a chart comparing how two selections portray the subject of tree kangaroos. Have students refer to their **Student Book pp. 174–189** and **194–199**.
ELA RI.5.3, RI.5.9 **ELD** ELD.PI.5.1

Selection Title	How Tree Kangaroos Are Portrayed
Quest for the Tree Kangaroo	The tree kangaroos are the subject of study. The animals have no personalities or "human" qualities.
Why Koala Has No Tail	Tree Kangaroo is a character in a fictional tale. She has emotions and a distinct personality.

Build Academic Sentence Structures To help students compare and contrast the way the two selections present tree kangaroos, ask: *How are the tree kangaroos the same in both selections? How are they different?* Provide sentence frames such as these:

- *Both selections feature <u>tree kangaroos</u>.*
- *The tree kangaroos in Papua New Guinea are <u>wild animals</u>.* **ELA** SL.5.1d **ELD** PI.5.1

Vocabulary Strategies

▶ SHARE OBJECTIVES
- Use the relationship between synonyms and antonyms to determine their meanings and better understand the words.
- Consult print and digital reference materials to clarify the meanings of words.

▶ SKILL TRACE

Synonyms and Antonyms	
Introduce	**T46–T47**
Differentiate	T76–T77
Reteach	T78
Test	Weekly Tests, Lesson 6

ENGLISH LANGUAGE SUPPORT

Preteach

All Proficiencies Explain to students that synonyms are words that have a similar meaning. Tell them that antonyms are words with opposite meanings. Provide students with example synonym and antonym pairs, such as *hot/steamy; hot/cold*.

Support Linguistic Transfer

Positive Transfer To help students whose first language is Spanish understand antonyms, provide examples, such as *joven/vieja* (young, old).

Apply Vocabulary Skills

Emerging Use gestures and pictures to demonstrate antonyms *hot* and *cold* as you say, *I am hot; I am cold.* Have students repeat each sentence.

Expanding Have students complete sentence frames: *Hot* means the same as _____ *steamy.* _____ is the opposite of *hot. Cold*

Bridging Have students write sentences using synonyms *hot* and *steamy* and antonyms *tidy* and *messy.*
ELD ELD.PI.5.8

Synonyms and Antonyms

1 Teach/Model

Terms About Language

antonyms words that have opposite meanings

synonyms words that share similar meanings

- Explain that **synonyms** are words that have similar meanings. Provide examples of familiar synonyms, such as *big / large, small / tiny, graceful / elegant*. Then tell students that **antonyms** are words that have opposite meanings. Provide examples that correspond to the synonyms already introduced: *small, large, clumsy*.

- Explain to students that they can use a print or digital reference work called a thesaurus to find synonyms and antonyms for different words. Display a sample thesaurus entry and read it aloud together.

- Tell students that often a familiar synonym or antonym appears in the same sentence or paragraph as an unknown word. Explain that using the relationships between these words can help students determine the meaning of the word they do not recognize.

- Write this sentence on the board: *The tree kangaroos easily elude the scientists; they have many tricks to avoid their traps*. Model how to define *elude* using the synonym *avoid*.

Think Aloud *I am not sure of the meaning of* elude. *But the second part of the sentence appears to restate the meaning of the first part. So, I can infer, or guess, that* avoid *is a synonym for* elude. *Recognizing this synonym helps me to understand that* elude *means "to escape from or avoid."*

2 Guided Practice

- Display the top half of Projectable 6.3 and read "The Tree Kangaroos" aloud.

- Point out the word *endearing* in the first sentence. Together with students, use a print or digital thesaurus to find a synonym and antonym for it. *lovable; hateful* Guide students to define *endearing*. *sweet, easy to love*

- Show students the bottom half of the projectable. Have them work in pairs to find synonyms, antonyms, and definitions for the words in the first column.

3 Apply

- Have partners look through a familiar selection in their **Student Book** and make a list of adjectives from the text. Have partners use a print or digital thesaurus to find synonyms as alternate word choices for each word. Then have them use the reference sources to find an antonym for each word. Have them exchange papers with another pair and define each other's adjectives based on their knowledge of the synonym and antonym.

- Have students use a print or digital dictionary to determine or clarify the meanings of any words that are unfamiliar. **ELA** L.5.4c, L.5.5c **ELD** ELD.PI.5.6b, ELD.PI.5.8

🖊 **Interactive Whiteboard Lesson** Use **Vocabulary Strategies: Synonyms and Antonyms** to reinforce how to use relationships between synonyms and antonyms to determine word meaning.

- Distribute to students Reader's Notebook page 63 or leveled practice in Grab-and-Go™ Resources to complete independently.

FORMATIVE ASSESSMENT  **RtI**

Are students able to use synonyms and antonyms to determine word meanings?

IF...	THEN...
students **struggle**,	▶ **Differentiate Vocabulary Strategies** for Struggling Readers, p. T76.
students are **on target**,	▶ **Differentiate Vocabulary Strategies** for On-Level Readers, p. T76.
students **excel**,	▶ **Differentiate Vocabulary Strategies** for Advanced Readers, p. T77.

SMALL GROUP options **Differentiate Vocabulary Strategies: pp. T76–T77** *Scaffold instruction to the English learner's proficiency level.*

ENGLISH LANGUAGE SUPPORT

Sentence Frames

Emerging Give students these sets of words: *sick/unwell/healthy; unhappy/sad/happy.* Then ask them to complete these sentence frames for each set: _____ *means the same as* _____ . _____ *means the opposite of* _____ .

Expanding Have students fill in these sentence frames with their own pairs of synonyms and antonyms: _____ *means the same as* _____ . _____ *means the opposite of* _____ .

Bridging Have partners use a print or digital thesaurus to find synonyms and antonyms for *warm, dangerous,* and *exact.* Ask them to write sets of two sentences that include each word and one of its antonyms and synonyms. **ELD** ELD.PI.5.6b, ELD.PI.5.8

DOMAIN: **Life Science**
LESSON TOPIC: Wild Animals

Extend the Topic

▶ **SHARE OBJECTIVES**
- Acquire and use domain-specific vocabulary.
- Conduct a short research project.

Words About the Topic: **Wild Animals**

- **adaptive** being able to change to fit the conditions of an environment
- **endangered species** a kind of animal whose numbers are so small it might become extinct
- **habitat** the environment where an animal or plant naturally lives
- **preservation** protection of a plant or animal species or of an environment
- **satellite tracking** a kind of technology that allows scientists to determine the exact location of wild animals

Domain-Specific Vocabulary

Introduce Words About the Topic Remind students that this week's topic is Wild Animals. Display the words shown in the left column. Tell students that these are words that can help them learn more about the study of wild animals. Read aloud the definition for each word and then have students respond to the following prompts:

- *Giant pandas and sea turtles need protection because they are both examples of this.* endangered species
- *If you bring home a plant or animal from another state, it might not thrive because it is no longer in its natural _____.* habitat
- *This helps scientists determine where humpback whales go in the winter.* satellite tracking
- *Experts hope that _____ efforts will keep American alligators from becoming extinct.* preservation
- *The white fur of a polar bear allows it to blend into the snow and stay hidden from prey. What kind of characteristic is this an example of?* adaptive

ENGLISH LANGUAGE SUPPORT For example, point out the white collar on page 187 and say: *This collar helps scientists follow an animal by using satellite tracking.*

Interact with the Words Have students work in small groups, using Graphic Organizer 6 (Four-Square Map) ⎘ to extend their understanding of each word about wild animals. Assign one word to each group, and have them follow these steps for completing the Four-Square Map with information about the word:

1 In the first corner, draw a picture that represents the word.

2 In the second corner, write the definition of the word.

3 In the third corner, write a sentence using the word.

4 In the fourth corner, write the word.

When groups have finished, have them share their completed Four-Square Maps with the class. **ELA** L.5.6 **ELD** ELD.PI.5.12a

Research and Media Literacy

Investigate Different Aspects of a Topic

Choose a Topic Have students revisit "Quest for the Tree Kangaroo." Generate a class list of related topics, such as *endangered species* and *desert habitats*. Have students choose a topic that interests them. Explain that they will use multiple sources to research different aspects of their topic and then present their findings.

Brainstorm and Identify Sources Have students create a Web for their topic, listing key words, phrases, and possible research questions in the outer circles. Then have students identify sources they can use to gather information, including digital and print reference sources, books, magazines, newspapers, almanacs, and websites.

Take Notes Explain to students that note-taking is a key element of integrating information from several sources on the same topic. Share the note-taking tips.
ELA W.5.7

- Write one piece of information per index card or sheet of paper and include the source.

- Summarize and paraphrase long passages of information; copy quotations accurately and place them in quotation marks right away so you will remember later that they are someone else's words.

- Identify notes by key words and source so that the information is easier to organize. **ELA** W.5.8

FOR STUDENTS WITH DISABILITIES Some students may need assistance to distinguish between the literal and figurative meaning of a word or phrase. Model using context clues to figure out the meaning. Instruct students on the use of the dictionary and thesaurus. Create a class notebook with examples of multiple-meaning words, their definitions, example sentences, and illustrations.

Prepare Outline Have students review their notes and decide which information they want to include in their presentation and how they want to present it. Tell them that they will integrate information from several sources into an outline that they will use as the basis for their presentation. Give students time to prepare their outline and practice using it to discuss their topic. **ELA** RI.5.9

Present Have students present their research findings to a small group or to the class. Tell them to use formal English and to speak clearly at an understandable pace. Remind them to maintain eye contact with their audience and to take time at the end of the presentation to answer questions. **ELA** SL.5.4b, SL.5.6 **ELD** ELD.PI.5.9

Skill Focus: Use Evidence Explain that when students conduct research and write reports, they will cite evidence to support conjectures or opinions based on prior knowledge and evidence collected and analyzed. Then provide the following scenario: A student is writing a research report about grizzly bears. He/she wrote an opinion in the report: *I think grizzly bears are the scariest creatures on Earth!* The student took these notes about grizzly bears: *Grizzly bears are brown bears with grizzled, or gray, fur. They are common in North America. Grizzlies can weigh over 800 pounds, and they have huge claws.* Which note supports the student's opinion?
ELA W.5.1b, W.5.8, W.5.9b

1	Choose Topic
2	Brainstorm and Identify Sources
3	Take Notes
4	Prepare Outline
5	Present

ENGLISH LANGUAGE SUPPORT To check students' understanding of the word *aspects*, say: *The aspects of a topic are the different ways you could look at it. For example, if the topic were trees, some aspects of that topic could be: How trees grow; Where trees can be found; What trees are used for.*

Fluency

▶ SHARE OBJECTIVES

- Read on-level texts orally with appropriate fluency.
- Read on-level texts orally with expression (prosody).

ENGLISH LANGUAGE SUPPORT

Peer-Supported Learning

All Proficiencies English learners who need additional support reading expressively in English can benefit from reading aloud with more fluent partners. If possible, pair each student with a more fluent partner. Ask students to practice proper expression as they read the text on **Student Book p. 179.** The more fluent reader can act as a coach for the less fluent reader, offering encouragement, help with difficult words, and feedback on expression. (If more fluent partners are not available, the instructor can act as the partner.) **ELD** ELD.PIII.5

HOUGHTON MIFFLIN HARCOURT

JOURNEYS

Cold Reads

Cold Reads: Support for fluent reading with comprehension

FORMATIVE ASSESSMENT   RtI

As student partners take turns reading the narrative on **Student Book p. 183,** circulate and spend time listening to each pair. If students have difficulty reading with expression, provide corrective feedback.

Model correct expression as you read the second section aloud to students, pointing out the punctuation cues, and have them choral- or echo-read with you.

Guide students to read another paragraph on their own, and provide feedback, as necessary. Tell students that their reading fluency will continue to improve as they work hard at improving their expression.

Expression

1 Teach/Model

- Tell students that good readers read with expression by changing the tone and volume of their voice and the pace of their reading. Good readers also use punctuation to help them read with expression.

- Have students follow along as you read aloud **Student Book p. 179,** using appropriate expression. Ask students to listen to how your expression changes based on what is happening.

- Then read several sentences in two ways: first with no expression and then with varying expression. Point out that it is not only more pleasant to listen to someone who reads with expression, but also more enjoyable for the reader.

2 Guided Practice

- Together, read aloud the first few paragraphs on **Student Book p. 180.**

- Work with students to adjust expression as necessary.

- If students are struggling with expression, have them turn to **Student Book p. 180.** Read several sentences aloud with appropriate expression. Then have students repeat each sentence after you, using similar expression.

- See also Instructional Routine 6.

3 Apply

- Tell students that with practice, they can improve their expression.

STANDARD ENGLISH LEARNERS Pronunciation Students may omit the final consonant in contractions such as *it's* or *don't*. They may pronounce *it's* as *it'* or *don't* as *don'*. Write this sentence on the board: *"Oh, no you don't,"* Tree Kangaroo said. Read the sentence aloud, emphasizing the final consonant sound in *don't*. Have students echo your reading several times.

- Have students choral-read the last section from **Student Book p. 183.** Remind them to read with appropriate expression. **ELA** RF.5.4a, RF.5.4b **ELD** ELD.PIII.5

Decoding

Common Beginning Syllables

1 | Teach/Model

Analyze Words with Common Beginning Syllables Tell students that many words share common first syllables, such as *a-* in *aboard* and *amuse*. Usually these syllables are unstressed, so many have a schwa vowel sound. Point out that looking for these common word parts can help in decoding a word.

- Write *aboard* and *amuse* on the board. Break the words into syllables (*a/board* and *a/muse*) and say them aloud.

- Point out to students that using knowledge of syllabication patterns to identify common beginning syllables in these words will help them to read the words accurately with correct pronunciation.

- Demonstrate identifying the syllables incorrectly by saying the words as *ab/oard* and *am/use*.

- Write the following words on the board and repeat the above process for each word: *contest, return,* and *distance.*

2 | Practice/Apply

Blend Words Display Lines 1–8 below and have students break each word into syllables, identify the first syllable, and say each word aloud. Provide corrective feedback as needed. Next point to words in random order. Ask students what strategies they used to read each one.

1. *compare   compete   computer   above   award   apology*

2. *research   repeat   repair   display   district   distance*

3. *comfortable   amazement   rearrange   discovery   reminder   competition*

4. *astound   regain   distress   discontinue   command   reflect*

5. *dishonest   compose   against   recalled   alive   combine*

Challenge Call on students who are ready for a challenge to read Line 6 and discuss the elements. Then have the class read the sentences in Lines 7 and 8 chorally.

6. *discard   reconsider   ashore   disease   compile   reassure*

7. *Raeanne complained of discomfort around her stomach and sought relief.*

8. *Paul remembers the distance of the commute when he traveled abroad to Europe.* **ELA** RF.5.3a **ELD** ELD.PIII.5

▶ SHARE OBJECTIVES

- Use knowledge of syllabication patterns to recognize words with common beginning syllables.

- Read accurately words with common beginning syllables.

FORMATIVE ASSESSMENT | **RtI**

If students have trouble decoding words with common beginning syllables, use the model below.

Correct the error. *Remember that common beginning syllables are usually unstressed.*

Model how to decode the words. *If I say the word* compete *with a beginning syllable of* comp-, *it doesn't sound right. I'll try again with the common beginning syllable* com-. *This is a word I know.*

Guide students to try shifting where they break the words into syllables to identify common beginning syllables. *What are the common beginning syllables in* repair *and* repeat, alive *and* against, *and* display *and* discard? re-, a-, *and* dis-

Check students' understanding. Read these word pairs. complain, compete; repair, repeat; alive, against; display, discard

Reinforce Have students repeat the process with the words *compose* and *astound.*

ENGLISH LANGUAGE SUPPORT

Linguistic Transfer

Use the transfer chart in the **Quick Start Pacing Guide** to determine whether your students will have difficulty due to transfer issues. As needed, preteach the skill. **ELD** ELD.PIII.5

Spelling Vowel + /r/ Sounds

▶ **SHARE OBJECTIVE**
- Spell grade-appropriate words with the vowel + /r/ sounds.

Spelling Words

Basic

glory	pardon	beware
aware	⭐ warn	absorb
carton	vary	armor
adore	barely	stairway
aboard	torch	perform
dairy	barge	former
ordeal	soar	

Review

board, repair, sharp, ⭐ square, compare

Challenge

discard, forfeit, orchestra, rarity, hoard

⭐ Forms of these words appear in "Quest for the Tree Kangaroo."

ENGLISH LANGUAGE SUPPORT

Preteach

Spanish Cognates Write and discuss these Spanish cognates for Spanish-speaking students.

adore • *adorar*

glory • *gloria*

Transfer Support Speakers of Asian languages, such as Korean, Hmong, Cantonese, and Mandarin, may have difficulty with vowel + /r/ sounds. Emphasize the /ôr/, /âr/, and /är/ sounds as you say *glory, dairy,* and *barge.* **ELD** ELD.PIII.5

Word Meanings Use Day 5 sentences to preview the meanings of spelling words.

DAY 1

❶ TEACH THE PRINCIPLE

- Administer the **Pretest**. Use the Day 5 sentences.
- Write *absorb* and *aboard* on the board. Identify the letters that make the /ôr/ sound. Repeat with /âr/ and /är/, using the chart below.

/ôr/	*or* as in *absorb* *oar* as in *aboard* *ore* as in *adore*
/âr/	*are* as in *beware* *air* as in *dairy*
/är/	*ar* as in *armor*

❷ GUIDED PRACTICE

Guide students to identify the sounds/spellings in the remaining Spelling Words.

Model a Word Sort Model sorting words based on the vowel + /r/ sound, /ôr/, /âr/, or /är/. Present the Model the Sort lesson on page 66 of the **Literacy and Language Guide**.

❸ APPLY

Distribute Reader's Notebook page 64 and have students complete it independently.

DAY 2

❶ TEACH WORD SORT

- Set up three rows as shown. Model adding a Spelling Word to each row.
- Have students copy the chart. Guide students to write each Spelling Word where it belongs.

/ôr/	soar
/âr/	vary
/är/	pardon

❷ GUIDED PRACTICE

- Have students add words to the chart from "Quest for the Tree Kangaroo."

Guided Word Sort Guide students to sort words according to the vowel + /r/ spelling patterns. Present the Guess My Category lesson on page 66 of the **Literacy and Language Guide**.

❸ APPLY

Distribute Reader's Notebook page 65 and have students complete it independently.

DAY 3

1 TEACH WORD FAMILIES

- **WRITE** *adore*. Define it: "to love or admire."

- **WRITE** *adorable*. Define it: "charming or lovable."

- **ASK** *What is the connection between these words? Both contain the word part* "ador;" *the meanings of both words connect to a feeling of affection.*

- With students, list and discuss more words related to *adore*. *samples:* adored, adoring, adoration

2 GUIDED PRACTICE

- **WRITE** *absorb*. Define it: "to soak up a liquid."

- **WRITE** *absorbent* and *absorption*. Ask students to look these words up in a dictionary or an electronic source.

- **ASK** *What is the connection among* absorb, absorbent, *and* absorption?

Have students write their answers.

3 APPLY

Independent Word Sort Have students sort and write words that a partner says aloud. Present the Blind Writing Sort lesson on page 67 of the **Literacy and Language Guide**.1

DAY 4

1 CONNECT TO WRITING

- Read and discuss the prompt below.

Informative Writing
Write a procedural composition about why it is important to learn about animals. Use what you learned from your reading this week.

2 GUIDED PRACTICE

- Guide students as they plan and write their procedural compositions.

- Remind students to proofread their writing and to consult print and digital references to confirm correct spelling. (See p. T60.) **ELA** L.5.2e

Speed Sort Have students sort words as quickly as they can. Present the Speed Sort lesson on page 67 of the Literacy and Language Guide.

3 APPLY

Distribute Reader's Notebook page 66 and have students complete it independently.

DAY 5

ASSESS SPELLING

- Say each boldfaced word, read the sentence, and then repeat the word.

- Have students write the boldfaced word. **ELA** L.5.2e

Basic

1. We enjoyed the **glory** of winning.
2. Juan was **aware** of the time.
3. Buy a **carton** of eggs.
4. I **adore** your new coat!
5. People came **aboard** the ship.
6. This **dairy** also bottles milk.
7. Traveling during the holidays can be an **ordeal**.
8. Please **pardon** my dirty room.
9. Alarms will **warn** of storms.
10. The menu may **vary** each day.
11. I can **barely** see in the fog.
12. A **torch** lit the dark cave.
13. A **barge** took away the trash.
14. Eagles **soar** overhead.
15. Always **beware** of lightning.
16. Black will **absorb** light.
17. Knights wore metal **armor**.
18. I fell in the dark **stairway**.
19. The band will **perform** a concert.
20. A **former** player is now a coach.

Grammar Verbs

▶ SHARE OBJECTIVES

- Identify main verbs, helping verbs, and linking verbs.
- Use main, helping, and linking verbs in writing and speaking.
- Use verb tenses to convey times, sequences, states, and conditions.

Terms About Language

linking verb connects a subject of a sentence to information about it • *verbo*

action verb tells what the subject does, did, or will do

main verb conveys the most important action, state, or condition in a sentence

helping verb adds detail to the main verb

verb tense a verb form that conveys time, sequence, state, or condition

ENGLISH LANGUAGE SUPPORT

Preteach: All Proficiencies

Explain the Language Term Point out the cognate in the list above. Then explain that:

• A verb is a word that usually expresses action.

Linguistic Transfer In Cantonese, Hmong, Vietnamese, Tagalog, and Haitian Creole, verbs do not change to show tense. Instead, adverbs or expressions of time indicate when an action has taken place.

Scaffolded Practice

Emerging Tell students that you are going to perform an action. Then, walk across the room. Point out that *walked* is a verb that describes that action. It is an action verb.	**Expanding** Demonstrate other actions, and help students identify the verbs for those actions	**Bridging** Write something on the board. Ask student volunteers to describe what you did in a complete sentence. *You have written on the board.* Explain that the word *have* in this answer is called a helping verb. The helping verb changes the tense of the word *write,* so that it represents an action taken in the past.

DAY 1 TEACH

DAILY PROOFREADING PRACTICE

Kangaroo are wild animal, so if you encounter one, be careful.
kangaroos; animals

① TEACH VERBS

- Display Projectable 6.4 ⌐⌐. Explain that a **verb** states the existence or action of a subject. **Linking verbs**, such as the verbs *be, become,* or *seem,* do not describe an action. Instead, they link the subject to more information about the subject, as in the sentence "I am cold." Linking verbs serve an important but limited purpose. Whenever possible, good writers try to use **action verbs,** which convey the subject's activities.

ENGLISH LANGUAGE SUPPORT Present the English terms for the types of verbs that students have learned: action verbs, linking verbs, main verbs, and auxiliary (helping) verbs. Note that the words *action* and *auxiliary* are cognates of the Spanish terms. Display the following sentences. Work with the group to identify each verb type.

- Many sea turtles swim long distances. *(action verb: swim)*
- Turtles are a kind of reptile. *(linking verb: are)*
- The vet has treated the turtle. *(auxiliary verb: has; main verb: treated)*
- Model identifying action verbs in this sentence: *The tree kangaroo climbed out on the branch.*

Think Aloud *To identify the action verb, I ask this Thinking Question:* **What has the subject of the sentence done?** *Climbed is what the subject, the tree kangaroo, did, so it is the action verb.*

② PRACTICE/APPLY

- Complete Projectable 6.4 ⌐⌐ with students.
- Write the verbs *run, walk, write, yell, perform,* and *sleep* on the board. Ask volunteers to think of other action verbs that could be synonyms for these words. Have them use the synonyms in sentences. **ELD** ELD.PII.5.3
- Have students complete Reader's Notebook p. 67 ⌐⌐ for practice with simple subjects and predicates.

DAY 2 TEACH

DAILY PROOFREADING PRACTICE

The man climb the tree to found the kangaroo. *climbed; find*

1 TEACH MAIN AND HELPING VERBS

- Display Projectable 6.5 ⌐. Explain that a **main verb** is the most important verb in a sentence. It tells what the subject is thinking or doing. **Helping verbs** come before main verbs and add details.

- Model identifying the main verb and helping verb in the following sentence: *We may go to the rain forest soon.*

> **Think Aloud** *To identify the helping verb and main verb, I ask this Thinking Question:* **Which verb describes the action and which verb helps it?** *May is the helping verb and go is the main verb because it describes the action of the subject.*

2 PRACTICE/APPLY

- Complete the other examples on Projectable 6.5 ⌐ with students.

- Have students choose three of the helping verbs on Projectable 6.5 ⌐ and write a sentence using each one. **ELD** ELD.PII.5.3

- Have students complete Reader's Notebook p. 68 ⌐ for practice with simple subjects and predicates.

DAY 3 TEACH

DAILY PROOFREADING PRACTICE

I were reading about wild animals yesterday when I find an article on tree kangaroos. *was; found*

1 TEACH VERB TENSES

- Display Projectable 6.6 ⌐. Explain that verbs appear in different tenses. Examples include the present tense—something happening right now—and the past tense, which is something that happened in the past. Explain that **verb tenses** can help convey time, sequence, condition, and states.

- Show how verb tenses can convey time, sequence, condition, or state using the examples on Projectable 6.6 ⌐.

> **Think Aloud** *To identify how tenses can be used to convey time, sequence, state, or condition, I ask this Thinking Question:* **Do the verb tenses help convey time, sequence, condition, or state?** *In the first example, the tense indicates time because searched is a past tense verb.*

2 PRACTICE/APPLY

- Complete the examples on Projectable 6.6 ⌐ with students.

- Ask students to write sentences that use verb tenses to convey time, sequence, condition, and states, then trade sentences with partners who will identify the way verb tenses are used. **ELA** L.5.1c **ELD** ELD.PII.5.3

- Have students complete Reader's Notebook p. 69 ⌐ for practice with simple subjects and predicates.

DAY 4 REVIEW

DAILY PROOFREADING PRACTICE

The biologists will traveled to the island on boat. *travel; by*

1 REVIEW VERBS

- Explain that a **linking verb** links the subject to additional information and an **action verb** conveys what the subject is doing, has done, or will do.

- Explain that a **main verb** is the most important verb in the sentence and it tells what the subject thinks or does.

- **Helping verbs** appear before main verbs and add detail to them.

- **Verb tenses** can help convey time, sequence, states, and conditions.

ENGLISH LANGUAGE SUPPORT Remind students that most verbs are action or linking. Provide examples of each such as: *ran, helped, saw* (action); *are, were, became* (linking).

2 SPIRAL REVIEW

- **Subjects and Predicates** Remind students that a complete sentence must include a subject and a predicate. The subject identifies what the sentence is about. The predicate tells what the subject is doing, or it tells something about the subject. Tell students that sentences missing a subject or a predicate are sentence fragments and cannot be used alone.

- Have students write three sentences and three fragments. Then ask students to exchange their sentences and fragments with a partner. Have partners identify the subjects and predicates in each other's sentences and rewrite the fragments as complete sentences.

Then have students complete Reader's Notebook p. 70 ⤴ for more practice with subjects, predicates, and complete sentences.

DAY 5 CONNECT TO WRITING

DAILY PROOFREADING PRACTICE

The scientist study animals on the forest. *studies; in*

1 INTERACTIVE WHITEBOARD LESSON

For cumulative review, use **Grammar: Verbs** to reinforce how to identify and use main verbs, linking verbs, and helping verbs.

2 CONNECT TO WRITING

- Explain that properly formed sentences help the reader understand the text and stay focused on the topic. Every properly formed sentence must contain a subject and a predicate.

- Point out that an important part of writing and editing is making sure that verbs are used correctly.

3 PRACTICE/APPLY

- Display the following sentences. Guide students in identifying the verbs and their types.

  David seemed pleased by the news about the new animal tracking devices.

  Louise had worked in the forest for years.

  I have read a magazine article about tree kangaroos.

- Have students turn to **Student Book p. 200**. Review the types of verbs and how verb tenses can help convey times, sequences, states, and conditions. Then have them complete the Try This! activity. **ELA** L.5.1c

- Have partners write a short narrative that includes verb tenses showing times, sequences, states, and conditions. Tell partners to exchange papers with another pair and check that verb tenses were used correctly. **ELA** L.5.1c **ELD** ELD.PII.5.3

- Have students complete Reader's Notebook p. 71 ⤴ for practice with combining sentences.

Grammar

Digital Resources
▶ Multimedia
Grammar Glossary

What Is a Verb? A **verb** is a word that can show action or state of being. Sometimes a verb is made up of more than one word—a main verb and a helping verb. **Verb tenses** can be used to convey various times, sequences, states, and conditions.

Verb Tenses Used to Convey Information
The trackers bark up the tree. The trackers barked up the tree. The trackers will bark up the tree.
Time Three tenses of *bark* are used to show action occurring in the past *(barked)*, present *(bark)*, and future *(will bark)*.
The trackers know that they made the right decision.
Sequence Verb tense shows the order of events. The trackers know now that they made the right decision earlier.
The scientists will examine the tree kangaroo if the trackers catch it.
Condition Verb tense shows that one action or state of being depends on a condition being met. The scientists will examine the animal in the future—but only if the trackers catch it in the present.
The trackers felt happy about their success.
State Tenses of linking verbs indicate when the subject is in a particular state of being. The trackers were in a state of happiness in the past.

 Try This! Work with a partner. Identify helping verbs and main verbs in the sentences. Then tell whether each verb conveys time, sequence, state, or condition.

❶ After I read the tree kangaroo article, I will watch the video.

❷ I will learn even more if I get that book from the library.

❸ The book includes many illustrations and explanations.

❹ I will be an expert on these fascinating animals.

You can make your writing strong by using verbs that convey details and information vividly and accurately.

Sentence with Vague Verb	Sentence with Exact Verb
 The tree kangaroo went up into a tree.	 The tree kangaroo scrambled up into a tree.
 The scientist watched the tree branches.	The scientist peered into the tree branches.

Connect Grammar to Writing

As you revise your procedural composition, replace vague verbs with exact verbs to show readers what you mean. Exact verbs will help clarify the actions and events you write about.

Try This!

1. *Main verb: watch; helping verbs: will; sequence*
2. *Main verb: learn; helping verbs: will; condition*
3. *Main verb: includes; state*
4. *Main verb: be; helping verb: will; time*

Connect Grammar to Writing

- Have students turn to **Student Book p. 201**. Reread the sentence at the top of the page with them.

- Read the sentences in the chart. Point out that the revised sentences on the right contain verbs that help readers see the action more clearly.

- Tell students that they should use exact verbs and strong word choice as they revise their procedural composition. ELD ELD.PII.5.3

ENGLISH LANGUAGE SUPPORT

Additional Grammar Practice

Teach/Model Display the picture of the man in the tree pointing.

Have a student describe the image. Ask: *What does the man do when he spots a tree kangaroo?*

- Write: *The man points at the tree kangaroo.* Remind students that *points* is a verb, or an action word.

Guided Practice Explain that an action verb shows what the subject does or did.

- Draw or have a student draw a simple diagram of a man pointing into some trees.

- Have students pantomime, or act out, the man pointing into the trees. Say: *The man points into the trees.* Stress the word *points.*

- Have students underline the verb. ELA L.5.1.c

Connect to Writing Have partners write a paragraph about "Why Koala Has No Tail" and exchange papers with another pair. Have them circle the verbs. ELD ELD.PI.5.2, ELD.PII.5.3

Informative Writing Focus Trait: Organization

▶ SHARE OBJECTIVES

- Prewrite, draft, and revise a procedural composition.
- Describe a process, or a series of events or steps.
- Develop the topic with facts, definitions, details, quotations, or other information.

Terms About Writing

procedural composition text that describes a process or a series of events or steps

ENGLISH LANGUAGE SUPPORT

Collaborative Writing

Explain that the class will work together to write a procedural composition.

- **Say:** *Let's imagine that we are planning a science experiment.* Discuss how to identify the steps in this process. *What is the first step we need to take? What is the second step?*
- **Ask:** *What is the best way to organize the steps in a process? in sequential order What are some words you can use to indicate that one step is leading to another? Examples include* next, then, *and* finally. Remind students that these are called *transition* words.
- **Say:** *It's also important to make your writing clear and interesting.* Review the composition and include suggestions to improve clarity and interest level. **ELD** ELD.PI.5.1

Read the completed composition aloud chorally.

Performance Task

my WriteSmart Have students complete the writing task through *my*WriteSmart. Students will read the prompt within *my*WriteSmart and have access to multiple writing resources, including the Student eBook, Writing Rubrics, and Graphic Organizers.

DAY 1 ANALYZE THE MODEL

❶ INTRODUCE PROCEDURAL COMPOSITION

- Tell students that they will be writing a **procedural composition** in this lesson.
- Display Projectable 6.7 ⬚ and read aloud Writing Model 1. Discuss the following.

What Is a Procedural Composition?

- It begins with a topic—an observation and a focus for the composition.
- It develops the topic with facts, definitions, details, quotations, or other examples.
- It explains each event or step in the procedure, providing illustrations or multimedia if useful.
- It includes a concluding statement or section.

- Use the annotations on Projectable 6.7 ⬚ to point out the way the writing model introduces the topic, develops the topic with details, and provides a step-by-step description of the procedure.

ENGLISH LANGUAGE SUPPORT How English Works As students study the model, point out how the writer's ideas are expressed in sequential order, using the transition words *First*, *Next*, and *Finish with*. Have students suggest additional transition words for their procedural compositions. **ELD** ELD.PII.5.1

❷ PRACTICE/APPLY

- Read aloud Writing Model 2 on Projectable 6.7 ⬚.
- Work with students to identify and label the different components of the writing model.

LESSON	FORM	FOCUS
6	Procedural Composition	Organization
7	Compare-Contrast Essay	Elaboration
8	Cause-and-Effect Essay	Evidence
9	Prewrite: Research Report	Evidence
10	Draft, Revise, Edit, Publish: Research Report	Conventions

WRITING

Additional support for Informative Writing appears in **the Common Core Writing Handbook,** Lesson 6.

DAY 2 TEACH

① INTRODUCE THE WRITING FOCUS

ORGANIZATION Explain that most procedural compositions are organized chronologically to show a sequence of steps. Review transition words such as *first, next, then,* and *finally* that signal order.

Connect to "Quest for the Tree Kangaroo"	
Instead of this . . .	**. . . the author wrote this.**
The animals are weighed in their burlap bags.	"First, while the animals are in their burlap bags, they are weighed." (p. 180)

- Point out how the author's sentence signals the beginning of a procedure. The word *while* identifies the conditions under which the step was begun. Remind students that verb tense can also be used to signal time and sequence.

🖉 🖿 *Annotate it!* Have students highlight other parts of the text in which the author uses transition words to signal time or sequence.

② PRACTICE/APPLY

- Have partners define the steps in a procedure. Encourage them to use transitions and verb tense to show sequence. Ask volunteers to write their responses on the board. *Sample answer: To cook rice, first, boil two cup of water. Then, stir in one cup of rice. Next, lower the heat and wait for the water to evaporate.* **ELA** W.5.4, W.5.5, W.5.10

- Have students discuss each example and suggest revisions that improve the organization and clarity. *Sample revisions: Heat two cups of water in a saucepan until boiling. Finally, remove the pan from the stove and serve.*

- Distribute Reader's Notebook page 72 ⧉ and have students complete it independently.

DAY 3 PREWRITE

① TEACH PLANNING A PROCEDURAL COMPOSITION

- Display Projectable 6.8 ⧉ and read aloud the prompt. Ask students to think about processes that they could describe in a procedural composition.

- Explain that a Flow Chart can help them identify the steps of a procedure and arrange them in sequence. They can use such a chart to plan their writing.

② PRACTICE/APPLY

- Point out the space for recording the topic at the top of Projectable 6.8 ⧉. Tell students that they will be introducing this topic in the first paragraph of their procedural composition.

- Work with students to complete the Flow Chart for an appropriate topic, such as how to write a great book report. Help them list the steps in the proper sequence.

- Distribute copies of **Graphic Organizer 4.** Encourage students to use the Flow Chart to plan their procedural compositions.

- Have students plan to include formatting, illustrations, or multimedia to help the audience understand their topic. **ELA** W.5.2a, W.5.4, W.5.5, W.5.10

ENGLISH LANGUAGE SUPPORT

How English Works: Productive

Connecting Ideas Before students begin drafting their procedural compositions, have them plan to use connecting words as they write. Tell students that writers use special words to connect, or put together, ideas in sentences. Give examples such as *however* and *therefore*. Provide model sentences such as *I thought I saw the bird, however, I was wrong. Therefore, I had to change my spot.* Help different proficiency levels build word banks of connecting words to use while drafting. **ELD** ELD.PII.5.6

DAY 4 DRAFT

1 BEGIN A DRAFT

- Have students use their Flow Charts to begin drafting their procedural compositions. Discuss with them the following.

```
┌─────────────────────────────────────────────────────┐
│ 1.  Introduce the topic—provide an observation and   │
│     focus for the composition to follow.             │
└─────────────────────────────────────────────────────┘
                          ↓
┌─────────────────────────────────────────────────────┐
│ 2.  Develop the topic with facts, definitions,       │
│     details, or other information and examples.      │
└─────────────────────────────────────────────────────┘
                          ↓
┌─────────────────────────────────────────────────────┐
│ 3.  Organize steps in a sequence that details the    │
│     process. Use verb tense to show sequence, and    │
│     link ideas using transitional words and phrases. │
│     Group related information.                       │
└─────────────────────────────────────────────────────┘
                          ↓
┌─────────────────────────────────────────────────────┐
│ 4.  Include illustrations and other media, as        │
│     appropriate.                                     │
└─────────────────────────────────────────────────────┘
                          ↓
┌─────────────────────────────────────────────────────┐
│ 5.  Conclude with statement or section that          │
│     summarizes the topic.                            │
└─────────────────────────────────────────────────────┘
```

2 PRACTICE/APPLY

- Have students draft their own procedural composition, using the proper formatting. Remind them to consult the Flow Chart that they completed for prewriting. **ELA** W.5.2a, W.5.2b, W.5.2c, W.5.2d, W.5.2e, W.5.4, W.5.10, L.5.1c

HANDWRITING TIP Have students write their final pieces in cursive, using their best handwriting. Tell them to be sure to leave the appropriate spaces between the letters and words. See also pp. R22–R27 for handwriting support.

DAY 5 ANALYZE THE MODEL

1 INTRODUCE THE STUDENT MODEL

- Remind students that good writers organize their procedural compositions carefully in order to make their meaning clear and precise.

- Read the top of **Student Book p. 202** with students. Discuss the revisions made by the student writer, Barry. Point out how Barry changed the organization and added transitional words to clarify the proper order of information in his composition.

- Have students explore Digital Lesson: Writing Informative Texts: Introduction ⬀ to develop their informative writing.

2 PRACTICE/APPLY

- Display Projectable 6.9 ⬀. Work with students to revise the rest of Barry's composition. Point out places where better organization might help make the composition clearer or more compelling.

- Work with students to answer the *Reading as a Writer* questions on **Student Book p. 203**.

- **Revising** Have students revise their own compositions using the Writing Checklist on **Student Book p. 202**.

- **Proofreading** For proofreading support, have students use the Proofreading Checklist Blackline Master ⬀. **ELA** W.5.4, W.5.5

ENGLISH LANGUAGE SUPPORT

Peer-Supported Learning

All Proficiencies See the Peer Conference Forms in the ELL Teacher's Handbook.

Informative Writing

Interactive Lessons
▶ Writing Informative Texts: Organize Your Information
▶ Writing Informative Texts: Introduction

*my*WriteSmart

☑ **Organization** In a **procedural composition**, you describe a process, or series of events or steps. You should begin by introducing the topic. Then explain each event in the order in which it happens or should happen. Using transition words such as *first, next, then,* and *finally* will make the order of events more clear to readers.

Barry wrote a procedural composition explaining how to plan a science fair project. Later, he reordered events and added transition words to link his ideas. Use the Writing Checklist below as you revise your writing.

Writing Checklist

☑ **Organization**
Did I explain events in order and use transitions to link ideas?

☑ **Purpose**
Did I express my ideas in a clear and interesting way?

☑ **Evidence**
Did I describe the steps in a process?

☑ **Elaboration**
Did I use specific nouns and strong verbs?

☑ **Conventions**
Did I use verbs correctly?
Did I use correct spelling, grammar, and punctuation?

Revised Draft

The next steps have to do with planning your experiment and gathering supplies.

Include a hypothesis, or what you think you
~~Second,~~
will discover. Make a list of supplies that you
~~First,~~
will need. Write out a plan for how you will do your experiment. Finally, think about any special requirements.

Final Copy

How to Plan a Science Fair Project
by Barry Williams

Entering a science fair is a big job for most fifth graders. They have to prepare carefully for their experiments. What does it take to have a winning science fair project?

Think about your favorite science topic and write two or three experiments that relate to it. For example, maybe you'd like to study moonlight and whether it affects plants. Once you have written your experiments, choose the one you like best.

The next steps have to do with planning your experiment and gathering supplies. First, write out a plan for how you will do your experiment. Include a hypothesis, or what you think you will discover. Second, make a list of supplies that you will need. Finally, think about any special requirements. Will you need a special location or other students to help you? Put all of this information in your plan and get your teacher to approve it.

After your plan is approved, it is time to experiment. Work carefully and take many notes about what happens. Even after all your planning, there is a chance you will face challenges—but don't worry. One of these challenges could lead you to a great scientific discovery!

Reading as a Writer

Which steps did Barry reorder? What transitions did he use to clarify sequence? How can you clarify the process in your own composition?

In my final paper, I reordered steps in the process and added transitions to make the sequence of events more clear. I also checked to see that I used verbs correctly.

202 **ELA** W.5.2a, W.5.2c, W.5.2d, W.5.4 **ELD** ELD.PI.5.10a, ELD.PII.5.1, ELD.PII.5.2

203

WRITING TRAITS SCORING RUBRIC

SCORE		4	3	2	1	NS
Purpose/Organization		The narrative is clear, focused, and well organized throughout. • Contains an effective and complete plot • Develops strong setting, narrator/characters • Includes a variety of transitions to connect ideas • Contains a logical sequence of events • Includes an effective introduction and conclusion	The narrative's organization is adequately maintained, and the focus is generally clear. • Plot is mostly effective/may contain small flaws • Develops setting, narrator/characters • Adequate use of transitions to connect ideas • Contains an adequate sequence of events	The narrative is somewhat organized and may be unclear in some parts. • Plot may be inconsistent • Minimal development of setting, narrator/characters • Contains inconsistent use of transitions to connect ideas • Sequence of events is weak or unclear • Introduction and conclusion need improvement	The narrative may be somewhat organized but unfocused. • Little or no plot • Little or no development of setting, narrator/characters • Contains few or inappropriate transitions and weak connections among ideas • Sequence of events is not organized • Introduction and/or conclusion may be missing	• Not intelligible • Not written in English • Not on topic • Contains text copied from another source • Does not address the purpose for writing
Development/Elaboration		The narrative includes effective elaboration using details, dialogue, and description. • Characters, setting, experiences, and events are well developed • Writer uses a variety of narrative techniques that strengthen the story or illustrate the experience • Contains effective sensory, concrete, and figurative language • Style is appropriate and effective	The narrative includes adequate elaboration using details, dialogue, and description. • Characters, setting, experiences, and events are adequately developed • Writer uses a variety of narrative techniques that generally move the story forward and illustrate the experience • Contains adequate sensory, concrete, and figurative language • Style is mostly appropriate	The narrative includes partial or ineffective elaboration using unclear or inconsistent details, dialogue, and description. • Characters, setting, experiences, and events lack consistent development • Writer uses inconsistent or weak narrative techniques • Contains weak sensory, concrete, and figurative language • Style is inconsistent or inappropriate	The narrative provides little or no elaboration using few or no details, dialogue, and description. • Very little development of characters, setting, experiences, and events • Writer's use of narrative techniques are minimal and may be incorrect • Little or no sensory, concrete, and figurative language • Little or no evidence of style	• Not intelligible • Not written in English • Not on topic • Contains text copied from another source • Does not address the purpose for writing

SCORE		2	1	0	NS
Conventions		The narrative demonstrates adequate command of conventions. • Consistent use of correct sentence structures, punctuation, capitalization, grammar, and spelling	The narrative demonstrates partial command of conventions. • Limited use of correct sentence structures, punctuation, capitalization, grammar, and spelling	The narrative demonstrates little or no command of conventions. • Rare use of correct sentence structures, punctuation, capitalization, grammar, and spelling	• Not intelligible • Not written in English • Not on topic • Contains text copied from another source

See also ***Writing Rubric Blackline Master*** and Teacher's Edition pp. R18–R21.

Formative Assessment

Weekly Tests

At the end of the lesson, administer the Weekly Test. This will give you a **snapshot of how students are progressing** with the Reading and Language Arts skills in this lesson and can give you **guidance on grouping, reteaching, and intervention.** Suggestions for adjusting instruction based on these results can be found on the next page.

Access Through Accommodations

When you administer the Weekly Test, some students may have problems accessing all or parts of the assessment. The purpose of the Weekly Test is to determine students' ability to complete the Reading and Language Arts tasks they learned in this lesson. Any barriers to them accessing the tasks demanded of them should be lowered so they can focus on skill demonstration.

When choosing accommodations, you will want to avoid invalidating the test results; if you are measuring a student's reading skill, for example, you will not want to read aloud the passage. The following accommodations, if needed, will not interfere with the Weekly Test's validity:

- Read aloud the assessment directions and item prompts. If students are English learners, read aloud the assessment directions and item prompts in the student's native language, if possible.

- Define any unknown words in the directions or item prompts that do not give away the answers to the items.

- Allow for a break during the assessment.

- Simplify the language of assessment directions and item prompts.

- Administer the assessment in a smaller group setting.

- Administer the assessment on a computer or other electronic device.

- Provide audio amplification equipment, colored overlays, or visual magnifying equipment to maintain visual/audio attention and access.

- Allow students to complete the assessment items orally or by having another person transcribe their responses.

Using Data to Adjust Instruction

Use students' scores on the Weekly test to determine Small Group placement, reteaching, and potential for Intervention.

☑ VOCABULARY AND COMPREHENSION

Cause and Effect; Quotes and Description; Domain-Specific Vocabulary; Anchor Text Target Vocabulary; Synonyms and Antonyms

IF STUDENT SCORES...	
...at acceptable,	**...below acceptable,**
THEN continue core instruction.	THEN use Reteach Comprehension Skill and Vocabulary Strategies lessons. For struggling students, administer the *Intervention Assessments* to determine if students would benefit from intervention.

☑ LANGUAGE ARTS

Verbs

IF STUDENT SCORES...	
...at acceptable,	**...below acceptable,**
THEN continue core instruction.	THEN use Reteach Language Arts lesson. For struggling students, administer the *Intervention Assessments* to determine if students would benefit from intervention.

☑ DECODING

Common Beginning Syllables

IF STUDENT SCORES...	
...at acceptable,	**...below acceptable,**
THEN continue core instruction.	THEN use Reteach Decoding lesson. For struggling students, administer the *Intervention Assessments* to determine if students would benefit from intervention.

☑ FLUENCY

Fluency Plan

Assess one group per week using the Fluency Tests ⟦ in the *Grab-and-Go™* Resources. Use the suggested plan at the right.

● Struggling Readers	Weeks 1, 3, 5
▲ On Level	Week 2
■ Advanced	Week 4

IF...	
...students are reading on-level text fluently,	**...students are reading below level,**
THEN continue core instruction.	THEN provide additional fluency practice using the **Student Book**, the **Cold Reads**, and the Leveled Readers. For struggling students, administer the *Intervention Assessments* to determine if students would benefit from intervention.

HOUGHTON MIFFLIN HARCOURT

JOURNEYS

Cold Reads

5

The **Cold Reads** passages increase gradually in Lexile® measures throughout the year, from below grade-level to above grade-level.

• Each passage is accompanied by several selected-response questions and one constructed-response prompt, requiring students to read closely, answer questions at substantial DOK levels, and cite text evidence.

• The *Cold Reads* may be used to provide practice in reading increasingly complex texts and to informally monitor students' progress.

• The *Cold Reads* may be used to estimate students' Lexile® levels in order to recommend appropriately challenging books for small-group instruction or independent reading.

Turn the page for more information about using FORMATIVE ASSESSMENT for ELD AND INTERVENTION.

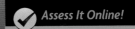
Assess It Online!

▶ Language Workshop Assessment Handbook

▶ Intervention Assessments

Formative Assessment for ELD and Intervention

Formative Assessment for English Learners

English learners should engage in the same rigorous curriculum and formative assessment as other students. However, it is important to remember that English learners face a dual challenge: they are strengthening their abilities *to use* English at the same time that they are learning challenging content *through* English. Use the following strategies and resources for ongoing assessment of English language development, in addition to the assessments you use with all students:

- A combination of **observational measures,** such as listening in as students read aloud or participate in collaborative conversations. Be prepared to provide **"just-in-time" scaffolding** to support students. For example, if students are retelling a story, you could help them use sentence structures with past-tense verbs and time-order transition words.

- **Constructive feedback** that focuses on communication and meaning-making. Avoid overcorrecting in a way that makes English learners reluctant to speak up. You might try recasting a child's statement more correctly, making a note to address the target form more directly during Designated ELD time.

- **Student self-assessment**, through students' own notes in their vocabulary notebooks or other learning journals. If possible, meet with each child to review his or her self-assessments and provide encouragement and feedback.

- **Formative assessment** notes that are integrated into the Language Workshop Teacher's Guide for use during Designated ELD.

- **Language Workshop Assessment Handbook** for longer-cycle assessment to make sure students are progressing in their English development.

Response to Intervention

Use the Weekly Tests and Benchmark and Unit Tests, along with your own observations, to determine if individual students are not responding to Tier I instruction and need additional testing to identify specific needs for targeted intervention.

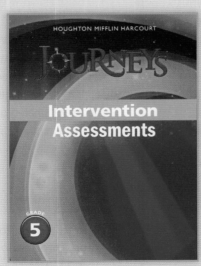

Intervention Assessments

Assessment for Intervention

Progress-Monitoring Assessments Administer this assessment to

- students in Tier II and Tier III Intervention to gauge progress towards exit from the intervention program.

- students who demonstrate lack of success with Weekly Tests, Benchmark and Unit Tests, and core instruction to determine if they might benefit from additional practice or intervention.

Weekly
Small Group Instruction

DAY 1

Vocabulary Reader
- *The Lost World of Papua New Guinea*, T68–T69

DAY 2

Differentiate Comprehension
- Target Skill: Cause and Effect, T70–T71
- Target Strategy: Question, T70–T71

DAY 3

Leveled Readers
- ● *Kangaroos*, T72
- ▲ *On the Trail of Rain Forest Wildlife*, T73
- ■ *Mad for Marsupials!* T74
- ◆ *Animals in the Rain Forest*, T75

DAY 4

Differentiate Vocabulary Strategies
- Synonyms and Antonyms, T76–T77

DAY 5

Options for Reteaching
- Vocabulary Strategies: Synonyms and Antonyms, T78
- Comprehension Skill: Cause and Effect, T78
- Language Arts: Verbs/Informative Writing, T79
- Decoding: Common Beginning Syllables, T79

Literacy Centers
Independent Practice
- Comprehension and Fluency, T6
- Word Study, T6
- Think and Write, T7

RtI Small Group Planner
Differentiated Instruction

		DAY 1	DAY 2	DAY 3
Teacher-Led	**Struggling Readers**	**Vocabulary Reader** *The Lost World of Papua New Guinea*, Differentiated Instruction, p. T68 **English Language Support**, p. T69	**Differentiate Comprehension** Cause and Effect; Question, p. T70 **English Language Support**, p. T71	**Leveled Reader** *Kangaroos*, p. T72 **English Language Support**, Leveled Reader Teacher's Guide, p. 5
	On Level	**Vocabulary Reader** *The Lost World of Papua New Guinea*, Differentiated Instruction, p. T68 **English Language Support**, p. T69	**Differentiate Comprehension** Cause and Effect; Question, p. T70 **English Language Support**, p. T71	**Leveled Reader** *On the Trail of Rain Forest Wildlife*, p. T73 *Animals in the Rain Forest*, T75 **English Language Support**, Leveled Reader Teacher's Guide, p. 5
	Advanced	**Vocabulary Reader** *The Lost World of Papua New Guinea*, Differentiated Instruction, p. T69 **English Language Support**, p. T69	**Differentiate Comprehension** Cause and Effect; Question, p. T71 **English Language Support**, p. T71	**Leveled Reader** *Mad for Marsupials!* p. T74 **English Language Support**, Leveled Reader Teacher's Guide, p. 5
What are my other students doing?	**Struggling Readers**	**Reread** *The Lost World of Papua New Guinea*	**Vocabulary in Context Cards** 51–60 *Talk It Over* Activities	**Listen** to Audio of "Quest for the Tree Kangaroo"; retell and discuss
	On Level	**Reread** *The Lost World of Papua New Guinea*	**Reread** "Quest for the Tree Kangaroo" with a partner	**Reread** Leveled Reader: *On the Trail of Rain Forest Wildlife* or *Animals in the Rain Forest* **Complete** Leveled Practice EL6.1
	Advanced	**Vocabulary in Context Cards** 51–60 *Talk It Over* Activities	**Reread and Retell** "Quest for the Tree Kangaroo"	**Reread** Leveled Reader: *Mad for Marsupials!*

For Strategic Intervention for this lesson, see pp. S2–S11.

DAY 4

Differentiate Vocabulary Strategies
Synonyms and Antonyms, p. T76
English Language Support, p. T77

Differentiate Vocabulary Strategies
Synonyms and Antonyms, p. T76
English Language Support, p. T77

Differentiate Vocabulary Strategies
Synonyms and Antonyms, p. T77
English Language Support, p. T77

- **Partners: Reread**
  Kangaroos
- **Complete** Leveled Practice SR6.1

- **Vocabulary in Context Cards**
  51–60 *Talk It Over* Activities
- **Complete** Reader's Notebook, p. 63

- **Reread** for Fluency: "Quest for the
  Tree Kangaroo"
- **Complete** Leveled Practice A6.1

DAY 5

Options for Reteaching,
pp. T78–T79

Options for Reteaching,
pp. T78–T79

Options for Reteaching,
pp. T78–T79

- **Reread** for Fluency: "Quest for the
  Tree Kangaroo"
- **Complete** Literacy Centers
- **Independent Reading**

- **Complete** Literacy Centers
- **Independent Reading**

- **Complete** Literacy Centers
- **Independent Reading**

English Language Support

*Use the Leveled Reader Teacher's Guide to support
ELs during differentiated instruction.*

- **Characteristics of the Text** (p. 1)
  Identify challenging language features, such as text
  structure, literary features, complex sentences, and
  vocabulary.

- **Cultural Support/Cognates/Vocabulary** (p. 5)
  Explain unfamiliar features of English and help ELs
  transfer first-language knowledge.

- **Oral Language Development** (p. 5)
  Check comprehension using dialogues that match
  students' proficiency levels.

Book Share
Use this routine at the end of the week to enable
students to demonstrate that they have become
experts on their Leveled Readers.

Step 1:
Have each student write a presentation based on his
or her Leveled Reader **Responding** page, using the
following guidelines:

- Briefly tell what your book is about.

- Show your Cause-and-Effect Diagram and explain
  what you added to complete it.

- Tell about your favorite part of the book, what you
  found most interesting in it, or what you learned
  from it.

Students should prepare to share their presentations
with a group.

Step 2:
Have students form groups in which each student has
read a different Leveled Reader.

Step 3:
Have students take turns sharing their book
presentations in their groups. Continue until all
students have finished sharing. Encourage students to
ask questions of the presenters. Provide frames such
as the following for support.

Can you tell me more about _____?

I wonder why _____.

What do you think about _____?

Vocabulary Reader
The Lost World of Papua New Guinea

Summary

Papua New Guinea, located in the Pacific region, is one of the last "lost worlds" on Earth, a place few outsiders have ever seen.

☑ **TARGET VOCABULARY**

dwarfed	**calculate**
presence	**snug**
procedure	**perch**
outfitted	**enthusiastic**
transferred	**beaming**

STRUGGLING READERS

ELA RI.5.4, RF.5.4a, L.5.4a, L.5.6 **ELD** ELD.PI.5.1, ELD.PI.5.6b

- Tell students that Papua New Guinea, which is located in the Pacific Ocean region, is called a "lost world" because it has been seen by only a few outsiders. This land is filled with wonders—rare birds, animals, sea creatures, and plants.

- Guide students to preview the Vocabulary Reader. Read aloud the headings. Ask students to describe the images, using Target Vocabulary when possible.

- Have students alternate reading pages of the text aloud. Guide them to use context to determine the meanings of unfamiliar words. As necessary, use the **Vocabulary in Context Cards** to review the meanings of vocabulary words.

- Assign the **Responding Page** and Blackline Master 6.4 . Have partners work together to complete the pages.

ON LEVEL

ELA RI.5.4, RF.5.4a, L.5.4a, L.5.6
ELD ELD.PI.5.1, ELD.PI.5.6b

- Explain to students that there are still areas on our planet that remain largely unknown to most people, such as Papua New Guinea. Then encourage them to create mental images of a "lost world" that is the size of California and the wonders it might contain. Guide students to preview the Vocabulary Reader.

- Remind students that context clues can help them determine the meaning of an unknown word. Tell students to use context clues to confirm their understanding of Target Vocabulary and to learn the meanings of new words.

- Have students alternate reading pages of the text aloud. Tell them to use context clues to determine the meanings of unknown words. As necessary, use the **Vocabulary in Context Cards** to review the meanings of the vocabulary words.

- Assign the **Responding Page** and Blackline Master 6.4 . Have partners work together to complete the pages.

ADVANCED

ELA RI.5.4, RF.5.4a, L.5.4a, L.5.6
ELD ELD.PI.5.1, ELD.PI.5.6b

- Have students preview the Vocabulary Reader and make predictions about what they will read, using information from the preview and prior knowledge.

- Remind students to use context clues to help them determine the meanings of unknown words.

- Tell students to read the Vocabulary Reader with a partner. Ask them to stop and discuss the meanings of unknown words as necessary.

- Assign the **Responding Page** and Blackline Master 6.4 ⬚. For the Write About It activity, encourage students to use sensory details in their journal entries so readers will have a vivid picture of this "lost world." Remind students to use words from their Webs in their entries.

The Lost World of Papua New Guinea, p. 15

ENGLISH LANGUAGE SUPPORT

ELA RI.5.4, RF.5.4a, L.5.4a, L.5.6
ELD ELD.PI.5.1, ELD.PI.5.6b

Provide Struggling Readers, On Level, and Advanced ELs proficiency-level support during differentiated instruction.

Emerging

Conduct a picture walk with students. Pause to read aloud the captions on pp. 6–7 and point to the images they describe or use simple synonyms to explain the terms *dwarfed* and *perch*. Remind students that they can use pictures or context clues to determine the meanings of unknown words.

Expanding

Use visuals, simplified language, and gestures to preteach the following selection vocabulary: *procedure, calculate, snug,* and *perch*. Have partners take turns using the words in oral sentences.

Bridging

Read aloud p. 14. Check students' understanding of unfamiliar words or expressions, such as *preserving, threatened,* or *over-logging*. Have them use the words in sentences.

Differentiate Comprehension
Cause and Effect; Question

STRUGGLING READERS

ELA RI.5.3, RF.5.4a
ELD ELD.PI.5.1, ELD.PI.5.5, ELD.PII.5.1

I DO IT

- Explain that understanding cause and effect means understanding how events happen. Tell students that asking questions as they read will help them understand the relationships between events.

- Read aloud **Student Book p. 179**. Model questioning to understand a cause-and-effect relationship.

  Think Aloud *What causes the tree kangaroo to climb higher?*

WE DO IT

- Read aloud p. 180.

- Guide students to identify the effect of the tree kangaroo's jump to the ground. *The trackers are able to grab hold of the tree kangaroo.*

- Work with students to record on a T-Map the causes and effects of the events leading to the tree kangaroo's capture.

YOU DO IT

- Distribute Graphic Organizer 10 (Story Map) ⬚. Have students record additional causes and effects for events on pp. 179–180 in their T-Maps.

- Ask students to explain how questioning helped them understand the cause-and-effect relationships.

ON LEVEL

ELA RI.5.3, RF.5.4a
ELD ELD.PI.5.1, ELD.PI.5.5, ELD.PII.5.1

I DO IT

- Read aloud **p. 180** of "Quest for the Tree Kangaroo."

- Explain to students that asking questions about cause-and-effect relationships can help them understand events.

- Model with a Think Aloud.

  Think Aloud *What is the effect of the tree kangaroo's jump to the ground?*

WE DO IT

- Have students read pp. 183–185 of "Quest for the Tree Kangaroo."

- Guide students to use the questioning strategy to identify cause-and-effect relationships on these pages. *Why do the scientists monitor the kangaroo's breathing and heart rate? They need to watch for dangerous effects of the anesthesia.*

YOU DO IT

- Distribute Graphic Organizer 10 (Story Map) ⬚. Have students work in pairs to complete a T-Map for "Quest for the Tree Kangaroo" by identifying the causes and effects of key events.

- Have partners share their T-Maps with other pairs and discuss the importance of each event to the overall outcome.

ADVANCED

ELA RI.5.3, RF.5.4a
ELD ELD.PI.5.1, ELD.PI.5.5, ELD.PII.5.1

I DO IT

- Remind students that asking questions about a text helps a reader understand cause-and-effect relationships, which may need to be inferred.

- Read aloud **Student Book p. 179–180**. As you read, point out how one event leads to another.

WE DO IT

- Read aloud pp. 187–189.

- Work together to identify causes and effects for the events on the pages. Help students use their questioning skills to infer any unstated causes or effects.

YOU DO IT

- Distribute Graphic Organizer 10 (Story Map) ⌐. Have students fill in their T-Maps with causes and effects from the text.

- Have students write a paragraph describing the success of the scientists' project and its possible effects on future research of the tree kangaroo.

- Invite students to use their completed T-Maps to question the cause-and-effect relationships in the text.

ENGLISH LANGUAGE SUPPORT

ELA RI.5.3, RF.5.4a
ELD ELD.PI.5.1, ELD.PI.5.5, ELD.PII.5.1

Provide Struggling Readers, On Level, and Advanced ELs proficiency-level support during differentiated instruction.

Display a T-Map with causes and effects from the selection to review the target skill. Choose one of the following activities for additional support, as appropriate.

Emerging

Display the terms *then, so, because*. Model how to use them to connect a cause and an effect. Write: *A tracker went closer to the tree kangaroo. So, the tree kangaroo moved higher up the tree.* Underline *so*. Explain that it connects the *cause* (the tracker went near the animal) to the *effect* (the animal moved away from the tracker). Repeat with other terms as needed.

Expanding

Display the phrases *due to, as a result, this leads to*. Tell students they can use the terms to connect the causes and effects they list on their T-Maps. Model with this example: *The scientists want to be sure the collar will fit on the tree kangaroo. As a result, they measure the animal's neck first.* Help students come up with other words they can use to explain cause and effect.

Bridging

Brainstorm with students transitional words and phrases they can use to link ideas in the text. Give them sentence starters they can use to construct an extended response. For example: *Due to anesthesia's harmful effects, scientists pay close attention when giving it to kangaroos. For instance, anesthesia can _____. As a result, scientists monitor _____.*

☑ **TARGET SKILL**
Cause and Effect

☑ **TARGET STRATEGY**
Question

☑ **TARGET VOCABULARY**

dwarfed	calculate
presence	snug
procedure	perch
outfitted	enthusiastic
transferred	beaming

Leveled Readers

ELA RI.5.3, RI.5.4, RF.5.4b, SL.5.1a
ELD ELD.PI.5.1, ELD.PI.5.6a, ELD.PII.5.1

STRUGGLING READERS

 ## Kangaroos

GENRE: INFORMATIONAL TEXT

Summary Kangaroos are strong jumpers who can move at thirty-five miles per hour. Their babies, or joeys, mature in the mother's pouch. Australia controls the animals' numbers but also protects them.

Introducing the Text

- Discuss key vocabulary from the selection. Tell students that kangaroos come in many varieties and sizes. They eat plants and often live in groups.

- Remind students that they can use a graphic organizer to track causes and their effects in a selection.

Supporting the Reading

- As you listen to students read, pause to discuss these questions.

  p. 5 *What might cause a kangaroo to stomp its feet loudly? A kangaroo might stomp if it saw a dangerous animal, to warn other kangaroos.*

  p. 12 *How did people's burning of forests affect kangaroos? More grass grew in the areas where trees had been burned. This created more food for kangaroos, so their numbers grew.*

Discussing and Revisiting the Text

CRITICAL THINKING After discussing *Kangaroos* together, have students read the instructions on the top half of **Responding** p. 15. Use these teaching points to guide them as they revisit the text.

- Ask a volunteer to read aloud the text in the graphic organizer.

- Have partners review the "Top Hopper" section starting on p. 4 to identify two more effects to complete Blackline Master 6.5.

FLUENCY: EXPRESSION Model reading the first page of *Kangaroos* aloud. Use your voice to express how amazing the facts about kangaroos are. Then have students echo-read another page with you.

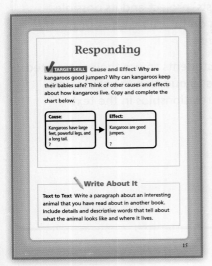

Responding

✓ TARGET SKILL Cause and Effect Why are kangaroos good jumpers? Why can kangaroos keep their babies safe? Think of other causes and effects about how kangaroos live. Copy and complete the chart below.

Cause:		Effect:
Kangaroos have large feet, powerful legs, and a long tail.	→	Kangaroos are good jumpers.
?		?

✏ **Write About It**

Text to Text Write a paragraph about an interesting animal that you have read about in another book. Include details and descriptive words that tell about what the animal looks like and where it lives.

15

Kangaroos, p. 15

ELA RI.5.3, RI.5.4, RF.5.4b, SL.5.1a
ELD ELD.PI.5.1, ELD.PI.5.6a, ELD.PII.5.1

ON LEVEL

 ## On the Trail of Rain Forest Wildlife

GENRE: INFORMATIONAL TEXT

Summary Rain forests are home to a huge and diverse range of animal species, most of which live high in the canopy. It is difficult and often dangerous for scientists to study these animals.

Introducing the Text

- Discuss key vocabulary from the selection. Tell students that the Amazon basin in South America has the world's largest rain forest. On a map, point out the Amazon River and its many tributaries, which define the basin.

- Remind students that keeping track of cause-and-effect relationships can help them understand a nonfiction selection.

Supporting the Reading

- As you listen to students read, pause to discuss these questions.

  p. 4 *Why is the rain forest floor a "dark and shadowy" place? The tops of the trees create a canopy that blocks sunlight.*

  p. 11 *What effect do the red-eyed tree frog's eyes have on predators? The big red eyes startle predators and may give the frog time to escape.*

Discussing and Revisiting the Text

CRITICAL THINKING After discussing *On the Trail of Rain Forest Wildlife* together, have students read the instructions on the top half of **Responding** p. 19. Use these teaching points to guide them as they revisit the text.

- Have partners read the first two events in the graphic organizer.

- Ask them to discuss two more effects that follow from these and write them on Blackline Master 6.6.

FLUENCY: EXPRESSION Have partners take turns reading paragraphs from the text with expression. Encourage them to share constructive feedback.

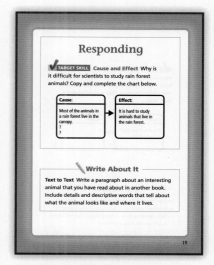

On the Trail of Rain Forest Wildlife, p. 19

☑ **TARGET SKILL**
Cause and Effect

☑ **TARGET STRATEGY**
Question

☑ **TARGET VOCABULARY**

dwarfed	calculate
presence	snug
procedure	perch
outfitted	enthusiastic
transferred	beaming

Leveled Readers

ELA RI.5.3, RI.5.4, RF.5.4b, SL.5.1a
ELD ELD.PI.5.1, ELD.PI.5.6a, ELD.PII.5.1

ADVANCED

 ## *Mad for Marsupials!*

GENRE: INFORMATIONAL TEXT

Summary Marsupials are mammals that carry their babies in pouches. Kangaroos are the best-known marsupials, but others include koalas, wombats, Tasmanian devils, and opossums.

Introducing the Text

- Discuss key vocabulary from the selection. Tell students that marsupials are a category of mammals known for carrying their babies in pouches.

- Tell students that noting cause-and-effect relationships can help them understand animal behavior and how human activity affects animals.

Supporting the Reading

- As you listen to students read, pause to discuss these questions.

   p. 6 *Why do kangaroos have a name from the Aboriginal language? The Aboriginal people were the first humans to encounter the animals.*

   p. 8 *What causes koalas to be able to eat poisonous eucalyptus leaves? Special bacteria in their intestines allow them to digest the leaves.*

Discussing and Revisiting the Text

CRITICAL THINKING After discussing *Mad for Marsupials!* together, have students read the instructions on the top half of **Responding** p. 19. Use these teaching points to guide them as they revisit the text.

- Have students work individually or in pairs to read the first cause in the graphic organizer and to identify three effects that follow from it.

- Students should write the effects on Blackline Master 6.7 ⌐.

FLUENCY: EXPRESSION Have partners take turns reading paragraphs from the text with appropriate expression. Suggest that they pay attention to places where the author is making a joke or sharing an amazing fact.

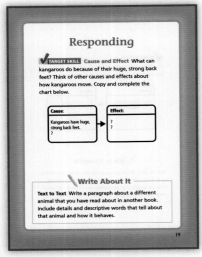

Mad for Marsupials!, p. 19

ELA RI.5.3, RI.5.4, RF.5.4b, SL.5.1a
ELD ELD.PI.5.1, ELD.PI.5.6a, ELD.PII.5.1

ENGLISH LANGUAGE SUPPORT

Animals in the Rain Forest

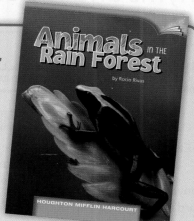

GENRE: INFORMATIONAL TEXT

Summary A vast number of unique animals live in the rain forest, from colorful frogs to big cats. Many live high in the tree tops, making it difficult and often dangerous for scientists to study them.

Introducing the Text

- Discuss key vocabulary from the selection. Tell students that a river basin is the area drained by a large river and all the smaller rivers that flow into it. On a map of South America, point out the Amazon basin. Explain that this region has the world's largest rain forest.

- Remind students that noting which events cause other events to happen will help them understand a nonfiction text.

Supporting the Reading

- As you listen to students read, pause to discuss these questions.

p. 9 *Many rain forest animals are active only at night. How does this affect the scientists who study the animals? It makes their work harder because they must track the animals in the dark.*

p. 15 *What causes predators to stay away from poison dart frogs? The frogs' bright coloring warns other animals that they are dangerous to eat.*

Discussing and Revisiting the Text

CRITICAL THINKING After discussing *Animals in the Rain Forest* together, have students read the instructions on the top half of **Responding** p. 19. Use these teaching points to guide them as they revisit the text.

- Ask a student to read aloud the cause and then the effect.

- Have partners identify two more causes, reviewing the text as needed. Encourage them to use complete sentences as they write the causes on Blackline Master 6.8 [↗].

FLUENCY: EXPRESSION Model reading aloud the first paragraph on p. 4 with expression. Note that exclamation marks indicate strong feelings. Have partners take turns reading aloud as you circulate and provide feedback.

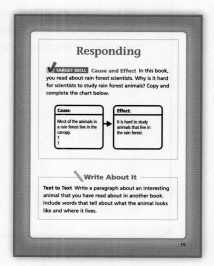

Responding

✓ **TARGET SKILL** Cause and Effect In this book, you read about rain forest scientists. Why is it hard for scientists to study rain forest animals? Copy and complete the chart below.

Cause:		Effect:
Most of the animals in a rain forest live in the canopy. ? ?	→	It is hard to study animals that live in the rain forest.

✎ Write About It

Text to Text Write a paragraph about an interesting animal that you have read about in another book. Include words that tell about what the animal looks like and where it lives.

19

Animals in the Rain Forest, p. 19

Differentiate Vocabulary Strategies
Synonyms and Antonyms

STRUGGLING READERS

ELA L.5.4a, L.5.5c, L.5.6
ELD ELD.PI.5.1, ELD.PI.5.6b, ELD.PI.5.12a

I DO IT

- Display **Vocabulary in Context Card 59:** *enthusiastic*.

- Explain to students that a synonym is a word that means the same as another word and an antonym is a word that has the opposite meaning.

- Tell students that knowing synonyms and antonyms for a word can help them understand the word's meaning more clearly.

WE DO IT

- Have students read aloud the context sentence on the front of the **Vocabulary in Context Card**.

- Guide students to identify a synonym for the word *enthusiastic* based on the sentence and the picture. Have a volunteer use the synonym to help define *enthusiastic*.

- Together, think of antonyms for the word *enthusiastic*. Demonstrate for students how to use a print or digital thesaurus to add more antonyms. *disinterested, unexcited, bored*

YOU DO IT

- Have pairs of students make a synonym/antonym card for *enthusiastic*. Have them write the Target Vocabulary word on the top of a sheet of paper.

- On one half of the paper, have them write a synonym and draw a picture illustrating the word.

- On the second half of the paper, have them write an antonym and illustrate its meaning.

ON LEVEL

ELA L.5.4a, L.5.5c, L.5.6
ELD ELD.PI.5.1, ELD.PI.5.6b, ELD.PI.5.12a

I DO IT

- Explain to students that a synonym is a word that means the same as another and an antonym is a word that has the opposite meaning.

- Display **Vocabulary in Context Cards 57:** *snug*, **51:** *dwarfed*, **59:** *enthusiastic*, **52:** *presence*

WE DO IT

- Help students identify a synonym for each word based on the sample sentence and the picture.

- Guide them to use a print or digital thesaurus to look up additional synonyms and antonyms and list them next to each word.

- Then call out a synonym or antonym. Have students respond with the correct Target Vocabulary word. Example: *Disinterested is an antonym for _____. enthusiastic*

YOU DO IT

- Have students then write two sentences for two of the Target Vocabulary words. One sentence in the set should include the vocabulary word and one of its synonyms; the other should include the vocabulary word and an antonym.

- Have them share their sentences with the class.

ADVANCED

ELA L.5.4a, L.5.5c, L.5.6
ELD ELD.PI.5.1, ELD.PI.5.6b, ELD.PI.5.12a

I DO IT

- Explain that a synonym is a word that means the same as another and an antonym is a word with the opposite meaning.

- Tell students that synonyms and antonyms can be clues to a word's meaning.

- Display **Vocabulary in Context Cards 57**: *snug*, **51**: *dwarfed*, **59**: *enthusiastic*, **52**: *presence*, and **58**: *perch*.

WE DO IT

- Read each sample sentence aloud. Have students identify a synonym for each word based on the sentence and the picture.

- Model how to use a print or digital thesaurus to look up additional synonyms as well as antonyms for the word *snug*.

- Then have students find additional synonyms and antonyms for the remaining words.

- Review the lists together.

YOU DO IT

- Have students then write new sentences for five of the Target Vocabulary words, using one synonym or antonym as a context clue to each word's meaning.

- Have students exchange sentences with a partner and define each word from the clue given.

ENGLISH LANGUAGE SUPPORT

ELA L.5.4a, L.5.5c, L.5.6
ELD ELD.PI.5.1, ELD.PI.5.6b, ELD.PI.5.12a

Provide Struggling Readers, On Level, and Advanced ELs proficiency-level support during differentiated instruction.

Emerging

Explain that a synonym means "the same as" and an antonym means "the opposite of". Read aloud this sentence: *The fans watching the game were enthusiastic.* Act out the meaning of *enthusiastic* and then the opposite emotion to elicit synonyms and antonyms from students. *excited; disinterested*. Repeat the strategy as needed for the other words students learn during the lesson.

Expanding

Help students use context to come up with synonyms and antonyms for words. Read **Vocabulary in Context Cards 57** *(snug)* and **59** *(enthusiastic)*. Work with students to identify synonyms from the context. Then place the word *not* in front of the words and their synonyms (example: *not excited*). Have students think of antonyms that have this opposite meaning.

Bridging

Have students work in pairs to use a thesaurus to find synonyms and antonyms for words they learn over the course of the lesson. On separate index cards, have them write each word, an accompanying synonym, and an accompanying antonym. Have them exchange their cards with a partner and match the sets.

Options for Reteaching

VOCABULARY STRATEGIES

ELA L.5.4a, L.5.4c, L.5.5c
ELD ELD.PI.5.1, ELD.PI.5.6b, ELD.PI.5.8

Synonyms and Antonyms

I DO IT

- Review the definitions of *synonyms* (words that have the same or nearly the same meaning) and *antonyms* (words that have opposite meanings).

- Write these words on the board: *nervous*, *calm*, and *worried*. Ask students to identify the two words that are synonyms (*nervous*, *worried*) and the one that is an antonym to the other two (*calm*).

- Remind students that if they see an unfamiliar word while reading, sometimes they can find a synonym or an antonym in the context that will help them define the unknown word.

WE DO IT

- Write these sentences from **Student Book p. 185** on the board: *"Respiration is thirty-two," says Christine. That means she's breathing thirty-two times a minute.*

- Model how to apply the vocabulary strategy to figure out the meaning of *respiration*.

> **Think Aloud** *The first sentence doesn't tell me what* respiration *means, but the next sentence restates the information in different words. Breathing and* respiration *must be synonyms. Now I understand that* respiration *means "the act of breathing."*

- Ask volunteers to give examples of activities that might affect their respiration.

YOU DO IT

- Have pairs locate these words in the selection: *scanned* (p. 179), *squirming* (p. 185), *frequency* (p. 189), and *beaming* (p. 189).

- Ask students to look at the context in which each word appears and identify an antonym for *squirming* and synonyms for the other words. scanned/look, squirming/relaxes, frequency/channel, beaming/smile

- Invite volunteers to explain how to use synonyms and antonyms from the context to figure out the meaning of each word.

COMPREHENSION SKILL

ELA RI.5.2
ELD ELD.PI.5.1, ELD.PI.5.5, ELD.PI.5.6a

Cause and Effect

I DO IT

- Remind students that recognizing causes and effects helps readers identify the connections between events.

- Remind students that authors sometimes use words such as *because, so, since, as a result,* and *therefore* to signal which events are causes and which are effects.

- Provide a few simple examples of cause and effect.

WE DO IT

- Read aloud the paragraph that begins with "It's 10:55 A.M." on **Student Book p. 185.**

- Model how to identify the cause-and-effect relationship in this passage.

> **Think Aloud** *The author doesn't state that one event caused another. However, I can infer how the events are related. Holly places a mask on the tree kangaroo that delivers the anesthesia, and then the animal falls asleep. I can infer that the anesthesia caused the animal to fall asleep.*

- Have students use a signal word to state the cause-and-effect relationship. *The animal fell asleep because of the anesthesia.*

YOU DO IT

- Distribute Graphic Organizer 4 .

- Read p. 187 aloud. In the top box of the graphic organizer, have students write: *Gabriel unties the top of the male kangaroo's bag.*

- Have student pairs fill in the chart with effects that follow from the first event.

- Review the completed graphic organizers.

ELA W.5.4, L.5.2b
ELD ELD.PI.5.1, ELD.PI.5.2

LANGUAGE ARTS

Verbs/Informative Writing

I DO IT

- Review with students that a verb is a word that can show action or a state of being.

- Remind students that verb tenses indicate when actions occur and in what order. Provide these examples of past, present, and future tenses: *Yesterday I rode my bike. I ride my bike every day. Tomorrow I will ride my bike.*

WE DO IT

- Point out that verb tenses can show the order in which the steps in a procedure must be done. On **Student Book p. 183,** Holly describes the procedure the team will follow with the first tree kangaroo: *We'll measure the neck, put on the radio collar, insert the ID chip, pluck fur for more testing, check the pouch—see if she has a baby.*

- Model how verb tenses can be used to clarify the sequence of steps in the procedure.

  Think Aloud *The first step in the procedure is to measure the animal's neck. Then the radio collar is put on. I could describe these steps by saying, "After they measure the animal's neck, the scientists will put on the radio collar." Measure is in the present tense, and will put is in the future tense. Measuring happens before putting on the collar.*

- Have students complete this sentence: *After the scientists _____ the radio collar, they _____ the ID chip. put on; will insert*

YOU DO IT

- Have students write a paragraph describing an ongoing task. Examples include reading a book, completing a project at home or at school, and learning to play a musical instrument. Instruct students to use past, present, and future verb tenses.

- Have students share their paragraphs and explain how they used verb tenses to show time order.

ELA RF.5.3a, RF.5.4a

DECODING

Common Beginning Syllables

I DO IT

- Remind students that many common beginning syllables are unstressed and have a schwa sound.

- Point out that looking for common beginning syllables can help readers decode a word and determine how to stress its syllables.

- Write *about* on the board and point out that the common first syllable in this word is unstressed.

WE DO IT

- Write these words from "Quest for the Tree Kangaroo" on the board: *exclaims, recalled, decided, because,* and *admired.*

- Model how to decode *exclaims.*

  Think Aloud *I recognize the first part of this word as a common prefix. I have seen many other words that begin with ex-, such as examine and explode. Knowing how to pronounce words that begin this way will be helpful. I break the first syllable apart as ex-. The stress goes on the second syllable, claims. I pronounce the word ex/CLAIMS.*

- Work with students to brainstorm other words with the common beginning syllable *ex-* and to decode them. *example, exit, exhaust, exhibit, extra*

YOU DO IT

- Have partners decode the remaining words.

- Have them identify the common beginning syllables and list and decode other words that begin with the same common syllables.

- Use the Corrective Feedback on p. T51 if students need additional help.

Teacher Notes

JOURNEYS

Anchor Text

Paired Selection

DIGITAL RESOURCES

Teacher Dashboard

Log onto the Teacher Dashboard and *my*SmartPlanner. Use these searchable tools to customize lessons that achieve your instructional goals.

Interactive Whiteboard Lessons

• Grammar: Direct and Indirect Objects
• Vocabulary Strategies: Adages and Proverbs

• Write About Reading
• Informative Writing: Compare-Contrast Essay

Interactive Lessons

▶ Participating in Collaborative Discussions
▶ Writing to Sources
▶ Informative Writing

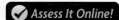 **Assess It Online!**

• Weekly Tests
• Assessment-driven instruction with prescriptive feedback

Student eBook

🖉 Annotate it! **Strategies for Annotation**

Guide students to use digital tools for close reading.

Students may also use the interactive features in their Student eBooks to respond to prompts in a variety of ways, including:

• short-answer response
• spoken response
• fill-in-the-blank
• drag-and-drop
• multiple choice

 High-Interest Informational Texts and Multimedia

Have students explore the FYI website for additional information about topics of study.

ENGLISH LANGUAGE SUPPORT

Culturally Responsive Teaching

Take a Trip to the Past Tell students that this week, they will be reading and thinking about historical fiction, and the ways that people in the past faced dangerous situations.

• Create a classroom display about enjoyable historical fiction titles and encourage students to add favorite titles to the display.

• Provide a text-rich environment with an array of historical fiction titles and resources for a variety of historical eras. Include titles for English learners in their home languages.

• During the week, have informal groups meet to discuss a variety of historical fiction titles and series that they have enjoyed. Encourage students to compare and contrast elements in different titles.

Scaffold Instruction Use visuals to present new concepts and information. For emerging English learners, use simple sentence and question structures. Provide word banks, as well as sentence and question frames, to help English learners respond, share ideas, and ask questions.

Language Support Card

Use the Lesson 7 Language Support Card to activate prior knowledge, frontload vocabulary, and teach academic English.

 Use the Text X-Ray on page T89 to review the language demands of "Old Yeller" with the needs of English learners in mind.

Language Workshop for Designated ELD

• Connection to Essential Question
• Vocabulary Network
• Focus on Interacting in Meaningful Ways
• Discussion Frames
• How English Works
• Word Learning Strategies

You may wish to use the following suggestions to modify instruction for some students, according to their needs.

Learner's Journal

Keeping a Learner's Journal can help students see themselves as successful, growing learners. Developing a sense of ownership in students can motivate them to reach their highest potential. Have students begin a Learner's Journal to help them keep track of their growing knowledge and skills. Depending on students' needs and skills, have them record information about what they are learning. Some examples:

- Day 1: Vocabulary: *frantic, lunging, stride, checking, wheeled, bounding, shouldered, strained, romp, picturing*
- Day 2: The title of the Anchor Text, "Old Yeller," and information about the text
- Day 3: Write about something new they learned about how dangerous situations bring people closer together. To help, you might want to discuss with students the Essential Question and their ideas about it.
- Day 4: Write several words they have learned to spell this week.
- Day 5: Write about how they are becoming better writers. For example, "I am learning to write a compare-contrast essay."

Student eBook

- **Audio** can be activated to support fluency, decoding, and comprehension.
- **Alternative Text** provides spoken information that can be used in place of the information provided in the book's images.
- **Vocabulary Pop-Ups** contain point-of-use definitions for selection vocabulary.

History-Social Science

U.S. States and Territories in 1850 Have partners work together to identify the states and territories that existed in 1850 and create a map to identify their locations and major geographical features.

- Prepare or select print and/or online resources students can use to locate information about U.S. states and territories in 1850.
- Remind students that "Old Yeller" takes place on the Texas frontier during the second half of the nineteenth century.
- Tell students that they will work with a partner to find information that will help them create a map about the U.S. states and territories that existed in 1850. Explain that their maps will indicate the names of the states and territories, their locations, and major geographical features, such as mountain ranges and principal rivers.
- Pair students with a partner and provide time for students to locate information and create their maps.
- Invite students to share and discuss their maps with a small group or the whole class.

LESSON 7 *Our* Focus Wall

ANCHOR TEXT

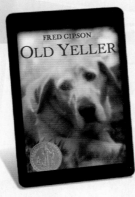

Old Yeller
Historical Fiction

What Makes It Good?
Persuasive Text

ESSENTIAL QUESTION

How can dangerous situations bring people closer together?

WRITING

Writing

Informative Writing:
Compare-Contrast Essay
Focus Trait: Word Choice

READING LITERATURE & INFORMATIONAL TEXT

Comprehension Skills and Strategies

☑ **TARGET SKILL**
- Understanding Characters
- Author's Word Choice
- Dialect

☑ **TARGET STRATEGY**
- Visualize

FOUNDATIONAL SKILLS

Fluency

Intonation

Decoding

Vowel + /r/ Sounds

LANGUAGE

☑ **Target Vocabulary**

frantic	bounding
lunging	shouldered
stride	strained
checking	romp
wheeled	picturing

Spelling

More Vowel + /r/ Sounds

earth	squirm
peer	weary
twirl	alert
burnt	murmur
smear	one-third
further	reverse
appear	worship
worthwhile	career
nerve	research
pier	volunteer

Grammar

Direct and Indirect Objects

Vocabulary Strategies

Adages and Proverbs

ANCHOR TEXT

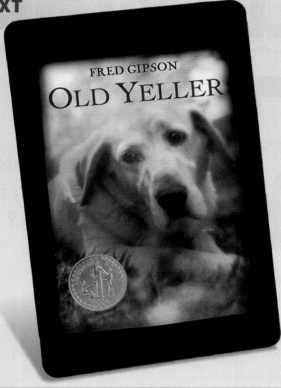

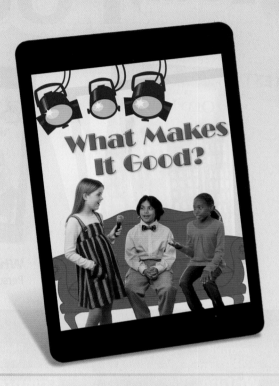

Old Yeller
GENRE: Historical Fiction

Prepare for Complex Texts For a comprehensive overview and analysis of key ideas and academic language features of this lesson's Anchor Text, see pages T88–T89.

What Makes It Good?
GENRE: Persuasive Text
21st Century Theme: Environmental Literacy

Digital Resources

▶ **eBook: Annotate It!**

▶ **Interactive Whiteboard Lessons**
  • Vocabulary Strategies: Adages and Proverbs
  • Grammar: Direct and Indirect Objects

▶ **Multimedia Grammar Glossary**

▶ **my**SmartPlanner

▶ **Parent Resource**

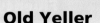 **Additional Resources**
  • Vocabulary in Context Cards 61–70
  • Reader's Notebook, pp. 73–84
  • Lesson 7 Blackline Masters
  • Literacy and Language Guide

Meaning Making

Language Development

Effective Expression

Content Knowledge

Foundational Skills

LINGUISTICALLY DIVERSE LEARNERS

⌄ Integrated English Language Support

● Interacting in Meaningful Ways

Classroom Conversations
- Think-Pair-Share, p. T97
- Collaborative Conversation, pp. T92, T108, T112, T123

Interactive and Collaborative Writing
- Visualize, p. T108
- Write About Reading, p. T113
- Compare-Contrast Essay, p. T132

Self-Selected Reading, p. T114

Sentence Frames for Speaking, p. T123

● Learning About How English Works

Scaffold the Texts
- Text X-Ray: Focus on Academic Language, p. T89
- Condensing Ideas, pp. T104, T112, T133

Language Detective
- Target Vocabulary, p. T94
- Text Cohesion, p. T109

Communicative Modes
- Write About Reading, p. T113
- Compare-Contrast Essay, p. T132

● Using Foundational Literacy Skills

Fluency: Intonation, p. T124
Decoding: Vowel + /r/ Sounds, p. T125

Apply Language Skills
- Direct and Indirect Objects, p. T128

Support Linguistic Transfer
- Adages and Proverbs, p. T120
- More Vowel + /r/ Sounds, p. T126
- Direct and Indirect Objects, p. T128

⌄ Standard English Learners

- Pronunciation: Voicing /th/, p. T103
- Direct and Indirect Objects, p. T130

ASSESSMENT

● Formative Assessment

- Target Vocabulary, p. T95
- Target Strategy: Visualize, pp. T102, T106
- Target Skill: Understanding Characters, p. T111
- Vocabulary Strategies: Adages and Proverbs, p. T121
- Decoding: Vowel + /r/ Sounds, p. T125
- Using Data to Adjust Instruction, p. T137

● ✓ Assess It Online!

- Weekly Tests

Performance Tasks
- Write About Reading, p. T113
- Write an Explanatory Essay, p. T364

Vocabulary Reader

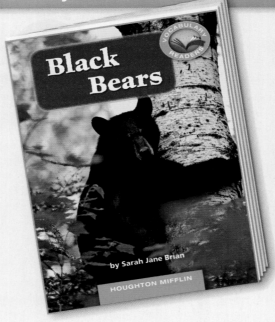

Black Bears
by Sarah Jane Brian
HOUGHTON MIFFLIN

 Vocabulary Reader
for all levels

Provide strategic scaffolding to support all students in reading on-level text and in acquiring general academic and domain-specific vocabulary. Use the instructional supports on pp. T142–T143 or the Leveled Reader Teacher's Guide.

Guided Reading Level: Q
Lexile: 630L
DRA: 40
Leveled Reader Teacher's Guide

Weekly Leveled Readers

Guide students to read and comprehend additional texts about the lesson topic. Use the instructional supports on pp. T146–T149 or the Leveled Reader Teacher's Guides.

Struggling Readers	On Level	Advanced	English Language Learners
Guided Reading Level: Q	**Guided Reading Level: T**	**Guided Reading Level: W**	**Guided Reading Level: T**
Lexile: 580L	Lexile: 750L	Lexile: 770L	Lexile: 430L
DRA: 40	DRA: 44	DRA: 60	DRA: 44
Leveled Reader Teacher's Guide	Leveled Reader Teacher's Guide	Leveled Reader Teacher's Guide	Leveled Reader Teacher's Guide

   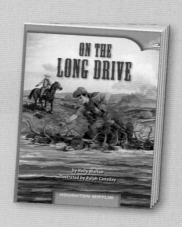   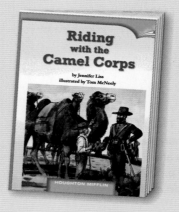   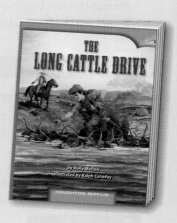

Young Eagle and His Horse
by Lisa Lunney
illustrated by Kristina Rodanas
HOUGHTON MIFFLIN

ON THE LONG DRIVE
by Holly Melton
illustrated by Ralph Canaday
HOUGHTON MIFFLIN

Riding with the Camel Corps
by Jennifer Liss
illustrated by Tom McNeely
HOUGHTON MIFFLIN

THE LONG CATTLE DRIVE
by Holly Melton
illustrated by Ralph Canaday
HOUGHTON MIFFLIN

Meaning Making

Language Development

Effective Expression

Content Knowledge

Foundational Skills

⌄ Language Workshop for Designated ELD

- Provides reteaching and practice in the key foundational skills for reading: print concepts, phonological/phonemic awareness, phonics and word recognition, and fluency.

- Explicit, sequential, and systematic instruction designed to bring students up to grade level.

- Screening and Diagnostic Assessments (within Intervention Assessments) place individual students within the system.

Lesson 7 Focus

Collaborate: Negotiate with Others in Conversations

Interpret: Describe Ideas and Text Elements

Produce: Write Informational Texts Independently

How English Works: Understand Text Cohesion

Vocabulary Network

⌄ Intervention

Strategic Intervention Tier II

Write-In Reader: *Nothing Ever Happens in the Country*

- Interactive worktext with selection that connects to the lesson topic
- Reinforces the lesson's vocabulary and comprehension
- Build skills for reading increasingly complex texts
- Online version with dual-speed audio and follow-text

Daily Lessons See this week's daily Strategic Intervention Lesson on pp. S12–S21.

- Preteach and Reteach daily instruction
- Oral Grammar
- Decoding
- Comprehension

- Fluency
- Grammar
- Written Response
- Unpack Meaning
- Return to Anchor Text

Decoding Power: Intensive Intervention

- Provides reteaching and practice in the key foundational skills for reading: print concepts, phonological/phonemic awareness, phonics and word recognition, and fluency.

- Explicit, sequential, and systematic instruction designed to bring students up to grade level.

- Screening and Diagnostic Assessments (within Intervention Assessments) place individual students within the system.

✓ Assess It Online!

▶ **Screening and Diagnostic Assessments** (within Intervention Assessments) place individual students within the system.

▶ **Progress-Monitoring Assessments** (within Intervention Assessments) ensure students are making satisfactory progress and provide a measure of student readiness to exit the system.

⌄ What My Other Students Are Doing

Digital Resources

▶ **Literacy Centers:** Word Study, Think and Write, Comprehension and Fluency

▶ **Interactive Lessons:** Writing to Sources, Writing Informative Texts: Organize Your Information, Participating in Collaborative Discussions

◉ Additional Resources

- Vocabulary in Context Cards 61–70
- Reader's Notebook, pp. 73–84
- Independent Reading
- Lesson 7 Blackline Masters

Literacy Centers

Managing Independent Activities

Comprehension and Fluency

Materials

- Student Book
- pencil or pen
- Reading Log

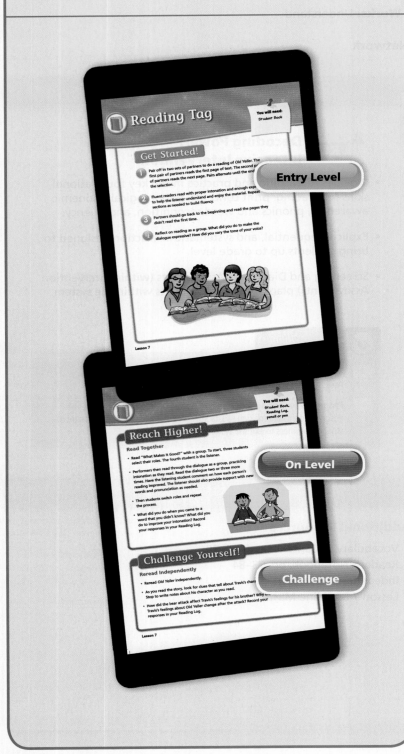

Reading Tag

You will need:
Student Book

Get Started!

1. Pair off in two sets of partners to do a reading of *Old Yeller*. The first pair of partners reads the first page of text. The second pair of partners reads the next page. Pairs alternate until the end of the selection.

2. Fluent readers read with proper intonation and enough expression to help the listener understand and enjoy the material. Repeat sections as needed to build fluency.

3. Partners should go back to the beginning and read the pages they didn't read the first time.

4. Reflect on reading as a group. What did you do to make the dialogue expressive? How did you vary the tone of your voice?

Entry Level

Lesson 7

Reach Higher!

Read Together

- Read "What Makes It Good?" with a group. To start, three students select their roles. The fourth student is the listener.

- Performers then read through the dialogue as a group, practicing intonation as they read. Read the dialogue two or three more times. Have the listening student comment on how each person's reading improved. The listener should also provide support with new words and pronunciation as needed.

- Then students switch roles and repeat the process.

- What did you do when you came to a word that you didn't know? What did you do to improve your intonation? Record your responses in your Reading Log.

You will need:
Student Book,
Reading Log,
pencil or pen

On Level

Challenge Yourself!

Reread Independently

- Reread *Old Yeller* independently.

- As you read the story, look for clues that tell about Travis's character. Stop to write notes about his character as you read.

- How did the bear attack affect Travis's feelings for his brother? Why did Travis's feelings about Old Yeller change after the attack? Record your responses in your Reading Log.

Challenge

Lesson 7

Word Study

Materials

- Reading Log
- computer with Internet access
- poster paper
- pencil or pen
- crayons or markers

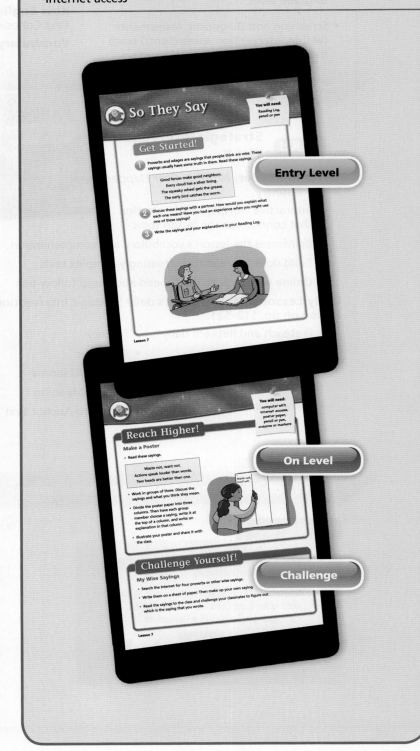

So They Say

You will need:
Reading Log,
pencil or pen

Get Started!

1. Proverbs and adages are sayings that people think are wise. These sayings usually have some truth in them. Read these sayings.

   Good fences make good neighbors.
   Every cloud has a silver lining.
   The squeaky wheel gets the grease.
   The early bird catches the worm.

2. Discuss these sayings with a partner. How would you explain what each one means? Have you had an experience when you might use one of these sayings?

3. Write the sayings and your explanations in your Reading Log.

Entry Level

Lesson 7

Reach Higher!

Make a Poster

- Read these sayings.

   Waste not, want not.
   Actions speak louder than words.
   Two heads are better than one.

- Work in groups of three. Discuss the sayings and what you think they mean.

- Divide the poster paper into three columns. Then have each group member choose a saying, write it at the top of a column, and write an explanation in that column.

- Illustrate your poster and share it with the class.

On Level

Challenge Yourself!

My Wise Sayings

- Search the Internet for four proverbs or other wise sayings.

- Write them on a sheet of paper. Then make up your own saying.

- Read the sayings to the class and challenge your classmates to figure out which is the saying that you wrote.

Challenge

Lesson 7

Meaning Making

Effective Expression

Language Development

Content Knowledge

Foundational Skills

Assign Literacy Center activities during small group time. Each center contains three activities. Students who experience success with the entry-level activity move on to the on-level and challenge activities, as time permits.

Think and Write

Materials

- old magazines
- colored markers
- pencil or pen
- library books
- encyclopedias
- paper

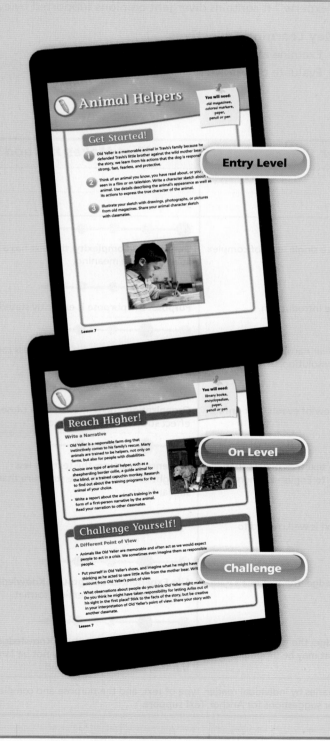

Entry Level

On Level

Challenge

Independent Reading

Student Choice Students who choose their own books will be more actively involved in the reading process.

- In a group discussion, ask students how they choose books. Record their responses on a chart, and display it in the classroom library.

- Then suggest questions students can ask themselves when selecting a book, such as these:

  - Do I want to read a make-believe story (fiction) or something with true facts (informational text)?

  - Have I already read this book? If I have, should I read it again?

  - Have I read other books by this author? Did I like them enough to read another one?

  - Am I interested in this topic?

  - Did someone else recommend this book? If so, am I usually happy when I take his or her recommendations?

See p. T114 for additional independent reading support.

ELA RL.5.10, RI.5.10

Anchor Text

Old Yeller
by Fred Gipson

GENRE: Historical Fiction

Why This Text?

Students regularly encounter historical fiction in literature anthologies and their own independent reading. This text is an excerpt from an American classic. It is written in the informal dialect of 1860s Texas.

Key Learning Objectives
- Build an understanding of characters in a story.
- Study the use of dialect in a story.
- Examine an author's word choice in a story.

Paired Selection

What Makes It Good?
by Cynthia Benjamin

GENRE: Persuasive Text

Why This Text?

Students encounter persuasive text in textbooks, magazines, and in the media. The text presents a movie review from the points of view of two "experts." It contains divergent opinions supported by evidence.

Key Learning Objectives
- Examine a persuasive text.
- Evaluate persuasive techniques.

▲ TEXT COMPLEXITY RUBRIC

		Old Yeller	*What Makes It Good?*
Quantitative Measures	Lexile	930L	NP
	Guided Reading Level	U	S
Qualitative Measures	Meaning and Purpose	**Density and Complexity:** the text has a single level of complex meaning. **Purpose:** the purpose is implied in the introduction.	**Density and Complexity:** the text has a single level of simple meaning. **Purpose:** the purpose is explicitly stated.
	Text Structure	**Organization:** the text follows a familiar narrative structure with a well-developed problem and resolution. **Narration:** the text offers a limited view of events that unfold during first-person narration	**Genre:** the interview structure is less common in informational text. **Organization:** the text contains a cause-and-effect structure within opinions.
	Language Features	**Standard English and Variations:** the text uses dialect that will be unfamiliar to some, especially to English learners. **Conventionality and Register:** the text is well crafted to create mood.	**Sentence Structure:** the text has less straightforward sentence structure than other similar texts.
	Knowledge Demands	**Life Experiences/Background Knowledge:** the text deals with unfamiliar life experiences. **Intertextuality and Cultural Knowledge:** the text is set in a historical period with experiences that may be unfamiliar.	**Life Experiences/Background Knowledge:** The text is in a familiar interview format. **Intertextuality and Cultural Knowledge:** the text refers to ideas that may not be familiar, but they are clearly explained.
Reader/Task Considerations		Determine using the professional judgment of the teacher. This varies by individual reader, type of text, and the purpose and complexity of particular tasks. See **Reader and Task Considerations** on p. T99 for suggestions for Anchor Text support.	

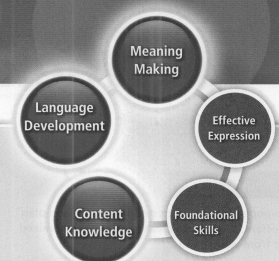

Meaning Making

Language Development

Effective Expression

Content Knowledge

Foundational Skills

TEXT X-RAY

ENGLISH LANGUAGE SUPPORT Use the Text X-Ray below to prepare for teaching the Anchor Text. Use it to plan, support, and scaffold instruction in order to help students understand the text's **key ideas** and **academic language features**.

Zoom In on Key Ideas
Students should understand these **key ideas** after reading *Old Yeller*.

Key Idea | pp. 210–211
In 1860s Texas, Travis takes on grown-up responsibilities while his father is on a cattle drive. His little brother, Arliss, takes in a mangy, yellow stray dog, but Travis doesn't like the dog. On Travis's way home from splitting logs, he hears the panicked screaming of his little brother. Travis runs through the woods towards the screaming. And then he hears a roar that he knows is the sound of a charging bear.

Key Idea | pp. 212–213
Travis finds Little Arliss is in a water hole, holding onto the hind leg of a bear cub. Arliss is too scared to do anything but scream. As Mama comes running from the cabin, the mother bear comes charging through the trees to save her cub. There seems to be no way that either Mama or Travis can get to Arliss in time to save him.

Key Idea | pp. 215–217
Travis is so panicked that he can't even scream. As the mother bear approaches Little Arliss, the yellow dog appears in a flash and attacks the much larger bear. The bear stands on its hind legs, with the dog hanging on to its throat. Travis is able to snatch Arliss out of the way and throw him into Mama's arms. He then turns back with his axe, hoping to swipe at the bear's head, but he can't swing because the yellow dog has managed to keep the bear from getting any closer. Mama calls out to Travis from close to the house and tells him to run. As soon as he runs, the dog follows suit and beats him to the house.

Key Idea | p. 189
Travis realizes now how much he loves his little brother, after nearly losing him to an angry bear. In addition, he can't help but love Old Yeller, the dog that saved Arliss's life.

Zoom In on Academic Language
Guide students at different proficiencies and skill levels to understand the structure and language of this text.

Focus: Word Level | pp. 210–211
Support English learners and others in understanding the author's use of **informal language**. Elicit from students that the story is narrated by Travis. Work with students to identify some informal words and phrases on these pages.

Focus: Text Level | pp. 210–211, 217, 219
Guide students to build an understanding of Travis, the story's **main character**. What do they know about Travis and the way he feels about Little Arliss? On p. 217, does Travis still think that Arliss is troublesome? Ask students to point out parts of the text that led them to their response.

Focus: Sentence Level | pp. 212–213
Support English learners and others in recognizing words that help to connect thoughts. In the first paragraph on p. 212, the sentence structure "I didn't know…, but I knew…" shows the relationship between Travis's thoughts.

Focus: Word Level | pp. 215, 219
Students might not make the connection between the story title and the yellow dog mentioned in the introduction on p. 210. Read aloud from the third paragraph, "It was that big yeller dog." Ask students what *yeller* means. Students may see a connection to the verb *yell* and think it means that the dog yells or makes noise. If so, read the sentence directly above it: "a flash of yellow came streaking out of the brush." On p. 219, it becomes clear that the dog now has a name, Old Yeller.

Content and Language Instruction Make note of additional **content knowledge** and **language features** students may find challenging in this text.

Weekly Planner

my SmartPlanner

Auto-populates the suggested five-day lesson plan and offers flexibility to create and save customized plans from year to year.

See **Standards Correlations** on p. C1. In your eBook, click the Standards button in the left panel to view descriptions of the standards on the page.

	DAY 1	**DAY 2**
	Materials • ELL Blackline Masters 7.2, 7.3 • Graphic Organizer 12 • Lesson 7 Language Support Card • Literacy and Language Guide p. 68 • Projectables 7.1, 7.4, 7.7 • Reader's Notebook pp. 76, 79 • Strategy Projectables S1–S8 • Student Book pp. 204–219 • Vocabulary in Context Cards 61–70	**Materials** • Graphic Organizer 12 • Interactive Lessons: Speaking Constructively, Writing to Sources • Literacy and Language Guide p. 68 • Projectables 7.2, 7.5 • Reader's Notebook pp. 77, 80, 84 • Student Book pp. 208–223

Whole Group

Oral Language
Listening
Comprehension

Teacher Read Aloud
"Annie's Pride," T92–T93

Turn and Talk, T112

Vocabulary
Text-Based Comprehension
• Skills and Strategies
• Craft and Structure

Research and Media Literacy

☑ **Introduce Vocabulary**
Vocabulary in Context, T94–T95
☑ **Read and Comprehend,** T96–T97
FIRST READ Think Through the Text
Read the Anchor Text: "Old Yeller," T98–T109

SECOND READ
☑ **Dig Deeper: How to Analyze the Text,** T110–T111
• Understanding Characters
• Author's Word Choice
• Dialect
• Text Cohesion
Analyze the Text
Reread the Anchor Text: "Old Yeller," T101, T105, T107
☑ **Your Turn,** T112–T113

Foundational Skills
• Fluency
• Decoding

☑ **Fluency**
Model Intonation, T92

☑ **Fluency**
Teach Intonation, T124
Practice Intonation, T103

Whole Group Language Arts

Spelling
Grammar
Writing

☑ **Spelling**
More Vowel + /r/ Sounds:
Pretest, T126
☑ **Grammar**
Daily Proofreading Practice, T128
Teach Direct Objects, T128
☑ **Informative Writing:**
Compare-Contrast Essay
Analyze the Model, T132

☑ **Spelling**
More Vowel + /r/ Sounds: Word Sort, T126
☑ **Grammar**
Daily Proofreading Practice, T129
Extend Direct Objects, T129
☑ **Informative Writing:**
Compare-Contrast Essay
Focus Trait: Word Choice, T133

Small Group

Suggestions for Small Groups (See pp. T140–T141.)

DAY 3

Materials
- Instructional Routine 7
- Literacy and Language Guide pp. 69, 128–129
- Projectables 7.6, 7.8
- Reading Log Blackline Master
- Reader's Notebook pp. 73–74, 81
- Student Book pp. 208–219

Classroom Conversation, T115

Independent Reading, T114
- Reader's Guide: "Old Yeller"
- Self-Selected Reading

Apply Vocabulary Knowledge, T115

☑ **Fluency**
Practice Intonation, T103
☑ **Decoding**
Vowel + /r/ Sounds, T125

☑ **Spelling**
More Vowel + /r/ Sounds: Word Families, T127
☑ **Grammar**
Daily Proofreading Practice, T129
Teach Indirect Objects, T129
☑ **Informative Writing:**
Compare-Contrast Essay
Prewrite, T133

DAY 4

Materials
- Interactive Whiteboard Lesson: Adages and Proverbs
- Literacy and Language Guide pp. 128–129
- Projectable 7.3
- Reader's Notebook pp. 75, 78, 82
- Student Book pp. 224–227

Classroom Conversation, T116

Connect to the Topic
- Read Persuasive Text: "What Makes It Good?" T116
- Think Through the Text, T118
☑ **Compare Texts,** T39
☑ **Vocabulary Strategies**
Adages and Proverbs, T120–T121

☑ **Fluency**
Practice Intonation, T117

☑ **Spelling**
More Vowel + /r/ Sounds: Connect to Writing, T127
☑ **Grammar**
Daily Proofreading Practice, T130
Review Direct and Indirect Objects, T130
☑ **Informative Writing:**
Compare-Contrast Essay
Draft, T134

DAY 5

Materials
- Cold Reads
- Graphic Organizer 6
- Interactive Lessons: Participate in Collaborative Conversations, Writing Informative Texts: Organize Your Information
- Interactive Whiteboard Lesson: Direct and Indirect Objects
- Projectable 7.9
- Proofreading Checklist Blackline Master
- Reader's Notebook p. 83
- Student Book pp. 228–231
- Writing Rubric Blackline Master

Speaking and Listening, T43

Extend the Topic: Responsibility
- Domain-Specific Vocabulary, T122
- Optional Second Read: "What Makes It Good?" T116

☑ **Fluency**
Progress Monitoring, T137

☑ **Spelling**
More Vowel + /r/ Sounds: Assess, T127
☑ **Grammar**
Daily Proofreading Practice, T130
Connect Grammar to Writing, T130–T131
☑ **Informative Writing:**
Compare-Contrast Essay
Revise for Word Choice, T134

 Tier II Intervention provides thirty minutes of additional daily practice with key parts of the core instruction. See pp. S12–S21.

Teacher Read Aloud

- Listen to fluent reading.
- Summarize a written text read aloud using compare-and-contrast sentence frames. **LANGUAGE**

ENGLISH LANGUAGE SUPPORT

Use Visuals

All Proficiencies To assist students with accessing the content and topic of the Teacher Read Aloud, discuss the High-Utility Words on the Lesson 7 Language Support Card ⬚.

☑ **PREVIEW**

Target Vocabulary

romp an energetic and noisy way to play

strained stretched to the limit, either physically or mentally

shouldered carried the weight

lunging making a sudden forward movement

wheeled turned quickly

frantic wild with excitement or worry

picturing creating a mental image of something

bounding leaping

checking limiting or controlling something

stride the rhythm of your walking and the length of your steps

Model Fluency

Intonation Explain that when good readers read aloud, they vary the pitch of their voice to emphasize meaning and to make the text interesting. This is called intonation.

- Display Projectable 7.1 ⬚. Read two or three sentences without intonation. Then reread the same sentences with proper intonation to demonstrate the difference.
- Point out that punctuation and context help determine when to vary the pitch of your voice.
- Reread the sentences together with students, modeling good intonation.

Listening Comprehension

Read aloud the story. Pause at the numbered stopping points to ask students the questions below. Discuss the meanings of the highlighted words, as needed, to support the discussion.

1 *Why does the author include details about the clothes Annie wore in Boston? These details show how privileged her family used to be.* **AUTHOR'S PURPOSE**

2 *When Annie says, "My face was never rough and sunburned from toiling outdoors," what does that tell readers about her character? She has been protected and has not had to work hard.* **UNDERSTANDING CHARACTERS**

3 *What problem does Annie face when she gets to the barn? Her brothers are in danger because a panicking horse has cornered them in a stall.* **IDENTIFY STORY STRUCTURE**

4 *What do readers learn about Annie's character from the way she rescues her brothers? She is stronger and braver than she thought. She might like her new life in Kansas after all.* **UNDERSTANDING CHARACTERS**

💬 Classroom Collaboration

Display these questions and have students discuss them in small groups: *What was Annie's life like a year ago? What is it like now?* Encourage them to organize their ideas using compare-and-contrast sentence frames. Then have have students share their answers with the class. Together, develop a brief summary of the story. **ELA** SL.5.2 **ELD** ELD.PI.5.1, ELD.PI.5.5

ENGLISH LANGUAGE SUPPORT

Read Aloud—Second Read Project the Target Vocabulary Preview. Introduce each word to students. Use visuals, gestures, or yes/no questions to help them understand the meaning of each word. Have students listen to the Read Aloud again and signal when they hear a Target Vocabulary Word. **ELD** ELD.PI.5.5

Annie's Pride

Today, a dry wind howls across the prairie under a blazing sun. Before breakfast, Father and Uncle Pete rode out to the far edge of the farm. It saddens me to watch Father ride off on his old chestnut mare. Back east, he traveled in style in a horse-drawn coach. That coach—and all our possessions—is long gone, sold after fire swept along the wharf and destroyed my father's trading ships.

I flap my apron at the chickens and call Wade and Charlie from the barn. When they do not answer, I march over. Brothers! When they finish their chores, they always play among the stalls in a loud **romp.** How different life is now. When we lived in Boston, I wouldn't think of leaving the house without wearing a bright bonnet and a magnificent strand of pearls. I could never have imagined myself on a Kansas farm, tossing handfuls of chicken feed from the pockets of my mud-stained apron. My face was never rough and sunburned from toiling outdoors; my clothes were never covered in dirt; I never **strained** my muscles with hard work. Sometimes, I hardly recognize myself.

When Father lost everything, Wade and Charlie were thrilled to move west. Even Father looked forward to farming here next to Uncle Pete. "A fresh start," he said. Mother has **shouldered** the burdens of our new life without complaint, but I believe she feels as I do—that farming is men's work.

Approaching the barn door, I hear a scream. One of the horses is **lunging** at the corner of its stall, where Charlie crouches, his arms shielding his head. "Down, Shadow—down!" shouts Wade. He runs to catch the horse's lead, but now the horse has **wheeled,** turning to kick its hooves at him. Suddenly, Wade too is down, huddling against the wall.

These foolish boys—playing in the barn, where strange, sudden noises can make these wild animals **frantic** with fear. I cannot be the one to calm this huge, frightened beast. But I close my eyes, **picturing** horses as I knew them just one year ago, trotting regally down the cobblestone streets of Boston, and without thinking, I am **bounding** across the barn.

Checking my **stride,** I stop, then tell the boys, "No yelling." Rearing up and whinnying, Shadow is almost on top of them. I call his name in a soft, singing tone, saying, "Shush, shush." I grab a carrot and stroke Shadow's flank. Soon, his eyes stop rolling, and he settles into a rocking motion. Finally, I grab his lead and wave my brothers to safety.

When I turn back to Shadow, he takes the carrot. For the first time, I look him in the eye, and he nuzzles me with his big black head. Suddenly, he looks smaller. Or perhaps I have grown, swollen with pride at what I have done, at the idea that I am worth something more than pearls and lace.

Introduce Vocabulary

▶ **SHARE OBJECTIVE**

- Acquire and use vocabulary.
- Use knowledge of linguistic context to determine the meaning of unknown words. LANGUAGE

Teach

Display and discuss the Vocabulary in Context Cards [↗], using the routine below. Direct students to use **Student Book pp. 204–205.**

1 **Read and pronounce the word.** Read the word once alone and then together.

2 **Explain the word.** Read aloud the explanation under *What Does It Mean?*

ENGLISH LANGUAGE SUPPORT Review this cognate with Spanish-speaking students.

- *frenético (frantic)*

3 **Discuss vocabulary in context.** Together, read aloud the sentence on the front of the card. Help students explain and use the word in new sentences.

4 **Engage with the word.** Ask and discuss the *Think About It* question with students.

Apply

Give partners or small groups one or two **Vocabulary in Context Cards.**

- Help students complete the *Talk It Over* activity on the back of each card.
- Have students complete the activities for all cards during the week.

🔍 **Language Detective** Tell students that verbs are action words and tell what a character is doing. Have partners find the verbs in the list of Vocabulary words. Have them use the words in a new sentence. Have them share their sentences with the class. **ELA** L.5.4a, L.5.6 **ELD** ELD.PI.5.12a, ELD.PII.5.3

Lesson 7

Vocabulary in Context

1 romp
For many kids in the 1800s, the trip West was a romp. For adults, it was a serious task.

2 strained
Gold-rush miners strained to sift gold from mounds of heavy soil.

🔍 **LANGUAGE DETECTIVE**

Talk About the Writer's Words
Verbs are words that name actions. Work with a partner. Find the Vocabulary words that are verbs. What are your clues? Use the verbs in new sentences.

3 picturing
In their imagination, many pioneers were picturing owning big cattle ranches.

4 wheeled
Teams of oxen wheeled the wagons around to form a circle for protection.

204   **ELA** L.5.4a, L.5.6   **ELD** ELD.PI.5.12a, ELD.PII.5.3

ENGLISH LANGUAGE SUPPORT

Use Gestures

Emerging Use actions and facial expressions to demonstrate the meanings of *romp, lunging,* and *stride.* Then have students perform the actions, saying each word as they do. **ELD** ELD.PI.5.12a

Expanding Use actions to demonstrate the meaning of *frantic* and say, *When I could not find my keys, I became frantic. Describe my behavior. Use a complete sentence.* **ELD** ELD.PI.5.12a

Bridging Have partners ask and answer questions about each vocabulary word. For example, *What might make you feel frantic?* **ELD** ELD.PI.5.1, ELD.PI.5.12a

► Study each Context Card.

► Use a thesaurus to find a synonym for each Vocabulary word.

5 shouldered

Pioneers may have shouldered newborn animals to carry them, just like this farmer.

6 frantic

Frightened by the storm, this frenzied herd of buffalo began a frantic stampede.

7 lunging

These goats, like the ones on farms, enjoy lunging, or dashing, at each other.

8 checking

Stopping, or checking, the wandering ways of sheep is the job of these farm dogs.

9 stride

Pioneers who walked had to match their stride, or step, to the pace of the wagons.

10 bounding

This man is cheered by his happy dog bounding forward to greet him.

205

FORMATIVE ASSESSMENT **RtI**

Are students able to understand and use Target Vocabulary words?

IF...	THEN...
students **struggle**,	► use **Vocabulary in Context Cards** and differentiate the **Vocabulary Reader**, *Black Bears*, for Struggling Readers, p. T142.
students are **on target**,	► use **Vocabulary in Context Cards** and differentiate the **Vocabulary Reader**, *Black Bears*, for On-Level Readers, p. T142.
students **excel**,	► differentiate the **Vocabulary Reader**, *Black Bears*, for Advanced Readers, p. T143.
SMALL GROUP Options	**Vocabulary Reader,** pp. T142–T143 *Scaffold instruction to the English Learner's proficiency level.*

ENGLISH LANGUAGE SUPPORT

Read and Write Together

Emerging/Expanding

Read Together Display ELL7.2 in Grab-and-Go™ Resources. Read aloud the title and have students repeat. Then, have students look at the images on the page and predict what they think the text will be about.

• As you read the text aloud, display Vocabulary in Context Cards for *bounding*, *lunging*, and *frantic*. Then, have students read the text reread it in pairs.

• Help students generate true and false statements that use the Vocabulary words. For example, *Puppies like to romp and play.*

(true) Allow students to include language from **ELL.7.2**. Write and display the sentences. **ELD** ELD.PI.5.12a

Write Together Display sentence frames, such as the following, and have partners use them to write complete sentences. **ELD** ELD.PI.5.2

1. The dog was *lunging* toward the angry bear.

2. The mother kept *checking* to make sure her children were safe. **ELD** ELD.PI.5.12a

Read and Comprehend

- Compare and contrast characters in a work of fiction.
- Use text details to visualize characters and events.
- Engage effectively in collaborative discussion. LANGUAGE

☑ TARGET SKILL

Understanding Characters

- Read the top section of **Student Book p. 206** with students. Tell students that they can learn about characters in a story by looking at their actions, traits, thoughts, and words

- Explain that when readers compare characters, they look at how their behaviors and traits are the same and different. For example, in "Old Yeller," the two characters Arliss and Travis react very differently to conflict. Using text evidence to compare and contrast the two characters helps readers understand each one more clearly.

- Draw students' attention to the T-Map on **Student Book p. 206.** Tell them that as they read the story, they will be recording important details about the actions and traits of Travis and Arliss.

- Explain that they will use these details to compare and contrast the two characters. **ELA** RL.5.3

ENGLISH LANGUAGE SUPPORT Scaffold Anchor Text Before reading the selection, distribute ELL7.3 in Grab-and-Go™ Resources ⬚. Read the page aloud, and then have students chorally reread it with you.

Review Understanding Characters Reread aloud the first paragraph.

- Explain that character traits are the qualities of a character. Characters' actions and traits help readers understand what characters are like.

Guided Practice Display a T-map. During reading, complete the chart with students.

- Explain to students that the T-map can help them understand story characters by charting key details about the character's actions and traits.

- Help students identify details about each main character. **ELD** ELD.PI.5.6a

---

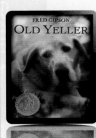

Read and Comprehend

☑ TARGET SKILL

Understanding Characters As you read "Old Yeller," note the ways in which the narrator, Travis, and his brother, Arliss, are similar and different. Look for text evidence to help you examine their **actions** and their **traits**. By comparing the two characters, you will learn more about who they are and why they behave as they do. Record your details in a graphic organizer like the one shown here.

Travis	Arliss

☑ TARGET STRATEGY

Visualize When you **visualize**, you use text details to form pictures in your mind. As you read "Old Yeller," use sights, sounds, and other details in the text to picture each scene. By visualizing what Travis experiences, you can better understand his actions.

Comprehensible Input

Emerging Briefly review a familiar story with students. On the board, list actions and traits of two of the characters. Discuss how they are the same and different.
ELD ELD.PI.5.1, ELD.PI.5.6a

Expanding Have students work with a partner to list details about two characters from a work they have previously read. Have pairs explain how the characters are the same and different.
ELD ELD.PI.5.1, ELD.PI.5.6a

Bridging Have partners compare and contrast two characters from a familiar story. Ask them to explain what they learn about each character through their comparison.
ELD ELD.PI.5.1, ELD.PI.5.6a

You may have heard someone described as having "a sense of responsibility." This sense has nothing to do with hearing, smelling, tasting, touching, or seeing. Rather, it means that the person is dependable. He or she does what needs to be done, even when tasks are hard or unpleasant.

Travis, the narrator of "Old Yeller," has a strong sense of responsibility. While his father is away, he takes on all of the chores needed to keep the family farm going. As you read the story, you will see that he also feels responsible for keeping his brother safe.

💬 Think | Pair | Share

Think about some of your daily responsibilities at home.
► What are they?
► Why are they important?
► Does anyone help you?
Share these with a partner. Then, discuss how your responsibilities and your partner's responsibilities are alike and different. Be sure to listen carefully to your partner and to take turns speaking.

207

COMPREHENSION STRATEGIES

Use the following strategies flexibly as you read with students by modeling how they can be used to improve comprehension. See scaffolded support for the strategy shown in boldface during this week's reading.

- **Monitor/Clarify**
- **Summarize**
- **Infer/Predict**
- **Visualize**
- **Analyze/Evaluate**
- **Question**

Use the Strategy Projectables S1–S8 ⤴, for additional support.

☑ TARGET STRATEGY

Visualize

- Read the bottom section of **Student Book p. 206** with students. Tell students that writers often use descriptive words and phrases to enable readers to "see" what is happening in the story.

- Explain that as they read, students should look for words and phrases that appeal to their senses. They should pause and form a mental picture in their minds of what is happening, who is involved, and where the action is taking place. **Visualizing** will help them form a better understanding of why the characters act as they do.

- Tell students that you will model how to use text details to visualize as you read "Old Yeller" together.

PREVIEW THE TOPIC

Responsibility

- Tell students that today they will begin reading "Old Yeller."

- Read the information at the top of **Student Book p. 207** with students.

- Discuss the concept of responsibility. Have students volunteer ways in which they show that they are responsible. Then, ask them how the image on **p. 207** illustrates the idea of responsibility.

Think-Pair-Share

- Before students have their discussion, display a list of common household responsibilities, such as washing dishes and taking out the trash. Have students add other responsibilities to the list.

- Then, have partners take turns talking about their responsibilities. Give partners time to discuss how their responsibilities are similar and different. Encourage students to ask their partners any questions they have and take turns when speaking.
ELA SL.5.1c **ELD** ELD.PI.5.1

ENGLISH LANGUAGE SUPPORT Access Prior Knowledge: All Proficiencies Use the image on Lesson 7 Language Support Card ⤴ to review the selection topic with students. Show the completed chart again and help students summarize its content.

FIRST READ

Read the Anchor Text

✓ GENRE

Historical Fiction

- Read the genre information on **Student Book p. 208** with students.

- Preview the story and model identifying characteristics of historical fiction.

Think Aloud *As I look through this story, I notice in the illustrations that the characters seem to live in a cabin or farmhouse, and they seem to be dressed in clothing from the past. In addition, the first paragraph includes expressions that don't sound modern. So, I think that this story is set in the past. It is historical fiction.*

- As you preview, ask students to identify other features of historical fiction.

ENGLISH LANGUAGE SUPPORT Access Prior Knowledge: All Proficiencies List characters, setting elements, and plot events from "Old Yeller" on the board. Distribute Story Maps to students. Have student pairs make story predictions by using items from the list to fill in their maps. During reading, have students check their predictions and continue to add to their Story Maps.

ELA RL.5.10 **ELD** ELD.PI.5.6a

Lesson 7

ANCHOR TEXT

✓ GENRE

Historical fiction is a story set in the past. It contains characters, places, and events that actually existed or happened, or that could have existed or happened. As you read, look for:
▶ realistic characters
▶ some made-up events
▶ details that show the story took place in the past

MEET THE AUTHOR

Fred Gipson

Fred Gipson was born in 1908 in Texas's Hill Country, which became the setting for many of his stories. He believed that *Old Yeller* was his best book. It won the 1957 Newbery Honor and was made into a movie. Although Gipson died in 1973, his books remain popular classics.

MEET THE ILLUSTRATOR

Marc Elliot

Like many kids, Marc Elliot loved to draw dinosaurs, only Marc was determined to draw them life-sized on taped-together cardboard in his living room. These days, Marc tries to keep his illustrations to a size that will fit between two book covers. He lives on a farm with sheep, two donkeys, and two crazy long-haired cats.

208   **ELA** RL.5.3, RL.5.10, RF.5.4a, RF.5.4b   **ELD** ELD.PI.5.6a

---

Scaffold Close Reading

Strategies for Annotation	Think Through the Text	Analyze the Text	Independent Reading
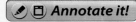 **Annotate it!** As you read the selection with students, look for ✎ 🖰 *Annotate it!* . It indicates opportunities for students to annotate the text independently.	**FIRST READ** Develop comprehension through • Guided Questioning • Target Strategy: Visualize • Vocabulary in Context	**SECOND READ** Support analyzing short sections of text: • Understanding Characters • Author's Word Choice • Dialect • Text Cohesion Use directed note-taking by working with students to complete a graphic organizer during reading. Distribute copies of Graphic Organizer 12 🖰.	• Students analyze the text independently, using the Reader's Guide on pp. 73–74 of the Reader's Notebook 🖰. (See p. T114 for instructional support.) • Students read independently in a self-selected trade book.

Old Yeller

by Fred Gipson
selection illustrated by Marc Elliot

ESSENTIAL QUESTION

How can dangerous situations bring people closer together?

209

READER AND TASK CONSIDERATIONS

Determine the level of additional support that students will need to read and comprehend "Old Yeller" successfully.

READERS

- **Motivate** Ask students to share what they hope to learn from reading the story.
- **Talk It Over** Use Lesson 7 Language Support Card ⬚ for a discussion about people and animals.
- **Access Knowledge and Experiences** Remind students of the information on **Student Book p. 207**. Ask them to share with a partner what they know about having responsibilities around the home.

TASKS

- **Increase Scaffolding** Guide students to use the Infer/Predict strategy as they read the text to help them gain a better understanding of characters' actions and plot events.
- **Foster Independence** Have students work in pairs to determine how the story would change if it were told from Little Arliss's point of view.

ESSENTIAL QUESTION

Read aloud the Essential Question on **Student Book p. 209**: *How can dangerous situations bring people closer together?* Then tell students to think about this question as they read "Old Yeller."

Predictive Writing

- Explain that students will write a paragraph to explain what they expect "Old Yeller" to be about. Ask them to think about how the Essential Question relates to what they noticed while previewing the selection or what they already know from their own experiences or past readings.

- Guide students to think about the genre of the selection to help them write.

Set Purpose

- Tell students that good readers set a purpose for reading, based on their preview of the selection, what they know about the genre, and what they hope to enjoy about the story.

- Model setting a reading purpose.

> **Think Aloud** *This story is historical fiction, which means I can learn about a particular time period while I enjoy reading the story. I would like to know more about life on the frontier in the 1800s. I want to know how people lived and what challenges they faced.*

- Have students set their own purpose for reading. Ask several students to share their purposes with the class. **ELA** RF.5.4a

ENGLISH LANGUAGE SUPPORT Preteach Academic English: Emerging/Expanding Guide students to complete the Academic English activities on Language Support Card 7.

Think Through the Text

Cite Text Evidence

① *What inference about Travis's character does the author want readers to make from these paragraphs? What details support this inference?* Readers infer from these paragraphs that Travis is a hard worker who pushes himself. Details include "The sweat poured off me" and "I was worn down to a nub." **ELA RL.5.1**

② *How does the author intensify suspense in the last two paragraphs on page 211?* Arliss's cry is more frantic. Travis can't identify the second sound but knows he should be able to place it. Then, he hears the roar of a charging bear.

ENGLISH LANGUAGE SUPPORT Tell students that the author uses figurative language to characterize the narrator, Travis. Point out the similes that compare Arliss's scream to "the gobble of a wild turkey" and Travis's movements to those of "a scared wolf." Ask volunteers to share what these descriptions tell them about Travis. *Sample answer: He is used to being outside and around wild animals.*

ELA RL.5.4 ELD ELD.PI.5.8

It is the late 1860s. Travis lives with his family on the Texas frontier. When Papa leaves home to drive their cattle to market in Kansas, Travis must take over Papa's responsibilities. All goes well until a stray yellow dog shows up. Travis's younger brother, Little Arliss, loves the dog, but Travis thinks the mangy animal is nothing but a "meat-stealing rascal." Then one day something happens that changes Travis's feelings about the dog forever.

Swinging that chopping axe was sure hard work. The sweat poured off me. My back muscles ached. The axe got so heavy I could hardly swing it. My breath got harder and harder to breathe.

An hour before sundown, I was worn down to a nub. It seemed like I couldn't hit another lick. Papa could have lasted till past sundown, but I didn't see how I could. I shouldered my axe and started toward the cabin, trying to think up some excuse to tell Mama to keep her from knowing I was played clear out.

That's when I heard Little Arliss scream.

210

ENGLISH LANGUAGE SUPPORT

Use Sentence Frames

Emerging Help students respond to the Think Through the Text questions by phrasing them as sentence frames. For example, for question 1, write on the board: *From the first two paragraphs, we learn that Travis is a _____.* hard worker

Expanding Reword each question in the form of a sentence frame. Have partners work together to provide answers.

Bridging Have students respond orally to the questions, providing details from the story as support.

Well, Little Arliss was a screamer by nature. He'd scream when he was happy and scream when he was mad and a lot of times he'd scream just to hear himself make a noise. Generally, we paid no more mind to his screaming than we did to the gobble of a wild turkey.

But this time was different. The second I heard his screaming, I felt my heart flop clear over. This time I knew Little Arliss was in real trouble.

I tore out up the trail leading toward the cabin. A minute before, I'd been so tired out with my rail splitting that I couldn't have struck a trot. But now I raced through the tall trees in that creek bottom, covering ground like a scared wolf.

Little Arliss's second scream, when it came, was louder and shriller and more frantic-sounding than the first. Mixed with it was a whimpering crying sound that I knew didn't come from him. It was a sound I'd heard before and seemed like I ought to know what it was, but right then I couldn't place it.

Then, from way off to one side came a sound that I would have recognized anywhere. It was the coughing roar of a charging bear. I'd just heard it once in my life. That was the time Mama had shot and wounded a hog-killing bear and Papa had had to finish it off with a knife to keep it from getting her. **2**

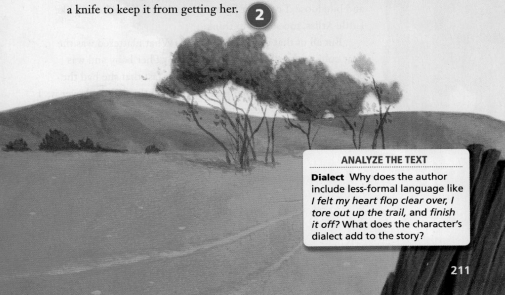

> **ANALYZE THE TEXT**
>
> **Dialect** Why does the author include less-formal language like *I felt my heart flop clear over, I tore out up the trail,* and *finish it off*? What does the character's dialect add to the story?

211

DOMAIN: Values

LESSON TOPIC: Responsibility

Cross-Curricular Connection Elicit from students their definition of the word *responsibility*. Then, ask them how Travis exhibits a sense of responsibility. *He is doing chores and helping to take care of the family farm; he runs to help his brother.* Point out that children who lived on farms in the 1800s often played an important role in keeping the farms running. Many were asked to perform household chores, care for crops and animals, and help keep an eye on younger children during the workday.

Analyze the Text

Dialect

- Read the Analyze the Text box on **Student Book p. 211** with students.

- Remind students that dialect is a form of language used by a group of people in a particular place or time. Discuss with them how the use of dialect makes a story more authentic or realistic. Point out that dialect also provides insight into a character's background and perspective and can add to readers' understanding of setting.

ENGLISH LANGUAGE SUPPORT Explain to students that they probably use a mix of formal and informal language every day. Point out that while they might speak to their friends in a natural dialect, full of slang and expressions and cultural references, they probably speak to teachers, doctors, grandparents, and other adults in a more formal way. Invite volunteers to share examples of when they would use dialect and when they might use formal English.

- Locate the expressions listed in the box. Together, rephrase each expression in more formal language. *I was shocked and afraid; I ran frantically along the trail; kill the bear.*

- Have students compare and contrast the formal language with Travis's. Tell them that authors use different varieties of English to define characters and to give narrators distinctive voices. Point out that the more formal language changes the narrator's voice and the impression of him that is conveyed through what he says.

- Discuss how the use of more formal language also removes clues to the setting; the story could be taking place anywhere and at any time.

- Have students find other examples of dialect throughout the story. Ask students to think about how each example adds to their understanding of character and setting.

ELA L.5.3b **ELD** ELD.PI.5.6a, ELD.PI.5.8

✏ 🖥 ***Annotate it!*** Have students highlight examples of dialect in the text.

FIRST READ

Think Through the Text

 Cite Text Evidence

3 *Why do you think the author chose first-person point of view to tell the story? The first-person point of view enables readers to feel Travis's fear and panic and heightens the suspense as they watch events unfold through his eyes.*

ELA RL.5.6

☑ **TARGET STRATEGY**

Visualize

Reread the third paragraph on **Student Book p. 212** aloud. Then model the strategy:

> **Think Aloud** *This paragraph includes details that appeal to my senses of sight and hearing. Arliss is "lying half in and half out of the water." The bear cub is "whimpering and crying and clawing." Arliss is screaming. Because of these details, I can picture exactly what is happening at the spring hole and where each character is.*

Tell students to practice using the Visualize strategy as they continue reading.

4 *How do Arliss's actions contrast with those of Travis? Arliss is unable to act, whereas Travis is rapidly responding to the situation.*

ELA RL.5.3 ELD ELD.PI.5.6a

ENGLISH LANGUAGE SUPPORT Ask this question in a different way. *How has Arliss responded to what's happening? In what way is Travis's response different?*

My heart went to pushing up into my throat, nearly choking off my wind. I strained for every lick of speed I could get out of my running legs. I didn't know what sort of fix Little Arliss had got himself into, but I knew that it had to do with a mad bear, which was enough.

The way the late sun slanted through the trees had the trail all cross-banded with streaks of bright light and dark shade. I ran through these bright and dark patches so fast that the changing light nearly blinded me. Then suddenly, I raced out into the open where I could see ahead. And what I saw sent a chill clear through to the marrow of my bones. **3**

There was Little Arliss, down in that spring hole again. He was lying half in and half out of the water, holding on to the hind leg of a little black bear cub no bigger than a small coon. The bear cub was out on the bank, whimpering and crying and clawing the rocks with all three of his other feet, trying to pull away. But Little Arliss was holding on for all he was worth, scared now and screaming his head off. Too scared to let go.

How the bear cub ever came to prowl close enough for Little Arliss to grab him, I don't know. And why he didn't turn on him and bite loose, I couldn't figure out, either. Unless he was like Little Arliss, too scared to think.

But all of that didn't matter now. What mattered was the bear cub's mama. She'd heard the cries of her baby and was coming to save him. She was coming so fast that she had the brush popping and breaking as she crashed through and over it. I could see her black heavy figure piling off down the slant on the far side of Birdsong Creek. She was roaring mad and ready to kill.

212

 **FORMATIVE ASSESSMENT** **3 2 1 RtI**

Visualize

IF students have difficulty applying the Visualize strategy... **THEN** use this model:

> **Think Aloud** *In the last paragraph on page 213, I am not sure exactly what is happening. I need to reread the details and look for words and phrases that help me see where the bear is and what she is doing.*

Have students use the details in the paragraph to describe the scene.

And worst of all, I could see that I'd never get there in time!

Mama couldn't either. She'd heard Arliss, too, and here she came from the cabin, running down the slant toward the spring, screaming at Arliss, telling him to turn the bear cub loose. But Little Arliss wouldn't do it. All he'd do was hang with that hind leg and let out one shrill shriek after another as fast as he could suck in a breath.

Now the she bear was charging across the shallows in the creek. She was knocking sheets of water high in the bright sun, charging with her fur up and her long teeth bared, filling the canyon with that awful coughing roar. And no matter how fast Mama ran or how fast I ran, the she bear was going to get there first!

4

213

Practice Fluency

SECOND READ

Intonation Read aloud the last three paragraphs on **Student Book p. 213** as students follow along. First read in a monotone, and then read the passage with intonation, using your hand to show the rise and fall of your voice.

- Discuss with students how the two readings differ. Ask them to identify which reading helped to bring out the suspenseful mood in the passage.

- Have students echo-read each sentence after you read it, using the correct intonation.

- Provide further modeling and practice using the Fluency lesson on p. T124. **ELA** RF.5.4b

FOR STANDARD ENGLISH LEARNERS Pronunciation Some students may need help mastering Standard English pronunciations when reading aloud or speaking in a more formal register. Students may have trouble voicing /th/ at the beginning of words such as *this* or *that*. They may pronounce the /th/ sound as /d/, saying "dis" for *this*. Write this sentence on the board: *There was Little Arliss, down in that spring hole again.* Read the sentence aloud, emphasizing the /th/ sound in *There* and *that*. Have students echo your reading several times.

FIRST READ

Think Through the Text

5 *How would you characterize Old Yeller, based on his actions in this part of the story? Old Yeller is brave and loyal; he does not hesitate to defend Arliss.* **ELA** RL.5.3 **ELD** ELD.PI.5.6a

6 *What context clues help you understand the phrase "Without ever checking my stride"? The clues "I didn't wait to see more" and "I ran in" reveal that the phrase means "moving swiftly and without pausing."* **ELA** RL.5.4 **ELD** ELD.PI.5.6a, ELD.PI.5.8

ENGLISH LANGUAGE SUPPORT Tell students that "checking my stride" is an idiom that means *watching my steps,* or *slowing down.* Explain that authors sometimes use idioms to show personality in a character's speech or thoughts.

7 *Look at the illustration on these pages. How does it support the action described on page 215? Possible answer: Old Yeller isn't "one-third as big and heavy as the she-bear." Both animals look angry. Travis is pulling Arliss away, just as the text describes.* **ELA** RL.5.7 **ELD** ELD.PI.5.6a

214

ENGLISH LANGUAGE SUPPORT

How English Works: Interpretive

Condensing Ideas As students read this selection, have them look for places where the author has written sentences that are detailed and that give exact messages. For example, sometimes the author needs to join two short sentences to be exact. Read aloud paragraph 4 on **Student Book p. 215,** emphasizing the following sentence: *As I raced past them, I saw the bear lunge up to stand on her hind feet like a man while she clawed at the body of the yeller dog hanging to her throat.* Write the sentence on the board and explain that it is made up of these three ideas: *I raced past them. I saw the bear lunge up to stand on her hind feet like a man. She clawed at the body of the yeller dog hanging to her throat.* Tell students that the author condensed ideas by using the pronouns *her* and *she.* Write these sentences on the baord: *I heard Arliss screaming. I saw Arliss holding on to the bear cub.* Have partners talk about how they can combine these sentences. *Sample answer: I heard Arliss screaming and saw him holding on to the bear cub.* **ELD** ELD.PII.5.7

I think I nearly went blind then, picturing what was going to happen to Little Arliss. I know that I opened my mouth to scream and not any sound came out.

Then, just as the bear went lunging up the creek bank toward Little Arliss and her cub, a flash of yellow came streaking out of the brush.

It was that big yeller dog. He was roaring like a mad bull. He wasn't one-third as big and heavy as the she bear, but when he piled into her from one side, he rolled her clear off her feet. They went down in a wild, roaring tangle of twisting bodies and scrambling feet and slashing fangs.

5

As I raced past them, I saw the bear lunge up to stand on her hind feet like a man while she clawed at the body of the yeller dog hanging to her throat. I didn't wait to see more. Without ever checking my stride, I ran in and jerked Little Arliss loose from the cub. I grabbed him by the wrist and yanked him up out of that water and slung him toward Mama like he was a half-empty sack of corn. I screamed at Mama. "Grab him, Mama! Grab him and run!" Then I swung my chopping axe high and wheeled, aiming to cave in the she bear's head with the first lick.

6

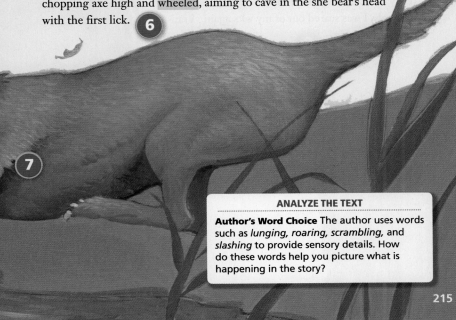

7

> **ANALYZE THE TEXT**
>
> **Author's Word Choice** The author uses words such as *lunging, roaring, scrambling,* and *slashing* to provide sensory details. How do these words help you picture what is happening in the story?

215

FOR STUDENTS WITH DISABILITIES Some students may have difficulty keeping their place on a page of text. Provide an index card with a cutout window so students see only one line of text at a time. Have them move the card down the page as they read.

Author's Word Choice

Analyze the Text

- Read the Analyze the Text box on **Student Book p. 215** with students.

- Remind students that sensory details appeal to the five senses and that authors use sensory details to give information and make events and characters' actions come alive.

- Ask students to identify the sense that each of the words listed in the box appeals to. *sight; hearing; sight; sight/touch* Discuss movements, sounds, and sensations associated with each.

- Then replace the words with *leaning, noisy, moving,* and *biting.* Read the sentences aloud with the new words.

- Have students explain the effect of the new words as compared to the images evoked by the use of the original words. *The new words do not create a mental picture; they are weaker words that do not show the intensity of the action.*

ENGLISH LANGUAGE SUPPORT Ask students the following series of questions. *What do you picture in your mind when you read these new words? Are they as vivid as the words the author uses in the text? Why or why not? How do the words chosen by the author help you picture what Travis sees, or feel what he feels?*

- Tell students to look for other sensory details as they read the story, and to think about how the author's word choice affects their ability to picture what Travis describes in each scene.
ELD ELD.PI.5.6a, ELD.PI.5.8

🖊️ 📱 ***Annotate it!*** Have students highlight words in the text that provide vivid, sensory details.

Think Through the Text

Cite Text Evidence

✓ TARGET STRATEGY

Visualize

Have students read the first paragraph on **Student Book p. 216** silently. Have them apply the Visualize strategy to picture the animals' movements and sounds in this part of the story. Call on volunteers to explain which words and phrases help them create a mental image of the action.

8 *Why does Travis suddenly feel frightened again? Arliss is out of danger, so he can think clearly and realize how close he came to having to defend Arliss against the bear.*

9 *Why does the author include the first paragraph on p. 217? The details in this paragraph explain what happened while Travis was running back to the cabin. They connect the events before and after Travis left the spring hole.* **ELA** RL.5.5 **ELD** ELD.PI.5.6a

ENGLISH LANGUAGE SUPPORT Break this question into parts. Ask: *What happens in the first paragraph on p. 217? Why do you think this paragraph is important to the story? What events does it connect?*

10 *How does Travis support his inference that Old Yeller thought the fight was fun? Old Yeller bounds in and licks everyone's face, barking excitedly.* **ELA** RL.5.1

But I never did strike. I didn't need to. Old Yeller hadn't let the bear get close enough. He couldn't handle her; she was too big and strong for that. She'd stand there on her hind feet, hunched over, and take a roaring swing at him with one of those big front claws. She'd slap him head over heels. She'd knock him so far that it didn't look like he could possibly get back there before she charged again, but he always did. He'd hit the ground rolling, yelling his head off with the pain of the blow; but somehow he'd always roll to his feet. And here he'd come again, ready to tie into her for another round.

I stood there with my axe raised, watching them for a long moment. Then from up toward the house, I heard Mama calling: "Come away from there, Travis. Hurry, son! Run!"

That spooked me. Up till then, I'd been ready to tie into that bear myself. Now, suddenly, I was scared out of my wits again. I ran toward the cabin. **8**

216

Visualize

IF students do not have a clear image of what happens in this part of the story… **THEN**, revisit the Visualize strategy by modeling how to use words and images to create a mental picture:

> **Think Aloud** *The first paragraph on page 216 includes several details that help me see what is happening. The bear takes "a roaring swing" at Old Yeller that "slap[s] him head over heels." But Old Yeller would "always roll to his feet" and get "ready to tie into her for another round." Old Yeller is standing up to the bear.*

Have students draw or describe the image that these details create.

But like it was, Old Yeller nearly beat me there. I didn't see it, of course; but Mama said that the minute Old Yeller saw we were all in the clear and out of danger, he threw the fight to that she bear and lit out for the house. The bear chased him for a little piece, but at the rate Old Yeller was leaving her behind, Mama said it looked like the bear was backing up. **9**

But if the big yeller dog was scared or hurt in any way when he came dashing into the house, he didn't show it. He sure didn't show it like we all did. Little Arliss had hushed his screaming, but he was trembling all over and clinging to Mama like he'd never let her go. And Mama was sitting in the middle of the floor, holding him up close and crying like she'd never stop. And me, I was close to crying, myself.

Old Yeller, though, all he did was come bounding in to jump on us and lick us in the face and bark so loud that there, inside the cabin, the noise nearly made us deaf.

The way he acted, you might have thought that bear fight hadn't been anything more than a rowdy romp that we'd all taken part in for the fun of it. **10**

> ### ANALYZE THE TEXT
>
> **Understanding Characters** How does Travis respond to the bear attacking Arliss? What does his response say about his feelings toward his brother?

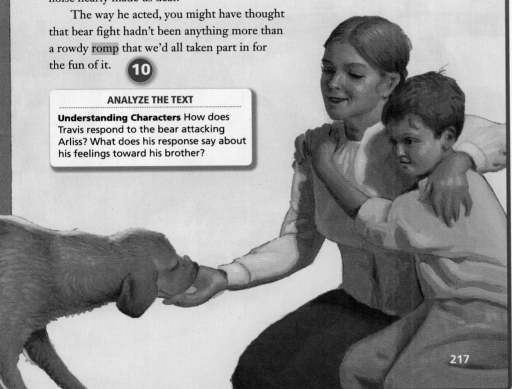

217

Understanding Characters

Analyze the Text

- Read the Analyze the Text box on **Student Book p. 217** with students. Then, distribute Graphic Organizer 12 .

- Remind students that comparing how two characters react to conflict can help readers see more clearly what each character is like.

- Display Projectable 7.2 . Tell students you will work together to complete the graphic organizer with text details.

- Have students reread **pp. 215–217**. Ask them to list details that describe Travis's reaction to the bear's attack. *He runs as fast as he can to the water hole; he pulls Arliss out; he prepares to go after the bear with his axe.* Ask what Travis's actions show about his character and his feelings toward his brother.

ENGLISH LANGUAGE SUPPORT Ask students to go back to the text and find one example each of something Travis does and something Arliss does. Have students explain what these actions show about each character. Provide these sentence frames to support participation. *In one part of the story, Travis _____. This action shows that he _____.*

- Have pairs add details to their T-Maps that show Arliss's response. *He screams; he can't move; he has to be pulled away by Travis.* Guide students to use the two characters' actions to compare and contrast them. **ELA** RL.5.1, RL.5.3 **ELD** ELD.PI.5.6a

---

✏ 🖥 *Annotate it!* Have students highlight details and character actions in the text that provide a better understanding of Arliss and Travis.

Think Through the Text

Cite
Text Evidence

11 *What contrast between the two boys do the details in this paragraph reveal?* Arliss spends his time playing and getting in the way of everyone who works on the farm, unlike Travis, who helps out however he can. Travis acts like a man, whereas Arliss is still a boy.
ELA RL.5.3 **ELD** ELD.PI.5.6a

12 *What does Travis mean when he says, "I knew then that I loved him as much as I did Mama and Papa, maybe in some ways even a little more"?* Arliss needs Travis, which may be why Travis loves him more. *How do Travis's feelings for Arliss contribute to the theme of the story?* When he sees Arliss in danger, he realizes how much he cares for him. He also feels responsible for him. **ELA** RL.5.2 **ELD** ELD.PI.5.6a

Classroom Conversation

Have students discuss "Old Yeller," either as a whole class or in small groups. Provide this prompt to focus their discussion: *Is Travis a good role model for his younger brother? Why or why not?* Have students revisit the text and use evidence from it to support their opinion. Remind students to respond to each other's comments and questions in complete sentences, to follow discussion rules, and to allow everyone a chance to share their thoughts.
ELA SL.5.1a, SL.5.1b, SL.5.1c **ELD** ELD.PI.5.1, ELD.PI.5.4

218

ENGLISH LANGUAGE SUPPORT

Collaborate: Visualize

Teach/Model Display the word *visualize* and explain its meaning. Remind students that visualizing story characters helps readers understand them. Use a Think Aloud to model visualizing events in "Old Yeller."

Think Aloud *Why would scientists need to capture a wild tree kangaroo in order to learn about it? How does capturing the animal help scientists study it?*

Guided Practice Assign students paragraphs from "Old Yeller" to read. Have students visualize the details and events in the text.

• Review **Teach Academic Language** on Lesson 7 Language Support Card.

• Remind students to pay attention to adjectives and quotations as they visualize the story and characters.

Till Little Arliss got us mixed up in that bear fight, I guess I'd been looking on him about like most boys look on their little brothers. I liked him, all right, but I didn't have a lot of use for him. What with his always playing in our drinking water and getting in the way of my chopping axe and howling his head off and chunking me with rocks when he got mad, it didn't seem to me like he was hardly worth the bother of putting up with. **11**

But that day when I saw him in the spring, so helpless against the angry she bear, I learned different. I knew then that I loved him as much as I did Mama and Papa, maybe in some ways even a little bit more. **12**

So it was only natural for me to come to love the dog that saved him. After that, I couldn't do enough for Old Yeller.

219

Scaffolded Practice and Application

Emerging Describe a scene and have students sketch the details as they visualize. Ask them to label the sketch with appropriate words and phrases.

Expanding Describe a scene and have students explain which details they visualize. Ask students to use phrases and sentences to explain what visualizing helps them understand.

Bridging Describe a scene and have students visualize it. Ask them to write several details that might help a reader get a clear picture of the scene.

Q Language Detective

Text Cohesion

- Point out to students that authors of stories often include a character's thoughts in a way that makes it seem as if that character is speaking to readers. In first-person narration, the person who tells the story is the main character, and he or she observes and describes the actions of others. Pronouns are often used in these descriptions to make the writing smooth and clear.

- Read aloud **Student Book p. 215.** Draw students' attention to paragraph 3. Ask: *What pronouns do you see here? it, he, her,* and *they What parts of the text do they refer back to? It refers to the flash of yellow Travis sees while he's watching the bear. He refers to Old Yeller. She refers to the bear. They refers to both the dog and the bear as they're fighting.* **Use the Think Aloud to model understanding text cohesion.**

> **Think Aloud** *This paragraph contains several pronouns that refer to things and animals in the text. If I replace the pronouns with what they refer to, I can see that the writing becomes choppy and confusing. If the narrator used "the bear" every time he referred to her, I would be overwhelmed by the repetition of this same phrase. Using the pronoun instead smooths out the narration while still clearly showing what's happening in the story.*

- Have partners or small groups revisit the text and look for places in which pronouns are used to clarify and smooth out the narration. Ask students to share and discuss their findings.
ELA RL.5.1, RL.5.6 **ELD** ELD.PII.5.2a

🖉 🗐 Annotate it! Have students highlight pronouns in the text and underline the people, places, things, or events they refer to.

Dig Deeper *Use Clues to Analyze the Text*

▶ SHARE OBJECTIVES

- Compare and contrast characters, drawing on specific text details.
- Examine the effect of the author's word choice.
- Understand the use of dialect in a story and what it can reveal about characters.
- Understand the use of pronouns in narrative text. LANGUAGE

ENGLISH LANGUAGE SUPPORT

Use Sentence Frames

Emerging Write these sentence frames on the board: *Travis _____ when he sees the bear. Arliss _____ when he sees the bear.* Using gestures and words, guide students to complete the sentence frames.

Expanding Have students write words and phrases to complete the sentence frames above.

Bridging Have students write two sentences that explain how each character reacts to the bear.

ELD ELD.PI.5.2

Text-Based Comprehension

1 Teach/Model

Terms About Literature

main character the most important person, animal, or imaginary creature taking part in a story's action

sensory language words and phrases that appeal to the senses of sight, hearing, touch, taste, and smell

dialect variety of English spoken in a particular place or time period by a particular group of people

pronoun a word that takes the place of and refers back to a noun in a text

---

- Remind students that they have just read a story about a conflict between a bear and a dog.

- Read **Student Book p. 220** with students. Tell them that Travis is both the **main character** and the narrator in the story. Readers learn about everything that happens from his perspective.

- Explain that Travis shares details about himself and Arliss that reveal their similarities and differences. Tell students that they should draw on these kinds of text details as they compare and contrast the two characters.

- Model for students how to identify ideas to record on the T-Map:

  Think Aloud *From the first part of the story, I learn that Travis is taking the place of his father while his father is away. That shows me he is responsible. Later in the story, on page 212, Travis says, "I didn't know what sort of fix Little Arliss had got himself into. . . ." This tells me that Arliss has a habit of getting into trouble.*

- Next, read **Student Book p. 221** with students. Explain that **sensory language** adds to the meaning of a story and makes the difference between a dull story and an exciting one. Demonstrate by having students identify which of these statements appeals to their senses: *The bear was mad. The bear snarled, saliva dripping from his exposed gums*.

- Explain that Travis's **dialect,** or his unique way of speaking, makes him believable as a character. Tell students that paying special attention to a character's use of dialect, and comparing and contrasting it with familiar varieties of English, can help them understand that character's background and traits.

Q **Language Detective: Text Cohesion** Tell students that authors use pronouns to refer to people or objects mentioned elsewhere in a text. Pronouns make writing smooth and easy to follow, and are often used in stories when a character is speaking, or being described by a narrator.

Dig Deeper

Use Clues to Analyze the Text

Use these pages to learn about Understanding Characters, Author's Word Choice, and Dialect. Then read "Old Yeller" again to apply what you learned.

Understanding Characters

The story of "Old Yeller" is told through the eyes of its **main character**, Travis. Readers learn not only what Travis does and says, but also what he thinks and feels.

In the selection, Travis and his little brother, Arliss, are caught in the same conflict. Readers learn about Arliss through his actions and what Travis tells about him. Comparing the two characters reveals more about each one's personality and their relationship.

Look closely for details that tell you about Travis and Arliss. Think about their different reactions to situations. What do you learn about Travis from his response to events? What do you learn about Arliss?

Travis	Arliss

Author's Word Choice

Sensory language is language that helps readers see, hear, and experience what happens in a story. Recall the scene from "Old Yeller" in which Travis first realizes that a charging bear is after Little Arliss. The author uses words and phrases such as "popping," "breaking," and "awful coughing roar" to build the intensity of the moment and to make readers feel as if they are in the scene with Travis.

Dialect

Dialect, a variety of English associated with a certain place or group of people, adds realism to historical fiction such as "Old Yeller." On page 210, Travis uses expressions such as "worn down to a nub" and "I couldn't hit another lick" to describe how tired he is after chopping wood. These expressions fit his character and the story's setting. They also help establish Travis's voice as he begins to narrate the story.

---

2 Guided Practice/Apply

Analyze the Text

Begin a second read of "Old Yeller" with students. Use the stopping points and instructional support to guide students to analyze the text:

- Understanding Characters, p. T103 **ELA** RL.5.3 **ELD** ELD.PI.5.6a
- Author's Word Choice, p. T105 **ELD** ELD.PI.5.7
- Dialect, p. T107 **ELA** L.5.3b **ELD** ELD.PI.5.7
- Text Cohesion, p. T109 **ELD** ELD.PII.5.2a

Directed Note Taking The graphic organizer will be completed with students during the second read on p. T103.

FORMATIVE ASSESSMENT △3 2 1 RtI

Are students able to understand characters?

IF...	THEN...
students struggle,	**Differentiate Comprehension** for Struggling Readers, p. T144.
students are on track,	**Differentiate Comprehension** for On-Level Readers, p. T144.
students excel,	**Differentiate Comprehension** for Advanced Readers, p. T145.

Differentiate Comprehension, pp. T144–T145
Scaffold instruction to the English Learner's proficiency level.

SECOND READ

Your Turn

Cite
Text Evidence

▶ SHARE OBJECTIVES

- Use quotations and other text evidence to support ideas in writing or discussion.
- Determine a story's theme.
- Prepare for and participate in group discussions.
- Write a response to the selection. LANGUAGE

RETURN TO THE ESSENTIAL QUESTION

As students discuss the Essential Question, remind them to bring in specific details and evidence from the text to support their insights. Tell them to summarize what others say in discussion to make sure they understand the points, and to elaborate on each others' remarks to deepen their analysis or to introduce new ways of thinking about the questions.

ELA RL.5.1, SL.5.1a, SL.5.1c **ELD** ELD.PI.5.1, ELD.PI.5.4, ELD.PI.5.6a

Classroom Conversation

Make sure students understand the terms *setting, narrator,* and *drawing conclusions.* Then, have them volunteer their answers to each question. Encourage them to comment constructively on points offered by other members of the class. See Digital Lesson: Speaking Constructively ⬀. **ELA** SL.5.1a, SL.5.1c **ELD** ELD.PI.5.1, ELD.PI.5.6a

ENGLISH LANGUAGE SUPPORT Use sentence frames, such as the following, to support discussion.

- *I think the setting affects what happens in the story because _____.*
- *I think Travis (is)/(is not) a good choice as narrator because _____.*
- *The conclusion I can draw about life on the frontier is _____.*

As students share their ideas, tell them to use text evidence to support their responses.

ELD ELD.PI.5.1, ELD.PI.5.4, ELD.PI.5.11a

Your Turn

RETURN TO THE ESSENTIAL QUESTION

Turn and Talk

Review the selection to prepare to discuss this question: *How can dangerous situations bring people closer together?* Take turns sharing your insights in a small group. Elaborate on each other's comments.

Classroom Conversation

Continue your discussion of "Old Yeller" by using text evidence to explain your answers to these questions:

1. How does the setting affect what happens in the story?

2. Is Travis a good choice for the narrator of this story? Explain.

3. What conclusions about life on the frontier can you draw from the story?

DISCUSS CHARACTER GROWTH

Partner Talk How do Travis's feelings toward his brother change during the story? With a partner, discuss how the incident with the bear affects Travis. Then evaluate whether his change in perspective is believable, based on your ideas about how real people react and feel in such situations. Share your observations with the class.

222   **ELA** RL.5.1, RL.5.2, W.5.9a, W.5.10, SL.5.1a, SL.5.1c **ELD** ELD.PI.5.1, ELD.PI.5.6a, ELD.PI.5.10a

ENGLISH LANGUAGE SUPPORT

How English Works

Condensing Ideas Before students begin their discussion, have them plan to use sentences that are detailed and that give exact messages. For example, sometimes speakers join two short sentences to be exact. Give the following examples: *The woman gave a performance. The woman is a singer.* Provide a revised sentence, and explain that the pronoun *who* is used to condense it. Help different proficiency levels build sentences about their discussion topics using the words *who, that,* or *which.* Have students use these sentences in their discussions. **ELD** ELD.PII.5.7

Performance Task

WRITE ABOUT READING

Response To determine the theme, or message, of a short story, think about how the main character responds to conflict. For example, how does Travis react when his brother is in danger? Write a paragraph explaining how Travis's actions reveal a general message about life or people. Support your ideas with quotations and other text evidence.

Writing Tip

Be sure to use quotation marks around phrases or sentences that you take directly from the text. Include only those details that support your main idea.

223

DISCUSS CHARACTER GROWTH

Direct students to the beginning and the end of the story to find details that describe Travis's feelings about his brother. Have them explain what he realizes through the incident with the bear. Ask them to think about a time when they almost lost something or someone and how they felt afterwards. Have them compare their reaction and feelings to Travis's in order to evaluate how realistic his change is.

ELA SL.5.1a **ELD** ELD.PI.5.1, ELD.PI.5.4, ELD.PI.5.6a

WRITE ABOUT READING   **Performance Task**

Remind students that what a character learns from overcoming a conflict often translates into the theme of a story. Have students review the story to find specific details describing Travis's reaction to the conflict. Point out how tired he is when the story opens and how he overcomes his exhaustion to act. Then, have them think about what lesson he takes from the experience. Ask them to write a paragraph stating this lesson as a universal theme, quoting accurately from the text to support their explanation and inferences.

ELA RL.5.1, RL.5.2, W.5.9a, W.5.10

ENGLISH LANGUAGE SUPPORT Tell students to state the theme of the story in the opening sentence. Provide this frame:

The theme of the story is _____.

Tell students to support their ideas using these frames:

*When his brother is in danger, Travis _____.
In addition, the text says _____.*

Remind students to use pronouns to condense their ideas in their paragraphs. See Digital Lesson: Writing to Sources 🔗.

ELD ELD.PI.5.6a, ELD.PI.5.10b, ELD.PII.5.7

Writing Tip Make sure students read the Writing Tip before they begin writing. Remind them that they can quote all or part of a sentence from the story.

*my*WriteSmart Have students complete the Write About Reading activity through *my*WriteSmart. Students will read the prompt within *my*WriteSmart and have access to multiple writing resources, including the Student eBook, Writing Rubrics, and Graphic Organizers.

ENGLISH LANGUAGE SUPPORT

Collaborative Writing

Step 1 Guide students to complete a web to determine the theme of the story and support it with reasons based in text evidence.

Step 2 Explain that you will work together as a class to write a response to reading by using the completed graphic organizer. Point out to students that they will say ideas and sentences, and you will write them down for the group to see and read.

Step 3 Have students develop the response by referring to the graphic organizer and answering questions such as these:

- What words will help begin this response?
- What information should we include? How do we say that in a sentence?
- What is the first reason that we should write?
- What text evidence will we use?

Step 4 Read the unfinished response aloud to students. Repeat, and have students read aloud with you. Ask students if they see or hear anything they would like to change.

Extra Scaffold Without purposely making mistakes, revise in the moment by using Think Alouds. **ELD** ELD.PI.5.2

Independent Reading

▶ SHARE OBJECTIVES

- Read and comprehend literature.
- Quote accurately from a text to support analysis and inferences.
- Read independently from a "just right" book.
- Ask and answer questions about key details. LANGUAGE

ENGLISH LANGUAGE SUPPORT

"Just Right" Books for English Learners

All Proficiencies When or if English learners abandon a book that they have chosen, this provides a great opportunity to get information. Talk with students about why they changed their minds about the book. Were the concepts in it unfamiliar? Was the language in it complex, and if so, how? Did the book have complex vocabulary or sentence structures? Use this information to make future recommendations and to guide students in selecting the right book the next time.

Reader's Guide

Use Text Evidence Tell students that they will read "Old Yeller" on their own to analyze key details about the story.

Have students use the Reader's Guide pages in their <u>Reader's Notebook, pp. 73–74</u> 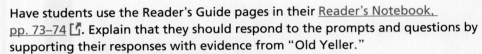. Explain that they should respond to the prompts and questions by supporting their responses with evidence from "Old Yeller."

Model Questioning Demonstrate generating a complex question about *Old Yeller* or a particular section of the story. For example, write this question on the board: *How does the first-person point of view contribute to your understanding of events?* Reread **Student Book pp. 211–212** with students, working together to respond to the question.

Generate Questions Have students work independently or collaboratively to generate questions about "Old Yeller." Ask students to share their questions. Begin a class discussion of questions that students have in common or that are most significant to their understanding of the story. **ELA** RL.5.1, RL.5.10, RF.5.4a, SL.5.1c **ELD** ELD.PI.5.1

Self-Selected Reading

Genres of Interest Review different genres with students. To explore genres of interest, suggest that students answer these questions: *What is your purpose for reading? What topics interest you most?*

Students should use their answers to select a genre and book. Ask students to use their <u>Reading Logs in Grab-and-Go™</u> to record their progress and thinking about the book.

Fluency

Partner Read Have students read aloud with expression to a partner, using passages from their self-selected reading books. Then have them give each other feedback and reread to apply it. **ELA** RF.5.4b

Apply Vocabulary Knowledge

✓ Review Target Vocabulary

💬 **Classroom Collaboration** Read aloud each of the following questions. Have students discuss their answers. Allow several students to respond to each question to provide a variety of possible responses for discussion.
ELA L.5.6 **ELD** ELD.PI.5.12a

1. When you are **picturing** the frontier, what do you see?

2. What parts of a bike are involved in **checking** its speed?

3. What kind of **stride** would be best for walking through a crowded classroom?

4. If you **shouldered** a backpack full of books, how might your back feel?

5. How might shoppers **frantic** for a bargain act?

6. If you were in a haunted house, what might you expect to come **lunging** out at you?

7. What kind of a **romp** might kindergartners enjoy?

8. How might you react if an unfamiliar dog came **bounding** out of a yard towards you?

9. What would you think if a teacher passed you in the hall and then **wheeled** around suddenly?

10. Why do you think families like Travis's **strained** to make a home on the frontier?

Quick Write Display the following prompt: *Explain the way of life that the story Old Yeller describes. Use the vocabulary words you have learned in your writing.*

Have students examine the challenges that Travis faces to help them describe life on the frontier as it appears in the story. Remind them to quote accurately. When they have finished writing, tell students to exchange papers with a partner and discuss whether they used the words correctly in their paragraphs.
ELA RL.5.1, L.5.6 **ELD** ELD.PI.5.1, ELD.PI.5.4

▶ **SHARE OBJECTIVES**
- Acquire and use vocabulary in speaking and writing. LANGUAGE
- Collaboratively respond to questions about familiar vocabulary. LANGUAGE

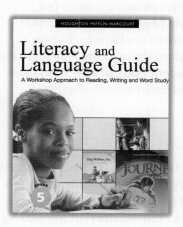

HOUGHTON MIFFLIN HARCOURT
Literacy and Language Guide
A Workshop Approach to Reading, Writing and Word Study
GRADE 5

For additional practice with the lesson's Target Vocabulary, use the activities on pages 128–129 of the **Literacy and Language Guide.**
- Word Associations
- Synonyms and Antonyms
- Act Out the Words
- Vocabulary Web

ENGLISH LANGUAGE SUPPORT

Use Graphic Organizers

All Proficiencies Have students plan their writing by completing a graphic organizer such as a chart with the heading **Travis's Challenges.** Then guide students to look through the text for details that describe life on the frontier. Have students include vocabulary words to their details and add them to the chart. **ELD** ELD.PI.5.4, ELD.PI.5.10b

⟡ **DOMAIN: Values**
LESSON TOPIC: RESPONSIBILITY

CONNECT TO THE TOPIC

Persuasive Text

Preview the Persuasive Text

- Tell students that this selection is a readers' theater in which the characters review a movie. Tell students that a movie review offers an opinion about a movie and often contains persuasive techniques. Ask students to read the title and cast of characters on **Student Book p. 224.** Then have students read the selection independently.
ELA RI.5.10

Discuss Persuasive Techniques

- Explain to students that authors of persuasive texts use techniques to try to convince readers to think or act in a certain way. Some of these techniques, such as exaggerated, contradictory, or misleading statements, give the reader false information.

- Have students look for exaggerated, contradictory, or misleading statements throughout the selection.
ELA RF.5.4a

exaggerated	makes an outlandish claim
contradictory	expresses opposite ideas
misleading	intends to deceive the reader

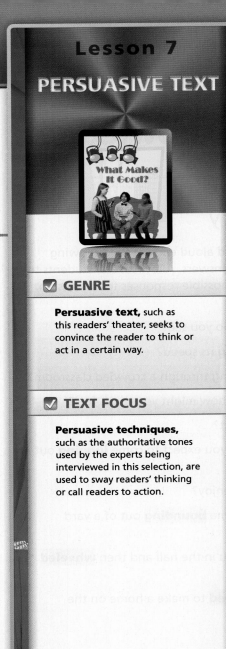

Lesson 7

PERSUASIVE TEXT

Readers' Theater

What Makes It Good?

by Cynthia Benjamin

☑ GENRE

Persuasive text, such as this readers' theater, seeks to convince the reader to think or act in a certain way.

☑ TEXT FOCUS

Persuasive techniques, such as the authoritative tones used by the experts being interviewed in this selection, are used to sway readers' thinking or call readers to action.

Cast of Characters
Television Host
Animal Expert Kay Nyne
Historian Lester Year

Host: Welcome to *What Makes It Good?*, the movie review show that asks the experts if a movie is accurate enough to be good. Today we are reviewing the film version of *Old Yeller*, and we have two experts with us. One is historian Lester Year, who writes about life on the nineteenth-century Texas frontier. The other is animal expert Kay Nyne.

First up is our animal expert. What makes *Old Yeller* good?

224   **ELA** RL.5.10, RF.5.4a, RF.5.4b   **ELD** ELD.PI.5.6a

---

ENGLISH LANGUAGE SUPPORT

Scaffold

Emerging Define *movie review*. Have students identify a favorite movie. Guide them to orally complete this sentence frame: *The movie is good because it _____.*

Expanding Pose simple questions about the movie review. Discuss with students their responses, and clarify understanding.
ELD ELD.PI.5.1, ELD.PI.5.6a

Bridging Have partners tell whether they think *Old Yeller* would be worth seeing. Have them use complete sentences and provide reasons for their opinions. **ELD** ELD.PI.5.1, ELD.PI.5.6a

Kay Nyne: The accurate portrayal of animals makes *Old Yeller* good. If the bear squeaked like a mouse, or if Old Yeller ran away from his owners, then you would not believe the story.

For instance, I loved the scene with Old Yeller bounding into the cabin to lick Arliss in the face! We know that dogs often lick their masters on the face or hand, so it makes sense that Old Yeller would lick the young boy after saving him.

I also thought the way Old Yeller went lunging at the attacking bear in a frantic attempt to save Arliss was very realistic. Dogs are loyal animals. In fact, dogs and people have lived together for more than ten thousand years! Mother bears are fiercely protective of their cubs. I have no problem picturing a bear attacking if she thought her cub were in danger. It is details like these that make the movie believable and exciting.

1

225

Practice Fluency

Intonation Have students follow along as you read aloud the second paragraph on **Student Book p. 225**.

- Remind students that good readers change the pitch of their voice as they read. Explain that using intonation makes the story more interesting for listeners and also gives clues about what is important. Reread the sentence with the exclamation point so students will hear the appropriate emphasis.

- Have students do repeated readings of the third paragraph on **Student Book p. 225**. Remind them to raise and lower their voices with the text, as appropriate. **ELA** RF.5.4b

---

⊘ **DOMAIN: Values**

LESSON TOPIC: Responsibility

Cross-Curricular Connection Discuss with students the responsibilities that people who work in the media have. Point out that people in the media include television and radio reporters, bloggers, and others.

Ask students what responsibilities movie reviewers have to their audience and to society. *They have a responsibility to be accurate and fair.* Ask students what they think the role of the media is today. For example, how can people in the media act responsibly while helping to improve government and society? *The media could investigate government and industry wrongdoings, as well as innovations that benefit society.*

Think Through the Text

Cite Text Evidence

Pause at the stopping points to ask students the following questions.

1 *Do you think Kay Nyne considers Old Yeller loyal? Why or why not? Sample answer: Yes, Old Yeller was loyal because he made a "frantic attempt" to save Arliss from the bear.*
ELA RI.5.1 **ELD** ELD.PI.5.6a

ENGLISH LANGUAGE SUPPORT Tell students that the word for *loyal* in Spanish is *leal*.

2 *What evidence does Lester Year point out to support his idea that pioneers needed their tools for survival? Sample answer: He notes that Travis used an ax and that having tools such as these handy was a matter of life or death.*
ELA RI.5.8 **ELD** ELD.PI.5.6a

3 *Summarize how Kay Nyne supports her main idea that the movie is scientifically accurate. How does Lester Year support his main idea? Sample answer: Kay focuses on details that portray animal behavior accurately, such as the bear trying to protect her cub. In contrast, Lester focuses on other details, such as the notches used in the cabin, to support his idea that historical accuracy is more important.*
ELA RI.5.2 **ELD** ELD.PI.5.10b

Classroom Collaboration

As a class, have students discuss their thoughts about books that become movies. Encourage them to cite examples of movies they have seen based on books they have read. Encourage students to respond to each others' examples and to add relevant details. **ELA** SL.5.1c, SL.5.1d **ELD** ELD.PI.5.1

Lester Year: Now wait a minute! That fight between Old Yeller and the bear was exciting, I admit. But what makes the movie truly great is its historical accuracy. If Travis had broken his stride, wheeled around and seen the bear, then dialed 9-1-1 on a cell phone, you would not believe it.

But he does not carry a cell phone. He has shouldered an ax. I hope you noticed the ax. It was an excellent example of an important 1860s tool. Living on the frontier was no romp on the playground, and pioneers depended on their tools for survival.

Ah, now that scene of Old Yeller licking Arliss after checking the bear's attack may be very accurate as far as dog behavior is concerned. But more important, the cabin looks very realistic, down to the notches holding the logs in place. If the cabin had wallpaper, you would have strained to believe the scene. That is why historical accuracy is more important.
Host: We are almost out of time. Let's summarize. *Old Yeller* is a good movie because it is . . .
Kay Nyne: Scientifically accurate.
Lester Year: Historically accurate.
Host: Well, they may never agree. Audience, I guess you have to decide for yourself what makes it good!

226

ENGLISH LANGUAGE SUPPORT

Peer-Supported Learning

All Proficiencies Organize students into small mixed-proficiency groups to generate ideas using lists. Have some of the groups make a list with the phrase *scientific accuracy* at the top. The other groups should make a list with the phrase *historical accuracy* at the top.

The list is passed from student to student, and each student adds an appropriate word or phrase from the text to the list. After each student has had a few turns to add to the list, invite each group to share their completed list with the class. Post the lists for use as anchor charts when students complete the Compare Texts writing tasks.

Compare Texts

TEXT TO TEXT

Analyze Viewpoint In "What Makes It Good?" Lester Year makes a clear argument about "Old Yeller" and provides evidence to support it. Identify Lester Year's viewpoint. Then make a list of all the ideas and text evidence from "Old Yeller" that supports his viewpoint. Include those that he mentions from the film, as well as those you find in the text. Use your list to write a sentence or two explaining how the ideas and text evidence work together to form a solid argument.

TEXT TO SELF

Write About an Animal Think about an experience you have had with an animal, or an experience you would like to have. Write a narrative paragraph about the experience. Include details that convey your thoughts and feelings. Draw a picture to accompany your paragraph, and provide a caption for your drawing.

Always view wildlife from far away.

TEXT TO WORLD

Compare Dialects The authors of "Old Yeller" and "Off and Running" (Lesson 3) use types of dialect to make their story characters realistic. With a partner, create a T-Map listing examples of dialect from each story. Compare and contrast the unique words and phrases found in each dialect. Discuss whether you think the dialect helps define the characters who use it, and why.

ELA RI.5.8, W.5.4, W.5.10, L.5.3b **ELD** ELD.PI.5.1, ELD.PI.5.6a, ELD.PI.5.8, ELD.PI.5.10b

227

Compare Texts

TEXT TO TEXT

Help students identify the details that show historical accuracy. Ask them to use an Idea-Support Map to organize the ideas and details that form Lester Year's viewpoint and argument.

ELA RI.5.8, W.5.4 **ELD** ELD.PI.5.6A, ELD.PI.5.11a

TEXT TO SELF

Display these sentence frames to help students write about an animal experience:

My favorite animal is _____

The best experience I had with an animal is _____.

The experience I would like to have is _____.

ELA W.5.10 **ELD** ELD.PI.5.4

TEXT TO WORLD

Have students start by creating a word bank of the dialect used in *Old Yeller* and *Off and Running* to place in their t-maps. Remind students that comparing and contrasting the varieties of English used in stories can give them insights into characters' traits and backgrounds and provide a clearer picture of the story's setting.

ELA L.5.3b **ELD** ELD.PI.5.1, ELD.PI.5.7

ENGLISH LANGUAGE SUPPORT

Compare Texts

Organize Concepts Help students complete a chart comparing story characters.
ELA RI.5.3, RI.5.9 **ELD** ELD PI.5.1

Character	When He or She Lives	Responsibilities	Goal
Television Host	present day	introducing guests	identify what makes a movie good
Travis	1860s	working on a farm	help his brother
James	1860s	cooking on a cattle drive	become a wrangler

Build Academic Sentence Structures To help students compare and contrast characters, ask questions such as: *What do Travis and James have in common? In what ways are their thoughts and goals different from those of the television host?* Provide sentence frames such as these:

- *Travis and James both* lived in the 1860s.
- *One difference between Travis and James is* their work.

Vocabulary Strategies

▶ **SHARE OBJECTIVES**

- Recognize and explain the meanings of adages and proverbs.
- Consult print and digital reference materials to determine or clarify the meanings of phrases.

▶ **SKILL TRACE**

Adages and Proverbs	
Introduce	**T120–T121**
Differentiate	T150–T151
Reteach	T152
Review	T194–T195, Unit 5
	T126–T127, Unit 6
Test	Weekly Tests, Lesson 7

ENGLISH LANGUAGE SUPPORT

Preteach

All Proficiencies Explain that adages are observations or situations that have been proven true over time, and proverbs are sayings that express wisdom in simple terms. Provide students examples and explanations of an adage and a proverb such as, *practice makes perfect* and *better late than never.*

Apply Vocabulary Skills

Emerging Say: *Look before you leap.* Then use gestures to show students the meaning of the proverb.

Expanding Discuss the meaning of the saying *Look before you leap.* Then guide students to complete this sentence frame: If you run somewhere before looking, you might _____.

Bridging Have partners discuss what the saying *Look before you leap* means. Have them share their ideas with the class. **ELD** ELD.PI.5.1, ELD.PI.5.8

Adages and Proverbs

1 Teach/Model

Terms About Language

adage a traditional expression that has proven to be true over time

proverb a saying that expresses common-sense wisdom in simple terms

---

- Tell students that **adages** are observations about situations or human nature that have been shown to be true. Provide these examples for students and explain their meanings: *"Haste makes waste." "Good things come in small packages."* Explain that **proverbs**, such as "Laughter is the best medicine," are short, memorable sayings that offer practical advice or wisdom.

- Discuss how some sayings are so familiar that students recognize their meanings immediately. Explain that when they see unfamiliar expressions, they should look for context clues and restate the saying in their own words to help clarify its meaning.

- Display the following sentences about "Old Yeller": *Living on the frontier taught Travis an important lesson: 'Never put off until tomorrow what you can do today.'* His family learned through experience that leaving jobs undone could lead to serious trouble. Model how to determine the meaning of the expression.

> **Think Aloud** *The context of the saying helps me to understand that it is about the risks of procrastinating. Putting tasks or decisions off can lead to big problems. For example, in the winter on the frontier, not chopping enough firewood could result in a family freezing if a storm moved in overnight.*

- Point out that if students are still unsure of a phrase's meaning after using context clues, they can consult digital reference sources to determine or clarify the precise meanings of many common adages and proverbs.

2 Guided Practice

- Display the top half of <u>Projectable 7.3</u> and read aloud "A Saying for Every Occasion."

- Point out the first expression, "Sharing is caring." Help students to understand its meaning by rephrasing it: *Sharing something with a friend shows that you care about him or her.*

- Work with students to determine the meanings of the remaining sayings. Remind them to look for context clues for help and to consult digital reference sources if they need further help to determine or clarify the meaning of a saying. **ELA** L.5.4c

3 Apply

- Have partners identify three or four other adages or proverbs that they have heard or read before. Suggest that they use the Internet or other print or digital references to locate and clarify the meaning of each phrase. Have each pair use the expression in a sentence that shows its meaning.

- Have pairs exchange sentences and identify and explain each saying.
ELA L.5.5b **ELD** ELD.PI.5.1, ELD PI.5.8

    Interactive Whiteboard Lesson Use **Vocabulary Strategies: Adages and Proverbs** to reinforce how to recognize and explain common adages and proverbs.

- Distribute to students <u>Reader's Notebook page 75</u> or <u>leveled practice in Grab-and-Go™ Resources</u> to complete independently.

FORMATIVE ASSESSMENT  **RtI**

Are students able to recognize and explain the meanings of adages and proverbs?

IF...	THEN...
students **struggle,**	▶ **Differentiate Vocabulary Strategies** for Struggling Readers, p. T150.
students **on target,**	▶ **Differentiate Vocabulary Strategies** for On-Level Readers, p. T150.
students **excel,**	▶ **Differentiate Vocabulary Strategies** for Advanced Readers, p. T151.

SMALL GROUP Options

Differentiate Vocabulary Strategies: pp. T150–T151 *Scaffold instruction to the English learner's proficiency level.*

ENGLISH LANGUAGE SUPPORT

Comprehensible Input

Emerging Discuss the meaning of the saying *"A dog is man's best friend."* Then have students illustrate a scene from "Old Yeller" that shows the truth of the expression.

Expanding Have students write a sentence or two discussing how the saying *"A dog is man's best friend"* applies to the story "Old Yeller." Prompt them with sentence frames as appropriate.

Bridging Have pairs of students choose a proverb or adage that they think applies to "Old Yeller." Have them write a few sentences explaining their choice.
ELD ELD.PI.5.8

DOMAIN: Values

LESSON TOPIC: Responsibility

Extend the Topic

▶ SHARE OBJECTIVES

- Acquire and use domain-specific vocabulary.
- Report on a text, speaking clearly at an understandable pace.
- Adapt speech to context, task, and purpose.

Words About the Topic: **Responsibility**

- **decisiveness** the ability to display little or no hesitation when making choices
- **devotion** strong dedication; great attachment to a cause or a person
- **maturity** adulthood; showing thoughtful, responsible behavior
- **obligation** a binding promise, contract, sense of duty
- **self-sacrificing** giving up one's interests or desires for the good of another

Domain-Specific Vocabulary

Introduce Words About the Topic Remind students that this week's topic is Responsibility. Display the words. Tell students that these are words that can help them learn more about responsibility. Read aloud the definition for each word and then have students respond to the following prompts:

- *If you choose not to watch your favorite TV program in order to help a friend, you are being _____ . self-sacrificing*

- *Which word describes a quality shown by people who are always quick to resolve an issue or find an answer? decisiveness*

- *When you spend time with your younger sister, you likely feel a sense of _____ to look out for her. obligation*

- *Which word refers to the behavior of someone who seems sensible and older than their age would suggest? maturity*

- *When someone stands by a friend, defending them when no one else will, they are displaying this quality. devotion*

ENGLISH LANGUAGE SUPPORT For example, point out the illustration on page 218 and say: *When he licks Little Arliss, Old Yeller is showing his devotion.*

Interact with the Words Have students work in small groups using Graphic Organizer 6 (Four-Square Map) 🖥 to extend their understanding of each word about responsibility. Assign one word to each group, and have them follow these steps for completing the Four-Square Map with information about the word:

1 In the first corner, draw a picture that represents the word.

2 In the second corner, write the meaning of the word.

3 In the third corner, write a sentence using the word.

4 In the fourth corner, write the word.

When groups have finished, have them share their completed Four-Square Maps with the class. **ELA** L.5.6 **ELD** ELD.PI.5.12a

Speaking and Listening [Performance Task]

Report on a Text

Select a Story Tell students that they will read a story related to the theme of "Old Yeller" and prepare an oral report about the story to share with the class. Have students revisit "Old Yeller." Discuss the themes in the story. Then ask students to select a story that deals with values and responsibility. Suggest that students browse a library or other online catalogue and speak with peers, teachers, parents, or a librarian to help identify an appropriate story.

Model Speaking Skills Ask students to listen as you model how to deliver a report on a text: *My report today is on a book that is very similar to* Old Yeller *because both books deal with handling responsibility.*

Read the Story Students should read the story carefully, taking notes as they go. They can keep track of characters and their relationships, the action and timing, figurative or sensory language, and their own responses to the story.

Organize Thoughts Suggest that students use one or more graphic organizers to help them organize their thoughts before preparing their report. They might use a concept web to illustrate ideas that relate to the central theme of values and responsibility or a flow chart like the one below to keep track of the plot.

| Papa is gone—Travis doing Papa's work | → | Little Arliss gets in trouble with the bear | → | Travis goes to help | → | Old Yeller saves them | → | Travis comes to love Little Arliss and Old Yeller |

Prepare a Report Display the tips on giving an oral report shown at right. Suggest that students use notes rather than writing out the report entirely. They might also use visual aids such as photographs or drawings to help illustrate important points. Remind them that they should know the story well enough to be able to answer questions about it at the end of their presentation.

Present Have students present their report. Remind them to speak clearly at an understandable pace and to maintain eye contact with their audience. Point out that they should adjust their speech to the task, using formal English to deliver their report. **ELA** SL.5.4b, SL.5.6 **ELD** ELD.PI.5.9

FOR STUDENTS WITH DISABILITIES To help students focus on an involved task, have them show their organization plans before they begin. For example, have them list key points of information they are looking for in their reading.

SPEAKING TIPS

1. Begin with an interesting fact, quote, or question.

2. Use your note cards when you need them, but keep your eyes on your audience.

3. Use a tone of voice that matches the topic and helps keep the audience interested.

4. End your report with a key point, fact, or idea that you want your audience to remember.

ENGLISH LANGUAGE SUPPORT Provide sentence frames for students to use while delivering their reports: *My report today is on a book titled _____. It was written by _____.*

Fluency

ENGLISH LANGUAGE SUPPORT

Intonation

All Proficiencies Speakers of Chinese and Vietnamese may need extensive modeling and practice to adjust to the patterns of stress and intonation of English. Cantonese, Mandarin, and Vietnamese are tonal languages, and tonal variation is used for each individual syllable, as part of expressing its meaning. In English, syllables within a word and words within a sentence get different amounts of stress. In addition to explicitly teaching and modeling patterns of oral language in English, you may wish to engage students in frequent choral readings, repeated readings, and partner reading activities. **ELD** ELD.PIII.5

Cold Reads: Support for fluent reading with comprehension

FORMATIVE ASSESSMENT · RtI

As students read **Student Book p. 217**, circulate and spend time listening to each pair. If students have difficulty reading with proper intonation, provide corrective feedback.

Model proper intonation as you read aloud the section to students, emphasizing the rise and fall of your voice, and have them choral- or echo-read with you.

Guide students to read another paragraph on their own, and provide feedback, as necessary. Tell students that their reading fluency will continue to improve as they work hard at improving their intonation.

Intonation

1 Teach/Model

- Tell students that intonation is the rise and fall of the pitch of their voice. Explain that their intonation should reflect the meaning of what is being read.
- Point out that the punctuation in each sentence can help guide students in expressing the correct intonation.
- Have students follow along as you read aloud **Student Book p. 213**. First, read the page aloud in a monotone. Then read it with appropriate intonation. Tell them that the second reading is an example of good intonation.

2 Guided Practice

- Together, read aloud the first paragraph on **Student Book p. 218**.
- Work with students to adjust intonation to reflect what is being read.
- If students are struggling, guide them by reading aloud from **Student Book p. 217** and pointing out how the action being described and the punctuation that is used can help guide intonation.
- See also Instructional Routine 7 .

3 Apply

- Tell students that with practice, they can improve their intonation.
- Have students echo-read **Student Book p. 217** with you, matching your intonation as you read. **ELA** RF.5.4a, RF.5.4b **ELD** ELD.PIII.5

Decoding

Vowel + /r/ Sounds

1 Teach/Model

Teach Vowel + /r/ Sounds Tell students that the letter *r* affects the pronunciation of vowels that come before it.

- Say the words *frontier* and *market* aloud to demonstrate.
- Point out that students should experiment and try different vowel sounds when they are decoding a word with a vowel followed by *r*. As they do this, they may realize that the word is a familiar one. Then they can adjust the sounds to pronounce the word more accurately.

2 Guided Practice

Blend Words Display Lines 1–8 below and have students break each word into syllables, identify the vowel + /r/ sound, and say each word aloud. Provide Corrective Feedback as needed. Next, point to words in random order. Ask students what strategies they used to read each one.

1. pier | cing   al | ert   be | fore   near | ly   up | stairs
2. argue   earth   roaring   weary   airplane
3. sharing   worship   appear   foreign   soaring
4. wordly   further   career   research   caring
5. murmur   dreary   reverse   twirling   yearn

Challenge Call on students who are ready for a challenge to read Line 6 and discuss the elements. Then have the class read the sentences in Lines 7 and 8 chorally.

6. cereal   durable   furious   interpret   encourage
7. The engineer was in charge of all external power outages.
8. The volunteer considered time spent helping others was worthwhile.
ELA RF.5.3a **ELD** ELD.PIII.5

▶ **SHARE OBJECTIVES**

- Use knowledge of morphemes to read accurately words with vowel + /r/ sound.
- Use knowledge of morphemes to read accurately longer words with vowel + /r/ sound.

FORMATIVE ASSESSMENT   RtI

If students have trouble decoding words with vowel + /r/ sounds, use the model below.

Correct the error. Say the word *sharing* aloud. *The word is* sharing.

Model how to decode the word. *I can try to pronounce the ar like the ar in* market. *This doesn't make a word I recognize, but when I pronounce the ar like the air in* airplane, *it sounds right.*

Guide students to pronounce the word. *Students should pronounce the word like the air in* airplane.

Check students' understanding. *What is the word?* sharing

Reinforce Have students repeat the process with the word *cereal*.

ENGLISH LANGUAGE SUPPORT

Linguistic Transfer

Use the transfer chart in the **Quick Start Pacing Guide** to determine whether your students will have difficulty due to transfer issues. As needed, preteach the skill. **ELD** ELD.PIII.5

Spelling More Vowel + /r/ Sounds

▶ **SHARE OBJECTIVE**
- Spell more grade-appropriate words that have the vowel + /r/ sounds.

Spelling Words

Basic

earth	worthwhile	thirsty
peer	nerve	reverse
twirl	pier	worship
burnt	squirm	career
smear	weary	research
further	alert	volunteer
⭐ appear	murmur	

Review

early, world, ⭐ rear, current, cheer

Challenge

yearn, engineer, interpret, dreary, external

⭐ Forms of these words appear in "Old Yeller."

ENGLISH LANGUAGE SUPPORT

Preteach

Spanish Cognates Write and discuss these Spanish cognates for Spanish-speaking students.

appear	•	aparecer
nerve	•	nervio
alert	•	alerta
volunteer	•	voluntario

Transfer Support The vowel + /r/ sound does not exist in many languages. Model the /ûr/ and /îr/ sounds in several words. Then, have students repeat the sounds and reread the words in this week's spelling list. **ELD** ELD.PIII.5

Word Meanings Use Day 5 sentences to preview the meanings of spelling words.

DAY 1

❶ TEACH THE PRINCIPLE

- Administer the **Pretest**. Use the Day 5 sentences.

- Write *earth*, *twirl*, and *burnt* on the board. Guide students to identify the letters in each word that spell the /ûr/ sound. *ear, ir, ur* Use the chart below to add additional words. Repeat with the sound /îr/.

/ûr/	ear as in earth ir as in twirl ur as in burnt or as in worship er as in alert
/îr/	eer as in peer ier as in pier

❷ GUIDED PRACTICE

Guide students to identify sounds/spellings in the remaining Spelling Words.

Model a Word Sort Model sorting words based on their /ûr/ or /îr/ sound. Present the Model the Sort lesson on page 68 of the **Literacy and Language Guide**.

❸ APPLY

Distribute Reader's Notebook page 76 ↗ and have students complete it independently.

DAY 2

❶ TEACH WORD SORT

- Set up two rows as shown. Model adding a Spelling Word to each row.

/ûr/	earth
/îr/	career

❷ GUIDED PRACTICE

- Have students add to the chart words from "Old Yeller."

Guided Word Sort Guide students to sort words according to the /ûr/ or /îr/ sound. Present the Pattern Sort lesson on page 68 of the **Literacy and Language Guide**.

❸ APPLY

Distribute Reader's Notebook page 77 ↗ and have students complete it independently.

DAY 3

1 TEACH WORD FAMILIES

- **WRITE** *worth*. Define it: "something's value, usefulness, or importance."

- **WRITE** *worthwhile*. Define it: "something that is worth the time, money, or effort spent on it."

- **ASK** *What is the connection between these words? Both contain the word* worth; *both meanings refer to something's value.*

- With students, list and discuss more words related to *worth*. samples: worthless, worthy, worthiness

2 GUIDED PRACTICE

- **WRITE** *appear*. Define it: "to have the impression of a certain quality."

- **WRITE** *appearance and disappear*. Ask students to look up these words in a dictionary or an electronic resource.

- **ASK** *What is the connection among* appear, appearance, *and* disappearance?

Have students write their answers.

3 APPLY

Independent Word Sort Have students sort words that a partner says aloud. Present the Blind Writing Sort lesson on page 69 of the **Literacy and Language Guide.**

DAY 4

1 CONNECT TO WRITING

- Read and discuss the prompt below.

Informative Writing
Write a compare-contrast essay about responsibility. Use what you've learned from your reading this week.

2 GUIDED PRACTICE

- Guide students as they plan and write their compare-contrast essays.

- Remind students to proofread their writing and to consult print and digital references to confirm correct spelling. (See p. T134.) **ELA** I.5.2e

Buddy Sort Have students sort words with the /ûr/ or /îr/ sound and compare with a partner. Present the Buddy Sort lesson on page 69 of the **Literacy and Language Guide.**

3 APPLY

Distribute Reader's Notebook page 78 and have students complete it independently.

DAY 5

ASSESS SPELLING

- Say each boldfaced word, read the sentence, and then repeat the word.

- Have students write the boldfaced word. **ELA** I.5.2e

Basic

1. Corn grew in the rich **earth**.
2. Microscopes let us **peer** at cells.
3. I will **twirl** the rope for Susan.
4. A **burnt** smell filled the air.
5. I got a **smear** of paint on my shirt.
6. Practice will **further** your skills.
7. They **appear** to be happy.
8. Winning made my effort **worthwhile**.
9. Lori had the **nerve** to dive in.
10. Marco tied his boat to the **pier**.
11. The dog may **squirm** under the fence.
12. The **weary** hikers rested.
13. Rangers stay **alert** for fires.
14. I listened to the **murmur** of water.
15. Drink water if you're **thirsty**.
16. To get home, **reverse** the directions.
17. We visited a temple of **worship**.
18. **Journalism** may lead to a career.
19. Scientists do **research** in labs.
20. People who **volunteer** are not paid.

Grammar Direct and Indirect Objects

▶ SHARE OBJECTIVES

- Identify direct and indirect objects.
- Create compound direct objects.
- Combine sentences for meaning and style.

Terms About Language

direct object the word that receives the action of the verb • *objeto directo*

compound direct object words that receive the action of the same verb

indirect object tells to or for whom or what the action is done

ENGLISH LANGUAGE SUPPORT

Preteach: All Proficiencies

Explain Terms About Language Point out the cognate in the list above. Then explain that:

- When a verb describes an action, the direct object is the person or thing that receives that action.

Linguistic Transfer In some languages, such as Spanish, direct objects can come before the verb, after the verb, and can even be attached to the end of the verb. Point out that in English, the direct object nearly always follows the verb.

Scaffolded Practice

Emerging Use the frames to demonstrate direct and indirect objects, respectively.	Expanding Use the frames to demonstrate direct and indirect objects. Guide students to generate sentences for each type of object. Then have them exchange sentences with another student and identify the direct and indirect objects in each other's sentences.	Bridging Provide students with the sentence frames below, and have them combine them into one sentence with a compound direct object.
Raul chopped _____ for the stove. wood		*Travis fed the _____ .*
Raul fed the _____ some food. chickens		*Travis then fed the _____ .*
Explain the difference between the two types of objects. Guide students to generate sentences with direct and indirect objects.		

DAY 1 TEACH

DAILY PROOFREADING PRACTICE

Since she prefer to feed the horses, Marta have asked Jane to switch chores. *prefers; asked*

1 TEACH DIRECT OBJECTS

- Display Projectable 7.4 ⌐. Explain that a **direct object** is a word in the predicate that receives the action of the verb.

ENGLISH LANGUAGE SUPPORT Review that a direct object is a word in the predicate that takes the action of a verb. A sentence can have one direct object or a compound direct object with *and* or *or*. An indirect object tells *to whom* or *to what* the action of the verb is done. Display sentences, such as the following. Work with students to identify each direct object and indirect object.

- Travis heard a scream. *(direct object)*
- The dog protected Arliss and Travis. *(compound direct object)*
- Mom gave her sons *(indirect object)* some food. *(direct object)*
- Model identifying the direct object in the example: *The boy helped his mother with the chores.*

Think Aloud *To identify the direct object, I ask the following Thinking Question:* **What word tells who or what receives the action of the verb?** *Mother is the direct object because it receives the action of the verb* helped.

2 PRACTICE/APPLY

- Complete items 1–8 on Projectable 7.4 ⌐ with students.
- Have students use the Thinking Question to identify the direct object of each sentence below:

  Travis liked Old Yeller. *Old Yeller*

  Old Yeller saved Travis's brother. *Travis's brother*

- Have students complete Reader's Notebook p. 79 ⌐ for practice with simple subjects and predicates.

DAY 2 TEACH

DAILY PROOFREADING PRACTICE

Wilma told he to help milk the cows. *told; him*

1 EXTEND DIRECT OBJECTS

- Display Projectable 7.5 [↗]. Tell students that when more than one word in a sentence receives the action of the verb, that sentence contains a **compound direct object**.
- Model identifying the compound direct object in the example sentence: *My dog Pete requires care and attention.*

Think Aloud *To identify the direct objects, I ask the following Thinking Question:* **What words tell who or what receives the action of the verb?** *Care and* attention *are the direct objects because they receive the action of the verb* requires.

2 PRACTICE/APPLY

- Complete items 1–8 on Projectable 7.5 [↗] with students.
- Write the following sentences on the board. Have students orally identify the compound direct object in each sentence.

Prairie settlers built cabins and barns. *cabins and barns*

Farm dogs stalked rabbits and badgers. *rabbits and badgers*

- Have students complete Reader's Notebook p. 80 [↗] for practice with simple subjects and predicates.

DAY 3 TEACH

DAILY PROOFREADING PRACTICE

We took Pete, she, and he with us to help clean. *her; him*

1 TEACH INDIRECT OBJECTS

- Display Projectable 7.6 [↗]. Explain that an **indirect object** usually tells to or for whom/what the action of the verb is done.
- Model identifying the indirect object in this sample sentence: *Old Yeller gave Arliss a lick.*

Think Aloud *To identify the indirect object, I ask the following Thinking Question:* **To whom or what or for whom or what is the action of the verb done?** *Gave is the verb. Old Yeller gave to Arliss a lick. Arliss is the indirect object.*

2 PRACTICE/APPLY

- Complete items 1–8 on Projectable 7.6 [↗] with students.
- Have volunteers generate sentences with indirect objects, and write them on the board. Then have other volunteers identify the indirect objects and explain the reasons for their choices.
- Have students complete Reader's Notebook p. 81 [↗] for practice with simple subjects and predicates.

DAY 4   REVIEW

DAILY PROOFREADING PRACTICE

Mama showed themselves and I the tools. *them; me*

❶ REVIEW DIRECT AND INDIRECT OBJECTS

• Remind students that a **direct object** is the word in the predicate that receives the action of a verb. A **compound direct object** is made up of two or more words that receive the action of the same verb. An indirect object usually tells to whom or what the action of the verb is done. Review the chart on **Student Book p. 228**. Then have students complete the **Try This!** activity.

ENGLISH LANGUAGE SUPPORT Remind students that the direct object is the person or thing that receives an action. Provide this example: The dog chewed the bone. *(direct object: bone)*

❷ SPIRAL REVIEW

KINDS OF SENTENCES Remind students that there are four kinds of sentences: **declarative, interrogative, imperative**, and **exclamatory**. Use the examples below to point out the different types and the proper punctuation for each.

> We hunted rabbits and wild turkeys.
>
> Did you chop that wood yet?
>
> Give Old Yeller some food.
>
> Mama needs help quick!

Write the following sentences on the board. Have students identify the type of sentence and how it should be punctuated.

> Come home now *imperative; period*
>
> The boy was scared *declarative; period*
>
> Did you see the bear *interrogative; question mark*
>
> Old Yeller is some dog *exclamatory; exclamation point*

Then have students complete Reader's Notebook p. 82 [↗] for more practice with kinds of sentences.

DAY 5   CONNECT TO WRITING

DAILY PROOFREADING PRACTICE

Did you bring she the necessary supplies. *her; supplies?*

❶ INTERACTIVE WHITEBOARD LESSON

For cumulative review, use **Grammar: Direct and Indirect Objects** to reinforce how to identify and use direct and indirect objects in sentences.

❷ CONNECT TO WRITING

• Tell students that combining sentences to create a compound direct object can improve the flow of their writing.

• Explain that an important part of revising is to eliminate choppy writing by combining sentences where it makes sense.

❸ PRACTICE/APPLY

• Display the following sentences. Guide students to combine them by creating compound direct objects. **ELA** L.5.3a

> We helped my mother plant lettuce. We also helped my mother plant peas. *We helped my mother plant lettuce and peas.*
>
> She built a fence around the yard. She made a separate dog exit from the house. *She built a fence around the yard and a separate dog exit from the house.*

• Using the samples above as models, ask volunteers to write pairs of sentences on the board that each contain direct objects. Then have all students combine the pairs to write sentences with compound direct objects. Call for volunteers to share their revised sentences. **ELA** L.5.3a

• Have students complete Reader's Notebook p. 83 [↗] for practice with combining sentences.

Grammar

Digital Resources
▶ Multimedia Grammar Glossary

What Is a Direct Object? A **direct object** is the word in the predicate that receives the action of the verb. It can be a noun or a pronoun, a word that takes the place of a noun. A **compound direct object** is made up of two or more words that receive the action of the same verb.

Verbs and Objects	What Receives the Action
action verb direct object The boy swung his axe.	*Axe* receives the action of the verb *swung*.
action verb compound direct object He chopped big logs and small branches.	*Logs* and *branches* receive the action of the verb *chopped*.

An **indirect object** usually tells to *whom* or to *what* the action of the verb is done. The indirect object comes between the verb and the direct object.

action verb indirect object direct object
The boy gave his brother a treat.

Brother tells to whom the treat was given.

> **Try This!** The action verb in each sentence is printed in bold type. Find the direct object. Then find the indirect object, if one is used.
>
> ❶ Mom **wrote** Dad a letter.
>
> ❷ She **described** the big fight.
>
> ❸ Our dog **protected** my brother and me.
>
> ❹ We **gave** our dog great praise.

You can improve the flow of your writing by combining sentences in which the direct objects receive the action of the same verb. First, identify the subject, verb, and direct object of each sentence. Then combine the sentences, using *and* or *or* to join the direct objects.

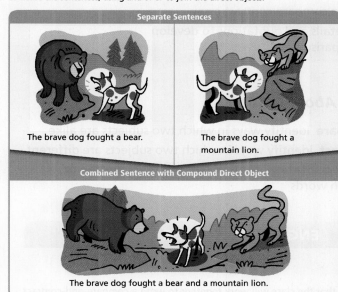

Separate Sentences

The brave dog fought a bear.

The brave dog fought a mountain lion.

Combined Sentence with Compound Direct Object

The brave dog fought a bear and a mountain lion.

Connect Grammar to Writing

As you revise your compare-contrast essay this week, see where you can create compound direct objects to combine sentences. Combining sentences will help make your writing smoother.

> **Try This!**
> 1. *direct object: letter; indirect object: Dad*
> 2. *direct object: fight*
> 3. *direct object: my brother and me*
> 4. *direct object: praise; indirect object: dog*

Connect Grammar to Writing

- Have students turn to **Student Book p. 229**. Read the first paragraph with them.
- Read aloud the sentences in the chart. Point out that the combined sentence with a compound direct object is smoother to read and less repetitive.
- Tell students that they should look for opportunities to combine direct objects as they revise their writing. **ELA L.5.3a**

ENGLISH LANGUAGE SUPPORT

Additional Grammar Practice

Teach/Model Remind students that a direct object is a noun or pronoun that receives the action of a verb.

- Write: *Travis shouldered an ax.* Underline *shouldered* and circle *ax.* Draw an arrow pointing from *shouldered* to *ax.* Explain that *shouldered* is the action word, and *ax* is the noun that receives the action. Ask: *What thing did Travis shoulder?* (the ax)

Guided Practice Write sentences that describe events from "Old Yeller." Help students identify each verb and direct object.

- Write: *Little Arliss grabbed the cub. The mother bear clawed Old Yeller.*
- Read the first sentence aloud. Ask: *What is the verb, or action word, in this sentence?* Take responses, and then confirm that the verb is *grabbed.*
- Ask: *What noun is affected by the verb?* Solicit responses, and then confirm that the noun is *cub.*
- Have students identify the verb and direct object in the next sentence.

Connect to Writing Ask students to choose one of the selections to describe in a paragraph. Have them include and underline three or four direct objects in the paragraph. **ELD ELD.PI.5.10a**

Direct and Indirect Objects (SB pp. 228–229) • **T131**

Informative Writing Focus Trait: Elaboration

▶ SHARE OBJECTIVES

- Write a compare-contrast essay.
- Use details and quotations to develop a comparison.

Terms About Writing

compare identify ways in which two subjects are alike

contrast identify ways in which two subjects are different

direct quotation another person's exact written or spoken words

ENGLISH LANGUAGE SUPPORT

Collaborative Writing

Explain that the class will work together to write a compare-and-contrast essay examining two characters from "Old Yeller"—Old Yeller and the mother bear.

- Ask: *In what ways are the two characters similar?* Help students find specific examples from the story. *Example: Both characters wanted to protect something they cared about. Both faced danger and were willing to fight. In what ways are the two characters different? The bear is much larger and stronger than Old Yeller.*

- Ask: *What are some details from the story that show how the animals are similar? Both animals make noise as they charge into the conflict. Both fight and don't back down. What are some details that show how the animals are different? The bear is easily able to swat away the challenges of Old Yeller.* **ELD** ELD.PI.5.1

Read the completed composition aloud chorally.

Performance Task

myWriteSmart Have students complete the writing task through *my*WriteSmart. Students will read the prompt within *my*WriteSmart and have access to multiple writing resources, including the Student eBook, Writing Rubrics, and Graphic Organizers.

DAY 1 ANALYZE THE MODEL

❶ INTRODUCE COMPARE-CONTRAST ESSAY

- Tell students that they will be writing a **compare-contrast essay** in this lesson.
- Display Projectable 7.7 and read aloud the Writing Model prompt. Discuss the following:

> #### What Is a Compare-Contrast Essay?
>
> - It shows how two subjects are the same and different.
> - It includes precise details and direct quotations to develop the comparison.
> - It presents details in a logical order linked by transitions.
> - It provides a strong conclusion that explains the importance of the comparison.

- Point out the topic sentence. Ask students what this sentence tells them. *The writer is comparing Travis and Mama and begins by showing how they are different.*

❷ PRACTICE/APPLY

- In the second model paragraph, work with students to label the topic sentence, details, direct quotations, and transitions.
- Ask students what the purpose of the second paragraph is. *to show similarities between the two characters*

ENGLISH LANGUAGE SUPPORT How English Works As students study the model, point out how the writer has expanded the verb *exhausted* with the verb phrase *from chopping wood*. Point out how this adds information to and enriches the sentence. Have students practice writing more verb phrases using the verb *exhausted*. **ELD** ELD.PII.5.5

LESSON	FORM	FOCUS
6	Procedural Composition	Organization
7	**Compare-Contrast Essay**	**Elaboration**
8	Cause-and-Effect Essay	Evidence
9	Prewrite: Research Report	Evidence
10	Draft, Revise, Edit, Publish: Research Report	Conventions

WRITING

Additional support for Informative Writing appears in **the Common Core Writing Handbook,** Lesson 7.

DAY 2 TEACH

❶ INTRODUCE THE WRITING FOCUS

ELABORATION Tell students that when they write a compare-contrast essay, they should include precise details and **direct quotations** to support their ideas and elaborate on their ideas.

Connect to "Old Yeller"	
Instead of this . . .	**. . . write this.**
Travis was working hard.	Travis was exhausted from the back-breaking hours of chopping wood. He says, "The sweat poured off me." (p. 210)

• Point out that instead of just telling readers that Travis was working hard, the precise detail and the direct quotation from the story create a vivid picture in readers' minds of what he was doing and how it affected him.

🖉 🗐 *Annotate it!* Have students highlight examples of the author's use of precise details. Then tell students to share their examples and discuss how the details help readers visualize story events.

❷ PRACTICE/APPLY

• Write these two sentences on the board: *Travis ran fast. Arliss didn't move.* Ask students to reword these sentences in a way that makes them more precise. *Sample answers: Travis flew over the ground, pumping his arms and legs as fast as he could. Arliss sat as if frozen in place.*

• Then have students find direct quotations from the story that they could use to convey the same ideas about the two characters. **ELA** W.5.2b, W.5.2d

• Distribute Reader's Notebook page 83 🗐 and have students complete it independently.

DAY 3 PREWRITE

❶ TEACH PLANNING A COMPARE-CONTRAST ESSAY

• Display Projectable 7.8 🗗. Read aloud the prompt. Have students think of two parts of a story that they would like to compare and contrast. They might choose two settings, two characters, two events, or even the language in two passages.

• Explain that using a Venn diagram can help them identify the differences and similarities that they want to include in their essays.

❷ PRACTICE/APPLY

• Point out the precise details included in the diagram on Projectable 7.8 🗗. Draw students' attention to the direct quotations. Discuss the importance of copying direct quotations exactly and enclosing them in quotation marks.

• Remind students that their goal is to help their readers understand the differences and similarities between the two elements of the story, not to just list them.

• Work with students to complete the Venn Diagram.

• Distribute **Graphic Organizer 14.** Have students then fill out the Venn Diagram for the two parts of a story that they are planning to compare. **ELA** W.5.5, W.5.10

ENGLISH LANGUAGE SUPPORT

How English Works: Productive

Condensing Ideas Before students begin drafting their compare-contrast essays, have them plan to use sentences that are detailed and that give exact messages. Explain that sometimes writers join two short sentences to be exact. Give the following examples: *The dog is mine. The dog is in the yard.* Provide this revised sentence: *The dog that is in the yard is mine.* Explain that the pronoun *that* is used to condense the two sentences. Help different proficiency levels build sentences about their writing topics, using the words *who, that,* or *which.* Have students use these sentences while drafting. **ELD** ELD.PII.5.7

DAY 4 DRAFT

① BEGIN A DRAFT

- Have students begin their drafts using their Venn Diagrams. Discuss with them the following:

---

1. **Introduce** the topic of your compare-contrast essay.

↓

2. **Organize** your essay logically, grouping details that develop the similarities and then the differences or vice versa.

↓

3. **Include** direct quotations and use precise language to illustrate similarities and differences.

↓

4. **Conclude** by explaining what you have learned from your comparison or why it is important.

---

② PRACTICE/APPLY

- Have students draft their compare-contrast essays. Remind them to refer to their Venn diagrams and to decide how they want to organize their details before they begin to write. **ELA** W.5.2a, W.5.4

- Tell them to link their ideas with transitional words and phrases, such as these: *similarly, in contrast, unlike, like,* and *in addition.* **ELA** W.5.2c

HANDWRITING TIP Have students write their final pieces in cursive, using their best handwriting. Tell them to be sure to leave the appropriate spaces between the letters and words. See also pp. R22–R27 for handwriting support.

DAY 5 ANALYZE THE MODEL

① INTRODUCE THE STUDENT MODEL

- Remind students that good writers include direct quotations to bring out important ideas in their comparisons.

- Read the top of **Student Book p. 230** with the class. Discuss the revisions made by Stefania. Point out the direct quotations that Stefania added to make her comparison more specific and clear.

- Have students explore Digital Lesson: Writing Informative Texts: Organize Your Information ⟋ to develop their informative writing.

② PRACTICE/APPLY

- Display Projectable 7.9 ⟋. Work with students to revise the rest of the student draft. Point out where more precise detail could strengthen the comparison and contrast between the two animals.

- Read Stefania's Final Copy on **Student Book p. 231** to the class. Work with students to answer the *Reading as a Writer* questions.

- **Revising** Have students revise their essays using the Writing Checklist on **Student Book p. 230**. **ELA** W.5.2b, W.5.2d, W.5.2e, W.5.5, W.5.10

- **Proofreading** For proofreading support, have students use the Proofreading Checklist Blackline Master ⟋.

ENGLISH LANGUAGE SUPPORT

Peer-Supported Learning

All Proficiencies See the Peer Conference Forms in the ELL Teacher's Handbook.

Informative Writing

Interactive Lessons
▶ Writing Informative Texts: Organize Your Information

myWriteSmart

✔ **Elaboration** The author of "Old Yeller" uses vivid descriptions and action to tell a great story. You can analyze descriptions and events in a story to compare and contrast parts of it in your writing.

Stefania drafted a **compare-contrast essay** to explain how Old Yeller and the bear are alike and different. Later, she added quotations and precise details from the text to support her ideas.

Use the Writing Checklist below as you revise your writing.

Writing Checklist

✔ **Elaboration**
Did I use precise words and details from the text?

✔ **Evidence**
Did I develop my topic with quotations and examples from the text?

✔ **Organization**
Did I explain each comparison and provide a conclusion?

✔ **Purpose**
Is my writing clear and informative?

✔ **Conventions**
Did I vary the structure of my sentences? Did I use correct spelling and grammar?

Revised Draft

The most exciting scene in "Old Yeller" is when Old Yeller fights the mother bear in order to protect Arliss. The author describes both animals as ready to fight. The bear is protecting her cub and "roaring mad and ready to kill." Old Yeller is protecting Little Arliss and "roaring like a mad bull." When Old Yeller sees that Little Arliss is in danger, he ~~takes action.~~

runs at the bear and knocks her off her feet

230   ELA W.5.2a, W.5.2b, W.5.2e, W.5.5   ELD ELD.PI.5.10a, ELD.PI.5.12a, ELD.PII.5.1, ELD.PII.5.2

Final Copy

Old Yeller and the Bear
by Stefania Almeida

The most exciting scene in "Old Yeller" is when Old Yeller fights the mother bear in order to protect Arliss. The author describes both animals as ready to fight. The bear is protecting her cub and "roaring mad and ready to kill." Old Yeller is protecting Little Arliss and "roaring like a mad bull." When Old Yeller sees that Little Arliss is in danger, he runs at the bear and knocks her off her feet. The bear stands her ground, as well. She keeps fighting until the end when Old Yeller outruns her and goes back to the family's house.

The main difference between the two animals is their size. The bear is much bigger and stronger than Old Yeller. This size difference does not scare Old Yeller, though. He acts on his protective instincts and takes on an animal three times his size. The bear is brave, as well. She believes her cub is in danger and is willing to do anything to protect it. Once Old Yeller knows that Arliss and the rest of the family are out of danger, he stops fighting. Though the bear chases him for a bit, she eventually gives up, too, and probably returns home with her cub. Both animals do what is necessary to protect those they care about.

Reading as a Writer

Which details made Old Yeller's and the bear's similarities and differences clear? Where in your writing can you make similarities and differences more clear?

In my final paper, I used quotations and precise details from the text to support my ideas.

231

WRITING TRAITS SCORING RUBRIC

SCORE	4	3	2	1	NS
Purpose/ Organization	**The narrative is clear, focused, and well organized throughout.** • Contains an effective and complete plot • Develops strong setting, narrator/characters • Includes a variety of transitions to connect ideas • Contains a logical sequence of events • Includes an effective introduction and conclusion	**The narrative's organization is adequately maintained, and the focus is generally clear.** • Plot is mostly effective/may contain small flaws • Develops setting, narrator/characters • Adequate use of transitions to connect ideas • Contains an adequate sequence of events	**The narrative is somewhat organized and may be unclear in some parts.** • Plot may be inconsistent • Minimal development of setting, narrator/characters • Contains inconsistent use of transitions to connect ideas • Sequence of events is weak or unclear • Introduction and conclusion need improvement	**The narrative may be somewhat organized but unfocused.** • Little or no plot • Little or no development of setting, narrator/characters • Contains few or inappropriate transitions and weak connections among ideas • Sequence of events is not organized • Introduction and/or conclusion may be missing	• Not intelligible • Not written in English • Not on topic • Contains text copied from another source • Does not address the purpose for writing
Development/ Elaboration	**The narrative includes effective elaboration using details, dialogue, and description.** • Characters, setting, experiences, and events are well developed • Writer uses a variety of narrative techniques that strengthen the story or illustrate the experience • Contains effective sensory, concrete, and figurative language • Style is appropriate and effective	**The narrative includes adequate elaboration using details, dialogue, and description.** • Characters, setting, experiences, and events are adequately developed • Writer uses a variety of narrative techniques that generally move the story forward and illustrate the experience • Contains adequate sensory, concrete, and figurative language • Style is mostly appropriate	**The narrative includes partial or ineffective elaboration using unclear or inconsistent details, dialogue, and description.** • Characters, setting, experiences, and events lack consistent development • Writer uses inconsistent or weak narrative techniques • Contains weak sensory, concrete, and figurative language • Style is inconsistent or inappropriate	**The narrative provides little or no elaboration using few or no details, dialogue, and description.** • Very little development of characters, setting, experiences, and events • Writer's use of narrative techniques are minimal and may be incorrect • Little or no sensory, concrete, and figurative language • Little or no evidence of style	• Not intelligible • Not written in English • Not on topic • Contains text copied from another source • Does not address the purpose for writing

SCORE	2	1	0	NS
Conventions	**The narrative demonstrates adequate command of conventions.** • Consistent use of correct sentence structures, punctuation, capitalization, grammar, and spelling	**The narrative demonstrates partial command of conventions.** • Limited use of correct sentence structures, punctuation, capitalization, grammar, and spelling	**The narrative demonstrates little or no command of conventions.** • Rare use of correct sentence structures, punctuation, capitalization, grammar, and spelling	• Not intelligible • Not written in English • Not on topic • Contains text copied from another source

See also ***Writing Rubric Blackline Master*** and Teacher's Edition pp. R18–R21.

Formative Assessment

Weekly Tests

At the end of the lesson, administer the Weekly Test. This will give you a **snapshot of how students are progressing** with the Reading and Language Arts skills in this lesson and can give you **guidance on grouping, reteaching, and intervention.** Suggestions for adjusting instruction based on these results can be found on the next page.

Access Through Accommodations

When you administer the Weekly Test, some students may have problems accessing all or parts of the assessment. The purpose of the Weekly Test is to determine students' ability to complete the Reading and Language Arts tasks they learned in this lesson. Any barriers to them accessing the tasks demanded of them should be lowered so they can focus on skill demonstration.

When choosing accommodations, you will want to avoid invalidating the test results; if you are measuring a student's reading skill, for example, you will not want to read aloud the passage. The following accommodations, if needed, will not interfere with the Weekly Test's validity:

- Read aloud the assessment directions and item prompts. If students are English learners, read aloud the assessment directions and item prompts in the student's native language, if possible.

- Define any unknown words in the directions or item prompts that do not give away the answers to the items.

- Allow for a break during the assessment.

- Simplify the language of assessment directions and item prompts.

- Administer the assessment in a smaller group setting.

- Administer the assessment on a computer or other electronic device.

- Provide audio amplification equipment, colored overlays, or visual magnifying equipment to maintain visual/audio attention and access.

- Allow students to complete the assessment items orally or by having another person transcribe their responses.

Using Data to Adjust Instruction

Use students' scores on the Weekly Test to determine Small Group placement, reteaching, and potential for Intervention.

☑ VOCABULARY AND COMPREHENSION

Understanding Characters; Dialect; Author's Word Choice; Anchor Text

Target Vocabulary; Adages and Proverbs

IF STUDENT SCORES...

...at acceptable,	...below acceptable,
THEN continue core instruction.	**THEN** use Reteach Comprehension Skill and Vocabulary Strategies lessons. For struggling students, administer the *Intervention Assessments* to determine if students would benefit from intervention.

☑ LANGUAGE ARTS

Direct and Indirect Objects

IF STUDENT SCORES...

...at acceptable,	...below acceptable,
THEN continue core instruction.	**THEN** use Reteach Language Arts lesson. For struggling students, administer the *Intervention Assessments* to determine if students would benefit from intervention.

☑ DECODING

Vowel + /r/ Sounds

IF STUDENT SCORES...

...at acceptable,	...below acceptable,
THEN continue core instruction.	**THEN** use Reteach Decoding lesson. For struggling students, administer the *Intervention Assessments* to determine if students would benefit from intervention.

☑ FLUENCY

Fluency Plan

Assess one group per week using the Fluency Tests in the *Grab-and-Go™* Resources. Use the suggested plan at the right.

● Struggling Readers	Weeks 1, 3, 5
▲ On Level	Week 2
■ Advanced	Week 4

IF...

...students are reading on-level text fluently,	...students are reading below level,
THEN continue core instruction.	**THEN** provide additional fluency practice using the **Student Book**, the **Cold Reads**, and the Leveled Readers. For struggling students, administer the *Intervention Assessments* to determine if students would benefit from intervention.

HOUGHTON MIFFLIN HARCOURT

JOURNEYS

Cold Reads

5

The **Cold Reads** passages increase gradually in Lexile® measures throughout the year, from below grade-level to above grade-level.

- Each passage is accompanied by several selected-response questions and one constructed-response prompt, requiring students to read closely, answer questions at substantial DOK levels, and cite text evidence.

- The *Cold Reads* may be used to provide practice in reading increasingly complex texts and to informally monitor students' progress.

- The *Cold Reads* may be used to estimate students' Lexile® levels in order to recommend appropriately challenging books for small-group instruction or independent reading.

Turn the page for more information about using FORMATIVE ASSESSMENT for ELD AND INTERVENTION.

Assess It Online!

► Language Workshop
Assessment Handbook

► Intervention
Assessments

Formative Assessment for ELD and Intervention

Formative Assessment for English Learners

English learners should engage in the same rigorous curriculum and formative assessment as other students. However, it is important to remember that English learners face a dual challenge: they are strengthening their abilities *to use* English at the same time that they are learning challenging content *through* English. Use the following strategies and resources for ongoing assessment of English language development, in addition to the assessments you use with all students:

- A combination of **observational measures,** such as listening in as students read aloud or participate in collaborative conversations. Be prepared to provide **"just-in-time" scaffolding** to support students. For example, if students are retelling a story, you could help them use sentence structures with past-tense verbs and time-order transition words.

- **Constructive feedback** that focuses on communication and meaning-making. Avoid overcorrecting in a way that makes English learners reluctant to speak up. You might try recasting a child's statement more correctly, making a note to address the target form more directly during Designated ELD time.

- **Student self-assessment**, through students' own notes in their vocabulary notebooks or other learning journals. If possible, meet with each child to review his or her self-assessments and provide encouragement and feedback.

- **Formative assessment** notes that are integrated into the Language Workshop Teacher's Guide for use during Designated ELD.

- **Language Workshop Assessment Handbook** for longer-cycle assessment to make sure students are progressing in their English development.

Response to Intervention  RtI

Use the Weekly Tests and Benchmark and Unit Tests, along with your own observations, to determine if individual students are not responding to Tier I instruction and need additional testing to identify specific needs for targeted intervention.

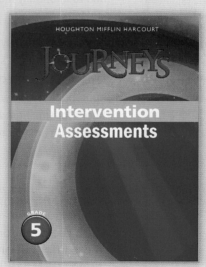

Intervention Assessments

Assessment for Intervention

Progress-Monitoring Assessments Administer this assessment to

- students in Tier II and Tier III Intervention to gauge progress towards exit from the intervention program.

- students who demonstrate lack of success with Weekly Tests, Benchmark and Unit Tests, and core instruction to determine if they might benefit from additional practice or intervention.

Vocabulary Reader
- *Black Bears*, T142–T143

Differentiate Comprehension
- Target Skill: Understanding Characters, T144–T145
- Target Strategy: Visualize, T144–T145

Leveled Readers
- ● *Young Eagle and His Horse*, T146
- ▲ *On the Long Drive*, T147
- ■ *Riding with the Camel Corps*, T148
- ◆ *The Long Cattle Drive*, T149

Differentiate Vocabulary Strategies
- Adages and Proverbs, T150–T151

Options for Reteaching
- Vocabulary Strategies: Adages and Proverbs, T152
- Comprehension Skill: Understanding Characters, T152
- Language Arts: Direct and Indirect Objects/Informative Writing, T153
- Decoding: Vowel + /r/ Sounds, T153

Literacy Centers
Independent Practice
- Comprehension and Fluency, T86
- Word Study, T86
- Think and Write, T87

Small Group Planner
Differentiated Instruction

		DAY 1	DAY 2	DAY 3
Teacher-Led	**Struggling Readers**	**Vocabulary Reader** *Black Bears,* Differentiated Instruction, p. T142 **English Language Support,** p. T143	**Differentiate Comprehension** Understanding Characters; Visualize, p. T144 **English Language Support,** p. T145	**Leveled Reader** *Young Eagle and His Horse,* p. T146 **English Language Support,** Leveled Reader Teacher's Guide, p. 5
	On Level	**Vocabulary Reader** *Black Bears,* Differentiated Instruction, p. T142 **English Language Support,** p. T143	**Differentiate Comprehension** Understanding Characters; Visualize, p. T144 **English Language Support,** p. T145	**Leveled Reader** *On the Long Drive,* p. T147 *The Long Cattle Drive,* p. T149 **English Language Support,** Leveled Reader Teacher's Guide, p. 5
	Advanced	**Vocabulary Reader** *Black Bears,* Differentiated Instruction, p. T143 **English Language Support,** p. T143	**Differentiate Comprehension** Understanding Characters; Visualize, p. T145 **English Language Support,** p. T145	**Leveled Reader** *Riding with the Camel Corps,* p. T148 **English Language Support,** Leveled Reader Teacher's Guide, p. 5
What are my other students doing?	**Struggling Readers**	**Reread** *Black Bears*	**Vocabulary in Context Cards** 61–70 *Talk It Over* Activities	**Listen** to Audio of "Old Yeller"; Retell and discuss
	On Level	**Reread** *Black Bears*	**Reread** "Old Yeller" with a partner	**Reread** for Fluency: *On the Long Drive* or *The Long Cattle Drive* **Complete** Leveled Practice EL7.1
	Advanced	**Vocabulary in Context Cards** 61–70 *Talk It Over* Activities	**Reread and Retell** "Old Yeller"	**Reread** for Fluency: *Riding with the Camel Corps*

 For Strategic Intervention for this lesson, see pp. S12–S21.

DAY 4	DAY 5	English Language Support

DAY 4

Differentiate Vocabulary Strategies
Adages and Proverbs, p. T150
English Language Support, p. T151

Differentiate Vocabulary Strategies
Adages and Proverbs, p. T150
English Language Support, p. T151

Differentiate Vocabulary Strategies
Adages and Proverbs, p. T151
English Language Support, p. T151

- **Partners: Reread** *Young Eagle and His Horse*
- **Complete** Leveled Practice SR7.1

- **Vocabulary in Context Cards**
  61–70 *Talk It Over* Activities
- **Complete** Reader's Notebook, p. 75

- **Reread** for Fluency: "Old Yeller"
- **Complete** Leveled Practice A7.1

DAY 5

Options for Reteaching,
pp. T152–T153

Options for Reteaching,
pp. T152–T153

Options for Reteaching,
pp. T152–T153

- **Reread** for Fluency: "Old Yeller"
- **Complete** Literacy Centers
- **Independent Reading**

- **Complete** Literacy Centers
- **Independent Reading**

- **Complete** Literacy Centers
- **Independent Reading**

English Language Support

Use the Leveled Reader Teacher's Guide to support ELs during differentiated instruction.

- **Characteristics of the Text** (p. 1)
  Identify challenging language features, such as text structure, literary features, complex sentences, and vocabulary.

- **Cultural Support/Cognates/Vocabulary** (p. 5)
  Explain unfamiliar features of English and help ELs transfer first-language knowledge.

- **Oral Language Development** (p. 5)
  Check comprehension using dialogues that match students' proficiency levels.

Book Share
Use this routine at the end of the week to enable students to demonstrate that they have become experts on their Leveled Readers.

Step 1:
Have each student write a presentation based on his or her Leveled Reader **Responding** page, using the following guidelines:

- Briefly tell what your book is about.

- Show your Column Chart and explain what you added to complete it.

- Tell about your favorite part of the book, what you found most interesting in it, or what you learned from it.

Students should prepare to share their presentations with a group.

Step 2:
Have students form groups in which each student has read a different Leveled Reader.

Step 3:
Have students take turns sharing their book presentations in their groups. Continue until all students have finished sharing. Encourage students to ask questions of the presenters. Provide frames such as the following for support.

Can you tell me more about _____?

I wonder why _____.

What do you think about _____?

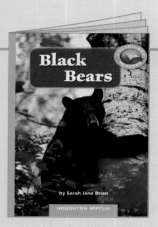

Summary

In this informational text, students will learn where black bears live and what they eat. Students will learn tips on how they can stay safe in bear country and how bears can also stay safe.

☑ **TARGET VOCABULARY**

romp	frantic
strained	lunging
picturing	checking
wheeled	stride
shouldered	bounding

👥 **SMALL GROUP OPTIONS**

Vocabulary Reader
Black Bears

STRUGGLING READERS

ELA L.5.4c
ELD ELD.PI.5.1, ELD.PI.5.6b

- Explain that black bears are generally afraid of people and that as more humans move into bear country, bears may feel threatened. Have students predict the problems that such a situation may cause.

- Guide students to preview the Vocabulary Reader. Read aloud the headings. Ask students to describe the images, using Target Vocabulary when possible.

- Have students alternate reading pages of the text aloud. Guide them to use context to determine the meanings of unfamiliar words. As necessary, use the **Vocabulary in Context Cards** to review the meanings of vocabulary words.

- Assign the **Responding Page** and <u>Blackline Master 7.4</u> 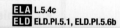. Have partners work together to complete the pages.

ON LEVEL

ELA L.5.4c
ELD ELD.PI.5.1, ELD.PI.5.6b

- Explain that black bears are generally afraid of people and that as more people move into bear country, bears may feel threatened. Guide students to preview the Vocabulary Reader.

- Remind students that they can use context clues to confirm their understanding of Target Vocabulary and to learn the meanings of new words and phrases.

- Have partners alternate reading pages of the text aloud. Tell them to use context clues to determine the meanings of unknown words.

- Assign the **Responding Page** and <u>Blackline Master 7.4</u> 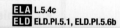. Have students discuss their responses with a partner.

ADVANCED

ELA L.5.4c
ELD ELD.PI.5.1, ELD.PI.5.6b

- Have students preview the Vocabulary Reader and make predictions about what they will read, using information from their preview and prior knowledge.

- Remind students to use context clues to help them determine the meanings of unknown words.

- Tell students to read the text with a partner. Ask them to stop and discuss the meanings of unknown words as necessary.

- Assign the **Responding Page** and Blackline Master 7.4 🔗. For the Write About It activity, remind students to use facts and details to support their ideas.

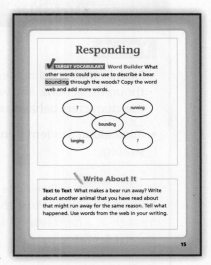

Black Bears, p. 15

ENGLISH LANGUAGE SUPPORT

ELD ELD.PI.5.1, ELD.PI.5.6b

Provide Struggling Readers, On Level, and Advanced ELs proficiency-level support during differentiated instruction.

Emerging

Use visuals, simplified language, and gestures to preteach the following Target Vocabulary words: *stride, wheeled, bounding,* and *romp.* Guide students to use use the words in oral sentences.

Expanding

Have students read aloud sentences from the Vocabulary Reader. Check students' understanding of the vocabulary words. Have students complete this sentence frame: *Black bears can be dangerous when ____.*

Bridging

As students read, have them list reasons why bears run away. Give them a variety of frames to complete to practice responding to the Write About It prompt: *Bears tend to run away because _____. For instance, they _____. In addition, _____.*

Differentiate Comprehension
Understanding Characters; Visualize

STRUGGLING READERS

ELA RL.5.3, RF.5.4a
ELD ELD.PI.5.1, ELD.PI.5.5, ELD.PI.5.6

I DO IT

- Explain that good readers use characters' thoughts, actions, and words to understand why the characters behave as they do.

- Read aloud **Student Book p. 210**. Model this strategy.

Think Aloud *Travis doesn't want his mom to know he is tired. I think that's because he wants to be seen as a hard worker like his dad. He must respect his father.*

WE DO IT

- Read pp. 212–213 with students. Ask them to visualize Travis's facial expressions and actions as they read.

- Have volunteers list adjectives that describe Travis based on the passages they just read. Have students add these to one column of a T-Map.

- Ask students to explain how visualizing helped them better understand Travis.

YOU DO IT

- Distribute Graphic Organizer 10 (Story Map) 🔗. Have student pairs work together to add Arliss's traits to their T-Maps.

- Review the charts together as a class. Have students tell how they determined what the traits were for the respective characters.

ON LEVEL

ELA RL.5.3, RF.5.4a
ELD ELD.PI.5.1, ELD.PI.5.5, ELD.PI.5.6

I DO IT

- Read aloud pp. 210–211 of "Old Yeller."

- Explain that students can determine a character's traits from the character's thoughts, actions, and words.

Think Aloud *Travis panics when he hears his brother screaming. This shows that he cares for him very much.*

WE DO IT

- Have students read pp. 212–213.

- Ask volunteers to list other traits of Travis based on the pages they have just read.

- Work together to add the characteristics of Travis to a T-Map.

YOU DO IT

- Distribute Graphic Organizer 10 (Story Map) 🔗. Ask students to identify the character traits of Arliss by visualizing his actions and what Travis tells about him. Then have them add these traits to their T-Maps.

- Have students share their T-Maps and discuss ways in which Travis and Arliss are similar and different.

ADVANCED

ELA RL.5.3, RF.5.4a
ELD ELD.PI.5.1, ELD.PI.5.5, ELD.PI.5.6

I DO IT

- Explain that students can determine a character's traits from the character's thoughts, actions, and words.

- Point out that characters can change their feelings and behavior over the course of a story, just as real people do.

- Explain that these changes happen because of key story events.

WE DO IT

- Have students read **Student Book pp. 211** and **218.**

- Discuss the changes in Travis's feelings toward Arliss. Ask students how Travis feels about Arliss in the beginning of the story. *Travis seems annoyed by Arliss.*

- Ask how Travis feels about Arliss at the end of the selection. *Travis realizes he loves Arliss very much.*

YOU DO IT

- Distribute Graphic Organizer 10 (Story Map). Have students use T-Maps to record traits of Travis and Arliss.

- Have students write a paragraph comparing and contrasting the two characters.

- Invite students to use their completed T-Maps to visualize events from the story.

ENGLISH LANGUAGE SUPPORT

ELA RL.5.3, RF.5.4a, L.5.3a
ELD ELD.PI.5.1, ELD.PI.5.5, ELD.PI.5.6

Provide Struggling Readers, On Level, and Advanced ELs proficiency-level support during differentiated instruction.

Emerging

Write the following sentence frames on the board. *Travis thinks _____. Travis says _____. Travis _____.* Complete these frames with students' help, guiding them to use an action verb for the last frame. Encourage students to use similar frames to tell about Arliss's traits.

Expanding

After students have added traits for either character or both characters to their T-Maps, have them use the words and phrases in complete sentences to describe the character/s. Have students check that their sentences are based on details in the text.

Bridging

Guide students to consult online or print thesauruses to find precise adjectives that describe story characters. Have them practice writing sentences about the characters using the words they find as well as details from the text to support their statements. Provide sentence frames as needed. For example: *I think that _____ is _____ because _____. He appears to be _____. The character's actions tell me that _____. At the end of the story, _____.*

☑ **TARGET SKILL**
Understanding Characters

☑ **TARGET STRATEGY**
Visualize

☑ **TARGET VOCABULARY**

frantic	bounding
lunging	shouldered
stride	strained
checking	romp
wheeled	picturing

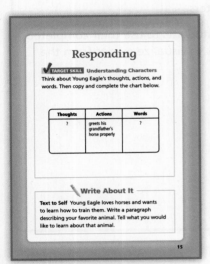

Responding

☑ **TARGET SKILL** Understanding Characters
Think about Young Eagle's thoughts, actions, and words. Then copy and complete the chart below.

Thoughts	Actions	Words
?	greets his grandfather's horse properly	?

✐ Write About It

Text to Self Young Eagle loves horses and wants to learn how to train them. Write a paragraph describing your favorite animal. Tell what you would like to learn about that animal.

15

Young Eagle and His Horse, p. 15

Leveled Readers

ELA RL.5.1, RL.5.3, SL.5.1a, SL.5.6
ELD ELD.PI.5.1, ELD.PI.5.5, ELD.PI.5.6a

STRUGGLING READERS

 Young Eagle and His Horse

GENRE: HISTORICAL FICTION

Summary Young Eagle is excited to prove he can train his grandfather's horse, Leaping Water. When the horse realizes a bear is nearby, it panics and ends up hurting its leg. All alone, Young Eagle must help Leaping Water.

Introducing the Text

• Discuss key vocabulary from the story. Explain that the Nez Perce Native American tribe is from the western United States. Horses were an important part of their lives in the 1800s, when this story takes place.

• Remind students that using a graphic organizer will help them understand characters by recording the characters' thoughts, actions, and words.

Supporting the Reading

• As you listen to students read, pause to discuss these questions.

p. 8 *What character traits can we infer about Young Eagle from the description of his search for the horse after it runs off? Young Eagle is smart, and he knows and cares about horses.*

p. 9 *How does Young Eagle look and act when he finds Leaping Water? He acts calmly. He talks to the horse quietly and moves slowly so that he won't scare him.*

Discussing and Revisiting the Text

CRITICAL THINKING After discussing *Young Eagle and His Horse* together, have students read the instructions at the top of **Responding** p. 15. Use these teaching points to guide students as they revisit the text.

• Have partners review the text together.

• Have partners complete Blackline Master 7.5 ⬚ by identifying character traits.

FLUENCY: INTONATION Model reading p. 8, and then have partners echo-read it. They should concentrate on varying the pitch of their voices.

ELA RL.5.1, RL.5.3, SL.5.1a, SL.5.6
ELD ELD.PI.5.1, ELD.PI.5.5, ELD.PI.5.6a

 ## *On the Long Drive*

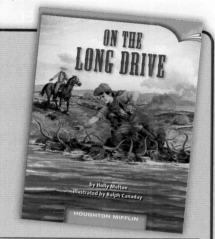

GENRE: HISTORICAL FICTION

Summary When his mother dies, young James Warner sets off on a cattle drive as a cook's helper. He soon learns that he will have to earn the cowboys' respect.

Introducing the Text

• Discuss key vocabulary from the story. Explain that a cattle drive could take months and involved thousands of cattle. The cowboys encountered many dangers along the way.

• Remind students that by focusing on what characters say, think, and do, they will better understand characters' motives and relationships.

Supporting the Reading

• As you listen to students read, pause to discuss these questions.

p. 7 *James looked forward to making friends on the cattle drive. How does Ben's reaction to the rattlesnake make him feel? James is humiliated and embarrassed.*

pp. 9–10 *James was shocked to find another rattlesnake, this time in his boot. After realizing Ben was playing a joke on him, how does James react? He is angry. After making a sarcastic remark to Ben, James cuts off the rattle and puts it in his hatband.*

Discussing and Revisiting the Text

CRITICAL THINKING After discussing *On the Long Drive* together, have students read the instructions at the top of **Responding** p. 19. Use these teaching points to guide students as they revisit the text.

• Have students work in pairs to review the text together.

• Have students complete Blackline Master 7.6 by identifying character traits.

FLUENCY: INTONATION Have students practice reading p. 9 aloud. They should concentrate on varying the pitch of their voices, especially when reading the dialogue.

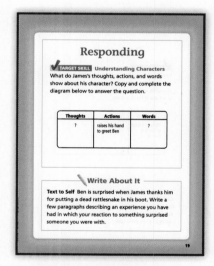

On the Long Drive, p. 19

RtI

☑ **TARGET SKILL**
Understanding Characters

☑ **TARGET STRATEGY**
Visualize

☑ **TARGET VOCABULARY**

frantic	bounding
lunging	shouldered
stride	strained
checking	romp
wheeled	picturing

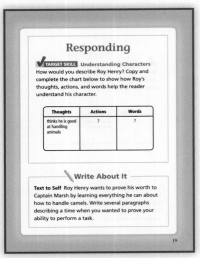

Riding with the Camel Corps,
p. 19

Leveled Readers

ELA RL.5.1, RL.5.3, SL.5.1a, SL.5.6
ELD ELD.PI.5.1, ELD.PI.5.5, ELD.PI.5.6a

ADVANCED

Riding with the Camel Corps

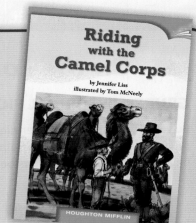

GENRE: HISTORICAL FICTION

Summary In this piece of historical fiction, Roy Henry wants to become part of the new Camel Corps and travel to the unexplored West. He soon learns that these foreign animals are stubborn and hard to train.

Introducing the Text

- Discuss key vocabulary from the story. Explain that the Camel Corps was part of a U.S. Army experiment for exploring the West. People believed that camels' strength and ability to go without food or water for days would make them well-suited to the dry, rugged desert terrain.

- Remind students that by focusing on what characters say, think, and do, they will better understand characters' motives and relationships.

Supporting the Reading

- As you listen to students read, pause to discuss these questions.

  p. 7 *Why does Roy feel disappointed when the camels eat his cactus fence? He had wanted to impress the captain. He's embarrassed because everything seems to go wrong.*

  p. 16 *When Roy goes after the stray camel, what is he able to finally see? He sees patches of green grass and a creek with reeds.*

Discussing and Revisiting the Text

CRITICAL THINKING After discussing *Riding with the Camel Corps* together, have students read the instructions at the top of **Responding** p. 19. Use these teaching points to guide students as they revisit the text.

- Have students work individually or in pairs to review the text.

- Have them identify character traits and list them on <u>Blackline Master 7.7</u>.

FLUENCY: INTONATION Have students practice reading paragraphs 3–5 on p. 7 aloud. They should concentrate on varying the pitch of their voices to make the reading interesting to the listeners.

ELA RL.5.1, RL.5.3, SL.5.1a, SL.5.6
ELD ELD.PI.5.1, ELD.PI.5.5, ELD.PI.5.6a

ENGLISH LANGUAGE SUPPORT

 ## *The Long Cattle Drive*

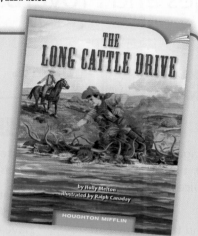

GENRE: HISTORICAL FICTION

Summary In this fictional account, James Warner works as a cook's helper on a cattle drive in the Old West. He soon meets adventure and must prove himself to earn the respect of the cowboys.

Introducing the Text

• Discuss key vocabulary from the story. Explain that in the mid-nineteenth century, much of the West was still wild. Cowboys traveled through rough and sometimes dangerous conditions to deliver their cattle.

• Remind students that using a graphic organizer will help them understand characters by recording characters' thoughts, actions, and words.

Supporting the Reading

• As you listen to students read, pause to discuss these questions.

p. 7 *What is Ben's reaction toward James when James finds a rattlesnake? He makes fun of James and calls him a beginner.*

pp. 15–16 *Describe the setting on the night of the storm. Lightning is lighting up the night and making blue balls of fire. The cattle are scared and lunging and running everywhere.*

Discussing and Revisiting the Text

CRITICAL THINKING After discussing *The Long Cattle Drive* together, have students read the instructions at the top of **Responding** p. 19. Use these teaching points to guide students as they revisit the text.

• Have students read aloud the text shown in the chart.

• Have them work individually or in pairs to identify character traits and enter them on Blackline Master 7.8 🔗.

FLUENCY: INTONATION Have partners echo-read p. 10. They should concentrate on varying the pitch of their voices.

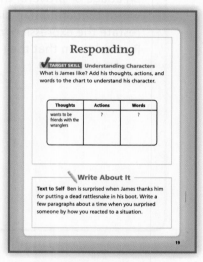

The Long Cattle Drive, p. 19

Differentiate Vocabulary Strategies
Adages and Proverbs

STRUGGLING READERS   **ELA** L.5.4c, L.5.5b   **ELD** ELD.PI.5.1

I DO IT

- Explain to students that an adage is an expression that has been proven true over time. A proverb is a saying that offers practical advice or wisdom in simple terms.

- Tell students that to understand the meaning of an adage or proverb, they should first define any words that are unfamiliar. Then they should restate the expression in familiar language. Remind them that they might also be able to use context clues.

WE DO IT

- Write this expression on the board: *Hindsight is always twenty-twenty*.

- Together, define *hindsight* as "understanding of events after they have occurred." Explain that *twenty-twenty* refers to perfect vision.

- Guide students to restate the expression in their own words. *It is easy to know what should have been done when looking back at events that have already happened.*

YOU DO IT

- Write these expressions on the board: *Haste makes waste. It is better to be safe than sorry.*

- Have students work in pairs to restate each saying. Remind them to use a print or digital dictionary if they need to define unfamiliar words.

- Have pairs share their restatements with the class.

ON LEVEL   **ELA** L.5.4c, L.5.5b   **ELD** ELD.PI.5.1

I DO IT

- Explain to students that an adage is an expression that has been proven true over time and that a proverb is a saying that offers practical advice or wisdom in simple terms.

- Tell students that to understand the meaning of an adage or proverb, they should define unfamiliar words and then restate the expression in familiar language. Remind them to use context clues if possible as well.

WE DO IT

- Write this expression on the board: *Hindsight is always twenty-twenty*.

- Model how to restate it.

Think Aloud   *I know that hindsight means to have an understanding of something after it happens. Twenty-twenty is perfect vision. So this means that it's easy to know what you should have done after a situation is over.*

- Have pairs apply a Think Aloud strategy to restate *Haste makes waste*.

YOU DO IT

- Write these expressions on the board: *Pride goes before a fall. Honesty is the best policy.*

- Have students work in pairs to rewrite each saying in their own words. Have them include a picture that illustrates each expression's meaning.

- Have pairs share their restatements and drawings.

ADVANCED

ELA L.5.4c, L.5.5b
ELD ELD.PI.5.1

I DO IT

- Explain to students that an adage is an expression that has been proven true over time. A proverb is a saying that offers practical advice or wisdom.

- Tell students that to understand the meaning of an adage or proverb, they should define unfamiliar words and then restate the expression in their own words. Remind them that they can also use context clues.

WE DO IT

- Write this expression on the board: *Pride goes before a fall.*

- Have students work together to rewrite the saying in their own words. Call on volunteers to share their restatements. *Being overconfident can lead you to make mistakes.*

- Then have students explain the meanings of these expressions: *Doubt is the beginning, not the end, of wisdom. Hindsight is always twenty-twenty.*

YOU DO IT

- Have pairs of students find additional adages and proverbs using digital and print resources.

- Ask them to rewrite each expression in their own words. Then have them list the sayings in one column and the restatements in random order in a second column.

- Have pairs exchange papers and complete each other's quizzes.

ENGLISH LANGUAGE SUPPORT

ELA L.5.4c, L.5.5b
ELD ELD.PI.5.1

Provide Struggling Readers, On Level, and Advanced ELs proficiency-level support during differentiated instruction.
Use the following activities for additional support, as appropriate.

Emerging

Explain that an adage is a popular saying that usually restates a truth. Tell students that rewriting adages and proverbs can help them understand their meaning. Work with students to restate *Honesty is the best policy*. Help students restate or rewrite other adages or proverbs they learn during the course of the lesson.

Expanding

Have students write a simple restatement of each new adage they learn. If possible, have them draw an illustration to summarize the gist of the saying. To check their understanding of the adage, give students an example and a non-example for the adage and have them choose the right one.

Bridging

Have students consult print or online resources that explain the meanings of adages they learn over the course of the lesson. Guide students to rewrite each adage in their own words. If appropriate, have them write or say a similar adage in their dominant language or another language they know as a way to reinforce understanding.

Options for Reteaching

ELA L.5.4a, L.5.5c, L.5.6
ELD ELD.PI.5.1, ELD.PI.5.6b, ELD.PI.5.12a

VOCABULARY STRATEGIES

Adages and Proverbs

I DO IT

- Review with students that an adage is a traditional saying that has proven to be true over time. An example is "Haste makes waste." It means that when you rush to complete something, it turns out badly and you may have to start all over again.

- Review that a proverb is a brief, simple expression of common-sense wisdom. "Laughter is the best medicine" is a proverb that advises people to take a break and have some fun when life gets stressful.

- Point out that recognizing adages and proverbs can help students understand what they read.

WE DO IT

- Write this sentence about "Old Yeller" on the board: *Travis never told his little brother that he loved him, but actions speak louder than words.*

- Model how to apply the strategy to interpret the adage.

  Think Aloud *I've heard the expression "Actions speak louder than words" many times. It's a common adage. What does it tell me about Travis in this sentence? I know from reading the story that Travis risks his life to save Arliss from a bear. His actions prove that he loves Arliss. So the adage is used here to mean that Travis's actions tell more about his true feelings than anything he might say.*

- Ask students to suggest other examples that apply to the adage "Actions speak louder than words."

YOU DO IT

- On the board, write the proverb "Don't judge a book by its cover."

- Have partners discuss how this proverb applies to Travis's opinion about the "big yeller dog." Ask each pair to use the proverb in a sentence about the selection.

- Invite pairs to share their sentences with the class.

ELA RI.5.3, RF.5.4a
ELD ELD.PI.5.1, ELD.PI.5.6a, ELD.PII.5.1

COMPREHENSION SKILL

Understanding Characters

I DO IT

- Remind students that they can understand a character's traits by analyzing the character's thoughts, actions, and words. In particular, they should pay attention to the way a character responds to conflict and challenges.

- Point out that comparing and contrasting two characters is another good way to analyze and understand them.

WE DO IT

- Have students turn to **Student Book pp. 210–211**. Read aloud the three paragraphs beginning with "An hour before sundown" and ending with "the gobble of a wild turkey."

- Model how to compare Travis and Arliss to gain a better understanding of Travis.

  Think Aloud *Travis is exhausted from chopping wood, yet he wants to make an excuse so his mother won't know how tired he is. Arliss, on the other hand, is "a screamer by nature." He wants everyone to know how he feels. This contrast helps me appreciate Travis's quiet, private nature.*

- Ask students to identify specific details in the text that support your comparison of Travis and Arliss.

YOU DO IT

- Distribute Graphic Organizer 12 🔼.

- Have one partner review "Old Yeller" for details about Travis while the other finds details about Arliss. Then have pairs work together to fill out both columns of the T-Map.

- Review the completed T-Maps. Discuss what the comparison of Travis and Arliss reveals about both characters.

ELA W.5.2a, W.5.2d, W.5.4, L.5.1c
ELD ELD.PI.5.1, ELD.PI.5.10a, ELD.PII.5.2a, ELD.PII.5.3

LANGUAGE ARTS

Direct and Indirect Objects/Informative Writing

I DO IT

- Remind students that a direct object receives the action of a verb and that an indirect object tells to whom or to what the action of the verb is done.

- Write on the board: *Old Yeller gave that bear a brave fight.* Model how to identify the direct and indirect objects.

Think Aloud *To find the direct object, I ask: What did the dog give? The dog gave a fight. To find the indirect object, I ask: To whom was the action done? The dog fought the bear.*

WE DO IT

- Work together to write sentences that contain a direct and an indirect object. Write the sentences on the board.

- Guide students to use the questions that were modeled in the Think Aloud to help them identify the direct object and the indirect object.

- For each sentence, have a volunteer come up to the board to underline the direct object and circle the indirect object.

YOU DO IT

- Have partners write paragraphs comparing and contrasting the actions of the dog and the mother bear in "Old Yeller." Tell them to be sure to include direct and indirect objects.

- Have partners trade paragraphs with another pair. Each pair should underline the direct objects and circle the indirect objects in the other pair's paragraph.

DECODING

ELA RF.5.3a

Vowel + /r/ Sounds

I DO IT

- Remind students that the letter *r* affects the pronunciation of vowels that come before it.

- Students should try different pronunciations of the vowel sound before *r*. Using the correct vowel sound may help them recognize a word.

- Tell students that they will practice decoding words with vowel + /r/ sounds.

WE DO IT

- Write *market, before, hardly,* and *poured* on the board.

- Help students write sentences containing these words.

- Model how to decode *market* step by step.

Think Aloud *I can try to pronounce the* ar *like the* ar *in* arrow, *but that doesn't make it sound like a word I recognize. So I will try a different word:* car. *When I pronounce the* ar *in* market *like the* ar *in* car, *it does make a word that I recognize.*

YOU DO IT

- Have partners decode the remaining words.

- Have them identify the vowel sound before each *r*.

- Use the Corrective Feedback on p. T125 if students need additional help.

Teacher Notes

JOURNEYS

Anchor Text

Paired Selection

DIGITAL RESOURCES

Teacher Dashboard

Log onto the Teacher Dashboard and *my*SmartPlanner. Use these searchable tools to customize lessons that achieve your instructional goals.

Interactive Whiteboard Lessons

- Grammar: Conjunctions
- Vocabulary Strategies: Prefixes *en-, re-, pre-, pro-*

my WriteSmart

- Write About Reading
- Informative Writing: Cause-and-Effect Essay

Interactive Lessons

- ▶ Participating in Collaborative Discussions
- ▶ Writing to Sources
- ▶ Informative Writing

✓ Assess It Online!

- Weekly Tests
- Assessment-driven instruction with prescriptive feedback

Student eBook

🖊 📱 Annotate it! **Strategies for Annotation**

Guide students to use digital tools for close reading.

Students may also use the interactive features in their Student eBooks to respond to prompts in a variety of ways, including:

- short-answer response
- spoken response
- fill-in-the-blank
- drag-and-drop
- multiple choice

High-Interest Informational Texts and Multimedia

Have students explore the FYI website for additional information about topics of study.

ENGLISH LANGUAGE SUPPORT

Culturally Responsive Teaching

Visit America's National Parks! Tell students that this week, they will be reading and thinking about wild and beautiful protected places in the United States, such as Everglades National Park in Florida.

- Invite students and family and community members to share their experiences visiting one of America's national parks.

- Provide a variety of resources that students can investigate to learn more about our country's national parks. If two or more students show an interest in a particular park, encourage them to learn together, collaborate, and share information.

- Display a map of the United States and invite students to place notes about where national parks are located, what they are like, and parks they would like to visit.

Use Multiple Levels of Questioning For emerging English learners, ask questions that can be answered nonverbally or with single words. Use *who, what, when,* and *where* questions for expanding English learners, progressing to *why* and *how* questions.

Language Support Card

Use the Lesson 8 Language Support Card to activate prior knowledge, frontload vocabulary, and teach academic English.

Use the Text X-Ray on page T163 to review the language demands of "Everglades Forever: Restoring America's Great Wetland" with the needs of English learners in mind.

Language Workshop for Designated ELD

- Connection to Essential Question
- Vocabulary Network
- Focus on Interacting in Meaningful Ways
- Discussion Frames
- How English Works
- Word Learning Strategies

You may wish to use the following suggestions to modify instruction for some students, according to their needs.

Learner's Journal

Keeping a Learner's Journal can help students see themselves as successful, growing learners. Developing a sense of ownership in students can motivate them to reach their highest potential. Have students add to their Learner's Journal for this lesson. Depending on students' needs and skills, have them record information about what they are learning. Some examples:

- Day 1: Vocabulary: *endangered, unique, adapted, vegetation, conserving, restore, guardians, attracted, regulate, responsibility*
- Day 2: The title of the Anchor Text, "Everglades Forever: Restoring America's Great Wetland," and information about the text
- Day 3: Write about something new they learned about protecting the environment. To help, you might want to discuss with students the Essential Question and their ideas about it.
- Day 4: Write several words they have learned to spell this week.
- Day 5: Write about how they are becoming better writers. For example, "I am learning to write a cause-and-effect essay."

Student eBook

- **Audio** can be activated to support fluency, decoding, and comprehension.
- **Alternative Text** provides spoken information that can be used in place of the information provided in the book's images.
- **Vocabulary Pop-Ups** contain point-of-use definitions for selection vocabulary.

Science

Develop Models of Interactions Between Systems Have partners use information from "Everglades Forever: Restoring American's Great Wetland" to develop a model that describes the interaction of two systems, such as a geosphere and a biosphere.

- Conduct a brief picture walk to have students identify different areas of the Everglades described in the selection.
- Tell students that they will work with a partner to use information from the selection to create a web, flow chart, or another type of graphic organizer about one area of the Everglades that explains how animals (the biosphere) and the land and water (the geosphere) interact and influence each other.
- Display examples of blank graphic organizers students might create, and briefly discuss the uses of each one.
- Pair students with a partner. Have students choose a region, or assign a region to each group. Regions might include a mangrove swamp, the slough on the Ashinga Trail, the Pinelands, or a sawgrass prairie.
- Have partners review information in the selection about their region and discuss ways to present it graphically. When students have completed their graphic organizers, have them share them with another pair or with a small group.

LESSON **8** *Our* **Focus Wall**

ANCHOR TEXT

Everglades Forever: Restoring America's Great Wetland
Narrative Nonfiction

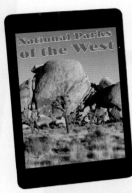

National Parks of the West
Informational Text

ESSENTIAL QUESTION

What reasons do people have for protecting the environment?

WRITING

Writing

Informative Writing:
Cause-and-Effect Essay
Focus Trait: Ideas

READING LITERATURE & INFORMATIONAL TEXT

Comprehension Skills and Strategies

☑ **TARGET SKILL**
• Author's Purpose
• Explain Scientific Ideas
• Domain-Specific Vocabulary

☑ **TARGET STRATEGY**
• Analyze/Evaluate

FOUNDATIONAL SKILLS

Fluency

Adjust Rate to Purpose

Decoding

Homophones

LANGUAGE

☑ Target Vocabulary

endangered	restore
unique	guardians
adapted	attracted
vegetation	regulate
conserving	responsibility

Spelling

Homophones

steel	manor
steal	manner
aloud	pedal
allowed	peddle
ring	berry
wring	bury
lesson	hanger
lessen	hangar
who's	overdo
whose	overdue

Grammar

Conjunctions

Vocabulary Strategies

Prefixes *en-, re-, pre-, pro-*

ANCHOR TEXT

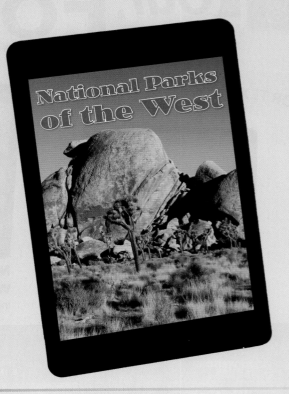

Everglades Forever
GENRE: Narrative Nonfiction

Prepare for Complex Texts For a comprehensive overview and analysis of key ideas and academic language features of this lesson's Anchor Text, see pages T162–T163.

National Parks of the West
GENRE: Informational Text
21st Century Theme: Environmental Literacy

Digital Resources

▶ **eBook: Annotate It!**

▶ **Interactive Whiteboard Lessons**
• Vocabulary Strategies: Prefixes *en-*, *re-*, *pre-*, *pro-*
• Grammar: Conjunctions

▶ **GrammarSnap Videos**
• Compound Sentences
• Coordinating: Conjunctions

▶ **Multimedia Grammar Glossary**

▶ *my*SmartPlanner

▶ **Parent Resources**

● Additional Resources

• Vocabulary in Context Cards 71–80
• Reader's Notebook, pp, 85–96
• Lesson 8 Blackline Masters
• Literacy and Language Guide

Meaning Making

Language Development

Effective Expression

Content Knowledge

Foundational Skills

LINGUISTICALLY DIVERSE LEARNERS

∨ Integrated English Language Support

● **Interacting in Meaningful Ways**

Classroom Conversations
- Think-Write-Pair-Share, p. T171
- Collaborative Conversation, pp. T166, T184, T188, T199

Interactive and Collaborative Writing
- Analyze/Evaluate, p. T184
- Write About Reading, p. T189
- Cause-and-Effect Essay, p. T208

Self-Selected Reading, p. T190

Sentence Frames for Speaking, p. T199

● **Learning About How English Works**

Scaffold the Texts
- Text X-Ray: Focus on Academic Language, p. T163
- Text Cohesion, pp. T176, T188, T209

Language Detective
- Target Vocabulary, p. T168
- Modifying to Add Details, p. T181

Communicative Modes
- Write About Reading, p. T189
- Cause-and-Effect Essay, p. T208

● **Using Foundational Literacy Skills**

Fluency: Adjust Rate to Purpose, p. T200
Decoding: Homophones, p. T201

Apply Language Skills
- Conjunctions, p. T204

Support Linguistic Transfer
- Prefixes *en-, re-, pre-, pro-*, p. T196
- Homophones, p. T202
- Conjunctions, p. T204

∨ Standard English Learners

- Pronunciation: Voicing /l/, p. T177
- Conjunctions, p. T206

ASSESSMENT

● **Formative Assessment**

- Target Vocabulary, p. T169
- Target Strategy: Analyze/Evaluate, pp. T178, T184
- Target Skill: Author's Purpose, p. T187
- Vocabulary Strategies: Prefixes *en-, re-, pre-, pro-*, p. T197
- Decoding: Homophones, p. T201
- Using Data to Adjust Instruction, p. T213

● ✅ *Assess It Online!*

- Weekly Tests

Performance Tasks
- Write About Reading, p. T189
- Write an Explanatory Essay, p. T364

Small Group/Independent Resources

LESSON 8

∨ Vocabulary Reader

Mangrove Swamp
by Elspeth Leacock

HOUGHTON MIFFLIN

● **Vocabulary Reader**
for all levels

Provide strategic scaffolding to support all students in reading on-level text and in acquiring general academic and domain-specific vocabulary. Use the instructional supports on pp. T218–T219 or the Leveled Reader Teacher's Guide.

Guided Reading Level: R
Lexile: 590L
DRA: 40
Leveled Reader Teacher's Guide

∨ Weekly Leveled Readers

Guide students to read and comprehend additional texts about the lesson topic. Use the instructional supports on pp. T222–T225 or the Leveled Reader Teacher's Guides.

Struggling Readers	**On Level**	**Advanced**	**English Language Learners**
Guided Reading Level: R	**Guided Reading Level: U**	**Guided Reading Level: V**	**Guided Reading Level: U**
Lexile: 590L	Lexile: 830L	Lexile: 980L	Lexile: 660L
DRA: 40	DRA: 44	DRA: 50	DRA: 44
Leveled Reader Teacher's Guide	Leveled Reader Teacher's Guide	Leveled Reader Teacher's Guide	Leveled Reader Teacher's Guide

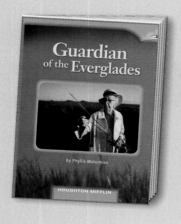  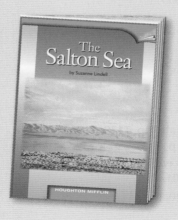 

Guardian of the Everglades
by Phyllis Waterman
HOUGHTON MIFFLIN

America's Urban Parks
by Thomas Pressel
HOUGHTON MIFFLIN

The Salton Sea
by Suzanne Lindell
HOUGHTON MIFFLIN

America's City Parks
by Thomas Pressel
HOUGHTON MIFFLIN

Language Workshop for Designated ELD

- Provides reteaching and practice in the key foundational skills for reading: print concepts, phonological/phonemic awareness, phonics and word recognition, and fluency.

- Explicit, sequential, and systematic instruction designed to bring students up to grade level.

- Screening and Diagnostic Assessments (within Intervention Assessments) place individual students within the system.

Lesson 8 Focus

Collaborate: Provide Counterarguments

Interpret: Ask and Answer Questions

Produce: Use Technology Where Appropriate

How English Works: Expand Noun Phrases

Vocabulary Network

Intervention

 Strategic Intervention Tier II

Write-In Reader: *Oil Spill in Alaska*

- Interactive worktext with selection that connects to the lesson topic
- Reinforces the lesson's vocabulary and comprehension
- Build skills for reading increasingly complex texts
- Online version with dual-speed audio and follow-text

Daily Lessons See this week's daily Strategic Intervention Lesson on pp. S22–S31.

- Preteach and Reteach daily instruction
- Oral Grammar
- Decoding
- Comprehension
- Fluency
- Grammar
- Written Response
- Unpack Meaning
- Return to Anchor Text

 Decoding Power: Intensive Intervention

- Provides reteaching and practice in the key foundational skills for reading: print concepts, phonological/phonemic awareness, phonics and word recognition, and fluency.

- Explicit, sequential, and systematic instruction designed to bring students up to grade level.

- Screening and Diagnostic Assessments (within Intervention Assessments) place individual students within the system.

✓ Assess It Online!

▶ **Screening and Diagnostic Assessments** (within Intervention Assessments) place individual students within the system.

▶ **Progress-Monitoring Assessments** (within Intervention Assessments) ensure students are making satisfactory progress and provide a measure of student readiness to exit the system.

What My Other Students Are Doing

Digital Resources

▶ **Literacy Centers:** Word Study, Think and Write, Comprehension and Fluency

▶ **Interactive Lessons:** Writing to Sources, Writing Informative Texts: Use Facts and Examples, Participating in Collaborative Discussions

◯ Additional Resources

- Vocabulary in Context Cards 71–80
- Reader's Notebook, pp. 85–96
- Independent Reading
- Lesson 8 Blackline Masters

Literacy Centers

LESSON 8

Managing Independent Activities

Comprehension and Fluency

Materials
- Student Book
- pencil or pen
- dictionary
- Reading Log
- Vocabulary Log

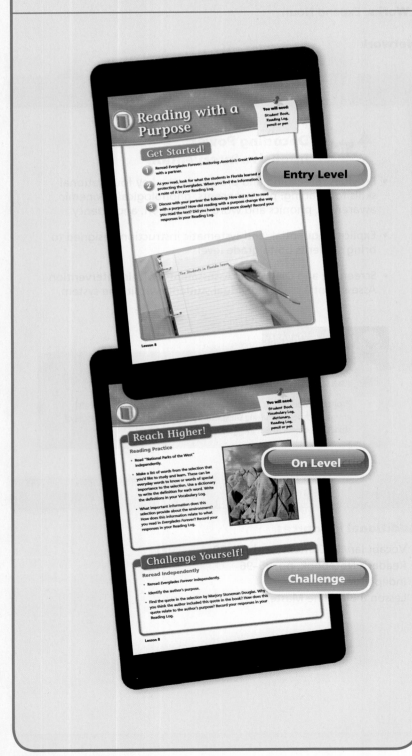

Reading with a Purpose

You will need: Student Book, Reading Log, pencil or pen

Get Started!

1. Reread *Everglades Forever: Restoring America's Great Wetland* with a partner.

2. As you read, look for what the students in Florida learned about protecting the Everglades. When you find the information, make a note of it in your Reading Log.

3. Discuss with your partner the following: How did it feel to read with a purpose? How did reading with a purpose change the way you read the text? Did you have to read more slowly? Record your responses in your Reading Log.

Entry Level

Lesson 8

Reach Higher!

Reading Practice
- Read "National Parks of the West" independently.
- Make a list of words from the selection that you'd like to study and learn. These can be everyday words to know or words of special importance to the selection. Use a dictionary to write the definition for each word. Write the definitions in your Vocabulary Log.
- What important information does this selection provide about the environment? How does this information relate to what you read in *Everglades Forever*? Record your responses in your Reading Log.

On Level

Challenge Yourself!

Reread Independently
- Reread *Everglades Forever* independently.
- Identify the author's purpose.
- Find the quote in the selection by Marjory Stoneman Douglas. Why do you think the author included this quote in the book? How does this quote relate to the author's purpose? Record your responses in your Reading Log.

Challenge

Lesson 8

Word Study

Materials
- dictionary
- pencil or pen
- paper

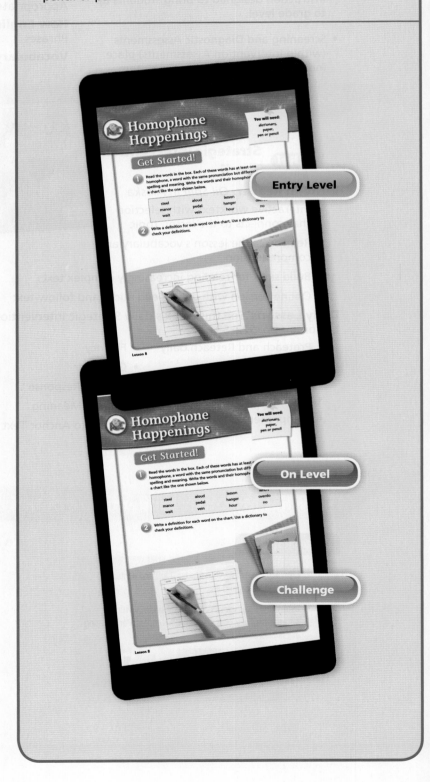

Homophone Happenings

You will need: dictionary, paper, pen or pencil

Get Started!

1. Read the words in the box. Each of these words has at least one homophone, a word with the same pronunciation but different spelling and meaning. Write the words and their homophones in a chart like the one shown below.

steel	aloud	lesson		
manor	pedal	hanger		no
wait	vein	hour		

2. Write a definition for each word on the chart. Use a dictionary to check your definitions.

Entry Level

Lesson 8

Homophone Happenings

You will need: dictionary, paper, pen or pencil

Get Started!

1. Read the words in the box. Each of these words has at least one homophone, a word with the same pronunciation but different spelling and meaning. Write the words and their homophones in a chart like the one shown below.

steel	aloud	lesson		
manor	pedal	hanger		overdo
wait	vein	hour		no

2. Write a definition for each word on the chart. Use a dictionary to check your definitions.

On Level

Challenge

Lesson 8

Assign Literacy Center activities during small group time. Each center contains three activities. Students who experience success with the entry-level activity move on to the on-level and challenge activities, as time permits.

Meaning Making

Language Development

Effective Expression

Content Knowledge

Foundational Skills

Think and Write

Materials

- library books
- encyclopedias
- paper
- pencil or pen

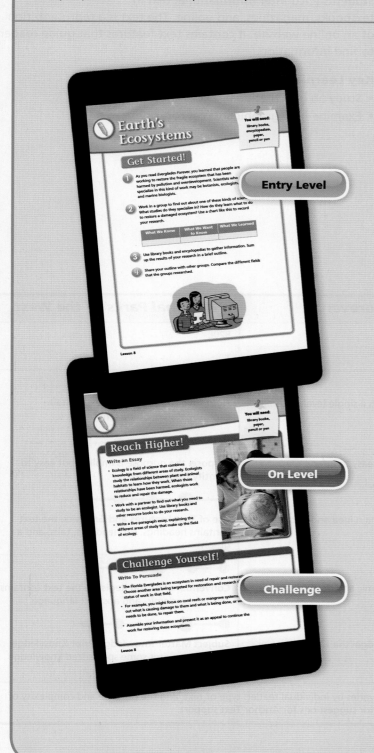

Entry Level

On Level

Challenge

Independent Reading

Opportunities for Social Interaction Discussing books with classmates gives students the opportunity to share what they know and to learn about other books. Schedule time for sharing opportunities like these:

- **Book Talks and Reviews** Students work in small groups to talk about their books. They show the book and give the title, the author, and a short summary. They tell what they liked or didn't like and whether they would recommend the book.

- **Book Sharing** Set up a basket or separate area in the library for sharing. Students place books they think others will like in this area.

- **Partner Reading** Partners read the same book. They alternate reading aloud sentences, paragraphs, or pages. Then they discuss what they have read.

- **Discussion Circles** Students who have read the same book or books on the same topic hold a discussion. You may want to appoint one group member to act as moderator to make sure that everyone has the opportunity to share.

See p. T190 for additional independent reading support.
ELA RL.5.10, RI.5.10

Prepare for Complex Texts

Anchor Text

Everglades Forever: Restoring America's Great Wetland
by Trish Marx

GENRE: Narrative Nonfiction

Why This Text?

Students regularly encounter narrative nonfiction in reading textbooks, magazines, and their own independent reading. This text explains some of the unique features of Florida's Everglades and efforts to preserve the ecosystem. It is written in an informal narrative style.

Key Learning Objectives
• Examine how an author conveys his or her purpose in a text.
• Explore how an author explains scientific ideas.
• Identify and learn domain-specific vocabulary.

Paired Selection

National Parks of the West

GENRE: Informational Text

Why This Text?

Students encounter informational text in textbooks, magazines, and online. The text is a representation of an online website. It contains text features that guide readers to find information.

Key Learning Objectives
• Study an informational text.
• Examine how graphic sources contribute to a text.

⚠ TEXT COMPLEXITY RUBRIC

		Everglades Forever	*National Parks of the West*
Quantitative Measures	Lexile	1190L	820L
	Guided Reading Level	W	T
Qualitative Measures	Meaning and Purpose	**Density and Complexity:** the text has a single level of complex meaning. **Purpose:** the purpose is implied but easy to infer.	**Figurative Language:** the text contains explicitly stated, literal language. **Purpose:** the purpose is implied but easy to identify from context.
	Text Structure	**Organization:** the organization of main idea and details is complex but largely explicit.	**Use of Text Features and Graphics:** the text contains headings, subheadings, tabs, and a graph.
	Language Features	**Vocabulary:** the text contains academic and domain-specific vocabulary.	**Conventionality and Register:** the text contains formal, academic, and abstract language.
	Knowledge Demands	**Intertextuality and Cultural Knowledge:** the text has one or two historical culture references.	**Subject Matter Knowledge/Prior Knowledge:** the text requires some specialized knowledge.
Reader/Task Considerations		Determine using the professional judgment of the teacher. This varies by individual reader, type of text, and the purpose and complexity of particular tasks. See **Reader and Task Considerations** on p. T173 for suggestions for Anchor Text support.	

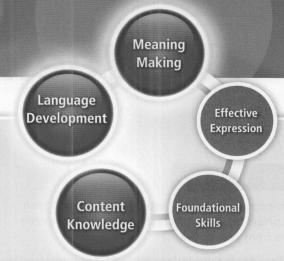

Meaning Making

Language Development

Effective Expression

Content Knowledge

Foundational Skills

TEXT X-RAY

ENGLISH LANGUAGE SUPPORT Use the Text X-Ray below to prepare for teaching the Anchor Text. Use it to plan, support, and scaffold instruction in order to help students understand the text's **key ideas** and **academic language features**.

Zoom In on Key Ideas
Students should understand these **key ideas** after reading *Everglades Forever*.

Key Idea | pp. 238–239
The Everglades is a vast wetland that covers the southern end of Florida. The Comprehensive Everglades Restoration Plan was started in 2000 to preserve the area and its water system. A fifth-grade class from nearby Homestead, Florida is taking a field trip to Everglades National Park, where Ranger Jim will be their tour guide.

Key Idea | pp. 240–241
Because it is the dry season, many types of animals converge on the deeper areas that still have water, because that is where they can feed. In addition to wet and dry seasons, the Everglades also has some areas that are wetter or drier than others due to their height, or elevation. The vegetation can be very different depending on just a few inches of elevation. The lowest-lying habitat is the mangrove swamp, an area where fresh water mixes with the salty water from the ocean.

Key Idea | pp. 244
Ranger Jim and Ms. Stone, the class teacher, talk with the students about the connections between all plant and animal life. The Miccosukee call this the "circle of life." Without the Everglades Restoration Plan to protect the area from the effects of development, would all of the interesting plants and animals here be able to survive?

Key Idea | pp. 246–249
At the end of their field trip, the students visit a finger glade, a small part of the sawgrass prairie that will remain dry and hard until the next wet season. The children are allowed to wander and explore the wide-open area as they wish. The students know that they play a part in preserving and protecting the Everglades.

Zoom In on Academic Language
Guide students at different proficiencies and skill levels to understand the structure and language of this text.

Focus: Text Level | pp. 238–249
Remind students that **graphic aids,** such as maps and photographs, can be very helpful in gaining a better understanding of the text. Have them study the map of South Florida on p. 238. Point out that Miami is a large city; then, guide students to use the color-coded map legend. This indicates that Everglades National Park itself is massive, and the overall conservation areas are enormous.

Focus: Word Level | pp. 239–240
Students may not be familiar with many of the animal or plant names in this text. While some are important to comprehension, others can be understood at a more general level, such as knowing that the anhinga, osprey, and cormorant are birds.

Focus: Sentence Level | p. 241
Support English learners and others in analyzing the **cause-and-effect structure** of the paragraph on p. 241. Guide them through the description of plants and animals that are specially adapted to life in a mangrove swamp. In the middle of the paragraph, read aloud, "If the brackish water in mangrove swamps changes, these animals cannot survive." Discuss with students the cause and the effect mentioned in this sentence.

Content and Language Instruction Make note of additional **content knowledge** and **language features** students may find challenging in this text.

Weekly Planner

my SmartPlanner

Auto-populates the suggested five-day lesson plan and offers flexibility to create and save customized plans from year to year.

See **Standards Correlations** on p. C1. In your eBook, click the Standards button in the left panel to view descriptions of the standards on the page.

Whole Group

Oral Language
Listening
Comprehension

Vocabulary
Text-Based Comprehension
- Skills and Strategies
- Craft and Structure

Research and Media Literacy

Foundational Skills
- Fluency
- Decoding

Whole Group Language Arts

Spelling
Grammar
Writing

Small Group

Suggestions for Small Groups (See pp. T216–T217.)

DAY 1

Materials
- ELL Blackline Masters 8.2, 8.3
- Graphic Organizer 7
- Lesson 8 Language Support Card
- Literacy and Language Guide p. 70
- Projectables 8.1, 8.4, 8.7
- Reader's Notebook pp. 88, 91
- Strategy Projectables S1–S8
- Student Book pp. 232–249
- Vocabulary in Context Cards 71–80

Teacher Read Aloud
"Attack of the Alien Species," T166–T167

☑ **Introduce Vocabulary**
Vocabulary in Context, T168–T169
☑ **Read and Comprehend,** T170–T171
FIRST READ Think Through the Text
Read the Anchor Text: "Everglades Forever," T172–T185

☑ **Fluency**
Model Adjust Rate to Purpose, T166

☑ **Spelling**
Homophones: Pretest, T202
☑ **Grammar**
Daily Proofreading Practice, T204
Teach Using *and, but,* and *or,* T204
☑ **Informative Writing: Cause-and-Effect Essay**
Analyze the Model, T208

DAY 2

Materials
- Graphic Organizer 7
- Interactive Lessons: Rules for a Good Discussion, Writing to Sources
- Literacy and Language Guide p. 70
- Projectables 8.2, 8.5
- Reader's Notebook pp. 89, 92, 96
- Student Book pp. 236–253

Turn and Talk, T188

SECOND READ
☑ **Dig Deeper: How to Analyze the Text,** T186–T187
- Author's Purpose
- Explain Scientific Ideas
- Domain-Specific Vocabulary
- Modifying to Add Details
Analyze the Text
Reread the Anchor Text: "Everglades Forever," T177, T183, T185
☑ **Your Turn,** T188–T189

☑ **Fluency**
Teach Adjust Rate to Purpose, T200
Practice Adjust Rate to Purpose, T179

☑ **Spelling**
Homophones: Word Sort, T202
☑ **Grammar**
Daily Proofreading Practice, T205
Teach Using *and, but,* and *or* to Combine Sentences and Ideas, T205
☑ **Informative Writing: Cause-and-Effect Essay**
Focus Trait: Ideas, T209

DAY 3

Materials
- Instructional Routine 7
- Literacy and Language Guide pp. 71, 130–131
- Projectables 8.6, 8.8
- Reading Log Blackline Master
- Reader's Notebook pp. 85–86, 93
- Student Book pp. 236–249

Classroom Conversation, T191

Independent Reading
- Reader's Guide: "Everglades Forever"
- Self-Selected Reading
Apply Vocabulary Knowledge, T191

☑ **Fluency**
Practice Adjust Rate to Purpose, T200
☑ **Decoding**
Homophones, T201

☑ **Spelling**
Homophones: Word Families, T203
☑ **Grammar**
Daily Proofreading Practice, T205
Teach Using Subordinating Conjunctions, T205
☑ **Informative Writing:
Cause-and-Effect Essay**
Prewrite, T209

DAY 4

Materials
- Interactive Whiteboard Lesson: Prefixes *en-*, *re-*, *pre-*, *pro-*
- Literacy and Language Guide p. 130–131
- Projectable 8.3
- Reader's Notebook pp. 87, 90, 94
- Student Book pp. 254–257

Classroom Conversation, T192

Connect to the Topic
- Read Informational Text: "National Parks of the West," T192
- Think Through the Text, T194
☑ **Compare Texts,** T195
☑ **Vocabulary Strategies**
Prefixes *en-*, *re-*, *pre-*, *pro-*, T196–T197

☑ **Fluency**
Practice Adjust Rate to Purpose, T193

☑ **Spelling**
Homophones: Connect to Writing, T203
☑ **Grammar**
Daily Proofreading Practice, T206
Review Conjunctions, T206
☑ **Informative Writing:
Cause-and-Effect Essay**
Draft, T210

DAY 5

Materials
- Cold Reads
- Graphic Organizer 6
- Interactive Lessons: Participate in Collaborative Conversations, Writing Informative Texts: Use Facts and Examples
- Interactive Whiteboard Lesson: Compound Sentences
- Projectable 8.9
- Proofreading Checklist Blackline Master
- Reader's Notebook p. 35
- Student Book pp. 106–109
- Writing Rubric Blackline Master

Speaking and Listening, T199

Extend the Topic: Conservation
- Domain-Specific Vocabulary, T198
- Optional Second Read: "National Parks of the West," T192

☑ **Fluency**
Progress Monitoring, T213

☑ **Spelling**
Homophones: Assess, T203
☑ **Grammar**
Daily Proofreading Practice, T206
Connect Grammar to Writing, T206–T207
☑ **Informative Writing:
Cause-and-Effect Essay**
Revise for Ideas, T210

 Tier II Intervention provides thirty minutes of additional daily practice with key parts of the core instruction. See pp. S22–S31.

Teacher Read Aloud

▶ **SHARE OBJECTIVES**
- Listen to fluent reading.
- Respond to a written text read aloud using domain-specific words. LANGUAGE
- Listen for the evidence presented to support a speaker's points.

ENGLISH LANGUAGE SUPPORT
Use Visuals

All Proficiencies To assist students with accessing the content and topic of the Teacher Read Aloud, discuss the High-Utility Words on the Lesson 8 Language Support Card ☐.

☑ **PREVIEW**
Target Vocabulary

endangered threatened; for plants and animals, threatened with extinction

responsibility a duty or job

conserving using only what you need of something and protecting it; not wasting something

regulate to control

unique unusual and special in some way

attracted drew attention and captured interest

adapted changed to survive or fit into new conditions

vegetation plants found in a particular area

guardians people who protect or take care of others

restore to return something to its original state

Model Fluency

Adjust Rate to Purpose Explain that good readers adjust their rate depending on their purpose for reading. They may read slowly when reading difficult text or read more quickly when reading for enjoyment.

- Display Projectable 8.1 ☐. As you read the passage, adjust your rate to model reading for different purposes.
- Demonstrate how to slow your reading speed for unfamiliar words and ideas or to emphasize certain parts of the text.
- Reread the passage with students. Adjust rate appropriately as you read.
  ELA RF.5.4a, RF.5.4b

Listening Comprehension

Read aloud the passage, using an appropriate rate. Then ask the following questions.

1 *What is the author trying to make readers understand about the Everglades? The Everglades is under attack from human activity and alien species.* **AUTHOR'S PURPOSE**

2 *What example does the author provide to convince readers that the ecosystem is out of balance in the Everglades? the Burmese python and the alligator competing for food* **CITE TEXT EVIDENCE**

3 *In one sentence, summarize how alien species harm the native species in a habitat like the Everglades. They compete for resources such as food and water, making it more difficult for the native species to survive.* **SUMMARIZE** **ELA** SL.5.2

💬 Classroom Collaboration

Ask students which example of an alien species they found most interesting or memorable and why. Have them cite domain-specific words that made these parts memorable. Then ask what else the author could have done to make the selection memorable to readers. *Sample answer: The author could have given more examples of native species struggling to survive.*
ELD ELD.PI.5.1, ELD.PI.5.5

ENGLISH LANGUAGE SUPPORT
Read Aloud—Second Read Project the Target Vocabulary Preview. Introduce each word to students. Use visuals, gestures, or yes/no questions to help them understand the meaning of each word. Have students listen to the Read Aloud again and signal when they hear a Target Vocabulary Word. **ELD** ELD.PI.5.5

Attack of the Alien Species

1 Florida's Everglades is under attack. Human activity has altered the landscape. Waterways have been drained and rerouted to pave the way for development. As their habitat shrinks, many plants and animals have become **endangered.** People who have the **responsibility** of **conserving** this natural resource are blaming a surprising element: the invasion of alien species.

No—space creatures have not landed in the Sunshine State. When wildlife experts talk about "alien species," they mean plants and animals that are not native to a particular habitat. Why is this a problem? Consider what happens in an ecosystem like the Everglades. Here, thousands of plants and animals coexist in harmony, each with its own role to perform. Birds and frogs thin out insect populations. Bees pollinate plants, helping replenish food supplies. One species cannot crowd others out, because checks and balances **regulate** this **unique** arrangement. Nonnative, or exotic, species upset this balance, destroying native species and eventually the habitat itself.

A few years ago, tourists visiting Everglades National Park watched as a huge Burmese python wrapped itself around an alligator. The two animals battled for more than 24 hours—until the snake broke free and slithered off into the marsh.

2 These snakes, which can grow to a length of more than 20 feet, live in Southeast Asia. So how did they get here? Burmese pythons are imported as pets. People may be **attracted** to the cute little hatchlings. But often, many owners dump them when they get too big. In the Everglades, pythons now compete for food with top predators such as the alligator. They were not **adapted** to live in this habitat when they first arrived, but they learned quickly how to survive here. Other invaders have done the same.

Large Cuban tree frogs are eating smaller native frogs. Wild hogs are pigging out on native plants, damaging landscapes as they root up **vegetation.** However, the most harmful exotic species here may be a plant called the melaleuca, or "paper tree." People brought this tree from Australia to Florida to plant in private yards. Winds quickly blow its seeds out to the wild. Here, they become dangerous as they grow close together, **3** soaking up almost five times more water than native trees. In the Everglades, dense areas of melaleuca shade out other plants and dry out the soil.

Many biologists believe that the best we can do is to contain these exotic species. Some national park **guardians** are asking for volunteers to help clear away invasive species. They also urge people to take these steps:

- Never release your pets into the wild.
- Avoid planting exotic species in your own garden.
- Urge your legislators to vote for conservation methods that can help **restore** the Everglades.

Introduce Vocabulary

Vocabulary in Context

▶ **SHARE OBJECTIVE**

- Acquire and use vocabulary.
- Use knowledge of linguistic context to determine the meaning of unknown words. LANGUAGE

Teach

Display and discuss the Vocabulary in Context Cards ⬀, using the routine below. Direct students to use **Student Book pp. 232–233.**

1 **Read and pronounce the word.** Read the word once alone and then together.

2 **Explain the word.** Read aloud the explanation under *What Does It Mean?*

ENGLISH LANGUAGE SUPPORT Review these cognates with Spanish-speaking students.

- *adaptar (adapted)*
- *conservar (conserving)*
- *guardas (guardians)*
- *responsabilidad (responsibility)*
- *único (unique)*
- *vegetación (vegetation)*

3 **Discuss vocabulary in context.** Together, read aloud the sentence on the front of the card. Help students explain and use the word in new sentences.

4 **Engage with the word.** Ask the *Think About It* question and discuss it with students.

Apply

Give partners or small groups one or two **Vocabulary in Context Cards.**

- Help students complete the *Talk It Over* activity on the back of each card.
- Have students complete the activities for all cards during the week.

Q **Language Detective** Tell pairs to choose two Vocabulary words, and have them write a sentence that uses both words. Have each pair read aloud their sentences to the class.
ELA L.5.4a, L.5.6 **ELD** ELD.PI.5.12a

Q LANGUAGE DETECTIVE

Talk About the Writer's Words
Work with a partner. Choose two Vocabulary words. Use them in the same sentence. Share your sentences with the class.

1 **conserving**
Saving, or conserving, natural habitats is a main goal of our national park system.

2 **restore**
Park workers restore harmed habitats by bringing them back to their original state.

3 **regulate**
Managers regulate, or control, access to an area. Fewer people cause less harm.

DUNES ARE FRAGILE KEEP OFF!

4 **vegetation**
Many animals survive by feeding on the vegetation, or plant life, in a habitat.

232 **ELA** L.5.4a, L.5.6 **ELD** ELD.PI.5.12a

ENGLISH LANGUAGE SUPPORT

Comprehensible Input

Emerging Say each Vocabulary word, and have students repeat it. Provide simple explanations of *attracted, unique,* and *regulate,* and help students use them in simple sentences. Provide sentence frames, such as the following, to help students use the words. *You can find vegetation in a garden or park.*
ELD ELD.PI.5.12a

Expanding Have partners ask and answer questions about each Vocabulary word. For example, *What is one responsibility of a pet owner?*
ELD ELD.PI.5.1, ELD.PI.5.12a

Bridging Ask students questions to confirm their understanding. For example, *I am conserving electricity at home. Why might I do this?*
ELD ELD.PI.5.1, ELD.PI.5.12a

▶ Study each Context Card.

▶ Use a thesaurus to find an alternate word for each Vocabulary word.

⑤ endangered

Damaged habitats put endangered animals at risk of dying out.

⑥ responsibility

Humans have a duty, or responsibility, to preserve and protect wild habitats.

⑦ attracted

Birds are attracted, or drawn to, habitats that can hide their nests from predators.

⑧ adapted

Gills are specially adapted features that let fish breathe in the water.

⑨ unique

Many habitats support unique plants and wildlife that are not found elsewhere.

⑩ guardians

One day some of these students may become guardians, or caretakers, of wild habitats.

233

FORMATIVE ASSESSMENT △ RtI

Are students able to understand and use Target Vocabulary words?

IF...	THEN...
students **struggle**,	▶ use **Vocabulary in Context Cards** and differentiate the **Vocabulary Reader,** *Mangrove Swamp,* for Struggling Readers, p. T218.
students are **on target**,	▶ use **Vocabulary in Context Cards** and differentiate the **Vocabulary Reader,** *Mangrove Swamp,* for On-Level Readers, p. T218.
students **excel**,	▶ differentiate the **Vocabulary Reader,** *Mangrove Swamp,* for Advanced Readers, p. T219.

SMALL GROUP Options

Vocabulary Reader, pp. T218–T219
Scaffold instruction to the English Learner's proficiency level.

ENGLISH LANGUAGE SUPPORT

Read and Write Together

Emerging/Expanding

Read Together Display ELL8.2 in Grab-and-Go™ Resources. Read aloud the title and have students repeat. Then, have students look at the images on the page and have them predict what they think the text will be about.

• As you read the text aloud, display Vocabulary in Context Cards for *conserving,* *responsibility,* and *endangered.* Then, have students read the text chorally with you.

• Tell students that habitats are places where animals live. Ask: *What would happen if a*

habitat was destroyed? The animals in it would be endangered. Allow students to include language from **ELL.8.2.**

Write Together Display sentence frames such as the following and have partners use them to write complete sentences.

1. It is our *responsibility* to conserve wetlands and forests.

2. If the vegetation in a forest dies, the animals in it will be *endangered*.

ELD ELD.PI.5.2, ELD.PI.5.4, ELD.PI.5.12a

Read and Comprehend

Read and Comprehend

☑ **TARGET SKILL**

Author's Purpose Every author has a specific reason, or **purpose**, for writing. The author of "Everglades Forever" writes about the Everglades region. As you read the selection, think about whether the author's purpose is to entertain, to inform, to describe, or to persuade. Use the graphic organizer shown below to record facts and other details that help you determine the author's purpose.

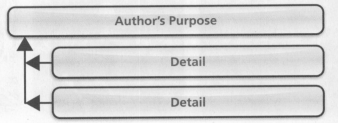

☑ **TARGET STRATEGY**

Analyze/Evaluate As you read "Everglades Forever," **analyze** the facts and other text evidence the author presents to support her points. **Evaluate** this evidence by asking yourself questions such as *Does this fact really support the author's ideas? Do I feel convinced by her argument? Why or why not?*

► **SHARE OBJECTIVES**

- Explain how an author uses reasons and evidence to support points.
- Quote accurately to support analysis and inferences.
- Engage effectively in collaborative discussion. LANGUAGE

☑ **TARGET SKILL**

Author's Purpose

- Read the top section of **Student Book p. 234** with students.

- Tell students that authors have a specific purpose, or reason, for writing. For example, they may write to inform, to entertain, to describe, or to persuade.

- Explain that in this selection, the author is writing about the Everglades region.

- Draw students' attention to the graphic organizer on **Student Book p. 234**. Tell them that using a graphic organizer like this one will help them determine the author's purpose and identify text evidence that supports it.

- Explain that students should record the author's purpose in the top box. Then, as they read, they should write down the facts, examples, descriptions, and other details that the author uses to convince readers to agree with her main points. **ELA** RI.5.1, RI.5.8

ENGLISH LANGUAGE SUPPORT Scaffold Anchor Text Before reading the selection, distribute ELL8.3 in Grab-and-Go™ Resources ⬈.

Review Author's Purpose Reread aloud the last paragraph.

- Tell students that in this paragraph, we learn the author's purpose, or what the author wants to persuade us to do. The author also gives reasons, or explanations, why the purpose is important.

Guided Practice Display an Idea-Support Map. During reading, complete the map with students.

- Have students look for details that support the author's purpose. **ELD** ELD.PI.5.6a

ENGLISH LANGUAGE SUPPORT

Use Sentence Frames

Emerging Display this sentence frame: *If my coach won't let me play _____, I will have to persuade him by _____.* Guide students to complete the sentence frame orally.	**Expanding** Have students write sentence frames describing a time when they convinced someone to change their mind about something. Have partners trade papers and complete each sentence frame.	**Bridging** Have students write a persuasive paragraph about a local issue of concern to them. **ELD** ELD.PI.5.10a

PREVIEW THE TOPIC

Conservation

The term *conservation* refers to any activity that helps protect wildlife and natural resources, such as water and soil. Conservation includes what people can do every day, such as walking instead of driving, or turning down the thermostat. It also includes large projects conducted by experts, such as reintroducing a species of animal to a particular habitat.

In "Everglades Forever," the author goes along on a field trip in southern Florida to learn about conserving the Everglades. By sharing the students' discoveries, the author also shows readers how they can help and why their efforts are necessary.

Think | Write | Pair | Share

What can people do to help protect the environment? Write a paragraph that explains your answer. Then share your writing with a partner. Discuss each other's ideas. Ask any questions you have and answer any questions your partner has.

235

COMPREHENSION STRATEGIES

Use the following strategies flexibly as you read with students by modeling how they can be used to improve comprehension. See scaffolded support for the strategy shown in boldface during this week's reading.

- **Monitor/Clarify**
- **Visualize**
- **Summarize**
- **Analyze/Evaluate**
- **Infer/Predict**
- **Question**

Use the Strategy Projectables S1–S8 ⤴, for additional support.

✓ TARGET STRATEGY

Analyze/Evaluate

- Read the bottom section of **Student Book p. 234** with students. Tell them that when they **analyze**, they closely examine the text and the details the author provides, and when they **evaluate**, they judge how well the author presents ideas.

- Explain that evaluating the text might include asking questions as they read.

- Tell students that you will demonstrate how to use the strategy when you read "Everglades Forever" together.

PREVIEW THE TOPIC

Conservation

- Tell students that today they will begin reading "Everglades Forever."

- Read the information at the top of **Student Book p. 235** with students.

- Point out that the Everglades is a wetlands in southern Florida that is home to many different species of plants and animals.

- Then, write on the board the terms *habitat* and *restoration*. Have students explain their understanding of these terms, using the information in the text and their own experiences.

- Ask students to consider how these terms might apply to the topic of conservation and to the photograph on **Student Book pp. 234–235**. **ELA** RI.5.3

Think-Write-Pair-Share

- Before students begin writing, provide sentence frames to get them started such as, *You can help your local environment by ____. You can help clean your community by____.*

- Have partners discuss any new ideas they learned from their partner. Encourage students to ask their partner questions. **ELA** W.5.10, SL.5.1c **ELD** ELD.PI.5.1

ENGLISH LANGUAGE SUPPORT Access Prior Knowledge: All Proficiencies Use the image on Lesson 8 Language Support Card ⤴ to review the selection topic with students. Show the completed web again and help students summarize its content.

Read and Comprehend (SB p. 235) • **T171**

FIRST READ

Read the Anchor Text

☑ **GENRE**

Narrative Nonfiction

- Read the genre information on **Student Book p. 236** with students.

- Preview the selection with students, and model identifying characteristics of narrative nonfiction.

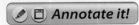 **Think Aloud** *The title and photographs make me think this selection will present facts about the Everglades. The text is nonfiction that tells a story.*

- As you preview, ask students to identify other features of narrative nonfiction.

ENGLISH LANGUAGE SUPPORT Access Prior Knowledge: All Proficiencies Write the following statements on the board.
1. Narrative nonfiction includes facts.
2. Narrative nonfiction is more entertaining than informational text.
3. Everyone can help conserve the environment.
4. It is easy to respect nature.
Have pairs take turns reading a statement to each other and sharing their opinions. Provide these frames for support: *The statement says _____. I agree/disagree because _____. What do you think?* Have students record their opinions to refer to later. During reading, have students check their opinions and note whether they have changed.
ELA RI.5.10 **ELD** ELD.PI.5.6a

Lesson 8

ANCHOR TEXT

EVERGLADES FOREVER

☑ **GENRE**

Narrative nonfiction tells about people, things, events, and places that are real. As you read, look for:
▶ factual information that tells a story
▶ features such as photographs and captions

236   **ELA** RI.5.3, RI.5.8, RI.5.10, RF.5.4a, RF.5.4b
ELD ELD.PI.5.6a

MEET THE AUTHOR

Trish Marx

Trish Marx travels to the people and places she writes about to get firsthand information for her nonfiction books. For *Everglades Forever*, she spent time studying and going on field trips with Ms. Jacquelyn Stone's fifth-grade class at Avocado Elementary School in Homestead, Florida.

MEET THE PHOTOGRAPHER

Cindy Karp

Cindy Karp has worked with Trish Marx on several books for children. She is also a photojournalist whose pictures have appeared in national magazines and newspapers. Karp is a resident of Miami, Florida, and has spent many days exploring the Everglades.

Scaffold Close Reading

Strategies for Annotation	Think Through the Text	Analyze the Text	Independent Reading
	FIRST READ	**SECOND READ**	
Annotate it! As you read the selection with students, look for ✎ 🗐 *Annotate it!* . It indicates opportunities for students to annotate the text independently.	Develop comprehension through • Guided Questioning • Target Strategy: Analyze/Evaluate • Vocabulary in Context	Support analyzing short sections of text: • Author's Purpose • Explain Scientific Ideas • Domain-Specific Vocabulary • Modifying to Add Details Use directed note-taking by working with students to complete Graphic Organizer 7 🗐 during reading.	• Students analyze the text independently, using the Reader's Guide on pp. 85–86 of the Reader's Notebook 🗐. (See p. T190 for instructional support.) • Students read independently in a self-selected trade book.

EVERGLADES FOREVER

RESTORING AMERICA'S GREAT WETLAND

by Trish Marx • photographs by Cindy Karp

237

ESSENTIAL QUESTION

What reasons do people have for protecting the environment?

READER AND TASK CONSIDERATIONS

Determine the level of additional support your students will need to read and comprehend "Everglades Forever" successfully.

READERS

- **Motivate** Ask students who enjoy reading about conservation or science texts to share what they hope to learn from the selection.
- **Talk It Over** Use Lesson 8 Language Support Card ⬈ for a discussion about the environment.
- **Access Knowledge and Experiences** Ask students to make connections between information in "Everglades Forever" and what they might learn in a science lesson on conservation and share with a partner.

TASKS

- **Increase Scaffolding** Guide students to identify unknown, domain-specific vocabulary in the text and to use context clues or reference sources to determine meaning.
- **Foster Independence** Have small groups of motivated readers read the text together. Tell them to think through the text by pausing to ask questions of themselves and each other to understand the text and its structure.

ESSENTIAL QUESTION

Read aloud the **Essential Question** on **Student Book p. 237**: *What reasons do people have for protecting the environment?* Then tell students to think about this question as they read "Everglades Forever."

Predictive Writing

- Explain that students will write a paragraph to explain what they expect "Everglades Forever" to be about. Ask them to think about how the Essential Question relates to what they noticed while previewing the selection or what they already know from their own experiences or past readings.

- Guide students to think about the genre of the selection to help them write.

Set Purpose

- Tell students that good readers set a purpose for reading, based on their preview of the selection, what they know about the genre, and what they want to learn from the selection.

- Model setting a reading purpose.

  Think Aloud *I know that narrative nonfiction gives real information in the form of a story. I'm curious about how a place can have a story to be told. One purpose for reading might be to learn why the Everglades may need saving.*

- Have students set their own purpose for reading. Ask several students to share their purpose for reading. **ELA** RF.5.4a

ENGLISH LANGUAGE SUPPORT Preteach Academic English: Emerging/Expanding Guide students to complete the Academic English activities on Language Support Card 8.

Think Through the Text

Cite Text Evidence

1 *What evidence in the text suggests that the author has a particular viewpoint about the Everglades? She describes the Everglades as an "amazing place."* **ELA** RI.5.1

ENGLISH LANGUAGE SUPPORT Ask this question another way. *How does the author describe the Everglades? What does this description reveal about her feelings toward the Everglades?*

2 *How does the landscape near the Everglades contrast with the landscape near Avocado School? The landscape near the school is full of houses and shopping centers, while the land near the Everglades is flat and grassy with nothing to block the view of the horizon.*

3 *Why are there so many birds at the beginning of the trail? There are many birds because there is a slough at the beginning of the trail that never dries up. The birds catch fish in the slough.* **ELA** RI.5.3 **ELD** ELD.PI.5.6a

In Homestead, Florida, the students in Ms. Stone's fifth-grade class have been learning about the Everglades, a vast natural wetland located on the southern tip of Florida. Since 2000, the Comprehensive Everglades Restoration Plan has helped to preserve this wetland and its natural water system. Now all of Ms. Stone's students are visiting the Everglades to experience this amazing place and learn what they can do to preserve it. The map on the right shows where Everglades National Park is located in Florida and the areas Ms. Stone's class explored.

On the morning of the field trip, the bus traveled west from Avocado School. The students saw the landscape change from houses and shopping centers to a flat, grassy prairie that met the horizon miles away. Soon they arrived at the Royal Palm Visitor Center, part of Everglades National Park.

South Florida

Lake Okeechobee
Miami
Gulf of Mexico
Pinelands Homestead
Anhinga Trail
Florida Bay ATLANTIC OCEAN
Key West
0   25   50 Miles
0   25   50 Kilometers

Legend
Everglades Agricultural Area
Water Conservation Area
Big Cypress National Preserve
Everglades National Park
■ Visited by Ms. Stone's Class

238

Comprehensible Input

Emerging Using the photographs, preview the selection with students. Help them name objects they recognize.

Expanding While reading the first paragraph, pause to explain these words: *vast, preserve,* and *explored.* Then, repeat the explanations as students match them to the appropriate words.

Bridging Have students read pp. 238–239. Then, have them restate ideas from the text and ask clarifying questions.

Overlooking sawgrass on Anhinga Trail

Ms. Stone had arranged for the class to meet Ranger Jim at the visitor center. From there the ranger led them to the start of the Anhinga Trail, a boardwalk circling into a slough (sloo). It was the dry season, which lasts from December through April, so the water levels were low. But there is a deep part of the slough at the beginning of the trail that never dries up. Around the edge of this part, large waterbirds called Anhingas sunned their wings. Anhingas hold out their wings to thermoregulate (thur moh REHG yuh layt), or regulate their body temperature, by soaking up the sun's energy to keep their bodies warm. An Osprey, a fish-eating hawk, waited in a tree for a flash of fish in the water. In the distance an egret stood in the sawgrass, and a flock of endangered wood storks flew overhead. **3**

239

⌐> **DOMAIN: Life Science**

LESSON TOPIC: Conservation

Cross-Curricular Connection Explain that food chains depict the flow of energy in the form of food through an ecosystem and that every ecosystem contains several food chains. Point out that wetlands provide an important habitat for different species of plants and animals and function as a nursery for many kinds of fish. Discuss the impact that the  disappearance of wetland areas would have on the food chain. *Plants and animals that depend on the wetlands would disappear. For example, there would be no fish for birds like the osprey to eat.* Guide students to understand that the disappearance of an ecosystem causes problems in the food chain and can even lead to the extinction of some plants and animals.

FIRST READ

Think Through the Text

Cite
Text Evidence

4 *Why might the author have chosen a park ranger to provide much of the narrative in this section of the text? Sample answer: The park ranger provides an expert's point of view and credible support for the author's points.*
ELA RI.5.8 **ELD** ELD.PI.5.6a

5 *What factors create different habitats within the Everglades? Both seasonal changes and changes in elevation affect how wet the soil is. In turn, the different moisture levels in the soil create unique habitats.* **ELA** RI.5.3 **ELD** ELD.PI.5.6a

6 *What clues in the text around the word* adapted *help you understand what it means?* "specially", "so they can live"
ELA RI.5.4, L.5.6 **ELD** ELD.PI.5.6b

ENGLISH LANGUAGE SUPPORT Tell students that the word *adapted* has a cognate in Spanish: *adaptado*. Remind students to look for cognates as they read to help them figure out the meanings of key words.

7 *Why does the author explain that the Restoration Plan regulates the amount of freshwater flowing during each season? Sample answer: The author wants readers to understand the value of the regulation. It helps to preserve the habitat by maintaining the level of brackish water, which is important for mangrove trees and the survival of many marine animals.* **ELA** RI.5.3

Great Blue Heron feeding on fish

"Right now you'll see many animals close together around the deeper water areas," said Ranger Jim. Fish and smaller water animals had migrated to these deep water areas to search for food. Wading birds, alligators, Ospreys, and Cormorants (large diving birds with bright green eyes) followed to feed on the fish and smaller animals. Alligators also use their tails, snouts, and feet to dig deep holes, which fill with water. These holes are places for alligators to cool off while they wait for a meal of the small animals that are attracted to the water-filled holes. During the wet season, which lasts from May through November, water covers much of the land. Then the animals spread out because the water that carries their food is spread out. **4**

The Everglades has wet and dry seasons, but it also has wetter and drier areas caused by how high the land is above the water level. Even a few inches of elevation can make a difference in how wet or dry the soil remains throughout the year. These differences in moisture help create unique habitats, each with its own special set of plants and animals. **5**

Mangrove trees

240

ENGLISH LANGUAGE SUPPORT

How English Works: Interpretive

Text Cohesion As students read this selection, have them look for places where the author refers the reader back in the text. Explain to students that sometimes an author needs a way to make readers connect to, or refer to, a part of the text that they have already read. For example, read aloud the second paragraph on **Student Book p. 240** while students follow along.

• Help students identify how the author refers the reader back in the text to the Everglades. *Sample answers: The author uses the pronoun* it.

• Tell students to identify other places in the text where the author uses pronouns to refer to nouns.

• Have students turn to a partner and discuss the ways they might use pronouns to refer the reader back in texts that they write.

• Collect samples from volunteers and write them on the board. **ELD** ELD. PII.5.2a

One of the lowest Everglades habitats is the mangrove swamp, which is named for the mangrove trees that line the islands and bays leading into the ocean. Fresh rainwater flows toward these areas and mixes with the salty ocean water, making the water in mangrove swamps brackish. The mangrove trees have specially adapted roots and leaves so they can live in this salty, muddy water. The swamps also serve as nurseries for shrimp, bonefish, and other marine animals that need a protected place to grow before they head to the ocean. If the brackish water in mangrove swamps changes, these animals cannot survive. Since two goals of the Restoration Plan are to allow Everglades water to flow more naturally to the ocean and to regulate the amount of freshwater flowing during each season, animals of the mangrove swamps—including pelicans, sea turtles, and the endangered American crocodiles and manatees—will be helped to survive. **7**

6

ANALYZE THE TEXT

Domain-Specific Vocabulary What domain-specific words does the author use on these two pages? How do these words help deepen your knowledge of the topic?

241

Domain-Specific Vocabulary   *Analyze the Text*

- Read the Analyze the Text box on **Student Book p. 241** with students.

- Tell students that authors of informational text often use domain-specific vocabulary to explain their topics. Point out that these precise and accurate terms help authors convey information effectively; at the same time, readers learn vocabulary associated with the particular subject area.

- Ask students to list some of the domain-specific terms that they see on pp. 240–241. *migrated, elevation, habitats, brackish, adapted* As a class, use the context of the words to define each. Then, have students use the words in original sentences.

- Ask students how these words and the other precise vocabulary used by the author help to deepen their knowledge of the topic. *These words have very specific meanings that cannot be misunderstood. They belong to the context of science; therefore, when they are used, readers know what is being discussed.*
  ELA RI.5.4, L.5.6 **ELD** ELD.PI.5.6b

  🖊️ 🖥️ *Annotate it!* Have students highlight domain-specific words and their context clues in the text.

STANDARD ENGLISH LEARNERS Pronunciation Some students may need help mastering Standard English pronunciations when reading aloud or speaking in a more formal register. Students may have trouble voicing /l/ in words, such as *people, myself,* and *help.* They may omit the /l/ sound and voice the words as *peopuh, myse'f,* and *he'p.* Write on the board and read aloud the last sentence on **Student Book p. 241,** emphasizing the /l/ sound in *animals, crocodiles,* and *turtles.* Have students echo your reading several times.

FIRST READ

Think Through the Text

Cite Text Evidence

8 *In the first paragraph, the author describes the various habitats the students saw as they walked the trail. What main idea does the author want to convey through these details? The Everglades is unique because of the number of varied habitats it supports. What main idea, developed in paragraph 3, is supported by the photograph on p. 243? The main idea is that the Pinelands is a completely different habitat from the Anhinga Trail. The photograph helps to illustrate these differences.* **ELA** RI.5.2, RI.5.8 **ELD** ELD.PI.5.6a

ENGLISH LANGUAGE SUPPORT Provide these sentence frames to support understanding. *The main idea the author wants to convey is _____. The photograph on p. 243 supports the main idea that _____.*

☑ TARGET STRATEGY

Analyze/Evaluate

Reread aloud the last paragraph on **Student Book p. 242**. Then model the strategy:

> **Think Aloud** *I ask myself if the author's descriptions of the plant and animal life support her argument that the Everglades should be protected. I reread the author's descriptions of snails under tree bark and spiders weaving webs. Her descriptions are interesting and make the wildlife seem important and worth saving.*

Tell students to practice using the Analyze/Evaluate strategy as they continue reading.
ELA RI.5.3, RI.5.8 **ELD** ELD.PI.5.6a

The class was too far from the ocean to see a mangrove swamp, but as they walked the Anhinga Trail, the students saw several of the Everglades habitats. The slough filled with slow-moving water stretched in the distance. A sawgrass prairie covered the shallow parts of the slough, and in the distance the rounded domes of hardwood hammocks rose above the surface of the water.

As the students came to the end of the Anhinga Trail, Ranger Jim pointed out a gumbo limbo tree. "It's also called a tourist tree," he said, "because the bark of the tree peels off, just like the skin of sunburned tourists." Then he directed the students back to the bus for a short ride to a pine forest called the Pinelands.

Ranger Jim took the class on a hike through the Pinelands, one of the driest habitats in the Everglades. The sunlight filtered through the trees. Everything was quieter than on the Anhinga Trail. The floor of the Pinelands is covered with cabbage palms, marlberry bushes, blue porter flowers, and other vegetation that help absorb sounds from the outside world. **8**

"This is where you'll find solution holes," Ms. Stone told the students. They searched the forest for the large holes that have been carved out of the limestone by tannic acid, a chemical formed when rainwater mixes with the pine needles and other leaves in the forest. Small animals live, feed, and raise their young in the solution holes. The students also watched as a tiny yellow tree snail nestled under the bark of a tree, eating a growth on the tree called lichen. They saw a Red-Shouldered Hawk swirl in the sky, and they waited for a golden orb spider to catch its next meal in its web close to the ground.

Hiking through the Pinelands

242

Analyze/Evaluate

IF students have difficulty applying the Analyze/Evaluate strategy ... **THEN**, use this model:

> **Think Aloud** *In the third paragraph, the author names different kinds of vegetation, or plants, in the Pinelands habitat and explains that they help to absorb sounds from the outside world. I'm going to stop and think about this. How does this statement help support the author's viewpoint that the Everglades needs to be protected? I think the author is saying that the vegetation helps to keep the Pinelands quiet and peaceful, both for the animals that live there and for the people who visit.*

Point out to students that the author's word choice also affects the persuasiveness of her writing.

"Perhaps even in this last hour . . . the vast, magnificent, subtle and unique region of the Everglades may not be utterly lost."

Marjory Stoneman Douglas

243

Practice Fluency

Adjust Rate to Purpose Read aloud the third paragraph on **Student Book p. 242** as students follow along.

- Remind students that reading for different purposes affects rate. Reading at a slower pace helps readers and listeners take in new facts or visualize a scene.

- *What are some new facts you learned in this paragraph? Sample answers: There are pine forests in the Everglades; vegetation in the pine forests helps to absorb sounds from the outside world.*

- Have students echo read the paragraph, mimicking your slow, thoughtful pace.

- The Fluency lesson on p. T200 provides further opportunities for modeling and practice with adjusting rate to purpose. **ELA** RF.5.4b

⌒ **DOMAIN: Life Science**

LESSON TOPIC: Conservation

Cross-Curricular Connection Remind students that the manatee is one of many endangered species that live in the Everglades. The manatee is Florida's state marine mammal. Display photographs of manatees, and have students discuss physical characteristics. Explain that manatees move slowly and feed often. Manatees have been seen body surfing and barrel rolling during play.  Although some manatees have been known to travel north, most spend the winter in the warmer waters along the Florida coastline. Primary threats to manatees include destruction of their habitats and boat strikes. Have students use their knowledge of Everglades conservation and manatees to predict some adaptive characteristics for manatee survival.

FIRST READ

Think Through the Text

Cite Text Evidence

9 *How might farming and development harm the Everglades? Both farming and development expand land use, which brings people closer to the Everglades. Both use a lot of water that comes from the Everglades. Both cause pollution.* **ELA** RI.5.2, RI.5.3 **ELD** ELD.PI.5.6a

10 *Why does the author ask a question about what would happen to the plants and animals instead of giving the answer? She wants to catch readers' attention and make them think about what they have learned.* **ELA** RI.5.8

As they walked through the Pinelands, the students talked with Ms. Stone and Ranger Jim about the circle of life—the Miccosukee (MIHK uh SOO kee) belief that all plant and animal and human life is connected. They had seen this today in the habitats they visited. The students also realized how terrible it would be if the habitats in this part of the Everglades were not protected from the effects of farming and development that were still putting the Everglades in danger. What would happen to all the unique plants and animals they had seen? Ranger Jim said they could help by conserving water, even when brushing their teeth or washing their faces, because most of the water used in southern Florida comes from the Everglades. With responsible water conservation, the Everglades Restoration Plan could, over the next thirty years, restore a healthy balance so all living things—plants, animals, and people—will be able to live side by side in the only *Pa-hay-okee*, "Grassy River," in the world.

It was the end of a long day for the class, but there was one more part of the Everglades to visit. Ms. Stone and Ranger Jim led the students into an open space hidden at the end of the hiking trail.

9

10

Flock of White Ibis

244

ENGLISH LANGUAGE SUPPORT

Comprehensible Input

Emerging Using simple language, explain how students can help preserve habitats by conserving water. Then, have students use actions to demonstrate the meaning of *conserve*.

Expanding Work with students to paraphrase "conserving water." Then, have partners draw pictures of ways that they could help to conserve water in their homes.

Bridging Have students identify clues that help them understand the meaning of "conserving water."

245

🔍 Language Detective

Modifying to Add Details

- Tell students that prepositional phrases are tools that authors use to add detail to sentences. The phrases can add information about people, places, things, or activities. Prepositional phrases give authors a way to tell where, when, or how.

- Remind students that prepositional phrases begin with a preposition, such as *on, under, at, in,* or *as.* The preposition is paired with a noun to make a prepositional phrase, such as *beside the river* or *in the forest.*

- Read aloud **Student Book p. 238.** Display this sentence from paragraph 2: *On the morning of the field trip, the bus traveled west from Avocado School.*

- Ask: *What is the prepositional phrase in the sentence? On the morning of the field trip What information does it add? It tells when the bus is traveling.*

- Now draw students' attention to the last sentence on **Student Book p. 239** and model the thinking.

> **Think Aloud** *I notice that this sentence contains a prepositional phrase: In the distance. The author is talking about an egret flying. The prepositional phrase adds information about where the bird is flying--not close by, but in the distance.*

- Assign partners a section of the text, and tell them to find other prepositional phrases that the author has used to add detail. Tell partners to discuss whether each phrase tells where, when, or how.

- Tell partners to write lines of dialogue showing a conversation between two people. Have students practice using prepositional phrases to tell where, when or how. **ELA** L.5.1a **ELD** ELD.PII.5.5

> ✏️ 🖥 ***Annotate it!*** Have students highlight examples of prepositional phrases in the text.

⟐ DOMAIN: Life Science

LESSON TOPIC: Conservation

Cross-Curricular Connection Remind students that the water cycle connects all of Earth's water, including the oceans, through evaporation and precipitation. Point out that water collects in the Everglades in two ways: first through precipitation, and second through the overflow of lakes, rivers, and streams into the Everglades. Explain that as water flows through the Everglades to the ocean, some of it seeps through the ground into underground caves called *aquifers.* Some of Florida's drinking water comes from these underground caves.

Think Through the Text

Cite Text Evidence

11 *What causes the finger glade to stay dry when the larger sawgrass prairie is wet? It is on higher ground.* ELA RI.5.3

12 *Based on the description of what students did in the finger glade, how large of an area do you imagine it to be? Sample answer: the size of a football field*

13 *The author includes Ms. Stone's words as she talks about the silence of the finger glade. What feeling is she creating by including this dialogue? Sample answer: The dialogue draws readers into the setting and helps create a feeling of awe and importance.* ELA RI.5.8 ELD ELD.PI.5.6a

"This is a finger glade," Ms. Stone said. "It's a small part of the sawgrass prairie that does not stay wet all year." During the wet season, the finger glade would be filled with water and fish. But now the ground, which is higher than the larger sawgrass prairies, was dry and hard. **11**

"For a few minutes you can walk as far as you like and enjoy the finger glade," said Ms. Stone.

The students fanned out. Some pretended they were birds, flying low overhead. Others studied the sawgrass, pretending to be explorers discovering the glade. Still others talked about how the hard ground on which they were walking would turn into a lake deep enough for fish to swim through during the wet season. And some just lay on their backs, looking at the sky and the ring of trees around the glade. **12**

246

ENGLISH LANGUAGE SUPPORT

Use Visuals

Emerging Show students a photograph of a sawgrass prairie covered with water and one of a finger glade. Guide students to compare and contrast the two.

Expanding Show students a photograph of a sawgrass prairie covered with water and one of a finger glade. Ask: How is the larger sawgrass prairie different from the finger glade?

Bridging Show students a photograph of a sawgrass prairie covered in water. Ask them to describe what they see, and then compare the larger sawgrass prairie to a finger glade.

When the students came back, they sat in a circle close to Ms. Stone.

"Close your eyes," said Ms. Stone, "and listen."

"Do you hear cars?" she whispered.

"Do you hear sirens?"

"Do you hear people?"

"What do you hear?"

Silence.

"You are not going to find silence like this anyplace else in the world," Ms. Stone said quietly. "This glade is protected by a circle of trees and marshes and natural wildlife. It is far from the noise of the outside world. It's full of *silence.* Any time you are in a sawgrass prairie like this one, stop and listen to the silence." **13**

ANALYZE THE TEXT

Explain Scientific Ideas Why do you think the author includes this description of the finger glade? What has it helped you understand about the sawgrass prairies of the Everglades? How does this area compare to the mangrove swamp and Pinelands habitats?

247

FOR STUDENTS WITH DISABILITIES Have students work in small, mixed ability groups to read "Everglades Forever." Group members take turns reading each section of the text aloud and discussing each section before moving on to the next. Have group members summarize each section and the entire text.

Explain Scientific Ideas

Analyze the Text

- Read the Analyze the Text box on **Student Book p. 247** with students.

- Remind students that to help their readers understand the information they are presenting, authors of scientific text show relationships between ideas or concepts. They may do this is by comparing and contrasting concepts or ideas and showing cause and effect.

- Have students reread Student Book p. 246. Ask: *How does the finger glade compare to the larger sawgrass prairie? The finger glade is dry, while the larger sawgrass prairie is wet. How does elevation help to shape each habitat? Sample answer: Higher areas are drier, so they contain plants that grow in drier places.*

ENGLISH LANGUAGE SUPPORT Tell students that in some informational texts, like this one, relationships between events or ideas are implied rather than explicitly stated. Remind students that they will sometimes need to look back through the text and make inferences about how different sections are connected. Provide these questions to help students think about or discuss the text: *What is this section about? What other information in the text does it seem to be related to? In what way(s)?*

- Have students compare the plants in the finger glade to the plants in the Pinelands habitat and the mangrove swamp. Ask: *How have the plants adapted to the conditions in their different environments? The finger glade contains grasses that grow in drier environments, whereas the mangrove swamp contains trees that have specially adapted roots and leaves that help the trees survive in brackish water. The Pinelands habitat is drier, allowing tall pine trees to grow.*

- As students finish reading the selection, have them explain the relationships between the most important scientific ideas the author presents in the text. **ELA** RI.5.2, RI.5.3 **ELD** ELD.PI.5.6a

✎ 🗋 **Annotate it!** Have students highlight details that help clarify the scientific ideas presented in the text.

Think Through the Text

Cite Text Evidence

✓ TARGET STRATEGY

Analyze/Evaluate

Tell students to practice the Analyze/Evaluate strategy as they read **Student Book p. 249** silently to themselves. Ask several students to point out where they used the strategy to help them analyze the text and evaluate the facts and details the author uses to support her argument.

14 *In what way are the students a part of the Everglades? Sample answer: The students live in Florida, and their habits and behavior affect the Everglades and the plants and animals that live there.* **ELA** RI.5.2, RI.5.3 **ELD** ELD.PI.5.6a

15 *What do you think the author believes people should do in taking responsibility for the Everglades? Sample answer: They should conserve water and not pollute. They should preserve and protect the unique habitats of the Everglades.* **ELA** RI.5.2, RI.5.3 **ELD** ELD.PI.5.6a

ENGLISH LANGUAGE SUPPORT Give students this sentence frame to support participation. *I think the author believes people should _____.*

💬 Classroom Conversation

Have students discuss "Everglades Forever," either as a whole class or in small groups. Provide this prompt to focus their discussion: *What information and experiences will the students on the field trip to the Everglades be able to share with their families and with other students at their school?* Have students revisit the selection and use text evidence to support their thoughts. Remind students to respond in complete sentences to each other's comments and questions, and to give everyone a chance to participate in the conversation. **ELA** SL.5.1a, SL.5.1b, SL.5.1c **ELD** ELD.PI.5.1, ELD.PI.5.4

248

Collaborate: Analyze/Evaluate

Teach/Model Write analyze and evaluate, and explain the terms. Remind students that when we evaluate a persuasive text, we decide whether the author did a good job of supporting an opinion with reasons and facts. Use a Think Aloud to model evaluating "Everglades Forever."

Think Aloud *The author believes that the Comprehensive Everglades Restoration Plan is important. When I read about the mangrove swamp, I understood why. She gave a good reason: the plan will regulate the swamp's freshwater and salt water.*

Guided Practice Read aloud **Student Book pp. 241 and 249.** Ask students to evaluate the author's opinion. Have them list reasons and facts the author uses to support her opinion.

• Review **Teach Academic English** on Lesson 8 Language Support Card 🗗. **ELD** ELD.PI.5.6a, ELD.PI.5.7

The sun was setting over the Everglades as the class walked back to the bus. Birds flew low over the sawgrass prairie. It was a peaceful time, a time for everything to settle down for the night. The students knew that for the near future the Everglades would look the same, and might even be almost the same. They also knew about the dangers facing the Everglades, and that it would not stay the same unless people watched over it and took care of it.

Restoring the Everglades will take a long time, and it may never be finished. But the students knew they could play a part as they grew older. They had learned that they too were a part of the Everglades, connected in the same circle of life with the tiniest insect and largest alligator. They knew that someday in the not-too-distant future, responsibility for the Everglades would pass on to them. They would become the guardians and protectors of the only Everglades in the world, helping this wild and wonderful place go on *forever*. **15**

ANALYZE THE TEXT

Author's Purpose Why might the author have written about a class field trip to the Everglades? Why do you think she included so many vivid details about the wetlands?

249

> **DOMAIN: Life Science**

LESSON TOPIC: Conservation

Cross-Curricular Connection Explain to students that another growing problem for Everglades habitats is the introduction of non-native or invasive species of plants and animals. Point out that invasive plants may compete with and crowd out native plants. Tell students that invasive species of wildlife also pose threats to the ecosystem. Wild  pigs are non-native animals that digs up native plants, disturbing habitats and killing vegetation. Also, a variety of snakes and exotic pets have been introduced into the Everglades as a result of pet owners releasing their animals into the wild. Huge boa constrictors and anacondas are reproducing in the Everglades, eating native animals and competing with other predators for food. Although park officials are trying to control this problem, the task is time-consuming and difficult.

Author's Purpose

Analyze the Text

- Read the Analyze the Text box on **Student Book p. 249** with students. Then distribute Graphic Organizer 7 .

- Remind students that the author provides details, reasons, and evidence to support particular points in the text. Point out that authors often include this kind of strong support when trying to convince readers to agree with a certain way of thinking.

- Display Projectable 8.2 . Read the author's purpose in the top box. Next, ask students to point out where in the selection they can find the first piece of evidence the author provides to support her argument. *pp. 239 and 240*

- Then, have students revisit the text to identify more details, reasons, and evidence the author uses to support her argument. Have students record this information in their maps.

- Work with students to explain how the author uses details, reasons, and evidence to support her argument. Have students identify which pieces of evidence support which key points. Then, discuss whether the author achieves her purpose.
  ELA RI.5.8 **ELD** ELD.PI.5.6a, ELD.PI.5.7

✎ 🖵 *Annotate it!* Have students highlight details throughout the text that show the author's purpose and support her argument.

Dig Deeper   *Use Clues to Analyze the Text*

▶ SHARE OBJECTIVES

- Identify and analyze reasons and other text evidence that support the author's purpose.
- Explain the relationships between ideas in a scientific text.
- Determine the meanings of and use of domain-specific words.
- Understand the use of prepositional phrases in informational text. LANGUAGE

ENGLISH LANGUAGE SUPPORT

Comprehensible Input

Emerging When Ranger Jim tells the students to conserve water when they brush their teeth, he is trying to persuade them. Help students understand the concept of persuasion and how it is being used here.

Expanding Write this sentence frame on the board: *Ranger Jim is trying to _____ the students to conserve water by _____.* Help students complete the sentence.

Bridging Have students locate the passage about water conservation on **Student Book p. 244,** and discuss its effectiveness with a partner. **ELD** ELD.PI.5.1

Text-Based Comprehension

1 Teach/Model

Terms About Informational Text

author's purpose an author's reasons for writing

domain-specific words words directly related to a topic

prepositional phrase a phrase that gives information about time or place

---

- Remind students that they have just read a work of narrative nonfiction about conservation.

- Read **Student Book p. 250** with students. Explain that authors of narrative nonfiction may write for different reasons. Remind students that the author of "Everglades Forever" wants to persuade her readers.

- Tell students that when they read persuasive text, they should first identify the details, reasons, and evidence the author uses to support particular points in the text. Once they have recorded important facts and other evidence, they can determine which pieces of evidence support which points, how convincing the author's argument is, and whether she achieves her purpose. Discuss how to use the graphic organizer to keep track of details in support of the **author's purpose**, using this model:

  Think Aloud *On page 241, readers learn how mangrove trees grow in salty water and act as nurseries for shrimp and small fish. These details show the uniqueness of the Everglades, supporting the author's point that it should be protected.*

  Next, read **Student Book p. 251** with students.

- Point out that to help readers understand important or complex scientific information, authors might choose to break down a broad idea into smaller parts, explain similarities or differences between ideas, or trace how one event causes another to happen. Tell students that as they read and analyze a scientific text, they should pause to identify and explain the relationships between important ideas.

- Tell students that authors of informational texts often use domain-specific words and phrases to explain a scientific concept or process. Point out that determining the meanings of these words in context will help students gain a deeper understanding of the text's topic, as well as learn to use the words in their own writing and discussions.

  🔍 Language Detective: Modifying to Add Details Tell students that authors use prepositional phrases to provide additional information about a noun or a verb. These phrases answer readers' questions about who, what, where, when, and why in informational text.

Dig Deeper

Use Clues to Analyze the Text

Use these pages to learn about Author's Purpose, Explaining Scientific Ideas, and Domain-Specific Vocabulary. Then read "Everglades Forever" again to apply what you learned.

Author's Purpose

Authors of narrative nonfiction, such as "Everglades Forever," have a variety of reasons for writing. They may want to share information, describe an event or a person, or persuade readers to agree with their position on an issue. In their writing, they include details such as facts, examples, and descriptions that will help them fulfill their purpose.

In "Everglades Forever," the **author's purpose** is to persuade. She wants to convince readers that it is important to protect the Everglades. She presents her argument and main points in the form of a narrative about a school field trip. This structure allows her to give reasons and evidence in a way that interests readers.

Look through the selection. What are the facts, examples, and other pieces of text evidence that help convince you the Everglades should be preserved?

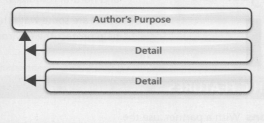

Author's Purpose
Detail
Detail

Explain Scientific Ideas

In "Everglades Forever," the author explains several important scientific ideas. For example, she talks about the migration of animals within the wetlands, their various habitats, and the need for water conservation. By thinking about the relationships between these different aspects of the same topic, readers can understand the author's argument more fully.

Domain-Specific Vocabulary

The author includes **domain-specific words** in her text. These are words directly related to the topic of Everglades conservation, such as *endangered, wetlands, habitat, thermoregulate,* and *slough.* Using domain-specific vocabulary allows textbook and informational text authors to explain things precisely and to show their knowledge of the subject. Domain-specific terms are often defined in the text. When they are not, readers can use context clues to figure out their meanings.

---

2   Guided Practice/Apply

Analyze the Text   Begin a second read of "Everglades Forever" with students. Use the stopping points and instructional support to guide students to analyze the text:

- Domain-Specific Vocabulary, p. T177   **ELA** RI.5.4, L.5.6 **ELD** ELD.PI.5.6b
- Modifying to Add Details, p. T181   **ELD** ELD.PII.5.5
- Explain Scientific Ideas, p. T183   **ELA** RI.5.3 **ELD** ELD.PI.5.6a
- Author's Purpose, p. T185   **ELA** RI.5.1, RI.5.8 **ELD** ELD.PI.5.6a

Directed Note Taking The graphic organizer will be completed with students during the second read on p. T185.

FORMATIVE ASSESSMENT    RtI

Are students able to identify reasons and evidence in the text that support the author's purpose?

IF...	THEN...
students struggle,	**Differentiate Comprehension** for Struggling Readers, p. T220.
students are on track,	**Differentiate Comprehension** for On-Level Readers, p. T220.
students excel,	**Differentiate Comprehension** for Advanced Readers, p. T221.

   Differentiate Comprehension, pp. T220–T221 *Scaffold instruction to the English learner's proficiency level.*

Your Turn

Cite Text Evidence

▶ SHARE OBJECTIVES

- Prepare for and participate in group discussions.
- Use illustrations and other graphic features to reinforce main ideas.
- Write an opinion paragraph that includes reasons and evidence as well as domain-specific vocabulary. **LANGUAGE**

RETURN TO THE ESSENTIAL QUESTION

Ask small groups to discuss the essential question, using text evidence to support their thinking. Have students sum up their discussion by explaining the key ideas they talked about.

ELA RI.5.1, SL.5.1a **ELD** ELD PI.5.1, ELD.PI.5.6a

 Classroom Conversation

Have partners continue their discussion of "Everglades Forever" by sharing their answers to each question. Remind them to clarify ideas by asking questions and adding comments to elaborate upon each others' remarks. See Digital Lesson: Rules for a Good Discussion 🔗.

ELA SL.5.1b, SL.5.1c **ELD** ELD.PI.5.1, ELD.PI.5.6a

ENGLISH LANGUAGE SUPPORT Use sentence frames, such as the following, to support discussion.

One of the habitats in the Everglades is _____.

This selection helps me understand the connections between people, animals, and natural resources because _____.

I can help protect the environment by _____.

As students share their ideas, tell them to use text evidence to support their responses.

ELD ELD.PI.5.1, ELD.PI.5.4, ELD.PI.5.6a, ELD.PI.5.11a

Your Turn

RETURN TO THE ESSENTIAL QUESTION

 Turn and Talk Review the selection to prepare to discuss this question: *What reasons do people have for protecting the environment?* Draw information from the text as well as your prior knowledge. Then share your ideas in a small-group discussion.

Save the Everglades

Classroom Conversation

Continue your discussion of "Everglades Forever" by using text evidence to answer these questions:

1. What are some of the habitats found in the Everglades?

2. How does the selection help you understand the connections between humans, plants, animals, and natural resources?

3. What are some ways that you can help protect the environment?

ADD GRAPHIC FEATURES

Write Captions With a partner, use the Internet or print resources to find additional graphic features for the selection. Look for photographs of Everglades animals, maps of the wetlands, or charts about the area's resources. Write a brief caption for each. Explain how the graphic feature supports an important idea in the text.

252   **ELA** RI.5.8, W.5.2d, W.5.9b, W.5.10, SL.5.1a, SL.5.1c **ELD** ELD.PI.5.1, ELD.PI.5.6a, ELD.PI.5.7, ELD.PI.5.10a, ELD.PI.5.11a, ELD.PI.5.12a

ENGLISH LANGUAGE SUPPORT

How English Works

Text Cohesion Before students begin their discussion, have them plan to make their responses cohesive by using pronouns to refer the listener back in the conversation. Provide a model such as, *Joseph is a scientist. He studies the Everglades.* Explain that *he* is a pronoun that refers back to *Joseph.* Help different proficiency levels think about their topics and build word banks of pronouns that can make their responses cohesive. **ELD** ELD.PII.5.2a

WRITE ABOUT READING

Response The author of "Everglades Forever" believes it is important to preserve the Everglades. What reasons and evidence does the author include to support her point? Write a paragraph to explain whether you agree or disagree with the author's argument. Use facts, examples, and other text evidence to support your position.

Writing Tip

Use precise language and domain-specific vocabulary as you present details to support your position.

253

ENGLISH LANGUAGE SUPPORT

Collaborative Writing

Step 1 Guide students to complete a web to build an opinion and support it with reasons based on facts, examples, and other evidence.

Step 2 Explain that you will work together as a class to write a response to reading by using the completed graphic organizer. Point out to students that they will say ideas and sentences, and you will write them down for the group to see and read.

Step 3 Have students develop the response by referring to the graphic organizer and answering questions such as these:

- What words will help begin this response?
- What information should we include? How do we say that in a sentence?
- What is the first reason that we should write?
- What text evidence will we use?

Step 4 Read the unfinished response aloud to students. Repeat, and have students read aloud with you. Ask students if they see or hear anything they would like to change.

Extra Scaffold Without purposely making mistakes, revise in the moment by using Think Alouds. **ELD** ELD.PI.5.2

ADD GRAPHIC FEATURES

Provide students with a list of Internet encyclopedias and websites that contain photographs of plants and animals, along with maps and charts about the Everglades. Discuss the types of graphic elements that could be used in this selection to support main ideas. After students have chosen theirs, have them indicate where each should be placed. Tell them that each caption should explain the relationship between the feature and the text.

ELA W.5.2d **ELD** ELD.PI.5.6a

WRITE ABOUT READING

Performance Task

Have students ask themselves whether they are convinced by the author's support for her argument, and why or why not. Tell them to state their opinion clearly and to provide reasons supported by facts, quotations, and other text evidence.

ELA RI.5.1, RI.5.8, W.5.1a, W.5.1b, W.5.9b, W.5.10

ENGLISH LANGUAGE SUPPORT Tell students to state the topic and their opinion in the opening sentence. Provide this frame:

> *I (agree)/(disagree) with the author's argument.*

Suggest that they add reasons for their opinion using these frames:

> *I think this because _____.*
> *The text says _____.*

Remind students to use pronouns correctly in their paragraph. See Digital Lesson: Writing to Sources. **ELD** ELD.PI.5.6a, ELD.PI.5.10a, ELD.PI.5.11a

Writing Tip Make sure students read the Writing Tip before they begin writing. Encourage them to include domain-specific words by working as a class to generate a list of the terms from the text. Remind them also to check their facts for accuracy.

ELA W.5.2d **ELD** ELD.PI.5.12a, ELD.PII.5.2a

myWriteSmart Have students complete the Write About Reading activity through *my*WriteSmart. Students will read the prompt within *my*WriteSmart and have access to multiple resources, including the Student eBook, Writing Rubrics, and Graphic Organizers.

Independent Reading

SHARE OBJECTIVES

- Read and comprehend informational text.
- Quote accurately from a text to support analysis and inferences.
- Read independently from a "just right" book.
- Ask and answer questions about key details.
LANGUAGE

ENGLISH LANGUAGE SUPPORT

"Just Right" Books for English Learners

All Proficiencies The "five-finger rule" may not always be the right approach for English learners. For example, a "just right" book for an English learner might be one that does not pass the five-finger rule but is an informational text that has many photos, illustrations, and terms defined in context.

Reader's Guide

Use Text Evidence Tell students that they will read "Everglades Forever" on their own to analyze important ideas in the text.

Have students use the Reader's Guide pages in their Reader's Notebook, pp. 85–86 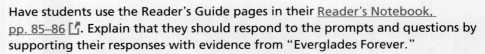. Explain that they should respond to the prompts and questions by supporting their responses with evidence from "Everglades Forever."

Generate Questions Have students work independently or collaboratively to generate questions about "Everglades Forever." Ask students to share their questions. Begin a class discussion of questions that students have in common or that are most significant to their understanding of the selection. **ELA** RI.5.1, RL.5.10, RF.5.4a, SL.5.1c **ELD** ELD.PI.5.1

Self-Selected Reading

Five-Finger Rule Use the steps below to review how to use the five-finger rule to choose an appropriate trade book.

- Open the book to a full page and read it aloud, holding up one finger each time you come to an unfamiliar word or chunk of words.

- When you finish the page, count how many fingers you are holding up. If the number is zero or one, the book may be too easy. If the number is two or three, the book may be just right. If you are holding up four or five fingers, the book may be too challenging.

Have students use the five-finger rule to help them choose a book for independent reading. Ask students to use their Reading Logs in Grab-and-Go™ 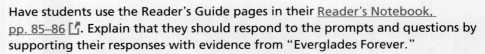 to record their progress and thinking about the book.

Fluency

Partner Read Have students read aloud with expression to a partner, using passages from their self-selected reading books. Tell them to give each other feedback and then reread to apply it. **ELA** RF.5.4b

Apply Vocabulary Knowledge

☑ Review Target Vocabulary

💬 **Classroom Collaboration** Read aloud each of the following questions. Have students discuss their answers. Allow several students to respond to each question to provide a variety of possible responses for discussion.

ELA L.5.6 **ELD** ELD.PI.5.12a

1. How can you personally take **responsibility** for **conserving** the Earth's resources?

2. What is a natural feature **unique** to your local region?

3. Why is it important to learn as much about **endangered** species as possible?

4. What kind of **vegetation** are animals such as deer and rabbits **attracted** to?

5. What does it mean to be **guardians** of the planet?

6. What is one way that desert plants and animals are **adapted** to the desert?

7. Would it be a good idea to **regulate** the number of visitors to fragile environments such as the Everglades? Why or why not?

8. What is one way that you **restore** your energy at the end of a long day?

Quick Write Display the following prompt: *Explain what makes the Everglades a unique place. Use the vocabulary words you have learned in your writing.*

Tell students to consider the physical features of the Everglades as well as the plant and animal life. Remind them to quote accurately. When they have finished writing, tell students to exchange papers with a partner and discuss whether they used the words correctly in their paragraphs

ELA RL.5.1, L.5.6 **ELD** ELD.PI.5.1, ELD.PI.5.4

▶ **SHARE OBJECTIVES**
- Acquire and use vocabulary in speaking and writing. LANGUAGE
- Collaboratively respond to questions about familiar vocabulary. LANGUAGE

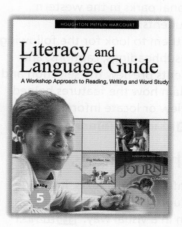

For additional practice with the lesson's Target Vocabulary, use the activities on pages 130–131 of the **Literacy and Language Guide.**

- Relating Words Questions
- Suffix *-ian*
- Word Sort
- Root Web

ENGLISH LANGUAGE SUPPORT

Use Sentence Frames

All Proficiencies Have students complete sentence frames such as these to help them use the vocabulary words in their writing.

The Everglades is a special, <u>unique</u> place. It is the home to an <u>endangered</u> species called the wood stork.

To help students discuss their partner's use of vocabulary in writing, provide discussion frames such as this one.

*You used the word **adapted** to describe _____.*

ELD ELD.PI.5.1, ELD.PI.5.4, ELD.PI.5.12a

○ **DOMAIN:** Life Science
LESSON TOPIC: CONSERVATION

CONNECT TO THE TOPIC
Informational Text

Preview the Informational Text

• Tell students that this informational text is a website about national parks in the western United States. As students read the text independently, tell them to look for the following features: headings, subheadings, captions, and graphics. Have students preview the selection and use a T-Map to explain how the features helped them gain an overview or locate information within the text. **ELA** RI.5.10, RF.5.4a **ELD** ELD.PI.5.6a

Discuss Graphic Sources

• Tell students that informational texts, including websites, often include graphic sources that present information in a visual way. **ELD** ELD.PII.5.1

• Remind students that a bar graph, such as the one on **Student Book p. 256,** is a feature that can show change over time.

• Define the key terms below and discuss how to use them to read a graph. Tell students that not all graphs include all of these features.

title	tells what the graph is about
variable	something that changes
x-axis	horizontal line that charts one of the variables
y-axis	vertical line that charts another variable

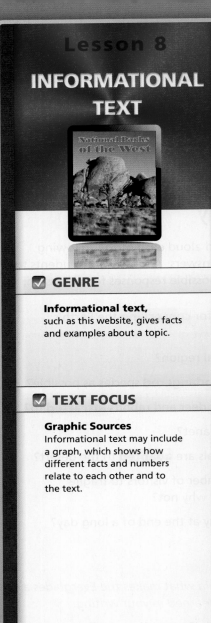

Lesson 8

INFORMATIONAL TEXT

☑ **GENRE**

Informational text, such as this website, gives facts and examples about a topic.

☑ **TEXT FOCUS**

Graphic Sources
Informational text may include a graph, which shows how different facts and numbers relate to each other and to the text.

254   **ELA** RL.5.10, RF.5.4a, RF.5.4b   **ELD** ELD.PI.5.6a

☐ **File**   **Edit**   **View**   **Favorites**

National Parks of the West

Big Bend National Park: Texas

Big Bend National Park is located along the Rio Grande, also called the Rio Bravo, the river that forms the boundary between Mexico and the United States. The park is open year-round. <u>more</u>

Wildlife and Vegetation

Big Bend is the home of more than 1,200 plant species, including 60 kinds of cactus, and more than 4,000 animal and insect species. This diversity is due to the park's many natural habitats, from the Chihuahuan Desert to the Chisos Mountains. <u>more</u>

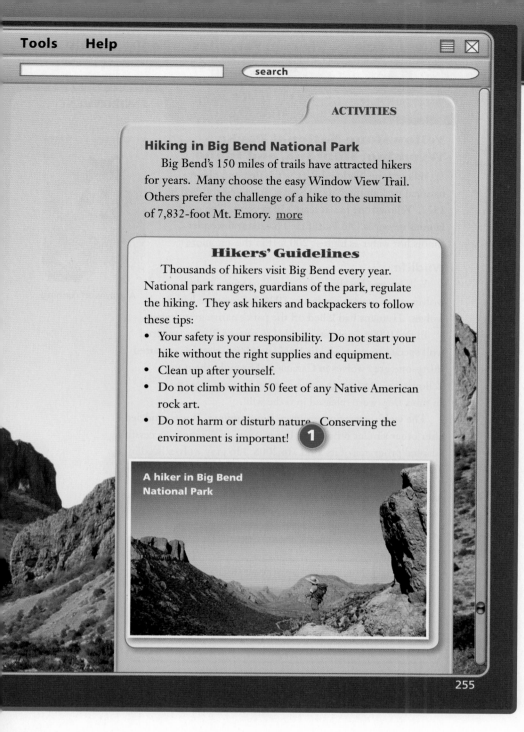

Tools   Help

search

ACTIVITIES

Hiking in Big Bend National Park

Big Bend's 150 miles of trails have attracted hikers for years. Many choose the easy Window View Trail. Others prefer the challenge of a hike to the summit of 7,832-foot Mt. Emory. <u>more</u>

Hikers' Guidelines

Thousands of hikers visit Big Bend every year. National park rangers, guardians of the park, regulate the hiking. They ask hikers and backpackers to follow these tips:

- Your safety is your responsibility. Do not start your hike without the right supplies and equipment.
- Clean up after yourself.
- Do not climb within 50 feet of any Native American rock art.
- Do not harm or disturb nature. Conserving the environment is important! **1**

A hiker in Big Bend National Park

255

Practice Fluency

Adjust Rate to Purpose Have students listen as you read aloud **Student Book p. 255**. First, read it quickly. Then, read it again at a slower pace. **ELD** ELD.PI.5.5

- Remind students that when a selection contains new words or information, slowing your reading rate helps you better understand the information.

- Have students partner-read each sentence on **Student Book p. 255**. Have them read slowly and accurately to understand the information. **ELA** RF.5.4b

DOMAIN: Life Science

LESSON TOPIC: Conservation

Cross-Curricular Connection Draw students' attention to this sentence on p. 255: "Conserving the environment is important!" Ask a volunteer to explain what it means to conserve the environment. Guide students to understand that conservation means leaving an area of land in its natural state and not changing it for human purposes. After students have read the selection, ask them to identify details in the text that show why conservation is important.

Sample answer: Natural places such as Big Bend National Park provide habitats for many species of plants and animals. National parks also provide a place for people to experience nature by hiking and by visiting natural wonders such as geysers.

Think Through the Text

Pause at the stopping points to ask students the following questions.

1. *Both this website and Everglades Forever discuss the topic of conservation. What ideas are conveyed by both selections?* Sample answer: National parks contain unique habitats where certain species of plants and animals can live. People must take action to conserve natural environments. National parks offer many opportunities for people to enjoy the natural world. **ELA** RI.5.6, RI.5.10 **ELD** ELD.PI.5.6a

2. *In one sentence, summarize the information in the section titled "Wildlife."* Sample answer: Because of a program started in 1995, wolves have been successfully restored to Yellowstone National Park. **ELA** RI.5.2 **ELD** ELD.PI.5.6a

3. *How does the information presented in the graph relate to the text?* Sample answer: The text is about restoring the wolf population to the park. The graph puts that information into numbers and shows how the wolves' numbers have changed over time. **ELA** RI.5.3

ENGLISH LANGUAGE SUPPORT Be sure students understand that there are two different kinds of numbers on the graph. Those on the left side describe wolves; those on the bottom describe years. **ELD** ELD.PI.5.6a

Classroom Collaboration

Why did the United States set aside land for national parks? As a class, have students discuss the benefits of places such as Big Bend and Yellowstone National Parks. Encourage them to use specific details from the selection in their discussions. **ELA** RI.5.1 **ELD** ELD.PI.5.1

File   Edit   View   Favorites   Tools   Help

ENVIRONMENT

Yellowstone National Park: Wyoming, Montana, and Idaho

Yellowstone National Park is the first and oldest national park in the United States. It was established in 1872. Yellowstone has at least 150 geysers. The most famous geyser is Old Faithful. This natural wonder shoots hot water as high as 200 feet in the air. more

A gray wolf running

Wildlife

Yellowstone has dozens of animal species. Today, wolves are among them, but in 1994, Yellowstone had no wolves. Humans had killed off the park's native gray wolves.

In the 1990s, scientists decided to restore this endangered wolf species to the park. In 1995 and 1996, scientists captured thirty-one gray wolves in Canada and brought them to Yellowstone. At first, the wolves lived in three large pens. In time, they were released into the wild.

The wolf restoration program is not unique. It was modeled after other similar programs. But it is one of the most successfully adapted programs of its kind. In 2006, 136 gray wolves lived in Yellowstone. They live in thirteen different areas of the park.

Analyze the graph below. In what year was the wolf population the highest? The lowest? How many wolves were there in each of these years?

Wolf Population

Year	Number of Wolves
2000	177
2001	218
2002	148
2003	174
2004	171
2005	118
2006	136

256

ENGLISH LANGUAGE SUPPORT

Use Visuals

Emerging Show students a photo of Old Faithful. Locate the word *geyser* on p. 256 and help students pronounce it. Point to the photo and ask, *What kind of natural wonder is this?* a geyser

Expanding Show students a photo of Old Faithful and identify it as a geyser. Ask students to complete this sentence: *Many people visit Yellowstone National Park to ____.* see a geyser **ELD** ELD.PII.5.3

Bridging Have students read about Old Faithful on p. 256 and examine a photo. Ask them to define *geyser* in a sentence. *A geyser is a natural fountain that shoots hot water into the air.* **ELD** ELD.PI.5.4

Compare Texts

TEXT TO TEXT

Compare and Contrast Texts With a partner, review "Everglades Forever" and "Quest for the Tree Kangaroo" (Lesson 6). Take notes on what you learn about wildlife conservation and human interaction with nature. Consider how the text structure, or overall organization of each text, affects your understanding of the topic. Discuss and compare the two selections.

TEXT TO SELF

Write an Informal Letter Write a letter to your classmates to persuade them to plan a field trip to the Everglades. Use facts and details from "Everglades Forever" to make a strong case.

TEXT TO WORLD

Identify Viewpoint Review the website features on pages 254–256. What viewpoint is presented? Think about how that viewpoint affects your interest in national parks. Then search the Internet for a website about another wildlife preserve similar to Yellowstone. Discuss with classmates your thoughts about the website's information and its viewpoint.

ELA RI.5.5, RI.5.7, W.5.4, W.5.10 **ELD** ELD.PI.5.1, ELD.PI.5.3, ELD.PI.5.6a, ELD.PI.10a

257

ENGLISH LANGUAGE SUPPORT

Compare Texts

Organize Concepts Help students complete a chart comparing how parks preserve the environment and ancient artifacts. Have students refer to their **Student Book** for specific evidence.
ELD ELD PI.5.1

Name of Park	Types of Habitats	Location	Animals and Plants
Everglades National Park	wetlands, mangrove swamp, prairie	Florida	wood storks, alligators, ibis, sawgrass, mangrove trees
Big Bend National Park	desert, mountains	Texas	cactus, other plant, animal, and insect species

Build Academic Sentence Structures To help students compare and contrast how parks preserve environments and artifacts, ask questions such as: *How are the parks alike? How are they different?* Provide sentence frames such as these:

• *Both Everglades National Park and Big Bend National Park preserve* <u>natural habitats</u>.

• <u>*Everglades National Park*</u> *protects endangered wood storks.*

Compare Texts

TEXT TO TEXT

To help students analyze the text structure of the two selections, display a Venn diagram with these labels: "Everglades Forever" (left); "Both" (center); "Quest for the Tree Kangaroo" (right). Guide students to fill in the diagram with elements such as *photographs* ("Both"), *captions* ("Both"), *footnotes* ("Quest for the Tree Kangaroo"), and *a called-out quotation* ("Everglades Forever").
ELA RI.5.5, RF.5.4a **ELD** ELD.PI.5.1, ELD.PI.5.3

TEXT TO SELF

Display these sentence frames to help students organize facts and details:

Everglades National Park is located in the state of _____ .

_____ *lead students on tours of the Everglades.*

Some animals to see in the Everglades are _____ .

Model for students the structure of an informal letter, if needed.
ELA W.5.4, W.5.10 **ELD** ELD.PI.5.4, ELD.PI.5.11a

TEXT TO WORLD

Work with students to identify text details that provide clues to the author's point of view. Provide a list of national parks, and guide students to websites where they can learn more about the national park they choose.
ELA RI.5.7 **ELD** ELD.PI.5.1

Vocabulary Strategies

▶ **SHARE OBJECTIVES**
- Learn and use words with the prefixes *en–*, *re–*, *pre–*, *pro–*.
- Use prefixes as clues to word meaning.

▶ **SKILL TRACE**

Prefixes	
Introduce	T122–T123, Unit 1
Differentiate	T226–T227
Reteach	T228
Review	**T196–T197**
	T348–T349, Unit 3
Test	Weekly Tests, Lesson 8

ENGLISH LANGUAGE SUPPORT

Preteach

All Proficiencies Tell students that a prefix is a word part that is added to a base word or word root to change its meaning. Write: *en-* = *"put into,"* *re-* = *"again,"* *pre-* = *"before,"* *pro-* = *"forward."* Then provide students examples, such as *endanger, review, preview,* and *propel.*

Support Linguistic Transfer

Positive Transfer With students whose first language is Spanish, explain that the English prefixes *pre-* and *re-* have the same function as the Spanish prefixes *pre-* and *re-*.

Apply Vocabulary Skills

Emerging Add a prefix to the word *view.* Make a word that means "to view again." *review*

Expanding Write the word *review* on the board. Then say: *The word* review *means _____. to view again*

Bridging Have students use the words *review, preview,* and *endanger* in sentences. Have partners trade papers and discuss how the meanings of the words *view* and *danger* changed when each suffix was added.

ELD ELD.PI.5.1, ELD.PI.5.6b, ELD.PI.5.12b

Prefixes *en-, re-, pre-, pro-*

1 Teach/Model

Terms About Language

affix a suffix or prefix attached to a base word, stem, or root that changes the meaning of the word

prefix an affix added before a base word that changes the word's meaning

base word a word to which prefixes and/or suffixes are added

word root a part of a word to which prefixes and/or suffixes are added

- Explain that an **affix** is a word part attached to a **base word** or **word root** that changes the meaning of the word. A **prefix** is an affix attached to the beginning of a word.
- Tell students that *en–* means "put in," *re–* means "again," *pre–* means "before," and *pro–* means "for" or "before." Point out that these prefixes are derived from Latin.
- Write on the board: *A park ranger can teach us about plant and animal species that are threatened or endangered.*

Think Aloud *I see the word* danger *in the word* endangered. *I know* danger *means "in harm's way." I also know that the prefix* en– *means "put in." The context tells me that an animal or plant that is* endangered *may be harmed in some way. I think the harm in this case is complete disappearance, or extinction.* Endangered *must mean "put in danger of extinction."*

- Tell students that in the word *reclaim, claim* is a base word meaning *to declare as one's own,* so to reclaim means *to take as one's own again.*
- Discuss with students what else they can do to figure out the meaning of a word if looking in and around the word doesn't help. *consult a dictionary*

Literacy and Language Guide
See pages 130-131 for further practice with
lesson vocabulary.

2 Guided Practice

- Explain to students that in the word *predict, dict* is a word root. Work with students to infer the meaning of the Latin word root *dict* to determine the meaning of *predict. predict = say before*

- Display the top half of Projectable 8.3 and read "A Visit from the Park Ranger" aloud.

- Ask students to identify the Vocabulary words in the passage. Circle or highlight the words.

- Work with students to add the word parts and meanings to the chart. Discuss how the prefixes provide clues to the meanings.

3 Apply

- Have students look through their **Student Book** to locate words with the prefixes *en-, re-, pre-, pro-*. Then have them apply Steps 1 and 2 of the strategy on Projectable S8 to list the base words/roots, prefixes, and meanings of the words, using a print or digital dictionary to determine or clarify the meanings of unfamiliar words as needed. **ELA** L.5.4b, L.5.4c **ELD** ELD.PI.5.6b, ELD.PI.5.12b

Interactive Whiteboard Lesson Use **Vocabulary Strategies: Prefixes *en-, re-, pre-, pro-*** to reinforce how to use prefixes and base words to determine word meaning and to recognize and read words with the prefixes *en-, re-, pre-,* and *pro-*.

- Distribute to students Reader's Notebook page 87 or leveled practice in Grab-and-Go™ Resources to complete independently.

Are students able to use the prefixes en-, re-, pre-, *and* pro- *to determine word meaning?*

IF...	THEN...
students **struggle,**	▶ **Differentiate Vocabulary Strategies** for Struggling Readers, p. T226.
students **on target,**	▶ **Differentiate Vocabulary Strategies** for On-Level Readers, p. T226.
students **excel,**	▶ **Differentiate Vocabulary Strategies** for Advanced Readers, p. T227.

SMALL GROUP Options

Differentiate Vocabulary Strategies: pp. T226–T227. *Scaffold instruction to the English learner's proficiency level..*

ENGLISH LANGUAGE SUPPORT

Comprehensible Input

Emerging Say that *re–* means "again," so *replace* means "to place again." Guide students to analyze the use of prefixes for these words: *proceed, preheat,* and *enact.*

Expanding Write *view* on the board and model adding prefixes to form *replace* and *prepay.* Help students use each word in a sentence to confirm their understanding.

Bridging Ask clarifying questions to confirm students' understanding of prefixes. For example: If *pre–* means "before", what does *preheat* mean? *to heat before* **ELD** ELD.PI.5.6b, ELD.PI.5.12b

DOMAIN: Life Science

LESSON TOPIC: Conservation

Extend the Topic

▶ **SHARE OBJECTIVES**

- Acquire and use domain-specific vocabulary.
- Analyze and explain how an author supports an argument.
- Participate in a group discussion.

Words About the Topic: Conservation

- **carbon footprint** the amount of carbon dioxide or other types of carbon released into the air by the activities of a person, company, country, etc.

- **ecosystem** a system involving the interactions between a community of living organisms in an area and its nonliving environment

- **natural resource** something found in nature that is necessary or useful to humans, such as a forest, a mineral deposit, fresh water, etc.

- **wilderness** a wild region, such as a forest or desert, which is uninhabited or inhabited only by wild animals

Domain-Specific Vocabulary

Introduce Words About the Topic Remind students that this week's topic is Conservation. Display the words. Tell students that these are words that can help them learn more about conservation. Read aloud the definition for each word and then have students respond to the following prompts:

- *When you ride to school on a bus or in a car, you are contributing to your _____.* carbon footprint

- *If you go to a natural park, you might visit one of the few remaining areas in the country that is still considered _____.* wilderness

- *Farmland, timber, fish, copper. Which word is a good title for this list?* natural resources

- *If you study a pond and the area around it, you are studying an _____.* ecosystem

ENGLISH LANGUAGE SUPPORT For example, point out the illustration on page 237 and say: *The Everglades and the animals in it form an ecosystem.*

Interact with the Words Have students work in small groups using Graphic Organizer 6 (Four-Square Map) ⬦ to extend their understanding of each word about conservation. Assign one word to each group and have them follow these steps for completing the Four-Square Map with information about the word:

1 In the first corner, draw a picture that represents the word.

2 In the second corner, write the meaning of the word.

3 In the third corner, write a sentence using the word.

4 In the fourth corner, write the word.

When groups have finished, have them share their completed Four-Square Maps with the class. **ELA** L.5.6 **ELD** ELD.PI.12a

Speaking and Listening [Performance Task]

Explain an Author's Argument

Review Author's Purpose Have students review what they have learned in this lesson about author's purpose and supporting key points in a text with reasons and evidence. Tell them that they will work with a small group to choose and analyze another short persuasive text or article and participate in a discussion about the author's argument.

Model Speaking Skills Ask students to listen as you model how to identify the core of an argument: *I believe the author's main argument is that we must all do more to protect wildlife.*

Identify Support Have groups read their chosen text together. Point out that they should identify the author's purpose, argument, and main points.

Organize Information Have students work independently to complete a graphic organizer like the one below to help them explain how the author uses reasons and evidence to support particular points or arguments. They should list important details, reasons, and evidence in the bottom boxes and summarize the author's argument in the top box. **ELA** RI.5.8

Prepare for Discussion Have students review their graphic organizers and edit them as necessary to prepare for discussion.

Participate in Discussion Share with students the discussion tips at right. Have students rejoin their groups and participate in a discussion of the author's argument. Remind students to come to the discussion prepared, explicitly drawing on the work they have done for the discussion and referring to the graphic organizer as appropriate. **ELA** RI.5.8, SL.5.1a, SL.5.1b, SL.5.1c, SL.5.3 **ELD** ELD.PI.5.1

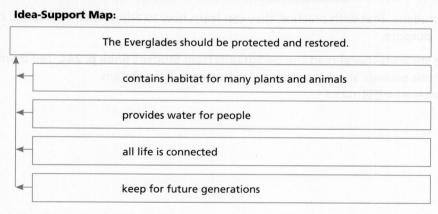

Idea-Support Map: _____

- The Everglades should be protected and restored.
  - contains habitat for many plants and animals
  - provides water for people
  - all life is connected
  - keep for future generations

FOR STUDENTS WITH DISABILITIES For students who have difficulty writing longer responses, have students fill in an outline and present their responses orally using the outline as a guide.

Skill Focus: Identify Ideas and Supporting Evidence Explain that authors often give reasons (the why) and evidence (the how) to support their ideas and opinions. Read aloud a portion of "Everglades Forever." Then have students summarize aloud the points the book makes by answering the following question: *Which details from the presentation support the idea that the Everglades should be preserved?* **ELA** SL.5.2, SL.5.3

DISCUSSION TIPS

1. **Before the discussion starts, decide which of the author's reasons you find most convincing.**

2. **During the discussion, remember to use the evidence you gathered to strengthen your points**

3. **Ask questions to clarify ideas or deepen the discussion, and make comments that build on others' ideas.**

4. **Remember to follow basic discussion rules.**

ENGLISH LANGUAGE SUPPORT Provide frames to help students separate the points of an argument:

- *The author's core argument is _____.*
- *The author's supporting reasons are _____.*

Fluency

- Read orally with appropriate rate.
- Read on-level text at a rate that reflects purpose for reading (prosody).

ENGLISH LANGUAGE SUPPORT

Audio Support

All Proficiencies Help English learners develop expression by having students listen to an audio recording of "Everglades Forever: Restoring America's Wetlands." Tell students to listen carefully to the different expressions used as the story is read. After listening to the recording, have students read **Student Book p. 239**. Listen as students read each sentence with the appropriate expression. **ELD** ELD.PIII.5

Cold Reads: Support for fluent reading with comprehension

FORMATIVE ASSESSMENT RtI

As students read **Student Book p. 244,** circulate and spend time listening to each student. If students have difficulty reading with proper phrasing, provide corrective feedback.

Model correct phrasing as you read aloud the section to students, pointing out the punctuation cues, and have them choral- or echo-read with you.

Guide students to read another paragraph on their own, and provide feedback, as necessary. Tell students that their reading fluency will continue to improve as they work hard at improving their phrasing.

Adjust Rate to Purpose

1 Teach/Model

- Tell students that good readers adjust their reading rate depending on their purpose for reading. For instance, skimming for facts and reading difficult material require different reading rates.

- Have students follow along as you read aloud **Student Book p. 239**. First, read the page quickly. Ask students to write what they remember. Then read the page slowly and purposefully. Again, ask students to write what they remember. Explain that your second reading was done at an appropriate rate for absorbing details from new material.

2 Guided Practice

- Together, read aloud the first paragraph on **Student Book p. 242**. Model reading slowly.

- Work with students to adjust their rate based on their purpose for reading.

- If students are having difficulty adjusting their rate to their purpose, reread with them the third paragraph on **Student Book p. 242**. Go over each sentence with students until they can read it fluently and at an appropriate rate. Ask questions to make sure students understand the content.

- See also Instructional Routine 7.

3 Apply

- Tell students that with practice, they can learn how to adjust their rate based on their purpose.

- Have students choral-read the paragraphs from **Student Book p. 244**. Tell them to read this passage slowly in order to understand all the details.
  ELA RF.5.4a, RF.5.4b **ELD** ELD.PIII.5

Decoding

Homophones

1 Teach/Model

Analyze Related Words Write the words *ceiling* and *sealing* on the board.

- Read the words aloud. Ask students what is the same about the two words. *They sound the same.* Point to the words and ask what is different about them. *They are spelled differently.*

- Underline the letters *ei* in *ceiling* and the letters *ea* in *sealing*. Guide students to use knowledge of letter-sound correspondences to understand that in both cases the letters stand for the long *e* sound.

- Explain that *ceiling* and *sealing* are homophones, two words that sound the same but have different spellings.

2 Practice/Apply

Blend Words Have students chorally read the following homophones. Then ask them to underline the spelling difference in each set of related words. Briefly define each word or have students check a dictionary.

over<u>due</u>   over<u>do</u>   allowed   aloud   profit   prophet

compliment   complement   bazaar   bizarre   flour   flower

site   sight   principle   principal   whether   weather

Use Context to Determine Meaning Write cloze sentences for the words above and other homophones. Have students select and spell aloud the correct word to finish each sentence. Ask students to explain context clues they used to determine the correct spelling. Use these and other sentences:

Lillian did not know _____ to ride her bike or take the bus. whether

To make the cookies, you will need sugar, chocolate, and _____. flour

If Christina does not practice, her chances of winning will _____. lessen

Dominic thinks the tree kangaroo is a _____-looking animal. bizarre

ELA RF.5.3a **ELD** ELD.PIII.5

▶ **SHARE OBJECTIVES**

- Use knowledge of letter-sound correspondences to recognize spelling changes in words that sound the same.

- Read accurately words that sound the same.

FORMATIVE ASSESSMENT  **RtI**

If students have difficulty decoding homophones, use the model below.

Correct the error. *Remember that homophones sound the same but have different spellings.*

Model how to decode the words. *Overdue and overdo start with the same /ō/ sound. They have /vər/ in the middle. Overdue has the ending -due, which stands for /do͞o/. Overdo ends in -do, which also stands for /do͞o/. I put them together. /ō vər do͞o/.*

Guide students to try different sounds to decode *overdue* and *overdo*.

Check students' understanding. *Which letters in each word stand for /do͞o/?* due, do *What are the words?* overdue, overdo

Reinforce Have students repeat the process with the words *lesson* and *lessen*.

ENGLISH LANGUAGE SUPPORT

Linguistic Transfer

Use the transfer chart in the **Quick Start Pacing Guide** to determine whether your students will have difficulty due to transfer issues. As needed, preteach the skill. **ELD** ELD.PIII.5

Spelling Homophones

▶ SHARE OBJECTIVE

- Spell grade-appropriate words that sound alike but have different meanings and spellings.

Spelling Words

Basic

steel	lessen	berry
steal	who's	bury
aloud	whose	hanger
⭐ allowed	manor	hangar
⭐ ring	manner	overdo
wring	pedal	overdue
lesson	peddle	

Review

⭐ wait, weight, vain, vane, vein

Challenge

canvass, canvas, site, sight, cite

⭐ Forms of these words appear in "Everglades Forever: Restoring America's Great Wetland."

ENGLISH LANGUAGE SUPPORT

Preteach

Spanish Cognates Write and discuss these Spanish cognates for Spanish-speaking students.

manner • *manera*

lesson • *lección*

Transfer Support Homophones can be very confusing for students who are learning English. To support students' understanding, help them create an illustrated list of common homophone pairs.

ELD ELD.PIII.5

Word Meanings Use Day 5 sentences to preview the meanings of spelling words.

DAY 1

① TEACH THE PRINCIPLE

- Administer the **Pretest**. Use the Day 5 sentences.
- Write *steel* and *steal* on the board. Remind students that homophones are words that sound alike but are spelled differently and have different meanings. Review the chart, explaining that students will have to memorize the different spellings of the words.

one syllable	steel/steal ring/wring
two syllables	aloud/allowed
three syllables	overdo/overdue

② GUIDED PRACTICE

Guide students to identify the sounds/spellings in the remaining Spelling Words.

Model a Word Sort Model sorting words based on the number of syllables in each word. Present the Model the Sort lesson on page 70 of the **Literacy and Language Guide**.

③ APPLY

Distribute Reader's Notebook page 88 ↗ and have students complete it independently.

DAY 2

① TEACH WORD SORT

- Set up three rows as shown. Model adding a Spelling Word to each row.
- Have students copy the chart. Guide students to write each Spelling Word where it belongs.

one-syllable homophones	who's/ whose
two-syllable homophones	manor/ manner
three-syllable homophones	overdo/ overdue

② GUIDED PRACTICE

- Have students add to the chart homophones from "Everglades Forever." Remind them to look carefully because homophones are often easily confused.

Guided Word Sort Guide students to sort words based on the number of syllables in each word. Present the Repeat the Sort lesson on page 70 of the **Literacy and Language Guide**.

③ APPLY

Distribute Reader's Notebook page 89 ↗ and have students complete it independently.

DAY 3

1 TEACH WORD FAMILIES

- **WRITE** *steal*. Define it: *to move somewhere quietly and in secret.*
- **WRITE** *stealth*. Define it: *to do something in a slow, quiet, and secretive way.*
- **ASK** *What is the connection between these words? Both contain the word* steal; *a person who steals into a room would probably be stealthy.*
- With students, list and discuss more words related to *steal*. *Sample:* stealthily, stealing

2 GUIDED PRACTICE

- **WRITE** *manner*. Define it: *the way you do something.*
- **WRITE** *mannerism* and *mannerly*. Have students look these words up in a dictionary or an electronic resource.
- **ASK** *What is the connection among* manner, mannerism, *and* mannerly?

Have students write their answers.

3 APPLY

Independent Word Sort Have students sort words as quickly as they can. Present the Speed Sort lesson on page 71 of the **Literacy and Language Guide.**

DAY 4

1 CONNECT TO WRITING

- Read and discuss the prompt below.

Informative Writing
Write a cause-and-effect essay about a natural area that you think needs to be protected. Use your writing to explain the effects of not protecting the area.

2 GUIDED PRACTICE

- Guide students as they plan and write their cause-and-effect essays.
- Remind students to proofread their writing and to consult print and digital references to confirm correct spelling. (See p. T210.) **ELA L.5.2e**

Open Sort Have students sort words according to categories of their choice. Present the Open Sort lesson on page 71 of the **Literacy and Language Guide.**

3 APPLY

Distribute Reader's Notebook page 90 and have students complete it independently.

DAY 5

ASSESS SPELLING

- Say each boldfaced word, read the sentence, and then repeat the word.
- Have students write the boldfaced word. **ELA L.5.2e**

Basic

1. Iron ore is used to make **steel**.
2. A thief may **steal** a diamond.
3. I read **aloud** to my little sister.
4. Skateboarding is not **allowed**.
5. She wore a beautiful **ring**.
6. **Wring** out your wet clothes.
7. Matt has a piano **lesson**.
8. Pain will **lessen** as you heal.
9. **Who's** bringing snacks?
10. I'll tell you **whose** bike that is.
11. The huge **manor** had twenty bedrooms.
12. Her proud **manner** annoyed me.
13. Mom stepped on the gas **pedal**.
14. Sellers **peddle** their goods.
15. This red **berry** tastes sweet.
16. **Bury** that in the ground.
17. Put your shirt on a **hanger**.
18. The airplane is in the **hangar**.
19. If you **overdo** it, you'll be tired.
20. She paid the **overdue** bill.

Grammar Conjunctions

▶ SHARE OBJECTIVES
- Explain the function of conjunctions.
- Use coordinating and subordinating conjunctions.
- Combine sentences using conjunctions.

Terms About Language

coordinating conjunction a conjunction that joins two words, groups of words, or sentences • *conjunción*

subordinating conjunction a conjunction that combines two clauses into a complex sentence

ENGLISH LANGUAGE SUPPORT

Preteach: All Proficiencies

Explain the Language Term Point out the cognate in the list above. Then explain that:

- A conjunction is a word that joins other words together.

Linguistic Transfer Explain to students that conjunctions serve the same function in many languages, which is to "connect."

Scaffolded Practice

Emerging Write this sentence on the board: *We enjoyed our trip to the park, but _____.* Have students complete the sentence in a way that creates a compound sentence.

Expanding Write sentence frames with *and* and *but* leaving out the words that follow the coordinating conjunction. Guide students to finish each sentence.

Bridging Have students write original compound sentences without the comma and coordinating conjunction. Have them exchange papers with a partner to complete.

DAY 1 TEACH

DAILY PROOFREADING PRACTICE

He gave Sylvia and I a tour, of the park. *me; tour of*

① TEACH USING *AND, BUT,* AND *OR*

- Display Projectable 8.4 🔗. Explain that **conjunctions** are words that connect other words or groups of words in a sentence.

ENGLISH LANGUAGE SUPPORT Present these examples of conjunctions. Coordinating Conjunctions: *and, but, or*; Subordinating Conjunctions: *because, if, although, when, as, since.* Have students identify the conjunction in each sentence below.

- Because the wetlands were endangered, people worked to restore them. *(because; subordinating)*

- An osprey is a kind of hawk, and it eats fish. *(and; coordinating)*

- Tell students that when *and, but,* and *or* connect sentence parts that are alike, they are called **coordinating conjunctions**. They can be used to connect similar words, phrases, or clauses within a sentence. They *also* can connect two sentences to make a compound sentence.

- Model identifying conjunctions in the example sentence: *Some desert animals are endangered and need our protection.*

Think Aloud *To identify coordinating conjunctions, I ask this Thinking Question:* **What word's function is to connect other words or groups of words in the sentence?** *The conjunction* and *joins two predicates:* are endangered *and* need our protection.

② PRACTICE/APPLY

- Complete the items on Projectable 8.4 🔗 with students.

- Write these sets of words and phrases on the board: took a trip to the park/listened to the ranger; the fifth grade/the sixth grade; informative/interesting. Have students join them with coordinating conjunctions and use them in sentences. **ELD** ELD.PII.5.6

- Have students complete Reader's Notebook p. 91 🔗 for practice with simple subjects and predicates.

DAY 2 TEACH

DAILY PROOFREADING PRACTICE

I read a book about alligators sawgrass marshes. *alligators and sawgrass marshes*

1 TEACH USING *AND, BUT,* AND *OR* TO COMBINE SENTENCES AND IDEAS

- Display Projectable 8.5 ⬀. Explain that coordinating conjunctions are used to create compound sentences. Tell students that two sentences with the same subject or related to the same idea can be joined with a comma and the coordinating conjunction *and.* Two sentences with contrasting ideas can be combined with a comma and the conjunction *but* or *or.*

- Model how to form a compound sentence using a conjunction to combine two ideas: *The Everglades is endangered by development. Alien species are also a threat.*

Think Aloud *To form a compound sentence, I ask these Thinking Questions:* **How are the two sentences related? What conjunction can I use to connect them?** *Both sentences relate to threats to the Everglades, so the conjunction* and *can be used to connect them.*

2 PRACTICE/APPLY

- Complete Projectable 8.5 ⬀ with students.

- Have volunteers write compound sentences on the board. Ask other students to explain the function of the conjunctions. **ELA** L.5.1a **ELD** ELD.PII.5.6

- Have students complete Reader's Notebook p. 92 ⬀ for practice with simple subjects and predicates.

DAY 3 TEACH

DAILY PROOFREADING PRACTICE

The Everglades is home to mangroves herons are often perch on them. *mangroves, and herons*

1 TEACH USING SUBORDINATING CONJUNCTIONS

- Display Projectable 8.6 ⬀. Explain that a **subordinating conjunction** makes one part of a sentence dependent on the other part. List common subordinating conjunctions: *while, because, although, if, since.* Tell students that connecting two sentences with a subordinating conjunction forms a complex sentence.

- Model identifying the dependent part of the sentence and the subordinating conjunction in this complex sentence: *Because the climate is dry, lizards thrive in the desert.*

Think Aloud *To identify a subordinating conjunction, I ask this Thinking Question:* **Which part of the sentence is dependent on the other part?** *Lizards thrive in the desert could form a complete sentence. It is not dependent. Because the climate is dry is dependent on the other part of the sentence, Because is the subordinating conjunction.*

2 PRACTICE/APPLY

- Complete Projectable 8.6 ⬀ with students.

- Have students write complex sentences using subordinating conjunctions. Have partners identify the conjunctions and dependent sentence parts. **ELA** L.5.1a **ELD** ELD.PII.5.6

- Have students complete Reader's Notebook p. 93 ⬀ for practice with simple subjects and predicates.

DAY 4 REVIEW

DAILY PROOFREADING PRACTICE

I took so many pictures, I am tired. *Because I took so many pictures, I am tired.*

1 REVIEW CONJUNCTIONS

- Remind students that conjunctions are words that connect other words or groups of words in a sentence. Have students turn to **Student Book p. 258**. Review coordinating and subordinating conjunctions and how they can be used to form compound and complex sentences. Then have students complete the **Try This!** activity.

ENGLISH LANGUAGE SUPPORT Remind students that conjunctions can be either coordinating or subordinating. Provide examples, such as *since* (subordinating), *and* (coordinating), *although* (subordinating), and *but* (coordinating).

2 SPIRAL REVIEW

COMPLETE SUBJECTS AND PREDICATES Review with students that all of the words in the subject make up the complete subject.

Remind students that the complete subject of an imperative sentence is *you*. In an imperative sentence, the word *you* is usually understood, not stated.

Explain that all of the words in the predicate make up the complete predicate.

Write these sentences on the board. Have students come to the board and underline the complete subjects and circle the complete predicates.

The piping hot pie (melted in my mouth)

The angry crowd (booed heartily.)

(Bike carefully!)

Then have students complete Reader's Notebook p. 94 for more practice with complete subjects and predicates.

DAY 5 CONNECT TO WRITING

DAILY PROOFREADING PRACTICE

When we visited the Everglades we had to. Dress for hot, dry, and wet weather. *Everglades, we had to dress*

1 INTERACTIVE WHITEBOARD LESSON

For cumulative review, use **Grammar: Conjunctions** to reinforce how to use coordinating and subordinating conjunctions to combine sentences.

2 CONNECT TO WRITING

- Remind students that using coordinating and subordinating conjunctions to connect short sentences can help make their writing flow more smoothly.

- Tell students that when they revise, they need to look for run-ons in their writing and correct them. Remind them that both types of conjunctions can be used to eliminate run-on sentences by forming compound or complex sentences.

3 PRACTICE/APPLY

- Display this run-on sentence on the board: The water flows from the Everglades to the ocean it does not flow naturally.

- Have students use coordinating and subordinating conjunctions to correct the run-on sentence. Have them share their new compound and complex sentences. **ELA** L.5.1a, L.5.3a

  (compound) The water flows from the Everglades to the ocean, but it does not flow naturally.

  (complex) Although the water flows from the ocean to the Everglades, it does not flow naturally.

- Have students write to a partner to explain the function of the coordinating and subordinating conjunctions in their sentences. **ELA** L.5.1a **ELD** ELD.PII.5.6

- Have students complete Reader's Notebook p. 95 for practice with simple subjects and predicates.

Grammar

Digital Resources
- Multimedia
  Grammar Glossary
- GrammarSnap
  Videos

What Is a Conjunction? A **conjunction** is a word that connects other words in a sentence. *And, but,* and *or* are **coordinating conjunctions**. They can connect two words, two groups of words, or two sentences. A sentence formed when a coordinating conjunction is used to connect two sentences is called a **compound sentence**. Words such as *if, because, although, after,* and *when* are **subordinating conjunctions**. A subordinating conjunction can connect a sentence and a dependent clause to form a **complex sentence**.

Coordinating Conjunction in a Compound Sentence

The egret stood in the sawgrass, and the osprey dived into the slough.

Subordinating Conjunction in a Complex Sentence

When the osprey dived, the egret flew away.

Try This! **Work with a partner. Identify each conjunction in the sentences below and tell whether it is coordinating or subordinating. Then explain the purpose of the conjunction in each sentence.**

1. Most plants cannot live in salty water, but mangrove trees thrive in it.
2. Where mangrove trees grow, shrimp and other marine animals can raise their young.
3. If the water in a swamp becomes too salty, some animals cannot survive there.
4. Fresh water is needed, and only rainfall can provide that.

258 **ELA** L.5.1a, L.5.3a **ELD** ELD.PII.5.6, ELD.PII.5.7

A good writer avoids run-on sentences. One way to correct a run-on sentence is to add a comma and a coordinating conjunction to turn the run-on sentence into a compound sentence. Another way to correct a run-on sentence is to add a subordinating conjunction to turn it into a complex sentence.

Run-On Sentence

The hikers entered the Pinelands the world became very quiet.

Compound Sentence	Complex Sentence
The hikers entered the Pinelands, and the world became very quiet.	When the hikers entered the Pinelands, the world became very quiet.

Connect Grammar to Writing

As you revise your cause-and-effect essay, look for run-on sentences. Correct a run-on sentence by dividing it into separate sentences or by using conjunctions to form a compound or complex sentence.

259

Try This!

1. *but; coordinating; to connect two complete sentences to form a compound sentence*
2. *Where; subordinating; to form a complex sentence with a dependent clause*
3. *If; subordinating; to form a complex sentence with a dependent clause*
4. *and; coordinating; to connect two complete sentences to form a compound sentence*

Connect Grammar to Writing

- Have students turn to **Student Book p. 259**. Read the top paragraph with students.

- Read aloud the first sentence in the chart. Point out that it is a run-on sentence made up of two independent thoughts. Then read the edited sentences. Point out that run-on sentences can be corrected with the use of commas and conjunctions.

- Tell students that they should look for opportunities to use conjunctions to form compound or complex sentences as they revise their paragraphs. **ELA** L.5.1a, L.5.3a **ELD** ELD.PII.5.6

ENGLISH LANGUAGE SUPPORT

Additional Grammar Practice

Teach/Model Point to the picture of the hiker on **Language Support Card 8**. Write: *The hiker sees water. The hiker sees trees.* Ask: *How can I combine these two sentences?*

- Write: *The hiker sees water and trees.* Underline *and* and say: *And is a connecting word. We use it to add extra information. Connecting words are called* conjunctions.

Guided Practice Write the following sentence frames. Have students add the conjunction that completes each sentence.

- We should conserve paper _____ plastic. *and*

- Should we throw away plastic bags, _____ should we recycle them? *or*

- Sometimes we remember to conserve, _____ at other times we forget. *but*

Connect to Writing Have students write sentences about their two favorite foods. Have them use all three of the conjunctions they learned.

ELA L.5.1a **ELD** ELD.PI.5.10a, ELD.PII.5.2b

Informative Writing Focus Trait: Evidence

▶ SHARE OBJECTIVES

- Write a cause-and-effect essay.
- Use specific facts and other details to develop the topic.

Terms About Writing

cause an event or circumstance that leads to another event

effect something that happens as the result of an earlier event

ENGLISH LANGUAGE SUPPORT
Collaborative Writing

Explain that the class will work together to write a cause-and-effect essay about the importance of protecting natural environments such as the Everglades.

- Say: *In this essay, what is the cause about which you will write?* **Help** students identify the cause. *the destruction of natural environments such as the Everglades What are some of the possible effects of this cause?* Help students find examples of possible effects if the cause—the destruction of the Everglades—were to happen. *Animals and plants would lose their habitat.*

- Ask: *What are some specific details or examples you could use from the anchor text to support your main idea? Examples include the key role of mangrove swamps in protecting certain fish and marine animals, such as shrimp and bonefish.* **ELD** ELD.PI.5.7

Encourage students to use clauses to link ideas and supporting details, and also to use precise words. Read the completed composition aloud chorally.

Performance Task

myWriteSmart Have students complete the writing task through *my*WriteSmart. Students will read the prompt within *my*WriteSmart and have access to multiple writing resources, including the Student eBook, Writing Rubrics, and Graphic Organizers.

DAY 1 ANALYZE THE MODEL

❶ INTRODUCE CAUSE-AND-EFFECT ESSAY

- Tell students that they will be writing a **cause-and-effect essay** in this lesson.
- Display Projectable 8.7 ⬈ and read aloud the Writing Model prompt. Discuss the following:

> #### What Is a Cause-and-Effect Essay?
> - It explains how one event leads to others.
> - It includes specific facts, relevant details, and precise language to explain the relationship.
> - It presents details in a logical order signaled by transitions.
> - It provides a strong conclusion that shows the importance of the cause-and-effect relationship.

- Point out the specific details and facts included in the first model paragraph. Discuss how they help to clarify the writer's main idea.

ENGLISH LANGUAGE SUPPORT How English Works As students study the model, explain that action verbs such as *bite, visit,* and *gather* are often part of verb phrases. Writers can build verb phrases by adding adverbs. Have students practice building more verb phrases with these action verbs. **ELD** ELD.PII.5.3

❷ PRACTICE/APPLY

- With students, label the cause, effects, facts, and details in the second paragraph.
- Ask students to identify transitional words and phrases in both paragraphs. As, When, during, resulting in, Only if; Well, When, leads to, So, next time

LESSON	FORM	FOCUS
6	Procedural Composition	Organization
7	Compare-Contrast Essay	Elaboration
8	**Cause-and-Effect Essay**	**Evidence**
9	Prewrite: Research Report	Evidence
10	Draft, Revise, Edit, Publish: Research Report	Conventions

WRITING

Additional support for Informative Writing appears in the **Common Core Writing Handbook**, Lesson 8.

DAY 2 TEACH

1 INTRODUCE THE WRITING FOCUS

EVIDENCE Tell students that when they write their cause-and-effect essay, they should present their supporting evidence in a logical order. Often writers choose to develop the cause first and then the effects.

Connect to "Everglades Forever"

Instead of this . . .	. . . the author wrote this.
The mangrove trees have adapted to unusual conditions.	"The mangrove trees have specially adapted roots and leaves so they can live in this salty, muddy water." (p. 241)

- Point out that the author's sentence includes specific details that tell about the mangrove's adaptation. Draw students' attention to the transition word *so,* which clarifies the cause-and-effect relationship in the sentence.

✎ 🗐 Annotate it! Have students highlight other supporting evidence in the text. Then have students share some examples and talk about how the author supports other statements with evidence.

2 PRACTICE/APPLY

- Write this sentence on the board: *The Restoration Plan will have a positive effect on the Everglades.* Have students find two specific facts or details that develop and explain the cause-and-effect relationship between the Restoration Plan and the Everglades. *Effects: the Everglades water will flow more naturally to the ocean; the amount of freshwater will be regulated; more animals will survive.* **ELA** W.5.2b

- Distribute Reader's Notebook page 96 🗐 and have students complete it independently.

DAY 3 PREWRITE

1 TEACH PLANNING A CAUSE-AND-EFFECT ESSAY

- Display Projectable 8.8 🗐. Read aloud the prompt. Have students think of a cause-and-effect relationship that they would like to explain. Help them identify topics by having them ask "why" questions about phenomena in nature, history, or science or the events they observe around them.

- Explain that their topic might have more than one cause for one effect or one cause that leads to several effects.

2 PRACTICE/APPLY

- Work with students to complete the cause-and-effect chart on Projectable 8.8 🗐.

- Distribute **Graphic Organizer 13**. Have students use the cause-and-effect chart to organize the causes and effects that they want to explain in their essays. **ELA** W.5.4, W.5.5, W.5.10

ENGLISH LANGUAGE SUPPORT

How English Works: Productive

Text Cohesion Before students begin drafting their cause-and-effect essays, have them plan to make their writing cohesive by using pronouns to refer readers back in their writing. Provide a model such as *The guide was a tall woman. She ducked under the tree branch.* Explain that *she* is a pronoun that refers back to *the guide.* Explain that using pronouns helps writers avoid repeating themselves. Help different proficiency levels think about their writing topics and build word banks of pronouns that can make their drafts cohesive. **ELD** ELD.PII.5.2a

DAY 4 DRAFT

① BEGIN A DRAFT

- Have students begin their drafts using their cause-and-effect charts. Discuss with them the following:

> 1. **Introduce** the topic of your essay clearly.

> 2. **Organize** your essay logically, exploring first the cause(s) and then the effect(s), or vice versa.

> 3. **Include** specific facts and details and use transitions to develop readers' understanding of the relationship(s).

> 4. **Conclude** by explaining the importance of the relationship(s).

② PRACTICE/APPLY

- Have students draft their cause-and-effect essays. Remind them to refer to their charts and to decide how they want to organize their details before they begin to write. **ELA** W.5.2a, W.5.2b, W.5.2e, W.5.4

- Have them reword details to make them more precise and to include facts where possible.

- Tell students to use transitions to link their ideas. List these examples on the board: *as a result, consequently, because,* **ELA** W.5.2c

HANDWRITING TIP Have students write their final pieces in cursive, using their best handwriting. Tell them to be sure to leave the appropriate spaces between the letters and words. See also pp. R22–R27 for handwriting support.

DAY 5 ANALYZE THE MODEL

① INTRODUCE THE STUDENT MODEL

- Remind students that good writers include specific facts and details.

- Read the top of **Student Book p. 260** with the class. Discuss the revisions made by Colin. Draw students' attention to the way in which Colin reworded details to make them more specific and meaningful. Point out where he states why the cause-and-effect relationship is important. Remind students that they, too, must show the significance of the relationship they have chosen.

- Have students explore Digital Lesson: Writing Informative Texts: Use Facts and Examples ⬈ to develop their informative writing.

② PRACTICE/APPLY

- Display Projectable 8.9 ⬈. Work with students to revise the rest of the student draft. Point out where more specific details and evidence could make the relationship between the alligators and the survival of other life in the Everglades clearer.

- Read Colin's Final Copy on **Student Book p. 261** to the class. Work with students to answer the *Reading as a Writer* questions.

- **Revising** Have students revise their essays using the Writing Checklist on **Student Book p. 260**. **ELA** W.5.2d, W.5.5

- **Proofreading** For proofreading support, have students use the Proofreading Checklist Blackline Master ⬈. **ELA** W.5.10

ENGLISH LANGUAGE SUPPORT

Peer-Supported Learning

All Proficiencies See the Peer Conference Forms in the ELL Teacher's Handbook.

Informative Writing

Interactive Lessons
► Writing Informative Texts: Use Facts and Examples
► Writing Informative Texts: Organize Your Information

myWriteSmart

✓**Evidence** The author of "Everglades Forever: Restoring America's Great Wetland" uses specific facts and details to inform readers about the Everglades habitat. When you revise your **cause-and-effect essay**, make sure your supporting details are specific.

Colin drafted an essay on what would happen if alligators disappeared from the Everglades. Later, he made his supporting details more specific so that his key points would be easy to follow.

Writing Checklist

✓ **Evidence**
Did I support my ideas with specific details?

✓ **Elaboration**
Did I use precise words?

✓ **Purpose**
Did I make relationships between causes and effects?
Is my writing clear and informative?

✓ **Organization**
Did I group related information logically?

✓ **Conventions**
Did I use correct spelling, grammar, and punctuation?
Did I use clauses effectively to link ideas?

Revised Draft

Alligators help create the habitats of other living things in the Everglades ^others. They dig deep holes, and the ^, which is part saltwater and part freshwater, holes fill with water. This brackish water^ ^that other animals depend on for food is home to young bonefish and shrimp.^

Final Copy

Protecting the Everglades

by Colin Diep

What would happen if alligators left the Everglades? In an ecosystem, every creature plays an important part in keeping the others alive. No part of life can be taken away or harmed without affecting other animals and plants.

Alligators help create the habitats of other living things in the Everglades. They dig deep holes, and the holes fill with water. This brackish water, which is part saltwater and part freshwater, is home to young bonefish and shrimp that other animals depend on for food. Many plants and animals gather in these wet alligator holes and use them to survive the dry season.

If alligators were to disappear, the life that depends on alligator holes in the dry season would not survive. The birds that feed on those plants and animals would have to find food elsewhere, or they would not survive either. By protecting alligators, we can help protect all life in the Everglades.

Reading as a Writer

How do specific details make the causes and effects more clear? Where can you strengthen words and details in your cause-and-effect essay?

In my final paper, I made my supporting details more specific. I also made clear connections between my ideas.

WRITING TRAITS SCORING RUBRIC

SCORE	4	3	2	1	NS
Purpose/ Organization	**The narrative is clear, focused, and well organized throughout.** • Contains an effective and complete plot • Develops strong setting, narrator/ characters • Includes a variety of transitions to connect ideas • Contains a logical sequence of events • Includes an effective introduction and conclusion	**The narrative's organization is adequately maintained, and the focus is generally clear.** • Plot is mostly effective/may contain small flaws • Develops setting, narrator/ characters • Adequate use of transitions to connect ideas • Contains an adequate sequence of events	**The narrative is somewhat organized and may be unclear in some parts.** • Plot may be inconsistent • Minimal development of setting, narrator/characters • Contains inconsistent use of transitions to connect ideas • Sequence of events is weak or unclear • Introduction and conclusion need improvement	**The narrative may be somewhat organized but unfocused.** • Little or no plot • Little or no development of setting, narrator/characters • Contains few or inappropriate transitions and weak connections among ideas • Sequence of events is not organized • Introduction and/or conclusion may be missing	• Not intelligible • Not written in English • Not on topic • Contains text copied from another source • Does not address the purpose for writing
Development/ Elaboration	**The narrative includes effective elaboration using details, dialogue, and description.** • Characters, setting, experiences, and events are well developed • Writer uses a variety of narrative techniques that strengthen the story or illustrate the experience • Contains effective sensory, concrete, and figurative language • Style is appropriate and effective	**The narrative includes adequate elaboration using details, dialogue, and description.** • Characters, setting, experiences, and events are adequately developed • Writer uses a variety of narrative techniques that generally move the story forward and illustrate the experience • Contains adequate sensory, concrete, and figurative language • Style is mostly appropriate	**The narrative includes partial or ineffective elaboration using unclear or inconsistent details, dialogue, and description.** • Characters, setting, experiences, and events lack consistent development • Writer uses inconsistent or weak narrative techniques • Contains weak sensory, concrete, and figurative language • Style is inconsistent or inappropriate	**The narrative provides little or no elaboration using few or no details, dialogue, and description.** • Very little development of characters, setting, experiences, and events • Writer's use of narrative techniques are minimal and may be incorrect • Little or no sensory, concrete, and figurative language • Little or no evidence of style	• Not intelligible • Not written in English • Not on topic • Contains text copied from another source • Does not address the purpose for writing

SCORE	2	1	0	NS
Conventions	**The narrative demonstrates adequate command of conventions.** • Consistent use of correct sentence structures, punctuation, capitalization, grammar, and spelling	**The narrative demonstrates partial command of conventions.** • Limited use of correct sentence structures, punctuation, capitalization, grammar, and spelling	**The narrative demonstrates little or no command of conventions.** • Rare use of correct sentence structures, punctuation, capitalization, grammar, and spelling	• Not intelligible • Not written in English • Not on topic • Contains text copied from another source

See also *Writing Rubric Blackline Master* and Teacher's Edition pp. R18–R21.

Formative Assessment

Weekly Tests

At the end of the lesson, administer the Weekly Test. This will give you a **snapshot of how students are progressing** with the Reading and Language Arts skills in this lesson and can give you **guidance on grouping, reteaching, and intervention.**

Suggestions for adjusting instruction based on these results can be found on the next page.

Access Through Accommodations

When you administer the Weekly Test, some students may have problems accessing all or parts of the assessment. The purpose of the Weekly Test is to determine students' ability to complete the Reading and Language Arts tasks they learned in this lesson. Any barriers to them accessing the tasks demanded of them should be lowered so they can focus on skill demonstration.

When choosing accommodations, you will want to avoid invalidating the test results; if you are measuring a student's reading skill, for example, you will not want to read aloud the passage. The following accommodations, if needed, will not interfere with the Weekly Test's validity:

- Read aloud the assessment directions and item prompts. If students are English learners, read aloud the assessment directions and item prompts in the student's native language, if possible.

- Define any unknown words in the directions or item prompts that do not give away the answers to the items.

- Allow for a break during the assessment.

- Simplify the language of assessment directions and item prompts.

- Administer the assessment in a smaller group setting.

- Administer the assessment on a computer or other electronic device.

- Provide audio amplification equipment, colored overlays, or visual magnifying equipment to maintain visual/audio attention and access.

- Allow students to complete the assessment items orally or by having another person transcribe their responses.

Using Data to Adjust Instruction

Use students' scores on the Weekly Test to determine Small Group placement, reteaching, and potential for Intervention.

☑ VOCABULARY AND COMPREHENSION

Author's Purpose; Explain Scientific Ideas; Domain-Specific Vocabulary; Anchor Text

Target Vocabulary; Prefixes *en-, re-, pre-, pro-*

IF STUDENT SCORES...	
...at acceptable,	**...below acceptable,**
THEN continue core instruction.	**THEN** use Reteach Comprehension Skill and Vocabulary Strategies lessons. For struggling students, administer the *Intervention Assessments* to determine if students would benefit from intervention.

☑ LANGUAGE ARTS

Conjunctions

IF STUDENT SCORES...	
...at acceptable,	**...below acceptable,**
THEN continue core instruction.	**THEN** use Reteach Language Arts lesson. For struggling students, administer the *Intervention Assessments* to determine if students would benefit from intervention.

☑ DECODING

Homophones

IF STUDENT SCORES...	
...at acceptable,	**...below acceptable,**
THEN continue core instruction.	**THEN** use Reteach Decoding lesson. For struggling students, administer the *Intervention Assessments* to determine if students would benefit from intervention.

☑ FLUENCY

Fluency Plan

Assess one group per week using the <u>Fluency Tests</u> 🔗 in the *Grab-and-Go™* Resources. Use the suggested plan at the right.

● Struggling Readers	Weeks 1, 3, 5
▲ On Level	Week 2
■ Advanced	Week 4

IF...	
...students are reading on-level text fluently,	**...students are reading below level,**
THEN continue core instruction.	**THEN** provide additional fluency practice using the **Student Book**, the **Cold Reads**, and the Leveled Readers. For struggling students, administer the *Intervention Assessments* to determine if students would benefit from intervention.

HOUGHTON MIFFLIN HARCOURT

JOURNEYS

Cold Reads

5

The ***Cold Reads*** passages increase gradually in Lexile® measures throughout the year, from below grade-level to above grade-level.

- Each passage is accompanied by several selected-response questions and one constructed-response prompt, requiring students to read closely, answer questions at substantial DOK levels, and cite text evidence.

- The *Cold Reads* may be used to provide practice in reading increasingly complex texts and to informally monitor students' progress.

- The *Cold Reads* may be used to estimate students' Lexile® levels in order to recommend appropriately challenging books for small-group instruction or independent reading.

Turn the page for more information about using FORMATIVE ASSESSMENT for ELD AND INTERVENTION.

✓ *Assess It Online!*

► **Language Workshop Assessment Handbook**

► **Intervention Assessments**

Formative Assessment for ELD and Intervention

Formative Assessment for English Learners

English learners should engage in the same rigorous curriculum and formative assessment as other students. However, it is important to remember that English learners face a dual challenge: they are strengthening their abilities *to use* English at the same time that they are learning challenging content *through* English. Use the following strategies and resources for ongoing assessment of English language development, in addition to the assessments you use with all students:

- A combination of **observational measures,** such as listening in as students read aloud or participate in collaborative conversations. Be prepared to provide **"just-in-time" scaffolding** to support students. For example, if students are retelling a story, you could help them use sentence structures with past-tense verbs and time-order transition words.

- **Constructive feedback** that focuses on communication and meaning-making. Avoid overcorrecting in a way that makes English learners reluctant to speak up. You might try recasting a child's statement more correctly, making a note to address the target form more directly during Designated ELD time.

- **Student self-assessment**, through students' own notes in their vocabulary notebooks or other learning journals. If possible, meet with each child to review his or her self-assessments and provide encouragement and feedback.

- **Formative assessment** notes that are integrated into the Language Workshop Teacher's Guide for use during Designated ELD.

- **Language Workshop Assessment Handbook** for longer-cycle assessment to make sure students are progressing in their English development.

Response to Intervention

Use the Weekly Tests and Benchmark and Unit Tests, along with your own observations, to determine if individual students are not responding to Tier I instruction and need additional testing to identify specific needs for targeted intervention.

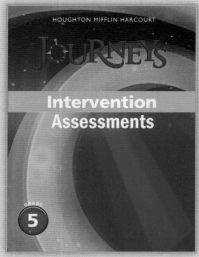

Intervention Assessments

Assessment for Intervention

Progress-Monitoring Assessments Administer this assessment to

- students in Tier II and Tier III Intervention to gauge progress towards exit from the intervention program.

- students who demonstrate lack of success with Weekly Tests, Benchmark and Unit Tests, and core instruction to determine if they might benefit from additional practice or intervention.

Vocabulary Reader
- *Mangrove Swamp*, T218–T219

Differentiate Comprehension
- Target Skill: Author's Purpose, T220–T221
- Target Strategy: Analyze/Evaluate, T220–T221

Leveled Readers
- ⬤ *Guardian of the Everglades*, T222
- ▲ *America's Urban Parks*, T223
- ■ *The Salton Sea*, T224
- ◆ *America's City Parks*, T225

Differentiate Vocabulary Strategies
- Prefixes *en-, re-, pre-, pro-*, T226–T227

Options for Reteaching
- Vocabulary Strategies: Prefixes *en-, re-, pre-, pro-*, T228
- Comprehension Skill: Author's Purpose, T228
- Language Arts: Conjunctions/Informative Writing, T229
- Decoding: Homophones, T229

Literacy Centers
Independent Practice
- Comprehension and Fluency, T160
- Word Study, T160
- Think and Write, T161

Teacher-Led

	DAY 1	DAY 2	DAY 3
Struggling Readers	**Vocabulary Reader** *Mangrove Swamp,* Differentiated Instruction, p. T218 **English Language Support,** p. T219	**Differentiate Comprehension** Author's Purpose; Analyze/Evaluate, p. T220 **English Language Support,** p. T221	**Leveled Reader** *Guardian of the Everglades,* p. T222 **English Language Support,** Leveled Reader Teacher's Guide, p. 5
On Level	**Vocabulary Reader** *Mangrove Swamp,* Differentiated Instruction, p. T218 **English Language Support,** p. T219	**Differentiate Comprehension** Author's Purpose; Analyze/Evaluate, p. T220 **English Language Support,** p. T221	**Leveled Reader** *America's Urban Parks,* p. T223 *America's City Parks,* p. T225 **English Language Support,** Leveled Reader Teacher's Guide, p. 5
Advanced	**Vocabulary Reader** *Mangrove Swamp,* Differentiated Instruction, p. T219 **English Language Support,** p. T219	**Differentiate Comprehension** Author's Purpose; Analyze/Evaluate, p. T221 **English Language Support,** p. T221	**Leveled Reader** *The Salton Sea,* p. T224 **English Language Support,** Leveled Reader Teacher's Guide, p. 5

What are my other students doing?

	DAY 1	DAY 2	DAY 3
Struggling Readers	**Reread** *Mangrove Swamp*	**Vocabulary in Context Cards** 71–80 *Talk It Over* Activities	**Listen** to Audio of "Everglades Forever"; retell and discuss
On Level	**Reread** *Mangrove Swamp*	**Reread** "Everglades Forever" with a partner	**Reread** for Fluency: *America's Urban Parks* or *America's City Parks* **Complete** Leveled Practice EL8.1
Advanced	**Vocabulary in Context Cards** 71–80 *Talk It Over* Activities	**Reread and Retell** "Everglades Forever"	**Reread** for Fluency: *The Salton Sea*

 **RtI** For Strategic Intervention for this lesson, see pp. S22–S31.

DAY 4

Differentiate Vocabulary Strategies
Prefixes *en-*, *re-*, *pre-*, *pro-*, p. T226
English Language Support, p. T227

Differentiate Vocabulary Strategies
Prefixes *en-*, *re-*, *pre-*, *pro-*, p. T226
English Language Support, p. T227

Differentiate Vocabulary Strategies
Prefixes *en-*, *re-*, *pre-*, *pro-*, p. T227
English Language Support, p. T227

- **Partners: Reread**
  Guardian of the Everglades
- **Complete** Leveled Practice SR8.1

- **Vocabulary in Context Cards**
  71–80 *Talk It Over* Activities
- **Complete** Reader's Notebook, p. 87

- **Reread** for Fluency: "Everglades
  Forever"
- **Complete** Leveled Practice A8.1

DAY 5

Options for Reteaching,
pp. T228–T229

Options for Reteaching,
pp. T228–T229

Options for Reteaching,
pp. T228–T229

- **Reread** for Fluency:
  "Everglades Forever"
- **Complete** Literacy Centers
- **Independent Reading**

- **Complete** Literacy Centers
- **Independent Reading**

- **Complete** Literacy Centers
- **Independent Reading**

English Language Support

Use the Leveled Reader Teacher's Guide to support ELs during differentiated instruction.

- **Characteristics of the Text** (p. 1)
  Identify challenging language features, such as text structure, literary features, complex sentences, and vocabulary.

- **Cultural Support/Cognates/Vocabulary** (p. 5)
  Explain unfamiliar features of English and help ELs transfer first-language knowledge.

- **Oral Language Development** (p. 5)
  Check comprehension using dialogues that match students' proficiency levels.

Book Share
Use this routine at the end of the week to enable students to demonstrate that they have become experts on their Leveled Readers.

Step 1:
Have each student write a presentation based on his or her Leveled Reader **Responding** page, using the following guidelines:

- Briefly tell what your book is about.

- Show your Inference Map and explain what you added to complete it.

- Tell about your favorite part of the book, what you found most interesting in it, or what you learned from it.

Students should prepare to share their presentations with a group.

Step 2:
Have students form groups in which each student has read a different Leveled Reader.

Step 3:
Have students take turns sharing their book presentations in their groups. Continue until all students have finished sharing. Encourage students to ask questions of the presenters. Provide frames such as the following for support.

Can you tell me more about _____?

I wonder why _____.

What do you think about _____?

 RtI

Summary

Mangrove swamps are habitats for baby sharks, pink shrimp, pelicans, raccoons, and alligators. The unique characteristics of the mangrove tree support this diverse ecosystem. Today, it is extremely important to help conserve these swamps.

☑ **TARGET VOCABULARY**

conserving	responsibility
restore	attracted
regulate	adapted
vegetation	unique
endangered	guardians

Vocabulary Reader
Mangrove Swamp

STRUGGLING READERS

ELA RI.5.4, L.5.4c
ELD ELD.PI.5.1, ELD.PI.5.6b

- Explain that mangroves are unusual trees that seem to be standing on their roots. In the United States, they can be found in the Florida Everglades, Louisiana, and Texas.

- Guide students to preview the Vocabulary Reader. Read aloud the headings. Ask students to describe the images, using Target Vocabulary when possible.

- Have students alternate reading pages of the text aloud. Guide them to use context to determine the meanings of unfamiliar words. As necessary, use the **Vocabulary in Context Cards** to review the meanings of vocabulary words.

- Assign the **Responding Page** and Blackline Master 8.4 🔗. Have partners work together to complete the pages.

ON LEVEL

ELA RI.5.4, L.5.4c
ELD ELD.PI.5.1, ELD.PI.5.6b

- Explain to students that mangroves, which are found mainly in the Florida Everglades in the United States, are protected by law. The trees are helpful to the environment because they feed and protect other living things.

- Remind students that context clues can help them determine the meaning of an unknown word. Tell students to use context clues to confirm their understanding of Target Vocabulary and to learn the meanings of new words.

- Have students alternate reading aloud pages of the Vocabulary Reader. Tell them to use context clues to determine the meanings of unknown words.

- Assign the **Responding Page** and Blackline Master 8.4 🔗. Have students discuss their responses with a partner.

ADVANCED

ELA RI.5.4, L.5.4c
ELD ELD.PI.5.1, ELD.PI.5.6b

- Have students preview the Vocabulary Reader and make predictions about what they will read, using information from the preview as well as prior knowledge.

- Remind students to use context clues to help them determine the meanings of unknown words.

- Tell students to read the text with a partner. Ask them to stop and discuss the meanings of unknown words as necessary.

- Assign the **Responding Page** and Blackline Master 8.4. For the Write About It activity, remind students to use facts and details from their reading to support their ideas.

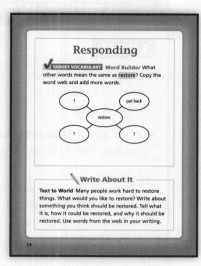

Mangrove Swamp, p. 14

ENGLISH LANGUAGE SUPPORT

ELD ELD.PI.5.1, ELD.PI.5.3, ELD.PI.5.6b

Provide Struggling Readers, On Level, and Advanced ELs proficiency-level support during differentiated instruction.

Emerging

Conduct a picture walk with students. Then read the Vocabulary Reader aloud with them. Pause at each Target Vocabulary word and ask students to give a meaning for the word.

Expanding

Use visuals, simplified language, and gestures to preteach the following selection vocabulary: *shallow, schedule, reptile,* and *guardian.* Have partners use the words in oral sentences.

Bridging

Have students look up synonyms for *restore* in preparation for the **Responding Page** activities. Encourage them to use each synonym in a sentence to practice writing their responses to the Write About It activity.

Differentiate Comprehension
Author's Purpose; Analyze/Evaluate

STRUGGLING READERS

ELA RI.5.1, RI.5.2, RI.5.8, RF.5.4a
ELD ELD.PI.5.1, ELD.PI.5.6a, ELD.PI.5.7, ELD.PII.5.1

I DO IT

- Explain that an author of a persuasive text tries to convince readers to feel, think, or act a certain way.

- Read aloud **Student Book p. 238** of "Everglades Forever" and model analyzing author's purpose.

  Think Aloud *The author calls the Everglades an "amazing place." She is probably trying to get me to feel a certain way about the Everglades.*

WE DO IT

- Have students read pp. 240–241 of "Everglades Forever."

- Guide them to name the author's purpose. *to persuade people to protect the Everglades*

- Start an Idea-Support Map on the board. Have students suggest facts and other details that support the author's purpose, and write them in the map.

YOU DO IT

- Distribute Graphic Organizer 10 (Story Map) ⬆. Have students create their own Idea-Support Maps for p. 242.

- Have students fill in evidence from that page that supports the author's purpose.

ON LEVEL

ELA RI.5.1, RI.5.2, RI.5.8, RF.5.4a, SL.5.1a
ELD ELD.PI.5.1, ELD.PI.5.6a, ELD.PI.5.7, ELD.PII.5.1

I DO IT

- Read aloud **Student Book pp. 238–240.**

- Explain that analyzing supporting reasons helps readers decide if the author has been effectively persuasive.

- Model analyzing author's purpose.

  Think Aloud *What is the author's goal? What facts and details support this goal?*

WE DO IT

- Have students read p. 244 of "Everglades Forever."

- Have a volunteer tell what the author is trying to persuade readers to do.

- Record the author's purpose in an Idea-Support Map.

YOU DO IT

- Distribute Graphic Organizer 10 (Story Map) ⬆. Have students fill in Idea-Support Maps with facts and details that support the author's purpose.

- Have students discuss whether the author provides effective persuasive support.

ADVANCED

ELA RI.5.1, RI.5.2
ELD ELD.PI.5.1, ELD.PI.5.6a

I DO IT

- Read aloud **Student Book pp. 238–240.**

- Explain that when an author is trying to persuade readers, he or she is expressing an opinion and arguing in favor of it. Point out that good persuasive writing is supported with facts and details.

WE DO IT

- Have students take turns reading aloud p. 244 of "Everglades Forever."

- Ask, *What is the author's opinion on this page? All life is connected. What facts support this? Farming and development put the plants and animals in danger; conservation of water would help save the area.*

YOU DO IT

- Distribute Graphic Organizer 10 (Story Map) . Have students complete an Idea-Support Map for "Everglades Forever."

- Then have students write a paragraph explaining how well they think the author uses facts to support her purpose.

- Invite students to use their completed Idea-Support Maps to analyze/evaluate the author's persuasive evidence.

ENGLISH LANGUAGE SUPPORT

ELD ELD.PI.5.1

Provide Struggling Readers, On Level, and Advanced ELs proficiency-level support during differentiated instruction.

Emerging

Review with students examples of persuasion in the text. Read aloud the text on p. 244. Write this sentence frame on the board: *Ranger Jim says that saving _____ will restore a healthy balance to all _____.* Help students complete the sentence and have them read it aloud. Ask students if Ranger Jim persuaded them.

Expanding

Review with students examples of persuasion in the text. Have students complete the following sentence frame with the word *persuasion. Jim easily convinced his friend to save water. He is good at _____.* If appropriate, help students state whether Ranger Jim succeeds in persuading them and why.

Bridging

Have students use the details they record in their Idea-Support Maps to write complete sentences that explain the author's purpose. If needed, provide the following frames: *The author's opinion about the topic is _____. She persuades readers to agree with her by offering details such as _____.*

☑ **TARGET SKILL**
Author's Purpose

☑ **TARGET STRATEGY**
Analyze/Evaluate

☑ **TARGET VOCABULARY**

endangered	restore
unique	guardians
adapted	attracted
vegetation	regulate
conserving	responsibility

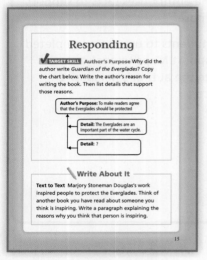

Guardian of the Everglades,
p. 15

 SMALL GROUP OPTIONS

Leveled Readers

ELA RI.5.1, RI.5.2, RI.5.8, SL.5.6
ELD ELD.PI.5.1, ELD.PI.5.5, ELD.PI.5.6a

STRUGGLING READERS

⬤ *Guardian of the Everglades*

GENRE: INFORMATIONAL TEXT

Summary Marjory Stoneman Douglas was an activist who worked to protect the Everglades for over 50 years. Though she had many opponents, Marjory persevered and brought attention to the cause.

Introducing the Text

- Discuss the key vocabulary in the story. Explain that the Everglades area is important because it provides both drinking water for people living in Florida and habitats for many animals.

- Remind students that using a graphic organizer can help readers use clues in the text to understand the author's purpose for writing, which might be to entertain, to inform, to express an opinion, or to persuade.

Supporting the Reading

- As you listen to students read, pause to discuss these questions.

  p. 7 *What reasons suggest that the author's purpose is to persuade readers of the Everglades' importance? The author states that the Everglades region is a huge source of water and that Earth only has a limited amount of water.*

  p. 8 *What will happen to the animals of the Everglades if they lose their habitats? The animals will disappear. Right now the Florida panther, the American crocodile, and the manatee are endangered.*

Discussing and Revisiting the Text

CRITICAL THINKING After discussing *Guardian of the Everglades* together, have students read the instructions at the top of **Responding** p. 15. Use these teaching points to guide them as they revisit the text.

- Have partners write the author's reasons and purpose on Blackline Master 8.5 ⬀.

FLUENCY: ADJUST RATE TO PURPOSE Have students choral-read p. 5. Explain that when they come to an unfamiliar word, they may slow their rate. Remind them to focus on reading accurately.

ELA RI.5.1, RI.5.2, RI.5.8, SL.5.6
ELD ELD.PI.5.1, ELD.PI.5.5, ELD.PI.5.6a

ON LEVEL

 ## *America's Urban Parks*

GENRE: INFORMATIONAL TEXT

Summary Many parks can be found amidst the tall buildings and busy roads of American cities. They provide habitats for plants and animals and offer humans a peaceful atmosphere in the middle of a bustling urban environment.

Introducing the Text

- Discuss key vocabulary from the story. Explain that some urban parks have been shaped by people over time, while other parks are natural habitats.

- Remind students that when an author's purpose is to persuade, he or she may express personal opinions, which should be supported by convincing facts.

Supporting the Reading

- As you listen to students read, pause to discuss these questions.

p. 4 *Why does the author ask you to imagine that you are hiking in an urban park? It brings the reader deeper into the story, letting the reader visualize the author's point and better understand the author's purpose for writing.*

p. 17 *Why do most cities require experts to examine a site before construction begins? Sometimes there are archaeological discoveries, such as a burial ground, that will put a halt to construction.*

Discussing and Revisiting the Text

CRITICAL THINKING After discussing *America's Urban Parks* together, have students read the instructions at the top of **Responding** p. 19. Use these teaching points to guide them as they revisit the text.

- Have students work individually or in pairs to fill in the author's reasons and purpose on Blackline Master 8.6 .

FLUENCY: ADJUST RATE TO PURPOSE Have students perform repeated readings of p. 5 aloud. Explain that they should adjust their rate when they find it difficult to understand information in the text.

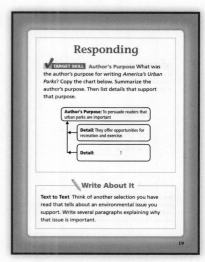

America's Urban Parks, p. 19

☑ **TARGET SKILL**
Author's Purpose

☑ **TARGET STRATEGY**
Analyze/Evaluate

☑ **TARGET VOCABULARY**

endangered	restore
unique	guardians
adapted	attracted
vegetation	regulate
conserving	responsibility

Leveled Readers

ELA RI.5.1, RI.5.2, RI.5.8, SL.5.6
ELD ELD.PI.5.1, ELD.PI.5.5, ELD.PI.5.6a

ADVANCED

 The Salton Sea

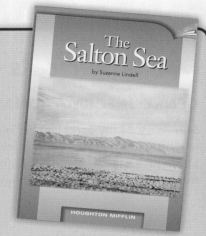

GENRE: INFORMATIONAL TEXT

Summary The Salton Sea is a habitat to many species, including birds and fish. Today the Salton Sea is in danger of drying up and becoming too salty to sustain life. A time line, a map, and diagrams illustrate the problem, and the author explains why action must be taken now.

Introducing the Text

- Discuss key vocabulary from the story. Explain that the Salton Sea's water source is excess irrigation water that is naturally salty. When the water evaporates, the salt remains since the sea has no outlet. This endangers the fish that live there.

- Remind students that when an author's purpose is to persuade, he or she may express personal opinions, which should be supported by convincing facts.

Supporting the Reading

- As you listen to students read, pause to discuss these questions.

  p. 13 *What reasons suggest that the author's purpose is to persuade readers that the Salton Sea should be saved? If something is not done soon, the fish will die, the birds will disappear, and people will be exposed to the salt, blown by desert winds.*

  p. 14 *Why isn't there more public awareness about this threat to the Salton Sea? The location of the Salton Sea is isolated, so many people cannot see its beauty or relate its problems to their own lives.*

Discussing and Revisiting the Text

CRITICAL THINKING After discussing *The Salton Sea* together, have students read the instructions at the top of **Responding** p. 19. Use these teaching points to guide them as they revisit the text.

- Have students identify the author's reasons and purpose on <u>Blackline Master 8.7</u> ⬀.

FLUENCY: ADJUST RATE TO PURPOSE Have students practice reading p. 9 aloud. Explain that they will need to read unfamiliar words carefully and that good readers read informational passages more slowly.

Responding

✓ **TARGET SKILL** Author's Purpose What was the author's purpose in writing *Salton Sea*? Copy the chart below. Summarize the author's purpose. Then list details that support that purpose.

Author's Purpose: To persuade readers that the Salton Sea is important and should be preserved

→ **Detail:** ?
→ **Detail:** ?

Write About It

Text to Text Think of another selection you have read that convinced you to do something about a particular issue. Write several paragraphs explaining why you think the issue is important.

The Salton Sea, p. 19

ELA RI.5.1, RI.5.2, RI.5.8, SL.5.6
ELD ELD.PI.5.1, ELD.PI.5.5, ELD.PI.5.6a

ENGLISH LANGUAGE SUPPORT

 America's City Parks

GENRE: INFORMATIONAL TEXT

Summary Many parks, such as San Francisco's Presidio and Washington D.C.'s Rock Creek National Park, can be found amidst the buildings and busy roads of American cities. They provide habitats for plants and animals and a peaceful retreat for humans.

Introducing the Text

• Discuss key vocabulary in the story. Explain that archaeology is the study of human history, usually through excavation, or digging. Important archaeological sites are sometimes preserved as parks.

• Remind students that using a graphic organizer helps identify an author's reasons and purpose. This can help them decide whether or not they agree.

Supporting the Reading

• As you listen to students read, pause to discuss these questions.

p. 7 *What do you think the author's purpose is for describing what happened to the Xerces Blue butterfly? How can you tell? The author wants us to feel sad about the extinction of the butterfly. He appeals to our emotions by using the word "sadly" and describing how people pushed out the butterflies.*

p. 11 *Why might you see a wild animal, such as a fox, in a public area? It's looking for food and travels along the city's greenways.*

Discussing and Revisiting the Text

CRITICAL THINKING After discussing *America's City Parks* together, have students read the instructions at the top of **Responding** p. 19. Use these teaching points to guide them as they revisit the text.

• Have students enter the author's reasons and purpose on Blackline Master 8.8.

FLUENCY: ADJUST RATE TO PURPOSE Have students echo-read p. 5. Explain that when they come to an unfamiliar word, they may need to slow their reading rate. Tell them to focus on reading carefully.

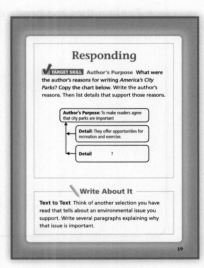

America's City Parks, p. 19

Differentiate Vocabulary Strategies
Prefixes *en-, re-, pre-, pro-*

STRUGGLING READERS

ELA L.5.4a, L.5.4b, L.5.4c
ELD ELD.PI.5.1, ELD.PI.5.6b

I DO IT

- Display **Vocabulary in Context Card 75:** *endangered*.

- Remind students that a prefix is a word part attached to the beginning of a base word or word root. A prefix changes the meaning of the word.

- Explain that the prefix *en-* means "put in/to."

WE DO IT

- Have students identify the prefix in the Target Vocabulary word *endangered*. *en-*

- Have a volunteer read the explanation on the back of the **Vocabulary in Context Card.**

- Have students restate the meaning of *endangered* using what they now know about the meaning of its prefix.

YOU DO IT

- Have students use their knowledge of the prefix *en-* to figure out the meaning of the word *entangle*. Then have them use a print or digital dictionary to check their definitions.

- Have students write a sentence that uses the word *entangle*.

- Have students look through "Everglades Forever" for words with the prefixes *en-, re-, pre-,* and *pro-*.

ON LEVEL

ELA L.5.4a, L.5.4b, L.5.4c
ELD ELD.PI.5.1, ELD.PI.5.6b

I DO IT

- Display **Vocabulary in Context Card 75:** *endangered*.

- Remind students that a prefix is an affix, or word part, attached to the beginning of a base word or word root. The prefix changes the meaning of the base word or word root.

- Explain that the prefix *en-* means "put in/to."

WE DO IT

- Have students use a print or digital dictionary to find the meaning of *endangered*. *in or put into danger*

- Guide students to think of words that begin with the prefixes *en-, re-, pre-,* and *pro-*. Write the words on the board, dividing them into columns according to prefix.

YOU DO IT

- Have students select one word from each column and write two sentences for each: one that uses the base word (if there is one) and another that uses the word with the prefix.

- Students should check a print or digital dictionary to be sure they are using the words correctly.

ADVANCED

ELA L.5.4a, L.5.4b, L.5.4c
ELD ELD.PI.5.1, ELD.PI.5.6b

I DO IT

- Write the following words on the board: *endangered, resubscribe, preschool, entrap, retraced, premature, prolong, remake,* and *proactive.*

- Remind students that a prefix is an affix that is added to the beginning of a base word or word root that changes the meaning of the word.

WE DO IT

- Discuss with students the meanings of the prefixes *en-, re-, pre-,* and *pro-.*

- Guide students to infer the meaning of each word on the board, using what they know about the base word and the prefix.

- Have students use a print or digital dictionary to verify meanings.

YOU DO IT

- Have students write sentences for each of the words on the board. Remind them to write sentences that give context to the meaning of each word, so that someone unfamiliar with the word might understand it.

- Students should then share their sentences with small groups.

ENGLISH LANGUAGE SUPPORT

ELD ELD.PI.5.1, ELD.PI.5.6b

Provide Struggling Readers, On Level, and Advanced ELs proficiency-level support during differentiated instruction.

Emerging

Display **Vocabulary in Context Card 75:** *endangered.* Have students listen for the word *endangered* as you read the sentence on the card. Point out and review the meaning of the prefix *en-* and the base word *danger.* Display other words with the prefixes *re-, pre-* and *pro-.* Ask students simple yes/no questions to help them guess or determine the meaning of each word.

Expanding

If students find it difficult to understand the meaning of a particular prefix or word, provide a simple definition, or use gestures and visuals to illustrate meaning. Then use the word in a question, relating the question, if possible, to "Everglades Forever." Have students answer based on their understanding of the prefix and its base word.

Bridging

Have students write a definition for each new word they learn over the course of the lesson. Then ask them to write a sentence for each word. Have students share and discuss their sentences with a partner.

Options for Reteaching

VOCABULARY STRATEGIES

ELA RF.5.3a, RF.5.4c, L.5.4a, L.5.6
ELD ELD.PI.5.1, ELD.PI.5.5, ELD.PI.5.6b

Prefixes *en-, re-, pre-, pro-*

I DO IT

- Review how to use prefixes to determine the meanings of unfamiliar words.

- Remind students that a prefix is an affix attached to the beginning of a base word or word root and that it changes the meaning of the word.

- Explain that *en-* means "put in/to," *re-* means "again," *pre-* means "before," and *pro-* means "for" or "before."

WE DO IT

- Write the following words with the prefixes *en-, re-, pre-,* and *pro-* on the board: *endangered, research, predict,* and *proclaim.*

- Model how to apply the vocabulary strategy to figure out the meaning of the word *endangered.*

  Think Aloud *If the prefix* en- *means "put in or into," then* endangered *must mean "put in danger." I can look it up in a dictionary to confirm my definition.*

- Have a volunteer look up *endangered* in a dictionary and read the definition aloud.

- Then have students define the other words on the board. Have volunteers look up the words to confirm the definitions.

YOU DO IT

- Have partners work together to write sentences using the words on the board. Have them exchange sentences with another pair to make sure they used the words correctly.

- Provide corrective feedback if students need additional support.

COMPREHENSION SKILL

ELA RI.5.1, RI.5.2, RF.5.4a, SL.5.1a
ELD ELD.PI.5.1, ELD.PI.5.5, ELD.PI.5.6a

Author's Purpose

I DO IT

- Remind students that authors write with a purpose in mind. The author of a nonfiction text must provide reasons and evidence to support his or her ideas. This will help the author achieve his or her purpose, whether that purpose is to inform or to persuade.

- Explain that readers should look for the evidence, such as facts and details, that the author includes. Good readers analyze the author's evidence and reasons to make sure they support the author's points.

WE DO IT

- Read aloud the two paragraphs on **Student Book pp. 240–241** that begin with "The Everglades has wet and dry" and end with "will be helped to survive." Model how to identify the evidence the author uses to support her points and accomplish her purpose.

  Think Aloud *I think the author's main point here is that the Everglades has unique habitats to which specific plants and animals have adapted. What facts does she include to support this? She gives details about the mangrove swamp, a habitat that supports mangrove trees, shrimp, bonefish, and other animals. She writes, "If the brackish water in the mangrove swamps changes, these animals cannot survive."*

- Discuss how the evidence supports the author's purpose, which is to persuade readers that the region is worth preserving.

YOU DO IT

- Distribute Graphic Organizer 7 🔗.

- Have students look on other pages to find evidence and reasons the author uses to support her main points.

- Have students work with partners to complete the graphic organizer.

- Review the completed graphic organizers. Have students discuss and evaluate how well the author's main points achieve her overall purpose.

ELA W.5.2a, W.5.4, W.5.10, L.5.1a, L.5.5c
ELD ELD.PI.5.10a

LANGUAGE ARTS

Conjunctions/Informative Writing

I DO IT

- Remind students that conjunctions are connecting words that join different words, groups of words, or sentences together.

- List common conjunctions on the board: *and, or, but, for, nor, so,* and *because.*

WE DO IT

- Write the following sentence on the board and model how to identify the conjunctions: *The Everglades has alligators and snakes, but it also has beautiful plants and birds.*

  Think Aloud *To identify a conjunction, I ask myself which word connects other words in the sentence. In this sentence, I can see that* and *joins two words, and* but *joins two groups of words. These must be conjunctions.*

- Have volunteers generate sentences that include conjunctions. Write them on the board. Then have other students identify the conjunctions.

YOU DO IT

- Have partners write a paragraph describing how people's actions can affect the Everglades, either positively or negatively.

- Encourage students to review the selection for details to show causes and effects.

- Have students review each other's paragraphs to find places where conjunctions could have been used to make the writing less choppy.

ELA RF.5.3a, L.5.4a, L.5.5c

DECODING

Homophones

I DO IT

- Remind students that homophones are words that sound the same but are spelled differently.

- Tell students that different letters can stand for the same sound.

WE DO IT

- Display these pairs of words: *weather/ whether; ceiling/sealing;* and *bolder/boulder.*

- Model how to determine the letters with the same sound in the first pair of homophones.

  Think Aloud *I see two differences in the spellings of* weather *and* whether. *The first is the letters* w *and* wh. *Both stand for the /w/ sound, but the* h *in* whether *is silent. The second difference is the letters* ea *and* e. *Both can stand for the short* e *sound. So the two words have the same pronunciation.*

- Have volunteers identify the letters in the other homophone pairs that have the same sounds.

YOU DO IT

- Have students generate sentences using the homophones on the board. Have them exchange sentences with another student to check that they are using the homophones correctly.

- Use the Corrective Feedback on **p. T201** if students need additional help.

Teacher Notes

Anchor
Text

Paired
Selection

Journeys

DIGITAL RESOURCES

Teacher Dashboard

Log onto the Teacher Dashboard and *my*SmartPlanner. Use these searchable tools to customize lessons that achieve your instructional goals.

Interactive Whiteboard Lessons

- Grammar: Complex Sentences
- Vocabulary Strategies: Greek and Latin Roots *tele, photo; scribe, rupt*

- Write About Reading
- Informative Writing: Research Report

Interactive Lessons

▶ Participating in Collaborative Discussions
▶ Writing to Sources
▶ Informative Writing

Assess It Online!

- Weekly Tests
- Assessment-driven instruction with prescriptive feedback

Student eBook

🖉 Annotate it! **Strategies for Annotation**

Guide students to use digital tools for close reading.

Students may also use the interactive features in their Student eBooks to respond to prompts in a variety of ways, including:

- short-answer response
- drag-and-drop
- spoken response
- multiple choice
- fill-in-the-blank

High-Interest Informational Texts and Multimedia

Have students explore the FYI website for additional information about topics of study.

ENGLISH LANGUAGE SUPPORT

Culturally Responsive Teaching

Readers' Theater Tell students that this week, they will be reading and thinking about acts of courage.

- Use "Storm Warriors" for a Readers' Theater activity. Choose sections of the selection with multiple roles and dialogue. Organize students into small groups, and assign a section to each group.

- Choose roles for students based on their current levels of fluency and English proficiency, so that they will be able to read their parts with ease.

- Allow students to practice reading aloud alone. Explain that they should practice reading aloud as if they were in a play. Then have small groups practice reading their section aloud together several times. Monitor groups to provide modeling, feedback, and support.

- Invite each group to present their reading to another small group.

Provide Modeling and Additional Practice As needed, support English learners by modeling fluent reading and allowing additional practice. Have students echo-read or read chorally after you model. Then have them practice reading aloud on their own, and provide additional support as needed.

Language Support Card

Use the Lesson 9 Language Support Card to activate prior knowledge, frontload vocabulary, and teach academic English.

Use the Text X-Ray on page T239 to review the language demands of "Storm Warriors" with the needs of English learners in mind.

Language Workshop for Designated ELD

- Connection to Essential Question
- Vocabulary Network
- Focus on Interacting in Meaningful Ways
- Discussion Frames
- How English Works
- Word Learning Strategies

You may wish to use the following suggestions to modify instruction for some students, according to their needs.

Learner's Journal

Keeping a Learner's Journal can help students see themselves as successful, growing learners. Developing a sense of ownership in students can motivate them to reach their highest potential. Have students add to their Learner's Journal for this lesson. Depending on students' needs and skills, have them record information about what they are learning. Some examples:

- Day 1: Vocabulary: *critical, secured, realization, annoyance, bundle, clammy, squalling, commotion, demolished, elite*
- Day 2: The title of the Anchor Text, "Storm Warriors," and information about the text
- Day 3: Write about something new they learned about acts of courage. To help, you might want to discuss with students the Essential Question and their ideas about it.
- Day 4: Write several words they have learned to spell this week.
- Day 5: Write about how they are becoming better writers. For example, "I am learning to write a research report."

Student eBook

- **Audio** can be activated to support fluency, decoding, and comprehension.
- **Alternative Text** provides spoken information that can be used in place of the information provided in the book's images.
- **Vocabulary Pop-Ups** contain point-of-use definitions for selection vocabulary.

Health

Accessing Help in an Emergency Have partners or small groups work together to investigate and compile a list of tips for accessing people who can help in an emergency. Students should also consider how to communicate information effectively during an emergency.

- Remind students of the dangerous situations they read about in "Storm Warriors," and that the elite life-saving crew bravely saved lives.
- Tell students that they will work with a partner or in a small group to investigate and compile a list of tips for contacting people who can help during an emergency at school, at home, or outdoors. Explain that they will also identify and discuss ways to communicate effectively with emergency personnel.
- Organize students into pairs or small groups. Have students work together to use print or online resources to find information.
- After students have completed their investigations, have them share their lists with the class or another small group.
- Encourage students to practice using the communication tips they identified by role-playing the parts of a caller to 9-1-1 and a 9-1-1 dispatcher.

DOMAIN: **Values**

LESSON TOPIC: **Courage**

LESSON **9** *Our* Focus Wall

ANCHOR TEXT

Storm Warriors
Historical Fiction

Pea Island's Forgotten Heroes
Informational Text

ESSENTIAL QUESTION

How can an act of courage reveal a person's true nature?

WRITING

Writing

Informative Writing:
Prewrite a Research Report

Focus Trait: Ideas

READING LITERATURE & INFORMATIONAL TEXT

Comprehension Skills and Strategies

☑ **TARGET SKILL**
- **Conclusions and Generalizations**
- **Point of View**
- **Characterization**

☑ **TARGET STRATEGY**
- **Infer/Predict**

FOUNDATIONAL SKILLS

Fluency

Phrasing: Punctuation

Decoding

Compound Words

LANGUAGE

☑ Target Vocabulary

critical	clammy
secured	squalling
realization	commotion
annoyance	demolished
bundle	elite

Spelling

Compound Words

wildlife	life preserver
uproar	barefoot
home run	part-time
headache	warehouse
top-secret	overboard
teammate	post office
wheelchair	outspoken
light bulb	up-to-date
well-known	awestruck
throughout	newscast

Grammar

Complex Sentences

Vocabulary Strategies

Greek and Latin Roots

ANCHOR TEXT

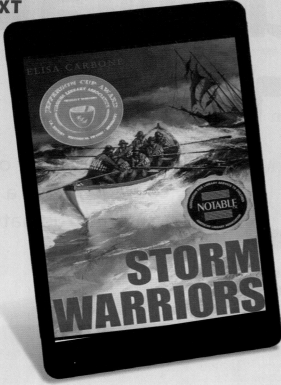

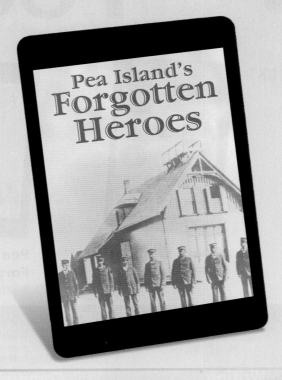

Storm Warriors
GENRE: Historical Fiction

Prepare for Complex Texts For a comprehensive overview and analysis of key ideas and academic language features of this lesson's Anchor Text, see pages T238–T239.

Pea Island's Forgotten Heroes
GENRE: Informational Text
21st Century Theme: Financial, Economic, Business and Entrepreneurial Literacy

Digital Resources

- ▶ **eBook: Annotate It!**
- ▶ **Interactive Whiteboard Lessons**
  - Vocabulary Strategies: Greek and Latin Roots *tele, photo; scribe, rupt*
  - Grammar: Complex Sentences
- ▶ **GrammarSnap Videos**
  - Complex Sentences

- ▶ **Multimedia Grammar Glossary**
- ▶ *my*SmartPlanner
- ▶ **Parent Resource**

Additional Resources

- Vocabulary in Context Cards 81–90
- Reader's Notebook, pp. 97–108
- Lesson 9 Blackline Masters
- Literacy and Language Guide

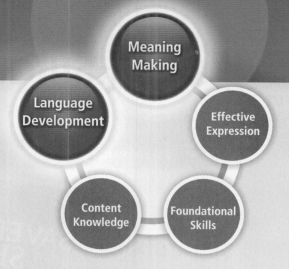

Meaning Making

Language Development

Effective Expression

Content Knowledge

Foundational Skills

LINGUISTICALLY DIVERSE LEARNERS

⌄ Integrated English Language Support

● **Interacting in Meaningful Ways**

Classroom Conversations
- Think-Pair-Share, p. T247
- Collaborative Conversation, pp. T242, T258, T262, T273

Interactive and Collaborative Writing
- Infer/Predict, p. T258
- Write About Reading, p. T263
- Prewrite a Research Report, p. T282

Self-Selected Reading, p. T264

Sentence Frames for Speaking, p. T273

● **Learning About How English Works**

Scaffold the Texts
- Text X-Ray: Focus on Academic Language, p. T239
- Using Noun Phrases, pp. T254, T262, T283

Language Detective
- Target Vocabulary, p. T244
- Verb Types, p. T259

Communicative Modes
- Write About Reading, p. T263
- Prewrite a Research Report, p. T282

● **Using Foundational Literacy Skills**

Fluency: Phrasing: Punctuation, p. T274
Decoding: Compound Words, p. T275

Apply Language Skills
- Complex Sentences, p. T278

Support Linguistic Transfer
- Greek and Latin Roots, p. T270
- Compound Words, p. T276
- Complex Sentences, p. T278

⌄ Standard English Learners

- Pronunciation: Final Consonant in Contraction, p. T257
- Complex Sentences, p. T280

ASSESSMENT

● **Formative Assessment**
- Target Vocabulary, p. T245
- Target Strategy: Infer/Predict, pp. T252, T256
- Target Skill: Story Structure, p. T261
- Vocabulary Strategies: Prefixes *re-, un-, dis-*, p. T271
- Decoding: VCV Syllable Pattern, p. T275
- Using Data to Adjust Instruction, p. T287

● ✓ *Assess It Online!*
- Weekly Tests

Performance Tasks
- Write About Reading, p. T263
- Write an Explanatory Essay, p. T364

Vocabulary Reader

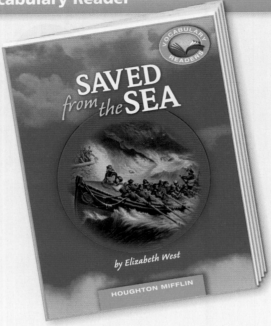

SAVED from the SEA

by Elizabeth West

HOUGHTON MIFFLIN

Vocabulary Reader
for all levels

Provide strategic scaffolding to support all students in reading on-level text and in acquiring general academic and domain-specific vocabulary. Use the instructional supports on pp. T292–T293 or the Leveled Reader Teacher's Guide.

Guided Reading Level: S
Lexile: 570L
DRA: 40
Leveled Reader Teacher's Guide

Weekly Leveled Readers

Guide students to read and comprehend additional texts about the lesson topic. Use the instructional supports on pp. T296–T299 or the Leveled Reader Teacher's Guides.

Struggling Readers	On Level	Advanced	English Language Learners
Guided Reading Level: R	**Guided Reading Level: T**	**Guided Reading Level: V**	**Guided Reading Level: T**
Lexile: 660L	Lexile: 840L	Lexile: 860L	Lexile: 410L
DRA: 40	DRA: 44	DRA: 50	DRA: 44
Leveled Reader Teacher's Guide	Leveled Reader Teacher's Guide	Leveled Reader Teacher's Guide	Leveled Reader Teacher's Guide

Sugaring Weather
by Roger Morrell
illustrated by Tony Sansevero
HOUGHTON MIFFLIN

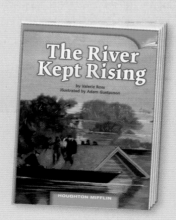

The River Kept Rising
by Valerie Ross
illustrated by Adam Gustavson
HOUGHTON MIFFLIN

Night of the Killer Waves
by Carmelia diMartini
illustrated by Anni Matsick
HOUGHTON MIFFLIN

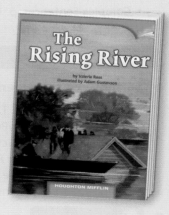

The Rising River
by Valerie Ross
illustrated by Adam Gustavson
HOUGHTON MIFFLIN

Meaning Making

Language Development

Effective Expression

Content Knowledge

Foundational Skills

Language Workshop for Designated ELD

- Provides reteaching and practice in the key foundational skills for reading: print concepts, phonological/phonemic awareness, phonics and word recognition, and fluency.

- Explicit, sequential, and systematic instruction designed to bring students up to grade level.

- Screening and Diagnostic Assessments (within Intervention Assessments) place individual students within the system.

Lesson 9 Focus

Collaborate: Persuade Others In Conversation

Interpret: Determine the Meanings of Unknown Words

Produce: Write Literary Texts Collaboratively

How English Works: Use Verbs and Verb Phrases

Vocabulary Network

Intervention

Strategic Intervention Tier II

Write-In Reader: *The Rescue Helicopter Team*

- Interactive worktext with selection that connects to the lesson topic
- Reinforces the lesson's vocabulary and comprehension
- Build skills for reading increasingly complex texts
- Online version with dual-speed audio and follow-text

Daily Lessons See this week's daily Strategic Intervention Lesson on pp. S32–S41.

- Preteach and Reteach daily instruction
- Oral Grammar
- Decoding
- Comprehension

- Fluency
- Grammar
- Written Response
- Unpack Meaning
- Return to Anchor Text

Decoding Power: Intensive Intervention

- Provides reteaching and practice in the key foundational skills for reading: print concepts, phonological/phonemic awareness, phonics and word recognition, and fluency.

- Explicit, sequential, and systematic instruction designed to bring students up to grade level.

- Screening and Diagnostic Assessments (within Intervention Assessments) place individual students within the system.

 Assess It Online!

▶ **Screening and Diagnostic Assessments** (within Intervention Assessments) place individual students within the system.

▶ **Progress-Monitoring Assessments** (within Intervention Assessments) ensure students are making satisfactory progress and provide a measure of student readiness to exit the system.

What My Other Students Are Doing

Digital Resources

▶ **Literacy Centers:** Word Study, Think and Write, Comprehension and Fluency

▶ **Interactive Lessons:** Writing to Sources, Writing as a Process: Plan and Draft, Participating in Collaborative Discussions

○ **Additional Resources**

- Vocabulary in Context Cards 81–90
- Reader's Notebook, pp. 97–108
- Independent Reading
- Lesson 9 Blackline Masters

Literacy Centers

Managing Independent Activities

Comprehension and Fluency

Materials
- Student Book
- Audio
- headphones
- tape recorder
- self-stick notes
- Reading Log
- pencil or pen

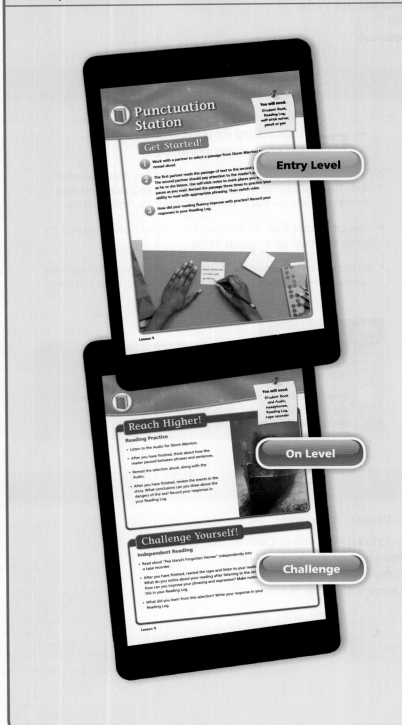

Word Study

Materials
- paper
- pencil or pen
- colored markers or pencils

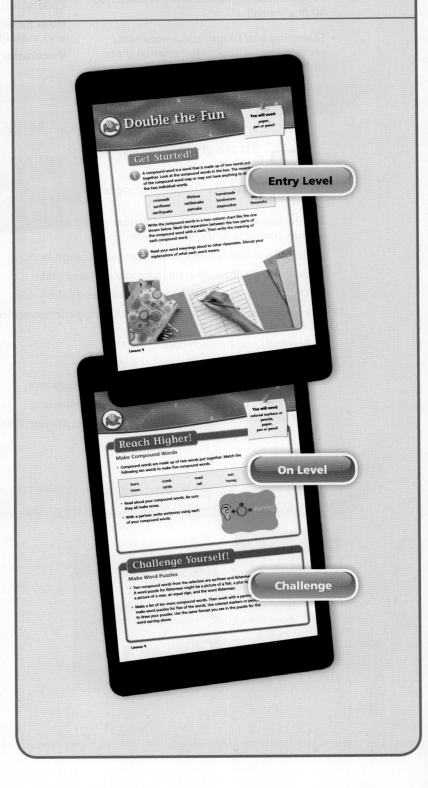

Assign Literacy Center activities during small group time. Each center contains three activities. Students who experience success with the entry-level activity move on to the on-level and challenge activities, as time permits.

Meaning Making

Language Development

Effective Expression

Content Knowledge

Foundational Skills

Think and Write

Materials
- colored markers or pencils
- paper
- pencil or pen
- library books

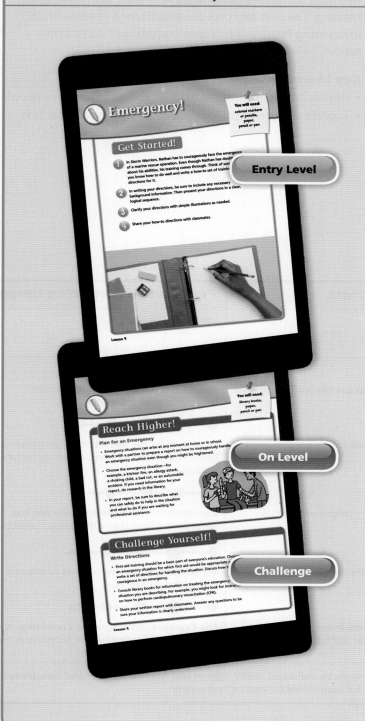

Entry Level

On Level

Challenge

Independent Reading

Writing in Response to Books Writing in response to texts prompts students to think more deeply about the text. Vary the kinds of writing you ask students to do to keep them engaged and motivated to write about their independent reading.

- **Planning for Book Talks** Students make brief notes or drawings to bring to Book Talk discussions. They can focus on a particular scene or a part that they really like.

- **Book Reviews** Students draw posters or make bookmarks to tell others about their books.

- **Reactions to Texts** Students write on index cards. They write the title, the author, and something they like or do not like about the book. They post it on a bulletin board near the classroom library.

- **Alternate Ending** Students draw or write a different ending to the book and tell a classmate how their ending is different from the book's real ending.

See p. T264 for additional independent reading support.
ELA RL.5.10, RI.5.10

Prepare for Complex Texts

Anchor Text

Storm Warriors
by Elisa Carbone

GENRE: Historical Fiction

Why This Text?

Students regularly encounter historical fiction in literature anthologies and their own independent reading. This text presents a fictional narrative of a dramatic, historical event. It contains vivid descriptions from a first-person point of view.

Key Learning Objectives

- Draw conclusions and make generalizations about a text.
- Study the use of point of view in a story.
- Examine how an author achieves characterization.

Paired Selection

Pea Island's Forgotten Heroes
by Cecelia Munzenmaier

GENRE: Informational Text

Why This Text?

Students encounter informational text in school textbooks, periodicals, and their own independent reading. The text explores the importance of research in uncovering history. It contains quotations from a primary source.

Key Learning Objectives

- Appreciate an informational text about courageous people.
- Explore the use of primary sources in informational text.

TEXT COMPLEXITY RUBRIC

		Storm Warriors	Pea Island's Forgotten Heroes
Quantitative Measures	Lexile	800L	790L
	Guided Reading Level	T	T
Qualitative Measures	Meaning and Purpose	**Density and Complexity:** the text has a single level of complex meaning.	**Figurative Language:** the text contains explicitly stated, literal language.
	Text Structure	**Narration:** the first-person narration is from a credible point of view.	**Organization:** the text has multiple transitions between past and present, as well as featured participants.
	Language Features	**Vocabulary:** the text contains literary language that may require use of context clues.	**Conventionality and Register:** the text has some formal language with abstract concepts.
		Sentence Structure: the text has more complex sentence structures.	**Sentence Structure:** the text has simple and compound sentences.
	Knowledge Demands	**Subject Matter Knowledge/Prior Knowledge:** the text requires some specialized knowledge and has historical culture references.	**Life Experiences/Background Knowledge:** the text deals with unfamiliar life experiences and a somewhat complex theme.
Reader/Task Considerations		Determine using the professional judgment of the teacher. This varies by individual reader, type of text, and the purpose and complexity of particular tasks. See **Reader and Task Considerations** on p. T249 for suggestions for Anchor Text support.	

Meaning Making

Language Development

Effective Expression

Content Knowledge

Foundational Skills

TEXT X-RAY

ENGLISH LANGUAGE SUPPORT Use the Text X-Ray below to prepare for teaching the Anchor Text. Use it to plan, support, and scaffold instruction in order to help students understand the text's **key ideas** and **academic language features**.

Zoom In on Key Ideas
Students should understand these **key ideas** after reading *Storm Warriors*.

Key Idea | pp. 268–269

In 1896 on North Carolina's Outer Banks, young Nathan's dream of becoming a member of a lifesaving crew is about to be tested. A ship has run aground and is sinking, but the surfmen are not able to use their usual equipment because of the stormy conditions. Two surfmen enter the wild and raging sea to attempt a rescue of the ship's passengers.

Key Idea | pp. 270–272

Nathan believes he would never have the courage being shown by the two surfmen who have entered the water. Still, he helps let out the rope that is attached to the rescuers. The surfmen reach the ship and turn back to shore.

The men have brought a young child ashore. The terrified child is passed from one man to the next and finally to Nathan, whose job is to quickly get the boy dry and warm. Soon, the surfmen bring the child's mother ashore, too. Then, there is a shout that they have brought an injured man.

Key Idea | pp. 274–275

Nathan, who has been studying medical books and life-saving techniques, is called on to help care for the injured sailor. Mr. Bowser is impressed by Nathan's abilities and leaves him to care for the patient, while he runs to help with the continuing rescue.

Key Idea | p. 277

The ship's captain finally is brought ashore. He thanks the surfmen for having saved the entire ship's crew.

Zoom In on Academic Language
Guide students at different proficiencies and skill levels to understand the structure and language of this text.

Focus: Word Level | pp. 268–277

English learners and others may have difficulty with **domain-specific words.** You may wish to preteach words and phrases, such as *hull, starboard, washed overboard, oilskin,* and life *preserver.*

Focus: Text Level | pp. 268, 269–277

Support students in analyzing the use of **point of view** in the story. After the introduction and first paragraph, ask students who the narrator is and how they know. Establish that the narrator is Nathan, who is described in the introduction.

Focus: Sentence Level | p. 270

Support English learners and others in drawing conclusions. Ask, On p. 270, why does Nathan say he would never be able to do what the surfmen are doing? Guide students through the paragraph: the surfmen's motto and what it implies and what Nathan thinks is his biggest obstacle.

Focus: Text Level | pp. 268–277

Guide students to examine how the author achieves **characterization** in the story. Point out key moments: the introduction, Nathan's realization that the men are walking into the stormy sea (p. 269), Nathan thinks he will not have enough courage (p. 270), he comforts the rescued child (p. 272), he recalls information he's read about treating wounds (p. 274), and he stands with the surfmen when the ship's captain thanks them for saving his crew (p. 277).

Content and Language Instruction Make note of additional **content knowledge** and **language features** students may find challenging in this text.

Weekly Planner

my SmartPlanner

Auto-populates the suggested five-day lesson plan and offers flexibility to create and save customized plans from year to year.

See **Standards Correlations** on p. C1. In your eBook, click the Standards button in the left panel to view descriptions of the standards on the page.

DAY 1

Materials
- ELL Blackline Masters 9.2, 9.3
- Graphic Organizer 8
- Lesson 9 Language Support Card
- Literacy and Language Guide p. 72
- Projectables 9.1, 9.4, 9.7
- Reader's Notebook pp. 100, 103
- Strategy Projectables S1–S8
- Student Book pp. 262–277
- Vocabulary in Context Cards 81–90

DAY 2

Materials
- Graphic Organizer 8
- Interactive Lessons: Listening and Responding, Writing to Sources
- Literacy and Language Guide p. 72
- Projectables 9.2, 9.5
- Reader's Notebook pp. 101, 104, 108
- Student Book pp. 266–281

Whole Group

Oral Language

Listening
Comprehension

DAY 1
Teacher Read Aloud
"A Watery Grave," T242–T243

DAY 2
Turn and Talk, T262

Vocabulary
Text-Based Comprehension
- Skills and Strategies
- Craft and Structure

Research and Media Literacy

DAY 1
☑ **Introduce Vocabulary**
Vocabulary in Context, T244–T245
☑ **Read and Comprehend,** T246–T247
FIRST READ **Think Through the Text**
Read the Anchor Text: "Storm Warriors," T248–T259

DAY 2
SECOND READ
☑ **Dig Deeper: How to Analyze the Text,** T260–T261
- Conclusions and Generalizations
- Point of View
- Characterization
- Verb Types
Analyze the Text
Reread the Anchor Text: "Storm Warriors," T253, T255, T257
☑ **Your Turn,** T262–T263

Foundational Skills
- Fluency
- Decoding

DAY 1
☑ **Fluency**
Model Phrasing: Punctuation, T242

DAY 2
☑ **Fluency**
Teach Phrasing: Punctuation, T274
Practice Phrasing: Punctuation, T251

Whole Group Language Arts

Spelling
Grammar
Writing

DAY 1
☑ **Spelling**
Compound Words: Pretest, T276
☑ **Grammar**
Daily Proofreading Practice, T278
Teach Complex Sentences, T278
☑ **Informative Writing: Prewrite a Research Report**
Analyze the Model, T282

DAY 2
☑ **Spelling**
Compound Words: Word Sort, T276
☑ **Grammar**
Daily Proofreading Practice, T279
Extend Complex Sentences, T279
☑ **Informative Writing: Prewrite a Research Report**
Focus Trait: Ideas, T283

Small Group

Suggestions for Small Groups (See pp. T290–T291.)

DAY 3

Materials
- Instructional Routine 9
- Literacy and Language Guide pp. 73, 132–133
- Projectable 9.6
- Reading Log Blackline Master
- Reader's Notebook pp. 97–98, 105
- Student Book pp. 266–277

Classroom Conversation, T265

Independent Reading, T264
- Reader's Guide: "Storm Warriors"
- Self-Selected Reading

Apply Vocabulary Knowledge, T265

☑ **Fluency**
Practice Phrasing: Punctuation, T274
☑ **Decoding**
Compound Words, T275

☑ **Spelling**
Compound Words: Word Families, T277
☑ **Grammar**
Daily Proofreading Practice, T279
Teach Correlative Conjunctions, T279
☑ **Informative Writing: Prewrite a Research Report**
Prewrite, T283

DAY 4

Materials
- Interactive Whiteboard Lesson: Greek and Latin Roots
- Literacy and Language Guide pp. 132–133
- Projectables 9.3, 9.8
- Reader's Notebook pp. 99, 102, 106
- Student Book pp. 282–285

Classroom Conversation, T266

Connect to the Topic
- Read Informational Text: "Pea Island's Forgotten Heroes," T266
- Think Through the Text, T268
☑ **Compare Texts,** T269
☑ **Vocabulary Strategies**
Greek and Latin Roots, T270–T271

☑ **Fluency**
Practice Phrasing: Punctuation, T267

☑ **Spelling**
Compound Words: Connect to Writing, T277
☑ **Grammar**
Daily Proofreading Practice, T280
Review Complex Sentences, T280
☑ **Informative Writing: Prewrite a Research Report**
Prewrite, T284

DAY 5

Materials
- Cold Reads
- Graphic Organizer 6
- Interactive Lessons: Participate in Collaborative Conversations, Writing as a Process: Plan and Draft
- Interactive Whiteboard Lesson: Complex Sentences
- Proofreading Checklist Blackline Master
- Reader's Notebook p. 107
- Student Book pp. 286–289
- Writing Rubric Blackline Master

Speaking and Listening, T273

Extend the Topic: Courage
- Domain-Specific Vocabulary, T272
- Optional Second Read: "Pea Island's Forgotten Heroes," T266

☑ **Fluency**
Progress Monitoring, T287

☑ **Spelling**
Compound Words: Assess, T277
☑ **Grammar**
Daily Proofreading Practice, T280
Connect Grammar to Writing, T280–T281
☑ **Informative Writing: Prewrite a Research Report**
Prewrite, T284

 Tier II Intervention provides thirty minutes of additional daily practice with key parts of the core instruction. See pp. S32–S41.

Teacher Read Aloud

▶ SHARE OBJECTIVES
- Listen to understand fluent reading by identifying commas and grouping words into phrases. LANGUAGE.
- Summarize a written text read aloud.

ENGLISH LANGUAGE SUPPORT

Use Visuals

All Proficiencies To assist students with accessing the content and topic of the Teacher Read Aloud, discuss the High-Utility Words on the Lesson 9 Language Support Card.

☑ PREVIEW
Target Vocabulary

clammy cold, sticky, and damp to the touch

elite something that has special skills or qualities that make it the best

commotion a lot of noise and confusion

annoyance something that is irritating

realization an awareness of something

secured fixed or held firmly in place

bundle to wrap something in many layers

critical something of great importance

demolished completely destroyed

squalling loud, harsh cries

Model Fluency

Phrasing: Punctuation Explain that good readers group words into phrases, using punctuation as a guide.

- Display Projectable 9.1. Model how to group words into phrases and pause at the end of a sentence.
- Point out that commas and end punctuation show where some, but not all, pauses should occur.
- Reread the sentences together with students, grouping the words into natural phrases and pausing where punctuation dictates. **ELA** RF.5.4a

Listening Comprehension

Read aloud the selection. Pause at the numbered stopping points to ask students the questions below. Discuss the meanings of the highlighted words, as needed, to support the discussion.

1 *Why were the waters surrounding the American colonies a good place for pirates to raid ships? The colonies had fewer laws to restrict the pirates' behavior than Britain did.* **SUMMARIZE**

2 *What do you think Blackbeard was like? He was greedy and fearless.* **MAKE INFERENCES**

3 *What do you think might happen to an inexperienced sailor in these waters? It would be almost impossible for an inexperienced sailor to navigate them safely.* **MAKE INFERENCES**

💬 Classroom Collaboration

Have pairs discuss why the author chose the title *A Watery Grave* for this selection. Then invite pairs to share their responses with the class. *The selection is about the waters around North Carolina's Outer Banks, which are treacherous for sailors. Many ships have been lost, and the waters have become a grave for many sailors.* **ELA** SL.5.2 **ELD** ELD.PI.5.1, ELD.PI.5.5

ENGLISH LANGUAGE SUPPORT

Read Aloud—Second Read Project the Target Vocabulary Preview. Introduce each word to students. Use visuals, gestures, or yes/no questions to help them understand the meaning of each word. Have students listen to the Read Aloud again and signal when they hear a Target Vocabulary Word. **ELD** ELD.PI.5.5

A Watery Grave

In 1996, on a cold, **clammy** November day, divers from a company called Intersal were finishing up for the day. Dedicated to finding and exploring shipwrecks, they were searching Beaufort Inlet off the North Carolina coast. According to historical records, here lay the *Queen Anne's Revenge*, once the flagship of the notorious pirate Blackbeard. Company divers had been surveying the area—unsuccessfully—for almost a decade. But today, the crew of **elite** shipwreck historians aboard the staging vessel heard a loud **commotion.** Divers had discovered a huge mound of cannons, anchors, and other artifacts—including a bronze bell inscribed with the date 1709. After inspecting these relics, underwater archaeologists agreed that this site probably contained the wreck of the *Queen Anne's Revenge.*

1 It's not surprising that the waters off North Carolina were once a draw for pirates. Britain's anti-smuggling laws restricted their activities, which was an **annoyance** to them. Across the Atlantic, however, the colonies posed no such problem. Emboldened by this **realization,** pirates found that North Carolina's Outer Banks were full of narrow bays and inlets—convenient for staging sneak attacks on merchant ships.

Historians have documented more than five thousand shipwrecks lost in North Carolina's waters, but no find has been as dramatic as the *Queen Anne's Revenge.* Much of this excitement comes from its role in the exploits of Blackbeard, the most feared pirate in history.

2 Blackbeard captured countless ships. The *Queen Anne's Revenge*, captured in Caribbean waters in 1717, was his prime weapon during the height of his reign as Pirate King. It was from the prow of this flagship in May of 1718 that Blackbeard commanded his most brazen act of piracy—the blockade of the port of Charleston. For an entire week, Blackbeard led three hundred pirates on four boats to attack merchant ships. Once **secured,** Blackbeard climbed aboard his prizes to raid their contents and **bundle** up stolen treasures.

However, the site of this campaign was also where both ship and pirate met their watery deaths. When his flagship sank in June of 1718, Blackbeard escaped—only to die in battle there a mere five months later.

3 The coastal waters that appealed to pirates posed many hazards. Sailors know that when they pass through Cape Hatteras, paying strict attention is of **critical** importance. Here, an area called the Diamond Shoals extends fourteen miles out, full of shifting sand bars that lurk under the shallow waters. These hidden dangers have caused many a ship to be **demolished.** The strong winds can toss salty spray a hundred feet into the air. A ship can be broken up, and no one would even hear it over the **squalling** of the stormy seas. In a book about the area's many shipwrecks, author David Stick writes: "You can stand on Cape Point at Hatteras on a stormy day and watch two oceans come together in an awesome display of savage fury. . . . Seafaring men call it the Graveyard of the Atlantic."

Introduce Vocabulary

▶ SHARE OBJECTIVE

- Acquire and use vocabulary.
- Use knowledge of linguistic context to determine the meaning of unknown words. LANGUAGE

Apply

Display and discuss the Vocabulary in Context Cards, using the routine below. Direct students to use **Student Book pp. 262–263.**

1 **Read and pronounce the word.** Read the word once alone and then together.

2 **Explain the word.** Read aloud the explanation under *What Does It Mean?*

ENGLISH LANGUAGE SUPPORT Review these cognates with Spanish-speaking students.

- *conmoción (commotion)*
- *crítico (critical)*
- *demolir (demolished)*

3 **Discuss vocabulary in context.** Together, read aloud the sentence on the front of the card. Help students explain and use the word in new sentences.

4 **Engage with the word.** Ask and discuss the *Think About It* question with students.

Apply

Give partners or small groups one or two **Vocabulary in Context Cards.**

- Help students complete the *Talk It Over* activity on the back of each card.
- Have students complete the activities for all cards during the week.

🔍 **Language Detective** Tell pairs to use the Vocabulary words to describe what they see in each photo. Have students read aloud their sentences to the class. Provide sentence frames to help students get started.

Over time, people have adapted to a new home.

ELA L.5.4a, L.5.6 **ELD** ELD.PI.5.12a

Lesson 9

Vocabulary in Context

🔍 **LANGUAGE DETECTIVE**

Talk About the Writer's Words
Work with a partner. Use the blue Vocabulary words in new sentences that tell about the photos. Write the sentences.

1 **critical**
Rescue workers can provide critical, or vital, aid when a hurricane strikes.

2 **demolished**
These people returned to search the ruins of their home after a tornado demolished it.

3 **elite**
Medals for bravery are given to an elite group of the best and most skilled lifeguards.

4 **commotion**
Rescue dogs are trained to stay calm in spite of chaos and commotion.

262 **ELA** L.5.4a, L.5.6 **ELD** ELD.PI.5.12a

ENGLISH LANGUAGE SUPPORT

Use Sentence Frames

Emerging Have students complete sentence frames for each Vocabulary word. For example, *The _____ is loud. commotion* **ELD** ELD.PI.5.12a

Expanding Have students complete sentence frames for each Vocabulary word. Then, have them trade frames with a partner and complete the other's frames. For example, *People sometimes feel clammy when _____.* **ELD** ELD.PI.5.12a

Bridging Have partners ask and answer questions about each Vocabulary word. For example, *What is critical to do before taking a test?* **ELD** ELD.PI.5.1, ELD.PI.5.12a

---

► Study each Context Card.

► Break each Vocabulary word into syllables. Use your glossary to check your answers.

5 bundle

Rescuers bundle, or wrap, injured skiers in blankets for warmth or to prevent shock.

6 annoyance

During a fire, people who get too close can distract firefighters and cause them annoyance.

7 secured

In mountain rescues, one person is secured to another by safety fasteners.

8 squalling

The squalling of a child can lead rescuers to the frightened, crying victim.

9 clammy

The protective clothing worn by firefighters can make them feel clammy and damp.

10 realization

The realization, or understanding, that rescuers save lives makes families proud.

263

FORMATIVE ASSESSMENT RtI

Are students able to understand and use Target Vocabulary words?

IF...	THEN...
students **struggle,**	► use **Vocabulary in Context Cards** and differentiate the **Vocabulary Reader,** *Saved from the Sea,* for Struggling Readers, p. T292.
students are **on target,**	► use **Vocabulary in Context Cards** and differentiate the **Vocabulary Reader,** *Saved from the Sea,* for On-Level Readers, p. T292.
students **excel,**	► differentiate the **Vocabulary Reader,** *Saved from the Sea,* for Advanced Readers, p. T293.

SMALL GROUP Options

Vocabulary Reader, pp. T292–T293 *Scaffold instruction to the English Learner's proficiency level.*

ENGLISH LANGUAGE SUPPORT

Read and Write Together

Emerging/Expanding

Read Together Display ELL9.2 in Grab-and-Go™ Resources. Read aloud the title and have students repeat. Then have students look at the images on the page and predict what they think the text will be about.

• As you read the text, display Vocabulary in Context Cards for *critical* and *demolished*. Then, have students read the text chorally with you.

• Help students generate true and false statements about the text on **ELL.9.2** that use the Vocabulary words. For example,

A fierce storm did not demolish the boat. false

Allow students to include language from the text on **ELL.9.2**. Write and display the sentences.

Write Together Display sentence frames, such as the following, and have partners use them to write complete sentences.

1. A storm *demolished* the ship.

2. The survivors needed *critical* help.

ELD ELD.PI.5.2, ELD.PI.5.4, ELD.PI.5.12a

FIRST READ

Read and Comprehend

▶ SHARE OBJECTIVES

- Draw conclusions and make generalizations in historical fiction.
- Infer and predict in historical fiction.
- Engage effectively in collaborative discussion. LANGUAGE

☑ TARGET SKILL

Conclusions and Generalizations

- Read the top section of **Student Book p. 264.**

- Tell students that when they read, they can use text details to draw conclusions and make generalizations to understand a text more fully.

- Remind students that conclusions are decisions or judgements that readers make based on information and details in the text. Generalizations are a type of conclusion; they are broad statements that are true most of the time.

- Draw attention to the graphic organizer on **Student Book p. 264.** Tell students that as they read, they can use a graphic organizer to record details from the text that will help them draw conclusions or make generalizations.

- Remind students that they should quote accurately from the text and use their own prior knowledge and experiences to support their conclusions. **ELA** RL.5.1

ENGLISH LANGUAGE SUPPORT Scaffold Anchor Text Before reading the selection, distribute <u>ELL9.3 in Grab-and-Go™ Resources</u> ⤴. Read the page aloud, and then have students chorally reread it with you.

Review Conclusions and Generalizations Reread aloud the first paragraph.

- Review with students that a conclusion is a guess about ideas not stated in the text. A generalization is a broad statement that is usually true.

Guided Practice Display an Inference Map. During reading, complete it with students.

- Have students use the Inference Map to record story details and a conclusion.

- Help students identify key story details, and work with them to draw a conclusion. **ELD** ELD.PI.5.6a

T246 • Unit 2 Lesson 9 (SB p. 264)

Read and Comprehend

☑ TARGET SKILL

Conclusions and Generalizations Using text evidence to figure out something in a story that isn't directly stated by the author is called drawing a **conclusion.** A **generalization**—a broad statement that is true most of the time—is a type of conclusion. As you read "Storm Warriors," notice the details the author provides about a rescue crew and the people on a ship called the *E.S. Newman.* Their actions and words can help you draw conclusions and make generalizations about the characters. Use a graphic organizer like this one to record a conclusion, as well as the details you used to draw your conclusion. Details may include quotes from the text.

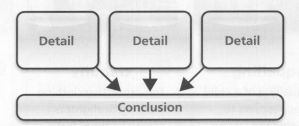

☑ TARGET STRATEGY

Infer/Predict As you read "Storm Warriors," make **inferences** based on details and characters' actions, and try to **predict** how the story will end.

264   **ELA** RL.1.1, SL.5.1c   **ELD** ELD.PI.5.1, ELD.PI.5.3, ELD.PI.5.6a

---

ENGLISH LANGUAGE SUPPORT

Comprehensible Input

Emerging Point to the illustrations, and use gestures to help students understand weather conditions. Ask students to describe the weather using short phrases. **ELD** ELD.PI.5.1

Expanding Using illustrations and text, have students identify clues in the story about weather conditions. Ask students to use complete sentences to make generalizations about the weather in "Storm Warriors." **ELD** ELD.PI.5.1

Bridging Ask students to tell how they know what the weather conditions are in "Storm Warriors." Encourage them to state details and make generalizations. **ELD** ELD.PI.5.1

PREVIEW THE TOPIC

Courage

Nearly everyone has an opinion on the topic of courage. Most people consider courage to be a positive character trait. But what does it mean to be courageous?

There are many different kinds of people and many unique situations that might require courage. So, it makes sense that there are many different ways to be courageous. In "Storm Warriors," you learn what one boy thinks about courage as he assists in rescuing people after a shipwreck. Reading this selection will help you expand your definition of courage.

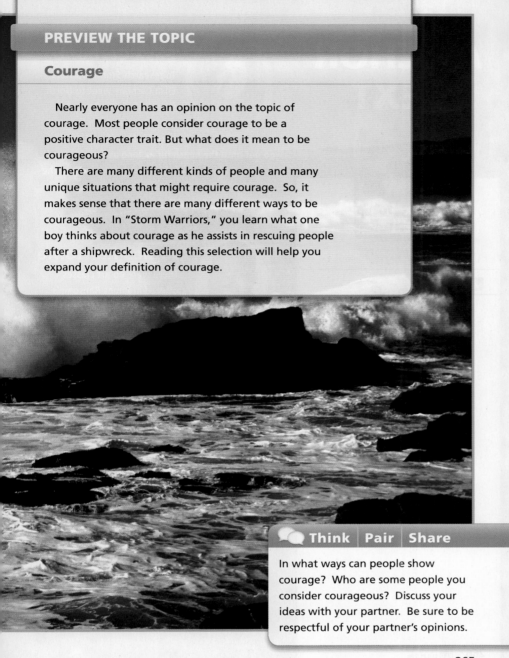

💬 Think | Pair | Share

In what ways can people show courage? Who are some people you consider courageous? Discuss your ideas with your partner. Be sure to be respectful of your partner's opinions.

265

COMPREHENSION STRATEGIES

Use the following strategies flexibly as you read with students by modeling how they can be used to improve comprehension. See scaffolded support for the strategy shown in boldface during this week's reading.

- • Monitor/Clarify
- • Summarize
- • **Infer/Predict**

- • Visualize
- • Analyze/Evaluate
- • Question

Use the Strategy Projectables S1-S8 ⌐, for additional support.

O— DOMAIN: **Values**
- - - - - - - - - - - -
LESSON TOPIC: Courage

☑ TARGET STRATEGY

Infer/Predict

- • Read the bottom section of **Student Book p. 264.** Remind students that making inferences and predictions while they read will give them a greater understanding of historical fiction.

- • Explain that when good readers **infer**, they determine something that is not directly stated by the author. They may use information in the text, or information they already know, to help them.

- • Explain that when good readers **predict**, they use text details to determine what might happen next in the story.

- • Then, explain that you will demonstrate how to use the strategy when you read "Storm Warriors" together. **ELA** RL.5.1 **ELD** ELD.PI.5.6a

PREVIEW THE TOPIC

Courage

- • Tell students that today they will begin reading "Storm Warriors."

- • Read the information at the top of **Student Book. p. 265** with students.

- • Have students discuss what the term *courage* means and what sort of behavior courage demands. Note that the title may help them predict the kind of courage someone would need during bad weather at sea.

Think-Pair-Share

- • Before partners begin their discussion, have the class suggest acts of courage that they have heard or read about. List these on the board.

- • Then, have partners take turns talking about their ideas. Give partners time to discuss how their opinions on the topic are similar and different. Remind students to be respectful of their partner's opinions. **ELA** SL.5.1c **ELD** ELD.PI.5.1, ELD.PI.5.3

ENGLISH LANGUAGE SUPPORT Access Prior Knowledge: All Proficiencies Use the image on Lesson 9 Language Support Card ⌐ to review the selection topic with students. Show the completed Flow Chart again and help students summarize its content.

Read and Comprehend (SB p. 265) • **T247**

FIRST READ

Read the Anchor Text

☑ GENRE

Historical Fiction

- Read the genre information on **Student Book p. 266** with students.
- Preview the selection with students, and model identifying the characteristics of historical fiction.

> **Think Aloud** *This selection has a setting that was a real time and place in the past. I see it features realistic characters and events. I understand that there are some made-up events and details, and they add to the realism of the dialogue and characters.*

- As you preview, ask students to identify other features of historical fiction.

ENGLISH LANGUAGE SUPPORT Access Prior Knowledge: All Proficiencies List characters, setting elements, and plot events from "Storm Warriors" on the board. Distribute Story Maps to students. Have student pairs make story predictions by using items from the list to fill in their maps. During reading, have students check their predictions and continue to add to their Story Maps.

ELA RL.5.10 **ELD** ELD.PI.5.6a

Lesson 9

ANCHOR TEXT

☑ GENRE

Historical fiction is a story in which characters and events are set in a real period of history. As you read, look for:
▶ a setting that is a real time and place in the past
▶ realistic characters and events
▶ some made-up events and details

266 | **ELA** RL.5.6, RL.5.10, RF.5.4a, RF.5.4b
ELD ELD.PI.5.6a

MEET THE AUTHOR
Elisa Carbone

To research *Storm Warriors*, Elisa Carbone went to North Carolina's Outer Banks to experience a storm for herself. She says, "I would go out onto the beach for as long as I could stand it, feeling the force of the wind, taking in all of the sensations. Then I'd . . . write it all down."

MEET THE ILLUSTRATOR
James Ransome

There were no art classes offered in James Ransome's school when he was a boy, so he studied books on how to draw. Then in high school and college, he had the chance to study painting, drawing, and film. Now he is the award-winning illustrator of over twenty-five books for children.

Scaffold Close Reading

Strategies for Annotation

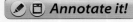 **Annotate it!**

As you read the selection with students, look for **✏ 🗎 Annotate it!**. It indicates opportunities for students to annotate the text independently.

Think Through the Text

FIRST READ

Develop comprehension through
- Guided Questioning
- Target Strategy: Infer/Predict
- Vocabulary in Context

Analyze the Text

SECOND READ

Support analyzing short sections of text:
- Conclusions and Generalizations
- Point of View
- Characterization
- Verb Types

Use directed note-taking to complete a graphic organizer during reading. Distribute Graphic Organizer 8 🗗.

Independent Reading

- Students analyze the text independently, using the Reader's Guide on pp. 97–98 of the Reader's Notebook 🗗 (See p. T264 for instructional support.)
- Students read independently in a self-selected trade book.

STORM WARRIORS

by Elisa Carbone
selection illustrated by James Ransome

ESSENTIAL QUESTION

How can an act of courage reveal a person's true nature?

267

READER AND TASK CONSIDERATIONS

Determine the level of additional support your students will need to read and comprehend "Storm Warriors" successfully.

READERS

- **Motivate** Have students read the story to understand the risks that were involved with being a member of the Pea Island crew.
- **Talk It Over** Use Lesson 9 Language Support Card for a discussion about water rescue.
- **Access Knowledge and Experiences** Ask students to make connections between information in "Storm Warriors" and what they might learn in a social studies text about the same time period and location.

TASKS

- **Increase Scaffolding** Guide students to visualize characters, settings, and story events as they read the text to gain a deeper understanding of story elements.
- **Foster Independence** Ask pairs of students to write on self-stick notes questions they have about the story. Have students discuss their questions after they have finished reading. Tell student pairs to share their questions with the class.

Read aloud the **Essential Question** on **Student Book p. 267**: *How can an act of courage reveal a person's true nature?* Tell students to think about this question as they read "Storm Warriors."

Predictive Writing

- Explain that students will write a paragraph to explain what they expect "Storm Warriors" to be about. Ask them to think about how the Essential Question relates to what they noticed while previewing the selection or what they already know from their own experiences or past readings.
- Guide students to think about the genre of the selection to help them write.

Set Purpose

- Tell students that setting a purpose for reading will make them better readers, particularly if they preview the selection, decide what they know about the genre, and determine what they hope to enjoy about the selection.
- Model setting a reading purpose.

Think Aloud *Historical fiction provides insight into the people who lived in a different time or place. My purpose for reading this story is to share the experiences of the characters and learn about how people lived during the time in which the story is set.*

- Have students set their own purpose for reading. Ask several students to share their purpose for reading. **ELA RF.5.4a**

ENGLISH LANGUAGE SUPPORT Preteach Academic English: Emerging/Expanding Guide students to complete the Academic English activities on Language Support Card 9.

FIRST READ

Think Through the Text

Cite Text Evidence

1 *What clues does the author give to explain the role of a surfman? It is defined by "lifesaving crew" and also in the next sentence as "rescuing people from shipwrecks."*
ELA RL.5.4 **ELD** ELD.PI.5.6b

2 *Quote from the text to explain why it might be helpful for Nathan to study medical books. The author says Nathan is learning "critical lifesaving skills." Perhaps medical knowledge is "as important as bravery" when it comes to rescues.* **ELA** RL.5.1

ENGLISH LANGUAGE SUPPORT *Ask this question in a different way. What is Nathan learning from studying medical books? What details in the text tell you that what Nathan's doing might be helpful?*

3 *What is the purpose of the first paragraph? Why is it printed in a different typeface? The first paragraph is an introduction that provides background for readers and puts the first scenes of the story in context. Putting the introduction in italics sets it apart and shows that it is not part of the actual story.* **ELA** RL.5.5

It's 1896 on Pea Island, part of North Carolina's Outer Banks. Nathan dreams of becoming a fearless surfman with Pea Island's elite African American lifesaving crew. However, his father, a fisherman, doesn't want Nathan to risk his life rescuing people from shipwrecks. Nevertheless, Nathan studies medical books and learns critical lifesaving skills. Then a hurricane hits the Outer Banks. The E.S. Newman runs aground in the storm. This is Nathan's chance to help the surfmen. As the storm rages, he begins to realize that knowledge is as important as bravery.

I stumbled forward and caught my balance on the side of the beach cart. I faced the sea and the wind. There was the sunken ship, hardly thirty yards from us. She was a mass of dark hull and white torn sails against the foaming sea, rocking on her side, her cabin and much of her starboard already demolished by the heavy surf. As I stood with my mouth open, panting, the wind blew my cheeks floppy and dried my tongue.

A cheer went up from the sailors aboard the ship. They'd spotted us and had high hopes that they would soon be rescued. I expected to hear the command "Action," to begin the breeches-buoy rescue, but heard nothing. It took me a moment to realize what Keeper Etheridge must already have figured out: our equipment was useless. There was no way to dig a hole for the sand anchor under these rolling waves, nowhere to set up the Lyle gun.

268

ENGLISH LANGUAGE SUPPORT

Use Visuals

Emerging Have students point out some of the weather details in the illustration. Ask: *Why is the ship so close to shore?* Accept one-word responses.

Expanding Have students refer to the illustrations to complete the sentence frame. *The ship is in trouble. The ship_____.* is sinking

Bridging Point to the men in the illustration. Ask: *What are the men doing?* Have students answer in complete sentences.

That's when I heard Mr. Meekins's voice above the din of wind and surf. "Those waves won't stop me from swimming through them—they're all blown over, hardly taller than a man," he said.

Swim? Swim out into that raging sea?

I stood rigid and watched as Mr. Etheridge pulled a large-sized shot line out of the beach cart and helped Mr. Meekins tie it around his waist. Mr. Pugh was tied in as well, and the heaving stick, attached to its own line, was secured to Mr. Meekins's body. The wind shoved at me and buffeted my ears. It was unthinkable, what these men were doing. Violence swirled around us—a deadly, churning mix of wind and sea. And these two surfmen were walking *into* it.

269

Practice Fluency

Phrasing: Punctuation Read aloud the first two paragraphs on **Student Book p. 269** while students follow along. As you read the text, model appropriate phrasing and using punctuation as a guide.

- Explain to students that proper phrasing involves breaking text into groups of words called phrases.

- Remind students to pause slightly after each phrase so that listeners have a chance to process what is being read.

- Review with students that punctuation marks show where a reader should pause, and also indicate the lengths of pauses needed, and where to pause for effect when reading quotations or dialogue.

> **Think Aloud** *When I read the beginning of the first paragraph, I pause when I get to the end of the first sentence. Then, I read what Mr. Meekins is saying as if he's speaking. Then, I pause again at the dash between "them" and "they're."*

- Have students choral read the paragraph, making sure to pause after each phrase or mark of punctuation.

- The Fluency lesson on p. T274 provides further opportunities for phrasing and practice with pausing for punctuation. **ELA** RF.5.4b

DOMAIN: Values

LESSON TOPIC: Courage

Cross-Curricular Connection Explain that the citizens who created the U.S. Lifesaving Service in 1871 went beyond their simple civic duties. These men patrolled the beaches and rescued shipwrecked crews. Remind students that the rescuers didn't have powerful boats. They saved people from the land using equipment, such as a Lyle gun, a cannon that shot a rope up to 300 yards to reach a ship, or a breeches buoy that was a life ring attached to a pair of pants. A victim climbed into the buoy and was then pulled by ropes to safety. These lifesavers also used sand anchors that could be buried in the sand and then tied to a rope attached to the ship. Have students discuss how these types of rescuers helped improve society.

FIRST READ

Think Through the Text

Cite Text Evidence

4 *How does the motto of the surfmen convey the dangers they face? It is a play on words for "going out" and "coming back." It is saying that the surfmen are required to go out and work to save people, but these's no guarantee that they themselves will survive the danger and make it back to the boat.*

ELA RL.5.4 **ELD** ELD.PI.5.6b

ENGLISH LANGUAGE SUPPORT Tell students that a motto is a short sentence or phrase that represents the beliefs or goals of a person or a group. Explain that the surfmen's motto shows both their dedication to rescues and the dangers they face by participating in them.

✅ **TARGET STRATEGY**

Infer/Predict

Reread aloud the last paragraph on **Student Book p. 270**. Then, model the strategy:

> **Think Aloud** *When I read that the narrator becomes sick over the realization that he will never be able to do what the others are doing, I infer that he has gained new respect for the surfmen. I cannot predict whether he will become a surfman but because he has special skills, I think he is going to help with the rescue in some way.*

Tell students to practice using the Infer/Predict strategy as they continue reading. **ELA** RL.5.1

5 *The narrator refers to "man the ropes" and at the start of Student Book p. 271, "paying out the ropes." What do these terms mean in the context of the story? The men on the beach control these ropes. To pay the rope out is to release length to allow someone tied to the rope to maneuver. To man the ropes is to have someone take hold and control them.*

ELA RL.5.4 **ELD** ELD.PI.5.6b

"Man the ropes," shouted Mr. Etheridge. "One of them goes down, we'll haul them both back in."

Mr. Meekins and Mr. Pugh were dark forms against the white foam, plodding into the surf. Powerful waves smacked them in the chest. They ducked their heads down and pushed forward.

I watched with a sick feeling in my stomach as the realization crept over me: I would never be able to do what these men were doing. The words of their motto ran through my head: "You have to go out, but you don't have to come back." In that moment I knew, with not a shred of doubt, that I did not have the courage to risk my life that way. The dream, and all the months of hoping, blew away as quickly as the foam off the waves. William and Floyd and Daddy were right. I would never be a surfman. **4**

270

FORMATIVE ASSESSMENT △ **3 2 1 RtI**

Infer/Predict

IF students do not check their understanding as they read… **THEN**, revisit the Infer/Predict strategy by modeling how to predict what Mr. Meekins is carrying instead of helping another sailor.

> **Think Aloud**  *From the way the narrator describes it, I can infer that Mr. Meekins is doing something unexpected by carrying something, instead of helping another sailor. Therefore, I can infer that something very valuable is in his arms. I predict that whatever he is carrying will become important to the narrator.*

Guide students to understand that whatever Mr. Meekins carries will be important to the plot.

There was no time for me to wallow in my loss. The men were paying out the ropes, and I was a fisherman—here to help. I took hold of one of the ropes. I turned my face sideways to the wind, but still it made my eyes blurry with tears. Blindly, I let the rope out, hand over hand, then squinted out toward the ship. A ladder had been lowered, and the sailors leaned over the side, waiting. Mr. Meekins and Mr. Pugh were almost there.

I heard another cheer from the men on the ship. When I peered out, Mr. Meekins was swinging the heaving stick and line. He let it fly and it landed on deck. The sailors would tie the line to the ship so that the rope could help steady the surfmen as they made their way from ship to shore and back again.

Soon we were hauling rope back in. The surfmen would be carrying one of the sailors between them now. I squinted into the spray. Where was the rescued sailor? Mr. Meekins and Mr. Pugh were on their way back, but without a third man between them. Mr. Meekins was carrying something a little larger than a Lyle gun.

5

ANALYZE THE TEXT

Conclusions and Generalizations
The narrator says that the men on the ship cheered. Why do you think they did this?

271

SECOND READ

Conclusions and Generalizations

Analyze the Text

- Read the Analyze the Text box on **Student Book p. 270** with students. Then distribute <u>Graphic Organizer 8</u> ⎃.

- Remind students that drawing conclusions and making generalizations as they read will help them figure out things not directly stated by the author and gain a more complete understanding of the story.

- Display <u>Projectable 9.2</u> ⎃ and tell students they will work together to analyze a section of the story.

- Have students find clues from the text on **p. 271** to conclude why the men cheered. "*Mr. Meekins was swinging the heaving stick and line …*"; *They cheer because they will soon be rescued.*

- Have students make a generalization based on these details as well. *People cheer to show happiness or encouragement.*

- Tell students that they can continue to draw conclusions and make generalizations as they read. **ELA** RL.5.1 **ELD** ELD.PI.5.6a

🖉 🔲 ***Annotate it!*** As students draw conclusions and make generalizations, have them highlight evidence from the text that supports their thoughts.

▷ **DOMAIN: Values**

LESSON TOPIC: Courage

Cross-Curricular Connection Point out that it takes great courage and being in peak physical condition to be a lifeguard. Have students discuss lifeguards they may have seen at beaches and pools, as well as some of the challenges these lifesavers face. Students should realize that swimming to rescue a drowning person can be very dangerous. A desperate, terrified victim can easily trap a lifeguard. Explain that the first lifeguards were police officers who were assigned to beaches after Americans first started bathing in the ocean in the 1800s. By the early 1900s, as many as 9,000 swimmers drowned each year, prompting communities to hire professionals. Today, lifeguards use jet skis, long boards, and other gear to keep swimmers safe.

Think Through the Text

Cite Text Evidence

6 *What simile does the author use to describe a screaming child? What does the simile mean, and why do you think the author chose it? Answers should quote accurately from the text. The author compares the child's crying to "the squalling of an alley cat." It means that the child's crying is high-pitched and loud. The author might have chosen it to help readers understand that the sound is wild and unexpected.*

ELA RL.5.1, RL.5.4, L.5.5a **ELD** ELD.PI.5.6a, ELD.PI.5.6b, ELD.PI.5.8

ENGLISH LANGUAGE SUPPORT Remind students that a simile compares something unfamiliar with something readers will be able to relate to. In this case, the author probably knows that babies can produce many different kinds of cries, and she wanted to make it very clear to readers what this one sounded like to Nathan.

7 *How do Nathan's actions in this scene begin to help you figure out the theme? Nathan is unsure at first, but his preparation and courage help him act to save the child's life.*

ELA RL.5.2 **ELD** ELD.PI.5.6a

8 *How does the illustration help the reader appreciate the emotions in the scene? It shows how much the mother loves and fears for her child. The lightning in the background also adds to the frightening tension in the scene.*

ELA RL.5.7

What in the world could be more important to save off that ship than the lives of the men on board? I shook my head and hauled rope. The surfmen were half walking, half swimming, pushing forward, the waves smacking against their backs and seeming to want to spit them out of the sea.

As the surfmen drew closer, I heard what sounded like the squalling of an alley cat. Mr. Meekins handed over his bundle and shouted, "Get it into dry blankets before it goes blue!" The bundle was passed from man to man, until it was handed to me and I found myself looking into the terrified eyes of a screaming child. **6**

Daddy put his arm around my shoulders. "The driving cart," he shouted over the din of the waves and wind. In the driving cart, which was nothing more than an open wagon, dry blankets were packed under oilskins.

We crouched next to the cart, and it gave us some protection from the storm. The child clung to my neck. He was drenched and shivering miserably. I tried to loosen his grip so I could get his wet clothes off, but he just clung tighter. He was crying more softly now. "Mamma?" he whimpered. **7**

I gave Daddy a pleading look. What if his mother had already been washed overboard and drowned? Daddy stood, cupped his hands around his eyes, and looked in the direction of the ship. "They're carrying a woman back now," he said.

"Your mamma is coming," I told the child. He looked to be about three or four years old, with pale white skin and a shock of thick brown hair. "Let's get you warm before she gets here."

We had the boy wrapped in a dry blanket by the time his mother came running to him, cried, "Thomas!" and clutched him to her own wet clothing with such passion that she probably got him half drenched again.

The lady, who told us her name was Mrs. Gardiner, said she'd be warm enough in her wet dress under blankets and oilskins. No sooner had we settled her with Thomas than we heard the cry "Ho, this man is injured!"

272 **8**

ANALYZE THE TEXT

Point of View How would the description of the story's events change if it were told from Mr. Meekins's third-person limited point of view?

273

Point of View

- Read the Analyze the Text box on **Student Book p. 273** with students.

- Review with students how the point of view of a story's narrator influences the ways in which events, characters, and feelings are described.

- Remind students that first-person point of view limits what the author can reveal, as only one character's experiences are told. Third-person allows a narrator to tell the story from the perspectives of a variety of characters.

  ENGLISH LANGUAGE SUPPORT Remind students that they can use a narrator's pronouns as a clue to the point of view of a story. Point out the use of the first-person pronouns *I, my,* and *we* on **Student Book p. 272**. Tell students that these pronouns indicate a first-person point of view.

- Have students read **Student Book p. 272** silently. Ask: *What paragraph describes Nathan's thoughts or opinions? Paragraph 1 tells what Nathan is thinking.* **Then ask:** *How would the story change if it were told from Mr. Meekins' point of view? Mr. Meekins would not be able to see what was going on between Nathan and the child on the shore because he is out in the surf. The story would be more focused on what's happening out in the water.* **ELA** RL.5.6 **ELD** ELD.PI.5.6a

✏️ 🖥 Annotate it! Have students highlight sections of the text that reveal the narrator's thoughts.

FOR STUDENTS WITH DISABILITIES Students may have difficulty comprehending narrative text with dialogue. Have students work in small groups, each taking the part of one character, and reading the text aloud. Have them pause after a page or two and summarize their character's thoughts and actions.

Think Through the Text

Cite Text Evidence

9 *What clues from the text tell the reader how Nathan learned about treating bleeding and hypothermia? Answers should quote accurately from the text. Nathan "recalled the words" about treating the injured "from the medical books."* **ELA RL.5.1**

10 *Mrs. Gardiner says, "He seems to know what to do, dear." How might Nathan's skills be different from those of the other surfmen? He has medical knowledge, and this is different from the surfmen who are strong and physically skilled.* **ELA RL.5.3 ELD ELD.PI.5.6a**

☑ **TARGET STRATEGY**

Infer/Predict

Tell students to practice the Infer/Predict strategy as they read **Student Book p. 274** silently to themselves. Ask several students to point out where they used the strategy to help them clarify information. **ELA RL.5.1**

I ran to see. A young sailor had just been delivered by the surfmen. Blood dripped from his head and stained his life preserver. His lips were a sickly blue. He took two steps, then collapsed face first into the shallow water. Mr. Bowser dragged him up by his armpits and pulled him toward the driving cart.

"George, take over my place with the ropes," he shouted to Daddy. "Nathan, come help me."

The sailor looked hardly older than me, with dirty blond hair that had a bloody gash the size of a pole bean running through it.

"Treat the bleeding first, then the hypothermia," I said as I recalled the words from the medical books and they comforted me with their matter-of-factness. **9**

Mr. Bowser grunted as we lifted the sailor into the driving cart. "You did study well, Nathan," he said.

Mr. Bowser sent me for the medicine chest, then I held a compress against the man's head wound while Mr. Bowser began to remove his wet clothes. That's when Mr. Bowser seemed to notice Mrs. Gardiner for the first time.

"Ma'am, we're going to have to . . ." He cleared his throat. "This boy's hypothermic, so his wet clothes have to . . ."

Mrs. Gardiner rolled her eyes in annoyance. "Oh, for heaven's sake!" she exclaimed. She immediately went to work to pull off the man's boots, help Mr. Bowser get the rest of his clothes off, and bundle him in a dry blanket.

"Are there any other injured on board?" Mr. Bowser **10** asked as he wrapped a bandage around the man's head.

"No, only Arthur," she said. "He took quite a fall when the ship ran aground."

274

FORMATIVE ASSESSMENT △ 3 2 1 **RtI**

Infer/Predict

IF students have difficulty applying the Infer/Predict strategy... **THEN**, use this model:

Think Aloud   *When I see Mr. Bowser become unable to speak in front of Mrs. Gardiner, I think of other times when people I know were like this, and I realize he is embarrassed. But I can predict that taking off the man's wet clothes will save his life, which is why Mrs. Gardiner ignores Mr. Bower's embarrassment. She knows a life is more important.*

Have students reread Student Book p. 275, and use the strategy to predict how Nathan will help other people.

Arthur groaned and his eyes fluttered open. "I'm cold," he complained.

Suddenly there was a commotion at the ropes. "Heave!" Mr. Etheridge shouted. "Haul them all in!"

"They've lost their footing!" I cried.

Mr. Bowser grasped me by the arms. "Take over here. I'm sure you know what to do." Then he ran to help with the ropes.

My hands felt clammy and shaky, but once again the words from the books came back to steady me: "Rub the legs and arms with linseed oil until warmth returns . . ." I rummaged in the medicine chest, found the linseed oil, and poured some into my palm.

"This will warm you, sir," I said loudly enough to be heard over the wind.

Arthur nodded his bandaged head and watched nervously as I rubbed the oil into his feet and calves, then his hands and arms. He gave Mrs. Gardiner a quizzical look. "Ain't he young to be a doctor?" he asked her.

She patted his shoulder and smoothed the hair off his forehead. "He seems to know what to do, dear," she said.

"I am warming up," he said.

I lifted the lantern to look at Arthur's face and saw that his lips were no longer blue.

ANALYZE THE TEXT

Characterization At first, Nathan was worried that he would not be helpful to the rescue effort. What evidence does the author give to show that Nathan is helpful after all?

275

Characterization

Analyze the Text

- Read the Analyze the Text box on **Student Book p. 275** with students.

- Review with students that characterization is an author's use of a character's actions, words, and thoughts to give readers insight into the character's traits, personality, and motivations.

- Tell students that strong characterization allows readers to feel as if they know the characters in a story. Explain that when a writer brings a character to life, readers are able to understand why that character does or says certain things, or has certain reactions or feelings.

- Ask: *How did the author let the reader know that Nathan doubted himself earlier? Earlier in the story, Nathan doubted his ability to be brave enough to walk into the waves like the other surfmen.*

ENGLISH LANGUAGE SUPPORT
Remind students that dialogue can be used to reveal character traits. Ask: *What dialogue does the author include to show that Nathan was helpful and wanted to be reassuring?*
Mr. Bowsers says to Nathan, "Take over here. I'm sure you know what to do." Nathan says to the injured man, "This will warm you, sir."

- *What other elements of characterization does the author include to make the characters come to life? Accept reasonable responses.*

ELA RL.5.1, RL.5.3 **ELD** ELD.PI.5.6a

🖉 🗐 ***Annotate it!*** Have students highlight dialogue in the story that helps characterize Nathan.

FOR STANDARD ENGLISH LEARNERS Pronunciation Some students may need help mastering Standard English pronunciations when reading aloud or speaking in a more formal register. Students may omit the final consonant in contractions such as *it's* or *don't*. They may pronounce *it's* as "it'" or *don't* as "don'." Write this sentence on the board: *"They've lost their footing!" I cried.* Read the sentence aloud, emphasizing the final consonant sound in *They've*. Have students echo your reading several times.

Think Through the Text

Cite Text Evidence

11 *What does the picture show you about what the characters are feeling?* It shows the gratitude of the captain and the pride in the faces of the surfmen. **ELA** RL.5.7

12 *What do you think would've happened to the crew if the surfmen hadn't helped them?* Their ship would have been smashed, and they would probably have died in the rough surf. **ELA** RL.5.1

ENGLISH LANGUAGE SUPPORT Provide these sentence frames to support participation. *If the surfmen hadn't helped, I think the crew's ship would have _____. This event probably would have caused _____.*

13 *How do you know that the captain is very grateful? What part of the text tells you this?* The author says, "his voice shaking," which means he is very emotional and can barely speak because "these good men" saved their lives. **ELA** RL.5.1 **ELD** ELD.PI.5.6a

14 *How does the beginning scene contrast with the final scene?* At the beginning, the weather is wild and people are in danger, but by the end, all the people are safe.
ELA RL.5.3, RL.5.5 **ELD** ELD.PI.5.6a

Classroom Conversation

Have students discuss "Storm Warriors," either in small groups or as a whole class. Use this prompt to focus their discussion: *What might Nathan be able to teach modern kids his age about courage?* Have students use text evidence and their own knowledge to support their thoughts. Remind students to respond to each other's comments and questions in complete sentences, to follow discussion rules, and to allow everyone a chance to share what they think. **ELA** SL.5.1a, SL.5.1b, SL.5.1c **ELD** ELD.PI.5.1, ELD.PI.5.4

276

Interactive Writing: Infer/Predict

Teach/Model Write *infer* and *predict*, and explain the meanings of the terms. Remind students that *infer* means to figure out details that are not stated in the text, while *predict* means to guess something in the text that will happen in the future. Use the Think Aloud to model inferring and predicting information from "Storm Warriors."

Think Aloud *I read that surfmen were an elite lifesaving team. I can infer that they were very good at what they did, and that they were very brave. I see the picture and predict that surfmen will be heroes in this story.*

Guided Practice Record details from "Storm Warriors" with the class, using text details to infer and predict information or events from the story. Remind students to use the future tense with *will* to write their predictions about the text.

• Review **Teach Academic Language** on Lesson 9 Language Support Card.

Just then a tall white man appeared, dressed in a captain's coat, his long hair flying in the wind. He reached up into the driving cart and pulled Mrs. Gardiner to him, pressing his cheek against hers. He must have asked about Thomas, because she pointed to him, bundled and sleeping in the cart. "They've saved the whole crew!" he cried. He looked around **12** at me and Arthur, and at the other rescued sailors and the surfmen who were now gathering around the driving cart in preparation for the long trip back through the storm to the station.

"My good men," he said, his voice shaking, "we owe you our lives." **13** **14**

277

Scaffolded Practice and Application

Emerging Have students write one prediction about the story. Provide this frame: *In this story, I think _____ will _____.*

Expanding Have students write one prediction about the story: *I think _____.* Remind students to use *will* as they record their prediction.

Bridging Have students write a prediction and one detail or piece of information they infer from the text.

🔍 Language Detective

Verb Types

- Explain to students that in most narratives, the author's focus is on events, characters, and what those characters do, think, and feel. Tell students that in order to show action and characters' thoughts and feelings, authors use a variety of verb types. Two types that help with character development are doing verbs and thinking verbs. Doing verbs allow writers to show what characters do and how they react to challenges. Thinking verbs allow writers to make clear what characters are thinking and feeling, and how they interact with others.

- Read aloud paragraph 5 on **Student Book p. 275** while students follow along. Ask: *What verbs does the author include in this paragraph? felt, came, steady, rub, rummaged, found, poured* Use the Think Aloud to model analyzing the functions of the verbs.

> **Think Aloud** *The text says that Nathan's hands felt clammy and that the knowledge he needed came back to him. The verbs felt and steady are thinking verbs that show his state of mind. The other verbs show action. He is remembering that he should rub the cold person's legs and arms with linseed oil to warm him up. Then he is searching for the oil, he finds it, and he pours some into his hand to start the treatment.*

- Have students choose a two-page section of the text and identify the verbs the author uses. Then have them determine whether the verbs are thinking verbs or doing verbs. Have students share their findings, and discuss with them how the different verb types give readers a complete picture of what's happening in the story.
ELA RL.5.1, L.5.1c **ELD** ELD.PII.5.3

🖊 📋 Annotate it! Have students highlight thinking verbs and underline doing verbs in the text as they read.

Dig Deeper *Use Clues to Analyze the Text*

▶ **SHARE OBJECTIVES**

- Draw conclusions and make generalizations about characters and events in a story.
- Determine author's point of view.
- Analyze characterization in a story.
- Understand the use of different verb types in narrative text. LANGUAGE

ENGLISH LANGUAGE SUPPORT

Comprehensible Input

Emerging Ask: *If students came into the classroom with wet umbrellas, could you say it is raining outside?* Show how this is a conclusion based on facts. Point out the facts of umbrellas and wetness.

Expanding Point out that when we say we "draw" a conclusion, we mean "come up with" or "describe." Have students complete this sentence frame. *A painter draws a _____ by describing something with paints and lines and shapes.*

Bridging Help partners understand something not directly stated in the text by identifying details that would allow them to draw a conclusion, or make a generalization or inference. **ELD** ELD.PI.5.1

Text-Based Comprehension

1 Teach/Model

Terms About Literature

conclusion a judgment based on text details

generalization a broad, usually true statement

first-person point of view one person tells the story as "I"

third-person limited point of view a narrator tells the story using "he," "she," "they"

characterization how a character is described by the author

verb a word that shows action or intention

- Remind students that they have just read a historical fiction piece about an African American lifesaving corps in 1896.

- Read **Student Book p. 278** with students. Tell them that authors provide details good readers can use to draw **conclusions** and make **generalizations**.

- Point out that each reader can draw slightly different conclusions or make different generalizations based on their prior knowledge or experiences and their interpretation of text evidence.

- Then, discuss the graphic organizer, using this model:

  Think Aloud *In the first paragraph, the author requires the reader to draw a conclusion about how this ship was wrecked. The details of it being just offshore and being pounded by surf and high winds suggest that a powerful storm has caused the accident.*

- Next, read **Student Book p. 279** with students.

- Tell students that the **point of view** an author chooses, whether it is **first-person** or **third-person limited,** greatly affects how a story is told. First-person limits what the author can reveal, as only one character's experiences are shared. Third-person limited allows a narrator to share a variety of perspectives about characters and events.

- Explain that good writers create memorable characters whose traits and personalities are clearly defined. Tell students that writers use elements of **characterization,** such as description, dialogue, and action, to bring characters to life.

🔍 **Language Detective: Verb Types** Explain to students that authors show action in stories by using different types of verbs. Paying close attention to verb types and what they show will help readers visualize character actions and plot events.

Q BE A READING DETECTIVE

Dig Deeper

Use Clues to Analyze the Text

Use these pages to learn about Conclusions and Generalizations, Point of View, and Characterization. Then read "Storm Warriors" again to apply what you learned.

Conclusions and Generalizations

Characters' actions and words can help you draw conclusions and make generalizations about a text in order to better understand it. A **conclusion** is a judgment reached by thinking about text details. A **generalization** is a broad statement that is true most of the time.

Authors do not always directly state information for readers to use in drawing conclusions or making generalizations. You can understand what is not directly stated in a story by using dialogue, details, and events to make **inferences.** As you read the selection again, use the text to draw conclusions and make generalizations about the characters' experiences. Remember to use quotations and evidence from the text to support your thoughts.

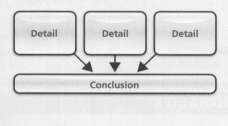

Detail	Detail	Detail

↓ ↓ ↓

Conclusion

278   **ELA** RL.5.1, RL.5.6, RF.5.4a, RF.5.4b   **ELD** ELD.PI.5.6a

Point of View

When an author writes in the **first-person point of view,** one character tells the story as he or she experiences it. Words such as *I, we, me,* and *mine* are used in first-person point of view. A **third-person limited point of view** means that a narrator tells what one character observes, feels, and knows. A third-person narrator is outside the story and uses words such as *he, she, him, his,* and *her* to discuss the characters.

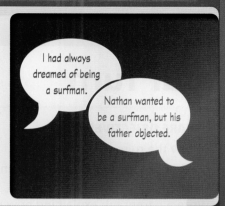

> I had always dreamed of being a surfman.

> Nathan wanted to be a surfman, but his father objected.

Characterization

An author describes a character's actions, words, and thoughts to help define the character's traits and personality. This technique is called **characterization.** In a story written from the first-person point of view, the narrator is a character in the story. The narrator's way of speaking, as well as thoughts about events and other characters in the story, helps characterize him or her.

279

---

2 Guided Practice/Apply

Analyze the Text

Begin a second read of "Storm Warriors" with students. Use the stopping points and instructional support to guide students to analyze the text:

- Conclusions and Generalizations, p. T253   **ELA** RL.5.1   **ELD** ELD.PI.5.6a
- Point of View, p. T255   **ELA** RI.5.6   **ELD** ELD.PI.5.6a
- Characterization, p. T257   **ELA** RL.5.3   **ELD** ELD.PI.5.6a
- Verb Types, p. T259   **ELD** ELD.PII.5.3

Directed Note-Taking The graphic organizer will be completed with students during the second read on p. T253.

FORMATIVE ASSESSMENT   RtI

Are students able to draw conclusions or make generalization and inferences in a text?

IF...	THEN...
students struggle,	**Differentiate Comprehension** for Struggling Readers, p. T294.
students are on track,	**Differentiate Comprehension** for On-Level Readers, p. T294.
students excel,	**Differentiate Comprehension** for Advanced Readers, p. T295.

Differentiate Comprehension, pp. T294–T295 *Scaffold instruction to the English Learner's proficiency level.*

SECOND READ

Your Turn

Cite Text Evidence

▶ **SHARE OBJECTIVES**
- Follow the rules of discussion.
- Provide text evidence to support analysis of story characters.
- Write a paragraph explaining how point of view influences descriptions in a story. **LANGUAGE**

RETURN TO THE ESSENTIAL QUESTION

Encourage students to work as partners to find text evidence that will support their discussion of the Essential Question. Have students define acts of courage and a person's nature.

ELA RL.5.1, SL.5.1a, SL.5.1c, SL.5.1d **ELD** ELD.PI.5.1, ELD.PI.5.6a

Classroom Conversation

Remind students that they should express their opinions as they answer the three questions, but they also should work with partners to find text evidence that supports what they believe. Review with students that good listeners ask thoughtful questions and respect the opinions of the speaker. See Digital Lesson: Listening and Responding ⤴.

ELA RL.5.1, SL.5.1a, SL.5.1c **ELD** ELD.PI.5.1, ELD.PI.5.6a

ENGLISH LANGUAGE SUPPORT Use sentence frames, such as the following, to support discussion.

I think Nathan's reasons for admiring the surfmen (are)/(are not) valid because ____.

What Nathan learns about courage is ____.

What Nathan has learned about himself might change his life by____.

As students share their ideas, tell them to use text evidence to support their responses.

ELD ELD.PI.5.1, ELD.PI.5.4, ELD.PI.5.6a, ELD.PI.5.11a

Your Turn

RETURN TO THE ESSENTIAL QUESTION

 Turn and Talk Review the selection to prepare to discuss this question: *How can an act of courage reveal a person's true nature?* As you discuss, take turns reviewing and explaining each other's key ideas. Ask questions to clarify points you don't understand.

Classroom Conversation

Continue your discussion of "Storm Warriors" by using text evidence to explain your answers to these questions:

1. What reasons does Nathan have for admiring the surfmen? Are his reasons valid? Why or why not?

2. What does Nathan learn about the nature of courage?

3. How might Nathan's life change because of what he learns about himself during the story?

WHO IS THIS CHARACTER?

Discuss Nathan Review the story to find evidence of Nathan's character traits. Look for examples of his intelligence, courage, kindness, and resourcefulness. Record the page numbers of the examples or passages you find. Then share your information with a partner. Work together to identify the best text evidence for each trait.

280   **ELA** RL.5.6, W.5.9a, W.5.10, SL.5.1a, SL.5.1c **ELD** ELD.PI.5.1, ELD.PI.5.3, ELD.PI.5.6a, ELD.PI.5.7, ELD.PI.5.10a, ELD.PI.5.11a, ELD.PII.5.2b

---

ENGLISH LANGUAGE SUPPORT

How English Works

Using Noun Phrases Before students begin their discussion, have them plan to add details about people, places, or things by building noun phrases. Provide a model, such as: *Some people have dangerous jobs.* Explain that *dangerous jobs* is a noun phrase. Point out the noun *job* and adjective *dangerous* to students. Help different proficiency levels build word banks to build noun phrases for their discussion. **ELD** ELD.PII.5.4

WRITE ABOUT READING ··············· *my*WriteSmart

Response "Storm Warriors" is written from the main character's—Nathan's—point of view. How does his point of view affect descriptions in the story? Think about what would be different if one of the surfmen or sailors told the story. Write a paragraph explaining how Nathan's point of view shapes the story and affects how you see events and other story characters. Use quotes and evidence from the text to support your ideas.

Writing Tip

Use conjunctions to combine sentences and help your readers understand the relationships between your ideas.

281

ENGLISH LANGUAGE SUPPORT

Collaborative Writing

Step 1 Guide students to complete a list of their ideas about the story's point of view and how it affects the readers' feelings and support it with text evidence.

Step 2 Explain that you will work together as a class to write a response to reading by using the completed graphic organizer. Point out to students that they will say ideas and sentences, and you will write them down for the group to see and read.

Step 3 Have students develop the response by referring to the graphic organizer and answering questions, such as these:

- What words will help begin this response?
- What information should we include? How do we say that in a sentence?
- What is the first reason that we should write?
- What text evidence will we use?

Step 4 Read the unfinished response aloud to students. Repeat, and have students read aloud with you. Ask students if they see or hear anything they would like to change.

Extra Scaffold Without purposely making mistakes, revise in the moment by using Think Alouds. **ELD** ELD.PI.5.2

WHO IS THIS CHARACTER?

Remind students that character is revealed in a story through details that show a character's words, thoughts, actions, and what other characters say about him or her. Point out that at first, Nathan doubts himself and then learns he is a valuable member of the team.
ELA RL.5.1 **ELD** ELD.PI.5.6a

WRITE ABOUT READING   *Performance Task*

Remind students that when an author tells a story from a single character's point of view, readers see descriptions and experience events and feelings through that character. Guide students to understand that if "Storm Warriors" were told from another character's perspective, or from an omniscient point of view, the descriptions and details included would be quite different. As they write, have students think about how Nathan's point of view influences what they see happening in the story. Remind them to use quotations and other text evidence to support their thoughts.
ELA RL.5.1, RL.5.6, W.5.9a, W.5.10

ENGLISH LANGUAGE SUPPORT Tell students to state their opinion in the opening sentence. Provide this frame:

I think Nathan's point of view shapes the story by ____.

Suggest that they add reasons for their opinion using these frames:

I believe this because ____.
The text says ____.

Remind students to use noun phrases correctly in their paragraphs. See Digital Lesson: Writing to Sources ⬏. **ELD** ELD.PI.5.10a, ELD.PII.5.4

Writing Tip Remind students to use conjunctions to help clarify the relationships between ideas. **ELA** L.5.3a **ELD** ELD.PII.5.2b

*my*WriteSmart Have students complete the Write About Reading activity through *my*WriteSmart. Students will read the prompt within *my*WriteSmart and have access to multiple writing resources, including the Student eBook, Writing Rubrics, and Graphic Organizers.

Independent Reading

▶ SHARE OBJECTIVES

- Read and comprehend literature.
- Quote accurately from a text to support analysis and inferences.
- Read independently from a "just right" book.
- Ask and answer questions about key details. LANGUAGE

ENGLISH LANGUAGE SUPPORT

"Just Right" Books for English Learners

All Proficiencies Sometimes an English learner may choose to reread a "just right" book. Use this opportunity to practice oral reading fluency or to practice applying a comprehension skill or strategy with the student. These practice times should take no more than five minutes, to respect the English learner's independent reading time.

Reader's Guide

Use Text Evidence Tell students that they will read "Storm Warriors" on their own to analyze key details about the story.

Have students use the Reader's Guide pages in their Reader's Notebook, pp. 97–98 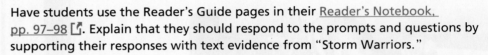. Explain that they should respond to the prompts and questions by supporting their responses with text evidence from "Storm Warriors."

Generate Questions Have students work independently or collaboratively to generate questions about "Storm Warriors." Ask students to share their questions. Begin a class discussion of questions that are most significant to their understanding. **ELA** RL.5.1, RL.5.10, RF.5.4a, SL.5.1c **ELD** ELD.PI.5.1

FOR STUDENTS WITH DISABILITIES To help students focus during group discussions, agree on a simple gesture, such as nodding three times or giving a thumbs-up, for students to use when they agree with another student's point during a discussion. Before the discussion, remind students about the gesture. Model the gesture when you agree with something someone adds to a discussion.

Self-Selected Reading

Read the Summary Remind students that a summary tells what a book is about. Point out that it is often found on the book jacket or on the back cover. Hold up a book that includes a summary and read it aloud. Model using the summary to decide whether to read the book: *Do I understand what this book is about? Does this topic interest me? Do I want to find out more, based on the summary?*

Explain that if students answer yes to these questions, then they will probably enjoy reading the book.

Have students read the summaries of a few books that might interest them and use the questions above to choose a book for independent reading. Ask students to use their Reading Logs in Grab-and-Go™ 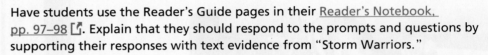 to record their progress and thinking about the book.

Fluency

Partner Read Have students read aloud with expression, using passages from their self-selected reading books. Tell them to provide each other with feedback and then reread to apply it. **ELA** RF.5.4b

Apply Vocabulary Knowledge

☑ Review Target Vocabulary

Classroom Collaboration Read aloud each of the following questions. Have students discuss their answers. Allow several students to respond to each question to provide a variety of possible responses for discussion.
ELA L.5.6

1. Why is it important to eliminate **commotion** during an emergency situation?

2. How might you quiet the **squalling** of a child?

3. If your bicycle was **secured** to a tree, what would you need to do to ride it?

4. How might **annoyance** affect someone's judgment in an emergency?

5. Why might a building damaged by fire need to be **demolished**?

6. If you see an accident, what **critical** step should you take immediately?

7. Why might a person feel **clammy**?

8. What are some modern-day **elite** groups that save lives?

9. What kind of **realization** might someone have after surviving a natural disaster?

10. What is a reason that you might **bundle** someone in a blanket?

Quick Write Display the following prompt: *Explain what* Storm Warriors *illustrates about the importance of teamwork. Use the vocabulary words you have learned in your writing.*

Tell students to think of the roles that each character took during the rescue operation. Remind them to quote accurately from the text. When they have finished writing, tell students to exchange papers with a partner and discuss whether they used the words correctly in their paragraphs.
ELA RL.5.1, L.5.6 **ELD** ELD.PI.5.1, ELD.PI.5.4

▶ SHARE OBJECTIVES

• Acquire and use vocabulary in speaking and writing. LANGUAGE

• Collaboratively respond to questions about familiar vocabulary. LANGUAGE

For additional practice with the lesson's Target Vocabulary, use the activities on pages 132–133 of the **Literacy and Language Guide.**

• Word Pairs

• Prefix *non-*

• Riddles

• Synonyms and Antonyms

ENGLISH LANGUAGE SUPPORT

Use Sentence Frames

All Proficiencies Have students complete sentence frames such as these to help them use the vocabulary words in their writing.

Nathan had the <u>realization</u> *that he would never be a surfman, but he was there to help.*

To help students discuss their partner's use of vocabulary in writing, provide discussion frames such as this one.

You used the word **squalling** *to describe _____.*
ELD ELD.PI.5.1, ELD.PI.5.4

⊃ DOMAIN: **Values**

LESSON TOPIC: COURAGE

CONNECT TO THE TOPIC
Informational Text

Preview the Informational Text

- Tell students that this selection is a magazine article about people who brought attention to the forgotten heroes of Pea Island. Ask students to read the title and headings and to preview the photographs. Have them read the text independently. **ELA** RI.5.10

Discuss Primary Sources

- Tell students that original documents or photographs from a period or an event are **primary sources**. Interviews can also be primary sources.

- Explain that primary sources give firsthand information. Researchers use them to understand events.

- Define key terms in the chart. Note that there are other types of primary sources. Then have students look for these types of primary sources as they read.

eyewitness	somebody who saw something happen
account	a report of something that has happened
document	a piece of writing that gives information

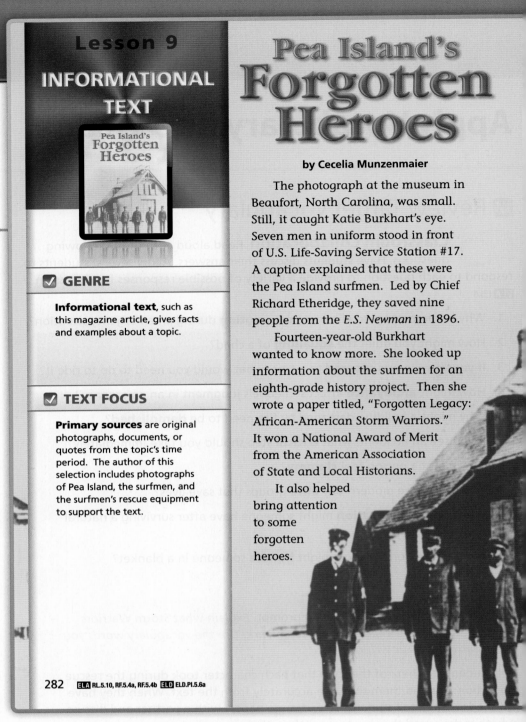

Lesson 9

INFORMATIONAL TEXT

Pea Island's Forgotten Heroes

☑ GENRE

Informational text, such as this magazine article, gives facts and examples about a topic.

☑ TEXT FOCUS

Primary sources are original photographs, documents, or quotes from the topic's time period. The author of this selection includes photographs of Pea Island, the surfmen, and the surfmen's rescue equipment to support the text.

282 **ELA** RI.5.10, RF.5.4a, RF.5.4b **ELD** ELD.PI.5.6a

by Cecelia Munzenmaier

The photograph at the museum in Beaufort, North Carolina, was small. Still, it caught Katie Burkhart's eye. Seven men in uniform stood in front of U.S. Life-Saving Service Station #17. A caption explained that these were the Pea Island surfmen. Led by Chief Richard Etheridge, they saved nine people from the *E.S. Newman* in 1896.

Fourteen-year-old Burkhart wanted to know more. She looked up information about the surfmen for an eighth-grade history project. Then she wrote a paper titled, "Forgotten Legacy: African-American Storm Warriors." It won a National Award of Merit from the American Association of State and Local Historians.

It also helped bring attention to some forgotten heroes.

Finding a Lost Story

Burkhart learned that Etheridge and his surfmen were an elite group. They were known for their skill and bravery. They were also the only African American group whose job was to save lives.

Then she came to a realization. Their bravery had never been officially recognized. "I immediately felt I had to do something about it," she says.

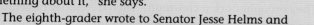

The eighth-grader wrote to Senator Jesse Helms and President Bill Clinton. She asked why the crew had not been given a medal. She learned that Coast Guard Officer Steve Rochon and graduate students David Zoby and David Wright were also trying to correct this wrong.

> *"Again and again, the crew went back through the raging sea."*

The Pea Island surfmen in about 1890

283

Practice Fluency

Phrasing: Punctuation Have students listen as you read aloud **Student Book p. 283**.

- Remind students that punctuation marks such as periods, commas, and colons indicate pauses. Tell them that certain punctuation marks, such as hyphens, do not require a pause. **ELD** ELD.PII.5.1

- Have students do repeated readings of the second paragraph on **Student Book p. 283** with a partner. Remind students to pause appropriately at punctuation marks. **ELA** RF.5.4a

---

▶ **DOMAIN: Values**

LESSON TOPIC: Courage

Cross-Curricular Connection Briefly review the informational text with students, and ask them to identify examples of courage by the Pea Island surfmen. Then have students review their social studies textbook or other informational texts to find more examples of courage. Discuss what makes an act courageous. *An act of courage is when a person goes beyond what we might expect, demonstrating bravery.* Guide students to see that acts of courage are ways ordinary people go beyond their basic civic responsibilities to help others and improve society.

Think Through the Text

Cite Text Evidence

Pause at the stopping points to ask students the following questions.

1 *What does realization mean as used in the text? What context clues help you determine its meaning? Sample answer: The word realization means "understanding." Through her research, Burkhart came to realize that the surfmen had never been honored for their deeds.* **ELA** RI.5.4

ENGLISH LANGUAGE SUPPORT Tell students that the word *real* has a cognate in Spanish: *real*. Remind students to look for cognates as they read to help them figure out the meanings of key words.

2 *Why did the surfmen ignore their own needs even though they were also cold and wet? Sample answer: The surfmen felt that it was their responsibility to rescue the people and take care of the people's needs first and foremost.* **ELA** RI.5.3

3 *Why did both Katie Burkhart and the descendants of the surfmen feel proud when the surfmen were finally recognized as heroes? Sample answer: The descendants must have been proud of their ancestors' courage, and Katie Burkhart must have been proud that her efforts were partly responsible for their recognition.* **ELA** RI.5.2

💬 Classroom Collaboration

Why do first responders such as the surfmen risk their lives to save others? As a class, have students discuss their thoughts on this topic. Encourage them to support their ideas with personal knowledge. **ELA** RI.5.1, SL.5.1d **ELD** ELD.PI.5.1, ELD.PI.5.6a

---

Reclaiming a Legacy

The researchers found Chief Etheridge's own account of what happened. He described the commotion of the hurricane that demolished the ship. "The storm was raging fearfully, the storm tide was sweeping across the beach, and the team was often brought to a standstill by the sweeping current," he wrote in the station log. Lending any help seemed impossible, yet they had to try.

Secured by a rope, two team members swam to the sinking ship. They brought back a crewman. Then a fresh team heard the squalling of the captain's baby and saved him. For six hours, they ignored their own needs. They were too busy to feel annoyance. Missed meals and clammy clothes were not important. As they saved people, they would bundle them into warm blankets at the station.

The research was critical in winning recognition for the team. One hundred years to the day after the rescue of the *E.S. Newman*, the Pea Island crew was awarded a Gold Lifesaving Medal. Katie Burkhart and several descendants of the surfmen listened with pride to the speech that described how "again and again, the Pea Island Station crew went back through the raging sea, literally carrying all nine persons from certain death to the safety of the shore."

Pea Island, 1917

Beach rescue equipment

284

ENGLISH LANGUAGE SUPPORT

Use Visuals

Emerging Clarify that the surfmen rescued the people from the ocean by showing the **online Picture Card** for "ocean." Ask: *Would it be easy or hard to save people from the ocean? hard* **ELD** ELD.PI.5.1

Expanding Show the **online Picture Card** for "ocean." *It would be difficult to rescue someone from the ocean because _____. the waves are rough; the water is deep* **ELD** ELD.PI.5.1

Bridging Show the **online Picture Card** for "ocean." Have students explain why it would be difficult to rescue someone from the ocean. Prompt them to use a complete sentence. *Sample answer: It is hard to swim in rough ocean waves.* **ELD** ELD.PI.5.1

Compare Texts

TEXT TO TEXT

Compare Texts About Heroes Talk with a partner about how heroes are portrayed in "Storm Warriors" and "Pea Island's Forgotten Heroes." After you have discussed your ideas, make a list describing the characteristics of heroes. For each characteristic, quote one detail or example from either text to support your generalizations about heroes.

TEXT TO SELF

Design a Medal The Pea Island crew members were awarded a Gold Lifesaving Medal for their heroism. Design a medal for a modern-day hero whom you admire. Include an image and a message to go on the medal. Write a short speech explaining why the person deserves the medal, and present your information to a partner.

TEXT TO WORLD

Research Hurricanes The Pea Island rescuers had to fight a hurricane in order to rescue the passengers and crew of the *E.S. Newman*. Work with a partner to brainstorm research questions about hurricanes or another kind of natural disaster you would like to learn more about. Then choose one of the questions and conduct research in print and digital sources to answer it.

ELA RI.5.1, RI.5.7, RI.5.9, W.5.7 **ELD** ELD.PI.5.1, ELD.PI.5.2, ELD.PI.5.6a, ELD.PI.5.10a

285

ENGLISH LANGUAGE SUPPORT

Compare Texts

Organize Concepts Help students complete a chart comparing natural disasters. Have students refer to their **Leveled Reader** and **Student Book pp. 266–277** and **282–284.** **ELD** ELD PI.5.1

Pea Island Shipwreck	Great Flood of 1927
hurricane	flood of the Mississippi River
People were stranded on a sinking ship.	People were stranded in homes and on rooftops.
Surfmen brought people to shore; Nathan helped survivors get warm.	Jimmy and Jess used a boat to transport people.

Build Academic Sentence Structures To help students compare and contrast natural disasters, ask questions such as: *What is similar about the Pea Island shipwreck and the Great Flood of 1927?* Provide sentence frames such as these:

• *Both the Pea Island shipwreck and the Great Flood of 1927* <u>were disasters</u>.

• *James and Jess were similar to the surfmen because they all* <u>rescued people in water</u>.

Compare Texts

TEXT TO TEXT

Display and model completing sentence frames such as the following for students to use as a guide for their comparisons.

A hero always _____.

A hero never _____.

Remind students to quote accurately from each text as they explain the portrayals of heroes in the two selections.

ELA RL.5.1, RI.5.1 **ELD** ELD.PI.5.1, ELD.PI.5.6a

TEXT TO SELF

Students may need help brainstorming ideas about modern-day heroes. If possible, guide them to print resources and websites where they can learn more about some heroic people and find ideas for an image and a message for their medal.

Display these sentence frames to help students organize their ideas:

The hero I admire is _____.

He/She deserves the medal because _____.

ELA W.5.7, W.5.10 **ELD** ELD.PI.5.9

TEXT TO WORLD

Discuss the types of print and Internet resources that would most likely contain accurate information. Then remind students to evaluate any website they intend to draw information from to ensure that it is reliable.

ELA RI.5.7, RI.5.9, W.5.7

Vocabulary Strategies

SHARE OBJECTIVES

- Use Greek and Latin roots *photo, tele, scrib,* and *rupt* as clues to word meaning.
- Use word-learning strategies independently.

SKILL TRACE

Greek and Latin Roots	
Introduce	T270–T271
Differentiate	T300–T301
Reteach	T302
Review	T272–T273, Unit 3 T174–T179, Unit 6
Test	Weekly Tests, Lesson 9

ENGLISH LANGUAGE SUPPORT

Preteach

All Proficiencies Explain that the root of a word can give clues to its meaning. Write on the board *geo* and *photo*. Explain that *geo* means "earth" and *photo* means "light." Work with students to determine the meanings of *geology* and *photographer*.

Support Linguistic Transfer

Positive Transfer Explain that many English and Spanish words have the same roots. Point out to students that the root *photo*, meaning "light," is used in the English word *photocopy* and the Spanish word *fotocopia*.

Apply Vocabulary Skills

Emerging Write the root *photo*. Make a word that means "to phone/call from a distance." *telephone*

Expanding Write the word *telephone* on the board. Then say: *The word* telephone *means _____. To call from a distance*

Bridging Have students use the words *televise* and *geography* in sentences. Have partners trade papers and discuss how the meanings of the roots *tele* and *geo* helped them determine them meaning of the words.

ELD ELD.PI.5.1, ELD.PI.5.6b

Greek and Latin Roots

1 Teach/Model

Terms About Language

root the base, or building block, of a word

- Explain that a **root** is the base, or building block, of a word to which a prefix or suffix may be added.

- Tell students that many English words have Greek or Latin roots. Point out that the Greek roots *tele* and *photo* mean "far" and "light," respectively. Tell students that the Latin roots *scrib* and *rupt* mean "write" and "break," respectively.

- Write: *The photograph of the Pea Island surfmen showed seven men in uniform on the beach.*

- Display the **Vocabulary Strategy** on Projectable S8 🔲. Model applying Steps 1 and 2 of the strategy to understand the meaning of the word *photograph.*

  Think Aloud *I see the root* photo *and know that it means "light." The context tells me that seven men are shown on the beach. A* photograph *is a picture made by a camera with light.*

- Ask: *What else can we do to figure out the meaning of a word if looking in and around the word doesn't help? consult a dictionary*

Roots		
Root	**Meaning**	**Examples**
photo	"light"	*photograph, photogenic*
tele	"from a distance"	*telephone, television, telescope*
scrib	"write"	*scribble, describe, prescribe*
rupt	"break"	*interrupt, disrupt*

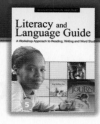

Literacy and Language Guide
See pages 132-133 for further practice with
lesson vocabulary.

2 Guided Practice

- Display the top half of <u>Projectable 9.3</u> and read "Nature's Fury" aloud.

- Display the Column Chart at the bottom of <u>Projectable 9.3</u> .

- Help students identify the words from the word list in the passage. Circle or highlight where these words appear in the passage.

- Guide students to identify the root of each word and write it in the proper column of the chart. Then work with students to use the roots to figure out the meanings of the words.

3 Apply

- Have students list words from a content-area textbook that contain the roots *tele, photo, scrib,* and *rupt.* Then have them use their knowledge of the roots to determine the meanings of the words and how each word's root affects the meaning.

- Have students use a print or digital dictionary to determine or clarify the meanings of any words that are still unfamiliar. **ELA** L.5.4b **ELD** ELD.PI.5.6b

 Interactive Whiteboard Lesson Use **Vocabulary Strategies: Greek and Latin Roots** to reinforce how to use Greek and Latin roots to determine word meaning.

- Distribute to students <u>Reader's Notebook page 99</u> or <u>leveled practice in Grab-and-Go™ Resources</u> to complete independently.

FORMATIVE ASSESSMENT ▲ RtI

Are students able to use the roots photo, tele, scrib, *and* rupt *to determine word meaning?*

IF...	THEN...
students **struggle,**	▶ **Differentiate Vocabulary Strategies** for Struggling Readers, p. T300.
students **on target,**	▶ **Differentiate Vocabulary Strategies** for On-Level Readers, p. T300.
students **excel,**	▶ **Differentiate Vocabulary Strategies** for Advanced Readers, p. T301.

SMALL GROUP Options **Differentiate Vocabulary Strategies:** pp. T300–T301. *Scaffold instruction to the English learner's proficiency level.*

ENGLISH LANGUAGE SUPPORT

Sentence Frames

Emerging Discuss the meanings of the example words in the chart on page T270. Then provide simple sentence frames for students to complete.

Expanding Guide students to use the meaning of the root *rupt* ("break") to determine the meaning of *disrupt.* Then have them write a sentence using the word.

Bridging Have pairs write sentence frames for the words *scribble, describe,* and *prescribe.* Have them exchange sentences with another pair and complete them with the correct word. **ELD** ELD.PI.5.6b

Extend the Topic

▶ **SHARE OBJECTIVES**

- Acquire and use domain-specific vocabulary.
- Engage in a collaborative discussion about literature, drawing on preparation and following agreed-upon rules.
- Pose and respond to discussion questions, and review others' key ideas, drawing conclusions based on knowledge gained from the discussion.

Words About the Topic: Courage

- **bold** not hesitating or fearful in the face of actual or possible danger; courageous and daring
- **competent** having suitable or sufficient skill, knowledge, and experience for some purpose; properly qualified
- **humility** the quality or condition of being humble; modest opinion or estimate of one's own importance or rank
- **purpose** determination; resoluteness
- **unflappable** not easily upset or excited, especially in a crisis; calm

Domain-Specific Vocabulary

Introduce Words About the Topic Remind students that this week's topic is Courage. Display the words shown at left. Tell students that these are words that can help them learn more about courage. Read aloud the definition for each word and then have students respond to the following prompts:

- *If your friend felt that recognition for her helping someone was unnecessary, she was likely showing _____. humility*
- *Which word should describe every doctor who practices medicine? competent*
- *If the fire alarm goes off and you do exactly what you are supposed to do, neither becoming upset nor frightened, you might be described as _____. unflappable*
- *Soldiers might win a medal when they take _____ action in a battle. bold*
- *If you studied for months for a placement test, you would be showing a strong sense of _____. purpose*

ENGLISH LANGUAGE SUPPORT For example, point out the illustration on pages 270–271 and say: *When Mr. Meekins and Mr. Pugh dove into the surf and swam out, they took bold action.*

Interact with the Words Have students work in small groups using Graphic Organizer 6 (Four-Square Map) ⌐ to extend their understanding of each word about courage. Assign one word to each group and have them follow these steps for completing the Four-Square Map with information about the word:

1 In the first corner, draw a picture that represents the word.

2 In the second corner, write the meaning of the word.

3 In the third corner, write a sentence using the word.

4 In the fourth corner, write the word.

When groups have finished, have them share their completed Four-Square Maps with the class. **ELA** L.5.6 **ELD** ELD.PI.5.12a

Speaking and Listening

Hold a Literature Discussion

Review Theme Point out that students should read a selection carefully and take notes to determine theme. Discuss how details about a character's qualities, motives, and actions may help readers identify a selection's theme.

Take Notes Have students revisit "Storm Warriors." Ask them to take notes on important actions, sensory language, and characters' qualities. Explain that they should take notes on all aspects of the story that might help them identify a theme.

ORGANIZE THOUGHTS Suggest that students use a graphic organizer to list details, such as Nathan's character, motives, and actions. Then have them use the details to determine the theme. **ELA** RL.5.2

Relate Theme to Topic Have students write a sentence or two that describes how the theme relates to the lesson topic of Courage. Students may also note personal experiences that illustrate the story's theme and how those experiences match Nathan's experience in displaying courage.

Model Speaking Skills Ask students to listen as you model how to take part in a literary discussion. Say: *I agree with your opinion, but I would take it a step further.*

Participate in Discussion Have small groups participate in a discussion about the story's theme. Assign roles to group members so that everyone is engaged and stays on task. Examples of group discussion roles include note-taker, leader, timekeeper, and presenter. Share the discussion rules shown at right, and have students complete the following steps:

- Come to discussions prepared, explicitly drawing on preparations such as notes and graphic organizers. Support your points with text evidence when possible.

- Follow the rules for a discussion, listening intently and taking turns speaking.

- Pose and respond to questions, make comments that contribute to the discussion, and elaborate on others' remarks to connect ideas.

- Wrap up by reviewing key ideas expressed and by drawing conclusions in light of each other's comments and the text evidence provided as support.
  ELA SL.5.1a, SL.5.1b, SL.5.1c, SL.5.1d **ELD** ELD.PI.5.1

FOR STUDENTS WITH DISABILITIES To help students focus during group discussions, agree on a simple gesture, such as nodding three times or giving a thumbs-up, for students to use when they agree with another student's point during a discussion. Before the discussion, remind students about the gesture. Model the gesture when you agree with something someone adds to a discussion.

DISCUSSION RULES

1. **Listen quietly while others are talking.**

2. **Respect the opinions of others.**

3. **Raise your hand before speaking.**

4. **Actively contribute to the conversation.**

ENGLISH LANGUAGE SUPPORT To check understanding of character, name a character the students know and ask: *What personal qualities make this character different from every other character?*

Fluency

Phrasing: Punctuation

- Read on-level text orally with appropriate fluency.
- Use punctuation to guide phrasing when reading text (prosody).

ENGLISH LANGUAGE SUPPORT

Use Language Models

All Proficiencies Help English learners develop phrasing and expression by modeling these skills while reading aloud from **Student Book p. 268.** You may also wish to mark up passages for students, using slashes to show where natural pauses should occur, such as after periods, commas, clauses, and phrases. **ELD** ELD.PIII.5

Cold Reads: Support for fluent reading with comprehension

FORMATIVE ASSESSMENT   RtI

As student partners read **Student Book p. 275,** circulate and spend time listening to each pair. If students have difficulty reading with expression, provide corrective feedback.

Model using expression as you read aloud the section to students, using appropriate emphasis, volume, and pace, and have them choral- or echo-read with you.

Guide students to read another paragraph on their own, and provide feedback, as necessary. Tell students that their reading fluency will continue to improve as they work hard at improving their expression.

1 Teach/Model

- Tell students that good readers pay attention to punctuation because it helps them break sentences into phrases. Breaking sentences into phrases helps readers and listeners better understand what is being read.

- Review with students the full range of punctuation marks, including quotation marks, dashes, and apostrophes.

- Have students follow along as you read aloud **Student Book p. 270.** First, read the page, ignoring any cues about phrasing that the punctuation would give you. Next, read the page, observing the punctuation.

- Ask students which reading was better and why. If needed, explain that the second reading was better because you used the punctuation to guide your phrasing.

2 Guided Practice

- Together, read aloud the first four paragraphs on **Student Book p. 275,** using punctuation to guide phrasing.

- Work with students to break the text into phrases using the punctuation.

- If students are struggling with using punctuation to guide phrasing, have students echo-read **Student Book p. 275** with you. Tell them to pay special attention to how you use punctuation to guide phrasing and pauses.

- See also <u>Instructional Routine 9</u> ⤴.

3 Apply

- Tell students that with practice, they can learn to recognize the punctuation that signals phrasing.

STANDARD ENGLISH LEARNERS Pronunciation Some students may need help mastering English pronunciations when reading aloud. Students may have trouble voicing /l/ in words such as *people*, *myself*, and *help*. They may omit the /l/ sound and voice the words as *peopuh*, *myse'f*, and *he'p*.

- Have students echo-read from **Student Book p. 275** with you, using the punctuation to guide their phrasing. **ELA** RF.5.4a **ELD** ELD.PIII.5

Decoding

Compound Words

1 Teach/Model

Recognize Compound Words Tell students that a compound word includes two or more words put together to make a new word.

- Students should look for familiar words within a compound word. For example, the compound word *wheelchair* includes the familiar words *wheel* and *chair*.

- Point out that students should divide compound words between the words or word parts that make up the compound.

2 Practice/Apply

Blend Words Display Lines 1–8 below and have students read Lines 1–5 chorally. Provide corrective feedback as needed. Then have them divide each word into separate words by indicating where the syllables break. Have students identify each smaller word and say each aloud.

1. *childlike   forever   goodbye   skateboard*

2. *keyboard   pancake   barefoot   headset*

3. *afternoon   ladybug   fireworks   sweatshirt*

4. *shipwreck   lifesaving   fisherman   sideways*

5. *wheelchair   awestruck   overboard   background*

Challenge Call on students who are ready for a challenge to read Line 6 and discuss the elements. Then have the class read the sentences in Lines 7 and 8 chorally.

6. *motorcycle   stomachache   blueprint   database*

7. *The newscaster was awestruck after the outspoken children talked about the political issue.*

8. *There was an uproar in the dugout among the teammates when the umpire called Luis's hit a foul instead of a home run.* **ELA** RF.5.3a **ELD** ELD.PIII.5

FORMATIVE ASSESSMENT   **RtI**

If students have trouble decoding compound words, use the model below.

Correct the error. Divide the word *surfman* between its parts. *The word is* surfman. *The parts are* surf *and* man.

Model how to decode the word. *I look for the two words in this word. I see* surf *and* man.

Guide students to identify the two words in *surfman*. *What is the first word?* surf *What is the second?* man

Check students' understanding. *What is the word?* surfman

Reinforce Have students repeat the process with the word *lifesaving*.

ENGLISH LANGUAGE SUPPORT

Linguistics Transfer

Use the transfer chart in the **Quick Start Pacing Guide** to determine whether your students will have difficulty due to transfer issues. As needed, preteach the skill. **ELD** ELD.PIII.5

Spelling Compound Words

▶ SHARE OBJECTIVE

• Spell grade-appropriate compound words as one word, a hyphenated word, or separate words.

Spelling Words

Basic

wildlife	light bulb	✪ overboard
uproar	well-known	post office
home run	throughout	outspoken
headache	✪ life preserver	up-to-date
top-secret	barefoot	awestruck
teammate	part-time	newscast
wheelchair	warehouse	

Review

goodbye, all right, forever, twenty-two, somebody

Challenge

motorcycle, overseas, quick-witted, stomachache, bulletin board

✪ Forms of these words appear in "Storm Warriors."

ENGLISH LANGUAGE SUPPORT

Preteach

Spanish Cognates Write and discuss these Spanish cognates for Spanish-speaking students.

light bulb • *bujía*

overboard • *por la borda*

Transfer Support Compound words may be especially difficult for ELLs. When possible, provide visuals such as photos to demonstrate the meaning of the smaller words that comprise the compound word.

ELD ELD.PIII.5

Word Meanings Use Day 5 sentences to preview the meanings of spelling words.

DAY 1

❶ TEACH THE PRINCIPLE

• Administer the **Pretest**. Use the Day 5 sentences.

• Write *outspoken, well-known,* and *light bulb* on the board. Guide students to see the different ways a compound word can be made from two words. Use the chart below.

one word	outspoken
with a hyphen	well-known
separate words	light bulb

❷ GUIDED PRACTICE

Guide students to identify the two or more words that make up each compound word in the remaining Spelling Words.

Model a Word Sort Model sorting words based on the spelling patterns of compound words. Present the Model the Sort lesson on page 72 of the **Literacy and Language Guide**.

❸ APPLY

Distribute Reader's Notebook page 100 ⌇ and have students complete it independently.

DAY 2

❶ TEACH WORD SORT

• Set up three rows as shown. Model adding a Spelling Word to each row.

• Have students copy the chart. Guide students to write each Spelling Word where it belongs.

one word	uproar
with a hyphen	part-time
separate words	post office

❷ GUIDED PRACTICE

• Have students add to the chart words from "Storm Warriors."

Guided Word Sort Guide students to sort words based on the number of syllables in each word. Present the Guess My Category lesson on page 72 of the **Literacy and Language Guide**.

❸ APPLY

Distribute Reader's Notebook page 101 ⌇ and have students complete it independently.

DAY 3

1 TEACH WORD FAMILIES

- **WRITE** *wild*. Define it: *describes animals or plants that are not looked after by people and live in natural surroundings.*
- **WRITE** *wildlife*. Define it: *animals that live in the wild.*
- **WRITE** *wilderness*. Define it: *an area of land which is not cultivated.*
- **ASK** *What is the connection between these words? All contain the base word* wild; *the meanings of all the words connect to living things that are not under the control of human beings.*
- With students, list and discuss more words related to *wild. Samples:* wildcat, wildflower, wildfire

2 GUIDED PRACTICE

- **WRITE** *news*. Define it: *information about events that is reported regularly.*
- **WRITE** *newsroom* and *newscast*. Ask students to look up these words in a dictionary or an electronic resource.
- **ASK** *What is the connection among* news, newsroom, *and* newscast*?*

Have students write their answers.

3 APPLY

Independent Word Sort Have students sort words that they find in their reading. Present the Word Hunt lesson on page 73 of the **Literacy and Language Guide**.

DAY 4

1 CONNECT TO WRITING

- Read and discuss the prompt below.

> **GUIDED PRACTICE**
> Gather information for a research report about acts of courage. Use what you've learned from your reading this week.

2 GUIDED PRACTICE

- Guide students as they plan and write their research reports.
- Remind students to proofread their writing and to consult print and digital references to confirm correct spelling. (See p. T284.) **ELA** L.5.2e

Speed Sort Have students sort words as quickly as they can. Present the Speed Sort lesson on page 73 of the **Literacy and Language Guide**.

3 APPLY

Distribute Reader's Notebook page 102 ↗ and have students complete it independently.

DAY 5

ASSESS SPELLING

- Say each boldfaced word, read the sentence, and then repeat the word.
- Have students write the boldfaced word. **ELA** L.5.2e

Basic

1. We saw **wildlife** such as deer.
2. The fans created an **uproar**.
3. Mark hit a **home run** today.
4. Loud noise gives me a **headache**.
5. The spy has a **top-secret** file.
6. Every **teammate** must play.
7. She used a **wheelchair** after surgery.
8. This **light bulb** is too dim.
9. A **well-known** chef cooked.
10. Clues are **throughout** the book.
11. He threw me a **life preserver**.
12. I walk **barefoot** on the beach.
13. Sheila has a **part-time** job.
14. The **warehouse** stores boxes.
15. Throw the anchor **overboard**.
16. The **post office** sells stamps.
17. When you're **outspoken**, people know what you think.
18. Lea wears **up-to-date** fashions.
19. I am **awestruck** by the comet.
20. We'll watch today's **newscast**.

Grammar Complex Sentences

▶ **SHARE OBJECTIVES**
- Identify and form complex sentences.
- Explain the function of subordinating conjunctions in complex sentences.
- Use correlative conjunctions.

Terms About Language

complex sentence a sentence containing a dependent and an independent clause joined by a subordinating conjunction
subordinating conjunction a conjunction that joins two clauses to form a complex sentence • *conjunction subordinante*
correlative conjunctions a pair of conjunctions that joins parallel words or phrases

ENGLISH LANGUAGE SUPPORT

Preteach: All Proficiencies

Explain Terms About Language Point out the cognate in the list above. Then explain that:

- A coordinating conjunction connects two simple sentence, but a subordinating conjunction connects a simple sentence and an incomplete thought.

Linguistic Transfer Explain to students that many languages contain subordinating conjunctions with meanings similar to those in English. Have students use bilingual dictionaries to find examples.

Scaffolded Practice

Emerging Write on the board the words *because* and *when,* and tell students these words are subordinating conjunctions. Explain that they are used to combine two related short sentences into a single, longer sentence. Use this model to demonstrate. *The rain stopped. The soccer game started.* _____ *the rain stopped, the soccer game started. When*

Expanding Use the same sentence frame to demonstrate how to form complex sentences. Help students identify the dependent and independent clauses. Prompt them with: *Which part of the sentence can stand on its own? Which part cannot?* Then help students form their own complex sentences, using subordinating conjunctions.

Bridging Provide students with pairs of short, related sentences that can be combined into complex sentences. Have partners combine the sentences and label the conjunction and the dependent clause in each.

DAY 1 TEACH

DAILY PROOFREADING PRACTICE

The condition of the sails decks masts showed the ship was deteriorating. *sails, decks, and masts*

❶ TEACH COMPLEX SENTENCES

- Display Projectable 9.4 ⬚. Explain that a **complex sentence** is formed by joining two groups of words, one of which expresses a complete thought. The other group of words adds meaning but does not express a complete thought. It begins with a **subordinating conjunction**, such as *because, although, when,* or *as.*

ENGLISH LANGUAGE SUPPORT Present the following subordinating conjunctions: *because, after, since, if, although, when, as, before.* Have students identify the dependent clause in each sentence below.

- Nathan searched for blankets because the young boy's clothes were soaked. *because the young boy's clothes were soaked*
- When the sailors saw the lifesaving team, they cheered loudly. *When the sailors saw the lifesaving team*
- Model identifying the elements of a complex sentence in the example sentence: *Because a storm had passed through the area, the waves were high.*

Think Aloud *To identify the elements of a complex sentence, I ask these Thinking Questions:* **Which part of the sentence cannot stand on its own? What word does it begin with?** *Because a storm had passed through the area cannot stand on its own; it begins with the subordinating conjunction* because.

❷ PRACTICE/APPLY

- Complete items 1–8 on Projectable 9.4 ⬚ with students.
- Have students create sentences with subordinating conjunctions. Then have them share their examples with the class and explain the function of each conjunction they have used.
  ELA L.5.1a **ELD** ELD.PII.5.6
- Have students complete Reader's Notebook p. 103 ⬚ for practice with simple subjects and predicates.

DAY 2 TEACH

DAILY PROOFREADING PRACTICE

After the ship sails. We will go home. *sails, we*

① EXTEND COMPLEX SENTENCES

- Display <u>Projectable 9.5</u> [↗]. Explain that a **dependent clause** cannot stand on its own as a complete thought and is usually introduced by a subordinating conjunction. An **independent clause** can stand on its own as a complete thought. A complex sentence is made up of an independent clause and one or more dependent clauses joined by a subordinating conjunction.

- Model identifying the dependent and independent clauses in the example sentence: *George went to the store after he heard about the hurricane*.

Think Aloud *To identify the dependent and independent clause, I ask these Thinking Questions: **Which part of the sentence can stand on its own? Which part just gives extra information?** George went to the store expresses a complete thought and can stand on its own. After he heard about the hurricane is extra information.*

② PRACTICE/APPLY

- Complete items 1–8 on <u>Projectable 9.5</u> [↗] with students.

- Have partners write three complex sentences. Then have them identify the independent and dependent clauses in another pair's sentences. **ELD** ELD.PII.5.6

- Have students complete <u>Reader's Notebook p. 104</u> [↗] for practice with simple subjects and predicates.

DAY 3 TEACH

DAILY PROOFREADING PRACTICE

Lita was awstruk she heard the news. *awestruck when*

① TEACH CORRELATIVE CONJUNCTIONS

- Display <u>Projectable 9.6</u> [↗]. Tell students that some conjunctions are always used in pairs. These are called **correlative conjunctions** because they correlate, or bring together, two similar words, phrases, or clauses in a sentence. Correlative conjunctions include *either/or, neither/nor, both/and, whether/or, not only/but also*.

- Model identifying correlative conjunctions in the example sentence: *Neither the crew nor the rescuers knew what to do*.

Think Aloud *To find the correlative conjunctions, I ask this Thinking Question: **What two words work together to connect parallel parts of the sentence?** The words Neither and nor link crew and rescuers. Therefore, they are correlative conjunctions.*

② PRACTICE/APPLY

- Review the rest of the examples on <u>Projectable 9.6</u> [↗] with students. Then work with them to complete items 1–5.

- Have students write three sentences using correlative conjunctions. Have them explain the function of the correlative conjunctions in each sentence. **ELA** L.5.1a, L.5.1e **ELD** ELD.PII.5.6

- Have students complete <u>Reader's Notebook p. 105</u> [↗] for practice with simple subjects and predicates.

DAY 4   REVIEW

DAILY PROOFREADING PRACTICE

Neither Ted or his brother, could jump the high waves. *nor his brother could*

① REVIEW COMPLEX SENTENCES

- Remind students that a **complex sentence** includes an independent clause and one or more dependent clauses. The clauses often are joined by a **subordinating conjunction**. Other conjunctions called correlative conjunctions connect parallel parts of a sentence.

  ENGLISH LANGUAGE SUPPORT Remind students that a subordinating conjunction connects a complete and an incomplete thought. Provide this example: *The sailors took cover when lightning struck the ship.*

② SPIRAL REVIEW

KINDS OF NOUNS Review with students that a **common noun** names any person, place, or thing. A **proper noun** names a particular person, place, or thing and is capitalized. Remind them that a **singular noun** names one person, place, or thing. A **plural noun** names more than one person, place, or thing. Explain that adding *s* or *es* to most nouns will create the plural form.

Guide students to identify the nouns in the sentence, determine their number, and decide whether they are common or proper. Then have them do the same for the second sentence independently. **ELD** ELD.PII.5.4

The surfmen of Pea Island are now receiving the honor they deserve. *common, plural: surfmen; common, singular: honor; proper: Pea Island*

The students will visit the museum in North Carolina. *common, plural: students; common, singular: museum; proper: North Carolina.*

Then have students complete Reader's Notebook p. 106 for more practice with nouns.

DAY 5   CONNECT TO WRITING

DAILY PROOFREADING PRACTICE

We enjoyed the exhibites at the national maritime museum. *exhibits; National Maritime Museum*

① INTERACTIVE WHITEBOARD LESSON

For cumulative review, use **Grammar: Complex Sentences** to reinforce how to identify and form compound and complex sentences.

② CONNECT TO WRITING

- Tell students that short sentences do not always show the relationship between ideas clearly.

- Explain that combining short sentences using subordinating or correlative conjunctions is a way to show the relationships between ideas. Tell students that an important part of revising is to determine which sentences could be linked to more effectively convey meaning.

③ PRACTICE/APPLY

- Display the following sentences. Guide students to use subordinating conjunctions or the correlative conjunctions in parentheses to combine the two ideas. **ELA** L.5.1e, L.5.3a

  The sail ripped. The wind blew so hard. *The sail ripped after the wind blew so hard.*

  The boat tilted. A man fell overboard. (not only/but also) *Not only did the boat tilt, but also a man fell overboard.*

  The mate spotted land. The captain ran to the deck. *Because the mate spotted land, the captain ran to the deck.*

- Have students turn to **Student Book p. 286**. Review subordinating conjunctions, complex sentences, and correlative conjunctions. Have students complete the **Try This!** activity. **ELD** ELD.PII.5.6

- Have students complete Reader's Notebook p. 107 for practice with simple subjects and predicates.

Grammar

Digital Resources
▶ Multimedia
  Grammar Glossary
▶ GrammarSnap
  Video

What Is a Complex Sentence? A **complex sentence** is made up of two clauses joined by a **subordinating conjunction**, such as *because*. The part of the sentence that contains the subordinating conjunction tells about the other part, and cannot stand on its own.

What Is a Correlative Conjunction? **Correlative conjunctions** work in pairs. Some examples are *both / and* and *neither / nor*. Correlative conjunctions can be used to join parallel words or phrases—for example, two nouns, two verbs, or two adjectives.

Complex Sentences and Correlative Conjunctions

can stand on its own — cannot stand on its own
The crew members were in danger because their ship had been wrecked.

cannot stand on its own — can stand on its own
Although the waves were big, two surfmen swam to the ship.

noun — noun
Both courage and knowledge are important in an emergency situation.

 Copy each sentence onto a sheet of paper. Circle the subordinating conjunctions. Underline the correlative conjunctions and the words or phrases they join.

❶ The surfmen could neither dig a hole for the sand anchor nor set up the Lyle gun.

❷ After the men rescued the child, Nathan took care of him.

❸ The child warmed up once he was wrapped in a dry blanket.

❹ Both Nathan and Mrs. Gardiner wanted to help the injured sailor.

286   ELA L.5.1a, L.5.1e   ELD ELD.PII.5.6, ELD.PII.5.7

Good writers establish clear relationships between ideas. Combining shorter sentences to form a complex sentence can show how ideas are linked or which idea is more important. Use a comma after the first part of a complex sentence if that part begins with a subordinating conjunction. Correlative conjunctions can also be used to combine related sentences.

Separate Sentences

The snow was dangerously deep.   The governor declared an emergency.

Subordinating Conjunction

Since the snow was dangerously deep, the governor declared an emergency.

Correlative Conjunctions

Neither the town nor the governor was prepared for the dangerously deep snow.

Connect Grammar to Writing

As you revise your research report next week, look for sentences with related ideas. Try using subordinating or correlative conjunctions to combine these related sentences.

287

Try This!

1. correlative conjunctions: neither, nor; dig a hole for the sand anchor, set up the Lyle gun
2. subordinating conjunction: after
3. subordinating conjunction: once
4. correlative conjunctions: both, and; Nathan, Mrs. Gardiner

Connect Grammar to Writing

- Have students turn to **Student Book p. 287**. Read the top paragraph with students.

- Read the sentences in the chart. Point out that the two shorter sentences at the top are combined into a complex sentence, using a subordinating conjunction, and a sentence with a compound subject is formed, using correlative conjunctions.

- Tell students that as they revise their writing, they should look for short sentences with related ideas that can be combined by using subordinating or correlative conjunctions. **ELD** ELD.PII.5.6

ENGLISH LANGUAGE SUPPORT

Additional Grammar Practice

Teach/Model Explain that a complex sentence is made up of two clauses joined by a subordinating conjunction. Examples of subordinating conjunctions include *since, after, because, when,* and *until*.

- Write and read aloud the following sentences: *Surfmen were heroes. They saved people's lives.* **Ask:** *What subordinating conjunction can we use to connect these sentences? (because)*

- *What complex sentence would this form? (Surfmen were heroes because they saved people's lives.)*

Guided Practice Have students read the sentences below and combine them into complex sentences using the conjunction in parentheses.

- Nathan wanted to be a surfman. He realized he was not brave enough to risk his life. (until).

- The injured soldier began to feel warm. Nathan rubbed linseed oil on the soldier's legs. (when).

Connect to Writing Have students write several complex sentences about one of the reading selections. Remind them to use subordinating conjunctions such as *since* and *because*. **ELA** L.5.1a **ELD** ELD.PII.5.2b

Informative Writing Prewrite a Research Report

▶ **SHARE OBJECTIVES**
- Plan a research report.
- Use print and digital sources to gather information.
- Practice organizational skills related to writing a research report.

Terms About Writing

paraphrase a quotation or an idea restated in your own words

summary the main ideas of a text, retold in your own words

source anything that supplies information

source list the names of all the resources from which information is taken for a report

ENGLISH LANGUAGE SUPPORT

Collaborative Writing

Tell the class that you will work together to plan a research report. Explain that the class will begin by exploring the topic of surfmen.

- Ask: *What are some questions you have to help focus your research?* Help students identify questions about the surfmen that they might like to answer, such as: *How were they trained? How were crews organized? What were some famous rescues?*

- Ask: *What kinds of sources might you use to help you answer your questions?* Remind students that it is important to use a variety of reliable resources. They can select from both print and digital sources.

- Ask: *What is the best way to organize the information we gather? It is useful to collect information on note cards. Then we must create an outline, with main topics and supporting details.*
  ELD ELD.PI.5.1

Go over the Writing Traits Checklist with students. Record students' suggestions for improving the story.

Performance Task

✔ my WriteSmart Have students complete the writing task through *my*WriteSmart. Students will read the prompt within *my*WriteSmart and have access to multiple writing resources, including the Student eBook, Writing Rubrics, and Graphic Organizers.

DAY 1 ANALYZE THE MODEL

❶ INTRODUCE RESEARCH REPORT

- Tell students that they will be preparing to write a research report in this lesson.
- Display Projectable 9.7 ⌐ and read aloud the Writing Model. Use the projectable to illustrate the following features of a research report. Note that the model is an excerpt without a conclusion.

What Is a Research Report?

- It explains a topic in depth.
- It presents logically organized information from a variety of print and digital sources.
- It includes **paraphrases** and **summaries** of facts and details as well as direct quotations.
- It provides a strong conclusion that sums up the significance of the facts presented.
- It includes a list of **sources**.

❷ PRACTICE/APPLY

- With students, label the second important idea, supporting facts, and a direct quotation.
- Point out the **source list,** which includes all the sources from which the writer took information: a website, an online magazine, and a book.

ENGLISH LANGUAGE SUPPORT How English Works As students study the model, point out how the writer established sequential order using transition words within the text such as *early life, then,* and *later*. Discuss with students how this use of transitions could be more challenging to readers than using sentence openers such as *First, Next,* and *Finally*. **ELD** ELD.PII.5.1

LESSON	FORM	FOCUS
6	Procedural Composition	Organization
7	Compare-Contrast Essay	Elaboration
8	Cause-and-Effect Essay	Evidence
9	**Prewrite: Research Report**	**Evidence**
10	Draft, Revise, Edit, Publish: Research Report	Conventions

WRITING

Additional support for Informative Writing appears in the **Common Core Writing Handbook**, Lesson 9.

DAY 2 TEACH

❶ INTRODUCE THE WRITING FOCUS

EVIDENCE Tell students that during research, they will take many notes about their topic, and they will need to organize those notes in a way that will help them present their evidence clearly.

Connect to "Pea Island's Forgotten Heroes"	
Main idea of paragraph	"Etheridge and his surfmen were an elite group." (p. 283)
Supporting details in paragraph	"They were known for their skill and bravery. They were also the only African American group whose job was to save lives." (p. 283)

• Point out that the author of the selection organized her information by main ideas and supporting details. The details she gathered during her research are grouped according to the topic or main idea they support.

🖉 📄 *Annotate it!* Have students highlight other supporting details in the story. Then have students share some examples and talk about how those details support the ideas in the text.

❷ PRACTICE/APPLY

• As a class, return to "Pea Island's Forgotten Heroes." Identify the main idea of each paragraph in the section "Reclaiming a Lost Legacy" (p. 284).

• Write the main ideas on the board and discuss how they relate to the overall topic of the selection.

• Distribute Reader's Notebook page 108 📑 and have students complete it independently.

DAY 3 PREWRITE

❶ TEACH EXPLORING A TOPIC

Display and discuss these steps for prewriting a research paper:

1. **Choose a topic.** Brainstorm ideas and select the one that is most interesting to you.

2. **Write research questions.** Decide what you want to know about your topic. Write each question down.

3. **Find sources.**

• Check the library for books or articles on your topic. Use the Internet to find websites or other online sources.

• Make sure your sources are trustworthy and provide relevant facts and details.

4. **Take notes.**

• Record information that answers your research questions. Rewrite facts and other details in your own words. Copy direct quotations exactly and put them in quotation marks.

• Record the source that each idea or quotation is taken from.

❷ PRACTICE/APPLY

• Explain to students that they will research and write a report on any topic related to this unit that interests them. For example, they might research other endangered species, courageous individuals, or maritime disasters.

• Tell students that reading general information about their topic will help them decide what their focus should be. Suggest that they start with encyclopedia articles or general websites.

• Have students work in groups to begin brainstorming their topics and identifying research questions before they locate sources and take notes. **ELA** W.5.5, W.5.8

ENGLISH LANGUAGE SUPPORT

How English Works: Productive

Using Noun Phrases Before students begin prewriting their research reports, have them plan to add details about people, places, or things by building noun phrases. Provide a model, such as: *High winds and heavy rains slowed us down.* Explain that both *high winds* and *heavy rains* are noun phrases. Point out the nouns and adjectives to students. Help different proficiency levels build word banks so that they can build noun phrases while drafting. **ELD** ELD.PII.5.4

DAY 4 PREWRITE

1 TEACH PLANNING A RESEARCH REPORT

- Review this organizational plan for a research report with students:

> 1. **Introduce** the topic of your research report and explain your particular focus.

> 2. **Organize** your report by developing each main idea in a separate paragraph.

> 3. **Include** facts, examples, and other details from print and digital sources as support for each main idea.

> 4. **Conclude** by stating the importance of the research you have presented.

2 PRACTICE/APPLY

- Display Projectable 9.8 ⬀. Explain that each Roman numeral in the outline shows a main idea. Each capital letter indicates a supporting detail. Have students refer back to the paired selection and Projectable 9.7 ⬀ to fill in missing details.

- Have partners sort their notes into groups and then work independently to outline their reports. **ELA** W.5.5, W.5.8

DAY 5 PREWRITE

1 TEACH PLANNING A RESEARCH REPORT

- Read the top of **Student Book p. 288** together. Then draw students' attention to the notes on the bottom part of the page. Point out the way in which the student writer used her questions to direct her research and how her notes help to answer each question.

- Ask students to identify the sources the writer used. Note the kinds of information she lists about each one.

- Have students explore Digital Lesson: Writing as a Process: Plan and Draft ⬀ to develop their informative writing.

2 PRACTICE/APPLY

- As a class, review the Outline on **Student Book p. 289**. Work with students to answer the *Reading as a Writer* questions.

- Ask students to review their outlines to make sure they have provided enough supporting details to fully develop each aspect of their topic. Have them work in small groups to make adjustments to their outlines. **ELA** W.5.5, W.5.7

- Then have students review the points listed in their outline and confirm that they have a source written in their notes for each one.

- Explain to students that it is always necessary to provide a source for words or ideas they use that are not their own, to avoid taking credit for others' work. **ELA** W.5.8

- **Proofreading** Have students use the Proofreading Checklist Blackline Master ⬀ for proofreading support.

ENGLISH LANGUAGE SUPPORT

Peer-Supported Learning

All Proficiencies See the Peer Conference Forms in the ELL Teacher's Handbook.

Reading-Writing Workshop: Prewrite

Informative Writing

Interactive Lessons
▶ Writing as a Process: Plan and Draft
▶ Writing Informative Texts: Organize Your Information

my WriteSmart

☑ **Evidence** To plan a **research report**, find reliable print and digital sources to answer your questions about your topic. Record facts and their sources on notecards. Then organize your notes into an outline, with details to support each main idea. Each main topic in your outline will become a paragraph in your report. Josie researched the sinking of the *Andrea Doria*. For her outline, she grouped her notes into four main topics.

Writing Process Checklist

▶ **Prewrite**
☑ Did I ask questions to focus my research?
☑ Did I choose a topic that will interest my audience and me?
☑ Did I gather facts from a variety of good sources?
☑ Did I organize facts into an outline with main topics and subtopics?

Draft
Revise
Edit
Publish and Share

Exploring a Topic

What happened to the Andrea Doria?
— captain did not slow ship's speed in the fog
— Stockholm's bow cut into the hull.
Ballard, Robert, and Rick Archbold. *Ghost Liners: Exploring the World's Greatest Lost Ships.* Boston, MA: Little, Brown and Company, 1998.

How were the passengers rescued?
— Stockholm rescued hundreds of passengers and crew from the Andrea Doria
— lifeboats were used *The Andrea Doria The Greatest Rescue of All Time.* 11 June 1998. ThinkQuest. 4 Feb. 2012. <http://library.thinkquest.org>

Outline

I. The accident
   A. July 25, 1956, off the coast of Massachusetts
   B. The *Andrea Doria* and the *Stockholm* hit each other.
II. Details of the crash
   A. Foggy night
   B. Both ships using radar to navigate
   C. The *Stockholm*'s bow hit the *Andrea Doria*'s side.
III. Help arrives
   A. Several ships came to the rescue.
   B. The *Ile de France* rescued passengers.
   C. The *Stockholm* was damaged but not sinking. It helped in the rescue.
IV. A historic rescue
   A. The *Andrea Doria* took 11 hours to sink.
   B. All but 46 people were rescued.

Reading as a Writer

Is Josie's outline well organized? Why do you think so? What parts of your outline can you organize better or make more complete?

In my outline, I organized facts into main topics and subtopics. I listed subtopics in logical order to support my main ideas.

WRITING TRAITS SCORING RUBRIC

SCORE	4	3	2	1	NS
Purpose/ Organization	The narrative is clear, focused, and well organized throughout. • Contains an effective and complete plot • Develops strong setting, narrator/ characters • Includes a variety of transitions to connect ideas • Contains a logical sequence of events • Includes an effective introduction and conclusion	The narrative's organization is adequately maintained, and the focus is generally clear. • Plot is mostly effective/may contain small flaws • Develops setting, narrator/ characters • Adequate use of transitions to connect ideas • Contains an adequate sequence of events	The narrative is somewhat organized and may be unclear in some parts. • Plot may be inconsistent • Minimal development of setting, narrator/characters • Contains inconsistent use of transitions to connect ideas • Sequence of events is weak or unclear • Introduction and conclusion need improvement	The narrative may be somewhat organized but unfocused. • Little or no plot • Little or no development of setting, narrator/characters • Contains few or inappropriate transitions and weak connections among ideas • Sequence of events is not organized • Introduction and/or conclusion may be missing	• Not intelligible • Not written in English • Not on topic • Contains text copied from another source • Does not address the purpose for writing
Development/ Elaboration	The narrative includes effective elaboration using details, dialogue, and description. • Characters, setting, experiences, and events are well developed • Writer uses a variety of narrative techniques that strengthen the story or illustrate the experience • Contains effective sensory, concrete, and figurative language • Style is appropriate and effective	The narrative includes adequate elaboration using details, dialogue, and description. • Characters, setting, experiences, and events are adequately developed • Writer uses a variety of narrative techniques that generally move the story forward and illustrate the experience • Contains adequate sensory, concrete, and figurative language • Style is mostly appropriate	The narrative includes partial or ineffective elaboration using unclear or inconsistent details, dialogue, and description. • Characters, setting, experiences, and events lack consistent development • Writer uses inconsistent or weak narrative techniques • Contains weak sensory, concrete, and figurative language • Style is inconsistent or inappropriate	The narrative provides little or no elaboration using few or no details, dialogue, and description. • Very little development of characters, setting, experiences, and events • Writer's use of narrative techniques are minimal and may be incorrect • Little or no sensory, concrete, and figurative language • Little or no evidence of style	• Not intelligible • Not written in English • Not on topic • Contains text copied from another source • Does not address the purpose for writing

SCORE	2	1	0	NS
Conventions	The narrative demonstrates adequate command of conventions. • Consistent use of correct sentence structures, punctuation, capitalization, grammar, and spelling	The narrative demonstrates partial command of conventions. • Limited use of correct sentence structures, punctuation, capitalization, grammar, and spelling	The narrative demonstrates little or no command of conventions. • Rare use of correct sentence structures, punctuation, capitalization, grammar, and spelling	• Not intelligible • Not written in English • Not on topic • Contains text copied from another source

See also ***Writing Rubric Blackline Master*** and Teacher's Edition pp. R18–R21.

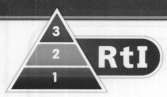

Formative Assessment

RtI

Weekly Tests

At the end of the lesson, administer the Weekly Test. This will give you a **snapshot of how students are progressing** with the Reading and Language Arts skills in this lesson and can give you **guidance on grouping, reteaching, and intervention**.

Suggestions for adjusting instruction based on these results can be found on the next page.

Access Through Accommodations

When you administer the Weekly Test, some students may have problems accessing all or parts of the assessment. The purpose of the Weekly Test is to determine students' ability to complete the Reading and Language Arts tasks they learned in this lesson. Any barriers to them accessing the tasks demanded of them should be lowered so they can focus on skill demonstration.

When choosing accommodations, you will want to avoid invalidating the test results; if you are measuring a student's reading skill, for example, you will not want to read aloud the passage. The following accommodations, if needed, will not interfere with the Weekly Test's validity:

- Read aloud the assessment directions and item prompts. If students are English learners, read aloud the assessment directions and item prompts in the student's native language, if possible.

- Define any unknown words in the directions or item prompts that do not give away the answers to the items.

- Allow for a break during the assessment.

- Simplify the language of assessment directions and item prompts.

- Administer the assessment in a smaller group setting.

- Administer the assessment on a computer or other electronic device.

- Provide audio amplification equipment, colored overlays, or visual magnifying equipment to maintain visual/audio attention and access.

- Allow students to complete the assessment items orally or by having another person transcribe their responses.

Using Data to Adjust Instruction

Use students' scores on the Weekly Test to determine Small Group placement, reteaching, and potential for Intervention.

☑ VOCABULARY AND COMPREHENSION

Conclusions and Generalizations; Point of View; Characterization; Anchor Text Target Vocabulary; Greek and Latin Roots

IF STUDENT SCORES...	
...at acceptable, THEN continue core instruction.	**...below acceptable,** THEN use Reteach Comprehension Skill and Vocabulary Strategies lessons. For struggling students, administer the *Intervention Assessments* to determine if students would benefit from intervention.

☑ LANGUAGE ARTS

Complex Sentences

IF STUDENT SCORES...	
...at acceptable, THEN continue core instruction.	**...below acceptable,** THEN use Reteach Language Arts lesson. For struggling students, administer the *Intervention Assessments* to determine if students would benefit from intervention.

☑ DECODING

Compound Words

IF STUDENT SCORES...	
...at acceptable, THEN continue core instruction.	**...below acceptable,** THEN use Reteach Decoding lesson. For struggling students, administer the *Intervention Assessments* to determine if students would benefit from intervention.

☑ FLUENCY

Fluency Plan

Assess one group per week using the <u>Fluency Tests</u> in the *Grab-and-Go*™ Resources. Use the suggested plan at the right.

● Struggling Readers	Weeks 1, 3, 5
▲ On Level	Week 2
■ Advanced	Week 4

IF...	
...students are reading on-level text fluently, THEN continue core instruction.	**...students are reading below level,** THEN provide additional fluency practice using the **Student Book**, the **Cold Reads**, and the Leveled Readers. For struggling students, administer the *Intervention Assessments* to determine if students would benefit from intervention.

HOUGHTON MIFFLIN HARCOURT

JOURNEYS

Cold Reads

5

The ***Cold Reads*** passages increase gradually in Lexile® measures throughout the year, from below grade-level to above grade-level.

- Each passage is accompanied by several selected-response questions and one constructed-response prompt, requiring students to read closely, answer questions at substantial DOK levels, and cite text evidence.

- The *Cold Reads* may be used to provide practice in reading increasingly complex texts and to informally monitor students' progress.

- The *Cold Reads* may be used to estimate students' Lexile® levels in order to recommend appropriately challenging books for small-group instruction or independent reading.

Turn the page for more information about using FORMATIVE ASSESSMENT for **ELD AND INTERVENTION**.

Formative Assessment for ELD and Intervention

Formative Assessment for English Learners

English learners should engage in the same rigorous curriculum and formative assessment as other students. However, it is important to remember that English learners face a dual challenge: they are strengthening their abilities *to use* English at the same time that they are learning challenging content *through* English. Use the following strategies and resources for ongoing assessment of English language development, in addition to the assessments you use with all students:

- A combination of **observational measures,** such as listening in as students read aloud or participate in collaborative conversations. Be prepared to provide **"just-in-time" scaffolding** to support students. For example, if students are retelling a story, you could help them use sentence structures with past-tense verbs and time-order transition words.

- **Constructive feedback** that focuses on communication and meaning-making. Avoid overcorrecting in a way that makes English learners reluctant to speak up. You might try recasting a child's statement more correctly, making a note to address the target form more directly during Designated ELD time.

- **Student self-assessment**, through students' own notes in their vocabulary notebooks or other learning journals. If possible, meet with each child to review his or her self-assessments and provide encouragement and feedback.

- **Formative assessment** notes that are integrated into the Language Workshop Teacher's Guide for use during Designated ELD.

- **Language Workshop Assessment Handbook** for longer-cycle assessment to make sure students are progressing in their English development.

Response to Intervention

Use the Weekly Tests and Benchmark and Unit Tests, along with your own observations, to determine if individual students are not responding to Tier I instruction and need additional testing to identify specific needs for targeted intervention.

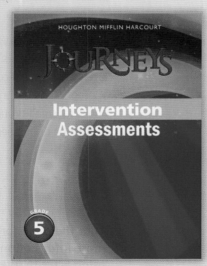

Intervention Assessments

Assessment for Intervention

Progress-Monitoring Assessments Administer this assessment to

- students in Tier II and Tier III Intervention to gauge progress towards exit from the intervention program.

- students who demonstrate lack of success with Weekly Tests, Benchmark and Unit Tests, and core instruction to determine if they might benefit from additional practice or intervention.

Weekly
Small Group Instruction

Vocabulary Reader
- *Saved from the Sea*, T292–T293

Differentiate Comprehension
- Target Skill: Conclusions and Generalizations, T294–T295
- Target Strategy: Infer/Predict, T294–T295

Leveled Readers
- ● *Sugaring Weather*, T296
- ▲ *The River Kept Rising*, T297
- ■ *Night of the Killer Waves*, T298
- ◆ *The Rising River*, T299

Differentiate Vocabulary Strategies
- Greek and Latin Roots, T300–T301

Options for Reteaching
- Vocabulary Strategies: Greek and Latin Roots, T302
- Comprehension Skill: Conclusions and Generalizations, T302
- Language Arts: Complex Sentences/Informative Writing, T303
- Decoding: Compound Words, T303

Literacy Centers
Independent Practice
- Comprehension and Fluency, T236
- Word Study, T236
- Think and Write, T237

RtI Small Group Planner
Differentiated Instruction

		DAY 1	DAY 2	DAY 3
Teacher-Led	**Struggling Readers**	**Vocabulary Reader** *Saved from the Sea*, Differentiated Instruction, p. T292 **English Language Support**, p. T293	**Differentiate Comprehension** Conclusions and Generalizations; Infer/Predict, p. T294 **English Language Support**, p. T295	**Leveled Reader** *Sugaring Weather*, p. T296 **English Language Support**, Leveled Reader Teacher's Guide, p. 5
	On Level	**Vocabulary Reader** *Saved from the Sea*, Differentiated Instruction, p. T292 **English Language Support**, p. T293	**Differentiate Comprehension** Conclusions and Generalizations; Infer/Predict, p. T294 **English Language Support**, p. T295	**Leveled Reader** *The River Kept Rising*, p. T297 *The Rising River*, p. T299 **English Language Support**, Leveled Reader Teacher's Guide, p. 5
	Advanced	**Vocabulary Reader** *Saved from the Sea*, Differentiated Instruction, p. T293 **English Language Support**, p. T293	**Differentiate Comprehension** Conclusions and Generalizations; Infer/Predict, p. T295 **English Language Support**, p. T295	**Leveled Reader** *Night of the Killer Waves*, p. T298 **English Language Support**, Leveled Reader Teacher's Guide, p. 5
What are my other students doing?	**Struggling Readers**	**Reread** *Saved from the Sea*	**Vocabulary in Context Cards** 81–90 *Talk It Over* Activities	**Listen** to Audio of "Storm Warriors"; retell and discuss
	On Level	**Reread** *Saved from the Sea*	**Reread** "Storm Warriors" with a partner	**Reread** for Fluency: *The River Kept Rising* or *The Rising River* **Complete** Leveled Practice EL9.1
	Advanced	**Vocabulary in Context Cards** 81–90 *Talk It Over* Activities	**Reread and Retell** "Storm Warriors"	**Reread** for Fluency: *Night of the Killer Waves*

For Strategic Intervention for this lesson, see pp. S32–S41.

DAY 4	DAY 5	English Language Support

DAY 4

Differentiate Vocabulary Strategies
Greek and Latin Roots, p. T300
English Language Support, p. T301

Differentiate Vocabulary Strategies
Greek and Latin Roots, p. T300
English Language Support, p. T301

Differentiate Vocabulary Strategies
Greek and Latin Roots, p. T301
English Language Support, p. T301

- **Partners: Reread**
  Sugaring Weather
- **Complete** Leveled Practice SR9.1

- **Vocabulary in Context Cards**
  81–90 *Talk It Over* Activities
- **Complete** Reader's Notebook, p. 99

- **Reread** for Fluency: "Storm Warriors"
- **Complete** Leveled Practice A9.1

DAY 5

Options for Reteaching,
pp. T302–T303

Options for Reteaching,
pp. T302–T303

Options for Reteaching,
pp. T302–T303

- **Reread** for Fluency: "Storm Warriors"
- **Complete** Literacy Centers
- **Independent Reading**

- **Complete** Literacy Centers
- **Independent Reading**

- **Complete** Literacy Centers
- **Independent Reading**

English Language Support

Use the Leveled Reader Teacher's Guide to support ELs during differentiated instruction.

- **Characteristics of the Text** (p. 1)
  Identify challenging language features, such as text structure, literary features, complex sentences, and vocabulary.

- **Cultural Support/Cognates/Vocabulary** (p. 5)
  Explain unfamiliar features of English and help ELs transfer first-language knowledge.

- **Oral Language Development** (p. 5)
  Check comprehension using dialogues that match students' proficiency levels.

Book Share
Use this routine at the end of the week to enable students to demonstrate that they have become experts on their Leveled Readers.

Step 1:
Have each student write a presentation based on his or her Leveled Reader **Responding** page, using the following guidelines:

- Briefly tell what your book is about.

- Show your Inference Map and explain what you added to complete it.

- Tell about your favorite part of the book, what you found most interesting in it, or what you learned from it.

Students should prepare to share their presentations with a group.

Step 2:
Have students form groups in which each student has read a different Leveled Reader.

Step 3:
Have students take turns sharing their book presentations in their groups. Continue until all students have finished sharing. Encourage students to ask questions of the presenters. Provide frames such as the following for support.

Can you tell me more about _____?

I wonder why _____.

What do you think about _____?

Vocabulary Reader
Saved from the Sea

Summary

Students learn about the dangers ships faced at sea during the nineteenth century. Descriptions of the U.S. Life-Saving Service's formation and the heroism of its workers are provided, along with details of the service's eventual merger with the Coast Guard.

☑ **TARGET VOCABULARY**

critical	annoyance
demolished	secured
elite	squalling
commotion	clammy
bundle	realization

STRUGGLING READERS

ELA RI.5.2, L.5.4a
ELD ELD.PI.5.1, ELD.PI.5.6b

- Explain that the U.S. Life-Saving Service was formed as a result of a number of deadly shipwrecks. Have students predict what kinds of things this service might do to save lives.

- Guide students to preview the Vocabulary Reader. Read aloud the headings. Ask students to describe the images, using Target Vocabulary when possible.

- Have students alternate reading pages of the text aloud. Guide them to use context to determine the meanings of unfamiliar words. As necessary, use the **Vocabulary in Context Cards** to review the meanings of vocabulary words.

- Assign the **Responding Page** and Blackline Master 9.4 ⤴. Have partners work together to complete the pages.

ON LEVEL

ELA RI.5.2, L.5.4a
ELD ELD.PI.5.1, ELD.PI.5.6b

- Explain to students that early systems to keep the ocean safe were not very effective. As a result, the government provided money, equipment, and training to make travel by ship less dangerous. Guide students to preview the Vocabulary Reader.

- Remind students that context clues can help them determine the meaning of an unknown word. Tell students to use context clues to confirm their understanding of Target Vocabulary and to learn the meanings of new words.

- Have partners alternate reading aloud pages of the text. Tell them to use context clues to determine the meanings of unknown words.

- Assign the **Responding Page** and Blackline Master 9.4 ⤴. Have students discuss their responses with a partner.

ADVANCED

ELA RI.5.2, L.5.4a
ELD ELD.PI.5.1, ELD.PI.5.6b

- Have students preview the Vocabulary Reader and make predictions about what they will read, using information from their preview and prior knowledge.

- Remind students to use context clues to help them determine the meanings of unknown words.

- Tell students to read the text with a partner. Ask them to stop and discuss the meanings of unknown words as necessary.

- Assign the **Responding Page** and Blackline Master 9.4 [⤴]. For the Write About It activity, remind students to use facts and details to support their ideas.

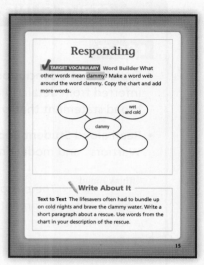

Saved from the Sea, p. 15

ENGLISH LANGUAGE SUPPORT

ELD ELD.PI.5.1, ELD.PI.5.6b

Provide Struggling Readers, On Level, and Advanced ELs proficiency-level support during differentiated instruction.

Emerging

Conduct a picture walk with students. Then read the Vocabulary Reader aloud with them, pausing to explain the Target Vocabulary words as necessary.

Expanding

Use visuals, simplified language, and gestures to preteach the following selection vocabulary: *clammy, squalling, commotion,* and *demolished.* Have partners use the words in oral sentences.

Bridging

Preview pp. 3–5 with students. Check their understanding of the terms *demolished, critical,* and *realization.* Have them complete these sentence frames: *I had the _____ that the situation was _____. The ship might be _____ in the storm!*

Differentiate Comprehension
Conclusions and Generalizations; Infer/Predict

STRUGGLING READERS

ELA RL.5.1, RF.5.4a, SL.5.1a
ELD ELD.PI.5.1, ELD.PI.5.6b

I DO IT

- Explain that a conclusion is a judgment that can be inferred from details in a text. A generalization is a broad statement that is true most of the time.

- Read aloud **Student Book p. 268** of "Storm Warriors" and model drawing a conclusion.

  Think Aloud *The passage says the seas were rough and the equipment useless. I can conclude that conditions were not good for surfmen to make a rescue.*

WE DO IT

- Read aloud pp. 274–275.

- Help students draw a conclusion about how Mr. Bowser regards Nathan. *Mr. Bowser trusts Nathan.*

- Ask students to give text details that support the conclusion, and write them on the board. *Mr. Bowser says Nathan studied well; he has Nathan take over, saying, "I'm sure you know what to do."*

YOU DO IT

- Distribute Graphic Organizer 10 (Story Map) ↪. Have students complete an Inference Map for p. 277. Ask them to record details that support a conclusion about how the tall man in the captain's coat feels.

- Have students discuss other conclusions and generalizations about the job of the surfmen, based on details in the text.

ON LEVEL

ELA RL.5.1, RF.5.4a, SL.5.1a
ELD ELD.PI.5.1, ELD.PI.5.6b

I DO IT

- Explain that good readers use details from the text to draw conclusions and make generalizations as they read.

- Read aloud pp. 268–269 of "Storm Warriors."

- Model how to draw a conclusion.

  Think Aloud *I can conclude that Nathan has some mixed feelings about being a surfman. It is his dream to become a surfman, but the idea of doing what the other surfmen do is "unthinkable" to him.*

WE DO IT

- Have students read pp. 274–275.

- Guide a volunteer to draw a conclusion about how Nathan feels as he's treating Arthur. *He's nervous.*

- Work together to find the text details that support the conclusion. Discuss whether the details offer the necessary support. *Nathan cries out; his hands are clammy and shaky.*

YOU DO IT

- Distribute Graphic Organizer 10 (Story Map) ↪. Have students complete an Inference Map for "Storm Warriors" using text details to draw a conclusion about the job of the surfmen.

- Have students take turns reading only the details on their maps to a partner. Partners should draw their own conclusions based on the details given. Have partners discuss the reasons for their conclusions.

ADVANCED

ELA RL.5.1, RF.5.4a, SL.5.1a
ELD ELD.PI.5.1, ELD.PI.5.6b

I DO IT

- Read aloud pp. 268–269 of "Storm Warriors."

- Explain that a generalization is a broad statement that is true most of the time, but not always. A reader bases a generalization on text details.

- Explain that an example of a generalization readers might make is that most young, inexperienced people often get nervous or scared when faced with a new challenge.

WE DO IT

- Have students read p. 277 independently.

- Ask students what conclusion they could draw about how the captain was feeling. *emotional and thankful* Ask what details support the conclusion. *When the captain saw that everyone was saved, his voice shook. He said the crew saved all of their lives.*

- Guide students to make a generalization based on these details. *Most rescued people are grateful to their rescuers.*

YOU DO IT

- Distribute Graphic Organizer 10 (Story Map) ⬆. Ask students to fill in an Inference Map with a conclusion about the surfmen and the necessary supporting details from "Storm Warriors."

- Then have them write a generalization based on the information from their maps.

- Finally, have them share their completed maps and discuss generalizations about the job of the surfmen with the group.

- Invite students to use their completed Inference Maps to analyze/evaluate the selection.

ENGLISH LANGUAGE SUPPORT

ELA RF.5.4a, RF.5.4c, L.5.4a, L.5.6
ELD ELD.PI.5.1, ELD.PI.5.6b

Provide Struggling Readers, On Level, and Advanced ELs proficiency-level support during differentiated instruction.

Emerging

Model for students how to use story details to draw conclusions. Choral-read **Student Book p. 269** with students. Ask yes/no questions to help them infer that Mr. Meekins is brave. Then work with them to identify specific words and phrases that tell the reader he is brave.

Expanding

Display the following sentence frame: *I can conclude that _____ because _____.* Guide students to complete the frame as a way to review examples of conclusions. Check students' understanding of why and how readers draw conclusions. If appropriate, ask them to read p. 269 and explain how they can conclude that Nathan is nervous about this rescue.

Bridging

Brainstorm with students general academic words and modal expressions they can use to express generalizations and conclusions. Alternately, prompt them with sentence starters such as *In my opinion …* or *I conclude from the details on p. x that ….* or *In general,* Have students complete the sentences with details from the text.

Leveled Readers

ELA RL.5.1, RF.5.4a, W.5.4, SL.5.1a
ELD ELD.PI.5.1, ELD.PI.5.5, ELD.PI.5.6a

☑ **TARGET SKILL**
Conclusions and Generalizations

☑ **TARGET STRATEGY**
Infer/Predict

☑ **TARGET VOCABULARY**

critical	clammy
secured	squalling
realization	commotion
annoyance	demolished
bundle	elite

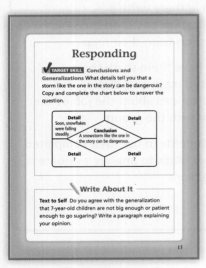

Sugaring Weather, p. 15

STRUGGLING READERS

 Sugaring Weather

GENRE: HISTORICAL FICTION

Summary Samuel and Pa head out to fill their barrel with sap from the sugar maples. Just as Ma warned them, a dangerous snowstorm comes along. Samuel remembers a cave he discovered in the summer where they can take cover until the snowstorm blows over.

Introducing the Text

- Discuss key vocabulary from the story. Explain that to gather maple sap, a farmer cuts holes in the tree trunks of sugar maples and then puts spiles, or wooden spouts, into the holes. After several days, buckets hanging from the spiles fill with sap.

- Remind students that using a graphic organizer can help them to see the details that support their conclusions about a story.

Supporting the Reading

- As you listen to students read, pause to discuss these questions.

  p. 3 *What can you conclude about Sam's relationship with his sister Phoebe? Why? They like to tease each other, but they're friendly; Sam kindly pats Phoebe on the head.*

  p. 8 *Why do Pa and Samuel decide to find shelter? They need to find shelter to stay safe from the storm. If they don't, they might freeze or get lost in the snow.*

Discussing and Revisiting the Text

CRITICAL THINKING After discussing *Sugaring Weather* together, have students read the instructions on **Responding** p. 15. Use these points to revisit the text.

- Have students read aloud the text shown in the graphic organizer.

- Have students work individually or in pairs to enter a conclusion and supporting details on Blackline Master 9.5 🔗. Discuss the conclusions with the class.

FLUENCY: PHRASING: PUNCTUATION Model using punctuation as a guide to correct phrasing. Then have partners echo-read p. 8 and focus on using punctuation to read with proper phrasing.

ELA RL.5.1, RF.5.4a, W.5.4, SL.5.1a
ELD ELD.PI.5.1, ELD.PI.5.5, ELD.PI.5.6a

ON LEVEL

 ## *The River Kept Rising*

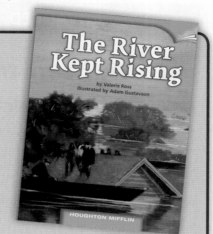

GENRE: HISTORICAL FICTION

Summary When the levees burst near Greenville, Mississippi, during the Great Flood of 1927, Jess and Jimmy Travers set out in their boat to search for people who need help.

Introducing the Text

• Discuss key vocabulary from the story. Explain that the Great Flood of 1927 was the most destructive river flood in U.S. history.

• Remind students that sometimes an author supplies details to explain ideas that may not be stated directly in the story.

Supporting the Reading

• As you listen to students read, pause to discuss these questions.

p. 6 *How difficult will it be to restore the town to its regular condition after the flood waters fall off? Why? It will take a long time; much of the town is destroyed, and you can only see the roofs of some houses.*

p. 14 *What do you think Jimmy and Jess will find when they go out on the boat? injured people who need to be rescued.*

Discussing and Revisiting the Text

CRITICAL THINKING After discussing *The River Kept Rising* together, have students read the instructions on **Responding** p. 19. Use these points to revisit the text.

• Have students review the text in pairs or small groups.

• Have students work individually or in pairs to enter a conclusion and supporting details on Blackline Master 9.6. Discuss selected conclusions and supporting text evidence with the class.

FLUENCY: PHRASING: PUNCTUATION Have partners read aloud their favorite parts of *The River Kept Rising,* using punctuation to guide their phrasing.

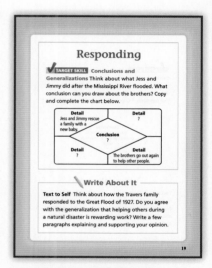

The River Kept Rising, p. 19

TARGET SKILL
Conclusions and Generalizations

TARGET STRATEGY
Infer/Predict

TARGET VOCABULARY

critical	clammy
secured	squalling
realization	commotion
annoyance	demolished
bundle	elite

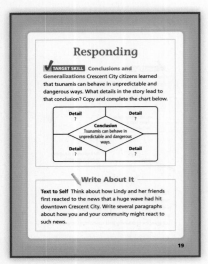

Night of the Killer Waves,
p. 19

Leveled Readers

ELA RL.5.1, RF.5.4a, W.5.4, SL.5.1a
ELD ELD.PI.5.1, ELD.PI.5.5, ELD.PI.5.6a

ADVANCED

 ## *Night of the Killer Waves*

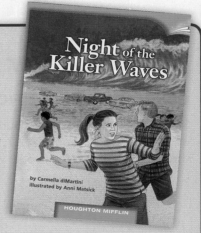

GENRE: HISTORICAL FICTION

Summary Lindy Morris and her friends were at a drive-in movie when they learned about the huge wave that had just flooded Crescent City, California. Little did they know, this was the first of four tsunami waves that would hit their town as the result of an earthquake off the coast of Alaska.

Introducing the Text

• Discuss key vocabulary from the story. Explain that the people of Crescent City knew about the first wave hours before it hit. They did not realize that more waves would come, the fourth being the deadliest.

• Remind students that sometimes an author supplies details to support a conclusion that may not be stated directly in a story.

Supporting the Reading

• As you listen to students read, pause to discuss these questions.

p. 4 *Why do you think Pete is hesitant to go downtown toward the flood? He doesn't want to damage his car.*

pp. 13–14 *When the sea was pulling back, what was about to happen? A bigger wave was coming. It caused a lot of destruction and then retreated, taking cars, buildings, and boats out to sea.*

Discussing and Revisiting the Text

CRITICAL THINKING After discussing *Night of the Killer Waves* together, have students read the instructions on **Responding** p. 19. Use these points to revisit the text.

• Have students work individually or in pairs to review the text.

• Have students work individually or in pairs to enter a conclusion and supporting details on Blackline Master 9.7 . Discuss selected conclusions and supporting text evidence with the class.

FLUENCY: PHRASING: PUNCTUATION Have small groups read aloud a page from *Night of the Killer Waves,* focusing on punctuation for phrasing.

ELA RL.5.1, RF.5.4a, W.5.4, SL.5.1a
ELD ELD.PI.5.1, ELD.PI.5.5, ELD.PI.5.6a

ENGLISH LANGUAGE SUPPORT

 ## *The Rising River*

GENRE: HISTORICAL FICTION

Summary The Great Flood of 1927 killed hundreds of people and destroyed thousands of homes. In this story, two boys from Greenville, Mississippi, help rescue people in their town.

Introducing the Text

- Discuss key vocabulary from the story. Then explain that floods can cause a lot of damage to people and their communities.

- Remind students that using a graphic organizer can help them organize their thoughts in order to draw conclusions.

Supporting the Reading

- As you listen to students read, pause to discuss these questions.

  p. 9 *What would you conclude about Jess and Jimmy's actions? Why? They were brave and heroic; they steered through dangerous waters to help people.*

  p. 17 *Why do you think Jess doesn't want to spend too much time looking for Moose? He's worried about Charley's grandma and doesn't want her to get sick while they look for Moose.*

Discussing and Revisiting the Text

CRITICAL THINKING After discussing *The Rising River* together, have students read the instructions on **Responding** p. 19. Use these points to revisit the text.

- Have students read aloud the text shown in the graphic organizer.

- Have students work in pairs to enter a conclusion and supporting details on Blackline Master 9.8. Discuss selected conclusions and supporting text evidence with the class.

FLUENCY: PHRASING: PUNCTUATION Remind students that punctuation helps them know when to pause while reading. Then have partners read a favorite part of *The Rising River*.

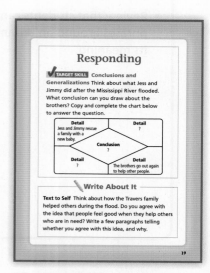

The Rising River, p. 19

Differentiate Vocabulary Strategies
Greek and Latin Roots

STRUGGLING READERS

ELA L.5.4a, L.5.4b, L.5.4c
ELD ELD.PI.5.1, ELD.PI.5.6b

I DO IT

- Write the word *telemarketer* on the board.

- Remind students that they learned several Greek and Latin roots in this lesson. Discuss how they can use the meanings of those roots to figure out the meanings of unknown words.

- Review that students can also use the words and phrases around an unfamiliar word to figure out its meaning.

WE DO IT

- Guide students to recall the meaning of the Greek root *tele*. *from a distance* Have a volunteer explain what a *marketer* is. *person who sells something*

- Help students combine the meanings of the word parts to find the meaning of *telemarketer*. *person who sells from a distance*

tele	marketer
from a distance	person who sells

YOU DO IT

- Have partners work together to come up with other words that have the root *tele*.

- Have students write definitions for the words based on the definitions of the word parts. Have them look up the words in a print or digital dictionary to confirm their definitions.

- Have students repeat the exercise for *photo*, *scrib*, and *rupt*.

ON LEVEL

ELA L.5.4a, L.5.4b, L.5.4c
ELD ELD.PI.5.1, ELD.PI.5.6b

I DO IT

- Review with students the meanings of the Greek and Latin roots *tele*, *photo*, *scrib*, and *rupt*.

- Tell students that knowing the meanings of roots will unlock the meanings of many unfamiliar words.

- Write the word *telescope* on the board. Model determining the meaning of the word.

  Think Aloud *I see the word* scope. *That is something you look through to see objects clearly. The root* tele *means "from a distance." So a* telescope *must let you see things from a distance.*

WE DO IT

- Write the word *photojournalist* on the board. Ask a volunteer to tell the meaning of the root *photo*. *relating to light* Point out that *photo* also appears in the word *photograph,* which means "an image made by capturing light."

- Ask students what a *journalist* is. *a person who writes for newspapers or magazines*

- Have volunteers come up with a definition for *photojournalist*. Then have them look up the word in a print or digital dictionary to confirm their definition.

YOU DO IT

- Have partners brainstorm a list of words with the roots *tele*, *photo*, *scrib*, and *rupt*.

- Ask them to create a definition for each word using what they know about the root.

- Have students look up their definitions in a print or digital dictionary. Then have them write a sentence using each word.

ADVANCED

ELA L.5.4a, L.5.4b, L.5.4c
ELD ELD.PI.5.1, ELD.PI.5.6b

I DO IT

- Write the roots *tele*, *photo*, *scrib*, and *rupt* on the board and provide their definitions.

- Remind students that knowledge of Greek and Latin roots will help them learn the meanings of unknown words.

- Explain that roots can sometimes be related and have similar meanings, such as *scrib* and *script*.

WE DO IT

- Help students use the meanings of the roots to figure out the meanings of *telecommunication*, *photocopy*, *prescribe*, and *bankrupt*.

- Help them separate the roots from the other word parts. Ask volunteers to define each word part and use the complete word in a sentence.

- Guide students to confirm the meanings in a print or digital dictionary.

YOU DO IT

- Have students brainstorm a list of words with the roots *tele*, *photo*, *scrib*, and *rupt*.

- Have student pairs write the word parts on separate pieces of paper or on index cards.

- Have partners spread their word parts across a desk and try to match them. Once they have made a match, they should say the definition of the word and confirm it using a print or digital dictionary.

ENGLISH LANGUAGE SUPPORT

ELA L.5.4a, L.5.4b, L.5.4c
ELD ELD.PI.5.1, ELD.PI.5.6b

Provide Struggling Readers, On Level, and Advanced ELs proficiency-level support during differentiated instruction.

Emerging

Help students break down words in order to focus on word roots. For example, display the word *telephone*. Underline "tele" and circle "phone." Tell students that *tele means* "from far away" and that *phone* means "voice or sound." Say: *A telephone lets you speak to someone from far away.* Repeat the activity with variations as needed for other words students learn in their respective groups.

Expanding

Have students write each word they are presented with in their respective groups on a piece of paper. Then have them underline the root in each word. Students should brainstorm or look up in a dictionary at least one more word for each root and give the meaning of each word.

Bridging

Display the words *telephone, photocopy, scribble,* and *interrupt*. Have students write each word on one side of an index card. Tell them to draw a line between the root and the other word part. On the other side of the card, have them write the root's meaning and then the meaning of the word.

Options for Reteaching

VOCABULARY STRATEGIES

Greek and Latin Roots

I DO IT

- Remind students that they can figure out the meanings of unfamiliar words by learning the meanings of many Greek and Latin roots.

- Review with students that *tele* means "from a distance," *photo* means "having to do with light," *scrib* means "write," and *rupt* means "to break apart."

WE DO IT

- Have students turn to **Student Book p. 274** and read aloud what Nathan says about the wounded sailor: "Treat the bleeding first, then the hypothermia."

- Model how to apply the vocabulary strategy to determine the meaning of *hypothermia*.

  Think Aloud Hypothermia *looks like a difficult medical term. However, I see that it contains two Greek roots.* Hypo *means "below" or "less than normal."* Therm *means "heat."* Hypothermia *must refer to something that is colder than normal. This sailor has just been dragged out of the ocean and is nearly freezing to death. So I think* hypothermia *means "a body temperature that is too low."*

- Have a volunteer look up *hypothermia* in a dictionary and read the definition aloud.

YOU DO IT

- Have partners think of other words with the roots *tele, photo, scrib, rupt, hypo,* and *therm.*

- Have them model using roots to determine the meanings of the words.

- Have them use dictionaries to verify their answers.

COMPREHENSION SKILL

Conclusions and Generalizations

I DO IT

- Remind students that a conclusion is a reasonable guess about ideas that are not stated in the text. A generalization is a broad statement about something that is true most of the time.

- Tell students that conclusions and generalizations should be supported by details in the text and by personal experience. Readers should infer, using what the author says in a passage, to draw conclusions.

WE DO IT

- Have students read p. 275 of "Storm Warriors." Guide them to draw conclusions and make generalizations based on details in the reading and their own personal experiences.

- Model how to identify supporting details and recall a personal experience in order to draw a conclusion or make a generalization.

  Think Aloud *I read that Nathan rubbed linseed oil on Arthur after the rescue. I know sometimes I rub my hands together to warm them. Arthur said, "I am warming up." This tells me that rubbing linseed oil on someone is a way of warming them up.*

- Help volunteers draw conclusions and make generalizations for another part of the story.

YOU DO IT

- Distribute <u>Graphic Organizer 8</u>.

- Have students draw a conclusion about the captain after reading p. 277.

- Have students work with partners to complete the graphic organizer with details from the text that support their conclusion.

- Review the completed graphic organizers.

LANGUAGE ARTS
ELA W.5.2a, W.5.2c, L.5.1e, L.5.3a
ELD ELD.PI.5.10a, ELD.PII.5.6, ELD.PII.5.7

Complex Sentences/Informative Writing

I DO IT

- Remind students that a complex sentence is an independent clause joined by a conjunction to one or more dependent clauses.

- Review that an independent clause forms a complete thought and can stand on its own.

- Review correlative conjunctions: pairs of conjunctions that work together, such as *both/and, either/or, neither/nor,* and *whether/or.* Correlative conjunctions can link two nouns, two verbs, or two adjectives.

WE DO IT

- Read aloud the following complex sentence from **Student Book p. 271:** *When I peered out, Mr. Meekins was swinging the heaving stick and line.*

- Model how to identify the dependent and independent clauses.

Think Aloud *The first clause in this sentence is "When I peered out." That can't stand alone as a sentence; it's not a complete thought. It's a dependent clause that begins with the conjunction* when. *The second clause is "Mr. Meekins was swinging the heaving stick and line." That's a complete sentence, so it's an independent clause.*

- Guide students to write a sentence about "Storm Warriors" that uses correlative conjunctions. *Sample answer: Nathan is both intelligent and brave.* Point out that using complex sentences and correlative conjunctions in their research reports will make their writing both clear and interesting to read.

YOU DO IT

- Have students review "Storm Warriors" for facts that they could use in a research report about the Pea Island surfmen. Ask them to take notes on these facts using complete sentences.

- When finished, have students exchange papers and underline any complex sentences. Ask them to circle any pairs of correlative conjunctions.

- Then have students look for simple sentences that could be combined or rewritten to form complex sentences, as well as sentences that could be rewritten with correlative conjunctions.

DECODING
ELA RF.5.3a, RF.5.4a

Compound Words

I DO IT

- Remind students that a compound word is two or more words put together.

- Compound words may be written as one word, hyphenated, or as two words.

- Model how to divide compound words.

Think Aloud *I can break the word* newsstand *into two separate words:* news *and* stand. *This is a compound word.*

WE DO IT

- Have students open to **Student Book p. 268.**

- Write *surfman, lifesaving, fisherman,* and *shipwrecks* on the board.

- Help students find the sentences on p. 268 containing those words.

- Guide students to decode *surfman* step by step.

- Have a volunteer draw a slash between the two words on the board.

YOU DO IT

- Have partners decode the remaining compound words on the board.

- Have students look through "Storm Warriors" for more compound words. Ask them to work with a partner to decode the words.

- Use the Corrective Feedback on **p. T275** if students need additional help.

Teacher Notes

JOURNEYS

Cougars Anchor Text

"Purr-fection" Paired Selection

Teacher Dashboard

Log onto the Teacher Dashboard and *my*SmartPlanner. Use these searchable tools to customize lessons that achieve your instructional goals.

Interactive Whiteboard Lessons

• Grammar: Quotations, Dialogue, and Interjections
• Vocabulary Strategies: Shades of Meaning

• Write About Reading
• Informative Writing: Research Report

Interactive Lessons

▶ Participating in Collaborative Discussions
▶ Writing to Sources
▶ Informative Writing

✔ Assess It Online!

• Weekly Tests
• Assessment-driven instruction with prescriptive feedback

Student eBook

✎ 🗖 Annotate it! **Strategies for Annotation**

Guide students to use digital tools for close reading.

Students may also use the interactive features in their Student eBooks to respond to prompts in a variety of ways, including:

• short-answer response
• spoken response
• fill-in-the-blank
• drag-and-drop
• multiple choice

High-Interest Informational Texts and Multimedia

Have students explore the FYI website for additional information about topics of study.

Culturally Responsive Teaching

The Big Cats Tell students that this week, they will be reading and thinking about animal behavior.

• Create a text-rich environment by providing a broad range of books, articles, and stories about "big cats" from all over the world. Provide books and resources in English learners' first languages in the collection.

• Have students identify and list as many types of "big cats" as they can. Encourage English learners to teach the class the words for these creatures in their home languages.

• Invite students to research a "big cat" in which they are especially interested. Encourage students to make their own choices about which animal they would like to learn about.

• During the week, invite students to be the "experts" and share what they have learned about their chosen creature.

Promote Oral Language Development Provide opportunities for English learners to develop and expand language production as they learn and share. Word banks and sentence frames can help English learners at all proficiency levels participate.

Language Support Card

Use the Lesson 10 Language Support Card to activate prior knowledge, frontload vocabulary, and teach academic English.

TEXT X-RAY Use the Text X-Ray on page T313 to review the language demands of "Cougars" with the needs of English learners in mind.

Language Workshop for Designated ELD

• Connection to Essential Question
• Vocabulary Network
• Focus on Interacting in Meaningful Ways
• Discussion Frames
• How English Works
• Word Learning Strategies

You may wish to use the following suggestions to modify instruction for some students, according to their needs.

Learner's Journal

Keeping a Learner's Journal can help students see themselves as successful, growing learners. Developing a sense of ownership in students can motivate them to reach their highest potential. Have students add to their Learner's Journal for this lesson. Depending on students' needs and skills, have them record information about what they are learning. Some examples:

- Day 1: Vocabulary: *unobserved, available, detecting, mature, ferocious, resemble, particular, vary, contentment, keen*
- Day 2: The title of the Anchor Text, "Cougars," and information about the text
- Day 3: Write about something new they learned about observing animal behavior. To help, you might want to discuss with students the Essential Question and their ideas about it.
- Day 4: Write several words they have learned to spell this week.
- Day 5: Write about how they are becoming better writers. For example, "I am learning to write a research report."

Student eBook

- **Audio** can be activated to support fluency, decoding, and comprehension.
- **Alternative Text** provides spoken information that can be used in place of the information provided in the book's images.
- **Vocabulary Pop-Ups** contain point-of-use definitions for selection vocabulary.

Dance

Convey Feeling and Expression Through Dance Have partners or small groups use gestures, posture, and movement to express ideas in poetry.

- Review the poems in "Purr-fection" with students and invite them to point out cat actions and roles that the poems describe.
- Tell students that they will work with a partner or a small group to use gestures, postures, and movements that illustrate and express the ideas in one of the poems, or in one of a poem's stanzas.
- Help students choose a partner or organize themselves into small groups. Explain that they will choose a poem or a stanza and then work together to create and use gestures, postures, and movements that express the ideas in the poem or stanza.
- Have groups work together to create their movements and practice them together a few times. Then have groups perform their movements for another group.

LESSON 10 *Our* Focus Wall

ANCHOR TEXT

Cougars
Informational Text

Purr-fection
Poetry

ESSENTIAL QUESTION

What can a scientist learn by observing the behaviors of a particular animal?

WRITING

Writing

Informative Writing: Write a Research Report

Focus Trait: Sentence Fluency

READING LITERATURE & INFORMATIONAL TEXT

Comprehension Skills and Strategies

☑ **TARGET SKILL**
- Main Ideas and Details
- Explain Scientific Ideas
- Domain-Specific Vocabulary

☑ **TARGET STRATEGY**
- Monitor/Clarify

FOUNDATIONAL SKILLS

Fluency

Stress

Decoding

Recognizing Schwa + /r/ Sounds

LANGUAGE

☑ Target Vocabulary

unobserved	resemble
available	particular
detecting	vary
mature	contentment
ferocious	keen

Spelling

Final Schwa + /r/ Sounds

cellar	tractor
flavor	thunder
cougar	pillar
chapter	border
mayor	calendar
anger	quarter
senator	lunar
passenger	proper
major	elevator
popular	bitter

Grammar

Direct Quotations and Interjections

Vocabulary Strategies

Shades of Meaning

ANCHOR TEXT

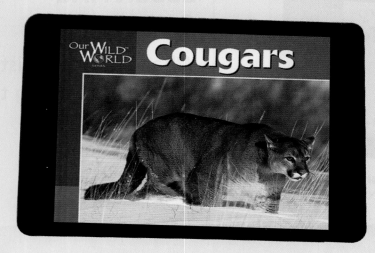

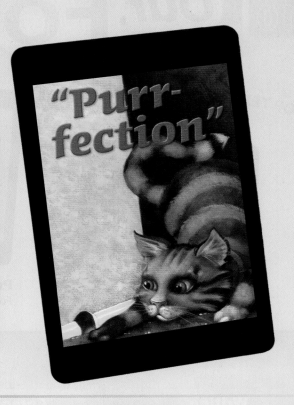

Cougars
GENRE: Informational Text

TEXT X-RAY

Prepare for Complex Texts For a comprehensive overview and analysis of key ideas and academic language features of this lesson's Anchor Text, see pages T312–T313.

"Purr-fection"
GENRE: Poetry
21st Century Theme: Environmental Literacy

Digital Resources

▶ **eBook: Annotate It!**

▶ **Interactive Whiteboard Lessons**
• Vocabulary Strategies: Shades of Meaning
• Grammar: Quotations, Dialogue, and Interjections

▶ **GrammarSnap Videos**
• Dialogue

▶ **Multimedia Grammar Glossary**

▶ *my*SmartPlanner

▶ **Parent Resource**

● **Additional Resources**

• Vocabulary in Context Cards 91–100
• Reader's Notebook, pp. 109–120
• Lesson 10 Blackline Masters
• Literacy and Language Guide

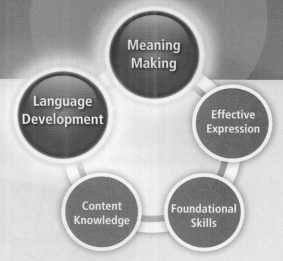

Meaning Making

Language Development

Effective Expression

Content Knowledge

Foundational Skills

LINGUISTICALLY DIVERSE LEARNERS

∨ Integrated English Language Support

● Interacting in Meaningful Ways

Classroom Conversations
- Talk About It, p. T321
- Collaborative Conversation, pp. T316, T332, T336

Interactive and Collaborative Writing
- Monitor/Clarify, p. T332
- Write About Reading, p. T337
- Revise a Research Report, p. T356

Self-Selected Reading, p. T338

Sentence Frames for Writing, pp. T347, T356

● Learning About How English Works

Scaffold the Texts
- Text X-Ray: Focus on Academic Language, p. T313
- Using Verb Tenses, pp. T324, T336, T357

Language Detective
- Target Vocabulary, p. T318
- Text Structure, p. T333

Communicative Modes
- Write About Reading, p. T337
- Revise a Research Report, p. T356

● Using Foundational Literacy Skills

Fluency: Stress, p. T348
Decoding: Recognizing Schwa + /r/ Sounds, p. T349

Apply Language Skills
- Direct Quotations and Interjections, p. T352

Support Linguistic Transfer
- Shades of Meaning, p. T344
- Final Schwa + /r/ Sounds, p. T350
- Direct Quotations and Interjections, p. T352

∨ Standard English Learners

- Pronunciation: Voicing /th/, p. T331
- Direct Quotations and Interjections, p. T354

ASSESSMENT

● Formative Assessment

- Target Vocabulary, p. T319
- Target Strategy: Monitor/Clarify, pp. T326, T330
- Target Skill: Story Structure, p. T335
- Vocabulary Strategies: Prefixes *re-, un-, dis-*, p. T345
- Decoding: VCV Syllable Pattern, p. T349
- Using Data to Adjust Instruction, p. T361

● ✅ Assess It Online!
- Weekly Tests

Performance Tasks
- Write About Reading, p. T337
- Write an Explanatory Essay, p. T364

LESSON 10 — Small Group/Independent Resources

∨ Vocabulary Reader

Big Cats
by Ellen L. Moore

HOUGHTON MIFFLIN

 Vocabulary Reader
for all levels

Provide strategic scaffolding to support all students in reading on-level text and in acquiring general academic and domain-specific vocabulary. Use the instructional supports on pp. T370–T371 or the Leveled Reader Teacher's Guide.

Guided Reading Level: P
Lexile: 780L
DRA: 38
Leveled Reader Teacher's Guide

∨ Weekly Leveled Readers

Guide students to read and comprehend additional texts about the lesson topic. Use the instructional supports on pp. T374–T377 or the Leveled Reader Teacher's Guides.

Struggling Readers
Guided Reading Level: R
Lexile: 600L
DRA: 40
Leveled Reader Teacher's Guide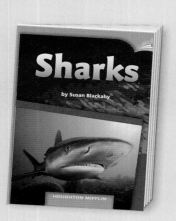

On Level
Guided Reading Level: S
Lexile: 870L
DRA: 40
Leveled Reader Teacher's Guide

Advanced
Guided Reading Level: V
Lexile: 950L
DRA: 50
Leveled Reader Teacher's Guide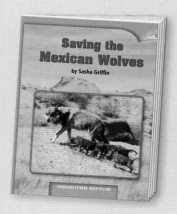

English Language Learners
Guided Reading Level: S
Lexile: 690L
DRA: 40
Leveled Reader Teacher's Guide

Language Workshop for Designated ELD

- Provides reteaching and practice in the key foundational skills for reading: print concepts, phonological/phonemic awareness, phonics and word recognition, and fluency.

- Explicit, sequential, and systematic instruction designed to bring students up to grade level.

- Screening and Diagnostic Assessments (within Intervention Assessments) place individual students within the system.

Lesson 10 Focus

Collaborate: Adapt Language Choices

Interpret: Evaluate an Author's Language Choices

Produce: Plan and Deliver Oral Presentations

How English Works: Expand Sentences to Add Detail

Vocabulary Network

Meaning Making
Language Development
Effective Expression
Content Knowledge
Foundational Skills

Intervention

 Strategic Intervention Tier II

Write-In Reader: *Bison Come Back to the Plains*

- Interactive worktext with selection that connects to the lesson topic
- Reinforces the lesson's vocabulary and comprehension
- Build skills for reading increasingly complex texts
- Online version with dual-speed audio and follow-text

Daily Lessons See this week's daily Strategic Intervention Lesson on pp. S42–S51.

- Preteach and Reteach daily instruction
- Oral Grammar
- Decoding
- Comprehension

- Fluency
- Grammar
- Written Response
- Unpack Meaning
- Return to Anchor Text

 Decoding Power: Intensive Intervention

- Provides reteaching and practice in the key foundational skills for reading: print concepts, phonological/phonemic awareness, phonics and word recognition, and fluency.

- Explicit, sequential, and systematic instruction designed to bring students up to grade level.

- Screening and Diagnostic Assessments (within Intervention Assessments) place individual students within the system.

✓ Assess It Online!

▶ **Screening and Diagnostic Assessments** (within Intervention Assessments) place individual students within the system.

▶ **Progress-Monitoring Assessments** (within Intervention Assessments) ensure students are making satisfactory progress and provide a measure of student readiness to exit the system.

What My Other Students Are Doing

Digital Resources

▶ **Literacy Centers:** Word Study, Think and Write, Comprehension and Fluency

▶ **Interactive Lessons:** Writing to Sources, Writing as a Process: Revise and Edit, Participating in Collaborative Discussions

◉ Additional Resources

- Vocabulary in Context Cards 91–100
- Reader's Notebook, pp. 109–120
- Independent Reading
- Lesson 10 Blackline Masters

Comprehension and Fluency

Materials
- Student Book
- stopwatch
- Reading Log
- pencil or pen
- paper

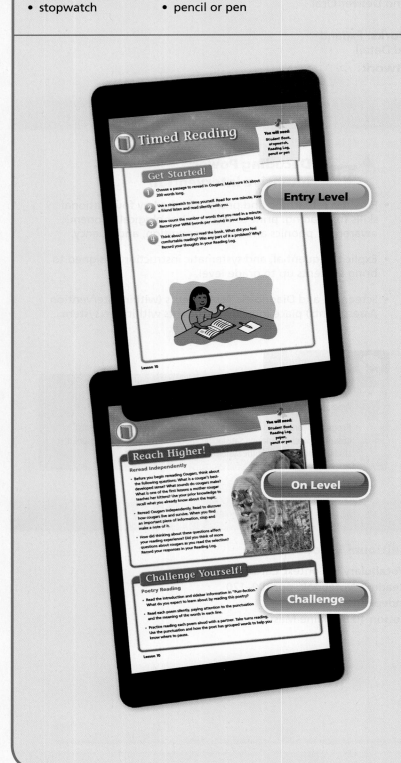

Word Study

Materials
- dictionary
- thesaurus
- computer with Internet access
- index cards
- paper
- pencil or pen

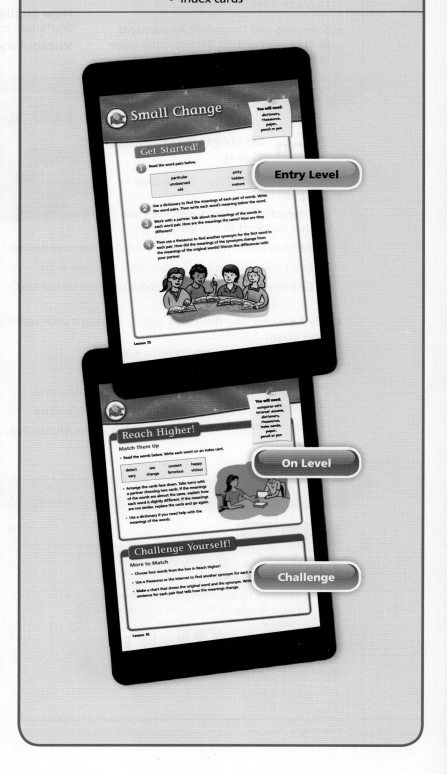

Assign Literacy Center activities during small group time. Each center contains three activities. Students who experience success with the entry-level activity move on to the on-level and challenge activities, as time permits.

Meaning Making

Effective Expression

Language Development

Content Knowledge

Foundational Skills

Think and Write

Materials
- computer with Internet access
- paper
- pencil or pen
- outline map of North and South America
- encyclopedia

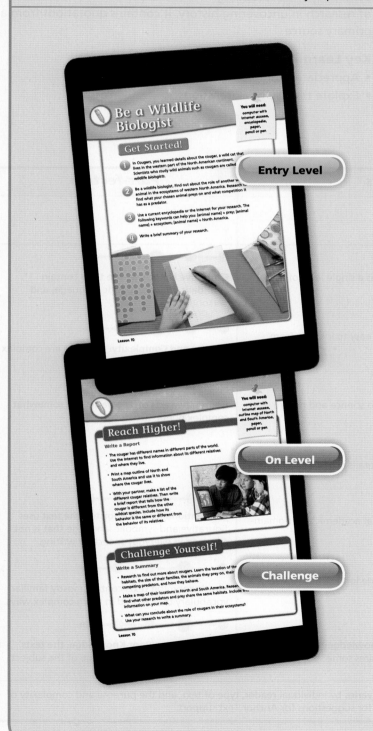

Entry Level

On Level

Challenge

Independent Reading

Teacher Modeling Modeling how to select appropriate books and books of interest is helpful to students who have difficulty choosing books. Select a book and do two brief Think Alouds—one in favor of reading the book and the other to demonstrate deciding not to read the book. Below are some example Think Alouds for a nonfiction book.

- **PRO**: *I'm interested in (topic). The title of this book has (topic) in it, so the whole book is probably about (topic). Each page has a picture with a caption that gives me more information. When I read the first two pages, I see a few words that are hard for me. I've read other books by this author, and I have enjoyed them. I think I'll give this book a try.*

- **CON**: *I'm interested in (topic). The title of this book includes (topic), but it also has other topics. Maybe the whole book isn't about what I want. When I read the first two pages, there are a lot of words that I don't know. I think this book might be too hard right now. I'll try another book.*

If a student consistently selects books that are too challenging for him or her, have the student explain why he or she has chosen a particular book before beginning to read. Guide the student to a more appropriate book, as necessary.

See p. T338 for additional independent reading support.
ELA RL.5.10, RI.5.10

Prepare for Complex Texts

Anchor Text

Cougars
by Patricia Corrigan

GENRE: Informational Text

Why This Text?

Students regularly encounter historical fiction in literature anthologies and their own independent reading. This text presents a fictional narrative of a dramatic, historical event. It contains vivid descriptions from a first-person point of view.

Key Learning Objectives

- Determine main ideas and details in a text.
- Understand and explain relationships between scientific ideas.
- Acquire and use domain-specific vocabulary.

Paired Selection

Purr-fection
by Various

GENRE: Poetry

Why This Text?

Students encounter informational text in school textbooks, periodicals, and their own independent reading. The text explores the importance of research in uncovering history. It contains quotations from a primary source.

Key Learning Objectives

- Appreciate examples of poetry related to cats.
- Explore the use of alliteration.

▲ TEXT COMPLEXITY RUBRIC

		Cougars	Purr-fection
Quantitative Measures	Lexile	960L	NP
	Guided Reading Level	V	T
Qualitative Measures	Meaning and Purpose	**Density and Complexity:** the text has a single level of literal meaning. **Purpose:** the purpose is implied but easy to identify from context.	**Figurative Language:** the texts contain abundant imagery, poetic language, and personification. **Density and Complexity:** the texts are complex and require inference.
	Text Structure	**Genre:** the text has traits common to science and nature essays. **Organization:** the main ideas and details organization is complex but largely explicit.	**Genre:** the texts offer a variety of somewhat complex poetic structures.
	Language Features	**Vocabulary:** the text contains general academic and domain-specific vocabulary. **Sentence Structure:** the text has some longer, descriptive sentences.	**Conventionality and Register:** the text uses figurative and symbolic language that is not common in everyday speech or writing. **Vocabulary:** the texts contain mostly familiar vocabulary that is used in more complex ways.
	Knowledge Demands	**Subject Matter Knowledge/Prior Knowledge:** the text offers general academic learning but requires some specialized knowledge.	**Subject Matter/Prior Knowledge:** the texts require some prior knowledge of the subject.
Reader/Task Considerations		Determine using the professional judgment of the teacher. This varies by individual reader, type of text, and the purpose and complexity of particular tasks. See **Reader and Task Considerations** on p. T323 for suggestions for Anchor Text support.	

JOURNEYS
TK–6 ELA/ELD

California Journeys scaffolds instruction for English learners in the critical areas of academic language, spelling, listening and reading comprehension, and knowledge and application of conventions.

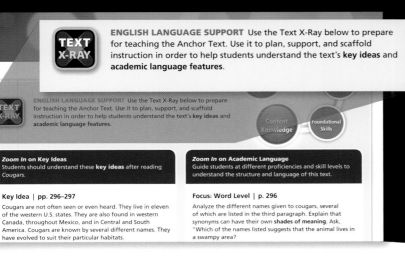

ENGLISH LANGUAGE SUPPORT Use the Text X-Ray below to prepare for teaching the Anchor Text. Use it to plan, support, and scaffold instruction in order to help students understand the text's **key ideas** and **academic language features**.

ENGLISH LANGUAGE SUPPORT Use the Text X-Ray below to prepare for teaching the Anchor Text. Use it to plan, support, and scaffold instruction in order to help students understand the text's key ideas and academic language features.

Zoom In on Key Ideas
Students should understand these **key ideas** after reading *Cougars*.

Zoom In on Academic Language
Guide students at different proficiencies and skill levels to understand the structure and language of this text.

Key Idea | pp. 296–297
Cougars are not often seen or even heard. They live in eleven of the western U.S. states. They are also found in western Canada, throughout Mexico, and in Central and South America. Cougars are known by several different names. They have evolved to suit their particular habitats.

Focus: Word Level | p. 296
Analyze the different names given to cougars, several of which are listed in the third paragraph. Explain that synonyms can have their own **shades of meaning**. Ask, "Which of the names listed suggests that the animal lives in a swampy area?"

Text X-Ray allows you to zoom in on aspects of complex text with specific instructional supports and scaffolds to help you guide students with varying proficiency and skill levels.

English Language Support boxes help teachers to actively engage students at **Emerging**, **Expanding**, and **Bridging** levels to acquire the knowledge and skills they need to access complex grade-level text.

Language Support Cards preteach concepts, build background vocabulary, and promote oral and academic language to help students connect with the core content.

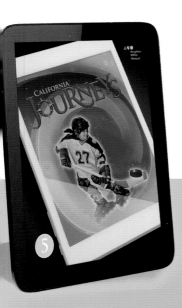

Online tools engage students in meaning making, drawing conclusions supported by text evidence through responding to questions at point of use, recording spoken responses, highlighting text, and taking notes.

Vocabulary in Context Cards deepen vocabulary knowledge by engaging with the photograph, context sentence, and definition for each word.

contentment
Like wild cats, house cats purr with contentment when they are satisfied.

conflicts
What Does It Mean?
When people have conflicts, they have problems or disagreements with each other.
Spanish cognate: conflictos

Think About It.
What do you think is the best way to solve conflicts?

Talk It Over.
Read each sentence to yourself. Then read aloud to a partner the sentences in which the word **conflicts** makes sense.

We resolved our _____ by talking through our problems.
Have those two countries always had _____?
Did you and Jose _____ the books?
I read about interesting ways to solve _____.
I saw many _____ in the phone book.

Collaborative Classroom Conversations /Talk About It

Dynamic Spoken Response Tools

Notes

Annotate it!

Highlight and annotate text.

Annotation ✕

◼ ◼ ◻ ◼ a a ○ ✉ Add Recipient

|

☐ Save to myNotebook   Delete   Save

resemble
Some house cats resemble, or look like, cougars, but cougars are much bigger.

HMH DECODING POWER
Intensive Reading Instruction

Decoding Power provides additional explicit, sequential instruction in foundational skills.

Language Workshop provides teachers and students with a full year of research-based, standards-aligned lessons and activities crafted for daily use during periods of designated English language instruction.

Weekly 5-Step lessons offer English learners at all proficiency levels— **Emerging**, **Expanding**, and **Bridging**—multiple opportunities to engage in challenging, purposeful, and scaffolded activities.

Designated ELD **Five Day** Lesson Plan

DAY 1 Connect to Text	Students revisit a critical selection from the *California Journeys* program, with an emphasis on comprehending and analyzing the author's use of English.
DAY 2 Collaborate	Students work with their peers to expand their knowledge of the vocabulary and to engage in meaningful conversations about the lesson topic and text.
DAY 3 Interpret	Focuses on developing students' interpretive skills as they apply to both text and vocabulary comprehension.
DAY 4 Produce	Dedicated to facilitating narrative, informational, or argumentative writing or speaking products that demonstrate an understanding of each language skill students have practiced.
DAY 5 Reflect	Guides students through the process of reflection about what they have learned over the course of the lesson.

Language Workshop Formative Assessments

support English learners in meeting ELD learning goals.

- **Language Workshop Assessment Handbook** measures English learners' progress in mastery of each proficiency level, as well as mastery of the English Language Development Standards.

- **Formative Assessment** opportunities for each lesson provide guidance for assessing student understanding and use of the skills covered.

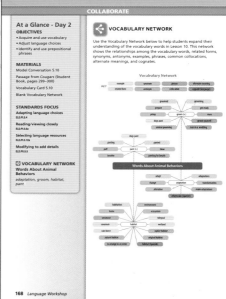

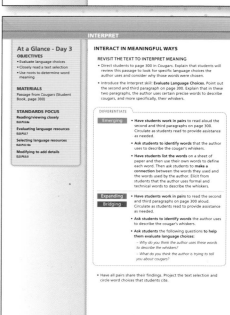

Houghton Mifflin Harcourt

Houghton Mifflin Harcourt™ is a trademark of Houghton Mifflin Harcourt.
© Houghton Mifflin Harcourt. All rights reserved. Printed in the U.S.A. 10/15 MS159124 F-1643793

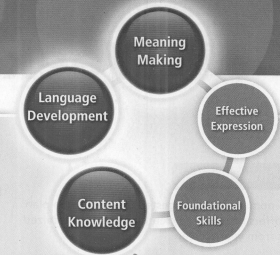

ENGLISH LANGUAGE SUPPORT Use the Text X-Ray below to prepare for teaching the Anchor Text. Use it to plan, support, and scaffold instruction in order to help students understand the text's **key ideas** and **academic language features**.

Zoom In on Key Ideas

Students should understand these **key ideas** after reading *Cougars.*

Key Idea | pp. 296–297

Cougars are not often seen or even heard. They live in eleven of the western U.S. states. They are also found in western Canada, throughout Mexico, and in Central and South America. Cougars are known by several different names. They have evolved to suit their particular habitats.

Key Idea | pp. 298–299

The cougar is a medium-sized and muscular wild cat. Their thick fur keeps them warm because they have little body fat. They do not sweat like humans do, but instead pant like dogs. Their eyesight is excellent both during the day and at night, which helps them hunt.

Key Idea | pp. 300–301

Cougars share many of the traits that are common in other cat species, such as keen senses of hearing and smell. They have sensitive whiskers that help them judge distance from objects. They have several vocalizations but cannot roar like lions do. Adults tend to live alone, needing as much as 200 square miles to roam.

Key Idea | pp. 302–303

Cougar kittens have spotted fur that helps camouflage them for about 8 months. They depend entirely on their mother for the first three months of life. The mother grooms them to disguise their scent and keep them safe from predators. At six months old, the kittens can eat prey and begin to explore away from their den. The kittens remain with their mother until they are about 18 months old. During this time, they learn survival skills from their mother. If they find a home with enough food and water, cougars can live for eight to ten years.

Zoom In on Academic Language

Guide students at different proficiencies and skill levels to understand the structure and language of this text.

Focus: Word Level | p. 296

Analyze the different names given to cougars, several of which are listed in the third paragraph. Explain that synonyms can have their own **shades of meaning**. Ask, "Which of the names listed suggests that the animal lives in a swampy area?"

Focus: Text Level | pp. 296–304

Remind students that an author can use different **text structures**. This text follows a main idea and details structure. On p. 296, point out the main idea in the first sentence of the third and fourth paragraphs. Have students look for details within the paragraphs that support the main idea. Repeat occasionally in other sections of the text.

Focus: Sentence Level | p. 296

Guide English learners and others in understanding how connecting words and phrases give a paragraph some structure. On p. 296, the phrases *Over time* and *For instance* link examples and details back to the main idea statement that cougars live in many habitats.

Focus: Word Level | pp. 300, 301

Remind students that they can often figure out the meaning of unfamiliar words by **using context**—looking for clues nearby. Provide an example from p. 300: "Like all cats, cougars groom themselves." *Grooming* is described later in the paragraph as using "their rough tongues to remove any loose hair and to untangle any matted hair."

Content and Language Instruction Make note of additional **content knowledge** and **language features** students may find challenging in this text.

LESSON 10 Weekly Planner

my SmartPlanner

Auto-populates the suggested five-day lesson plan and offers flexibility to create and save customized plans from year to year.

See **Standards Correlations** on p. C1. In your eBook, click the Standards button in the left panel to view descriptions of the standards on the page.

DAY 1

Materials
- ELL Blackline Masters 10.2, 10.3
- Graphic Organizer 15
- Lesson 10 Language Support Card
- Literacy and Language Guide p. 74
- Projectables 10.1, 10.4
- Reader's Notebook pp. 112, 115
- Strategy Projectables S1–S8
- Student Book pp. 290–305
- Vocabulary in Context Cards 91–100

DAY 2

Materials
- Graphic Organizer 15
- Interactive Lessons: Listening and Responding and Writing Opinions: Support Your Argument
- Literacy and Language Guide p. 64
- Projectables 5.2, 5.5
- Reader's Notebook pp. 53, 56, 60
- Student Book pp. 294–309

Whole Group

Oral Language
Listening
Comprehension

DAY 1
Teacher Read Aloud
"Who Tamed the Cat?" T316–T317

DAY 2
Turn and Talk, T336

Vocabulary
Text-Based Comprehension
- Skills and Strategies
- Craft and Structure

Research and Media Literacy

DAY 1
☑ **Introduce Vocabulary**
Vocabulary in Context, T318–T319
☑ **Read and Comprehend,** T320–T321
FIRST READ **Think Through the Text**
Read the Anchor Text: "Cougars," T322–T333
Research/Media Literacy, T347

DAY 2
SECOND READ
☑ **Dig Deeper: How to Analyze the Text,** T334–T335
- Main Ideas and Details
- Domain-Specific Vocabulary
- Explain Scientific Ideas
- Cause and Effect
Analyze the Text
Reread the Anchor Text: "Cougars," T325, T327, T331
☑ **Your Turn,** T336–T337

Foundational Skills
- Fluency
- Decoding

DAY 1
☑ **Fluency**
Model Stress, T316

DAY 2
☑ **Fluency**
Teach Stress, T348
Practice Stress, T329

Whole Group Language Arts

Spelling
Grammar
Writing

DAY 1
☑ **Spelling**
Final Schwa + /r/ Sounds: Pretest, T350
☑ **Grammar**
Daily Proofreading Practice, T352
Teach Quotations, T352
☑ **Informative Writing: Write a Research Report**
Draft, T356

DAY 2
☑ **Spelling**
Final Schwa + /r/ Sounds: Word Sort, T350
☑ **Grammar**
Daily Proofreading Practice, T353
Teach Text Quotations, T353
☑ **Informative Writing: Write a Research Report**
Draft, T357

Small Group

Suggestions for Small Groups (See pp. T368–T369.)

T314 • Unit 2 Lesson 10

DAY 3

Materials
- Instructional Routine 8
- Literacy and Language Guide pp. 75, 134–135
- Projectable 10.6
- Reading Log Blackline Master
- Reader's Notebook pp. 109–110, 117
- Student Book pp. 294–305

Classroom Conversation, T339

Independent Reading, T338
- Reader's Guide: "Cougars"
- Self-Selected Reading

Apply Vocabulary Knowledge, T339
Research/Media Literacy, T347

☑ **Decoding**
Recognizing Schwa + /r/ Sounds, T349
☑ **Fluency**
Practice Stress, T329

☑ **Spelling**
Final Schwa + /r/ Sounds: Word Families, T351
☑ **Grammar**
Daily Proofreading Practice, T353
Teach Interjections and Dialogue, T353
☑ **Informative Writing: Write a Research Report**
Draft, T357

DAY 4

Materials
- Interactive Whiteboard Lesson: Shades of Meaning
- Literacy and Language Guide p. 134–135
- Projectable 10.3
- Reader's Notebook pp. 111, 114, 118
- Student Book pp. 310–313

Classroom Conversation, T340

Connect to the Topic
- Read Poetry: "Purr-fection," T340
- Think Through the Text, T342
☑ **Compare Texts,** T343
☑ **Vocabulary Strategies**
Shades of Meaning, T344–T345
Research/Media Literacy, T347

☑ **Fluency**
Practice Stress, T341

☑ **Spelling**
Final Schwa + /r/ Sounds: Connect to Writing, T351
☑ **Grammar**
Daily Proofreading Practice, T354
Review Direct Quotations and Interjections, T354
☑ **Informative Writing: Write a Research Report**
Revise, T358

DAY 5

Materials
- Cold Reads
- Graphic Organizer 6
- Interactive Lessons: Participate in Collaborative Conversations, Writing as a Process: Revise and Edit
- Interactive Whiteboard Lesson: Direct Quotations and Interjections
- Projectable 10.7
- Proofreading Checklist Blackline Master
- Reader's Notebook p. 119
- Student Book pp. 314–317
- Writing Rubric Blackline Master

Speaking and Listening, T347

Extend the Topic: Animal Behaviors
- Domain-Specific Vocabulary, T346
- Research/Media Literacy, T347
- Optional Second Read: "Purr-fection," T340

☑ **Fluency**
Progress Monitoring, T361

☑ **Spelling**
Final Schwa + /r/ Sounds: Assess, T351
☑ **Grammar**
Daily Proofreading Practice, T354
Connect Grammar to Writing, T354–T355
☑ **Informative Writing: Write a Research Report**
Revise, Edit, and Publish, T358

Tier II Intervention provides thirty minutes of additional daily practice with key parts of the core instruction. See pp. S42–S51.

Teacher Read Aloud

- Listen to fluent reading.
- Summarize a written text read aloud by condensing ideas. LANGUAGE

ENGLISH LANGUAGE SUPPORT
Use Visuals

All Proficiencies To assist students with accessing the content and topic of the Teacher Read Aloud, discuss the High-Utility Words on the Lesson 10 Language Support Card 🔗.

☑ PREVIEW
Target Vocabulary

available ready to be used or taken

particular specific or special

keen sharp and alert

detecting working to discover something

mature to grow and develop over time

vary to change something

resemble to be or to look similar to something or someone

unobserved hidden or unnoticed

ferocious very aggressive and scary

contentment happiness

Model Fluency

Stress Explain that good readers emphasize certain words in a sentence to enhance meaning.

- Display Projectable 10.1 🔗. Read each sentence and model how stressing, or emphasizing, certain words or syllables affects the meaning.
- Demonstrate how stressing certain words or syllables adds emphasis and helps a sentence make sense.
- Reread the passage together. Guide students to stress certain words to help enhance meaning. **ELA** RF.5.4a

Listening Comprehension

Read aloud the selection. Pause at the numbered stopping points to ask students the questions below. Discuss the meanings of the highlighted words, as needed, to support the discussion.

1 *Based on the first paragraph, what central idea do you think will be explained in this selection? Cats have been tame for much longer than people once believed.* **MAIN IDEA AND DETAILS**

2 *What text evidence supports the idea that cats were tame at least 9,500 years ago? One cat was found buried with its owner in a grave that was 9,500 years old.* **CITE TEXT EVIDENCE**

3 *What did scientists learn from studying the genetic material of domestic cats from around the world? They learned that all the cats had common ancestors from the Fertile Crescent.* **SUMMARIZE**

4 *Why did cats become tame only after people began farming? Before people stored grain from farming, there were no cats around because there were no rodents to catch. When the cats came to chase the rodents, people could begin to tame them.* **SEQUENCE OF EVENTS**

💬 Classroom Collaboration

Ask students to describe the process by which wild cats became tame pets, condensing their ideas into a short summary. *Wild cats came to human communities because they could catch rodents there. People saw the cats were useful and encouraged them to stay by feeding them. The calmer, friendlier cats were taken into people's homes and became pets.* **ELA** SL.5.2 **ELD** ELD.PI.5.1, ELD.PI.5.5, ELD.PI

ENGLISH LANGUAGE SUPPORT
Read Aloud—Second Read Project the Target Vocabulary Preview. Introduce each word to students. Use visuals, gestures, or yes/no questions to help them understand the meaning of each word. Have students listen to the Read Aloud again and signal when they hear a Target Vocabulary Word. **ELD** ELD.PI.5.5

Who Tamed the Cat?

1 You might have heard that Ancient Egyptians first tamed the cat about 4,000 years ago. But new evidence suggests that the history of the domesticated cat dates back to an earlier time—maybe as far back as 12,000 years.

Historians began to think past Ancient Egypt when archaeologists, digging on the Mediterranean island of Cyprus, uncovered many cat bones. They were able to determine that these bones were 9,000 years old. Yet even after gathering all **available** data, scientists couldn't tell whether these cats were wild or tame. Then researchers stumbled upon the remains of one **particular** cat. It wasn't the bones themselves that made scientists so excited about this find and ready to turn their **keen** minds to discovering the facts. It was the way they had been buried.

2 This cat's grave lay just a few feet from a 9,500-year-old human grave. After some more **detecting,** new details came to light. Scientists believe this cat died at about eight months old, before it could **mature** to full adulthood. Both cat and human had been prepared for burial in the same manner. And both lay in the same position, with heads pointing to the west. Researchers believe these factors suggest that the cat was buried near its owner so that it could accompany him to the afterlife.

This discovery offered solid proof that Ancient Egyptians were not the first to coexist with cats. Meanwhile, researchers at England's Oxford University were coming to the same conclusion. There, a team of scientists studied genetic material from domestic cats around the world. They knew these cats would **vary** in size and appearance. But the cats did **resemble** each other in one important way: they had the **3** same ancestors. This species comes from a single location: the Fertile Crescent, which includes modern-day Iraq.

To historians, this evidence makes sense. It was here that, about 12,000 years ago, humans first began settling into permanent homes and villages. Previously, humans had wandered from place to place. As people began farming, they needed to stay in one place to tend their crops.

Where do cats come in? They followed the mice. After a harvest, farmers stored baskets of grain in barns and homes. Cats probably slunk around these stores, **unobserved,** waiting to pounce on rodents who got into the food. Cats had proven their usefulness, so people worked to keep them around, setting out fish scraps or saucers of milk. People began selecting certain cats as pets, passing over wild or **ferocious** individuals and bringing calmer creatures into their homes. Here, the **4** relationship brought joy and **contentment** to both animal and owner.

Today, some people still keep cats for their usefulness. Farmers let them prowl around barns, keeping rodents away from cows and horses. But most people just enjoy cats' companionship. It's safe to say that, as far as cats go, not much has changed in 12,000 years.

Introduce Vocabulary

Vocabulary in Context

▶ **SHARE OBJECTIVE**
- Acquire and use vocabulary.
- Use knowledge of linguistic context to determine the meaning of unknown words. LANGUAGE

Teach

Display and discuss the Vocabulary in Context Cards, using the routine below. Direct students to use **Student Book pp. 290–291.**

1 **Read and pronounce the word.** Read the word once alone and then together.

2 **Explain the word.** Read aloud the explanation under *What Does It Mean?*

ENGLISH LANGUAGE SUPPORT Review these cognates with Spanish-speaking students.

- *feroz (ferocious)*
- *particular (particular)*
- *variar (vary)*

3 **Discuss vocabulary in context.** Together, read aloud the sentence on the front of the card. Help students explain and use the word in new sentences.

4 **Engage with the word.** Ask and discuss the *Think About It* question with students.

Apply

Give partners or small groups one or two **Vocabulary in Context Cards.**

- Help students complete the *Talk It Over* activity on the back of each card.

- Have students complete the activities for all cards during the week.

🔍 **Language Detective** Explain that a *synonym* is a word that means the same or almost the same thing as another word. Have parnters rewrite one of the sentences using a synonym in place of a Vocabulary word. Tell them to share their new sentences with the class, explaining how the sentences are alike and different.

ELA L.5.4a, L.5.5c, L.5.6 **ELD** ELD.PI.5.8, ELD.PI.5.12a

🔍 **LANGUAGE DETECTIVE**

Talk About the Writer's Words
Work with a partner. Choose one of the sentences. Take out the Vocabulary word. Put in a word that means the same or almost the same thing. Tell how the sentences are the same and different.

290 **ELA** L.5.4a, L.5.5c, L.5.6
ELD ELD.PI.5.8, ELD.PI.5.12a

1 **resemble**
Some house cats resemble, or look like, cougars, but cougars are much bigger.

2 **detecting**
Excellent eyesight and a good sense of smell help lions in finding, or detecting, their prey.

3 **keen**
All cats have sharp, keen night vision. It is a great aid to them when hunting.

4 **vary**
The color of tiger stripes can vary from black and orange to black and white.

ENGLISH LANGUAGE SUPPORT

Comprehensible Input

Emerging Give students descriptions to which they can respond with each Vocabulary word. For example, a person *standing behind the door.* *unobserved* **ELD** ELD.PI.5.12a

Expanding Ask students questions to confirm their understanding. For example, *How do pencils resemble pens?* **ELD** ELD.PI.5.4, ELD.PI.5.12a

Bridging Have partners ask and answer questions about each Vocabulary word. For example, *How might you describe a barking dog?* **ELD** ELD.PI.5.1, ELD.PI.5.12a

▶ Study each Context Card.

▶ Use a dictionary to determine the part of speech of each Vocabulary word.

5 unobserved

Hiding under the rug, this kitten is unobserved, or unseen, by its owner.

6 mature

As cougars mature from cubs to adults, their eyes change from blue to greenish-yellow.

7 particular

A house cat may prefer a particular, or certain, brand of food. It will eat only that kind.

8 available

Big cats can live only where plenty of food is available, or obtainable.

9 ferocious

The savage, ferocious roar of a tiger signals that the animal is angry.

10 contentment

Like wild cats, house cats purr with contentment when they are satisfied.

291

FORMATIVE ASSESSMENT · RtI

Are students able to understand and use Target Vocabulary words?

IF...	THEN...
students **struggle**,	▶ use **Vocabulary in Context Cards** and differentiate the **Vocabulary Reader**, *Big Cats*, for Struggling Readers, p. T370.
students are **on target**,	▶ use **Vocabulary in Context Cards** and differentiate the **Vocabulary Reader**, *Big Cats*, for On-Level Readers, p. T370.
students **excel**,	▶ differentiate the **Vocabulary Reader**, *Big Cats*, for Advanced Readers, p. T371.

 Vocabulary Reader, pp. T370–T371 *Scaffold instruction to the English Learner's proficiency level.*

ENGLISH LANGUAGE SUPPORT

Read and Write Together

Emerging/Expanding

Read Together Display <u>ELL10.2 in Grab-and-Go™ Resources</u> ⌐. Read aloud the title and have students repeat. Then, have students look at the images on the page and predict what they think the text will be about.

• As you read the text, display Vocabulary in Context Cards for *particular, available, ferocious,* and *contentment*. Then, have partners read it together.

• Help students generate statements that use the Vocabulary words. For example, *Predators hunt for a particular kind of food.*

Allow students to include language from the text on **ELL.10.2**. Write and display the sentences.

Write Together Display sentence frames, such as the following, and have partners use them to write complete sentences.

1. Predators can be *ferocious.*

2. Cougars have very *keen* eyesight.

ELD ELD.PI.5.2, ELD.PI.5.4, ELD.PI.5.12a

FIRST READ

Read and Comprehend

▶ SHARE OBJECTIVES

- Determine main ideas and supporting details in informational text.
- Use main ideas to summarize a text.
- Monitor and clarify understanding of the relationships between ideas in a text.
- Engage effectively in collaborative discussion. LANGUAGE

☑ TARGET SKILL

Main Ideas and Details

- Read the top section of **Student Book p. 292** with students.

- Explain to students that the key to understanding an informational text is to identify the main idea of each paragraph within that text. Point out that a main idea may be stated directly or implied.

- Tell students that authors provide details to support each main idea. Supporting details may include facts, examples, and descriptions that relate to the main idea.

- Point out the graphic organizer on **Student Book p. 292**. The web shows the relationship between a main idea and its supporting details, which may include people, events, ideas, or concepts.

- Explain that completing a web can help prepare students to summarize a text. **ELA** RI.5.2, RI.5.3

ENGLISH LANGUAGE SUPPORT Scaffold Anchor Text Before reading the selection, distribute <u>ELL10.3 in Grab-and-Go™ Resources</u> ⬀. Read the page aloud and then have students chorally reread it with you.

Review Main Ideas and Details Reread aloud the third paragraph. Point out the first sentence.

- Tell students that in this paragraph, the first sentence tells the most important idea, or main idea. Explain that the other sentences add supporting details about the main idea.

Guided Practice Display a Web. During reading, complete the web with students.

- Have students identify the main idea and write it in the center of the web. Work with students to identify the supporting details. **ELD** ELD.PI.5.6a

T320 • Unit 2 Lesson 10 (SB p. 292)

Read and Comprehend

☑ TARGET SKILL

Main Ideas and Details As you read "Cougars," look for the **main ideas**, or most important points, that the author makes about cougars and their habitats. Each main idea is supported by **details**, such as facts, examples, and descriptions. You can use these main ideas and important details to **summarize** part or all of a text. To keep track of the main ideas in each part of the selection, use a graphic organizer like this one.

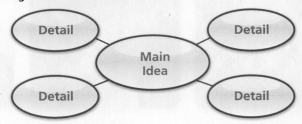

☑ TARGET STRATEGY

Monitor/Clarify As you read "Cougars," remember to **monitor**, or notice, how well you understand the text. If there is something you do not understand, pause to **clarify** it, or make it clear.

292   **ELA** RI.5.2, RI.5.3, SL.5.1c **ELD** ELD.PI.5.1, ELD.PI.5.6a

---

ENGLISH LANGUAGE SUPPORT

Comprehensible Input

Emerging Help students understand the word *main* by presenting some words or phrases that have similar meanings, such as *key, most important,* and *central.*

Expanding Invite students to identify words and phrases that have the same meaning as the word *main.*

Bridging Have partners page through an informational text they have read recently to identify the main idea. Ask them to explain how they identified it as the main idea. **ELD** ELD.PI.5.1, ELD.PI.5.6a

PREVIEW THE TOPIC

Animal Behaviors

Have you ever seen a dog trample the ground in circles before it settles down to sleep? Have you noticed how squirrels drop nuts from trees to crack the shells? Behaviors like these teach us about animals' intelligence and adaptability. Observing the behaviors of wild animals helps us find ways to protect both the animals and their habitats.

In "Cougars," the author shares many details about the behavior of these wild cats. Although cougars are not easy to study, scientists have tried to learn as much as they can about them. In certain regions, cougars are an important part of the ecosystem and play a crucial role in the chain of life.

💬 Talk About It

What kinds of animal behaviors have you noticed? What do you think they mean? Write your answers. Then share your ideas with your classmates.

293

COMPREHENSION STRATEGIES

Use the following strategies flexibly as you read with students by modeling how they can be used to improve comprehension. See scaffolded support for the strategy shown in boldface during this week's reading.

- **Monitor/Clarify**
- **Summarize**
- **Infer/Predict**
- **Visualize**
- **Analyze/Evaluate**
- **Question**

Use the Strategy Projectables S1-S8 ⌐, for additional support.

☑ TARGET STRATEGY

Monitor/Clarify

- Read the bottom section of **Student Book p. 292** with students. Explain that the Target Strategy has two parts. The first is **monitoring**, which allows students to detect problems in understanding. The second part is **clarifying**—seeking answers to questions that arise.

- Tell students that they can monitor their reading by stopping periodically to confirm their understanding of a text. Students can clarify information by rereading parts of the text and identifying details that support the main ideas.

- Tell students that you will demonstrate how to use the strategy when you read "Cougars" together.

PREVIEW THE TOPIC

Animal Behaviors

- Tell students that today they will begin reading "Cougars."

- Read the information at the top of **Student Book p. 293** with students.

- Explain that the animals shown—a cougar and its baby—are the subject of the text.

- Tell students that the photo shows one of the ways cougar mothers care for and protect their young. A mother's care is critical, because cougar babies are not able to protect themselves at birth. They depend on their mothers for survival.

Talk About It

- To prepare students for discussion, ask: *What are some animal behaviors you have noticed?* Have students use the questions to think about the types of animal behaviors they have seen or read about.

- Create a list of the students' replies. Guide students to ask questions about any new information they learned from other students. Have students make comments that contribute to the discussion and link to the remarks of others. **ELA** SL.5.1c **ELD** ELD.PI.5.1

ENGLISH LANGUAGE SUPPORT Access Prior Knowledge: All Proficiencies Use the image on Lesson 10 Language Support Card ⌐ to review the selection topic with students. Show the completed web again and help students summarize its content.

Read and Comprehend (SB p. 293) • **T321**

FIRST READ

Read the Anchor Text

GENRE

Informational Text

- Read the genre information on **Student Book p. 294** with students.

- Preview the selection with students, and model identifying characteristics of informational texts.

> **Think Aloud** *Each section seems to discuss a new main idea about cougars. The text has domain-specific vocabulary, photographs, and captions that enhance the text.*

- As you preview, ask students to identify other features of informational texts.

ENGLISH LANGUAGE SUPPORT Access Prior Knowledge: All Proficiencies Write the following statements on the board.
1. All informational texts follow the same format.
2. Informational texts are always easy to understand.
3. Wild animals have traits that help them survive.
4. Cougars don't take good care of their young.
Have pairs take turns reading a statement to each other and sharing their opinions. Provide these frames for support: *The statement says _____. I agree/disagree because _____. What do you think?* Have students record their opinions to refer to later. During reading, have students check their opinions and note whether they have changed.

ELA RI.5.10 **ELD** ELD.PI.5.6a

Lesson 10

ANCHOR TEXT

Cougars

GENRE

Informational text gives facts and details about a topic. As you read, look for:
▶ information that is clearly organized
▶ domain-specific vocabulary that aids understanding
▶ photographs and captions that enhance the text

294 **ELA** RI.5.2, RI.5.4, RI.5.10, RF.5.4a, RF.5.4b
ELD ELD.PI.5.6a, ELD.PI.5.12a

MEET THE AUTHOR

PATRICIA CORRIGAN

Patricia Corrigan began writing for her local newspaper while she was still in high school. Since then, she has been a writer for the *St. Louis Post-Dispatch* and has published numerous magazine articles, nonfiction books for adults, and nature books for children. She loves to travel and has taken trips to Argentina and Egypt.

Scaffold Close Reading

Strategies for Annotation

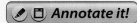

Annotate it!

As you read the selection with students, look for **Annotate it!** . It indicates opportunities for students to annotate the text independently.

Think Through the Text

FIRST READ

Develop comprehension through
- Guided Questioning
- Target Strategy: Monitor/Clarify
- Vocabulary in Context

Analyze the Text

SECOND READ

Support analyzing short sections of text:
- Main Ideas and Details
- Explain Scientific Ideas
- Domain-Specific Vocabulary
- Text Structure

Use directed note-taking by working with students to complete a graphic organizer during reading. Distribute copies of Graphic Organizer 15.

Independent Reading

- Students analyze the text independently, using the Reader's Guide on pp. 109–110 of the Reader's Notebook . (See p. T338 for instructional support.)

- Students read independently in a self-selected trade book.

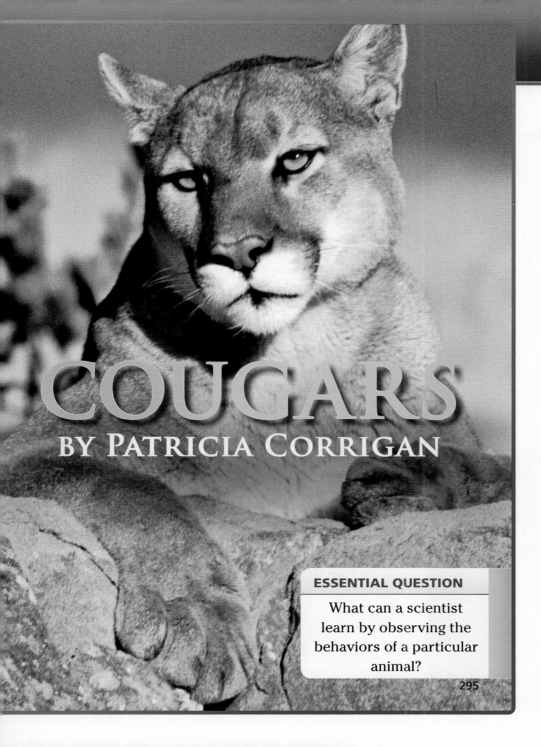

COUGARS

BY PATRICIA CORRIGAN

ESSENTIAL QUESTION

What can a scientist learn by observing the behaviors of a particular animal?

295

READER AND TASK CONSIDERATIONS

Determine the level of additional support your students will need to read and comprehend "Cougars" successfully.

READERS

- **Motivate** Ask students to share what they hope to learn from the selection.

- **Talk It Over** Use Lesson 10 Language Support Card ⬀ for a discussion about predatory animals.

- **Access Knowledge and Experiences** Remind students of the information on **Student Book p. 293**. Ask them to write one other thing they know about animal behaviors.

TASKS

- **Increase Scaffolding** Guide students to use the Question strategy as they read the text. Have students pause to ask and answer questions they have about the behaviors of cougars.

- **Foster Independence** Have small groups of motivated readers read the text together. Have them think about and discuss the text information from the point of view of an animal conservationist.

ESSENTIAL QUESTION

Read aloud the Essential Question on **Student Book p. 295**: *What can a scientist learn by observing the behaviors of a particular animal?* Then tell students to think about this question as they read "Cougars."

Predictive Writing

- Tell students that they will write a paragraph to explain what they expect "Cougars" to be about. Ask them to think about how the Essential Question relates to what they noticed while previewing the selection or what they already know from their own experiences or past readings.

- Guide students to think about the genre of the selection to help them write.

Set Purpose

- Tell students that good readers set a purpose for reading based on their preview of the selection, what they know about the genre, and what they want to learn from the selection.

- Model setting a reading purpose.

Think Aloud *Informational text provides factual information about a topic, such as cougars. One purpose for reading would be to learn more about this animal or about how wild animals generally survive and adapt to different environments.*

- Have students set their own purpose for reading. Ask several students to share their purposes for reading. **ELA** RF.5.4a

ENGLISH LANGUAGE SUPPORT **Preteach Academic English: Emerging/Expanding** Guide students to complete the Academic English activities on Language Support Card 10.

Think Through the Text

Cite Text Evidence

1. *What text evidence can you use to conclude that cougars are rarely seen by humans? Sample answer: They are good at concealing themselves, avoiding danger, and sneaking up on prey.*

2. *What do the examples of nicknames used for cougars suggest about them? They are ghostlike—quiet, stealthy, and capable of appearing and disappearing quickly.* **ELA** RI.5.3

3. *What evidence does the author present to support the point that cougars are good at adapting to different conditions? Quote accurately from the text to support your answer. They live in many types of environments, from mountains to forests to grassy plains. The author says that "cougars that live in northern mountains tend to . . . have a thicker coat of fur," have "learned to climb trees," and "can swim if necessary."* **ELA** RI.5.1, RI.5.2, RI.5.8 **ELD** ELD.PI.5.6a

ENGLISH LANGUAGE SUPPORT Break this question into parts. *What point does the author make about cougars and their ability to adapt? What evidence from the text supports her point?*

Cougars are seldom seen and rarely heard. In fact, they often live their entire lives unobserved by humans!

But we do know that these members of the cat family live in eleven western U.S. states. They are found from the southernmost tip of Alaska down to where the California border meets Mexico and east all the way to the edge of Texas. Their cousins, Florida panthers, live in Florida. In Canada, cougars are found in British Columbia and parts of Alberta. Cougars also live throughout Mexico, Central America, and South America.

In different areas of the world, cougars have different names. They may be called mountain lions, wildcats, pumas, painters, fire cats, swamp lions, or catamounts. In Mexico, Spanish for cougar is *el león* (leh OHN), which means "the lion." And sometimes they are known by nicknames like "ghost of the wilderness" and "ghost walker."

Fortunately, cougars are able to live in many different habitats. Over time, they have adapted, or evolved, for living in places such as snow-capped mountains, jungles thick with vegetation, cool pine forests, grassy plains, and murky swamps. For instance, cougars that live in northern mountains tend to be larger and have a thicker coat of fur than cougars that live elsewhere. They learned to climb trees. And they also can swim if necessary, but usually prefer to stay dry—like their relative, the house cat!

296

ENGLISH LANGUAGE SUPPORT

How English Works: Interpretive

Using Verb Tenses As students read this selection, have them look at the verb tenses that the author uses. Remind students that authors use verb types and tenses that match their writing purpose and topic. For example, authors might use the past tense to retell a story or the present tense for a science explanation. Read aloud the paragraph on **Student Book p. 297** while students follow along in the text.

• Help students identify the verbs and their tenses and explain their functions. Sample answers: *measures, stands, weigh (present tense); These verbs describe cougar traits in the present tense and help the author explain the size of wild cougars.*

• Have students turn to partners and practice using verbs and verb tenses in sentences of their own.

• Collect examples from volunteers and write them on board.
ELD ELD.PII.5.3

The average cougar measures from 3.3 to 5.3 feet long and stands about 2 feet high at the shoulder. Adult male cougars weigh up to 225 pounds, and adult females usually are slightly smaller. A cougar's tail may measure up to 32 inches, almost two-thirds the length of the animal's body.

ANALYZE THE TEXT

Main Ideas and Details What is the topic of this selection? How do you know? Choose a paragraph on one of these two pages. State its main idea and explain how it is supported by details.

Cougars don't hunt from trees, but a high branch makes a good lookout spot.

297

Main Ideas and Details

Analyze the Text

- Read the Analyze the Text box on **Student Book p. 297** with students. Ask students to identify the topic of the selection and tell how they know. *The topic is cougars. All of the information in the text is related to cougars.*

- Remind students that main ideas in a text, either stated or implied, are supported by details.

- Display Projectable 10.2 ⤢, and tell students that you will work together to complete the graphic organizer using information from the text. Then, distribute Graphic Organizer 15 ⤢.

- Read aloud the fourth paragraph on p. 296. Work with students to state its main idea. Record it in the web, and have students add supporting details from the text.

- Have students continue identifying main ideas and details in small sections of the text. Have them think about the text's overall main idea as they read. **ELA** RI.5.2, RI.5.3, RI.5.8 **ELD** ELD.PI.5.6a

> 🖉 📄 ***Annotate it!*** As students read the text, have them underline the main ideas and highlight the details that support those ideas.

FIRST READ

Think Through the Text

Cite Text Evidence

4 *What is the relationship between cougars and animals, such as the bobcat, lynx, tiger, and lion?* All of these animals are cats. Each one is a different species of cat.

ENGLISH LANGUAGE SUPPORT Ask this question another way. *What does the cougar have in common with the bobcat, lynx, tiger, and lion? In what ways are these animals different?*

☑ TARGET STRATEGY

Monitor/Clarify

Read aloud the second paragraph on **Student Book p. 298**. Then, model the strategy:

> **Think Aloud** *There is something that is not completely clear as I monitor my reading. The author says that cougars have little fat, which is a common insulation for animals. I was confused until I read that instead of fat, cougars have fur coats. This explains how cougars keep warm in cold climates even though they have little fat.*

Tell students to practice using the Monitor/Clarify strategy as they continue reading. **ELA** RI.5.10

5 *How might the differences in cougars' coloring be related to the habitats in which they live?* Their coloring varies so they can blend in with their particular surroundings **ELA** RI.5.3 **ELD** ELD.PI.5.6a

Cougars have good balance and can easily leap over fallen trees and onto rocks without slowing down.

4 The cougar is one species (SPEE sees), or kind, of wild cat. Cougars are medium-sized, along with bobcats and lynxes. Tigers, lions, and leopards all are larger and heavier.

Cougars are muscular and sleek, with little fat on their bodies. Fat usually serves as excellent insulation and keeps an animal's body warm. But because cougars have little of this kind of insulation, they have another natural defense against the cold: their fur coats keep them warm.

The layer of hair closest to the skin, called the underfur, is woolly and short. The top layer is made up of longer hairs, called guard hairs. These hairs are hollow and trap the air to keep cold temperatures from reaching the animal's skin.

Unlike humans, cougars have no sweat glands, so the cougars that live in warm climates cool themselves the same way dogs do, by panting to release heat from their bodies.

> **ANALYZE THE TEXT**
>
> **Domain-Specific Vocabulary** The author defines several domain-specific words on pages 298–299. How does the author's use of these words help strengthen the text? Does she seem more or less credible as a science writer? Why?

298

FORMATIVE ASSESSMENT ▲ 3 / 2 / 1 **RtI**

Monitor/Clarify

IF students do not check their understanding as they read… **THEN**, revisit the Monitor/Clarify strategy by modeling how to think about the differences in how cougars appear.

> **Think Aloud** *The text describes how cougars look, but it also explains that there is variety in their coloring. I wonder why this is true. As I keep reading, I see that the author writes, "Their coloring helps them blend in with their surroundings." Since cougars live in different habitats, I think their coloring depends on where they live.*

Guide students to understand that while all cougars share the same basic features, individual animals may vary, with some variations based on habitat.

Cougars' coats are usually tawny, or orange-brown. They also may be gray, sandy brown, reddish-brown, and tan. All adult cougars have black markings on the sides of the muzzle, or snout, where the whiskers are. Some people say this area looks as if the cougar has a "mustache." If cougars were less secretive, scientists might be able to tell individual animals apart by the dark patterns on the muzzles, but few of the animals are ever seen.

The chin is white, as is the area right under the pinkish-brown nose. The tips of their tails also are black. The underside of most cougars is light, sometimes nearly white. At first glance, adult cougars resemble female lions.

Their coloring helps them blend in with their surroundings. It is good camouflage (KAM uh flahj) and helps them hide from their prey (PRAY), or the animals they hunt for food.

Cougars have good eyesight. In fact, vision is their best-developed sense. Researchers believe that they can see moving prey from long distances. The cougar's yellow eyes have large, round pupils that take in all available light. That helps the animal see at night almost as well as during the day.

299

Domain-Specific Vocabulary

 Analyze the Text

- Remind students that informational texts often include vocabulary that is specific to the topic or subject. This domain-specific vocabulary may include unfamiliar words, as well as familiar words that have a special meaning within the context of the selection.

- Read the Analyze the Text box on **Student Book p. 298** with students. Have students review the text on pp. 298–299.

- To help students answer the questions about domain-specific vocabulary, ask: *What are some examples of domain-specific vocabulary on these pages? Examples include* underfur *and* guard hairs. *How does the use of these words strengthen the text? It provides detailed information that is new to the reader. Does the use of domain-specific vocabulary make the text more credible? Sample answer: Yes. It makes the author seem knowledgeable about her subject.*

ELA RI.5.4, L.5.6 **ELD** ELD.PI.5.6a, ELD.PI.5.6b, ELD.PI.5.7

✏ 📄 Annotate it! As they read the text, have students highlight domain-specific vocabulary and the context clues that help them understand it.

DOMAIN: Life Science

LESSON TOPIC: Animal Behaviors

Cross-Curricular Connection Animal camouflage takes many forms. Cougars have colors and patterns that help them blend in to their surroundings. Other animals can actively change their appearance depending on their surroundings. Still others have an appearance that can trick a predator into staying away. For example, some insects have markings that make them look larger and more fearsome than they actually are. Others look like another animal, such as a toxic snake.

Think Through the Text

Cite Text Evidence

6 *Why do you think cougars have developed such strong senses of hearing and smell, as well as sight? Use text evidence to support your answer. These senses aid the cougar in avoiding danger and finding prey.* **ELA** RI.5.3

7 *What do human beings use to collect the kind of information cougars collect through their whiskers? Human beings mainly use their hands and fingers to collect information through touch.*

8 *What conclusion can you draw from the fact that cougars have several different types of teeth? Cougars use their teeth for different purposes. These may include killing prey, taking meat from prey, and chewing food.*

ENGLISH LANGUAGE SUPPORT Provide these sentence frames to support participation. *Cougars use their teeth to _____. I think this means they have different types of teeth because _____.* **ELD** ELD.PI.5.6a

A keen sense of hearing is important for cougars. They even can move their small, rounded ears to take in sounds coming from different directions. Cougars also have a strong sense of smell, which can really be useful when following prey. Still, their sense of smell is not as well developed as their senses of sight or hearing.

6

Like all of their cat relatives, cougars have whiskers. These sensitive hairs are also called vibrissae (vy BRIHS ee). They grow on either side of the animal's nose and mouth, above the eyes, and sometimes on the chin.

These whiskers vary in length, but most of the whiskers found on the muzzle are long enough to stretch past the side of the face and back to the edge of the ear. The cougar uses whiskers to gather information through touch. With its whiskers, a cougar can determine the height of the grass, the width of the space under a rock, and whether a bush would be easy or difficult to push through.

7

Cougars make a variety of sounds, or vocalizations. Their meow, which is a sign of contentment, is much louder than that of a pet cat. They also purr when they are contented. Cougars hiss first and then growl when they feel threatened. Unlike lions, cougars cannot roar.

Like all cats, cougars groom themselves. Grooming helps keep their coats clean. They use their rough tongues to remove any loose hair and to untangle any matted hair. Female cougars groom their babies constantly, and young siblings have been seen grooming one another.

Mothers pick up their kittens by the scruff of the neck to move them one at a time to a new den site.

300

Expand Language Production

Emerging For questions, accept one-word responses and then expand them. For example, if students answer question 7 with the word *fingers*, expand it by saying, "Yes, humans use their fingers to touch and feel."

Expanding Provide a sentence frame for each answer and have students complete it. Then, have students read the complete response.

Bridging Encourage students to respond to the questions in complete sentences. Provide corrective feedback as needed.

When a cougar sees an enemy nearby, it may try to look ferocious and scare it away by showing its teeth and growling.

Cougars have very strong jaws. And they have three kinds of teeth, 24 in all. The carnassial (kar NASS ee uhl) teeth are located on both the top and bottom jaws. They are long and sharp, used for slicing or shearing. The canine (KAY nyn) teeth are thick and sharp, used for puncturing. The incisors (ihn SYZ ohrz) are small and straight, used for cutting and some chewing. But cougars don't chew their food very well. They mostly gulp down large chunks. **8**

Most adult cougars are solitary, which means they live alone. They protect their territory from intruders, including other cougars. Each cougar needs a lot of space, an average of as much as 200 square miles for adult males and less than half that for adult females. They may walk as far as 30 miles in a day, searching for food or patrolling their territory.

301

SECOND READ

Practice Fluency

Stress Read aloud the text on **Student Book p. 300** while students follow along. As you read the text, model placing appropriate stress on key words, phrases, and ideas.

- Tell students that stressing key words, phrases, and ideas can help listeners recognize the main ideas that the author is trying to convey. It is also appropriate to stress words that highlight a key supporting detail.

- Have students echo read each sentence after you read it. Make sure they apply the appropriate stress.

- Have students explain what techniques they used to stress key words, phrases, and ideas. The Fluency lesson on p. T348 provides further opportunities for modeling and practice with stress. **ELA** RF.5.4a

> **DOMAIN: Life Science**

LESSON TOPIC: Animal Behaviors

Cross-Curricular Connection Scientists have long argued about how and to what extent animals "talk" or use language. Today, we know that animals often use sounds to communicate a variety of complicated ideas. Some species appear to have the ability to communicate through sounds in a way that is not unlike human language. Discuss with students why the ability to share information and ideas verbally might be important to a species.

Think Through the Text

Cite Text Evidence

9 *Quote details from the text that show how young cougars look different from adults. Why do you think camouflage for young animals might be different than for adult animals? Baby cougars' fur is "speckled with brown spots," and they "have curly tails" and "blue eyes," which turn yellow as they get older. Adult cougars are likely to be active in hunting and pursuing animals, while baby cougars are likely to be trying to avoid detection by predators.*

ELA RI.5.1 **ELD** ELD.PI.5.6a

✓ TARGET STRATEGY

Monitor/Clarify

Tell students to practice the Monitor/Clarify strategy as they read **Student Book pp. 302–303** silently. Invite volunteers to explain places where they experienced confusion or a lack of clarity and how they resolved it. **ELA** RI.5.10

10 *How does a mother cougar help her kittens survive their first months of life? She keeps their fur clean so they won't be located by predators. She also provides milk and shelter for the kittens, moving them to new places when she senses danger.* **ELA** RI.5.2, RI.5.3 **ELD** ELD.PI.5.6a

Males and females look alike, but it is the female that cares for the young.

Newborn kittens have soft, fluffy-looking fur that is speckled with brown spots. This coloring helps camouflage them.

The spots disappear when the kittens are about eight months old. Kittens also have curly tails, which straighten out as they get older.

9 The kittens are born with blue eyes, which stay closed for about the first two weeks. Their eye color soon changes to yellow.

Kittens are totally dependent on their mother for food. They nurse for up to three months. Immediately after birth, and often in the next few weeks, the female licks the kittens to clean their fur. This helps them stay safe from enemies that might find the den site by detecting the scent of the newborn kittens.

If a female cougar thinks that her kittens are in danger in a particular spot, she often finds a new hiding place and moves them. A mother cougar will do whatever is necessary to keep the kittens away from dangerous predators, or enemies, such as wolves.

302

FORMATIVE ASSESSMENT — 3 2 1 RtI

Monitor/Clarify

IF students have difficulty applying the Monitor/Clarify strategy… **THEN**, use this model:

Think Aloud *On p. 303, I'm not sure why the author writes, "The mother makes no special effort to catch small prey for her small offspring." I'm going to stop and think about this. Why is the author making this point? How does it relate to the discussion of the mother's treatment of her babies? I think the author is pointing out how the mother teaches her babies important survival skills.*

Have students read the last sentence in the paragraph, and use the strategy to explain how cougar mothers teach their young.

When the mother leaves to hunt for food, the kittens stay hidden and quiet at the den site. When the kittens are about two months old, their teeth have grown and they nurse less. Their mother begins to bring them food every two or three days. The mother makes no special effort to catch small prey for her small offspring. At first, the young kittens just want to play with the food, no matter what she brings. One of the first lessons the mother teaches her kittens is how to eat this new food.

By example, she shows them how to bite, how to tear meat off the bone, and how to chew. She also teaches the kittens that their rough tongues are good for cleaning the meat off bones. After about six months the kittens are good at eating this food, and they begin to explore away from the den site. **10**

> **ANALYZE THE TEXT**
>
> **Explain Scientific Ideas** What ideas has the author shared about cougar kitten development on these two pages? How do these ideas relate to what you have learned about the lives of adult cougars?

This young cougar still has some of its baby spots. It is practicing stalking its prey.

303

FOR STANDARD ENGLISH LEARNERS Pronunciation Some students may need help mastering Standard English pronunciations when reading aloud or speaking in a more formal register. Students may have trouble voicing /th/ at the beginning of words, such as *this* or *that*. They may pronounce the /th/ sound as /d/, saying "dis" for *this*. Write this sentence on the board: *She also teaches the kittens that their rough tongues are good for cleaning the meat off bones.* Read the sentence aloud, emphasizing the /th/ sound in *that*, *their*, and *the*. Have students echo your reading several times.

Explain Scientific Ideas

- Read the Analyze the Text box on **Student Book p. 303** with students.

- Remind students that in general, the author of an informational text seeks to inform readers about a particular topic.

- Explain that in a science-related text, an author may use descriptive details that will help readers clearly understand scientific ideas and concepts. Tell students that identifying and being able to explain the relationships between the ideas and concepts in a text is an important step in understanding the text as a whole.

ENGLISH LANGUAGE SUPPORT Tell students that in informational texts, authors might rely heavily on transitional words and phrases to show readers how details or ideas are related. Point out the author's use of *At first, By example,* and *After about six months* on **Student Book p. 303**, and talk with students about how these phrases help tie together the information about mother cougars teaching their cubs about food.

- Guide students to explain the key ideas the author presents about cougar kitten development. Ask: *Which aspects of cougar growth and development does the author provide details about on these pages? What types of changes does the author describe? The author describes the appearance of a cougar kitten and its changing relationship with its mother—from total dependence at first to gradual independence. The text gives the specific example of food, beginning with nursing and progressing to letting babies eat their own food. How does this information relate to what you've already learned about adult cougars? The author has explained that cougars grow up to be solitary animals, and they must hunt for their food and eat raw meat. By teaching the kittens how to eat meat at a young age, the mother is helping them learn to thrive in the wild.* **ELA** RI.5.2, RI.5.3 **ELD** ELD.PI.5.6a

✎ 🖥 *Annotate it!* Have students highlight key details that help them understand the scientific ideas presented in the text.

Think Through the Text

Cite Text Evidence

11 *For what purpose do cougar kittens remain with their mothers? The young cougars need to learn certain life skills, such as how to hunt, from their mothers.* **ELA** RI.5.2, RI.5.3 **ELD** ELD.PI.5.6a

12 *What factors influence the life span of a cougar? Cougars' life spans are affected by the quality of the habitat in which they are able to settle, such as the amount of food and water available.* **ELA** RI.5.2, RI.5.3 **ELD** ELD.PI.5.6a

13 *What is the main idea of this page? Sample answer: Cougar kittens learn survival skills from their mothers.* **ELA** RI.5.2 **ELD** ELD.PI.5.6a

Classroom Conversation

Have students discuss "Cougars," either in small groups or as a whole class. Provide this prompt to focus their discussion: *How might learning about an animal inspire people to protect it?* Have students use text evidence to support their thoughts. Remind students to follow the rules for collaborative discussions, to respond to each other in complete sentences, and to thoughtfully answer each other's questions. **ELA** SL.5.1a, SL.5.1b **ELD** ELD.PI.5.1, ELD.PI.5.4

The kittens stay with their mother for about eighteen months. During this time, she teaches them many things about surviving in their habitat. As the kittens mature, the mother cougar takes them hunting. They learn how to find and carefully follow prey. This is called stalking.

They also learn when to pounce, or jump out suddenly, to capture the prey. They are taught how to hide their kill and protect it from other animals. With a
11 lot of practice, they learn to hunt for themselves.

Then, the young cougars go out on their own to find a territory and a mate. If they find a good habitat with plenty of prey animals and water in the area, cougars
12 **13** may live about eight to ten years.

304

ENGLISH LANGUAGE SUPPORT

Collaborate: Monitor/Clarify

Teach/Model Write *monitor* and *clarify*, and explain the meanings of the terms. *When we monitor our reading, we pay attention to whether we are understanding what we read in a text. When we clarify, we reread or ask questions to make the meaning clear.* Use a Think Aloud to model monitoring and clarifying understanding of "Cougars."

Think Aloud *When I read about how cougars use their whiskers, I monitored my reading. I did not understand at first. Then I reread that paragraph to clarify my understanding. I realized the cougars must brush their whiskers around something to figure out how big it is.*

Guided Practice Have pairs of students read the paragraph about grooming on Student Book p. 300. Have them monitor and clarify their understanding. Remind students to look for main ideas and details as they clarify.

- Review **Teach Academic Language** on <u>Lesson 10 Language Support Card</u> ⤤. **ELD** ELD.PI.5.6a

Cougar eyesight may be five times better than human eyesight.

305

🔍 Language Detective

Text Structure

- Remind students that while all informational texts are built around main ideas and details, they may also be structured in ways that show relationships between ideas. Review some of these text structures, such as cause and effect and sequential order, with students.

- Point out that authors may imply relationships between ideas or events, or they may use signal words to clearly state those relationships. Read aloud the following examples, and have students identify the relationship each signal word indicates:

  The ground is wet because it rained earlier. (cause and effect)
  After school, we went to the library. (sequence)
  Since it isn't cold out today, we can leave our coats at home. (cause and effect)

- Read **Student Book p. 304** with students and model the thinking.

  Think Aloud *The first sentence of the last paragraph says, "Then, the young cougars go out on their own to find a territory and a mate." I know that then is a sequence signal word. I think it is showing a relationship between the cougars venturing out on their own, and the growth steps they take beforehand. The text is saying that the cougars look for their territories and mates after they have matured and learned to hunt.*

- Have partners or small groups reread pp. 302–304. Tell them to look for sequence signal words and phrases that show relationships between ideas. Have students share their findings and explain how the text's structure helps them understand its key points. Provide the following examples of sequence signal phrases if students need help. *Soon after that in a few months when they have finished.* **ELA** RI.5.3, RI.5.5 **ELD** ELD.PI.5.6a

  🖊️ 🗐 **Annotate it!** Have students highlight signal words and phrases that indicate text structure or show relationships between ideas in the text.

Scaffolded Practice and Application

Emerging Read another page from the selection with students. Pause after each paragraph. Ask: *Is there anything you don't understand? Should I read it again? Are there any words you don't know?* Guide students to clarify the information.

Expanding Have partners read a page from the selection together. Tell them to pause after each paragraph and ask: *Do I understand this paragraph? Should I read it again? Are there any words I don't know? How can I clarify the information?*

Bridging Have partners read two pages from "Cougars" together. Tell them to pause after each paragraph to monitor and clarify their understanding.

Dig Deeper *Use Clues to Analyze the Text*

▶ SHARE OBJECTIVES

- Determine main ideas and explain how they are supported by details.
- Understand and explain relationships between ideas in a text.
- Acquire and use domain-specific words.
- Understand and analyze text structure.

ENGLISH LANGUAGE SUPPORT

Use Sentence Frames

Emerging Discuss with students some of the details on **Student Book p. 302**. Work with students to complete the following sentence frame based on the details: *These details are mainly about _____.*

Expanding Have students use p. 302 to fill in this sentence frame: *Two details about cougar kittens on this page are _____ and _____.*

Bridging Have students use the information on p. 302 to complete this sentence frame: *The main idea that the details on this page support is _____.* **ELD** ELD.PI.5.6a

---

Text-Based Comprehension

1   Teach/Model

Terms About Informational Text

main ideas major points an author wants readers to understand

supporting details facts, examples, descriptions, and other evidence used to develop main ideas

scientific ideas concepts or principles that relate to science

domain-specific words vocabulary specific to a content area

text structure the way information is organized in a nonfiction text

---

- Remind students that they have just read an informational text about cougars.

- Read **Student Book p. 306** with students, and remind them that **main ideas** in a text may be either stated or implied, and that readers may need to infer implied main ideas using **supporting details**. Tell students that supporting details may provide examples of a main idea, or evidence of it.

- Model how to apply the skill of identifying main ideas and details, using the third paragraph of **Student Book p. 296**.

  Think Aloud *To identify the main idea, I ask myself, "What is this paragraph about?" It's about different names being used for cougars in different parts of the world. The text provides these details to support the main idea: Cougars may be called* mountain lions, wildcats, pumas, painters, fire cats, swamp lions, *or* catamounts.

- Next, read **Student Book p. 307** with students.

- Explain that authors of science-related informational texts must explain **scientific ideas** with their audience in mind, describing concepts, relationships, and principles in ways that are clear and accessible without assuming too much background knowledge.

- Point out that informational texts may contain some unfamiliar vocabulary. These **domain-specific words** show the author's expertise and help expand the reader's knowledge of the subject.

  🔍 **Language Detective: Cause and Effect** Explain to students that information in nonfiction texts can be structured in several different ways. For example, an informational text may be organized in a way that shows events in chronological order, or that shows relationships between events or between causes and effects.

Dig Deeper

Use Clues to Analyze the Text

Use these pages to learn about Main Ideas and Details, Explaining Scientific Ideas, and Domain-Specific Vocabulary. Then read "Cougars" again to apply what you learned.

Main Ideas and Details

Informational texts, such as "Cougars," contain several main ideas and supporting details. A **main idea** is a major point brought out in the text or in a section of the text. Sometimes, a main idea is stated directly. If it is not stated directly, the reader must look at the information in that part of the text to infer, or guess, the main idea.

Supporting details are key facts, examples, descriptions, and other text evidence used to develop each main idea. For example, the main idea of the third paragraph on page 298 is that cougars have different layers of hair. The supporting details name and explain the purpose of each layer. As you revisit "Cougars," identify main ideas and details, and use them to summarize the text.

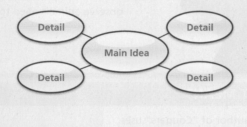

Explain Scientific Ideas

The purpose of most informational texts is to inform, or to share knowledge about a topic with readers. When that topic is related to science, the author carefully explains scientific ideas in ways that will help readers gain a solid understanding. For example, the author of "Cougars" uses clear, descriptive details to explain the ideas of cougar behavior and development.

Domain-Specific Vocabulary

Authors of informational texts often use **domain-specific words.** These are words from the content area that they are writing about— such as social studies, art, or science. Using domain-specific vocabulary enables authors to explain ideas precisely. It also shows the author's expertise or familiarity with the subject and lends credibility to his or her writing.

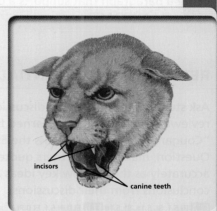
incisors
canine teeth

---

2 Guided Practice/Apply

Analyze the Text

Begin a second read of "Cougars" with students. Use the stopping points and instructional support to guide students to analyze the text:

- Main Ideas and Details, p. T325 ELA RI.5.2 ELD ELD.PI.5.6a
- Domain-Specific Vocabulary, p. T327 ELA RI.5.4, L.5.6 ELD ELD.PI.5.6b
- Explain Scientific Ideas, p. T331 ELA RI.5.3 ELD ELD.PI.5.6a
- Text Structure, p. T333 ELA RI.5.5 ELD ELD.PI.5.6a

Directed Note Taking The graphic organizer will be completed with students during the second read on p. T325.

FORMATIVE ASSESSMENT △ RtI

Are students able to identify main ideas and supporting details?

IF...	THEN...
students struggle,	**Differentiate Comprehension** for Struggling Readers, p. T372.
students are on track,	**Differentiate Comprehension** for On-Level Readers, p. T372.
students excel,	**Differentiate Comprehension** for Advanced Readers, p. T373.

Differentiate Comprehension, pp. T372–T373
Scaffold instruction to the English Learner's proficiency level.

SECOND READ

Your Turn

Cite Text Evidence

▶ **SHARE OBJECTIVES**

- Pose and respond to questions about scientific observation, using text evidence as support.
- Determine the meanings of domain-specific words and phrases.
- Write a paragraph that supports a clearly stated opinion. LANGUAGE

RETURN TO THE ESSENTIAL QUESTION

Ask students to prepare for discussion by reviewing what they have learned from "Cougars." While they discuss the Essential Question, make sure partners quote text evidence accurately as they review key ideas and draw conclusions from their discussions.

ELA RI.5.1, SL.5.1a, SL.5.1d **ELD** ELD.PI.5.1, ELD.PI.5.6a

Classroom Conversation

Have the class continue the discussion by explaining their answers to the three questions. Encourage students to make comments that contribute to the discussion and to elaborate on each other's remarks. See Digital Lesson: Speaking Constructively 🗗.

ELA SL.5.1a, SL.5.1c **ELD** ELD.PI.5.1

ENGLISH LANGUAGE SUPPORT Use sentence frames such as the following to support discussion.

I think the author feels _____ about cougars because _____.

I was surprised by_____.

I think scientists need _____ qualities to observe animals because _____.

As students share their ideas, tell them to use text evidence to support their responses.

ELD ELD.PI.5.1, ELD.PI.5.4, ELD.PI.5.11a

Your Turn

RETURN TO THE ESSENTIAL QUESTION

 Turn and Talk Review the selection to prepare to discuss this question: *What can a scientist learn by observing the behaviors of a particular animal?* As you discuss, take turns reviewing each other's key points.

Classroom Conversation

Continue your discussion of "Cougars" by using text evidence to explain your answers to these questions:

1. How do you think the author feels about cougars? Why?

2. What did you learn about cougars in this selection that surprised you?

3. What qualities do scientists who observe animals need to have?

WHAT DOES IT MEAN?

Look It Up The author of "Cougars" uses many domain-specific words. These words, such as *prey, whiskers, muzzle, vocalizations, matted, carnassial,* and *canine,* are directly related to the subject of cougars. Choose five domain-specific words from the text. Look them up in a print or digital dictionary. Write a new sentence for each word. Then share your sentences with a partner.

ENGLISH LANGUAGE SUPPORT

How English Works

Using Verb Types Before students begin their discussion, have them think about the verb types and verb tense for their discussion topic and purpose. Review some verb types with students: *learn, observe* (doing verbs). Help different proficiency levels think about their topics and build word banks of verbs for their discussion. Have students identify the verb types that they will use in their discussion. **ELD** ELD.PII.5.3

Performance Task

WRITE ABOUT READING

my WriteSmart

Response The last section of the text is about mother cougars and their kittens. Would you agree that one of the main ideas of this section could be stated as "mother cougars know best"? Write a paragraph explaining your opinion about the main ideas of this section of text. Show how the details in the text support the main ideas. Use specific quotations to develop your paragraph.

Writing Tip

State your opinion at the beginning of your paragraph. Be sure to include a conclusion that restates this opinion and makes it memorable for readers.

309

ENGLISH LANGUAGE SUPPORT

Collaborative Writing

Step 1 Guide students to complete a web to build an opinion and support it with reasons based in text evidence.

Step 2 Explain that you will work together as a class to write a response to reading by using the completed graphic organizer. Point out to students that they will say ideas and sentences and you will write them down for the group to see and read.

Step 3 Have students develop the response by referring to the graphic organizer and answering questions such as these:

- What words will help begin this response?
- What information should we include? How do we say that in a sentence?
- What is the first reason that we should write?
- What text evidence will we use?

Step 4 Read the unfinished response aloud to students. Repeat, and have students read aloud with you. Ask students if they see or hear anything they would like to change.

Extra Scaffold Without purposely making mistakes, revise in the moment by using Think Alouds. **ELD** ELD.PI.5.2

WHAT DOES IT MEAN?

Review the definition of *domain-specific words.* Choose one of the words listed on p. 308 and work with students to use a print or digital dictionary to look it up. Note the pronunciation and identify the appropriate definition of the word, if the entry lists more than one. Point out that noting the part of speech in the entry will help students use the word correctly in a sentence. Help students develop a sentence that conveys the meaning of the word. Then have students complete the activity independently. **ELA** RI.5.4, L.5.4c, L.5.6 **ELD** ELD.PI.5.12a

---

WRITE ABOUT READING

Performance Task

Guide students through the activity. As they review the reading to gather supporting evidence for their paragraph, remind them that they must quote the text and restate main ideas and details accurately. **ELA** RI.5.1, RI.5.2, W.5.9b, W.5.10

ENGLISH LANGUAGE SUPPORT Tell students to state the topic and their opinion in the opening sentence. Provide this frame:

> *One of the main ideas of the last section of the text (is)/(is not) "mother cougars know best."*

Tell students to add reasons for their opinion using these frames:

> *I think this because ____.*
> *The text supports this by saying ____.*

Remind students to use verb tenses correctly in their paragraphs. See Digital Lesson: Writing to Sources. **ELD** ELD.PI.5.6a, ELD.PI.5.11a, ELD.PII.5.3

Writing Tip Make sure that students read the Writing Tip before beginning their paragraph. Their introductory statement should clearly identify the topic and state their opinion. Their conclusion should express a final thought about their opinion. **ELA** W.5.1a, W.5.1d, W.5.9b, W.5.10 **ELD** ELD.PI.5.11a

---

my WriteSmart Have students complete the Write About Reading activity through *my*WriteSmart. Students will read the prompt within *my*WriteSmart and have access to multiple writing resources, including the Student eBook, Writing Rubrics, and Graphic Organizers.

Independent Reading

▶ **SHARE OBJECTIVES**

- Read and comprehend informational text.
- Quote accurately from a text to support analysis and inferences.
- Read independently from a "just right" book.
- Ask and answer questions about key details. **LANGUAGE**

ENGLISH LANGUAGE SUPPORT

"Just Right" Books for English Learners

All Proficiencies Create a home-school partnership for independent reading. Encourage students to talk about their books with caregivers. To get started, send home a book in the student's first language on the theme being studied in class. Suggest that students read and discuss the book with family members.

Reader's Guide

Use Text Evidence Tell students that they will read "Cougars" on their own to analyze important ideas in the text.

Have students use the Reader's Guide pages in their Reader's Notebook, pp. 109–110 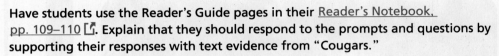. Explain that they should respond to the prompts and questions by supporting their responses with text evidence from "Cougars."

Generate Questions Have students work independently or collaboratively to generate questions about "Cougars." Ask students to share their questions. Begin a class discussion of questions that students have in common or that are most significant to their understanding of the selection. **ELA** RL.5.1, RL.5.10, RF.5.4a, SL.5.1c **ELD** ELD.PI.5.1

FOR STUDENTS WITH DISABILITIES Students may have particular difficulty comprehending expository text. Remind them to stop after reading a section, several paragraphs, or a page to check their understanding. Provide prompts such as: *Who/what is this part about? What new information does this part give? How does it connect to what you've already read?* Generate additional questions to help students understand sequential and cause-effect relationships in the text.

Self-Selected Reading

Topics of Interest Tell students that nonfiction books in a library are classified by number according to topic. Provide an overview of the classification system, holding up several books from different categories. Point out that a librarian can help students locate books by topic.

Explain that students can also use computers to find both fiction and nonfiction books on different topics. They can use an online library catalog and type in search terms, such as "North American cougars."

Once students have found books on their chosen topic, ask them to scan the book titles, covers, and summary information to select a book for independent reading. Ask students to use their Reading Logs in Grab-and-Go™ 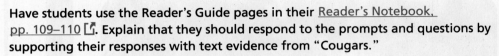 to record their progress and thinking about the book.

Fluency

Partner Read Have students read aloud with expression to a partner, using passages from their self-selected reading books. Have them give each other feedback as they listen. **ELA** RF.5.4b

Apply Vocabulary Knowledge

☑ Review Target Vocabulary

Classroom Collaboration Read aloud each of the following questions. Have students discuss their answers. Allow several students to respond to each question to provide a variety of possible responses for discussion. **ELA** L.5.6

1. When might a wild animal turn **ferocious**?

2. How do you **vary** your daily routine on the weekend?

3. What are some of the survival behaviors that most animals learn as they **mature**?

4. In what ways might family members **resemble** each other?

5. What technology would enable scientists to study animals while remaining **unobserved**?

6. Which of your senses would you describe as **keen**? Why?

7. How might humans express a feeling of **contentment**?

8. How can you tell if a dog is **detecting** an interesting scent?

9. Is there a **particular** route you like to take to school?

10. Which **available** afterschool activities would you like to participate in?

Quick Write Display the following prompt: *Explain why cougars are such excellent predators. Use the vocabulary words you have learned in your writing.*

Tell students that they might want to make a list of the cougar's physical traits and behaviors before writing and then describe the cougar's particular characteristics. Remind them to quote accurately if using text evidence from *Cougars*. When they have finished writing, tell students to exchange papers with a partner and discuss whether they used the words correctly in their paragraphs. **ELA** RI.5.1, L.5.6 **ELD** ELD.PI.5.1, ELD.PI.5.4

▶ **SHARE OBJECTIVES**

• Acquire and use vocabulary in speaking and writing. LANGUAGE

• Collaboratively respond to questions about familiar vocabulary. LANGUAGE

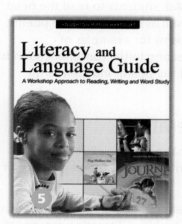

For additional practice with the lesson's Target Vocabulary, use the activities on pages 134–135 of the **Literacy and Language Guide.**

• Word Associations
• Suffix -ment
• Analogies
• Four-Square Map

ENGLISH LANGUAGE SUPPORT

Use Sentence Frames

All Proficiencies Have students complete sentence frames such as these to help them use the vocabulary words in their writing.

Cougars have a <u>keen</u> sense of hearing.

To help students discuss their partner's use of vocabulary in writing, provide discussion frames such as this one.

*You used the word **ferocious** to describe _____.*

DOMAIN: **Life Science**

LESSON TOPIC: ANIMAL BEHAVIORS

CONNECT TO THE TOPIC
Poetry

Preview the Poetry

- Tell students that this selection is a collection of poems about cats. Ask students to read the head "Purr-fection," as well as the titles of the poems, and preview the poems for examples of alliteration, or repeating initial consonant sounds. Have students read the poems independently.

  ELA RL.5.10

Discuss Alliteration

- Remind students that poets use alliteration by repeating consonant sounds at the beginnings of words.

- Explain that alliteration makes poetry more interesting and enjoyable. Alliteration can create strong, vivid images that appeal to the senses.

Lesson 10
POETRY

"Purr-fection"

Have you ever wondered how a cat uses its keen eyesight and hearing for detecting mice? Have you ever wished you could be a cat, napping in perfect contentment? From ferocious tigers to timid tabbies, cats have always fascinated people. The reasons may vary from person to person and culture to culture.

There are few animals that have inspired poets as much as cats. As you read the following poems, notice how the poets have tried to capture the particular way cats move, their mysterious nature, and their entertaining antics.

☑ GENRE

Poetry uses the sounds and rhythms of words to suggest images and express feelings in a variety of forms.

☑ TEXT FOCUS

Alliteration Poets often use repeating consonant sounds at the beginnings of words. Doing so draws attention to vivid images that appeal to the senses.

Tiger
by Valerie Worth

The tiger
Has swallowed
A black sun,

In his cold
Cage he
Carries it still:

Black flames
Flicker through
His fur,

Black rays roar
From the centers
Of his eyes.

①

310   **ELA** RL.5.10, RF.5.4a, RF.5.4b   **ELD** ELD.PI.5.6a

---

ENGLISH LANGUAGE SUPPORT

Comprehensible Input

Emerging Explain alliteration to students. Have students listen as you say examples such as *cold cage* and *rays roar* from "Tiger."
ELD ELD.PI.5.8

Expanding Write three sentences on the board that each include an example of alliteration. Have students identify the alliteration and say each example aloud.
ELD ELD.PI.5.8

Bridging Have students form complete sentences starting with "A tomcat is" and ending with a line or two from the poem on page 311. They may need to add words such as *a* and *an*.
ELD ELD.PII.5.6

A Tomcat Is
by J. Patrick Lewis

Nightwatchman of corners
Caretaker of naps
Leg-wrestler of pillows
Depresser of laps

A master at whining
And dining on mouse
Designer of shadows
That hide in the house

The bird-watching bandit
On needle-point claws
The chief of detectives
On marshmallow paws

A crafty yarn-spinner
A stringer high-strung
A handlebar mustache
A sandpaper tongue

The dude in the alley
The duke of the couch
Affectionate fellow
Occasional grouch

3

As male cats mature from kittens to tomcats, they take on different traits. The imagery in this poem describes all the different things a tomcat can resemble.

311

Practice Fluency

Stress Have students listen as you read aloud the poem on **Student Book p. 310.** **ELD** ELD.PI.5.5

- Remind students that when reading poems, good readers stress important literary elements, such as alliteration, or the repetition of sounds at the beginnings of words.

- Have students memorize the poem. Have them read aloud the poem with expression and at an appropriate rate. Remind them to also use the same stress that you used. **ELA** RF.5.4a, SL.5.4b

DOMAIN: Life Science

LESSON TOPIC: Animal Behaviors

Cross-Curricular Connection Point out that all animals, both wild and domestic, have behaviors or typical actions that make them unique. Have students recall what they learned about cougar behavior in *Cougars,* and explain that the three poems in this selection all describe how cats behave. Ask which poem describes a cat that is most like a cougar. *"Tiger" describes a big, wild cat, although this one lives in a cage.* Invite students to tell which descriptions in the poems match what they have observed in cats. Then have the class discuss ways in which house cats' behaviors are similar to and different from tigers' and cougars' behaviors.

Think Through the Text

Cite Text Evidence

Pause at the stopping points to ask students the following questions.

1 *Reread the last two stanzas of "Tiger." What theme or message about wildness is conveyed by the details in these lines?* Sample answer: A wild animal remains wild even if it is captured and put in a cage by humans.
ELA RL.5.2 **ELD** ELD.PI.5.6a

ENGLISH LANGUAGE SUPPORT To check that students understand that a stanza is a section of a poem, ask them to complete this frame: *There are _____ stanzas in the poem "Tiger."* four

2 *Who is the narrator of this poem? How does this point of view affect how the tomcat is described?* The narrator is a person who has watched how cats behave. The cat's actions are described in human terms; the cat is not literally a nightwatchman or a caretaker.
ELA RL.5.6 **ELD** ELD.PI.5.6a

3 *How do the stanzas in this poem fit together to form the overall structure of the poem? For example, do the stanzas describe how the tomcat faces a conflict and finally resolves it at the end?* The poem does not tell a story or have a plot. Instead, each stanza adds more examples to the list of things a tomcat is or does.
ELA RL.5.5 **ELD** ELD.PII.5.1

4 *How does the image on page 312 help you understand the poem?* Sample answer: The image shows me how a cat would look if it were disturbed while taking a nap.

Classroom Collaboration

How might three poems about dogs be different from three poems about cats? As a class, have students discuss the differences and similarities between the two animals. You may wish to use a Venn diagram to show a graphic display of those differences and similarities. **ELA** RL.5.3 **ELD** ELD.PI.5.6a

4

Disturbed, the cat
Lifts its belly
On to its back.

—Karai Senryū

Write Using Alliteration

Write a poem using alliteration. Use "Tiger" on page 310 as a model. Choose the subject of your poem and think of unusual details that are available to describe it. Create imagery that will reveal things that may go unobserved by most people. For each image, focus on a single repeating initial consonant sound. Alliteration can draw attention to unique imagery in a poem and make reading it exciting.

312

ENGLISH LANGUAGE SUPPORT

Peer-Supported Learning

All Proficiencies Place students in five mixed-proficiency groups and assign each group a stanza from "A Tomcat Is." Each group should read their stanza carefully, helping each other with vocabulary and using a dictionary to look up any unfamiliar words. When they have clarified the meaning of each image and how it relates to cat behavior, have them select one image to illustrate. They might draw a picture or plan how to act it out. Bring the class together and have each group present their stanza, explaining what the lines mean and sharing their illustrations. **ELD** ELD.PI.5.1, ELD.PI.5.12a, ELD.PI.5.12b

Compare Texts

TEXT TO TEXT

Analyze Writers' Approaches The author of "Cougars" and the poets in "Purr-fection" write about the traits and behaviors of cats. Compare and contrast the representations of cats in "Cougars" and in one of the "Purr-fection" poems. Use evidence from both selections to support your points. Pay special attention to the writers' uses of sensory details, figurative language, and sound.

TEXT TO SELF

Respond to a Poem Rhyme is a technique used by many poets. Quietly read the poem "A Tomcat Is" to yourself a few times. What rhyming words do you hear, and where? How do the rhymes affect the way you read the poem? Do you think they enhance the poem's imagery? How might you use this technique when writing your own poems? Discuss these questions with a partner.

TEXT TO WORLD

Compare and Contrast Texts Both "Quest for the Tree Kangaroo" (Lesson 6) and "Cougars" contain information about wild animals. How is the presentation of concepts, information, and other details in "Quest for the Tree Kangaroo" different from or similar to the presentation of these elements in "Cougars"? Support your answer with specific references to both texts. What did you learn about animals in the wild that you didn't know before?

ELA RI.5.5 RI.5.9 **ELD** ELD.PI.5.1, ELD.PI.5.6a, ELD.PI.5.8

313

Compare Texts

TEXT TO TEXT

To help students identify similarities and differences between house cats and cougars, suggest that they use a Venn diagram to list characteristics of the two types of cats. Remind them to keep track of sensory details and figurative language. **ELA** RI.5.9 **ELD** ELD.PI.5.8

TEXT TO SELF

Display these sentence frames to help students organize their thoughts about the poem:

In "Tomcat," I hear the rhyming words _____ .

The rhyming words are always placed at _____ .

In my own poem, I might place rhyming words at _____ .

Have students work with partners to discuss their conclusions about rhyme. **ELD** ELD.PI.5.1, ELD.PI.5.5

TEXT TO WORLD

To help students compare and contrast the two selections, display a two-column chart with the headings *Quest for the Tree Kangaroo* and *Cougars*. Guide students to fill in the diagram with information and details from each selection.

Have students work in pairs to discuss how each selection presents information and to identify details to support their ideas. **ELA** RI.5.5, RI.5.9 **ELD** ELD.PI.5.6a

Vocabulary Strategies

▶ **SHARE OBJECTIVES**

- Recognize different shades of meaning among synonyms.
- Use context clues to determine the meanings of words.

▶ **SKILL TRACE**

Shades of Meaning	
Introduce	T344–T345
Differentiate	T378–T379
Reteach	T380
Review	T46–T47, Unit 5
Test	Weekly Tests, Lesson 10

ENGLISH LANGUAGE SUPPORT

Preteach

All Proficiencies Remind students that a synonym is a word that has the same or almost the same meaning as another word. Explain that synonyms can have different shades of meaning. Provide students with examples that show shades of meaning such as *large* and *massive*. Discuss the meaning of each word.

Apply Vocabulary Skills

Emerging Write and say: *small* and *tiny*. Display a small object, such as a book, and say: *This book is small.* Then display a paperclip and say: *This paperclip is tiny.*

Expanding Have students complete sentence frames with synonyms that have different shades of meaning, such as *A cat is _____, but a kitten is _____.* small; tiny

Bridging Give students words such as *small, large* and *cold.* Have them work with a partner to create a list of synonyms for each word that shows different shades of meaning. **ELD** ELD.PI.5.8

Shades of Meaning

1   Teach/Model

Terms About Language

synonym a word that has the same or almost the same meaning as another word

context words and sentences around a word that give readers clues to its meaning

thesaurus reference source that lists synonyms for words

- Remind students that if they encounter an unfamiliar word, they should review the **context** in which it appears. Explain that there may be information in a nearby sentence that will provide a clue to the unfamiliar word's meaning.

- Review the definition of **synonyms**. Provide examples, such as *happy/joyful, smart/clever,* and *tired/exhausted.* Remind students that writers use synonyms to make their meaning more precise and to vary the way they express their ideas.

- Tell students that a **thesaurus** lists synonyms for words. Explain how to use both a print and a digital thesaurus. Then tell students that although there may be several synonyms for one word, not all of them will convey the exact same meaning.

- Write this sentence from **Student Book p. 298** on the board: *"Cougars are muscular and sleek, with little fat on their bodies."* Model how to find synonyms for the word *sleek.* Then show students how to choose the word that is closest to its meaning.

> **Think Aloud**   *When I look up the word* sleek *in my thesaurus, I find several possible synonyms. They are* glassy, polished, smooth, *and* glossy. *To help me decide which one conveys a similar meaning to* sleek, *I look back at the context sentence. It is describing the cougar's appearance. I think the words* glassy *and* polished *refer to things rather than living creatures.* Glossy *might work, but* smooth *is better because it conveys the idea of being trim or with little fat, which is what the sentence says cougars are.*

- Remind students that if they are not sure of the exact meaning of a synonym, they can clarify it by consulting a print or digital dictionary.

Literacy and Language Guide
See pages 134-135 for further practice with lesson vocabulary.

2 Guided Practice

- Display the top half of Projectable 10.3  and read the sentences about cougars aloud.

- Point out the word *slinks* in the first sentence. Tell students it is a verb that means "to move in a silent way." Explain that its connotation is "to move without disturbing anything." Then, together, look up the verb in a thesaurus and list several of its synonyms. *prowls, slips, slithers*

- Help students identify the context clues "cougar" and "noiselessly" in the sentence. Guide them to use these clues as well as their understanding of the meaning of *slinks* to choose the most accurate synonym. *slips*

- Display the bottom half of Projectable 10.3. Have partners use the above strategy to complete the chart. Discuss their choices.

3 Apply

- Have students work in pairs. Assign one partner to write sentences using these words: *prance, smirk, scary, tragic*. Have the other partner write sentences using these words: *jolly, magical, stroll, demolish*.

- Have partners exchange their sentences. Ask them to identify alternate word choices by finding a synonym for the key word in each sentence. Have them use a thesaurus for reference. Then have students discuss the different shades of meaning conveyed by their synonym choices. Remind them that they should use context or a print or digital dictionary to clarify the meanings of any unfamiliar words. **ELA** L.5.4a, L.5.4c, L.5.5c **ELD** ELD.PI.5.8

Interactive Whiteboard Lesson Use **Vocabulary Strategies: Shades of Meaning** to reinforce how to recognize different shades of meaning among synonyms.

- Distribute to students Reader's Notebook page 111 or leveled practice in Grab-and-Go™ Resources to complete independently.

Are students able to distinguish shades of meaning among synonyms?

IF...	THEN...
students **struggle,**	▶ **Differentiate Vocabulary Strategies** for Struggling Readers, p. T378.
students **on target,**	▶ **Differentiate Vocabulary Strategies** for On-Level Readers, p. T378.
students **excel,**	▶ **Differentiate Vocabulary Strategies** for Advanced Readers, p. T379.

SMALL GROUP Options **Differentiate Vocabulary Strategies:** pp. T378–T379 *Scaffold instruction to the English learner's proficiency level.*

ENGLISH LANGUAGE SUPPORT

Comprehensible Input

Emerging Write the words *warm, hot,* and *burning* on the board. Explain that the words have similar but not the same meanings. Then use gestures or pictures to illustrate each degree of heat.

Expanding Display these words in random order: *chilly, cold, frigid; warm, hot, burning.* Draw a continuum labeled *less* on the left side and *more* on the right. Have students place the words on the continuum.

Bridging Give students words such as *happy, sad,* and *strong.* Have pairs generate synonyms for each word that show different shades of meaning. Ask them to place each set of synonyms on a continuum. **ELD** ELD.PI.5.8

Extend the Topic

▶ **SHARE OBJECTIVES**

- Acquire and use domain-specific vocabulary.
- Integrate information from several texts on the same topic.
- Use technology to produce writing that includes illustrations and graphic features.

Words About the Topic: Animal Behaviors

- **adaptation** a natural change in an organism that makes the organism better fitted to survive and multiply in its environment
- **development** growth; progress
- **instinctive** natural; unlearned
- **observation** an act of viewing or noting a fact or occurrence for a scientific purpose
- **trait** a distinguishing characteristic or quality

Domain-Specific Vocabulary

Introduce Words About the Topic Remind students that this week's topic is Animal Behaviors. Display the words in the left column and tell students that these words can help them learn more about animal behaviors. Read aloud the definition for each word and then have students respond to the following prompts:

- *Being nocturnal, or active at night, is a _____ that bats and owls share.* trait
- *Which word can describe a section of a scientific lab report?* observation
- *A caterpillar changes into a butterfly in a later stage of _____.* development
- *When you raise your arm automatically to protect your face from a falling object, you have demonstrated this kind of action.* instinctive
- *Which word describes something that some animals could not achieve to help them survive?* adaptation

ENGLISH LANGUAGE SUPPORT For example, point out the illustration on page 301 and say: *When a cougar sees an enemy, its instinctive response is to growl.*

Interact with the Words Have students work in small groups using Graphic Organizer 6 (Four-Square Map) ⤢ to extend their understanding of each word about animal behaviors. Assign one word to each group and have them follow these steps for completing the Four-Square Map with information about the word:

1 In the first corner, draw a picture that represents the word.

2 In the second corner, write the meaning of the word.

3 In the third corner, write a sentence using the word.

4 In the fourth corner, write the word.

When groups have finished, have them share their completed Four-Square Maps with the class. **ELA** L.5.6 **ELD** ELD.PI.5.12a

Research and Media Literacy

Integrate Information from Multiple Texts

Review Selections Explain that pairs of students will be preparing a pamphlet and a short speech to teach about an aspect of nature and wildlife preservation. Their first step is to review the informational texts in Lessons 6, 8, and 10. Students should take brief notes on main ideas, facts, and key details in the texts and use the information they collect in their notes to identify two or three strong research questions related to the topic. **ELA** RI.5.9, W.5.9b

Conduct Research Have partners choose one of their research questions and conduct research to answer it, integrating information from several texts and other reliable print and digital sources. Students should take notes on interesting and important information that will help them teach about the topic. Encourage students to use a graphic organizer to organize the information. **ELA** RI.5.7

Create a Pamphlet Have pairs follow these guidelines to create an educational pamphlet to share what they have learned.

- Think about pamphlets or brochures you have seen. You may choose to use a combination of text, bullets, and graphics or diagrams to make the information focused and easy for your audience to follow.

- Remember that your audience may be unfamiliar with the topic of your pamphlet. Organize facts and details clearly and provide context or definitions for any domain-specific words.

- Use computer software to add art or colorful headings, or include hand-drawn illustrations, to enhance the main idea or message of your pamphlet.

Prepare a Speech Tell pairs that they will prepare a short speech to present their pamphlet to the class. Remind them to cover all points mentioned in the pamphlet, to provide additional information, and to be prepared to answer any questions.

Present Have students report on their chosen topic, speaking clearly at an understandable pace. They should adapt their speech to the context and task, using formal English in presenting the information and answering any questions. Remind listeners to be respectful and to pay attention to each speaker's key points. **ELA** SL.5.4b, SL.5.6 **ELD** ELD.PI.5.9

FOR STUDENTS WITH DISABILITIES To help students remember information, have them write down or say a few key words or main ideas at the end of the lesson. Before starting the next lesson on the same topic, review the main points from the previous lesson.

Skill Focus: Interpret Information from Text Source Explain that when students conduct research and write reports, they must integrate information from digital and/or print sources to support a given purpose. Then provide the following scenario: *A student is writing a report about migrating birds. He/She looked online and found facts about wind and temperatures that affect migrating birds. The student's report will include sections on weather, migratory routes, and seasons. In which part of the student's report would the facts from the source best fit?* **ELA** W.5.8, W.5.9a

1 **Review Selections**

2 **Conduct Research**

3 **Create a Pamphlet**

4 **Prepare a Speech**

5 **Present**

ENGLISH LANGUAGE SUPPORT To check students' understanding of *pamphlet*, say: *A pamphlet is a small publication, smaller than a book or a magazine.*

Fluency

▶ **SHARE OBJECTIVES**
- Read on-level text orally with appropriate fluency and expression.
- Use stress for appropriate expression and phrasing when reading aloud (prosody).

ENGLISH LANGUAGE SUPPORT

Audio Support

All Proficiencies Help English learners develop expression by having students listen to an audio recording of "Cougars." Tell students to listen carefully to the different expressions used as the story is read. After listening to the recording, have students read **Student Book p. 298.** Listen as students read each sentence with the appropriate expression. **ELD** ELD.PIII.5

Cold Reads: Support for fluent reading with comprehension

FORMATIVE ASSESSMENT

 **RtI**

As student partners read **Student Book p. 298,** circulate and spend time listening to each pair. If students have difficulty reading accurately and self-correcting, provide corrective feedback.

Model accurate reading as you read aloud the section to students and have them choral- or echo-read with you.

Guide students to read another paragraph on their own and provide feedback, as necessary.

Tell students that their reading fluency will continue to improve as they work hard at improving their accuracy.

Stress

1 Teach/Model

- Remind students that good readers stress, or emphasize, certain words as they read. Using stress properly helps readers understand and enjoy a text.
- Have students follow along as you read aloud **Student Book p. 298,** using appropriate stress. Ask them to listen for the words that you stress, or emphasize, as you read.
- Reread several sentences using no stress. Point out that a lack of stress when reading can make it difficult to understand the meaning of the text. Then repeat the same sentences, using stress. Discuss the words you stress in each sentence and why.

2 Guided Practice

- Remind students that reading with no stress or incorrect stress can make it difficult for listeners to understand the meaning of a text. Together, read aloud the first paragraph on **Student Book p. 300,** paying special attention to stress.
- Work with students to adjust the words they are stressing as needed to help make sense of the text.
- If students have difficulty with the concept of stress, break down sentences into phrases and have them echo-read each phrase. Work with students to identify words that should be stressed.
- See also Instructional Routine 8 ⬀.

3 Apply

- Tell students that with practice, they can make their reading more enjoyable and easier to understand by using appropriate stress.
- Have students choral-read from **Student Book p. 303.** Encourage them to emphasize, or stress, words appropriately as they read. **ELA** RF.5.4a **ELD** ELD.PIII.5

Decoding

Recognizing Schwa + /r/ Sounds

1 | Teach/Model

Analyze Words with Unstressed Syllables Remind students that knowledge of syllabication patterns can help them decode words. Point out that a multisyllable word will have one stressed syllable that sounds the strongest; other syllables are unstressed. In many two-syllable words with an *r*-controlled vowel in the second syllable, the first syllable is stressed, and the vowel and *r* in the second syllable make a schwa + /r/ sound.

- Explain that an *r*-controlled unstressed syllable makes a schwa + /r/ sound. Write these words on the board and read them aloud, identifying the words' unstressed second syllables and schwa + /r/ sounds: *dollar, polar,* and *tremor.*

- Point out that the schwa + /r/ sound rule doesn't apply to a stressed syllable. Note that *compartment,* for example, does not have the schwa + /r/ sound in its stressed second syllable.

- Write the word *explorer* on the board and read it aloud to students. Identify the word's stressed and unstressed syllables: ex / **plor** / er. Point out that the schwa + /r/ sound appears in the last unstressed syllable.

2 | Guided Practice

Blend Words Display Lines 1–8 below and have students break each word into syllables, identify the schwa + /r/ sound, and say each word aloud. Provide Corrective Feedback as needed. Next, point to words in random order. Ask students what stategies they used to read each one.

1. *color   cellar   doctor   cougar   bother*
2. *wonder   favor   flicker   anchor   manner*
3. *clamor   whisker   thunder   anger   major*
4. *pillar   stellar   quarter   tractor   flavor*
5. *passenger   calendar   popular   elevator   senator*

Challenge Call on students who are ready for a challenge to read Line 6 and discuss the elements. Then have the class read the sentences in Lines 7 and 8 chorally.

6. *particular   senator   muscular   survivor   circular*
7. *The mayor is seen as a pillar in our community.*
8. *My calendar shows the lunar patterns broken down by quarters.*
   ELA RF.5.3a **ELD** ELD.PIII.5

▶ **SHARE OBJECTIVES**

- Use knowledge of syllabication patterns to recognize stressed and unstressed syllables.
- Use knowledge of syllabication patterns to apply the schwa + /r/ sound to unstressed *r*-controlled syllables.

FORMATIVE ASSESSMENT

If students have trouble decoding words with the schwa + /r/ sound, use the model below.

Correct the error. *Remember that the part of a word that sounds strongest is the stressed syllable. Other syllables are unstressed.*

Model how to decode the words. *When I say the word* endure *with the first syllable stressed, it doesn't work. I can tell that the second syllable sounds stronger. That means the second syllable is stressed, so the r-controlled vowel does not have the schwa + /r/ sound.*

Guide students to say the words *color* and *flicker. Which syllable is unstressed in each of these words?* the last syllable *Does that mean that the last syllable has the schwa + /r/ sound?* yes

Check students' understanding. *Read these two words.* color, flicker

Reinforce Have students repeat the process with the words *anchor* and *certain.*

ENGLISH LANGUAGE SUPPORT

Linguistic Transfer

Use the transfer chart in the **Quick Start Pacing Guide** to determine whether your students will have difficulty due to transfer issues. As needed, preteach the skill. **ELD** ELD.PIII.5

Spelling Final Schwa + /r/ Sounds

▶ **SHARE OBJECTIVE**

- Spell grade-appropriate words that have the final schwa + /r/ sounds.

Spelling Words

Basic

cellar	passenger	calendar
flavor	major	quarter
⭐ cougar	popular	lunar
chapter	tractor	proper
mayor	thunder	elevator
anger	pillar	bitter
senator	⭐ border	

Review

collar, honor, doctor, enter, answer

Challenge

stellar, clamor, tremor, circular, adviser

⭐ Forms of these words appear in "Cougars."

ENGLISH LANGUAGE SUPPORT

Preteach

Spanish Cognates Write and discuss these Spanish cognates for Spanish-speaking students.

passenger • *pasajero(a)*
quarter • *cuarto*

Transfer Support Explain that many English nouns ending in *or* have Spanish cognates. For example, the English noun *tractor* corresponds with the Spanish noun *tractor*. **ELD** ELD.PII.5.4, ELD.PIII.5

Word Meanings Use Day 5 sentences to preview the meanings of spelling words.

DAY 1

❶ TEACH THE PRINCIPLE

- Administer the **Pretest.** Use the Day 5 sentences.
- Explain that the final schwa + /r/ sound can be a tricky one to spell because there can be three different spellings: *-ar, -er,* and *-or.* Point out that there are no good rules that determine which of the vowels comes before the *r* in a word, so students will have to memorize the spellings.

Sound	Spellings
schwa + /r/	*-ar, -er, -or*

❷ GUIDED PRACTICE

Guide students to identify the final schwa + /r/ sounds/spellings in the Spelling Words.

Model a Word Sort Model sorting words based on the spelling of their final schwa + /r/ sound. Present the Model the Sort lesson on page 74 of the **Literacy and Language Guide.**

❸ APPLY

Distribute Reader's Notebook page 112 ↗ and have students complete it independently.

DAY 2

❶ TEACH WORD SORT

- Set up three rows as shown. Model adding a Spelling Word to each row.
- Have students copy the chart. Guide students to write each Spelling Word where it belongs.

final /r/ spelled –ar	pillar
final /r/ spelled –er	quarter
final /r/ spelled –or	elevator

❷ GUIDED PRACTICE

- Have students add to the chart words from "Cougars."

Guided Word Sort Guide students to sort words based on the spelling of their final schwa + /r/ sound. Present the Repeat the Sort lesson on page 74 of the **Literacy and Language Guide.**

❸ APPLY

Distribute Reader's Notebook page 113 ↗ and have students complete it independently.

DAY 3

❶ TEACH WORD FAMILIES

- **WRITE** *popular*. Define it: *liked by a lot of people.*
- **WRITE** *popularity*. Define it: *the state of being liked by a lot of people.*
- **ASK** *What is the connection between these words? Both contain the word* popular; *both words connect to the idea of being liked by a lot of people.*
- With students, list and discuss more words related to *popular*. *Samples:* popularize, populate, populism

❷ GUIDED PRACTICE

- **WRITE** *bitter*. Define it: *sharp and unpleasant.*
- **WRITE** *bitterness* and *bitterly*. Ask students to look up these words in a dictionary or an electronic resource.
- **ASK** *What is the connection among* bitter, bitterness, *and* bitterly?

Have students write their answers.

❸ APPLY

Independent Word Sort Have students sort words according to their parts of speech. Present the Concept Sort lesson on page 75 of the **Literacy and Language Guide**.

DAY 4

❶ CONNECT TO WRITING

- Read and discuss the prompt below.

> **Informative Writing**
> Write a research report about animal behavior. Use what you've learned from your reading this week. Revise your report. Make sure you used precise language and included a concluding statement.

❷ GUIDED PRACTICE

- Guide students as they write and revise their research reports.
- Remind students to proofread their writing and to consult print and digital references to confirm correct spelling. (See p. T358.) **ELA** L.5.2e

Blind Writing Sort Have students sort and write words that a partner says aloud. Present the Blind Writing Sort lesson on page 75 of the **Literacy and Language Guide**.

❸ APPLY

Distribute Reader's Notebook page 114 and have students complete it independently.

DAY 5

ASSESS SPELLING

- Say each boldfaced word, read the sentence, and then repeat the word.
- Have students write the boldfaced word. **ELA** L.5.2e

> ### Basic
> 1. The storm sent us down to the **cellar**.
> 2. I enjoy the **flavor** of vanilla.
> 3. A **cougar** pounced from the rock.
> 4. Read the book's first **chapter**.
> 5. The **mayor** runs the city.
> 6. Jill's face showed **anger**.
> 7. A **senator** serves in Congress.
> 8. The **passenger** wore a seat belt.
> 9. Route 12 is a **major** highway.
> 10. The **popular** movie was crowded.
> 11. A **tractor** pulled the trailer.
> 12. Loud **thunder** woke me.
> 13. This **pillar** supports the roof.
> 14. We crossed Ohio's **border** to Indiana.
> 15. Check the day on the **calendar**.
> 16. I earned a **quarter** for doing that chore.
> 17. We watched the **lunar** eclipse.
> 18. It is **proper** to say, "Please."
> 19. Take the stairs or the **elevator**.
> 20. This fruit tastes **bitter**.

Grammar Direct Quotations and Interjections

▶ SHARE OBJECTIVES

- Use and explain the function of interjections.
- Recognize and use proper capitalization and punctuation for direct quotations.

Terms About Language

direct quotation the exact words a character or person says

quotation marks punctuation marks at the beginning and end of a direct quotation

interjection single word or group of words used to express a feeling or emotion • *interjección*

ENGLISH LANGUAGE SUPPORT

Preteach: All Proficiencies

Explain the Language Term Point out the cognate in the list above. Then explain that:

- An interjection is a word that expresses feelings.

Linguistic Transfer It is common when printing dialogue in Spanish to dispense with quotation marks and use a long dash (—), sometimes known as an *em* dash (*raya* in Spanish), to indicate the beginning and end of the quotation or a change in speaker.

Scaffolded Practice

Emerging Say: *I like this class.* Then write the sentence on the board, explaining that it is a direct quotation because you said it. Place quotation marks in the proper spots. Then say and write another direct quotation on the board and have students explain where they would put the quotation marks.

Expanding Flip through a story with dialogue that students have already read and guide them to read the direct quotations, explaining that the characters said those exact words.

Bridging Have students copy a short section of dialogue from a story, leaving out the quotation marks and other punctuation. Then have partners exchange sentences and add the correct punctuation marks.

DAY 1 TEACH

DAILY PROOFREADING PRACTICE

A cugar's fur coat keeps it warm, it has little fat. *cougar's; warm because it*

❶ TEACH QUOTATIONS

- Display Projectable 10.4 ⬚. Explain that a **direct quotation** is the exact words of a speaker or writer. Tell students that **quotation marks** are placed at the beginning and end of a direct quotation. End punctuation marks for the quotations——periods, exclamation points, and question marks——are placed inside the quotation marks. Quotations that are complete sentences are capitalized.

ENGLISH LANGUAGE SUPPORT Display the following examples without the internal punctuation. Help students identify the words of dialogue and add the missing punctuation.

- "Cougars are a species of wild cat," said my teacher.
- She added, "A cougar can weigh more than a person."

- Model how to punctuate direct quotations, using this example sentence: *"The zoo has five new cougar kittens," the veterinarian reported.*

> **Think Aloud** *To identify and punctuate the direct quotation, I ask these Thinking Questions:* **Does the sentence give a speaker's exact words? How can I separate the exact words from the rest of the sentence?** *A comma and quotation mark are used to separate the speaker's exact words from the rest of the sentence.*

❷ PRACTICE/APPLY

- Complete the items on Projectable 10.4 ⬚ with students.
- Hold a conversation with a volunteer. Have other students write down what is said and punctuate the quotations correctly.
- Have students complete Reader's Notebook p. 115 ⬚ for practice with simple subjects and predicates.

DAY 2 TEACH

DAILY PROOFREADING PRACTICE

The other passengir said I think I saw a cougar. *passenger; said,
"I think; cougar."*

1 TEACH TEXT QUOTATIONS

- Display <u>Projectable 10.5</u> ⬈. Remind students that direct
  quotations include someone else's words. Explain that they can
  use direct quotations when using text evidence in their writing
  to support a key point. Words, phrases, or sentences copied
  directly from another source always appear in quotation marks.

- Use this example from the projectable to model how students
  can weave parts of a direct quotation into their own writing:
  The article stated that they are "seldom seen."

> **Think Aloud**   *To decide how to include a direct quotation
> from a source, I ask these Thinking Questions:* **What part of the
> text do I want to quote? How can I include it smoothly in my
> writing?** *The words "seldom seen" are taken directly from the
> text to describe the cougars. This phrase cannot stand alone and
> must be built into the writer's own sentence.*

2 PRACTICE/APPLY

- Complete the items on <u>Projectable 10.5</u> ⬈ with students.

- Have students work in pairs to take direct quotations from
  "Cougars" and present them in their own sentences. Have
  volunteers write their sentences on the board.

- Have students complete <u>Reader's Notebook p. 116</u> ⬈ for practice
  with simple subjects and predicates.

DAY 3 TEACH

DAILY PROOFREADING PRACTICE

Cougars are often described as, "apex predators." *as "apex
predators."*

1 TEACH INTERJECTIONS AND DIALOGUE

- Display <u>Projectable 10.6</u> ⬈. Tell students that **interjections** are
  words or phrases that show emotion. When these words occur in
  dialogue, they usually appear at the beginning of a sentence
  and are followed either by an exclamation point or by a comma.

- Explain that sometimes writers split dialogue into two parts.
  Both parts begin and end with quotation marks. Unless the
  second part begins with a proper noun, the first word is not
  capitalized.

- Mention that in between the two parts of a split quotation, the
  writer usually tells who is speaking, what the speaker is doing,
  or how he or she is speaking.

- Point out in the last example that the interjection forms the first
  part of the split quotation. Model how to punctuate a split
  quotation correctly, using the Thinking Questions on the
  projectable.

2 PRACTICE/APPLY

- Complete the items on <u>Projectable 10.6</u> ⬈ with students.

- Have students return to the projectable and identify the
  function of each interjection. *grabs attention; shows excitement;
  shows enthusiasm; shows strong agreement* **ELA** L.5.1a

- Have students complete <u>Reader's Notebook p. 117</u> ⬈ for practice
  with simple subjects and predicates.

DAY 4 REVIEW

DAILY PROOFREADING PRACTICE

Unbelievable. That cougar can run so fast said Kevin.
"Unbelievable!; fast,"

1 REVIEW DIRECT QUOTATIONS AND INTERJECTIONS

Have students turn to **Student Book p. 314**. Review how to punctuate direct quotations with students. Remind them that if a quoted sentence is split into two parts, a comma and quotation marks end the first part. A comma, space, and then quotation marks follow the interrupting phrase. Then read the information on interjections aloud. Discuss the various functions of interjections in sentences.

ENGLISH LANGUAGE SUPPORT Remind students that when writing quotations, the punctuation—commas, periods, exclamation points, and question marks—should be placed inside the quotation marks.

2 SPIRAL REVIEW

KINDS OF VERBS Remind students that **action verbs** show mental or physical activity. **Linking verbs** connect the subject to adjectives, nouns, or pronouns that follow the verb. Verbs may include **helping verbs** that clarify the meaning of the main verb and help to show tense. Review with students how **verb tense** can be used to convey time, sequence, state, and condition.

Have students write sentences using helping and linking verbs and tenses that show time, sequence, states, and conditions. Use these sentences as models. **ELA** L.5.1c **ELD** ELD.PII.5 3

The photographer was happy. *was, linking; past, state*
We will go to the park. *will, helping; will go, action; future, time*

Then have students complete Reader's Notebook p. 118 for more practice with verb tenses.

DAY 5 CONNECT TO WRITING

DAILY PROOFREADING PRACTICE

If we will write a caption under the picture, it is better. *wrote; would be*

1 INTERACTIVE WHITEBOARD LESSON

For cumulative review, use **Grammar: Quotations, Dialogue, and Interjections** to reinforce how to identify and properly write quotations, dialogue, and interjections.

2 CONNECT TO WRITING

- Explain that good writers make sure they have punctuated their direct quotations correctly. An important part of revising is inserting commas, quotation marks, and other punctuation marks where they are needed.

- Remind students that including direct quotations from texts or other sources will lend support to their key points. These quotations must be copied exactly and punctuated accurately.

- Point out that interjections also must be punctuated correctly. Those that convey strong emotion are followed by an exclamation point. Others can be set off by a comma.

3 PRACTICE/APPLY

- Have students turn to **Student Book p. 314**. Have them complete the **Try This!** activity. **ELA** L.5.1a

- Then ask student pairs to write dialogue that includes the correct spacing, quotation marks, and punctuation, as well as interjections. Have volunteers write their dialogue on the board and explain the function of the interjections that they used.

- Have students complete Reader's Notebook p. 119 for practice with simple subjects and predicates.

Grammar

Digital Resources
► Multimedia
Grammar Glossary
► GrammarSnap
Video

Direct Quotations **Direct quotations** give a speaker's or an author's exact words. They can be used when writing story dialogue and when quoting from a text to support ideas in an essay or a research report. Capitalize the first word, and use a comma and quotation marks to set off a direct quotation from the other words in a sentence. At the end of a direct quotation, put a comma or other punctuation inside the quotation marks.

Interjections To show a speaker's strong emotion, or to make a character's voice more lively, include an **interjection** such as *Hey* or *Wow,* and punctuate it with a comma or an exclamation point.

Direct Quotations and Interjections

Ravindra said, "I can recognize cougar tracks." He was on a hike with his friends Paula and Bethany.

"Draw a sketch of a print," said Paula. She handed Ravindra her sketch pad and a pencil.

"Hey, I see a cougar print!" shouted Bethany.

 Try This! With a partner, talk about what you would capitalize and punctuate in these sentences. Then identify each interjection and explain its function in the sentence.

1. Sam asked are you sure it's a cougar print
2. Belinda replied it looks just like the one in the book.
3. Wow we have to tell people about this exclaimed Andre.
4. I will take a photo of the print said Nell.

314   ELA L.5.1a   ELD ELD.PI.5.1

To let readers know which words are a speaker's exact words, make sure quotation marks, commas, and end punctuation are placed correctly. When you are writing dialogue, start a new paragraph each time the speaker changes, making sure to indent the first line. Any interjections can be set off with a comma or can stand alone with an exclamation point.

Incorrect	Correct
I saw a cougar, Tom said.	"I saw a cougar," Tom said.
"Where was it? asked Lin."	"Where was it?" asked Lin.
Pete said "you just saw a housecat"	Pete said, "You just saw a housecat."
Tom yelled", No It was a cougar"!	Tom yelled, "No! It was a cougar!"

Connect Grammar to Writing

As you edit your research report, make sure you have written direct quotations and interjections correctly. Check for both capitalization and punctuation errors. Correct any errors you find.

315

Try This!

1. *Sam asked, "Are you sure it's a cougar print?"*
2. *Belinda replied, "It looks just like the one in the book."*
3. *"Wow! We have to tell people about this," exclaimed Andre.* interjection: *Wow;* shows excitement
4. *"I will take a photo of the print," said Nell.*

Connect Grammar to Writing

- Have students turn to **Student Book p. 315.** Read the top paragraph with students.
- Read the sentences in the *Incorrect* column first. Point out that the punctuation in the sentences is missing or misplaced. Those mistakes have been corrected in the *Correct* column.
- As they edit their reports, have students look for places to add quotations to support their main ideas.

ENGLISH LANGUAGE SUPPORT

Additional Grammar Practice

Teach/Model Review that a direct quotation shows someone's exact words. An interjection is a word or phrase that shows emotion. Interjections are often found in quotations. Write: *"Wow!" Tony said. "Cougars are awesome predators."*

- Ask: *What were Tony's exact words? How do you know?*
- Circle the quotation marks in the quotation. Say: *These are quotation marks. We put one set to show where a quotation starts. We put the other set to show where the quotation ends.*

Guided Practice Ask two students what they learned about cougars this week. Write their names and their responses. Have partners use these sentence frames to write quotations based on what each student said:

- _____ said, "_____."
- "_____," said _____.

Connect to Writing Have students write a paragraph that summarizes the main ideas of "Cougars." Have them use one quotation from the selection in their summary. ELD ELD.PI.5.10b

Informative Writing Write a Research Report

▶ SHARE OBJECTIVES

- Draft, revise, and edit a research report.
- Publish final drafts.

Terms About Writing

paraphrase restate an idea in your own words

summarize retell the main ideas of a text

source list written record of sources from which a writer has gathered information for a report

plagiarism passing off someone else's work or ideas as your own

ENGLISH LANGUAGE SUPPORT

Collaborative Writing

Explain that the class will work together to write a research report about a wild animal.

- **Ask:** *What should be in the first paragraph? The first paragraph should introduce the animal in an interesting way.* Remind students that they have used sources to collect information for the research report. When they write, they must be sure to use their own words to restate what appeared in the source. Explain that students can use synonyms to change the wording of their sources. Remind them to be aware of how synonyms often have different shades of meaning.

- **Say:** *We will write one paragraph for each main idea in the outline.* Work with students to write one body paragraph about a wild animal. Start with a topic sentence that states a main idea. Then encourage students to use facts and details to support the main idea.

- **Ask:** *What goes at the end of a research report? a conclusion that summarizes the main ideas* **ELD** ELD.PI.5.1

Go over the Writing Traits Checklist with students. Record students' suggestions for improving the story.

Performance Task

myWriteSmart Have students complete the writing task through *my*WriteSmart. Students will read the prompt within *my*WriteSmart and have access to multiple writing resources, including the Student eBook, Writing Rubrics, and Graphic Organizers.

DAY 1 DRAFT

❶ TEACH DRAFTING

- Tell students that they will be writing drafts of the research report they planned in Lesson 9. Review the following:

What Is a Research Report?

- It explains a topic in depth.
- It presents logically organized information from a variety of print and digital sources.
- It includes paraphrases and summaries of facts and details, as well as direct quotations.
- It provides a strong conclusion that sums up the significance of the facts presented.
- It includes a list of sources.

- Point out that the introduction should catch readers' attention as well as identify the specific focus of the report.

- Discuss this sample introduction:
  Who hasn't heard of the sinking of the Titanic *in the Atlantic Ocean on April 15, 1912? It is the most well-known disaster in maritime history. However, many lives could have been saved with more efficient emergency procedures and more lifeboats.*

- Point out that it begins with a broad question that captures readers' attention and that the last sentence tells readers exactly what the report will explain.

ENGLISH LANGUAGE SUPPORT How English Works As students work on their research reports, remind them that the information in their reports must be presented clearly. To do so, the reports should be structured in a way that helps readers understand the flow of information. Suggest that students review their organizational structures before they begin. **ELD** ELD.PII.5.1

❷ PRACTICE/APPLY

- Have students use their outlines and notes from Lesson 9 to begin drafting their reports. Remind them to keep their task, audience, and purpose in mind. **ELA** W.5.4

- Tell students to make sure their introductory paragraphs identify the focus of their report and engage their readers. **ELA** W.5.2a

LESSON	FORM	FOCUS
6	Procedural Composition	Organization
7	Compare-Contrast Essay	Elaboration
8	Cause-and-Effect Essay	Evidence
9	Prewrite: Research Report	Evidence
10	**Draft, Revise, Edit, Publish: Research Report**	**Conventions**

WRITING

Additional support for Informative Writing appears in **the Common Core Writing Handbook,** Lesson 10.

DAY 2 DRAFT

1 INTRODUCE THE WRITING FOCUS

CONVENTIONS Explain that students will **paraphrase** or **summarize** most of the information they take from their sources, using their own words to restate ideas.

- Tell students that if they copy words or phrases, they must use quotation marks. They can use transitional words, phrases, or clauses to make quotations fit smoothly into their sentences.

Connect to "Cougars"

Original Source	Paraphrase and Quotation
"Unlike humans, cougars have no sweat glands, so the cougars that live in warm climates cool themselves the same way dogs do, by panting to release heat from their bodies." (p. 298)."	Cougars cannot sweat. In warm weather, they cool down "the same way dogs do, by panting."

- Point out that the passage with the quotation also paraphrases the original source. The words *In warm weather* provide a transition. ELA W.5.2a, W.5.2c

Annotate it! Have students underline key passages in the text that could be used in a summary or research report.

2 PRACTICE/APPLY

- Work with students to summarize another passage. ELA W.5.8

- As students continue drafting, remind them to develop each aspect of their topic in a separate paragraph with facts, examples, and details. ELA W.5.2b

- Distribute Reader's Notebook page 120 and have students complete it independently.

ENGLISH LANGUAGE SUPPORT

How English Works: Productive

Using Verb Types As students draft their research reports, have them think about the verb types that they can use in their writing. Review some verb types with students—action verbs: *drove, walked, ran*; linking verbs: *is, was, became*; helping verbs: *can, will, have*. Help different proficiency levels think about their topics and build word banks of verbs to use while drafting. ELD ELD.PII.5.3

DAY 3 DRAFT

1 TEACH SOURCE LISTS

- Remind students that to avoid **plagiarism,** they must include a **source list** at the end of their research report. Tell students that this list should include all the sources from which they took information, so that the original writers get credit for their ideas.

- Explain that students need to put the details about each source in a specific format, depending upon what type of resource it is. Display the examples below.

Book by one author:

Last name of author, First name of author. Title of book. City of publication: Publisher, Copyright date.

Print encyclopedia article:

Last name of author, First name of author. "Title of article." Name of encyclopedia. Edition. Date.

Online encyclopedia:

"Title of article." Name of encyclopedia. Copyright date. Publisher. Date of access <URL>.

Website:

Title of the site. Date of last update of site. Sponsor of site. Date of access <URL>.

- Explain each example and what it includes. Point out the punctuation between components of the citations and the indentation of the second line. Make sure students know that "date of access" means when they used the source on the Internet.

2 PRACTICE/APPLY

- Have students take turns giving the details about one of their sources. Work together to create an entry for each one.

- Have students work on their source lists, arranging the sources in alphabetical order. ELA W.5.8, W.5.10

DAY 4 REVISE

1 TEACH/MODEL

- Review the organizational plan of a research report from Lesson 9, Day 4. Remind students that their report should present their ideas in a clear, focused, and orderly way. Emphasize the importance of using transitions to link ideas. **ELA** W.5.2a, W.5.2c

- Tell students that their conclusion should sum up their main points and show readers the importance of the information presented.

2 PRACTICE/APPLY

- Have students revise their drafts to make sure their details are in a logical order. Suggest that they use the highlighting tool in a word processing program to identify the main idea sentence in each paragraph. If they cannot, work with them to add to or strengthen their main ideas. **ELA** W.5.6

- Tell students to look for vague words in their drafts that could be replaced with precise language or with vocabulary that is specific to their topic. Have them consult print or digital reference materials to find alternate word choices. Have students revise as necessary to add transitions that will link related ideas. **ELA** W.5.2d, L.5.4c

- Remind students to make sure that any quotations in their report are formatted correctly and set off with quotation marks and proper punctuation.

- Then have students work with a partner to strengthen their conclusion. **ELA** W.5.2e, W.5.5

- Distribute the **Writing Conference Form**. Have student pairs evaluate their own and each other's reports. Have them use the feedback to continue their revisions.

DAY 5 REVISE, EDIT, AND PUBLISH

1 INTRODUCE THE STUDENT MODEL

- Read the top of **Student Book p. 316** together. Draw students' attention to the revisions made by the student writer. Point out that she avoided plagiarism by rewriting several sentences in her own words.

- Have students explore Digital Lesson: Writing as a Process: Revise and Edit ⌐ to develop their informative writing.

2 PRACTICE/APPLY

- Display Projectable 10.7 ⌐. Then have students read the Final Copy of Josie's report on **Student Book p. 317**. Have them compare the text on the projectable to the final copy. Ask them what Josie changed and why.

- Discuss the *Reading as a Writer* questions.

- **Proofreading** For proofreading support, have students use the Proofreading Checklist Blackline Master ⌐.

- **Publish** Have students create a final copy of their reports. Provide these publishing options:

  Illustrated Report Have students use word processing software to produce an illustrated version of their reports, incorporating graphics. See also Keyboarding Lessons on pp. R28–R32.

  Webpage Have students publish their report as a page on the school's website.

  Multimedia Report Have students add sound effects, music, and visuals to their reports and present them to the class. **ELA** W.5.6, W.5.2a

---

ENGLISH LANGUAGE SUPPORT

Peer-Supported Learning

All Proficiencies See the Peer Conference Forms in the ELL Teacher's Handbook.

Reading-Writing Workshop: Revise

Informative Writing

Interactive Lessons
► Writing as a Process: Revise and Edit

✔ Conventions In a **research report**, good writers are careful not to copy sentences or phrases from their sources. As you revise your report, use synonyms—different words with similar meanings—to help you rephrase quotes from your sources.

Josie drafted her report on the sinking of the *Andrea Doria*. Later, she rephrased sentences that she had accidentally copied and she made sure her spelling, grammar, and punctuation were correct. She made other revisions to improve her writing, as well.

Revised Draft

The night was foggy, and each ship was using its radar to navigate.

~~The Andrea Doria was surrounded by a fog~~

~~bank. When radar showed another ship (the~~
The Andrea Doria's radar showed the
~~Stockholm) nearby, she continued her course.~~
Stockholm nearby, but the crew decided not to turn the ship.
Eventually, the ships got close enough to see

each other through the fog, and the captains

realized they were too close to avoid a crash.
The bow, or front end, of the Stockholm
"slammed into the
~~The Stockholm's bow ripped into the side of~~

~~Andrea Doria's side."~~
~~the Andrea Doria.~~

Writing Process Checklist

Prewrite
Draft
► Revise

☑ Does my first paragraph introduce the main ideas in an interesting way?

☑ Did I use correct spelling, grammar, and punctuation?

☑ Did I develop my topic with facts, details, and examples?

☑ Did I use transitions to link ideas?

☑ Did I use quotations and domain-specific words and their definitions?

☑ Does my conclusion sum up my main ideas?

☑ Did I include an accurate list of sources?

316   ELA W.5.2a, W.5.2b, W.5.2c, W.5.2d   ELD ELD.PI.5.10a, ELD.PI.5.12a, ELD.PII.5.1, ELD.PII.5.2a, ELD.PII.5.2b, ELD.PII.5.6, ELD.PII.5.7

Final Copy

A Successful Rescue

by Josie Teicher

It was the night of July 25th, 1956. A terrible accident was about to happen. An Italian ship, the *Andrea Doria*, and a Swedish ship, the *Stockholm*, were headed straight for each other.

The night was foggy, and each ship was navigating by radar. The *Andrea Doria*'s radar showed the *Stockholm* nearby, but the crew decided not to turn the ship. Eventually, the ships got close enough to see each other through the fog, and the captains realized they were too close to avoid a crash. The bow, or front end, of the *Stockholm* "slammed into the *Andrea Doria*'s side."

The *Andrea Doria* put out an SOS, which is a radio call for help. The *Ile de France* arrived just three hours after the crash. It was able to rescue hundreds of *Andrea Doria* passengers. Even the *Stockholm* was able to rescue people because it was damaged but not sinking.

Partly because the *Andrea Doria* took so long to sink, all but forty-six of the 1,706 people on board were saved. This sea rescue was one of the most successful in history.

Reading as a Writer

In what other ways could Josie have reworded the sentences she copied? How can you reword any copied sentences in your report?

In my final paper, I included facts, definitions, details, and a quotation. I also made sure to avoid plagiarism by rephrasing sentences I had copied from sources during my research.

317

WRITING TRAITS SCORING RUBRIC

SCORE	4	3	2	1	NS
Purpose/ Organization	The narrative is clear, focused, and well organized throughout. • Contains an effective and complete plot • Develops strong setting, narrator/ characters • Includes a variety of transitions to connect ideas • Contains a logical sequence of events • Includes an effective introduction and conclusion	The narrative's organization is adequately maintained, and the focus is generally clear. • Plot is mostly effective/may contain small flaws • Develops setting, narrator/ characters • Adequate use of transitions to connect ideas • Contains an adequate sequence of events	The narrative is somewhat organized and may be unclear in some parts. • Plot may be inconsistent • Minimal development of setting, narrator/characters • Contains inconsistent use of transitions to connect ideas • Sequence of events is weak or unclear • Introduction and conclusion need improvement	The narrative may be somewhat organized but unfocused. • Little or no plot • Little or no development of setting, narrator/characters • Contains few or inappropriate transitions and weak connections among ideas • Sequence of events is not organized • Introduction and/or conclusion may be missing	• Not intelligible • Not written in English • Not on topic • Contains text copied from another source • Does not address the purpose for writing
Development/ Elaboration	The narrative includes effective elaboration using details, dialogue, and description. • Characters, setting, experiences, and events are well developed • Writer uses a variety of narrative techniques that strengthen the story or illustrate the experience • Contains effective sensory, concrete, and figurative language • Style is appropriate and effective	The narrative includes adequate elaboration using details, dialogue, and description. • Characters, setting, experiences, and events are adequately developed • Writer uses a variety of narrative techniques that generally move the story forward and illustrate the experience • Contains adequate sensory, concrete, and figurative language • Style is mostly appropriate	The narrative includes partial or ineffective elaboration using unclear or inconsistent details, dialogue, and description. • Characters, setting, experiences, and events lack consistent development • Writer uses inconsistent or weak narrative techniques • Contains weak sensory, concrete, and figurative language • Style is inconsistent or inappropriate	The narrative provides little or no elaboration using few or no details, dialogue, and description. • Very little development of characters, setting, experiences, and events • Writer's use of narrative techniques are minimal and may be incorrect • Little or no sensory, concrete, and figurative language • Little or no evidence of style	• Not intelligible • Not written in English • Not on topic • Contains text copied from another source • Does not address the purpose for writing

SCORE	2	1	0	NS
Conventions	The narrative demonstrates adequate command of conventions. • Consistent use of correct sentence structures, punctuation, capitalization, grammar, and spelling	The narrative demonstrates partial command of conventions. • Limited use of correct sentence structures, punctuation, capitalization, grammar, and spelling	The narrative demonstrates little or no command of conventions. • Rare use of correct sentence structures, punctuation, capitalization, grammar, and spelling	• Not intelligible • Not written in English • Not on topic • Contains text copied from another source

See also **Writing Rubric Blackline Master** and Teacher's Edition pp. R18–R21.

Formative Assessment

Weekly Tests

At the end of the lesson, administer the Weekly Test. This will give you a **snapshot of how students are progressing** with the Reading and Language Arts skills in this lesson and can give you **guidance on grouping, reteaching, and intervention.** Suggestions for adjusting instruction based on these results can be found on the next page.

Access Through Accommodations

When you administer the Weekly Test, some students may have problems accessing all or parts of the assessment. The purpose of the Weekly Test is to determine students' ability to complete the Reading and Language Arts tasks they learned in this lesson. Any barriers to them accessing the tasks demanded of them should be lowered so they can focus on skill demonstration.

When choosing accommodations, you will want to avoid invalidating the test results; if you are measuring a student's reading skill, for example, you will not want to read aloud the passage. The following accommodations, if needed, will not interfere with the Weekly Test's validity:

- Read aloud the assessment directions and item prompts. If students are English learners, read aloud the assessment directions and item prompts in the student's native language, if possible.

- Define any unknown words in the directions or item prompts that do not give away the answers to the items.

- Allow for a break during the assessment.

- Simplify the language of assessment directions and item prompts.

- Administer the assessment in a smaller group setting.

- Administer the assessment on a computer or other electronic device.

- Provide audio amplification equipment, colored overlays, or visual magnifying equipment to maintain visual/audio attention and access.

- Allow students to complete the assessment items orally or by having another person transcribe their responses.

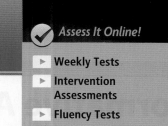
Using Data to Adjust Instruction

Use students' scores on the Weekly Test to determine Small Group placement, reteaching, and potential for Intervention.

☑ VOCABULARY AND COMPREHENSION

Main Ideas and Details; Explain Scientific Ideas; Domain-Specific Vocabulary; Anchor Text Target Vocabulary; Shades of Meaning

IF STUDENT SCORES...	
...at acceptable,	**...below acceptable,**
THEN continue core instruction.	**THEN** use Reteach Comprehension Skill and Vocabulary Strategies lessons. For struggling students, administer the *Intervention Assessments* to determine if students would benefit from intervention.

☑ LANGUAGE ARTS

Direct Quotations and Interjections

IF STUDENT SCORES...	
...at acceptable,	**...below acceptable,**
THEN continue core instruction.	**THEN** use Reteach Language Arts lesson. For struggling students, administer the *Intervention Assessments* to determine if students would benefit from intervention.

☑ DECODING

Recognizing Schwa + /r/ Sounds

IF STUDENT SCORES...	
...at acceptable,	**...below acceptable,**
THEN continue core instruction.	**THEN** use Reteach Decoding lesson. For struggling students, administer the *Intervention Assessments* to determine if students would benefit from intervention.

☑ FLUENCY

Fluency Plan

Assess one group per week using the <u>Fluency Tests</u> in the *Grab-and-Go™* Resources. Use the suggested plan at the right.

● **Struggling Readers**	**Weeks 1, 3, 5**
▲ **On Level**	**Week 2**
■ **Advanced**	**Week 4**

IF...	
...students are reading on-level text fluently,	**...students are reading below level,**
THEN continue core instruction.	**THEN** provide additional fluency practice using the **Student Book**, the **Cold Reads**, and the Leveled Readers. For struggling students, administer the *Intervention Assessments* to determine if students would benefit from intervention.

HOUGHTON MIFFLIN HARCOURT

JOURNEYS

Cold Reads

5

The **Cold Reads** passages increase gradually in Lexile® measures throughout the year, from below grade-level to above grade-level.

- Each passage is accompanied by several selected-response questions and one constructed-response prompt, requiring students to read closely, answer questions at substantial DOK levels, and cite text evidence.

- The *Cold Reads* may be used to provide practice in reading increasingly complex texts and to informally monitor students' progress.

- The *Cold Reads* may be used to estimate students' Lexile® levels in order to recommend appropriately challenging books for small-group instruction or independent reading.

Turn the page for more information about using FORMATIVE ASSESSMENT for ELD AND INTERVENTION.

✓ Assess It Online!

▶ Language Workshop Assessment Handbook

▶ Intervention Assessments

Formative Assessment for ELD and Intervention

Formative Assessment for English Learners

English learners should engage in the same rigorous curriculum and formative assessment as other students. However, it is important to remember that English learners face a dual challenge: they are strengthening their abilities *to use* English at the same time that they are learning challenging content *through* English. Use the following strategies and resources for ongoing assessment of English language development, in addition to the assessments you use with all students:

- A combination of **observational measures,** such as listening in as students read aloud or participate in collaborative conversations. Be prepared to provide **"just-in-time" scaffolding** to support students. For example, if students are retelling a story, you could help them use sentence structures with past-tense verbs and time-order transition words.

- **Constructive feedback** that focuses on communication and meaning-making. Avoid overcorrecting in a way that makes English learners reluctant to speak up. You might try recasting a child's statement more correctly, making a note to address the target form more directly during Designated ELD time.

- **Student self-assessment,** through students' own notes in their vocabulary notebooks or other learning journals. If possible, meet with each child to review his or her self-assessments and provide encouragement and feedback.

- **Formative assessment** notes that are integrated into the Language Workshop Teacher's Guide for use during Designated ELD.

- **Language Workshop Assessment Handbook** for longer-cycle assessment to make sure students are progressing in their English development.

Response to Intervention

Use the Weekly Tests and Benchmark and Unit Tests, along with your own observations, to determine if individual students are not responding to Tier I instruction and need additional testing to identify specific needs for targeted intervention.

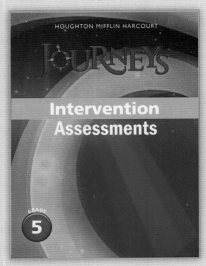

Intervention Assessments

Assessment for Intervention

Progress-Monitoring Assessments Administer this assessment to

- students in Tier II and Tier III Intervention to gauge progress towards exit from the intervention program.

- students who demonstrate lack of success with Weekly Tests, Benchmark and Unit Tests, and core instruction to determine if they might benefit from additional practice or intervention.

Performance Task

Discuss Writing to a Prompt

Point out the Task label on **Student Book p. 318.** Tell students that often they will be given a writing task that begins with a prompt that explains the writing task. Explain to students that the prompt tells exactly what students have to do and that it is important to understand all the parts of the prompt before beginning to write. Tell students that they can follow the steps below to help them respond to writing prompts.

1 Read the prompt carefully.

2 Ask yourself, "What is the prompt asking me to do? What am I supposed to write?" Make sure you understand whether you are being asked to write a story, an opinion essay, or an informational essay.

3 Restate the prompt in your own words to make sure you understand it.

4 Decide which text(s) you may need to look back at to use in your writing.

5 Complete the parts of the writing process: plan, draft, revise, and present.

ENGLISH LANGUAGE SUPPORT Help students identify the prompt on **Student Book p. 318,** or project it from the **eBook,** and read it aloud. Model how to break apart the prompt and highlight the key words to help students figure out the task. Underline key words as you think aloud. Vertical slash marks indicate individual parts to focus on and discuss one at a time.

Think about the information in the texts you just read. / Now write an essay that explains what people have done to protect natural areas and wildlife. / Use ideas from Quest for the Tree Kangaroo, Everglades Forever, and National Parks of the West in your essay.

Think Aloud *The first sentence of the prompt tells me to think about the information I just read in these three texts. The next sentence tells me to write an essay. There are many kinds of essays, but I will write an informational essay. I know that an informational essay explains about a topic. It is based on fact. My task is to write about what people have done to protect natural areas and wildlife. In the last sentence, I read that I will use ideas from the three texts in my essay.*

▶ SHARE OBJECTIVES

- Learn and apply strategies for writing to a prompt.

- Write an informational essay that clearly introduces the topic, uses facts to develop the topic, presents information in an organized way, and concludes with a summary.

- Gather information from sources to use in writing.

- Follow the steps of the writing process: plan, draft, revise, and present.

Unit Performance Tasks
Unit 1: Write a Story
▶ Unit 2: Write an Informational Essay
Unit 3: Write an Opinion Essay
Unit 4: Write a Literary Analysis
Unit 5: Write a Response to Literature

To support students before they start this task, use the following digital resources.

▶ Interactive Lessons: Writing to Sources. Writing Informative Texts: Use Facts and Examples. Writing Informative Texts: Organize Your Information

▶ Interactive Whiteboard Lessons: Text Analysis: Parts 1 and 2. Informational Writing

Write an Informational Essay

- Introduce the Performance Task on **Student Book p. 318** by reading the task with students. Help them identify the key parts of the prompt. Use Steps 1–4 on p. T363 to guide students in analyzing the prompt.

Plan

- Page through *Quest for the Tree Kangaroo* with students. Ask them to identify ways that people are protecting nature, and write students' responses on the board. Do the same with *Everglades Forever* and with *National Parks of the West.* Point out that each of these books tells about a different region. Remind them that they will write a clear introduction to the overall topic before they begin presenting facts about each region.

- Tell students to decide which region they will tell about first, second, and third. Have students think about which efforts at protecting wildlife interest them the most. Suggest that they start with that.

> **Think Aloud** *I've looked through* Quest for the Tree Kangaroo, Everglades Forever, *and* National Parks of the West. *I see that all these texts have the same topic in common—protecting nature—so I will think of an introduction that discusses that and fits with all three regions. I know that an informational essay should be clear and well organized. I've chosen the Everglades as the first area I will discuss in my essay and national parks of the West as the second area. I think my readers will be more familiar with these areas.*

- Distribute <u>Graphic Organizer 15</u> to students. Guide them to complete the idea web with examples of living things and environments that people are trying to protect. **ELA** L.5.6 **ELD** ELD.PI.5.12a, ELD.PII.5.1, ELD.PII.5.2b, ELD.PII.5.6

Write an Informational Essay

TASK In *Quest for the Tree Kangaroo*, you read about how a group of research scientists study and work to protect a rare animal. In *Everglades Forever*, you read about a group of students who explore the Everglades in order to learn how they can help preserve it. You have also read about preserving natural environments in *National Parks of the West*.

Think about the information in the texts you just read. Now, write an essay that explains what people have done to protect natural areas and wildlife. Use ideas from *Quest for the Tree Kangaroo*, *Everglades Forever*, and *National Parks of the West* in your essay. Your essay will be read by your classmates and your teacher.

Make sure your essay

- clearly introduces your topic.
- is organized by grouping related information logically.
- develops your topic with facts, details, and other information related to the topic.

> **PLAN** ▣ myNotebook

Gather Information What are some places people have tried to protect? What are some of the animals that need protecting? Revisit the texts to find this information.

Use the annotation tools in your eBook to gather evidence to support your ideas.

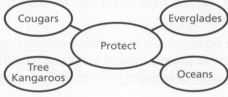

ENGLISH LANGUAGE SUPPORT

Unpack the Prompt

Emerging To help students complete the idea web, have them work with a partner to complete these sentence frames:

I write the _____ in the center of the web.

_____ is my main topic.

I write _____ in the center of this idea web.

I will tell how the _____ are protected.

I write _____ in one of the balloons.

I will do the same for the other _____.

Expanding Have students fill out the sentence frames independently. In mixed-ability groups, have them discuss their sentences and exchange suggestions before completing their idea webs. **ELD** ELD.PI.5.1

Bridging Have students discuss with a partner which ideas to include in their informational essay and why. Then have students discuss how to clearly introduce the topic and how to organize information logically. **ELD** ELD.PI.5.1, ELD.PII.5.1

Write Your Essay Now begin working on your essay. Use the flow chart and what you have already learned about writing an informational essay to write your draft.

Write your rough draft in *my*WriteSmart. Focus on getting your ideas down rather than perfecting your word choices.

BEGINNING

Write the beginning of your essay. Introduce your **topic** clearly and explain the particular **focus** of the essay. Be sure to **organize** related information logically. Make sure each **main idea** has its own paragraph.

MIDDLE

Develop your topic with **facts** and **definitions** related to the topic. Use **details** and **evidence** from the texts to support your **ideas**. Remember to use **quotation marks** to indicate words or phrases that are directly from the text. Use **transitions** to link your ideas. Use **precise language** and include **domain-specific vocabulary** to explain your topic.

ENDING

Provide a strong **conclusion** for your essay. Be sure to sum up the important facts that you presented and show how they relate to your topic.

319

Draft

Write Your Informational Essay Read aloud the information on **Student Book p. 319** with students, one section at a time. Remind them to use the information in their completed idea webs to help them follow the steps for drafting their informational essay.

- Tell students that at the beginning of their informational essay, they should introduce the topic clearly and explain the focus of the essay. Tell them that the whole essay should be organized logically and that each main idea has its own paragraph.

- Each essay topic should be developed with details and evidence from the text. Students should use domain-specific vocabulary and precise language. They should include definitions if necessary. Words or phrases directly from the text should be set off with quotation marks. Students should use transitions to link ideas in the essay.

- Explain to students that the essay needs a strong conclusion. They should summarize important facts and show how these relate to the overall topic.

Circulate, as needed, to provide assistance while students write their drafts. **ELA** W.5.2, W.5.2a, W.5.2b, W.5.2c, W.5.2d, W.5.2e, W.5.4, W.5.5, W.5.8, W.5.9a, W.5.10, L.5.3 **ELD** ELD.PI.5.4, ELD.PI.5.10a, ELD.PI.5.12a, ELD.PII.5.1, ELD.PII.5.2b

ENGLISH LANGUAGE SUPPORT As a class, work together to apply understanding of how ideas, events, or reasons are linked throughout a text, using such terms as *first, next, at the beginning, for example,* and *as a result.* Have students look back through the texts to find examples of these terms or other terms that show connection and progress of ideas. Have students share their examples with classmates. **ELD** ELD.PII.5.2b

Revise

Review Your Draft Read the top of p. 320 with students.

- Have partners read aloud each other's essays. They should pay attention to whether the essay is organized logically and whether it presents facts and other evidence from the text, uses domain-specific vocabulary, and sets off exact phrases from the text with quotation marks.

- Remind partners to ask questions to clarify the organization of the essay, if necessary. Encourage partners to brainstorm ways to revise.

ENGLISH LANGUAGE SUPPORT Model a conversation to help students with the peer review.

> **Think Aloud** *I see that after your opening, you discuss the Everglades and then national parks. Then you discuss tree kangaroos. You clearly present your facts, using specific vocabulary such as* carbon footprint, ecosystem, natural resource, *and* wilderness. *You used transitional phrases to connect ideas.*

> Provide sentence frames as needed, such as: *The fact that you tell about _____ is very powerful. Did it come from _____? Did you use a new _____ for each new topic?*

- As students revise, remind them to make their writing clearer by using specific vocabulary and defining it if necessary.

- If students have difficulty organizing, have them create an idea web for each topic they present. Remind them to use transitional phrases to show connection and progress of ideas.

- Remind students to proofread their drafts for correct spelling, capitalization, and punctuation. As needed, review word choice from Lesson 6.

  ELA W.5.2a, W.5.2b, W.5.2c, W.5.2d, W.5.2e, L.5.4c, L.5.6
  ELD ELD.PI.5.10a, ELD.PI.5.12a, ELD.PII.5.4

- To evaluate student writing, see **Writing Traits Scoring Rubric: Narrative Writing Rubric Blackline Master,** p. R14.

Present

Create a Finished Copy If students read their stories to classmates, remind them to read loudly, slowly, and clearly so that listeners can hear the facts and technical terms in the essay.

If students choose to publish their essays on the school website or blog, guide them to write a few sentences introducing themselves and asking for feedback from readers. **ELA** W.5.4 **ELD** ELD.PI.5.9

Review Your Draft Remember that the revision and editing steps give you a chance to look carefully at your writing and make changes. Work with a partner to determine whether your informational essay clearly introduces your topic, organizes information logically, develops the topic using facts and details, and provides a concluding section that sums up the facts presented.

> Have your partner review your essay in *my*WriteSmart and note where the essay is not clear. Discuss how to make improvements.

Purpose and Organization	Evidence and Elaboration	Conventions
✔ Did I introduce my topic clearly?	✔ Did I develop my topic with facts and details?	✔ Does my essay include a variety of complete sentences?
✔ Did I explain the focus of my essay?	✔ Are my ideas supported by details and evidence from the texts?	✔ Have I used quotation marks to show that the words are directly from the text?
✔ Is my information organized in a logical way?	✔ Did I use transitions to link my ideas?	✔ Is my spelling, punctuation, and capitalization correct?
✔ Do I have a strong conclusion that sums up my ideas?	✔ Have I used precise language and domain-specific vocabulary?	

PRESENT

Create a Finished Copy Write or type a final copy of your essay. You may want to include photographs or other graphics. Choose a way to share your essay with your classmates. Consider these options.

1. Read aloud your essay to your classmates. Be sure to speak clearly and at an understandable pace.

2. Publish your essay on a school website or blog and ask for feedback from readers.

3. Publish your essay using presentation software. Make it available for your classmates to view.

320

Weekly
Small Group Instruction

Vocabulary Reader
- *Big Cats,* T370–T371

Differentiate Comprehension
- Target Skill: Main Ideas and Details, T372–T373
- Target Strategy: Monitor/Clarify, T372–T373

Leveled Readers
- ● *Sharks,* T374
- ▲ *The Return of the Yellowstone Grizzly,* T375
- ■ *Saving the Mexican Wolves,* T376
- ◆ *Grizzly Bears Return to Yellowstone,* T377

Differentiate Vocabulary Strategies
- Shades of Meaning, T378–T379

Options for Reteaching
- Vocabulary Strategies: Shades of Meaning, T380
- Comprehension Skill: Main Ideas and Details, T380
- Language Arts: Direct Quotations and Interjections/
  Informative Writing, T381
- Decoding: Recognizing Schwa + /r/ Sounds, T381

Literacy Centers
Independent Practice
- Comprehension and Fluency, T310
- Word Study, T310
- Think and Write, T311

RtI Small Group Planner
Differentiated Instruction

		DAY 1	DAY 2	DAY 3
Teacher-Led	**Struggling Readers**	**Vocabulary Reader** *Big Cats*, Differentiated Instruction, p. T370 **English Language Support,** p. T371	**Differentiate Comprehension** Main Ideas and Details; Monitor/Clarify, p. T372 **English Language Support,** p. T373	**Leveled Reader** *Sharks*, p. T374 **English Language Support,** Leveled Reader Teacher's Guide, p. 5
	On Level	**Vocabulary Reader** *Big Cats*, Differentiated Instruction, p. T370 **English Language Support,** p. T371	**Differentiate Comprehension** Main Ideas and Details; Monitor/Clarify, p. T372 **English Language Support,** p. T373	**Leveled Reader** *The Return of the Yellowstone Grizzly*, p. T375 *Grizzly Bears Return to Yellowstone*, p. T377 **English Language Support,** Leveled Reader Teacher's Guide, p. 5
	Advanced	**Vocabulary Reader** *Big Cats*, Differentiated Instruction, p. T371 **English Language Support,** p. T371	**Differentiate Comprehension** Main Ideas and Details; Monitor/Clarify, p. T373 **English Language Support,** p. T373	**Leveled Reader** *Saving the Mexican Wolves*, p. T376 **English Language Support,** Leveled Reader Teacher's Guide, p. 5
What are my other students doing?	**Struggling Readers**	**Reread** *Big Cats*	**Vocabulary in Context Cards** 91–100 *Talk It Over* Activities	**Listen** to Audio of "Cougars"; retell and discuss
	On Level	**Reread** *Big Cats*	**Reread** "Cougars" with a partner	**Reread** for Fluency: *The Return of the Yellowstone Grizzly* or *Grizzly Bears Return to Yellowstone* **Complete** Leveled Practice EL10.1
	Advanced	**Vocabulary in Context Cards** 91–100 *Talk It Over* Activities	**Reread and Retell** "Cougars"	**Reread** for Fluency: *Saving the Mexican Wolves*

For Strategic Intervention for this lesson, see pp. S42–S51.

DAY 4

Differentiate Vocabulary Strategies
Shades of Meaning, p. T378
English Language Support, p. T379

Differentiate Vocabulary Strategies
Shades of Meaning, p. T378
English Language Support, p. T379

Differentiate Vocabulary Strategies
Shades of Meaning, p. T379
English Language Support, p. T379

- **Partners: Reread** *Sharks*
- **Complete** Leveled Practice SR10.1

- **Vocabulary in Context Cards**
  91–100 *Talk It Over* Activities
- **Complete** Reader's Notebook, p. 111

- **Reread** for Fluency: "Cougars"
- **Complete** Leveled Practice A10.1

DAY 5

Options for Reteaching,
pp. T380–T381

Options for Reteaching,
pp. T380–T381

Options for Reteaching,
pp. T380–T381

- **Reread** for Fluency: "Cougars"
- **Complete** Literacy Centers
- **Independent Reading**

- **Complete** Literacy Centers
- **Independent Reading**

- **Complete** Literacy Centers
- **Independent Reading**

English Language Support

Use the Leveled Reader Teacher's Guide to support ELs during differentiated instruction.

- **Characteristics of the Text** (p. 1)
  Identify challenging language features, such as text structure, literary features, complex sentences, and vocabulary.

- **Cultural Support/Cognates/Vocabulary** (p. 5)
  Explain unfamiliar features of English and help ELs transfer first-language knowledge.

- **Oral Language Development** (p. 5)
  Check comprehension using dialogues that match students' proficiency levels.

Book Share
Use this routine at the end of the week to enable students to demonstrate that they have become experts on their Leveled Readers.

Step 1:
Have each student write a presentation based on his or her Leveled Reader **Responding** page, using the following guidelines:

- Briefly tell what your book is about.

- Show your Web and explain what you added to complete it.

- Tell about your favorite part of the book, what you found most interesting in it, or what you learned from it.

Students should prepare to share their presentations with a group.

Step 2:
Have students form groups in which each student has read a different Leveled Reader.

Step 3:
Have students take turns sharing their book presentations in their groups. Continue until all students have finished sharing. Encourage students to ask questions of the presenters. Provide frames such as the following for support.

Can you tell me more about _____?

I wonder why _____.

What do you think about _____?

Vocabulary Reader
Big Cats

Summary

There are eight different kinds of big cats. They all are beautiful, fierce, and amazing hunters. But they also have interesting traits that make them distinct from one another.

☑ **TARGET VOCABULARY**

resemble	mature
detecting	particular
keen	available
vary	ferocious
unobserved	contentment

STRUGGLING READERS

ELA L.5.4a
ELD ELD.PI.5.1, ELD.PI.5.6b

- Explain that big cats come in different sizes and colors. They are some of the strongest, fastest animals on Earth.

- Guide students to preview the Vocabulary Reader. Read aloud the headings. Ask students to describe the images, using Target Vocabulary when possible.

- Have students alternate reading pages of the text aloud. Guide them to use context to determine the meanings of unfamiliar words. As necessary, use the **Vocabulary in Context Cards** to review the meanings of vocabulary words.

- Assign the **Responding Page** and Blackline Master 10.4. Have partners work together to complete the pages.

ON LEVEL

ELA L.5.4a
ELD ELD.PI.5.1, ELD.PI.5.6b

- Explain to students that big cats live in many places throughout the world. The environments they live in affect how the cats live, hunt, and raise their families. Guide students to preview the Vocabulary Reader.

- Remind students that context clues can help them determine the meaning of an unknown word. Tell students to use context clues to confirm their understanding of Target Vocabulary and to learn the meanings of new words.

- Have students alternate reading aloud pages of the text. Tell them to use context clues to determine the meanings of unknown words.

- Assign the **Responding Page** and Blackline Master 10.4. Have students discuss their responses with a partner

ADVANCED

ELA L.5.4a
ELD ELD.PI.5.1, ELD.PI.5.6b

- Have students preview the Vocabulary Reader and make predictions about what they will read, using information from the preview as well as prior knowledge.

- Remind students to use context clues to help them determine the meanings of unknown words.

- Tell students to read the text with a partner. Ask them to stop and discuss the meanings of unknown words as necessary.

- Assign the **Responding Page** and <u>Blackline Master 10.4</u> 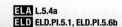. For the Write About It activity, remind students to use facts and details from the text.

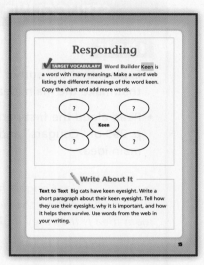

Big Cats, p. 15

ENGLISH LANGUAGE SUPPORT

ELD ELD.PI.5.1, ELD.PI.5.6b

Provide Struggling Readers, On Level, and Advanced ELs proficiency-level support during differentiated instruction.

Emerging

Conduct a picture walk with students. Then read the Vocabulary Reader aloud with them, pausing to explain the Target Vocabulary words as necessary.

Expanding

Use visuals, simplified language, and gestures to preteach the following selection vocabulary: *predator, stalk,* and *flexible.* Have partners use the words in oral sentences.

Bridging

Read aloud p. 5. Check students' understanding of unfamiliar words. Discuss the page with students before asking them to identify the main idea and supporting details orally.

Differentiate Comprehension
Main Ideas and Details; Monitor/Clarify

STRUGGLING READERS

ELA RI.5.2
ELD ELD.PI.5.1, ELD.PI.5.5, ELD.PI.5.6a

I DO IT

- Explain that the author uses facts and examples that make the main idea clear to readers.

- Read aloud the first paragraph on **Student Book p. 299** of "Cougars" and use details to identify the main idea.

> **Think Aloud** *Cougars have different colors but similar markings on the sides of their muzzles. The main idea is that they look similar but not identical.*

WE DO IT

- Read aloud pp. 298–300.

- Help students clarify what the main idea is. *Cougars' bodies help them survive.*

- Have students identify supporting details that they could include in a Web. Write the details on the board. *Two layers of hair keep cougars warm. Coloring helps them blend into surroundings.*

YOU DO IT

- Distribute Graphic Organizer 10 (Story Map) ↱. Have students read p. 302 and fill in a Web.

- Remind them that they should identify details that support the main idea and put those ideas in the outer circles.

- Ask volunteers to state the main idea and share details from the text that support it.

ON LEVEL

ELA RI.5.2
ELD ELD.PI.5.1, ELD.PI.5.5, ELD.PI.5.6a

I DO IT

- Read aloud p. 298 of "Cougars."

- Explain that understanding the details that support the main idea of a selection helps readers clarify meaning.

> **Think Aloud** *I learned that cougars have little fat on their bodies. They have layers of hair that keep them warm. Also, cougars don't have sweat glands, so they pant to cool down. These supporting details seem related. They describe ways in which the cougar's body characteristics help keep it at the right temperature.*

WE DO IT

- Have students read pp. 298–300.

- Have a volunteer name the main idea of this section. *Cougars have traits that help them survive.*

- Work together to find the text details that support the main idea. List them on the board. *Two layers of hair keep them warm. Coloring helps them blend into surroundings.*

- Discuss whether the details offer the necessary support.

YOU DO IT

- Distribute Graphic Organizer 10 (Story Map) ↱. Have students independently identify the main idea for a section of "Cougars." Have them enter it into a Web along with the supporting details.

- Have students read only the details in their Web to a partner and see if their partner can figure out the main idea.

ADVANCED

ELA RI.5.2
ELD ELD.PI.5.1, ELD.PI.5.5, ELD.PI.5.6a

I DO IT

- Read aloud p. 298 of "Cougars."

- Explain that a well-developed main idea will have strong supporting details.

- Explain that the main idea might not be obvious. Readers may have to analyze details in order to infer it.

- Add that a selection may be made up of several main ideas that, together, support a central main idea.

WE DO IT

- Have students read p. 302 independently.

- Ask students what is described on this page. *how newborn kittens change their appearance as they grow* Ask students what details support this. *description of their fur and how it changes over time; how their eyes change color; curly tails straighten*

- Guide students to infer the unstated main idea by connecting the details. *Kittens change as they grow older.*

YOU DO IT

- Distribute Graphic Organizer 10 (Story Map) ↱. Have partners choose a passage from the selection, infer its main idea, and identify the supporting details. Ask students to fill in a Web with this information.

- Then have students write a paragraph telling how their Webs helped them clarify meaning.

- Invite students to use their completed Webs to monitor/clarify their understanding of the text.

ENGLISH LANGUAGE SUPPORT

ELD ELD.PI.5.1, ELD.PI.5.5

Provide Struggling Readers, On Level, and Advanced ELs proficiency-level support during differentiated instruction.

Emerging

Help students understand what a main idea is and how details support it. Write: *My cat is pretty. She has green eyes and long, gray fur. Her fur is soft.* Ask for the main idea. *My cat is pretty.* Ask for details. *green eyes, long, gray, soft fur*

Expanding

Review with students how to locate and express a main idea. Display this sentence fram: *I know that cougars are _____ because they _____.* Complete it with student input to review an example of a main idea and details. Read pp. 298–300 of "Cougars" aloud. Ask students what the section is mostly about. *cougar survival traits* Guide them to understand this is the main idea. Repeat the activity with a different sentence frame to elicit supporting details. Tell students to use similar friends as they read the selection in their respective groups.

Bridging

Have students consult print and online dictionaries and thesauruses to find synonyms for the details they record in their Webs. Model how to find and use words and phrases that mean the same thing as *mature*. Write *mature* in a Web and guide students to find and add synonyms such as *develop, grow up, become an adult, reach adulthood*. Have students practice using the synonyms in sentences that give details about the main idea: *Kittens mature over time.*

Leveled Readers

ELA RI.5.2, RF.5.4a, W.5.1a, W.5.4, SL.5.1a
ELD ELD.PI.5.1, ELD.PI.5.5, ELD.PI.5.11a

✓ **TARGET SKILL**
Main Ideas and Details

✓ **TARGET STRATEGY**
Monitor/Clarify

✓ **TARGET VOCABULARY**

unobserved	resemble
available	particular
detecting	vary
mature	contentment
ferocious	keen

STRUGGLING READERS

 Sharks

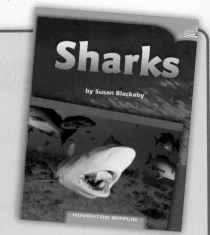

GENRE: INFORMATIONAL TEXT

Summary Sharks are fish at the top of the ocean food chain. This selection tells about how sharks use their five senses and how they are essential to keeping a balanced ocean ecosystem.

Introducing the Text

- Discuss key vocabulary from the text. Explain that sharks have been known to attack humans. However, this is often because the shark mistakes the human for a seal, which is its usual food.

- Remind students that a Web can help them organize and understand the supporting details for each main idea.

Supporting the Reading

- As you listen to students read, pause to discuss these questions.

  pp. 5–6 *What are some details that tell how all sharks are alike? They are fish, have backbones, are always growing new teeth, and breathe using gills.*

  p. 12 *We think of sharks as a threat to humans. How are humans a threat to sharks? Humans hunt sharks for their meat or for other uses. Sharks also get caught in fishing nets or tangled in garbage.*

Discussing and Revisiting the Text

CRITICAL THINKING After discussing *Sharks* together, have students read the instructions on **Responding** p. 15. Use these teaching points to guide them as they revisit the text.

- Have partners discuss the main idea of how sharks use their senses to hunt.

- Ask them to locate supporting details and enter them on <u>Blackline Master 10.5</u>.

FLUENCY: STRESS Model stressing words appropriately. Have students echo-read p. 12, reminding them that italics often indicate that a word should be stressed.

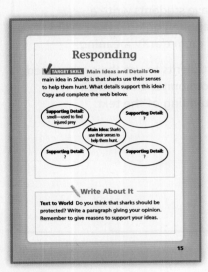

Sharks, p. 15

ELA RI.5.2, RF.5.4a, W.5.1a, W.5.4, SL.5.1a
ELD ELD.PI.5.1, ELD.PI.5.5, ELD.PI.5.11a

ON LEVEL

 ## *The Return of the Yellowstone Grizzly*

GENRE: INFORMATIONAL TEXT

Summary As settlers ventured west in the 1800s, they killed grizzlies because the bears were a threat to their animals and crops. In 1975, the grizzly bear was listed as a threatened species. Today their numbers have returned to healthy levels.

Introducing the Text

• Discuss key vocabulary from the text. Explain that Yellowstone Park once had a set of bleachers so people could sit and watch the grizzlies dig through garbage. This was a mistake!

• Remind students that a good reader always tries to identify the main idea of the paragraph and the details that support it.

Supporting the Reading

• As you listen to students read, pause to discuss these questions.

p. 7 *The pioneers thought the grizzly was a threat to them. What details does the author give to support this idea? Pioneers used traps and other methods to try to get rid of the bears.*

p. 9 *What was the result of people feeding bears? The grizzlies associated people with food, so they sought them out. Some bears became a danger to people and had to be removed from the park.*

Discussing and Revisiting the Text

CRITICAL THINKING After discussing the selection together, have students read the instructions on **Responding** p. 18. Use these teaching points to guide them as they revisit the text.

• Have students review the text individually or in pairs.

• Have students enter four details that support the main idea on Blackline Master 10.6 .

FLUENCY: STRESS Have students practice rereading p. 11, paying close attention to where they should use stress as they read.

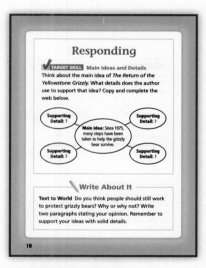

The Return of the Yellowstone Grizzly, p. 18

TARGET SKILL
Main Ideas and Details

TARGET STRATEGY
Monitor/Clarify

TARGET VOCABULARY

unobserved	resemble
available	particular
detecting	vary
mature	contentment
ferocious	keen

Leveled Readers

ELA RI.5.2, RF.5.4a, W.5.1a, W.5.4, SL.5.1a
ELD ELD.PI.5.1, ELD.PI.5.5, ELD.PI.5.11a

ADVANCED

 ## *Saving the Mexican Wolves*

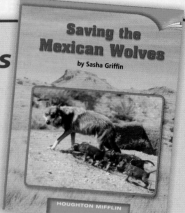

GENRE: INFORMATIONAL TEXT

Summary American settlers in the 1800s disliked the Mexican wolf, which attacked their livestock. By 1970, hunting had completely eliminated the Mexican wolf population in the United States. Slowly, the Mexican Wolf Recovery Plan has brought these wolves back.

Introducing the Text

- Discuss key vocabulary from the text. Explain that wolves are at the top of the food chain and that they are vital for a healthy ecosystem.

- Remind students that a good reader monitors text details in order to figure out the main idea.

Supporting the Reading

- As you listen to students read, pause to discuss these questions.

  p. 5 *Wolves are carnivores, yet they are part of a food chain that includes plants. What detail helps to explain this fact? The wolves feed on deer and elk, and the deer and elk feed on plants.*

  pp. 7–8 *For centuries, people disliked wolves. What details support this statement? Over the years folktales have depicted wolves as enemies of people. In the past, wolves and humans competed for some of the same foods, such as deer and elk.*

Discussing and Revisiting the Text

CRITICAL THINKING After discussing *Saving the Mexican Wolves* together, have students read the instructions on **Responding** p. 19. Use these teaching points to guide students as they revisit the text.

- Have students share their completed Web with a partner or in a small group.

- Have students work individually to list the main idea of the selection and the details that support it on Blackline Master 10.7.

FLUENCY: STRESS Have students practice reading their favorite parts of the book, paying attention to placing stress in the correct places.

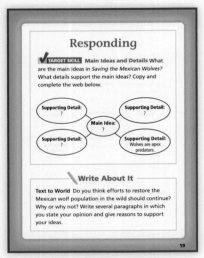

Saving the Mexican Wolves, p. 19

ENGLISH LANGUAGE SUPPORT

RI.5.2, RF.5.4a, W.5.1a, W.5.4, SL.5.1a
ELD.PI.5.1, ELD.PI.5.5, ELD.PI.5.11a

Grizzly Bears Return to Yellowstone

GENRE: HISTORICAL FICTION

Summary Due in part to a bad relationship with the early settlers, by the 1970s the grizzly bear was listed as a threatened species. After the protection of these animals became law in 1975, their numbers grew. Today they are no longer considered threatened.

Introducing the Text

- Discuss key vocabulary in the story. Explain that Yellowstone Park, located in Wyoming, is the oldest U.S. national park.

- Remind students that a Web can help them organize the supporting details that will help in determining the main idea(s).

Supporting the Reading

- As you listen to students read, pause to discuss these questions.

  pp. 4–5 *What details of a grizzly's appearance might make it seem frightening? It can weigh over 1,000 pounds, has four-inch claws, and can stand nine feet tall on its back legs.*

  p. 9 *Why is it important to keep grizzlies and humans apart?. When grizzlies are in contact with people, they also find garbage. When bears associate humans with food, they can learn to seek out humans.*

Discussing and Revisiting the Text

CRITICAL THINKING After discussing *Grizzly Bears Return to Yellowstone* together, have students read the instructions on **Responding** p. 18. Use these teaching points to guide students as they revisit the text.

- Have a student read aloud the main idea shown in the Web. Then have students work in pairs to enter details that support the main idea on Blackline Master 10.8.

FLUENCY: STRESS Have students read their favorite parts of *Grizzly Bears Return to Yellowstone*, placing stress in the correct places.

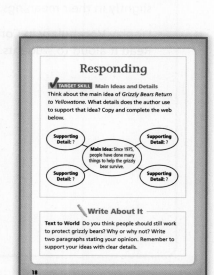

Grizzly Bears Return to Yellowstone, p. 18

Differentiate Vocabulary Strategies
Shades of Meaning

STRUGGLING READERS

ELA RF.5.4c, SL.5.1a, L.5.4a, L.5.4c, L.5.5c, L.5.6
ELD ELD.PI.5.1, ELD.PI.5.6b, ELD.PI.5.8

I DO IT

- Remind students that synonyms are words that have similar meanings.

- Tell students that not all synonyms are a precise match for each other. Explain that they might vary slightly in their meanings.

- Display **Vocabulary in Context Card 99**: *ferocious*. Read it aloud to students.

WE DO IT

- Work with students to define *ferocious* using context clues.

- Then guide students to use a print or digital thesaurus to find synonyms for *ferocious*. cruel, fierce, frightful

- Discuss how each synonym has a different shade of meaning. cruel: *deliberately mean;* fierce: *wild and savage;* frightful: *causing shock* **Return to the Vocabulary in Context Card.** Ask students which word most closely matches the shade of meaning of *ferocious*. fierce

YOU DO IT

- Display and read **Vocabulary in Context Card 93**: *keen*. Discuss the meaning of *keen* with students.

- Have pairs then use a thesaurus to find synonyms for *keen*. Remind them to look up unknown words in a dictionary. Have them choose the one with the same shade of meaning. Tell them to substitute their synonym for the word in the context sentence to confirm their choice.

- Have pairs share their synonyms.

ON LEVEL

ELA RF.5.4c, SL.5.1a, L.5.4a, L.5.4c, L.5.5c, L.5.6
ELD ELD.PI.5.1, ELD.PI.5.6b, ELD.PI.5.8

I DO IT

- Remind students that synonyms are words that have similar meanings. Explain that they might vary slightly in their meanings, making one a better match for the way the original word is used than another.

- Display **Vocabulary in Context Card 99**: *ferocious*.

WE DO IT

- Have students use context clues to define *ferocious*.

- Then guide them to find synonyms in a print or digital thesaurus. Discuss the connotation, or underlying shade of meaning, of each word. Ask volunteers which choice best fits the meaning of *ferocious* on the **Vocabulary in Context Card**.

YOU DO IT

- Write these words on the board: *keen* and *contentment*. Discuss their meanings.

- Have students write a sentence for each word.

- Then have students exchange sentences with a partner. Ask them to find a synonym for each Target Vocabulary word that conveys the same shade of meaning. Encourage them to use a thesaurus as needed.

ADVANCED

ELA RF.5.4c, SL.5.1a, L.5.4a, L.5.4c, L.5.5c, L.5.6
ELD ELD.PI.5.1, ELD.PI.5.6b, ELD.PI.5.8

I DO IT

- Remind students that synonyms are words that have similar meanings. Explain that they might vary in their connotations, or shades of meaning, making one a better match for the way the original word is used than another.

- Display **Vocabulary in Context Cards 93**: *keen,* **100**: *contentment,* and **99**: *ferocious.*

WE DO IT

- Guide students to use the context of each Target Vocabulary word to help them determine its meaning and connotation.

- Then elicit possible synonyms for each word, directing students in the use of a print or digital thesaurus as required.

- List the synonyms on the board. Have students volunteer which they think are the best matches for the Target Vocabulary words and why.

YOU DO IT

- Write these words on the board: *sleek, predators, pounce, strong,* and *sensitive.*

- Have students write a paragraph about cougars including each of the words.

- Then have them exchange paragraphs. Ask partners to replace the words with synonyms. Have pairs then discuss whether the synonym matches the shade of meaning of each original word.

ENGLISH LANGUAGE SUPPORT

ELA RF.5.4c, SL.5.1a, L.5.4a, L.5.4c, L.5.5c, L.5.6
ELD ELD.PI.5.1, ELD.PI.5.6b, ELD.PI.5.8

Provide Struggling Readers, On Level, and Advanced ELs proficiency-level support during differentiated instruction.

Emerging

Review that synonyms are words that have similar meanings. Model with the term *ferocious.* Display the image on **Vocabulary in Context Card 99** and explain that the cougar's expression is ferocious. Display a word web with the word *ferocious* in the center. Elicit synonyms for *ferocious* by asking students yes/no or either/or questions. For example: *Does* ferocious *mean* fierce *or* shy*? Which word means the same as* ferocious: angry *or* happy*? Does* ferocious *mean the same thing as* wild*? Add correct responses to the web.

Expanding

Guide students to create their own Vocabulary in Context Cards for other new words they are introduced to in their respective groups. Work with them to find synonyms or simple definitions in dictionaries and thesauruses.

Bridging

Ask students to use each new word and any accompanying synonyms they learn in a complete sentence. Remind students that using the words in meaningful sentences will help them remember the meaning of the words and also help them expand their vocabulary. If appropriate, have them find and list antonyms for each new word they learn as a way to contrast word meanings.

Differentiate Vocabulary Strategies • **T379**

Options for Reteaching

VOCABULARY STRATEGIES

ELA L.5.4a, L.5.6
ELD ELD.PI.5.1, ELD.PI.5.5, ELD.PI.5.6b

Shades of Meaning

I DO IT

- Remind students that synonyms are words that have similar meanings. A thesaurus is a reference source that students can use to look up synonyms for a word.

- Point out that synonyms usually have different shades of meaning. As a result, writers choose their words carefully, selecting the synonym that conveys just the right meaning.

- Explain that readers can use context to understand the shades of meaning of words.

WE DO IT

- Display this phrase from **Student Book p. 296** that describes cougar habitats: *snow-capped mountains, jungles thick with vegetation, cool pine forests, grassy plains, and murky swamps.*

- Model how to find synonyms for *murky* and determine which has the closest meaning in this context.

  Think Aloud *When I look up* murky *in a thesaurus, I see two entries with synonyms that could work in this context. One entry includes* grimy *and* muddy. *The other includes* gloomy *and* bleak. *I don't think the swamp would feel* gloomy *or* bleak *to a cougar.* Grimy *doesn't seem right, either—it makes me think of a dirty window.* Muddy *is the synonym with the best shade of meaning in this context.*

- Ask students to think of synonyms for *thick* and *cool,* and discuss which ones best fit the context.

YOU DO IT

- Have students locate the word *secretive* on p. 299.

- Have students work in pairs or small groups to look up *secretive* in a thesaurus. Each student should choose two synonyms and write a sentence using each one.

- Have students exchange sentences and use context clues to determine the exact shade of meaning of each synonym for *secretive.*

- As a class, discuss the various synonyms and their meanings.

COMPREHENSION SKILL

ELA RI.5.1, RI.5.2
ELD ELD.PI.5.1, ELD.PI.5.5

Main Ideas and Details

I DO IT

- Remind students that main ideas are the major points that a nonfiction author wants to make. A main idea may be stated directly, or readers may need to infer it.

- Remind students that main ideas are supported by details in the text. If a main idea is not stated directly, readers can use the supporting details to infer it.

- Point out that identifying the main ideas and important details helps readers summarize the text.

WE DO IT

- Have students read the last paragraph on **Student Book p. 299.**

- Model how to use supporting details to infer a main idea.

  Think Aloud *The author explains that eyesight is the cougar's strongest sense. Cougars can see long distances, and because of their large pupils, they see almost as well at night as they do during the day. I can infer from the details that cougars' eyesight is important to their success in hunting and surviving. I think that's the main idea.*

- Help volunteers infer main ideas in other passages from the selection.

YOU DO IT

- Distribute <u>Graphic Organizer 15</u>.

- Have students identify the main idea of the last paragraph on p. 301 after identifying supporting details. *Most adult cougars are solitary.*

- Have students work with partners to complete the graphic organizer.

- Review the completed graphic organizers. As a class, develop a sentence that summarizes the paragraph.

LANGUAGE ARTS

ELA W.5.2a, W.5.4, L.5.1a, L.5.5c ELD ELD.PI.5.10a

Direct Quotations and Interjections/Informative Writing

I DO IT

- Review that when students quote directly from a text, they must use quotation marks around the other writer's words.

- Explain that quotation marks are also used around the exact words spoken by a person or character.

- Remind students that interjections are words that express strong or sudden emotion, such as *wow* or *hey*. They are set off from a person or character's other words by a comma or exclamation point.

WE DO IT

- Remind students that when they write a research report, they may want to include direct quotations from their sources.

- Tell students that they will be writing a paragraph about how the cougar has adapted to its environment. Model finding a direct quotation on **Student Book p. 296**.

> **Think Aloud** *One excerpt that I might quote directly is "cougars that live in northern mountains tend to be larger and have a thicker coat of fur than cougars that live elsewhere." Since I am quoting the author's exact words, I need to use quotation marks and an attribution.*

- Have volunteers tell you where to put the punctuation as you write the quotation and attribution (such as "Patricia Corrigan explains") on the board.

YOU DO IT

- Have one partner write a paragraph about how well cougars are adapted to their environment, using direct quotations from pp. 298–301.

- Have another partner use interjections to write a dialogue between people who are sharing amazing facts about cougars.

- Have pairs exchange papers and review them for correct punctuation.

DECODING

ELA RF.5.3a, L.5.4a, L.5.5c

Recognizing Schwa + /r/ Sounds

I DO IT

- Remind students that in a two-syllable word with an *r*-controlled vowel in the second syllable, the first syllable is stressed.

- Explain that the vowel and *r* in the second syllable make a schwa + /r/ sound.

- Review the examples of *color* and *flicker*.

- Break the words into syllables for students and overemphasize the stressed first syllables. Guide them to focus on the schwa + /r/ sounds in the unstressed second syllables.

WE DO IT

- Write *whiskers, cougars, patterns,* and *leopards* on the board.

- Help students find sentences on **Student Book pp. 298–299** that contain the words.

- Model how to decode *cougars* step by step.

> **Think Aloud** *Most words with an unstressed second syllable have the schwa + /r/ sound. The word* cougars *fits this pattern because the stress is on the first syllable. If I'm not sure or I want to confirm the pronunciation, I can look up* cougars *in a dictionary.*

- Have volunteers look up *cougars* in a dictionary to confirm the pronunciation.

YOU DO IT

- Have partners decode the other words on the board. Then have them look on pp. 302–303 for two other schwa + /r/ words and decode them.

- Use the Corrective Feedback on p. T349 if students need additional help.

Teacher Notes

REALISTIC FICTION

EXEMPLAR

Students will read *Hound Dog True* to

- identify and analyze story themes.

- analyze characters and their development.

- study how a story is structured.

Summary

About to be the new girl at school yet again, Mattie Breen is dreading the start of the school year. She hopes to avoid the awkwardness of having no friends during recess and lunchtime by making herself indispensable to her uncle Potluck, who is a custodian at the school. Mattie uses her budding writing skills to compile in a journal what her uncle teaches her about "the custodial arts." In the process, she also learns a lot about herself, her family, and the meaning of friendship.

About the Author

Share the following information with students.

Linda Urban first discovered that she was a writer when she was in elementary school, but she put the ambition aside for many years. After years of working in a California bookstore selling the work of other authors, she returned to her first love and became a writer. She now lives and works in Vermont.

Prepare for Complex Texts

TRADE BOOK

Hound Dog True
by Linda Urban

GENRE: Realistic Fiction

Why This Text?

Students learn valuable lessons about situations that could actually happen by reading realistic fiction books. Inherently, students will benefit from exposure to the many various types of fiction. This author inspires others to take notice of the little things in life that are important. This fictional story shows how small acts of bravery and kindness positively impact a developing friendship.

Key Learning Objectives

- Read to analyze and understand characters and their development.
- Analyze the purpose of figurative language.
- Use information from the text to summarize important ideas and themes.
- Examine story structure and plot relationships.

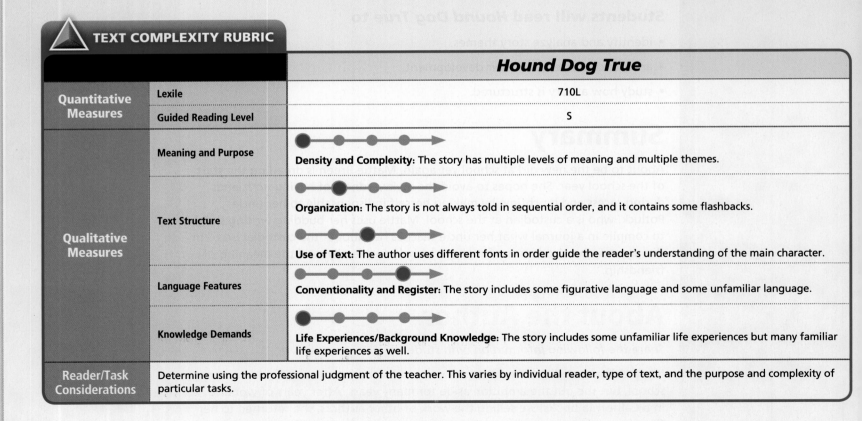

TEXT COMPLEXITY RUBRIC

		Hound Dog True
Quantitative Measures	Lexile	710L
	Guided Reading Level	S
Qualitative Measures	Meaning and Purpose	**Density and Complexity:** The story has multiple levels of meaning and multiple themes.
	Text Structure	**Organization:** The story is not always told in sequential order, and it contains some flashbacks.
		Use of Text: The author uses different fonts in order guide the reader's understanding of the main character.
	Language Features	**Conventionality and Register:** The story includes some figurative language and some unfamiliar language.
	Knowledge Demands	**Life Experiences/Background Knowledge:** The story includes some unfamiliar life experiences but many familiar life experiences as well.
Reader/Task Considerations		Determine using the professional judgment of the teacher. This varies by individual reader, type of text, and the purpose and complexity of particular tasks.

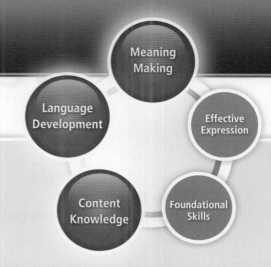

 ENGLISH LANGUAGE SUPPORT Use the Text X-Ray below to prepare for teaching the trade book *Hound Dog True*. Use it to plan, support, and scaffold instruction in order to help students understand the text's **key ideas** and **academic language features**.

Zoom *In* on Key Ideas
Students should understand these **key ideas** after reading *Hound Dog True*.

Key Idea | Segment 1, Introduction, pp. 1–22

Mattie intently regards her uncle Potluck's work and plans to be the custodial apprentice to Uncle Potluck. As the apprentice, Mattie hopes to escape from any awkward moments that often come with being new to a school. Later, at home, Quincy, the renter's niece, turns up at her uncle's house, and Mattie gets worried when her silver notebook is discovered. Mattie remembers Star, the last girl who found her notebook of stories and destroyed it.

Key Idea | Segment 2, pp. 23–50

Mattie refuses to invite Quincy for a sleepover because she feels uncomfortable having an older girl over. That afternoon, Quincy tries not to startle Mattie when she comes out to draw. They write and draw in silence, respecting one another. Mattie agrees to a sleepover. Out of modesty, Mattie puts on her pajamas before Quincy arrives but then feels embarrassed. She hopes no one will notice her babyish pajamas, but Quincy points out that Mattie's top mouse button is missing. "Poor Moe," thinks Mattie.

Key Idea | Segment 3, pp. 51–72

Quincy quizzes Mattie on what "Poor Moe" means. Reluctantly, Mattie explains that it's like saying *That stinks!* After Quincy falls asleep, Mattie writes the story of Poor Moe in her silver notebook. The next day, when Mattie gets home, Quincy and her aunt Crystal are all made up to go somewhere. Quincy says she does not want Mattie to go with them. When Mattie goes to her room, she sees her notebook on her bed. She is convinced that Quincy read it and that is why she refused to invite Mattie along.

Zoom *In* on Academic Language
Guide students at different proficiencies and skill levels to understand the structure and language of this text.

Key Idea | Segment 1, Introduction, pp. 1–22

Students should realize that realistic fiction tells a story about something that really can happen. Students review the first segment of the book, taking note of the words in italics and in a different font. Explain to students that the author uses italics to show what Mattie is thinking but does not say and that the author uses a different font to show what Mattie writes in her notebook.

Key Idea | Segment 2, pp. 23–50

Support English language learners and others as they analyze how the author develops the characters. On p. 25, Mattie claims that Quincy looks older than twelve. Ask students to identify the examples Mattie gives to support her inference about Quincy's age. Discuss why Mattie doesn't just ask Quincy how old she is.

Key Idea | Segment 3, pp. 51–72

Draw students' attention to the phrase *loud as a gunshot* in the second to last sentence on p. 54. Remind students that a simile uses the words *like* or *as* to make a comparison between two different things. Ask students why they think Mattie described the clock ticking like a gunshot. Then ask students to complete the following simile frames:

* *Mattie seems lonely as a _____.*

* *Poor Moe was twisted like a _____.*

* *Aunt Crystal makes Quincy up like a _____.*

This Text X-Ray continues on p. T427.

WeeklyPlanner

Daily Integrated ENGLISH LANGUAGE SUPPORT	DAY 1	DAY 2
	Materials • Trade Book: *Hound Dog True* • Reader's Notebook, pp. 139–144 • Interactive Lessons: Writing to Sources, Writing Narratives: Dialogue and Description • GrammarSnap Videos: Dialogue, Complex Sentences	**Materials** • Trade Book: *Hound Dog True* • Reader's Notebook, pp. 121–126, 145–150 • Interactive Lessons: Writing to Sources, Writing Narratives: Organize Your Ideas • GrammarSnap Videos: Complete Sentences and Sentence Fragments • Multimedia Grammar Glossary

First Week

	DAY 1	DAY 2
Project Development **Speaking and Listening** **Research and Media Literacy**	**Launch,** T392 Building Bridges **Teacher Read Aloud** "Assignment Notebook Friends," T388–T389 **Preview the Topic,** T390	**Discuss,** T396 Focus on Collaboration
Vocabulary **Close Reading**	**Preview Content Vocabulary,** T388 **Introduce the Trade Book,** T391	**Content Vocabulary,** T394 **Segment 1:** First Read, T394 **Segment 1:** Second Read, T395
Integrated Language Arts *Review* • Writing • Grammar • Spelling	**Writing / Grammar / Spelling,** T393 **Write About Media** Descriptions Dialogue Spelling Review	**Writing / Grammar / Spelling,** T397 **Write About Reading** Narratives Complete Sentences Spelling Review

Second Week

	DAY 1	DAY 2
Project Development **Speaking and Listening** **Research and Media Literacy**	**Prepare,** T412 Create Materials	**Prepare,** T416 Develop the Presentation
Vocabulary **Close Reading**	**Content Vocabulary,** T410 **Segment 4:** First Read, T410 **Segment 4:** Second Read, T411	**Content Vocabulary,** T414 **Segment 5:** First Read, T414 **Segment 5:** Second Read, T415
Integrated Language Arts *Review* • Writing • Grammar • Spelling	**Writing / Grammar / Spelling,** T413 **Write About Reading** Cause and Effect Complex Sentences Spelling Review	**Writing / Grammar / Spelling,** T417 **Write About Reading** Summarize Common and Proper Nouns Spelling Review

DAY 3

Materials
- Trade Book: *Hound Dog True*
- Reader's Notebook, pp. 127–132, 151–156
- Interactive Lessons: Writing to Sources, Writing Informative Texts, Writing Narratives
- Multimedia Grammar Glossary

Prepare, T400
Plan Roles and Tasks
Manage Time and Resources

Content Vocabulary, T398
Segment 2: First Read, T398
Segment 2: Second Read, T399

Writing / Grammar / Spelling, T401
Write About Reading
Compare and Contrast
Direct Objects
Spelling Review

Present, T420
Deliver the Presentation

Content Vocabulary, T418
Segment 6: First Read, T418
Segment 6: Second Read, T419

Writing / Grammar / Spelling, T421
Write About Reading
Short Story
Punctuation
Spelling Review

DAY 4

Materials
- Trade Book: *Hound Dog True*
- Reader's Notebook, pp. 133–138
- Interactive Lessons: Writing to Sources, Writing Informative Texts, Writing Narratives
- GrammarSnap Videos: Complete Sentences and Sentence Fragments, Compound Sentences
- Multimedia Grammar Glossary

Prepare, T404
Initiate Research

Content Vocabulary, T402
Segment 3: First Read, T402
Segment 3: Second Read, T403

Writing / Grammar / Spelling, T405
Write About Reading
Procedural Composition
Compound Sentences
Spelling Review

Assess, T423
Score the Project

Your Turn, T422

Write About Reading, T422

DAY 5

Materials
- Interactive Lessons: Writing Narratives: Dialogue and Description, Writing Informative Texts: Organize Your Information
- GrammarSnap Videos: Dialogue
- Multimedia Grammar Glossary

Prepare, T408
Discuss Peer Critiques
Evaluate Progress

Independent Reading, T406
Extend the Topic, T407
Domain-Specific Vocabulary

Writing / Grammar / Spelling, T409
Write About Reading
Dialogue
Punctuation
Spelling Review

Reflect, T426
Reflect on the Project

Independent Reading, T424
Compare Texts

Writing / Grammar / Spelling, T425
Write About Reading
Procedural Composition
Singular and Plural Nouns
Spelling Review

Teacher Read Aloud

▶ SHARE OBJECTIVES

- Listen to fluent reading.
- Paraphrase portions of a text read aloud. LANGUAGE
- Make inferences and draw conclusions. LANGUAGE

ENGLISH LANGUAGE SUPPORT

Use Visuals and Gestures

All Proficiencies Introduce each word to students. Use visuals, gestures, or yes/no questions to help them understand the meaning of each word. Have students listen to the Read Aloud again and signal when they hear a Target Vocabulary Word. **ELD** ELD.PI.5.1

☑ PREVIEW

Content Vocabulary

Students will encounter these content vocabulary words in the trade book.

postpone delay or reschedule

matter-of-fact something that is true and cannot be denied

scrutiny careful examination or observation

taut pulled or stretched tightly

disposition an inclination to act in a particular way

pouty showing displeasure or sulkiness

expertise expert skill or knowledge beyond criticism

impeccable perfect or flawless; beyond criticism

instincts strong, natural feelings

Model Fluency

Accuracy and Self-Correction Explain to students that when reading aloud, it is important to accurately, or correctly, read each word. Suggest that when students incorrectly read a word, they pause and reread the word accurately.

- Project the read aloud passage. Read the second paragraph aloud, mispronouncing the word *taut* as *taunt*. Pause and self-correct your pronunciation.

- Tell students that by pausing and correcting themselves when they incorrectly pronounce a word, they will help both them and their listeners to better comprehend the text.

- Reread the sentences together, guiding them to pause and self-correct when necessary. **ELA** RF.5.4c

Listening Comprehension

Read aloud the passage. Pause at the numbered stopping points to ask students the questions below. Discuss the meanings of the highlighted words, as needed, to support the discussion.

1 *From whose point of view is this story told?* Sample answer: Jackie seems to be telling the story and uses the word I, so this story is told from the first-person point of view. **POINT OF VIEW**

2 *How are Mama and Jackie different from one another?* Sample answer: Jackie is pouty and doubtful. Mama is upbeat and energetic. **COMPARE AND CONTRAST**

3 *Why does the petite, impeccably dressed girl give Jackie an assignment notebook?* Sample answer: The girl gives Jackie an assignment notebook because she wants to be friends. **INFER/PREDICT**

💬 Classroom Collaboration

Tell student to paraphrase the story and retell it to a partner. **ELA** RI.5.1, RI.5.2, SL.5.2

ENGLISH LANGUAGE SUPPORT

Use Sentence Frames Provide sentence frames such as these to supports students as they paraphrase and retell the passage: *Jackie does not want to _____ because _____. Jackie and Mama go school supply shopping, but Jackie does not get a _____ because _____. When Jackie goes to school, _____.*

ELD ELD.PI.5.5

Assignment Notebook Friends

"Jackie, you know that just because you haven't gone shopping for your school supplies, they won't **postpone** the first day of school," Mama hollered.

School would start tomorrow and I would once again be the new kid facing more **scrutiny** than I could stand, to be perfectly **matter-of-fact**. A lack of supplies would only cause others to scrutinize me even more, so I slipped on my shoes, pulled the laces **taut,** and raced out to Mama's car.

"We'll wind our way through the store, filling our cart with all the items on your school supply list. We will conquer the fifth grade one way or another."

Mama's **disposition** is definitely the polar opposite of mine. She is always highly energized and remarkably cool. Me, I am just **pouty** and doubtful most of the time—I wish I had a little more of Mama in me. When Mama's car door slammed, I was jolted back into reality. "We're here, Jackie, so let the shopping begin!"

Remarkably, most of the school supplies weren't picked over, even though we'd saved school shopping for the last minute. As I pitched items into the cart, Mama checked them off the list, and just when it seemed we'd handled this challenge with the **expertise** of master school supply shoppers, we hit a bump!

Without even looking up, Mama rattled off the next item on the list, "One 4 x 6 weekly assignment notebook." I turned around once, twice, three times and finally spotted the last assignment notebook in the aisle. But just as I reached up to grab it, a swift set of hands snatched the notebook right from underneath my nose. "It's the last thing on my list, and this looks like the last one. Sorry I got to it before you, but I heard they are selling them at Dan's Dime Store if you really need one," blurted out this petite young lady with **impeccable** hair and clothes.

"Seems they are out, but that girl said we should try Dan's Dime Store."

"Then off we go to check out and spin by Dan's Dime Store," Mama stated matter-of-factly as we headed toward the registers.

Of course, just my luck, no notebooks at Dan's Dime Store. So I set off to school the next morning, lacking vital school supplies and stressing out about whom I'd have to sit beside and what the teacher would say when he realized I didn't have a notebook.

As I shoved all my junk into my locker, I was startled by a *tap, tap, tap* on my shoulder. "Whoa, you spooked me!" I said as I turned around and found myself face to face with the impeccably dressed petite girl from the store.

"My **instincts** were right! I figured you would need a notebook, because my mom said she grabbed the last one at Dan's Dime Store yesterday. Guess it's your lucky day because I now have an extra assignment book and I want to give it to you. Here you go, and just in case you care, I wrote my number and e-mail address in it. "

And just like that she disappeared. I was glad to know I'd at least have someone to sit with at lunch today, if I could find her!

Hound Dog True • **T389**

Preview the Topic

- Gain background knowledge related to the lesson topic and project.
- Develop listening comprehension skills.
- Respond to multimedia. LANGUAGE
- Participate in a collaborative group discussion. LANGUAGE

ENGLISH LANGUAGE SUPPORT

Use Visuals

All Proficiencies Use visuals showing friendly acts to preview the trade book topic and the audio link with students. Enhance understanding by working with students to say or write short sentences about the topic and to produce answers to the questions. Provide sentence frames as necessary. **ELD** ELD.PI.5.10b

Building Bridges

Discuss the Topic Explain to students that they will be reading a trade book, called *Hound Dog True,* about the challenges that go with being the new kid at school and trying to make new friends. Tell students that they will have the opportunity to use the trade book, as well as other sources, to create a project related to this topic.

Point out that in any given year, many students are anxious about their first day of school, but the prospect is even more difficult when you also are new to the town. Some schools have set up ambassador programs for new students and their families. Current students at the school serve as ambassadors who provide helpful information and support to the new students and their families. Ask students to share what sort of information about their school they think would have been beneficial to know before their first day. **ELA** SL.5.1c

Access Prior Knowledge

Ask students what government ambassadors do to build bridges both nationally and internationally. Have volunteers explain what ambassadors at their school might do to build bridges between current and incoming students, even before the first day of school. **ELA** SL.5.1d

Explain to students that the ambassadors from the United States work to spread good will and advocate for the interests of the United States and its citizens. Help students realize that by serving as ambassadors, they will be spreading goodwill and positively representing their school to new students and their families. Give students time to discover more about ambassadors in history by looking at a website such as this one:
http://diplomacy.state.gov/discoverdiplomacy/diplomacy101/people/170341.htm
ELA SL.5.1c

View Multimedia

Tell students that they are going to listen to an audio clip from 1971. Explain that relations between China and United States had been difficult since the 1950s. Tell students they are going to hear about how a most unlikely situation spurred a change in the relations between the two countries. After listening to the clip related to the topic, students will discuss it in small groups.
http://www.history.com/speeches/ping-pong-diplomacy-in-china#ping-pong-diplomacy-in-china

💬 Classroom Collaboration

Place students in small groups and have them discuss the following questions. Circulate to encourage collaboration and productive feedback.

- Why was this Ping-Pong match monumental?
- What did United States officials hope would come out of the event?
- Who served as ambassadors in this situation?
- How did the Ping-Pong match build bridges between the two countries?
  ELA SL.5.1a, SL.5.1c

Introduce the Trade Book

EXEMPLAR

TRADE BOOK

Hound Dog True

Discuss Genre Display the book and read the title together. Tell students that this is a realistic fiction story about a shy girl who naturally finds it difficult to make friends. Review with students that realistic fiction tells about events that can actually happen.

Have students page through the book and examine the sections that appear in a different kind of type. Then use the following prompts to engage students in discussion:

- What does the image on the cover show?
- Why do you think some text is in a different kind of type?
  ELA SL.5.1a, SL.5.1c, SL.5.1d

Predictive Writing

Display the Essential Question and ask students to write it on their papers. Tell students they will write a paragraph to tell about things that people can do to make a new friend. Guide students to reflect on their preview of the selection for ideas for their writing. **ELA** W.5.2b, W.5.4, W.5.10

Set Purpose

Tell students that good readers think about their reasons for reading based on what they hope to learn. Then model setting a reading purpose. Invite students to share their personal reading purposes and record them in their journals.

> **Think Aloud**   *It isn't always easy to make new friends or be the new student in the classroom. I will read this book to get a better understanding of the qualities of a good friend.*

ESSENTIAL QUESTION

- *What can someone do to make a new friend?*

Hound Dog True is broken into six instructional segments.

- Complete the First Read and Second Read instruction for each segment before moving to the next one.
- Then have students read independently and complete the Reader's Notebook pages.

SEGMENT 1
Introduction,
pp. 1–22

SEGMENT 2
pp. 23–50

SEGMENT 3
pp. 51–72

SEGMENT 4
pp. 73–94

SEGMENT 5
pp. 95–122

SEGMENT 6
pp. 123–145,
Conclusion

Scaffold Close Reading

Think Through the Text **FIRST READ**	Analyze the Text **SECOND READ**	Independent Reading
Develop comprehension through: • Guided Questioning • Comprehension Strategies • Vocabulary in Context	Students apply what they have learned about analyzing text through collaboration and by generating their own discussion questions. Use directed note taking by working with students to complete a graphic organizer during reading. Distribute copies of Graphic Organizer 10.	Students analyze the text independently, using Reader's Notebook pp. 121–132.

Options for Reading

- **Independent/Partner** Students read and complete the Reader's Notebook pages independently or with a partner.
- **Supported** Students read a segment and complete the Reader's Notebook pages with teacher support and then reread the segment with a partner. Use students' responses to prompts to determine whether or not they need additional support.
- **Read Aloud** Students listen to the text read aloud and answer the questions for each segment in order to build knowledge.

Launch

▶ SHARE OBJECTIVES

- Gather relevant information from print and digital sources
- Build knowledge through topic investigation
- Collaborate with a group to initiate a project plan. LANGUAGE

Building Bridges

✔	Set the Stage
✔	Introduce the Task
✔	Clarify Project Requirements
✔	Form Teams

Set the Stage

You may wish to use ideas such as these to immerse students in the topic during the course of the project.

- Take students of a virtual field trip of famous ambassadors in history such as Shirley Temple, Eleanor Roosevelt, and Andrew Young Jr.
- Invite a veteran teacher or the principal to speak about the school history or policies.
- Gather informative pamphlets about the community.

Introduce the Task

As students read *Hound Dog True* over the next two weeks, they will gather important information and details about how to make friends and connect with others. They will also research the answer to the following Essential Question: *What can someone do to make a friend?*

Display the following project prompt: *You and your classmates have been invited to server as ambassadors to the new students and families entering our school. As ambassadors, you will need to design a pamphlet for new students and their families about the school history, school policies, school facts, and the community. You will present your pamphlet to new students and their families during your presentation.*

Tell students that they will use the trade book and two other sources of their choice to develop their pamphlets and presentations. **ELA** RI.5.9, W.5.2b, W.5.2c, W.5.2d, W.5.2e, W.5.7, W.5.8

Clarify Project Requirements

Tell students that they will work in small teams over the next two weeks to manage the development of their project and then present it to an audience. Explain to students that as a team, they will choose their own visuals for the project presentation.

Tell students that the purpose of the project should answer the Essential Question in a way that teaches their audience about their topic. Work with students to brainstorm essential information to include in the pamphlet and the presentation. Discuss with students the ideas, listed below, and encourage students to add their own ideas. **ELA** W.5.2c, SL.5.1c, SL.5.1D

A Comprehensive Pamphlet Includes . . .	An Informative Presentation . . .
<ul><li>the school's history and traditions</li><li>school policies</li><li>school facts</li><li>important dates and times</li><li>community details</li><li>a school map</li></ul>	<ul><li>introduces key administrators or faculty members</li><li>highlights some important members of the community</li><li>points out some crucial dates and times from the pamphlet</li><li>allows for questions and answers</li></ul>

Form Teams

Break students into groups of three to six. Explain to students that they will work with their team members to gather information and resources necessary to create their pamphlets and give their presentations to new students and their family members. Tell students that each team member will be expected to contribute to the project and presentation. Explain that students will be evaluated both as a team and individually.

ENGLISH LANGUAGE SUPPORT Ensure that all students are included in teams in which they can be supported as well as challenged. Students at all proficiency levels can contribute to all aspects of research, but students at the Emerging and Expanding levels may feel more comfortable working with an English-proficient team member to present their findings. **ELD** ELD.PI.5.2, ELD.PI.5.9, ELD.PI.5.10a

Point out that time management and prioritizing tasks are important responsibilities that are built into the assignment. Tell students that they must manage their time in order to meet their goals. Then give students time to discuss the project components and how they might approach each one.

INTEGRATED LANGUAGE ARTS REVIEW

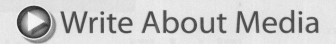 Write About Media

Digital Resources ▶

To support students before they start this task, use the following digital resources.

▶ Interactive Lesson: Narrative Writing: Dialogue and Description

▶ GrammarSnap Videos: Dialogue

INTRODUCE THE TASK

After students listen to the audio clip, tell them that they will respond to *Ping-Pong Diplomacy* by writing a diary entry.

- The diary entry should be written as though the writer were a member of the 1971 Ping-Pong team.
- The writer will describe his emotions and experiences.
- Remind students that the writer's language should sound natural and informal and that they should include dialogue to bring the event to life.

DISCUSS THE PROCESS

Remind students that their narrative should include personal details and dialogue.

- Ask students to think of what it would have been like to be one of the athletes playing in the match.
- Ask students to identify who they will be in their diary entry and what part of the experience they will write about.
- Discuss strategies for organizing the details and experiences in a logical manner.
- Brainstorm dialogue, details, and words that reveal the athlete's feelings and personality.

PLAN AND DRAFT

Tell students to write a narrative diary entry about the audio clip they heard. Student narratives should

- develop this event with relevant facts, details, and dialogue.
- clearly introduce the situation and support the purpose with relevant information.
- include interesting details about the importance of this monumental event.

REVISE AND EDIT

Ask students to work in pairs to review their diary entries. Guide the class to generate a checklist partners can use. For example:

- Have I conveyed the importance of this event?
- What other details can I add to my entry?
- Did I use the proper punctuation with the direct quotations?
- Have I corrected any spelling errors?

See the Narrative Writing Rubric, p. R16.

SHARE

Compile students' entries to create a newspaper page about this day in history.

ELA RL.5.7, W.5.3a, W.5.3b, W.5.3c, W.5.3d, W.5.3e, W.5.4, W.5.5, W.5.10

▶ SHARE OBJECTIVES

- Write a narrative diary entry. LANGUAGE
- Cite evidence from a media source.
- Use correct punctuation and spelling.

▶ SKILLS REVIEW

Review the following skills, as needed, before students begin to write their response.

- **Writing:** Narrative (Lessons 1–5)
- **Grammar:** Direct Quotations (Lessons 10)
- **Spelling:** Short, Long, and Other Vowel Sounds (Lessons 1–7), Homophones (Lesson 8), Compound Words (Lesson 9), Final Schwa Vowels (Lesson 10)

ENGLISH LANGUAGE SUPPORT

Sentence Frames

Emerging Say: *I am an American.* Then write the sentence on the board, explaining that it is a direct quotation because you said it. Place quotation marks in the proper spots. Then say and write another direct quotation on the board and have students insert the quotations in the correct spots.

Expanding Flip through *Hound Dog True* and guide students to read the direct quotations, explaining that the characters said those exact words.

Bridging Copy the following sentence frames on the board. Ask students to complete them and then add the correct punctuation marks. *When we saw _____ I said _____ and my mom said _____. I bet my best friend would've been just as amazed as we were.*

SEGMENT 1
INTRODUCTION, PP. 1–22

▶ **SHARE OBJECTIVES**

- Read to analyze and understand characters. LANGUAGE
- Read to make inferences and draw conclusions. LANGUAGE
- Identify cause-and-effect relationships.

Content Vocabulary

Display the words from the trade book listed below. Read each word with students and discuss its meaning.

potluck, Introduction, a choice of whatever is available

custodial, p. 3, related to the work of a custodian or janitor

traitorous, p. 7, disloyal or treacherous

apprentice, p. 11, someone who is being trained to do a job

COMPREHENSION STRATEGIES

Use the following strategies flexibly as you read with students by modeling how they can be used to improve comprehension.

- **Monitor/Clarify**
- Summarize
- Infer/Predict
- Visualize
- Analyze/Evaluate
- Question

FIRST READ

Think Through the Text

Read Segment 1, pages 1–22

- Periodically pause to check students' understanding. Examples of key concepts and vocabulary for selected pages follow. Base any additional discussion on students' needs.

pp. 1–4

- *Why does Mattie focus on the caution sign on Uncle Potluck's ladder instead of the classroom they are in? Possible response: She is trying not to think about being a student in that classroom and having to introduce herself to her new classmates.*

pp. 7–8

- *Why have Mattie and her mother moved to live in Uncle Potluck's house? Uncle Potluck needs surgery on his "traitorous" knee, and Mattie and her mother will help to care for him after the operation.*

pp. 13–15

- *Why does Mattie plan to be a "custodial apprentice" once school begins? She wants to be able to go to help Uncle Potluck during recess and lunch so that she will not have to be with the other students in her class.*

ENGLISH LANGUAGE SUPPORT Ask paired yes/no questions about story events to confirm understanding. For example, *Does Mattie like the idea of being Uncle Potluck's custodial apprentice? yes Does Uncle Potluck realize why Mattie is observing him so closely? no* **ELD** ELD.PI.5.1

pp. 20–22

- *What happens in the chapter in which Star discovers Mattie's notebook? Star is taking coins from coats and backpacks when she finds Mattie's notebook. Star tries to read what Mattie has written and destroys the notebook when she realizes Mattie has been watching her.* **ELA** RL.5.5

✓ TARGET STRATEGY

Monitor/Clarify

Review with students that good readers monitor their understanding as they read. Explain that when they find they don't understand a situation or idea, they work to clarify it. Point out that rereading or reading ahead may help clear up areas of confusion. Model the thinking:

> **Think Aloud** *I'm confused by the words in italic type the author uses on p. 16: Thumpthumpthump. Thump-thump-thump. Thump. Thump. Thump. I'm going to read the first five paragraphs slowly to be sure I understand what the author means.*

Tell students to practice using the Monitor/Clarify strategy as they continue reading.
ELA RF.5.4a, RF.5.4c

SECOND READ

Analyze the Text

Analyze the Text

Dig Deeper

- Model deeper thinking. Ask: *Why is Mattie frightened by Star?* Explain that to answer the question, you'll need to look back at details in the text.

- Read pp. 20–22 aloud, and ask students to listen for details that can help you answer the question. *The text says that Mattie has always been shy and that school makes her feel "skittish and small." When Star starts to read Mattie's notebook, Mattie thinks that it will make Star understand her and that they can be friends. Instead, Star destroys the notebook, making her appear far stronger and more powerful than Mattie.* Point out the different type used to show words that Mattie has written in the notebook, and as needed, explain that words written in that type reveal Mattie's private thoughts and ideas.

- Ask the question below. Guide students to look back at pp. 15–16 to find the answer. Have them reread the appropriate sections, and ask volunteers to share their answers. *How does the situation described in Chapter 5 connect to the way Mattie reacts when Quincy asks what she is writing? Use details from the text to support your response. Possible responses: Quincy surprises Mattie in a way that reminds her of the encounter with Star. She doesn't want to be in a situation in which she has to share her writing.* **ELA** RL.5.1

ENGLISH LANGUAGE SUPPORT Use these sentence frames to support participation: *Mattie feel uncomfortable about sharing _____ her writing with _____ Quincy because of what happened in fourth grade with _____. Star*

Classroom Collaboration

Divide the class into small groups. Ask the question below and have students discuss it. You might also choose to have students generate a question of their own for discussion.

On the first page of the book, what does Uncle Potluck mean when he says something is "hound dog true"? Possible responses: He means it is an obvious truth, as obvious as a trail is to a hound following a scent. The phrase may also refer to the obvious way in which a dog shows its emotions, without any effort to hide them.

Reconvene as a whole group and have the group share their answers. **ELA** RL.5.4, L.5.5a

ENGLISH LANGUAGE SUPPORT

Sentence Frames

Emerging Reframe questions to present choices, such as *Is Star friendly or mean?* Then have students use the word to complete a pair of sentences, such as *Star is _____ mean. She rips Mattie's notebook.*

Expanding Reframe questions to present choices, such as *Is Star friendly or mean?* Then have students locate evidence in the text that supports their responses and form a complete sentence to tell about it.

Bridging Have students use complete, complex statements to respond to questions. Encourage students to use the word *because* to help explain their reasoning. **ELD** ELD.PI.5.11a

INDEPENDENT READING

Have students read the introduction and pp. 1–22 independently and complete pp. 121–126 in their Reader's Notebooks Notebooks ⬚. Have students share their responses with the class.

Discuss

▶ **SHARE OBJECTIVES**

- Collaborate with a group to create a project plan. LANGUAGE
- Engage appropriately in discussion groups.
- Generate questions for research. LANGUAGE

Focus on Collaboration

✔	Discuss Collaboration
✔	Generate Discussion Rules
✔	Introduce Discussion Roles
✔	Have a Discussion
✔	Reflect on the Discussion

Discuss Collaboration Talk with students as a whole class about working in groups. Ask: *What does* collaboration *mean? working well together; contributing to a shared outcome* Share with students the importance of respecting and appreciating each other's ideas, efforts, and input. Point out that a group is most successful when everyone contributes equally.

Generate Discussion Rules Remind students that before they begin a discussion, they should agree on specific rules that will make their discussions more effective and enjoyable. Point out the following:

- Students should prepare for a discussion by reading and organizing their research notes and bringing any new questions they have.
- During discussion, students should take turns speaking, express their ideas clearly, and give details that explain their ideas.
- Students should listen carefully to elaborate on others' ideas or ask questions to clarify ideas.

Guide students to list discussion rules they feel are important to keep during the course of the project. You may want to start with this list and have students add to it. **ELA** SL.5.1b

	Discussion Rules
1	Be prepared for the discussion.
2	Carry out assigned roles.
3	Take turns speaking.
4	Clearly explain ideas.
5	Elaborate on other people's ideas.
6	Ask and respond to questions.

Introduce Discussion Roles Tell students that when group members have specific roles, or jobs, the group discussions run smoothly:

- **leader:** starts and guides the discussion, keeps it on track
- **recorder:** takes notes about key ideas to share with group members
- **timekeeper:** makes sure the discussion starts and ends on time
- **group members:** participate in the discussion

Have a Discussion Have students work in their groups to discuss the focus of their seminar by using the following prompts:

- *What information might new students need to know about this school?*
- *In which part of the project is it most natural to convey the necessary information?*
- *What should the sections of the pamphlet be?*
- *What ideas should be the focus of our presentation?*

Before groups begin their discussions, assign roles. Remind students to apply the discussion rules during their discussion. **ELA** SL.5.1a, SL.5.1b, SL.5.1c, SL.5.1d

See Collaborative Conversations Rubric, p. R25.

Reflect on the Discussion Have students reflect on the content and process of the discussion, using the following prompts:

- *Did you agree on what information needs to by shared with new students and families?*
- *Did you follow the discussion rules?*
- *What was the best part of the discussion?* **ELA** SL.5.1b

ENGLISH LANGUAGE SUPPORT Use these sentence frames to support participation: *The two most important things I think new students need to know about school are _____ when school starts and _____. what supplies you need It would be easiest to share this information _____. in the pamphlet* **ELD** ELD.PI.5.3, ELD.PII.5.1

INTEGRATED LANGUAGE ARTS REVIEW

Write About Reading

Digital Resources ▶

To support students before they start this task, use the following digital resources.

▶ Interactive Lesson: Writing Narratives: Organize Ideas

▶ GrammarSnap Video: Complete Sentences and Sentence Fragments

INTRODUCE THE TASK

After students have reread Segment 1, tell them that they will respond to the text by writing a short narrative about the difficulties that come with being in a new situation.

- Orally brainstorm new situations and the difficulties that come from them.
- Tell students they will have to go back to the text to find details to include in their narratives.

DISCUSS THE PROCESS

Remind students that a narrative short story introduces a conflict and solves it by the conclusion of the story.

- Ask students to identify who their main character will be and what challenging situation the character will face.
- Discuss how students should develop their main character's personality through the use of sensory details, dialogue, and action.

PLAN AND DRAFT

Have students write a narrative about the challenges that come with new situations. Students' narratives should include

- a main character who faces a challenge due to an unfamiliar situation.
- a beginning, middle, and end.
- a resolution to the challenge.
- details and dialogue that develop the characters, setting, and action.

REVISE AND EDIT

Have student pairs review their narratives. Guide the class to generate a checklist partners can use to revise each other's work, for example:

- Does my story include a problem that the main character or narrator must solve?
- Did I include appropriate dialogue and details so the reader can easily follow along?
- Does my story include a conclusion to the problem?
- Did I use correct spelling, grammar, and punctuation?

See the Narrative Writing Rubric, p. R16.

SHARE

Allow students to share their short stories in small groups. Have listeners identify the new situation and problem each character faced.

ELA W.5.3a, W.5.3b, W.5.3c, W.5.3d, W.5.3e, W.5.4, W.5.5, W.5.10, L.5.2e

▶ SHARE OBJECTIVES

- Write a narrative. LANGUAGE
- Cite evidence from the text.
- Use correct punctuation and spelling.

▶ SKILLS REVIEW

Review the following skills, as needed, before students begin to write their response.

- **Writing:** Narrative (Lesson 1–5)
- **Grammar:** Sentences (Lessons 1–3)
- **Spelling:** Short, Long, and Other Vowel Sounds (Lessons 1–7), *R*-Controlled Vowels (Lessons 6, 7, 10), Homophones (Lesson 8)

ENGLISH LANGUAGE SUPPORT

Sentence Frames

Emerging Help students orally brainstorm words associated with their topics. Then work with them to complete the following sentence frames: *My main character is feeling _____ because _____. _____ will help my main character overcome this new challenge.*

Expanding Have students orally describe their short story ideas while their partner scripts what they are saying, using complete sentences.

Bridging As students prewrite, have them use resources, such as print or electronic thesauruses, to find interesting words to describe their experiences.

ELD ELD.PI.5.8, ELD.PI.5.10a, ELD.PI.5.12a

SHARE OBJECTIVES

- Read to analyze character development.
- Read to make inferences and draw conclusions.
- Summarize important ideas and themes.
LANGUAGE

Content Vocabulary

Display the words from the trade book listed below. Read each word with students and discuss its meaning.

disposition, p. 31, an inclination to act in a particular way

posterity, p. 32, people in the future

solitary, p. 35, done alone or in private

pursuit, p. 35, a pastime, hobby, or leisure activity

matter-of-fact, p. 47, something that is true and cannot be denied

COMPREHENSION STRATEGIES

Use the following strategies flexibly as you read with students by modeling how they can be used to improve comprehension.

- Monitor/Clarify
- Summarize
- Infer/Predict
- **Visualize**
- Analyze/Evaluate
- Question

FIRST READ

Think Through the Text

Cite Text Evidence

Read Segment 2, Pages 23–50

- Periodically pause to check students' understanding. Examples of key concepts and vocabulary for selected pages follow. Base any additional discussion on students' needs.

pp. 24–26

- *What do you learn about Mattie from her decision not to have a sleepover with Quincy? Possible responses: Mattie is shy and feels uncertain about how to behave with girls who are older. Mattie is very observant about her mother.*

ENGLISH LANGUAGE SUPPORT Write the word *shy* on the board to describe Mattie. Invite students to identify other adjectives that mean the same thing as *shy. Possible responses: cautious, wary, nervous, afraid, fearful, reluctant, timid* Discuss how there are shades of meanings in these words. Ask students which words they listed best describe Mattie. **ELD** ELD.PI.5.8

pp. 31–33

- *What does Mattie write in her notebook? She lists tasks that need to be done; she describes how Uncle Potluck does his work.*

pp. 38–40

- *How is the way Quincy approaches Mattie different from their earlier meeting? Quincy tries to be noisy so she won't surprise Mattie.*

pp. 44–46

- *In Chapter 10, what do you learn about Mama from her story about her first job at a hospital? When she is worried or scared, she pretends to be strong and smart until it seems to be true.* **ELA** RL.5.1

✓ TARGET STRATEGY

Visualize

Review with students that they can use descriptions in the text to help them form a mental image of a scene, characters, or an event. Explain that visualizing helps readers better understand what a scene looks like or what is taking place.

ENGLISH LANGUAGE SUPPORT Reread the first full paragraph on p. 28 to students. Ask them what words the author uses to help them visualize Mattie at this moment. *Possible response: "Mattie keeps her face to the notebook page"* Finish reading p. 28 aloud and ask students to explain why Mattie describes the teachers as she does. *Possible response: She was looking down, so all she saw were their shoes. What does this tell you about Mattie? Possible response: She is too shy to look up at the teachers and principal.*

Tell students to practice using the Visualize strategy as they continue reading.

SECOND READ

Analyze the Text

Dig Deeper

- Model deeper thinking. Ask: *What does the author mean by saying that "Mattie tries on being matter-of-fact"?* **Explain that to answer the question, you'll need to look at the text.**

- **Return to pp. 46–47 and ask students to listen for details that can help you answer the question.** *The author describes the details that Quincy shares about her family and says Quincy isn't upset by the details. She is matter-of-fact. Mattie looks up "matter-of-fact" in a dictionary and thinks what it would be like to act in that way. Mattie decides to pretend to be matter-of-fact. She tries it on, like she might try on clothing in a store.*

ENGLISH LANGUAGE SUPPORT Explain to students that when something is said in a *matter-of-fact* way, the speaker does not show any emotion. Help students understand why being matter-of-fact does not quite fit Mattie's personality. Ask: *Is Mattie an emotional young girl? yes Is Mattie often worried about the details? yes Do you think Mattie's emotions make it difficult for her to be matter-of-fact? yes* **ELD** ELD.PI.5.1

- **Ask the question below. Guide students to look back at p. 23 and at p. 48 to find the answer. Have them review the text and ask volunteers to share their answers.** *Why does Mattie say "Poor Moe" when she buttons her pajamas? Use details from the story to support your answer. She has named the buttons on her pajamas Eenie, Meenie, Miney, and Moe. The button that was Moe has been lost, so she says "Poor Moe" when she leaves the last button unbuttoned. Something about that button seems important to her.* **ELA** RL.5.1

💬 Classroom Collaboration

Divide the class into small groups. Ask the questions below and have students discuss them. You might also choose to have students generate a question of their own for discussion. *How does the passage about Star at the beginning of Chapter 9 connect to the information about her in Chapter 5? How does it connect to Mattie's second meeting with Quincy? Possible response: The passage shows how Star used a word she'd read in the notebook to intimidate Mattie after Star destroyed the notebook. It shows why Mattie is reluctant to share anything about what she is writing with Quincy.*

Reconvene as a whole group and have the group share their answers. **ELA** RL.5.5

ENGLISH LANGUAGE SUPPORT Have students work with a partner to orally summarize and connect the information from Chapters 5 and 9. Provide sentence frames: *Star used _____ the word* ogre *to intimidate Mattie after she _____* tore apart **the notebook.** *Now Mattie is _____ anxious about sharing her stories with Quincy.*

ENGLISH LANGUAGE SUPPORT

Sentence Frames

Emerging For each question, accept one-word responses and expand them. For example, ask: *Is Mattie nervous about Quincy coming for a sleepover? yes* Then expand it by saying: *Yes, Mattie is nervous about Quincy coming for a sleepover.* Then ask: *Does Mattie usually speak in a matter-of-fact manner? no* And again expand it by saying: *No, Mattie does not usually speak in a matter-of-fact manner.*

Expanding Encourage students to answer questions about story events and characters using complete sentences. Provide corrective feedback as necessary.

Bridging Have students tell how they know the answer to each question based on evidence from the story.

INDEPENDENT READING

Have students read pp. 23–50 independently and complete pp. 127–132 in their Reader's Notebooks. Have students share their responses with the class.

Prepare

▶ SHARE OBJECTIVES

- Understand and assign project roles.
- Develop a manageable list of tasks and due dates.
- Determine how to manage time and resources.

Plan Roles and Tasks

| ✔ | Assign Roles |
| ✔ | Develop Task Checklist |

Assign Roles Assign each team member a role for the project. If students are familiar with project work, you may want to allow them to choose their own roles once they have had a chance to discuss the project. Roles for this project may include the following:

- **Designer:** responsible for determining how the pamphlet will be laid out

- **Writer:** responsible for writing the text in the pamphlet

- **Researcher:** responsible for finding accurate information

- **Organizer:** responsible for organizing the presentation

Discuss the responsibilities of each role with students and ensure that they are comfortable with their assignments. Identify which activities are better suited for speakers and which are better suited for writers. Encourage students to consider their strengths and weaknesses when determining who is comfortable taking on various roles to complete the project.

Develop Task Checklist Have students work together to list the tasks they have as a group to complete the project. If possible, you may want to have students use a task-management app to develop and keep track of their task checklists. Prompt students with questions such as these:

- *What products do you need to create? Describe them.*

- *What materials will you need to create these products?*

- *What resources will you use to produce these products?*

Then guide students to break these tasks into discrete steps. Point out to students that knowing exactly what is involved in a task will help them develop a realistic plan for completing their work on time. **ELA** RI.5.9, W.5.7, SL.5.1a, SL.5.1b, SL.5.1c, SL.5.1d

ENGLISH LANGUAGE SUPPORT Use this sentence frame to support participation. *I think I would feel most comfortable working on the _____ design of the pamphlet because _____. I am comfortable formatting documents on the computer.* **ELD** ELD.PI.5.3, ELD.PI.5.5

Manage Time and Resources

✔	Define Schedule and Milestones
✔	Develop a Realistic Schedule
✔	Determine Resource Needs

Define Schedule and Milestones Use a calendar to map out the two weeks of the project, noting that Days 1, 2, and 3 have all been introductory. You may want to provide students with a blank calendar to complete with you.

Guide students to begin populating Days 4–7 of the calendar with the tasks from their checklist. Tasks should include conducting research, receiving peer and teacher feedback, creating products and other materials, and rehearsing the presentation. Point out that on Days 8 and 9, they will be delivering their presentations and being assessed and that Day 10 will be a time for reflection and celebration.

Develop a Realistic Schedule Guide students to estimate how long it will take them to realistically complete each task for their project. In some cases, it maybe necessary to scale back or change tasks if they will not fit within the allotted time frame. Encourage students to check their schedules on a regular basis in order to stay on track to finish the project.

Determine Resource Needs Guide students to make sure they have the materials they need to create the pamphlet for their presentations. For example, prompt them to consider how many copies of their pamphlet they will need to present to their audience. Also encourage them to consider what resources, including technological resources, they may need to give and display their presentation. Then have students plan how to gather the necessary materials and resources in the allotted time frame. Help them understand that if they are not able to secure the items they need in a timely manner, they will need to revise their expectations or use some creative problem solving to stay on track. **ELA** SL.5.1a, SL.5.1b, SL.5.1c, SL.5.1d, SL.5.5

INTEGRATED LANGUAGE ARTS REVIEW

Write About Reading

Digital Resources ▶

To support students before they start this task, use the following digital resources.

▶ Interactive Lessons: Writing Informative Texts: Use Facts and Examples

INTRODUCE THE TASK After students have reread Segment 2, tell them they will respond to the text by writing a comparison-and-contrast essay about two characters in the book.

- Prompt students to identify appropriate characters from *Hound Dog True* to compare and contrast in a short essay.
- Tell students that they will have to go back into the text to find facts and details to include in their essays.

DISCUSS THE PROCESS Tell students that a comparison-and-contrast essay explores the similarities and differences between two or more things.

- Prompt students to complete a Venn diagram to identify similarities and differences between the characters.
- Discuss how to logically organize the information about the two characters, such as by grouping the similarities and the differences about the characters.
- Students should go back into the text to find details to illustrate similarities and differences.
- Remind students that they should conclude their essays by explaining what they learned from the comparisons.

PLAN AND DRAFT Have students write informative compare-contrast essays after reading Segment 2. Informative essays should contain

- facts about the characters they can support with details from the book.
- direct quotations from the book.
- similarities and differences between the characters being compared.
- a concluding statement to explain the importance of the comparison.
- comparison words to easily link ideas in the essay.

See the Analytic Writing Rubric, p. R15.

SHARE If possible, have students partner with another student who wrote an essay comparing the same two characters. Have students discuss the similarities and differences they identified about the characters in their essays.

ELA RL.5.1, RL.5.3, W.5.2a, W.5.2c, W.5.2d, W.5.2e, W.5.4, W.5.5, W.5.8, W.5.9a, W.5.10

▶ SHARE OBJECTIVES

- Write an informative essay. **LANGUAGE**
- Cite evidence from the text.
- Use correct punctuation and spelling.
- Make comparisons.

▶ SKILLS REVIEW

Review the following skills, as needed, before students begin to write their response.

- **Writing:** Informative Writing: Compare-Contrast Essay (Lesson 7)
- **Grammar:** Direct and Indirect Objects (Lesson 7)
- **Spelling:** Short, Long, and Other Vowel Sounds (Lessons 1–7), Compound Words (Lesson 9)

ENGLISH LANGUAGE SUPPORT

Sentence Frames

Emerging Work as a group to compare two similar objects such as a soccer ball and a football using a Venn diagram.

Expanding Students use sentence frames to begin working on their essay: *[A] and [B] are similar because _____. [A] and [B] are different because _____.*

Bridging Write two sentences on the board such as: *Mattie has a difficult time talking to people. Quincy talks a lot.* Have students join the sentences using a comparison word or phrase. *Quincy has an easier time talking to people than Mattie does.* **ELD** ELD.PI.5.6a, ELD.PII.5.6

SEGMENT 3
PP. 51–22

▶ SHARE OBJECTIVES

• Read to make inferences and draw conclusions. LANGUAGE

• Read to compare and contrast story events.

• Use information from the text to summarize important ideas and events. LANGUAGE

Content Vocabulary

Display the words from the trade book listed below. Read each word with students and discuss its meaning.

pouty, p. 59, showing displeasure or sulkiness

postpone, p. 64, to delay or reschedule

scrutiny, p. 64, careful examination or observation

instincts, p. 65, strong, natural feelings

deterioration, p. 65, the amount of wear and tear or weakening in something

COMPREHENSION STRATEGIES

Use the following strategies flexibly as you read with students by modeling how they can be used to improve comprehension.

• Monitor/Clarify   • Visualize

• Summarize   • Analyze/Evaluate

• Infer/Predict   • **Question**

Think Through the Text
Cite Text Evidence

Read Segment 3, Pages 51–72

• Periodically pause to check students' understanding. Examples of key concepts and vocabulary for selected pages follow. Base any additional discussion on students' needs.

pp. 52–54

• *In Chapter 12, what does Mattie tell Quincy to explain her use of the phrase "Poor Moe"? Mattie says that she uses the phrase out of habit, from a time when she was younger and lost the button she'd named Moe. She claims that she uses the phrase the way that others say "Darn!" or "That stinks!"*

ENGLISH LANGUAGE SUPPORT Pronounce the word *habit* and have students repeat. Explain that when you do something over and over with out thinking, such as turn off the light when you leave a room, it is a habit. Have students identify something they do out of habit.

pp. 56–57

• *In Chapter 13, what does Mattie write in her notebook to explain what happened to Moe? She explains that she twisted the button when she was worried. All of the twisting weakened the thread holding the button, and when the pajamas were washed, the thread snapped. The button was washed away.* **ELA** RL.5.1

pp. 63–65

• *Why does Mattie have to try to remember everything Uncle Potluck tells her about fixing a leaky pipe? She has forgotten to bring her notebook with her because she was distracted by putting up a tent and by the possibility that she and Quincy might be friends.*

pp. 71–72

• *Why is Mattie upset when she finds her notebook out on her bed? Mattie had left the notebook under her pillow. She believes that Quincy read the notebook when she was in Mattie's room that morning and that now Quincy does not want to be her friend.*

☑ TARGET STRATEGY

Question

Remind students that good readers ask themselves questions before they read, while they read, and after they read. Explain that students will sometimes need to reread or read ahead to answer their questions.

Tell students to practice using the Question strategy as they continue reading.

SECOND READ

Analyze the Text

Analyze the Text

Dig Deeper

- Model deeper thinking. Ask: *How might the story about Moe on pp. 56–57 connect to earlier story events?* Explain that to answer the question, you'll need to review the text.

- Return to pp. 56–57, and ask students to listen for details that can help you answer the question. *The text says that one night the girl could not fall asleep and that she twisted Moe as she worried and worried. If I think about the things Mattie might have worried about from earlier in the story, the events that come to mind are those about Star destroying Mattie's notebook in Chapter 5 and saying "og-ree" to force Mattie to move in Chapter 9. I'll read on to see if I am right.*

ENGLISH LANGUAGE SUPPORT Use prompts such as *first, next,* and *then* to support students as they connect the events in Mattie's life to the story about Moe. *Possible response: First, Star destroys Mattie's notebook. Next, Star torments Mattie by saying "og-ree." Then, Mattie worried so much she twisted Moe and the thread snapped.* **ELD** ELD.PII.5.2b

- Ask the question below. Have students return to pp. 63–64 to find details that answer the question. Have them reread the appropriate sections and ask volunteers to share their answers. *What bit of the "custodial wisdom" that Uncle Potluck shares could also be advice for Mattie about life? Possible responses: His statement that it is "best to fix things when they're small, before they get too big for fixing" applies to leaking pipes, but it could also apply to the way someone deals with other people. Mattie tries to hide from things that bother her, so those things take on greater importance than if she had dealt with them right away.* **ELA** RL.5.5

ENGLISH LANGUAGE SUPPORT Provide students with sentence frames to guide them as they identify the "custodial wisdom," for example: *Uncle Potluck says that when things are _____ small they are _____ easier to fix than when they are _____. bigger* **ELD** ELD. PI.5.1

Classroom Collaboration

Divide the class into small groups. Ask the question and have students discuss it. You might also choose to have students generate a question of their own for discussion. *Why is Mattie so much more comfortable with Uncle Potluck than she is with other people? Use evidence from the text to support your response. Possible response: Potluck seems to understand Mattie's shyness, and he uses custodial information and humor to defuse awkward situations for her. For example, he tells her about the "Miss Custodial America" competition when he notices she is too distracted to pay attention to what he is doing to fix a leaky pipe.*

Reconvene as a whole group and have the group share their answers. **ELA** RL.5.1

ENGLISH LANGUAGE SUPPORT

Expand Language Production

Emerging Guide students to choose between simple responses, such as *Are Mattie's stories about Moe the same? Are they different?* Then expand their responses, such as *Mattie's stories about Moe are different.*

Expanding Encourage students to respond to the questions in complete sentences. Provide corrective feedback as needed.

Bridging Have students use complete sentences to respond to the questions. Encourage them to include the word *because* to fully explain an idea. **ELD** ELD.PI.5.1, ELD.PII.5.6

INDEPENDENT READING

Have students read pp. 51–72 independently and complete pp. 133–138 in their Reader's. Have students share their responses with the class.

Prepare

▶ **SHARE OBJECTIVES**

- Use purpose and audience to focus topic.
- Generate research questions collaboratively.
  LANGUAGE
- Understand how to take notes effectively.

Initiate Research

✔	Focus the Topic
✔	Generate Research Questions
✔	Plan the Research Process
✔	Find Credible Sources
✔	Take Notes

Focus the Topic Remind students that this project has the real-world purpose of building bridges between the school and new students and their families. Have groups brainstorm questions that students and families not familiar with the school might have. Ask students how they might find answers to those questions and then use them to focus their projects.

Generate Research Questions Discuss with students some of the ways that they can build bridges by using what they know to connect with someone who is unfamiliar in a new situation. Ask students to talk about any questions they had about ambassadors and friends that were answered by the audio clip and by the trade book so far. Explain to students that asking questions and using texts or other reliable sources to find answers are good ways to focus both their reading and their research.

Work with students to generate several questions that school ambassadors need to be able to confidently answer when educating others about the school. Then help students evaluate the questions and choose the ones that seem most important and most likely to be useful to incoming students or their families. **ELA** W.5.8, SL.5.1a, SL.5.1b, SL.5.1c, SL.5.1d

Plan the Research Process Have groups start identifying ideas from the trade book that they would like to incorporate in their project. For example, would it have helped Mattie to have a map of the school or a schedule of the school day before the first day of school? Explain that as they continue to read the book, they may come across details they want to use in their projects.

Have students also begin listing the other information they will search for, either on a classroom set of computers or at the school library. Remind students that even though they are each assigned a role of their own, it is important to share what they find and to work together to create the best possible product. **ELA** RL.5.1, RI.5.9

Find Credible Sources Tell students that they will use the Internet to find two sources that answer the questions the group has chosen as the most likely questions to be asked by their new students and their families.

Remind students that the Internet can be a good source of information but that some websites are more reliable than others. Point out that blog postings and private sites may contain inaccurate information and should not be used as research sources. Tell students that websites ending in .edu, .org, and .gov are official sites run by schools, experts, or government officials and therefore are credible sources of information. **ELA** RI.5.8, RI.5.9

Take Notes After students have located their two sources, tell them to take notes about the information presented. Discuss these **Note-Taking Tips:**

- Use index cards to keep track of relevant information.
- Use one card for each important point.
- Include details and examples that support the important points.
- Write down the source information.

Tell students to keep these notes and use them as a model when they start doing research for other aspects of their project. **ELA** RI.5.8, RI.5.9

ENGLISH LANGUAGE SUPPORT Direct students to begin their research by using a district and/or school website to identify what schools feel it is most important to share with students and families. Provides students with index cards of two different colors. Explain to them that they should use one color index card per source. **ELD** ELD.PI.5.9, ELD.PI.5.10a

INTEGRATED LANGUAGE ARTS REVIEW

Write About Reading

Digital Resources ▶

To support students before they start this task, use the following digital resources.

▶ Interactive Lessons: Writing Informative Texts: Organize

▶ GrammarSnap Videos: Compound Sentences

INTRODUCE THE TASK
After students have reread Segment 3, tell them that they will respond to the text by writing a procedural composition to help Mattie recall how to fix a leaky pipe since she forgot her notebook at home.

- Prompt students to explain the importance of organization in a procedural composition.
- Tell students they will have to look back in the book to find the steps in the process used to fix the pipe.

Review the Model Display the model procedural composition from **Student Book p. 203** and review the transition words and phrases used to describe the steps in the process.

PLAN AND DRAFT
Have students write a procedural essay about fixing a leaky pipe after reading Segment 3. Students' essays should include

- an introduction to the topic and some details about it.
- details about each step in the procedure.
- transitional words and verbs to clearly describe the steps in the process.
- illustrations or media to complement the steps in the process.
- a conclusion that summarizes the topic.

REVISE AND EDIT
Have student pairs revise their procedural compositions. Guide students to generate a checklist partners can use to review each other's work. For example:

- Did I clearly describe the steps in the process?
- Did I organize the steps in sequential order?
- Did I use verbs correctly and incorporate appropriate transitional words and phrases?
- Did I use correct spelling, grammar, and punctuation?

See the Analytic Writing Rubric, p. R15.

SHARE
Have students pass their procedural compositions to the person seated on their right-hand side. Students read their neighbor's composition and identify two sequential words the author used in his or her composition. Hang students' compositions on a bulletin board for others to read.

ELA RL.5.1, RI.5.10, W.5.2a, W.5.2b, W.5.2c, W.5.2d, W.5.2e, W.5.4, W.5.5, W.5.8, W. 5.10, L.5.1c, L.5.2e

▶ SHARE OBJECTIVES
- Write a procedural composition. LANGUAGE
- Cite evidence from the text.
- Use correct punctuation and spelling.

▶ SKILLS REVIEW
Review the following skills, as needed, before students begin to write their response.

- **Writing:** Procedural Composition Lesson 6
- **Grammar:** Sentences (Lessons 1–3)
- **Spelling:** Short, Long, and Other Vowel Sounds (Lessons 1–7), *R*-Controlled Vowels (Lessons 6, 7, 10), Homophones (Lesson 8), Compound Words (Lesson 9), Final Schwa Vowels (Lesson 10)

ENGLISH LANGUAGE SUPPORT

Sentence Frames

Emerging Brainstorm a classroom procedure that students use daily, such as getting ready for lunch. Write *Step 1, Step 2,* and *Step 3* on the board. As one student acts out each step of the procedure ,write each action as a step in the procedure.

Expanding Students identify a procedure they use daily, such as leaving the house or getting ready for bed. They write *First, Next, Then,* and *Last* on a paper divided into four sections. Students draw each step of the procedure in the proper section.

Bridging Students identify a procedure they use daily, such as leaving the house or getting ready for bed. They write *First, Next, Then,* and *Last* on a paper divided into four sections. Students write each step of the procedure in the proper section. **ELD** ELD.PII.5.2b

Independent Reading

▶ **SHARE OBJECTIVES**

- Read and comprehend biographies or autobiographies.
- Refer to details and examples to analyze a text independently.
- Read independently from a "just right" text.
- Read with accuracy and self-correct as needed.

ENGLISH LANGUAGE SUPPORT

"Just Right" Texts

All Proficiencies Provide Emerging English learners with a choice of shorter but appropriately challenging books to read. Students at the Bridging proficiency level usually have more stamina and can be successful with a much longer book that they can read over time.

ELD ELD.PII.5.1

Read to Connect

Share and Compare Texts If students have already demonstrated comprehension and analysis of the first three segments of *Hound Dog True,* have them read in print or online a biography or autobiography about an ambassador. Ask students to use their Reading Logs ⎘ to record their progress and thinking about their reading. Have partners who have read the same selection ask and answer questions such as *What was the author's purpose? What did you learn from this selection? How can I use this information in my project? What more do I want to learn?*

ELA RI.5.1, RI.5.7, RI.5.9, RI.5.10

Self-Selected Reading

Extending the Project Topic Have students select an independent reading book. To help students select a book, guide them to generate a list of topics that supports this unit, such as famous ambassadors, becoming an ambassador, international relations, or diplomacy. Ask students to use their Reading Logs ⎘ to record their progress and thinking about their reading.

Fluency

Partner Read Have students practice reading aloud with accuracy and using self-correction, using their self-selected reading books. Tell them to select a passage or page and read it to their partner. Have them listen to the partner's feedback about accuracy and self-correction. Then have them reread aloud with their partner's comments in mind. **ELA** RF.5.4a, RF.5.4c

Extend the Topic

Domain-Specific Vocabulary

Discuss Words About the Topic Have students review in their journals the list of content vocabulary words and meanings they have encountered so far in *Hound Dog True*. Then display the words shown to the right. Tell students that these words can help them learn more about ambassadors. Read aloud the meaning of each word. Then have students respond to the following prompts:

- *A person serving as an _____ for the United States is often appointed by the President. ambassador*
- *A person selected to be ambassador is often consider a _____ in their community. touchstone*
- *As a member of the school welcoming committee, he will _____ the school to new students and families. promote*
- *Marianne will use _____ when welcoming the new members to the program. diplomacy* **ELA** RI.5.4, L.5.4a

ENGLISH LANGUAGE SUPPORT Support meaning of the content vocabulary word *promote* by asking students to make a sign that promotes something interesting or unique about their school. For example: *Gardenview School, Home of District Spelling Bee Finalists!* Invite students to explain how their sign promotes the school. **ELD** ELD.PI.5.12a

Interact with the Words Have students work in small groups, using Graphic Organizer 6 (Four-Square Map) to extend their understanding of each word about helping others. Assign one word to each group, and have them follow these steps for completing the Four-Square Map with information about the word:

1. In the first corner, draw a picture that represents the word.

2. In the second corner, write the meaning of the word.

3. In the third corner, write a sentence using the word.

4. In the fourth corner, write the word.

When groups have finished, have them share their completed Four-Square Maps with the class. **ELA** RI.5.4

▶ **SHARE OBJECTIVE**
- Acquire and use domain-specific vocabulary.

Words About the Topic: Ambassador

- **touchstone** an outstanding representation of a wider group
- **ambassador** a top-ranking official who lives in a foreign country while representing his/her own government
- **diplomacy** dealing with others in a delicate and effective manner
- **promote** to present information for the purpose of education or publicity

Prepare

▶ **SHARE OBJECTIVES**
- Respect one another and each person's work.
- Provide focused suggestions or compliments.
- Problem-solve solutions to overcome challenges.

Discuss Peer Critiques

✔ Learn About Peer Critiques
✔ Develop Evaluation Criteria
✔ Scheduling Peer Critiques

Learn About Peer Critiques Explain to students that peer critiques are not about fault-finding; they are meant to be helpful tips and ideas from other points of view about how you might improve your work. Identify and discuss the key elements of peer critiques for students: be nice, be clear, and be constructive.

Students can identify an aspect of the project they are having trouble with and work in small groups to identify and discuss possible solutions to the problems. This strategy works well during the initial preparation and drafting stages of the project. Students also can work in pairs to evaluate each other's work in more depth. This strategy works well during the later stages of the project, as students begin to finalize their presentations. FInally, students can hold a gallery walk by showing some of their work. The class can spend a few minutes at each student's work, providing suggestions, ideas, and feedback. This strategy works well during the initial preparation and drafting stages.

ELA SL.5.1b, SL.5.1c

Develop Evaluation Criteria Show the class an informational pamphlet. Have students discuss its characteristics and qualities. Write their ideas on the board. Encourage students to use this list of qualities as a touchstone against which their work will be evaluated. Remind students that this is not a checklist of necessary elements that each brochure must contain; it is simply a list of suggestions of elements students should consider.

Scheduling Peer Critiques To make sure students keep on track with their project work, you may wish to schedule some informal peer critiques during the preparation stage to help students as they draft their materials. The later stages of the project, including rehearsing the presentations, provide a good opportunity for more formal critiques as students finalize their work. At the end of the project, when students are reflecting on their work, they will have an opportunity for formal peer critiques (see page T426).

ENGLISH LANGUAGE SUPPORT Use these sentence frames to support participation. *This note says _____. I think there is too much white space on your pamphlet How can I solve this problem?* **ELD** ELD.PI.5.1, ELD.PI.5.3, ELD.PI.5.9, ELD.PI.5.11a

Evaluate Progress

✔ Check Student Progress
✔ Clarify Expectations
✔ Look Ahead

Check Student Progress Meet with each student individually to check on his/her progress. Ask students to explain what their role is in the group and what they have done to complete their tasks so far. Look over students' work with them and discuss any questions or concerns they have. Offer additional suggestions as needed and review timelines and deadlines as well.

ELA SL.5.1a, SL.5.1c, SL.5.1d

Clarify Expectations Bring students back together as a class and remind them of the project components: a pamphlet and presentation to new students and their families. Remind students that they are expected to work cooperatively to complete the project. Explain that they will be evaluated as a group after they deliver their presentations.

Look Ahead Regroup students with their project groups and give them a few minutes to discuss the critiques they heard and their progress so far. Ask groups to list any concerns or questions they have about going forward. Then meet with each group individually to review their progress on each task. If students have lost focus, guide them to revisit the project requirements. If students are struggling with time management, work with them to make a plan for meeting the project deadline.

ELA SL.5.1a, SL.5.1b, SL.5.1c, SL.5.1d

Digital Resources ▶

To support students before they start this task, use the following digital resources.

▶ Interactive Lesson: Writing Narratives: Dialogue and Description

▶ GrammarSnap Videos: Dialogue

INTEGRATED LANGUAGE ARTS REVIEW

Write About Reading

INTRODUCE THE TASK
After students complete their Independent Reading, tell them they will respond to the text by writing an imagined dialogue that could have occurred between the ambassador and a news anchor.

• Prompt students to think about what an ambassador would speak to the news anchor about.
• Tell students they will have to go back into the text to find facts and details to include in their dialogues.

DISCUSS THE PROCESS
Tell students that a dialogue consists mainly of the words people say to one another, not what a person is thinking.

• Ask what sorts of information the news anchor might want to discuss with an ambassador.
• Prompt students to write questions to gather the desired information.
• Remind students that they should not include their own opinions in the dialogue.

PLAN AND DRAFT
Have students write a dialogue they imagine took place between an ambassador and news anchor. Students' dialogues should include

• an introductory statement from the news anchor.
• a cohesive discussion between a news anchor and an ambassador.
• a concluding statement from one of the speakers about the purpose of the discussion.

REVISE AND EDIT
Have pairs review their dialogues. Guide the class to generate a checklist partners can use to review each other's work. For example:

• Does the dialogue seem natural and appropriate?
• Have I used complete sentences?
• Does the dialogue conclude by restating the main topic?
• Have I corrected any spelling or punctuation errors?

See the Analytic Writing Rubric, p. R15.

SHARE
Have partners take on the role of either news anchor or ambassador and present the dialogues to the class.

ELA RF.5.4a, W.5.3a, W.5.3b, W.5.3c, W.5.3d, W.5.3e, W.5.4, W.5.5, W.5.9b, W.5.10, L.5.2e

▶ SHARE OBJECTIVES
• Write a dialogue. LANGUAGE
• Cite evidence from the text.
• Use correct punctuation and spelling.

▶ SKILLS REVIEW
Review the following skills, as needed, before students begin to write their response.

• **Writing:** Dialogue (Lesson 3)
• **Grammar:** Punctuation (Lesson 3)
• **Spelling:** Short, Long, and Other Vowel Sounds (Lessons 1–7), Homophones (Lesson 8), Compound Words (Lesson 9)

ENGLISH LANGUAGE SUPPORT

Sentence Frames

Emerging Help students understand how dialogue sounds. Then work with them to complete the following sentence frames:

Mr. Johnson asked Shirley Temple, "_____ ."

Ms. Temple replied, "_____ ."

Expanding Have students write a pair of sentence frames like those above and exchange them with a partner to complete.

Bridging As students prewrite, have them focus on making the dialogue sound natural and appropriate to the speaker.

SEGMENT 4
PP. 73–94

▶ **SHARE OBJECTIVES**

- Read to analyze characters and their traits.
- Read to make inferences and draw conclusions. LANGUAGE
- Analyze cause-and-effect relationships. LANGUAGE

Content Vocabulary

Display the words from the trade book listed below. Read each word with students and discuss its meaning.

impeccable, p. 81, perfect or flawless; beyond criticism

visage, p. 81, someone's face

propriety, p. 81, displaying behaviors that are believed to be correct or appropriate

expertise, p. 83, expert skill or knowledge

consequences, p. 91, something that follows as a result

COMPREHENSION STRATEGIES

Use the following strategies flexibly as you read with students by modeling how they can be used to improve comprehension.

- Monitor/Clarify
- Summarize
- **Infer/Predict**
- Visualize
- Analyze/Evaluate
- Question

Think Through the Text

Read Segment 4, Pages 73–94

- Periodically pause to check students' understanding. Examples of key concepts and vocabulary for selected pages follow. Base any additional discussion on students' needs.

pp. 75–77

- *How did Uncle Potluck get his "traitorous knee"? When he was in the army, he trained a dog named Stella to be a tracker. Stella was frightened by thunder and tried to run. Potluck ran after her and caught his foot in a gopher hole. When he fell, he hurt his knee badly.*

ENGLISH LANGUAGE SUPPORT Point out the suffix *-ous* in the word *traitorous.* Remind students that the suffix *-ous* means "full of," and explain that when *-ous* is added to a noun, the noun becomes an adjective. Tell students that *traitorous* means "full of disloyalty." Ask students what is being described at traitorous. *Uncle Potluck's knee* Discuss how a knee can be traitorous, or full of disloyalty. **ELD** ELD.PI.5.6b

pp. 84–86

- *How is Mattie locked in the principal's office? She tries to fix a doorknob by herself, and she puts it on backwards.*

pp. 87–89

- *Why does Mattie believe that Uncle Potluck's fall in the principal's office is her fault? She left the vacuum cleaner plugged in, and Uncle Potluck tripped over the cord.*

p. 93

- *What are some "small brave things" that Principal Bonnet does before she climbs a mountain? She takes classes, climbs hills and small peaks, and does practice runs.*

ENGLISH LANGUAGE SUPPORT Encourage students to respond to questions in complete sentences. Provide corrective feedback as needed.

✓ TARGET STRATEGY

Infer/Predict

Remind students that good readers use information from a story and their own knowledge to understand things that are not stated directly in the text. Guide students to use their inferences to make predictions about upcoming story events and developments.

Tell students to practice using the Infer/Predict strategy as they continue reading. Have students pause occasionally to think about how each chapter builds on the previous one and to infer connections between Mattie's past and the experiences she is now having. **ELA** RL.5.5

Analyze the Text

Dig Deeper

- Model deeper thinking. Ask: *What does Principal Bonnet mean when she says, "You can't have brave without scared"?* Explain that to answer the question, you'll need to look at the text.

- Read pp. 92–94 aloud, and ask students to listen for details that can help you answer the question. *Principal Bonnet explains that what is scary for one person might not be scary for another. One example is petting a dog. It is brave for someone who is scared of dogs to pet a dog. It is not brave at all for someone who is not scared of dogs. Real bravery involves doing something even when you are afraid.*

ENGLISH LANGUAGE SUPPORT Use pictures and familiar examples to help students understand what the terms *brave* and *scared* mean. Say/ask: *Dogs scare some people. Is it brave for these people to pet a dog? yes* **ELD** ELD.PI.5.1

- Ask the question below. Guide students to look back at p. 93–94 to look for clues that will help them answer the question. Have them reread the text, and ask volunteers to share their answers. *What problem does Mattie have when she tries to decide what "small brave thing" she should do? Possible response: She is not sure what she is afraid of, so she cannot figure out how to start addressing her fears.* **ELA** RL.5.1

Classroom Collaboration

Divide the class into small groups. Ask the question below and have students discuss it. You might also choose to have students generate a question of their own for discussion. *Why do you think Principal Bonnet told Mattie her story about climbing a mountain? Use details from earlier chapters to support your answer. Possible response: Principal Bonnet noticed that Mattie was shy when they were introduced, and she noticed that Mattie carried a notebook like one that she had at Mattie's age (pp. 28–29). She may understand that Mattie is afraid of something because she was also afraid of things at Mattie's age.*

Reconvene as a whole group and have the group share their answers. **ELA** RL.5.1

INDEPENDENT READING

Have students read pp. 73–94 independently and complete pp. 139–144 in their Reader's Notebooks 🗗. Have students share their responses with the class.

Prepare

▶ **SHARE OBJECTIVES**

- Complete revised drafts of final project and presentation materials. LANGUAGE
- Gather materials necessary for the presentation.
- Outline the agenda for the final presentation.

Create Materials

✔ Discuss Digital Tools
✔ Plan Materials
✔ Draft and Revise the Pamphlet
✔ Create the Pamphlet

Discuss Digital Tools Remind students that there are many digital tools students can use to help them create professional-looking pamphlets. Have students identify digital tools they are familiar with that they think might be useful for this project. If necessary, go over some examples of tools students might use:

- **Word Processing or Page Composition Software** Students can use software to lay out the text and visuals in their pamphlets. Students can experiment with a variety of fonts, type sizes, and colors and even include clip art and other graphics.

- **Image Processing Software** Students can use image processing software to create or touch up visuals in the pamphlet.

- **Audiovisual Processing Software** Students can use software to create short animations or videos to include in their presentations.

Plan Materials Encourage students to review their task checklists to recall what products they are responsible for providing based on their assigned roles. Students can reconsider their roles and responsibilities if they find that the remaining workload is not distributed equally among team members.

Discuss how students will disseminate information during their presentation. Ask them if they will project their pamphlet for the audience to see using presentation software or if it would it be more useful for each audience member to have a copy of the pamphlet. Remind students to plan ahead if they need to make copies or gather materials for their presentation. Have students consult the milestones on their chart in regard to materials and be sure that they are on target.

Draft and Revise the Pamphlet Have students continue working on their pamphlets, using ideas and information from *Hound Dog True* and from the other sources they have identified.

Emphasize to students that the pamphlet will be the basis for their presentations and that they should use a style and a tone appropriate to their audience. Tell students that they may find it helpful to pause frequently and read aloud what they have written so that they can hear how it might sound to an audience. Have students revise their work as necessary, and circulate to offer suggestions and feedback.
ELA W.5.2a, W.5.2b, W.5.2c, W.5.2d, W.5.2e, W.5.4, W.5.5, W.5.6, W.5.7, W.5.8, W.5.10

Create the Pamphlet Tell students that the format they choose for their pamphlets should support and enhance the information they believe will help new students and their families. Explain that the pamphlet might include elements such as a school map, bulleted facts/key points, and illustrations. Point out that the text they include should be carefully written and free of mistakes and that each piece of information should have a clear relationship to the presentation. Allow students to use the Internet to locate examples of pamphlets or templates they might use as inspiration and models. Then have groups begin creating their pamphlets.
ELA W.5.2a, W.5.4, SL.5.5

ENGLISH LANGUAGE SUPPORT Use these sentence frames to support participation: *I think our pamphlet should be _____ one page, front and back* **long because** *_____. if we give people too much information, it will be overwhelming* **ELD** ELD.PI.5.3

INTEGRATED LANGUAGE ARTS REVIEW

Write About Reading

Digital Resources ▶

To support students before they start this task, use the following digital resources.

▶ Interactive Lessons: Writing to Sources

▶ GrammarSnap Videos: Complex Sentences

INTRODUCE THE TASK After students have reread Segment 4, tell them that they will respond to the text by writing a letter to Uncle Potluck from Mattie.

- Prompt students to identify what the parts of a letter are.
- Tell students that they will have to go back to the text to find facts and details to include in their letters.

PLAN AND DRAFT Have students write a letter to Uncle Potluck from Mattie after reading Segment 4. Letters should include:

- details about Uncle Potluck's relationship with Mattie.
- a logical explanation of the cause and effect for Mattie's actions in this segment of the book.
- sequential and transitional words to clearly identify the relationship between the events.
- a conclusion that explains what Mattie learned from the incident.
- the proper format for a letter.

REVISE AND EDIT Students review their letters in pairs. Guide the class to generate a checklist partners can use to review each other's work.

- Does my letter include a date, address, body, closing, and signature?
- Does my letter outline the nature of Uncle Potluck and Mattie's relationship?
- Is my letter written from Mattie's point of view?
- Does my letter include at least one cause and effect?
- Does my letter include a lesson learned by Mattie?

See the Analytic Writing Rubric, p. R15.

SHARE Students trade letters with a partner and write a short response from Uncle Potluck's perspective. Allow partners to verbally share their correspondences. **ELA** RL.5.1, RL.5.5, RL.5.6, W.5.3a, W.5.3b, W.5.3c, W.5.3d, W.5.3e, W.5.4, W.5.5, W.5.6, W.5.10, L.5.1a, L.5.2e, L.5.4a

▶ **SHARE OBJECTIVES**
- Write a letter. LANGUAGE
- Cite evidence from the text.
- Use correct punctuation and spelling.

▶ **SKILLS REVIEW**

Review the following skills, as needed, before students begin to write their response.

- **Writing:** Narrative Writing (Lessons 1–5 and 8)
- **Grammar:** Complex Sentences (Lesson 9)
- **Spelling:** Homophones (Lesson 8), Compound Words (Lesson 9), Final Schwa Vowels (Lesson 10)

ENGLISH LANGUAGE SUPPORT

Sentence Frames

Emerging Help students use subordinating conjunctions by writing the following sentences on the board: *When Mattie's mom brings out the tent, Mattie helps set it up. Mattie forgot her notebook at home because she was tired and preoccupied with setting up the tent.* Ask students to identify the subordinating conjunction in each sentence. when; because

Expanding Using the above sentences, ask students to identify the dependent and independent clauses.

Bridging Have students complete the following sentence frames and identify the subordinating conjunctions, dependent clause, and independent clause in each sentence: *Mattie thinks Uncle Potluck tripped because ____. When Uncle Potluck is with the doctor, Mattie ____.* **ELD** ELD.PII.5.6

SEGMENT 5
PP. 95–122

▶ SHARE OBJECTIVES

- Read to make inferences and draw conclusions. LANGUAGE
- Read to determine story themes and key ideas. LANGUAGE
- Examine story structure and plot relationships. LANGUAGE

Content Vocabulary

Display the words from the trade book listed below. Read each word with students and discuss its meaning.

versus, p. 102, against, especially in a competition or court case

lunge, p. 103, a sudden forward movement; part of an attack

nickname, p. 110, an invented or shortened name, often related to an event or characteristic

taut, p. 112, pulled or stretched tightly

mum, p. 122, saying nothing; silent

COMPREHENSION STRATEGIES

Use the following strategies flexibly as you read with students by modeling how they can be used to improve comprehension.

- Monitor/Clarify
- Visualize
- **Summarize**
- Analyze/Evaluate
- Infer/Predict
- Question

FIRST READ

Think Through the Text

Read Segment 5, Pages 95–122

- Periodically pause to check students' understanding. Examples of key concepts and vocabulary for selected pages follow. Base any additional discussion on students' needs.

p. 95

- *How does Mattie's decision to have a Popsicle connect to events in the last chapter?* She had joked with Principal Bonnet about it being brave to eat Popsicles if you were afraid of them. Mattie is trying to practice doing small brave things.

pp. 102–105

- *Why do Mattie and Quincy act out the story of "Moe Versus the Lint"?* At first, Mattie is trying to provide a model so Quincy can draw a picture to go with the story. As they act out the story, they start to have fun pretending to do brave things.

p. 110

- *How did Uncle Potluck get his nickname?* When he was young, he stole his own birthday cake but claimed a bear had eaten it. His mother said that he was "as unpredictable as a potluck supper." **ELA RL.5.1**

ENGLISH LANGUAGE SUPPORT Point out the two parts of the compound word *Potluck* as *pot* and *luck*. Tell students that the word originated in 1775 when what came out of a pot was considered a matter of chance or luck.

pp. 112–118

- *What does Mattie learn about Mama when they talk on the tin can telephone and later in Mattie's room?* Mattie learns that it was Mama who read her notebook, not Quincy, that Mama didn't know how difficult it was for Mattie to move so often, and that they would be staying in Uncle Potluck's house for a long time.

ENGLISH LANGUAGE SUPPORT Provide an illustration or demonstration of how a tin can telephone works and display a sentence frame such as: *When Mattie talks, she _____.* puts her mouth to the can *When Mattie _____,* listens she puts her ear to the can.

☑ TARGET STRATEGY

Summarize

Have students reread page 104. Remind students that they can use their own words to summarize story events and ideas. Point out that summarizing as they read will help them better understand what they read. Model the thinking:

Think Aloud *This page describes an important moment in the relationship between Mattie and Quincy. The author says, "Mattie does not think. She thwacks back." This means that Mattie is starting to enjoy the story she and Quincy are acting out.*

Tell students to practice using the Summarize strategy as they continue reading.

Prepare

Analyze the Text

Dig Deeper

- Model deeper thinking. Ask: *How is "Moe Versus the Lint" different from the story "Moe" on pp. 56–57?* Explain that to answer the question, you'll need to look at the text.

- Read aloud the stories on pp. 56–57 and p. 102, and ask students to listen for details that can help you answer the question. *In the earlier story, Moe is timid. He is washed away and doesn't fight back or call for help. In "Moe Versus the Lint," Moe decides to fight back against the Lint and finds a bobby pin to use as a sword. In this story, Moe is braver and takes charge to defend himself.*

- Ask the questions below. Guide students to review the text on pp. 102–103 to help them think about how they might respond. Ask volunteers to share their thoughts.

Why is it an important statement for Mattie when she says, "I'm Moe"? Possible response: She stands up for herself with Quincy and firmly says what she wants instead of running away.

What does this show about Mattie? Possible response: Like Moe in the stories she has written, Mattie has become braver. **ELA** RL.5.5

ENGLISH LANGUAGE SUPPORT Use sentence frames to support student responses, for example: *Mattie is feeling _____ braver. Instead of running away from Quincy, Mattie _____. tells her matter-of-factly what she wants Mattie acts like _____. Moe* **ELD** ELD.PI.5.1

Classroom Collaboration

Divide the class into small groups. Ask the question below and have students discuss it. You might also choose to have students generate a question of their own for discussion. *On p. 121, why does Mattie tell the moon she is sorry? Possible response: She doesn't want to talk to the moon in front of Quincy for fear that it will "mess up" their new friendship. She is telling the moon she is sorry that she cannot share any secrets that night.*

Reconvene as a whole group and have the group share their answers.

ENGLISH LANGUAGE SUPPORT

Sentence Frames

Emerging Break down story events into simple sentences, such as: *The girls act out a fight. The girls have fun. The girls are friends.* Then ask questions, such as: *Is Quincy Mattie's friend?*

Expanding Break down story events into simple sentences, such as: *The girls act out a fight. The girls have fun.* Then have students complete sentence frames, such as: *The girls are _____.*

Bridging Have students use complete, complex statements to respond to questions. Encourage students to use the word *because* to help explain their reasoning. **ELD** ELD.PI.5.1

INDEPENDENT READING

Have students read pp. 95–122 independently and complete pp. 145–150 in their Reader's Notebooks. Have students share their responses with the class.

Prepare

▶ SHARE OBJECTIVES

- Fine-tune the beginning, middle, and end of the presentation. LANGUAGE
- Actively listen and appropriately participate as audience members.
- Rehearse and modify the presentation as necessary.

Develop the Presentation

✔	Making a Strong Presentation
✔	Questions and Answers
✔	Audience Responsibilities
✔	Planning, Rehearsal, and Delivery

Making a Strong Presentation Tell students that strong presentations are well organized and engaging. Have students think about successful speeches and presentations they have seen, either in real life or in movies or media coverage of special events. If possible, show a video or invite a guest speaker to come to class and demonstrate. Ask students to list techniques the speakers use, such as eye contact, hand gestures, facial expressions, and tone. Tell students that it is important to capture and maintain the audience's attention and interest and to share information in a way that is easy to understand and remember. Display and discuss the following suggestions. **ELA** SL.5.2, SL.5.4a, SL.5.5, SL.5.6

Begin your presentation with . . .	• a question for the audience to think about. • an entertaining story. • a quote from a faculty member or famous ambassador.
During your presentation, try . . .	• organizing information in a logical way. • emphasizing important details or dates. • including visuals or multimedia. • using gestures and other appropriate visual cues.
Conclude by . . .	• restating key important dates. • summarizing important details. • teaching the audience a school or community tradition.

Questions and Answers Tell students that many presentations end with question-and-answer sessions with audiences. Explain that answering questions shows the audience that a speaker is knowledgeable about and confident in his or her work. It also provides an opportunity to elaborate on key points. Provide the following tips for asking and answering questions after a presentation:

- Call on a variety of audience members.
- Restate the question and ask for clarification if necessary.
- Answer questions honestly, and if you do not know the answer, say so. **ELA** SL.5.1a, SL.5.1b, SL.5.1c, SL.5.1d, SL.5.2, SL.5.6

Audience Responsibilities Remind students that during a presentation, they should give speakers their full attention. Tell students that they should listen carefully for ideas or information they might like to ask about. Explain that speaking in front of an audience can be challenging or even a bit frightening and that they can help each other succeed by being quiet, interested, and supportive audience members. Guide students to understand that public speaking is a valuable real-world skill and that both practicing it and watching other people do it will help prepare them for a variety of careers. **ELA** SL.5.1a, SL.5.1b, SL.5.1c, SL.5.1d

Planning, Rehearsal, and Delivery Tell students that in a group presentation, it's important to plan who will say what and when. Point out that it also important to prepare the venue and to decide when visuals will be shown and which pieces of information will be emphasized or reviewed. Remind students that they will provide a pamphlet during their presentation and will need to choose whether to distribute it at the beginning, during a pause in the middle, or at the end of their presentation. Remind students not to read their pamphlets to the audience but rather to highlight the important information. Have groups review their roles and scripts while making an outline of their presentations. Give students time to create note cards if needed and to rehearse their presentation. Circulate to help groups sort out any concerns or difficulties. Then have students practice delivering their presentations. Remind them to use eye contact and to speak clearly and at an appropriate pace. Provide the audience with an opportunity to ask questions or give positive feedback at the end of each lecture.
ELA SL.5.1a, SL.5.1b, SL.5.1c, SL.5.1d, SL.5.5, SL.5.6

ENGLISH LANGUAGE SUPPORT Use these sentence frames to support participation. *I am glad you highlighted _____ the cost of lunch items in your pamphlet. That information will help new students and/or their families _____. decide if they want to buy lunch at school or not* **ELD** ELD.PI.5.3

Digital Resources ▶

To support students before they start this task, use the following digital resources.

▶ Interactive Lesson: Writing to Sources

INTEGRATED LANGUAGE ARTS REVIEW

Write About Reading

INTRODUCE THE TASK After students reread Segment 5, tell them that they will respond to the text by writing a summary of Mattie's stories about Moe.

- Prompt students to think about how the stories about Moe change during *Hound Dog True*.
- Tell students that they will have to go back in the text to find details to include in their summaries.

DISCUSS THE PROCESS Tell students that a summary includes only the most important information in the text.

- Ask: *How do you know what information to include in a summary and what information to leave out?*
- Have students revisit the stories about Moe to note the details that are most important to understanding the main idea.
- Remind students that they should not include their own opinions in their summaries.

PLAN AND DRAFT Have students write a summary of Mattie's stories about Moe after reading Segment 5. Student summaries should include

- a topic sentence based on the main idea of the stories.
- two or three sentences that support the main idea.
- a concluding sentence to restate the main idea.
- proper use of common and proper nouns.

REVISE AND EDIT Have student pairs review their summaries. Guide the class to generate a checklist partners can use to review each other's work. For example:

- Does my topic sentence express the main idea of the stories?
- Have I included only the most important details?
- Does my conclusion restate the main idea?
- Have I properly used common and proper nouns?
- Have I corrected any spelling and punctuation errors?

See the Informative/Explanatory Writing Rubric, p. R17.

SHARE Have students share their summaries of Mattie's stories about Moe with a small group, comparing their topic sentences and details. Have students explain their choices.

ELA RL.5.1, RL.5.2, RL.5.5, W.5.4, W.5.5, W.5.9a, W.5.10, L.5.2e

▶ **SHARE OBJECTIVES**

- Write a summary of a set of short stories. LANGUAGE
- Cite evidence from the text.
- Use correct punctuation and spelling.

▶ **SKILLS REVIEW**

Review the following skills, as needed, before students begin to write their response.

- **Writing:** Summarize
- **Grammar:** Common and Proper Nouns (Lesson 4)
- **Spelling:** Short, Long, and Other Vowel Sounds (Lessons 1–7), *R*-Controlled Vowels (Lessons 6, 7, 10), Homophones (Lesson 8), Compound Words (Lesson 9), Final Schwa Vowels (Lesson 10)

ENGLISH LANGUAGE SUPPORT

Sentence Frames

Emerging Write a list of words from the trade book on the board. For example: *Mattie, custodian, tell, Quincy, nervous, shy, knee, tent, moon.* Ask students to sort the list into nouns and other words. Then point out that some of the nouns start with capital letters, revealing that they are proper nouns.

Expanding Write the following sentences on the board. Ask students to fill one with a common noun and the other one with a proper noun. *They brought a _____ to Arthur. We went to _____ on vacation.*

Bridging Have partners write two sentences on a sheet of paper. Tell partners to exchange papers and identify the nouns in the sentences. Ask them to tally how many common and how many proper nouns their partner used in their sentences.

SEGMENT 6
PP. 123–145, CONCLUSION

Think Through the Text

Cite Text Evidence

SHARE OBJECTIVES

- Read to make inferences and draw conclusions. LANGUAGE
- Read to determine story themes and key ideas.
- Use information from the text to summarize important ideas and events. LANGUAGE

Content Vocabulary

Display the words from the trade book listed below. Read each word with students and discuss its meaning.

potential, p. 124, possible, but as yet not actual

retrieve, p. 125, to reclaim or get something back

ponder, p. 129, think over or consider carefully

prognostication, p. 130, a prediction of future events

prone, p. 135, inclined to do or be affected by something

COMPREHENSION STRATEGIES

Use the following strategies flexibly as you read with students by modeling how they can be used to improve comprehension.

- Monitor/Clarify
- Summarize
- Infer/Predict
- Visualize
- **Analyze/Evaluate**
- Question

Read Segment 6, Pages 123–145, Conclusion

- Periodically pause to check students' understanding. Examples of key concepts and vocabulary for selected pages follow. Base any additional discussion on students' needs.

pp. 128–129

- *Why does Principal Bonnet salute Uncle Potluck? What earlier event does the salute connect to? Uncle Potluck always salutes Principal Bonnet's picture when he passes her office, but he thinks no one has seen him. She salutes to show that she has seen the salutes.*

ENGLISH LANGUAGE SUPPORT Use visuals or gestures to remind students what a salute is. Ask: *Do military persons in uniform salute the President of the United States? yes Do you salute the flag when you watch it being raised or lowered? yes* Ask students to describe how they salute the flag when they watch it being raised or lowered. *Possible response: by putting my right hand on my heart*

p. 135

- *What small brave thing does Mattie do after Quincy runs out of the house? At first, she waits for one of the adults to follow Quincy, but when no one does, she stands up and goes after Quincy.* **ELA RL.5.2**

pp. 139–140

- *What story does Mattie tell the moon? How does Quincy react to the story? Mattie tells the moon about Star destroying her notebook and later tormenting her with the word "og-ree." Quincy says that what Star did was bad but that Mattie's telling of the story shows what a good writer she is.* **ELA RL.5.5**

pp. 147–149

- *How does Mattie introduce herself to her new classmates? She says her name clearly and tells everyone that she is a writer.*

✓ TARGET STRATEGY

Analyze/Evaluate

Remind students that when they stop to analyze and evaluate what they are reading, they read carefully to form opinions about the text. Have students review the ending of the story to evaluate how Mattie has changed. Ask volunteers to share their ideas. **ELA RL.5.5**

ENGLISH LANGUAGE SUPPORT Prompt students to use connecting words or phrases such as *at the beginning, first/next,* and *for example* when describing how Mattie has changed throughout the course of the book. **ELD ELD.PI.5.11a, ELD.PII.5.2b**

Tell students to practice using the Analyze/Evaluate strategy as they continue reading.

SECOND READ

Analyze the Text

Dig Deeper

- Model deeper thinking. Ask: *At the end of Chapter 28, what is Mattie thinking of when she says "Hound dog true"?* **Explain that to answer the question, you'll need to look at the text.**

- Read the text on pp. 126–127 aloud, and ask students to listen for details that can help you answer the question. *Uncle Potluck describes what happens when Stella leads some MPs back to him when he injured his knee. While Miss Sweet says the dog had been lazy by not seeming able to track, Quincy comments that maybe the dog was misunderstood. Those comments make Mattie think that perhaps even Stella didn't know what she was capable of until she had to do it. That is what she is thinking of when she says "Hound dog true," as if what she is thinking is obvious and true.*

ENGLISH LANGUAGE SUPPORT Point out the prefix *mis-* in the word *misunderstood*. Tell students that *mis-* means "incorrectly" or "not." The word *misunderstood* means "incorrectly understood." Work together to list and define other words with the prefix *mis-*. *Possible responses:* misalign, misbehave, misspell, mistreat **ELD** ELD.PI.5.6b

- Ask the question below. Guide students to review how Mattie has changed over the course of the book and look back at pp. 139–140 to help them think about how they might respond. Ask volunteers to share their thoughts. After students have responded to the question, have them discuss how they think the later chapters connect to events in the earlier chapters and help complete the structure of the story.

Why does Mattie reveal her story about Star backwards, starting with the end of the story? Possible responses: Star seemed so powerful to her that Mattie may have only been able to reveal a little at a time. She may have described the events in reverse because it felt safer, like a "small brave thing." As a writer, she may have wanted to build suspense as she moved toward the first time she saw Star. **ELA** RL.5.5

Classroom Collaboration

Divide the class into small groups. Ask the question below and have students discuss it. You might also choose to have students generate a question of their own for discussion.

At the end of the story, Mattie introduces herself to her new classmates and tells them she is a writer. How does this show how she has changed since the beginning of the story? Possible response: In Chapter 1, when she introduced herself to the class, she was flustered and said she was "not a Buddhist." By the end of the book, she is more composed and tells what she is rather than what she is not.

Reconvene as a whole group and have the group share their answers. **ELA** RL.5.5

ENGLISH LANGUAGE SUPPORT

Peer-Supported Learning

All Proficiencies Organize students into mixed-proficiency small groups to generate important ideas as a team. Each group should create a web with the heading *Hound Dog True*. Each member of the group will add ideas to the web, either with words or phrases or by drawing a picture that illustrates a related idea. When they are done, have groups share and discuss their webs.

INDEPENDENT READING

Have students read pp. 123–149 independently and complete pp. 151–156 in their Reader's Notebooks. Have students share their responses with the class.

Present

▶ SHARE OBJECTIVES

- Deliver presentation to the audience.
- Monitor presentation in order to stay within time limits. LANGUAGE
- Answer questions from the audience.
- Be a supportive audience member

Deliver the Presentation

✔ Set Up Expectations
✔ Record the Event
✔ Discuss Audience Responsibilities
✔ Archive Products

Set Up Expectations Schedule project teams across one or two days, as needed. Use the Assessment strategies and rubric on p. T423 to assess groups and individuals as they deliver their presentations.

Determine how much time each group will have to present, and set a timer or appoint a timekeeper from another team. You may want to set up five- or ten-minute warnings to let teams know how much time they have left.

Record the Event Explain to students that their presentations will be recorded using a handheld video camera. Remind students to speak clearly and audibly while presenting their information. Tell students that they should always maintain the attention of the audience, rather than focusing on the recording device.

Discuss with students why recording their presentations is valuable. Ask students to consider how much more effective it is to see yourself on a recording than to just hear a peer's critique of their presentations. Explain that by recording their presentations throughout the year, it will be possible to see how students' public speaking skills and projects develop.

Discuss Audience Responsibilities Remind students that during a presentation, they should give speakers their full attention. Tell students that they should listen carefully for ideas or information they might like to ask about.

Explain that speaking in front of an audience can be challenging or even a bit frightening and that they can help each other succeed by being quiet, interested, and supportive audience members. Guide students to understand that public speaking is a valuable real-world skill and that both practicing it and watching other people do it will help prepare them for a variety of careers. **ELA** SL.5.1a, SL.5.1b, SL.5.1c, SL.5.1d

Archive Products Ask each group to take photographs of any displays or visuals they created for their presentations. Guide students to create an online presentation folder. Each student should include project photographs, PDFs of any drafts and final documents they used for their presentations and pamphlets, debriefing summaries, and recorded presentations in their online folders. In addition, teachers could upload peer critiques, teacher notes, rubric scores, and final assessments to this folder. Explain to students that by archiving these products, students will have access to an online portfolio of their presentations. By occasionally reviewing these files, students and teachers can get a real-time view of how students' project and presentations have developed throughout the course of the year. Also explain that the teacher may use these archived products as models in the future.

ENGLISH LANGUAGE SUPPORT Use these sentence frames to support participation. *During _____* Brent's presentation, I *wondered about _____.* how long recess is *Therefore, at the end of the presentation, I asked _____.* You said each grade takes recess, but how long will fifth grade recess be? **ELD** ELD.PI.5.5

Digital Resources ▶

To support students before they start this task, use the following digital resources.
- ▶ Interactive Lesson: Writing to Sources
- ▶ Interactive Lesson: Writing Narratives: Dialogue and Description

INTEGRATED LANGUAGE ARTS REVIEW

Write About Reading

INTRODUCE THE TASK
After students have read Segment 6, tell them that they will respond to the text by writing the next story about Moe in Mattie's notebook.

- Prompt students to describe what adventure or challenge Moe might face next.
- Tell student that they can go back in the text to find appropriate details about Moe to include in their short stories.

Review the Model Display the model short story in **Student Book p. 43** and review the importance of adding sensory details, active verbs, and dialogue to the narrative to make it more engaging.

PLAN AND DRAFT
Have students write a short story about Moe after reading Segment 6. Students' short stories should include
- a new challenge for Moe to solve.
- details and dialogue to develop Moe's character and the action.
- a beginning, a middle, and an end in a logical order.
- a resolution to the challenge Moe faces.

REVISE AND EDIT
Have student pairs review their short stories. Guide the class to generate a checklist partners can use to revise each other's work, for example:
- Do the events in my story unfold in an organized manner?
- Does my story include a problem that Moe must solve?
- Did I include appropriate dialogue and details so the reader can easily follow along?
- Does my story include a conclusion to the problem?
- Did I use correct spelling, grammar, and punctuation?

See the Narrative Writing Rubric, p. R16.

SHARE
Allow students to create a picture to support their short stories. Compile the stories into a book titled *Moe's Adventures*. Have listeners identify the problems Moe faced and how Moe overcame the challenging situation.

ELA W.5.3a, W.5.3b, W.5.3c, W.5.3d, W.5.3e, W.5.4, W.5.5, W.5.10, L.5.1a, L.5.2e

▶ SHARE OBJECTIVES
- Write a short story. LANGUAGE
- Cite evidence from the text.
- Use correct punctuation and spelling.

▶ SKILLS REVIEW
Review the following skills, as needed, before students begin to write their response.
- **Writing:** Short Story (Lesson 1)
- **Grammar:** Punctuation (Lesson 3)
- **Spelling:** Short, Long, and Other Vowel Sounds (Lessons 1–7), *R*-Controlled Vowels (Lessons 6, 7, 10,) Homophones (Lesson 8), Compound Words (Lesson 9), Final Schwa Vowels (Lesson 10)

ENGLISH LANGUAGE SUPPORT
Sentence Frames

Emerging Help students orally brainstorm words associated with their topics. Then work with them to complete the following sentence frames:

Moe could be described as both _____ and _____.
Moe becomes _____.

Expanding Guide students as they use the sentence frames above to begin drafting their short stories.

Bridging As students prewrite, have them use resources, such as print or electronic thesauruses, to find more interesting words to describe their experiences.

ELD ELD.PI.5.8

Your Turn

Cite Text Evidence

▶ SHARE OBJECTIVES

• Prepare to participate in classroom discussions by drawing on information about the topic.

• Examine and analyze how chapters fit together and provide story structure.

• Write a story that follows a clear sequence of events and reaches a conclusion.

ENGLISH LANGUAGE SUPPORT

Comprehensible Input

Emerging Use simple sentences to share important lessons, such as *Be kind to others*. Invite students to create drawings that illustrate their ideas for a story that could explain a lesson. Ask students yes/no questions to help them tell about their drawings.

Expanding After choosing a lesson, encourage students to sketch or write ideas for their stories. Remind students to use complete sentences in their writing. Have students share their ideas with a small group.

Bridging After choosing a lesson, encourage students to brainstorm ideas for their stories with a small group. Remind students to use complete, complex sentences in their writing.

RETURN TO THE ESSENTIAL QUESTION

Remind students of the Essential Question: *What can someone do to make a friend?* Before partners discuss the Essential Question, have them review the text and make notes about the ways different characters try to act as friends. In their discussion, have students cite examples from the text that support their ideas. At the end of the discussion, ask students to review the key ideas they discussed. **ELA** W.5.9a, SL.5.1a, SL.5.1d

ENGLISH LANGUAGE SUPPORT Remind students that one way to organize their notes is to make a T-chart. Students list an idea on one side of the chart and the supporting evidence from the trade book on the other side of the chart. Students can reference the chart when they write their story. **ELD** ELD.PI.5.10b

Classroom Collaboration
Remind students that Mattie comes to terms with her experience with Star over the course of the book and that the stories Mattie writes help her to shape her understanding of that experience. Point out that Mattie's story unfolds over a series of chapters and that it weaves stories that Mattie has written with the "custodial wisdom" she learns from Uncle Potluck.

Divide the class into small groups and have them discuss what Mattie learns. Ask them to identify her conflict and its resolution. Have groups choose three of their favorite chapters and talk about how they build on each other to provide story structure and connect to Mattie's stories or to the "custodial wisdom" she writes about.

Then reconvene as a whole group and have students share their responses. Have students explain in a few sentences how the book's chapters fit together to provide its structure. **ELA** RL.5.5, SL.5.1a, SL.5.1d

WRITE ABOUT READING

Performance Task

Remind students of the stories different characters shared about themselves in *Hound Dog True* and the lessons the characters learned from their stories. Have students think of an important lesson to share with others and then, using a character from *Hound Dog True*, write a story to share that lesson.

Writing Tip Remind students to set up some context that will help readers understand what is taking place in the story. Explain that their story's conclusion should clearly illustrate the story's message or lesson. **ELA** W.5.3a, W.5.3e

Assess

Score the Project

Scoring the Project Work with students to review the project requirements they were given during the launch and preparation stages. Share the rubric below, and tell students that you will work with them to score their project. As you assess and meet with each group, draw attention to project strengths, and talk with individual students about areas in which they excelled and in which they could have done a better job.

	Collaboration	Research and Text Evidence	Content	Presentation
4	• Students made valuable contributions to each task within the project. • Students provided constructive feedback and input during preparation steps and check-ins. • Discussions were polite and productive. • Group members demonstrated clear understanding of the role of collaboration in project success	• Information is organized in a clear and logical way. • Students chose a variety of reliable print and digital resources. • Research is carefully documented. • Text evidence is used successfully throughout the project.	• Content maintains a clear focus throughout. • Written portions of the project are well thought out and answer the project question thoroughly. • Visuals or multimedia are useful and enhance the product. • All parts of the project are free of errors.	• The presentation is dynamic and engages the audience. • Information is shared in an effective way. • The presentation is well organized. • Students are able to give thoughtful answers to questions from the audience.
3	• Students somewhat contributed to each task within the project. • Students provided some useful feedback and input during preparation steps and check-ins. • Discussions were polite but sometimes got off-track. • Group members demonstrated a basic understanding of the role of collaboration in project success.	• Information is mostly organized in a clear and logical way. • Students chose a few reliable print and digital resources. • Research is documented but disorganized or unclear. • Text evidence is used successfully in some parts of the project.	• Content is focused but may stray at times. • Written portions of the project are well thought out and address the project question. • Visuals or multimedia are useful. • All parts of the project contain minimal errors.	• The presentation is engaging. • Information is shared in an effective way. • The presentation has parts that could be better organized. • Students are able to answer questions from the audience.
2	• Students made partial contributions to tasks within the project. • Students had trouble providing useful feedback and input during preparation steps and check-ins. • Discussions led to disagreements or were frequently off-topic. • Group members made little effort to collaborate.	• Information is somewhat organized. • Students chose only print or only digital resources. • Research is not documented. • Text evidence is weak or used in a limited way.	• Content is unfocused in some areas. • Written portions of the project provide some information, but lack purpose. • Visuals or multimedia are not useful. • The project contains some errors throughout.	• The presentation is helpful but could be more engaging. • Information is shared but confusing at times. • The presentation lacks clear organization. • Students struggle to answer questions about their presentation.
1	• Students made few or no contributions to tasks within the project. • Students were unable to provide useful feedback and input during preparation steps and check-ins. • Discussions did not take place, or students had trouble interacting with each other. • Group members did not work as a team.	• Information has little to no organization. • There is no evidence of the use of reliable sources. • Research was limited or not conducted. • Text evidence has not been used.	• Content is haphazard throughout. • Written portions of the project are unclear and do not address the project question. • Visuals or multimedia are not present. • The project contains major errors.	• The presentation is off topic or not taken seriously. • The information shared is irrelevant or confusing. • The presentation is disorganized. • Students are unable to answer questions about their presentation.

For a student-friendly version of this rubric, see p. R21.

Independent Reading

▶ **SHARE OBJECTIVES**

- Research additional texts on a topic.
- Read independently.
- Compare and contrast texts on a topic.

ENGLISH LANGUAGE SUPPORT

Use Sentence Frames

Emerging Guide students to locate texts that have a high level of photographic support. Have students work in pairs. Guide them to complete their charts.

Expanding Before students respond in writing, provide these frames for their topic sentences: Hound Dog True *is similar to* _____ *in these two ways:* _____.

Hound Dog True *is different from* _____ *in these two ways:* _____.

Bridging Have partners share and discuss the information in their charts before writing their paragraphs. **ELD** ELD.PI.5.6a

Compare Texts

Research Texts on a Topic After students have completed reading *Hound Dog True*, have them research additional texts on the topic of making friends. Encourage students to research the topic on approved websites or locate book titles such as the following:

- *How Kids Make Friends: Secrets for Making Lots of Friends No Matter How Shy You Are* by Lonnie Michelle

- *Ellie McDoodle: New Kid in School* by Ruth McNally Barshaw

- *Diary of a Social Detective: Real-Life Tales of Mystery, Intrigue and Interpersonal Adventure* by Jeffery E. Jessum

Have students select one longer text or two shorter texts to compare to *Hound Dog True*. They should make notes using a chart such as the following. Encourage students to cite at least two ways each text or other source is similar to and different from *Hound Dog True*. **ELA** RL.5.3, RL.5.9, RI.5.6, RI.5.7, RI.5.9

Title Source:	Title Source:
How is this book similar to *Hound Dog True?* 1. 2.	How is this book similar to *Hound Dog True?* 1. 2.
How is it different from *Hound Dog True?*	How is it different from *Hound Dog True?*
Information I learned from this text:	Information I learned from this text:

INTEGRATED LANGUAGE ARTS REVIEW

Write About Reading

Digital Resources ▶

To support students before they start this task, use the following digital resources.

▶ Interactive Lesson: Writing Informative Texts: Introduction

▶ Interactive Lesson: Writing Informative Texts: Organize Your Information

INTRODUCE THE TASK After students complete their Independent Reading, tell them they will respond to the text by writing a procedural composition about how to make friends.

• Prompt students to think about the most important steps that go into making a friend.

• Tell students they will have to go back into the texts to find facts and details to include in their compositions.

Review the Model Display the model procedural composition from **Student Book p. 203** and review how the writer organizes the information in the procedural composition.

PLAN AND DRAFT Have students write a procedural essay about how to make a friend after completing their independent reading. Students' essays should include

• an introduction to the topic and some details about the topic.

• details about each step in the procedure.

• transitional words and verbs to clearly describe the steps in the process.

• illustrations or media to complement the steps in the process.

• a conclusion that summarizes the process.

REVISE AND EDIT Have student pairs revise their procedural compositions. Guide students to generate a checklist partners can use to review each other's work. For example:

• Did I clearly describe the steps in the process?

• Did I organize the steps in sequential order?

• Did I use verbs correctly and incorporate appropriate transitional words and phrases?

• Did I form plural nouns correctly?

• Did I use correct spelling, grammar, and punctuation?

See the Analytic Writing Rubric, p. R15.

SHARE Collect procedural compositions and then randomly distribute them. Students read the composition they receive and identify their favorite step in the procedure for making friends. Allow students to share their favorite steps while recording them on the board. Conclude by discussing whether making friends is really something that you can follow a manual to do or not.

ELA RL.5.1, RI.5.1, RI.5.7, RI.5.9, W.5.2a, W.5.2b, W.5.2c, W.5.2d, W.5.2e, W.5.4, W.5.5, W.5.8, W.5.10

▶ SHARE OBJECTIVES

• Write a procedural composition about making friends. LANGUAGE

• Cite evidence from the text.

• Use correct punctuation and spelling.

▶ SKILLS REVIEW

Review the following skills, as needed, before students begin to write their response.

• **Writing:** Procedural Composition (Lesson 6)

• **Grammar:** Singular and Plural Nouns (Lesson 5)

• **Spelling:** Short, Long, and Other Vowel Sounds (Lessons 1–7), Homophones (Lesson 8), Compound Words (Lesson 9)

ENGLISH LANGUAGE SUPPORT

Sentence Frames

Emerging Use the following sentence frame to demonstrate how to change singular nouns into plural nouns. For example:

Landon bought one _____ of bread, and Shana bought two _____ of bread. loaf; loaves

Expanding Have pairs of students write sentence frames similar to the one above. Partners exchange the frames and check to see if plurals are formed correctly. Encourage them to use both regular plurals and those that change forms.

Bridging Have students make lists of five other words that have irregular plurals. As needed, provide them with some examples, such as *foot, knife, child,* and *woman.*

ELD ELD.PI.5.6a, ELD.PI.5.10a, ELD.PI.5.12a, ELD.PII.5.1, ELD.PII.5.2b

Reflect

SHARE OBJECTIVES

- Reflect on the process and the product. LANGUAGE
- Make suggestions on how to improve the next project. LANGUAGE
- Celebrate completion of the project.

Reflect on the Project

✔	Debrief the Presentation
✔	Debrief the Project
✔	Celebrate!

Debrief the Presentation Remind students that discussion has played an important role in completing their projects. Tell students that they will now have the opportunity to come together as a group once again and discuss the parts of the process they think were most successful and the parts that could be improved for next time.

Explain that assessing not only the product they made, but also the ways in which they worked together to make it, will help students master real-world skills such as time management and problem solving. Point out that this kind of self-assessment will also help students learn to look critically at their own work and determine whether it has met expectations.

As you place students in their groups, guide them to create a T-map and use it to list positive aspects of the project experience and aspects that need improvement. You may wish to have students turn in these lists to you so the responses can be used to evaluate performance or inform future group assignments.

ELA SL.5.1a, SL.5.1b, SL.5.1c, SL.5.1d

ENGLISH LANGUAGE SUPPORT Use these sentence frames to support participation. *The most difficult part of the presentation was _____. My favorite part of the project was _____. During the next project, I would like to _____.* **ELD** ELD.PI.5.1

Debrief the Project Guide students in a discussion about what they learned from this project. Ask students to explain what they learned about ambassadors and how that relates to them. Students also should reflect on their work on the project. Suggest that they explore the following questions:

- *What aspects of the collaborative process were the most rewarding?*
- *What aspects of the collaborative process were the most challenging?*
- *How did I carry out all the tasks required of my role?*
- *What did I learn from this experience that I can apply toward doing a better job on my next project?*

Celebrate! Tell students that after all their hard work, it is important to celebrate their accomplishments. Work together with students to identify various appropriate ways to celebrate what they learned about being ambassadors and welcoming others to a new setting. For example, students might celebrate by playing team-building games that strengthen relationships. Once a variety of ideas have been generated, allow students to anonymously vote on their ideal celebration. After the nature of the celebration has been established, invite students to take part in planning the actual event and preparing/gathering the necessary materials. Take time at the celebration to highlight what students learned and achieved throughout the course of the project.

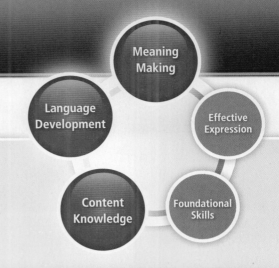

Meaning Making

Language Development

Effective Expression

Content Knowledge

Foundational Skills

 TEXT X-RAY

ENGLISH LANGUAGE SUPPORT Use the Text X-Ray below to prepare for teaching the trade book *Hound Dog True*. Use it to plan, support, and scaffold instruction in order to help students understand the text's **key ideas** and **academic language features**.

Zoom *In* on Key Ideas
Students should understand these **key ideas** after reading *Hound Dog True*.

Key Idea | Segment 4, pp. 73–94

As Mattie frets over Quincy reading her notebook, like Star did, she occupies her time by working in the garden with Uncle Potluck. Uncle Potluck falls and has to be taken to the hospital. While waiting at the hospital with the principal, Mattie learns from Principal Bonnet that being scared is part of being brave. Principal Bonnet explains how she did "small brave things" before she climbed a mountain. Mattie thinks about what she is afraid of and what "small brave things" she can do to overcome her fears.

Key Idea | Segment 5, pp. 95–122

Mattie's mom offers Quincy a Popsicle and asks her to deliver the silver notebook to Mattie. When Quincy gives Mattie the notebook, she happens to read about sad and lonely Moe. She inquires about Moe's demeanor and encourages Mattie to write Moe as adventurous and brave. Mattie challenges Quincy to draw something other than a still life. Both girls accept the challenges and end up acting out brave, adventurous Moe. When they wear themselves out, Mattie tells Quincy that "Uncle Potluck says when he talks to the moon, the moon talks back," but "you have to trust the moon for it to trust you." Quincy suggests the girls sleep in the tent and tell a secret to the moon so it will trust them. Mattie agrees.

Key Idea | Segment 6, pp. 123–145, Conclusion

When Mattie finds Quincy at the rock, Mattie tells the moon a story, not the one she intended to tell, but the moon seems to listen. So then Mattie tells her secret story, about Star reading her notebook. Quincy says she already told the moon all about her family. The girls go back to the tent and listen to the moon while drawing and writing. In the morning, Mattie rereads the beginnings of the story she wrote. When school eventually starts, Mattie introduces herself and finds the courage to say that she is a writer.

Zoom *In* on Academic Language
Guide students at different proficiencies and skill levels to understand the structure and language of this text.

Key Idea | Segment 4, pp. 73–94

Remind students that a cause is why something happened and an effect is what happened as a result. Reread the third paragraph on p. 91. Ask students to identify what caused Mattie to be so careless. *Mattie was tired from worrying all night about someone reading her notebook.* Then ask students what the effect was. *Mattie forgot to wind up the vacuum cord.* Have students identify other cause-and-effect relationships in the story.

Key Idea | Segment 5, pp. 95–122

Remind students that when they summarize a passage, they use their own words to retell what happened. Explain to students that summarizing helps the reader better understand how the events in a story fit together. Ask students to reread p. 99. Students can pair off and work together to verbally summarize what happens between Mattie and Quincy on this page.

Key Idea | Segment 6, pp. 123–145, Conclusion

Point out the title of this book to students: *Hound Dog True*. Ask students to describe what this phrase means. Then ask students to describe two things Mattie believes are "hound dog true."

Teacher Notes

Unit 2 Strategic Intervention

Lesson 6
"Will the American Chestnut Survive?" (Write-In Reader pages 54–60)

Target Vocabulary: *dwarfed, perch, presence, procedure, transferred*

Cause and Effect

Question

Lesson 7
"Nothing Ever Happens in the Country" (Write-In Reader pages 64–70)

Target Vocabulary: *bounding, frantic, lunging, picturing, romp*

Understanding Characters

Visualize

Lesson 8
"Oil Spill in Alaska" (Write-In Reader pages 74–80)

Target Vocabulary: *endangered, regulate, responsibility, restore, vegetation*

Author's Purpose

Analyze/Evaluate

Lesson 9
"The Rescue Helicopter Team" (Write-In Reader pages 84–90)

Target Vocabulary: *bundle, clammy, commotion, critical, demolished*

Conclusions and Generalizations

Infer/Predict

Lesson 10
"Bison Come Back to the Plains" (Write-In Reader pages 94–100)

Target Vocabulary: *available, detecting, ferocious, keen, unobserved*

Main Ideas and Details

Monitor/Clarify

INTRODUCE THE WRITE-IN READER

"Be a Reading Detective!"
Write-In Reader pages ii–iii

- Have students open their **Write-In Readers** to pages ii–iii.

- Point out that a police detective looks for clues to solve a crime. A reading detective looks for clues to understand a story or a nonfiction selection.

- Explain that looking for clues can make reading easier and more fun.

- Read page ii with students. Say: *What will you do as you read your* Write-In Reader? (look for clues; stop, think, and write)

TRY IT YOURSELF!

- Read the first part of page iii with students. Say: *What questions are you going to ask?* (Who is the story about? Where and when does the story take place? What is happening?)

- Say: *What kind of clues are you going to look for as you read?* (clues that answer the questions)

- Then have students read the passage, looking for clues.

- Circulate and offer feedback as students answer Question 1. If they have difficulty, remind them to look back at the text.

 Classroom Collaboration

- Use Question 2 to discuss the clues students found and how they helped answer Question 1.

- Explain that students will be reading detectives as they read each selection in the **Write-In Reader.**

RETURN TO THE ANCHOR TEXT

At the end of each lesson, students will return to the Anchor Text and look for clues to deepen their understanding. (See the "A" and "B" pages at the end of each lesson in the **Write-In Reader.**)

SHARE OBJECTIVES

- Identify the adjective or noun that is linked to a subject.
- Discuss the story of the American chestnut tree.
- Read to build meaning for Target Vocabulary words.

MATERIALS

Write-In Reader pages 52–53

TERMS ABOUT READING/ LANGUAGE ARTS

verb	subject	pronoun
adjective	linking verb	

ENGLISH LANGUAGE SUPPORT

Day 1

Vocabulary Help students build a word bank of linking verbs like those introduced in the Warm Up activity, for example: *I am, I was, I will be; We are, We were, We will be; They are, They were, They will be.* **ELD** ELD.PII.5.3

Sentence Frames Review the term *linking verb* with students. Guide students cto use frames such as the following to construct sentences that use linking verbs to describe the subject. *When I was very young, I was _____ . Now I am _____.* **ELD** ELD.PII.5.3

Oral Language Direct students' attention to the discussion of Target Vocabulary words on page 53. Work with them to make up new sentences that illustrate the multiple meanings of *perch* and *dwarfed*. Write the sentences on the board and have students choral-read them. **ELD** ELD.PIII.5

Warm Up

Oral Grammar

Linking Verbs

- Write on the board or a pad the present-tense forms of to be: *am, is, are, was, were.* Tell students that these verbs can be used to describe the subject. Say: *I am a teacher. I am [tall]. The pronoun* I *is the subject. The verb* am *links the subject to a noun* (teacher) *that describes the subject. It also links the subject to an adjective* [tall] *that describes the subject.*

- Say each sentence below. Then prompt students to supply the subject and the adjective or noun that describes it.

Teacher says, then asks, *Subject? Adjective or Noun?*	Students respond	
	Subject	**Adjective/Noun**
My students are energetic.	My students	Adjective: energetic
We were all students.	We	Noun: students
My pets are all dogs.	My pets	Noun: dogs
The trees in this forest are old.	The trees	Adjective: old

- Explain that when the verbs *am*, *is*, and *are* link the subject to a noun or adjective, they are called linking verbs.

Talk About It

Help focus students' attention on trees. Ask: *Why is it important to study and protect trees?*

Discuss the question, emphasizing these points:

- Protecting different kinds of native trees helps to keep forests healthy.

- Many different kinds of animals, including birds and squirrels, rely on the trees for food and shelter.

- Understanding the fungus that has killed the trees helps scientists put in place measures to protect other plants and animals from disease.

- Native trees such as the American chestnut are beautiful shade trees that have been valued and admired by generations in this country.

Target Vocabulary

Write-In Reader pages 52–53

- Read and discuss the selection. Then discuss the meaning of each Target Vocabulary word. Suggest that students underline words or phrases that provide clues to meaning. Also point out the following:

   Point out that as a verb, the word *perch* means "to alight or settle on something," as in *The parrot would perch on the top bar of the cage.* Explain that *perch* is also a noun that refers to a resting place or vantage point, as in *The bird would not leave its perch in the trees.* Point out that a perch is also a kind of fish.

   Contrast the meaning of *dwarfed* in the selection, "caused to appear smaller," with another meaning of *dwarfed,* "to restrict or stunt the growth of something," as in *The tomato plants were dwarfed by the unusually cold weather.*

- Allow time for students to write their responses. Then ask students to choose an answer they would like to read aloud. **ELA** RI.5.4, RF.5.4c, L.5.4a, L.5.5c, L.5.6 **ELD** ELD.PIII.5

   Responses:

   1. dwarfed
   2. perch
   3. presence
   4. transferred
   5. procedure

Quick Check | Target Vocabulary

Ask each student to use one of the Target Vocabulary words in a sentence. **ELA** W.5.2d

---

✔ TARGET VOCABULARY

If something is **dwarfed**, it is made to appear smaller by something else that is much bigger.

To **perch** means to rest or settle on a higher spot.

If you follow a **procedure**, you follow a series of steps done in a specific order to accomplish a goal.

If something is **transferred**, it is moved from one place to another.

Presence describes the fact or state of being present, or nearby and within sight.

EXTRA PRACTICE

Build Fluency Have students read **Write-In Reader** pages 52–53 with a partner or a family member.

DAY 2

SHARE OBJECTIVES

- Read words with open syllables.
- Determine cause-and-effect relationships.
- Read on-level text to apply skills and strategies.

MATERIALS

Write-In Reader pages 54–57

TERMS ABOUT READING/ LANGUAGE ARTS

cause   effect

ENGLISH LANGUAGE SUPPORT

Day 2

Vocabulary Help students build a word bank of words used to show cause-effect relationships to use during the Quick Check activity. Sample words: *because, since, so, as a result of.*

Sentence Frames Guide students to use sentence frames that show cause-effect relationships when responding to the Turn and Talk activity; for example, *The American chestnut is endangered because _____. Scientists hoped that the effect of introducing the Chinese chestnut would be _____.* **ELD** ELD.PII.5.6

Oral Language After students respond to the Quick Check, ask them to identify any words or phrases that they used to show a cause-effect relationship. **ELD** ELD.PI.5.1

Multisyllable Words

Focus: Open Syllables

Write these words on the board or on a pad.

1	ruby	lady	photo
2	solo	crazy	icy
3	baby	ego	crazy

Row 1: Say: *These words have a vowel-consonant-vowel letter pattern (known as a VCV letter pattern).* Remind students that the *y* at the end of a word acts like a vowel with a long *e* vowel sound. Demonstrate by identifying the VCV letter pattern.

Explain: *When a word has a VCV letter pattern, we first try dividing the word after the first vowel.* Draw a line: *ru / by, la / dy, pho / to.* Read each word, and say: *These words sound correct.* Say: *When a syllable ends in a vowel, it is called an open syllable. Most open syllables have a long vowel sound.*

Row 2: Have volunteers identify the VCV pattern and divide the word after the first vowel. Choral-read the words.

Row 3: Listen to each student read the words. Make corrections as needed. Record your findings. **ELA** RF.5.3a **ELD** ELD.PIII.5

RETEACH

Cause and Effect

- Show students an image that illustrates or suggests a cause-and-effect relationship. For example, show a picture of a car stalled along the side of the road or someone getting a trophy. Ask: *What does this picture show? Why did it happen?* Draw a chart to show how the events are related.

- Explain that sometimes one event causes another event to happen. Add a third box to the chart and label it *Effect.* Say: *What might happen as a result of the car not working?* (The driver might be late for work.)

- Emphasize that noting cause-and-effect relationships can help students understand how story events are related.

Quick Check Comprehension

Have students share a real-life experience in which one event caused another. Add a few student examples to the chart.

READ

"Will the American Chestnut Survive?"

Write-In Reader pages 54–57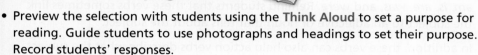

- Preview the selection with students using the **Think Aloud** to set a purpose for reading. Guide students to use photographs and headings to set their purpose. Record students' responses.

Think Aloud *The title of this selection is "Will the American Chestnut Survive?" The title and the photographs tell me that this selection is about an endangered tree. What other clues help you to figure out what the selection might be about?*

- Review the steps to the Question strategy, **Write-In Reader** page 305. As needed, guide students in applying the strategy.

READ

Ask students to read to confirm their predictions about the selection. Choral read page by page with students. Discuss, confirm, and revise student predictions based upon text details.

REREAD

Call on students to read aloud. Stop to discuss each question. Allow students to write their responses. Sample answers are provided.

Page 54: Why do you think the author introduced this article with these lines from a famous poem? (to show how common and celebrated the American chestnut tree used to be)

Help unpack meaning, if needed, by asking: *When was the poem written?* (in the 1800s) *How does the poet describe the tree?* (It is spreading, tall, and strong, providing shade. It is dependable.)

Unpack Meaning: For questions on pages 55–57, you may want to use the notes in the right-hand column. **ELA** RI.5.4, RF.5.4a **ELD** ELD.PIII.5

Page 55: How do the killer spores get into the tree trunk? (They fly through the air and are transferred to animals. When the animals perch on the trees, the spores settle in the cracks in the bark.)

Turn and Talk **Page 56:** Why might the American chestnut become extinct one day? (Even if roots survive the fungus, the fungus can still kill new trees that grow from the roots.) Have partners discuss the question and then share their responses with the group. **ELA** RI.5.10, RF.5.4a **ELD** ELD.PIII.5

Page 57: Why did scientists of the 1930s believe that the Chinese chestnut could help solve the problem? (It resists the fungus.)

UNPACK MEANING

Use prompts such as these if students have difficulty with a **Stop•Think•Write** question:

Page 55: *How do the spores get on animals?* (The spores are carried on the air and are transferred to animals.) *What causes the spores to be transferred from animal fur or feathers to the tree?* (Animals climb or land on the tree, and the spores are brushed off the fur or feathers into cracks in the tree bark.) *How might the cracks in the bark help the spores attack the tree?* (They provide an opening to the tree.) **ELA** RI.5.3, RI.5.8, RI.5.10, RF.5.4a **ELD** ELD.PIII.5

Page 56: *What happens to the roots of a tree that is killed by the fungus?* (They survive and grow into a new tree.) *What is the effect if the fungus attacks the new tree?* (The new tree dies.) *Do you think the roots would survive forever if new growth was continually killed by a fungus?* (probably not) **ELA** RI.5.10, RF.5.4a **ELD** ELD.PIII.5

Page 57: *How is the Chinese chestnut different from the American chestnut?* (It has a built-in protection against the fungus that kills the American chestnut.) *Why would having a built-in protection against the fungus help a tree?* (It could prevent the tree from getting sick and dying.) **ELA** RI.5.2, RI.5.10, RF.5.4a **ELD** ELD.PIII.5

EXTRA PRACTICE

Build Fluency Have students read **Write-In Reader** pages 54–57 with a partner or a family member.

DAY 3

ENGLISH LANGUAGE SUPPORT

Day 3

Vocabulary Review the term *expression*. Help students build a bank of words and phrases to use in the Fluency activity. Sample words and phrases: *too much emotion, flat, dramatic, appropriate inflection.*

Sentence Frames Guide students to respond to the first question on page 58 by using this frame: *During the 1930s, scientists _____. In contrast, Dr. Burnham _____. Because he did this, his trees_____.*
ELD ELD.PI.5.6b

Oral Language Support students' retelling of the end of "Will the American Chestnut Survive?" by guiding them to use this summary frame: *The American chestnut tree became endangered when _____. People tried to save the tree by _____. In the future, American chestnuts _____.* Guide students to choral-read the finished summary until they can read it fluently. **ELD** ELD.PI.5.10b

Oral Grammar
Helping Verbs

- Write on the board or on a pad the present- and past-tense forms of *to be*: *am, is, are, was,* and *were.* Remind students that these verbs sometimes link the subject to an adjective or noun that tells about the subject.
- In addition, these verbs can also help action verbs describe what the subject is doing. Read the sentence, and ask students to name the helping verb and the main verb.

Teacher says, then asks, *Helping verbs? Main verbs?*	Students respond	
	Helping verb	**Main verb**
My students are working now.	are	working
That boy is playing a game.	is	playing
The trees were tumbling over.	were	tumbling

- Explain that the verbs *am, is, are, was,* and *were* can help the main verb describe the action of the subject.

RETEACH

Fluency: Expression
Write-In Reader page 58

Explain that you are going to read from page 58 and that you want students to evaluate your reading.

- First, read in an expressionless tone, avoiding inflection and emotion as you read. Then, read the paragraph a second time with too much expression, adding inflection and emotion to words that don't warrant it, such as *the, was, young,* and *crossed.*

- Ask: *What did you think of my first reading? Explain. Was my second reading better? Explain.* Be sure students recognize how difficult it is to grasp meaning when someone reads with too much or too little expression.

- Reread the paragraph a third time. Use an appropriate level of expression, adding appropriate inflection and emotion. Then have students practice reading aloud the remaining paragraphs, focusing on reading with expression.

READ

"Will the American Chestnut Survive?"

Write-In Reader pages 58–60

Review the first part of the selection with students. Ask: *What have we learned about the American chestnut tree so far?* Then preview today's reading. Have students look for clues to help them predict how this selection will end.

READ

Ask students to read to confirm their predictions. Choral-read page by page with students. Discuss, confirm, and revise predictions based upon text details. Ask if there was anything about the way the selection ended that surprised them.
ELA RI.5.2, RI.5.10, RF.5.4a **ELD** ELD.PIII.5

REREAD

Call on individuals to read aloud while others follow along. Stop to discuss each question. Allow time for students to write their responses before proceeding. Sample answers are provided.

Page 58: How was Dr. Burnham's <u>procedure</u> different than the one used in the 1930s? (Instead of simply crossing American chestnuts with Chinese chestnuts, Dr. Burnham crossed trees that were half Chinese and half American with American chestnut trees, doing so over and over so that the resulting trees were more like American chestnuts but were stronger.) **ELA** RI.5.3, RI.5.4, RI.5.10, RF.5.4a, RF.5.4c, L.5.4a, L.5.5c, L.5.6 **ELD** ELD.PI.5.6b, ELD.PIII.5

Help unpack meaning, if needed, by asking: *What steps did scientists take?* (They crossed American chestnut trees with Chinese chestnuts.) *What steps did Dr. Burnham take?* (He repeatedly crossed American-Chinese chestnuts with American chestnuts.) **ELA** RI.5.3, RI.5.4, RI.5.10, RF.5.4a **ELD** ELD.PI.5.6b, ELD.PIII.5

Unpack Meaning: For questions on pages 59–60, you may want to use the notes in the right-hand column.

Page 59: What happens after the trees are bred? (They are put back in forests using a process called reforestation.)

Page 60: What detail supports the idea that the survival of the American chestnut is still uncertain? (Reforestation is a huge task.)

Quick Check Retelling

Have students retell the end of the article. Support the retelling by asking: *Why did most of the American chestnut trees disappear? What does the future look like for the American chestnut tree?*

UNPACK MEANING

Use prompts such as these if students have difficulty with a **Stop•Think•Write** question:

Page 59: *What comprehension skill do you think this question relates to?* (sequence of events) *What signal word in the sentence gave you a clue?* (after) *What other word in the text might mean the same things as after?* (once) *Why is looking for words like once a good strategy for finding the answer?* (If I find the word once, it will probably appear in a sentence that explains what happened after the trees were bred.) **ELA** RI.5.3, RI.5.10, RF.5.4a **ELD** ELD.PI.5.6a, ELD.PIII.5

Page 60: *What clue word tells you the author is asking for evidence to support the author's point that the American chestnut has an uncertain future?* (detail) *How might you find the answer to this question?* (by looking for evidence that supports the author's point) **ELA** RI.5.2, RI.5.8, RI.5.10, RF.5.4a **ELD** ELD.PIII.5

EXTRA PRACTICE

Build Fluency Have students reread **Write-In Reader** pages 58–60 with a partner or a family member.

DAY 4

SHARE OBJECTIVES

- Read words with open syllables.
- Identify action verbs.
- Support answers to questions with evidence from the text.

MATERIALS

Write-In Reader pages 54–61

TERMS ABOUT READING/ LANGUAGE ARTS

action verb

ENGLISH LANGUAGE SUPPORT

Day 4

Vocabulary Warm Up words such as *solo, hazy,* and *halo* may be unfamiliar to students. Use visuals, examples, and simple explanations to support understanding.

Sentence Frames Guide students to use their knowledge of word structure to determine the meaning of *reforestation.* Use frames such as the following: *Re-means "_____" so I know that reforest means "_____." Reforestation could help save the American chestnut because _____.* **ELD** ELD.PI.5.6b

Oral Language Support students' discussion of the Turn and Talk activity on page S9 by helping them understand the relationship between the deadly fungus and the American chestnut. Encourage them to use a frame such as this: *A fungus is _____. The fungus discovered in 1904 hurts American chestnut trees by _____. Chinese chestnut trees _____ the fungus.* Then discuss whether the verbs used in the frame are seen or unseen. **ELD** ELD.PII.5.6

Warm Up

Multisyllable Words
Focus: Open Syllables

Write these words on the board or on a pad.

1	hazy	silo	cozy
2	navy	solo	gravy
3	tidy	lazy	halo

Row 1: Say: *These words have a vowel-consonant-vowel letter pattern (known as a VCV letter pattern).* Demonstrate by identifying the VCV letter pattern.

Ask: *Where do we divide a word with a VCV letter pattern?* (try dividing after the first vowel) *What is this syllable called?* (an open syllable) *What kind of vowel sound do most open syllables have?* (long vowel)

Point to and read each syllable, and then blend the syllables to read *hazy.* Follow the same procedure with the remaining words.

Row 2: Have volunteers identify the VCV pattern and divide the word after the first vowel. Choral read the words.

Row 3: Listen to each student read the words. Make corrections as needed. Record your findings. **ELA** RF.5.3a **ELD** ELD.PIII.5

RETEACH

Action Verbs

- Review that an action verb expresses an action. Remind students that actions can be seen *(run, jump, swim)* and unseen *(believe, hope, understand).* Then have students read page 59.

- Ask: *What are some examples of action verbs in these lines? Are they seen or unseen actions?*

Turn and Talk Have students read the first paragraph of page 60 and write examples of seen and unseen action verbs.

Possible Answers: *reforested* (seen); *appear* (unseen); *needed* (unseen); *know* (unseen); *survive* (seen); *takes* (unseen)

Quick Check | Grammar

Have students find other action verbs in the selection and identify whether they are seen or unseen.

Look Back and Respond

Write-In Reader pages 54–61

Help students complete the Look Back and Respond page. Model how to use the hint in Question 1 to find evidence that can be used to support answers.

- Explain that evidence is proof, clues, or information.

- Remind students that they can circle or underline the specific words in the selection that they used as evidence for their answers.

1. What happened to the American chestnut tree in the early 20th century? (It was nearly wiped out by a fungus.) **ELA** RI.5.2, RI.5.3, RI.5.10, RF.5.4a **ELD** ELD.PI.5.6a, ELD.PIII.5

Help unpack meaning, if needed, by asking: *What happened after the fungus was discovered at the Bronx Zoo in 1904?* (Within two years, all of the chestnut trees at the zoo were dead or dying.) *What happened in another fifty years?* (The fungus killed four billion trees across the eastern United States.)
ELA RI.5.1, RI.5.3, RI.5.10, RF.5.4a **ELD** ELD.PI.5.6a, ELD.PIII.5

Turn and Talk Have students work independently on Questions 2–4. When students have completed the page, have partners discuss their responses and then share them with the group. Sample responses are provided. Accept reasonable responses. **ELA** SL.5.1b, SL.5.1d **ELD** ELD.PI.5.1

Unpack Meaning: For Questions 2–4, you may want to use the notes in the right-hand column to guide the discussion about student responses.

2. How does the fungus kill the trees? (The fungus grows around the trees and strangles them.) **ELA** RI.5.2, RI.5.3, RI.5.10, RF.5.4a **ELD** ELD.PI.5.6a, ELD.PIII.5

3. What makes the Chinese chestnut such a good choice for cross-breeding? (The Chinese chestnut cannot get sick.) **ELA** RI.5.3, RI.5.8, RI.5.10, RF.5.4a **ELD** ELD.PIII.5

4. What are the goals of the American Chestnut Foundation? (The goals are to support Dr. Burnham's program of developing trees that resist the fungus and to put those trees back into the forests.) **ELA** RI.5.10, RF.5.4a **ELD** ELD.PIII.5

UNPACK MEANING

Use prompts such as these if students have difficulty with a question.

2. *How might a tree be harmed by having a fungus grow around it?* (The fungus might constrict the tree's growth or prevent nutrients from moving from the roots to the leaves.) *What does the author's use of the word* strangled *tell you about the fungus's effect on the trees?* (The word *strangled* makes me think of constricting or squeezing something so that air and nutrients can't pass. This must be what happens to the trees.) **ELA** RI.5.10, RF.5.4a **ELD** ELD.PIII.5

3. *Where does the Chinese chestnut come from?* (the same region as the fungus) *How does coming from the same region as the fungus help the Chinese chestnut?* (It has a built-in protection against the fungus.) **ELA** RI.5.3, RI.5.10, RF.5.4a **ELD** ELD.PIII.5

4. *What program did Dr. Burnham start?* (He started a program cross-breeding chestnut trees that were half American and half Chinese back with American chestnuts.) *How does the word* hopeful *help you identify the foundation's goals?* (The word *hopeful* implies actions that the foundation wants to achieve, which is a definition of *goals*.) **ELA** RI.5.3, RI.5.10, RF.5.4a **ELD** ELD.PIII.5

EXTRA PRACTICE

Retell Have students retell "Will the American Chestnut Survive?" to a partner or a family member. **ELA** RI.5.2

DAY 5

SHARE OBJECTIVES

- Read words with open syllables.
- Demonstrate understanding of Target Vocabulary words.
- Preview Understanding Characters and the Visualize strategy.

MATERIALS

Context Cards: *beaming, calculate, dwarfed, enthusiastic, outfitted, perch, presence, procedure, snug, transferred*

Write-In Reader pages 54–60

Leveled Reader: *Kangaroos*

TERMS ABOUT READING/ LANGUAGE ARTS

character   visualize

☑ TARGET VOCABULARY

If you are **outfitted**, you are equipped or supplied with the right tools.

When something is **snug**, it is tight but not so tight as to be uncomfortable.

A person who is **enthusiastic** about something is eager and excited about it.

A **beaming** person is happy and smiling.

To **calculate**, you find an answer by performing a mathematical operation.

ENGLISH LANGUAGE SUPPORT

Day 5

Vocabulary Help students build a bank of words they could use to complete the Write About It activity. Ask them to suggest words and phrases that describe the benefits of trees. Sample words and phrases: *shade, beauty, clean the air, keep soil in place*.

Multisyllable Words
Cumulative Review

- Write these sentences on the board or on a pad.
    1. The photo shows a baby turtle.
    2. The eggs are cozy and warm in the sand.
    3. The lady sees what happens to the eggs.
- Have student volunteers circle the words with a VCV letter pattern and then place a line after the first vowel. Assign students to work with a partner to practice reading the sentences. Then listen to each student read one sentence. Make corrections as needed. Record your findings. **ELA** RF.5.3a **ELD** ELD.PIII.5

REVIEW

Target Vocabulary

Context Cards

- Display the **Context Cards** for *outfitted, snug, enthusiastic, beaming*, and *calculate*. Review the meanings of these words. Then have students use the words in oral sentences about trees.

- Add the **Context Cards** for *dwarfed, perch, presence, procedure*, and *transferred*. Give one card to each student. Have students imagine they are writing a report about the American chestnut tree. Have students work together to create a list of facts about the history of the tree over the last hundred years, with each student contributing a fact that includes his or her vocabulary word. Have students read their lists aloud. **ELA** RF.5.4c, L.5.4a, L.5.5c, L.5.6 **ELD** ELD.PI.5.6b, ELD.PIII.5

WRITE ABOUT IT

- Ask students to write about the importance of healthy trees and forests. Have them explain why we should value trees, using the word *presence* in their explanations. **ELA** W.5.2d

PRETEACH
Understanding Characters
Visualize
Write-In Reader pages 54–60

- Introduce skill and strategy. Say: *In the next lesson, we are going to focus on understanding the characters in a story. We'll also work on ways to visualize what we read.*

- Explain: *The characters of a story are the people or animals who the story is about. Understanding the characters can help you better understand the story and its message.*

- Ask: *What are some adjectives you would use to describe Dr. Charles Burnham?* (*driven, curious, intelligent*) **ELA** RI.5.3 **ELD** ELD.PI.5.6a

- Have students help you make a list on the board of details from the selection that the author uses to reveal a little more about Dr. Burnham.

   Page 58: Dr. Burnham teamed up with a chestnut farmer. (cooperative)

   Page 58: He used a procedure in which he crossed trees that were half-American and half-Chinese with American chestnuts. (intelligent, thorough, curious)
   ELA RI.5.3, RI.5.10, RF.5.4a **ELD** ELD.PI.5.6a, ELD.PIII.5

- Turn to and review the Visualize strategy, found on page 305 in the **Write-In Reader**. Then have students identify words and phrases in the text they used to visualize how the fungus killed the trees and how Dr. Burnham developed healthy new trees.
   ELA RI.5.3, RI.5.4, RI.5.10, RF.5.4a **ELD** ELD.PIII.5

APPLY READING SKILLS

- Introduce *Kangaroos*. Choral-read the first few pages with students. Depending on their abilities, have students continue reading with partners or as a group.

Quick Check Fluency

Listen to individual students as they read the **Write-In Reader** selection. Make specific notes about words that presented difficulty to them.

● **Leveled Reader**

RETURN TO THE ANCHOR TEXT

"Be a Reading Detective!"
Student Book pages 175–189
Write-In Reader pages 61A–61B

- Page through "Quest for the Tree Kangaroo" with students, and review the important ideas.

- Remind students about the target skill: **cause and effect.** Point out that one event, the cause, leads to another event, the effect.

- Have students answer the first question in the **Write-In Reader.** Remind them that a reading detective looks for clues.

- Circulate to offer assistance and to make sure that students are taking notes about evidence from the text.

- Have students write their responses.

SPIRAL REVIEW

- Review the skill **main ideas and details** with students. Remind them that an informational text presents many main ideas. The ideas are supported by details that give examples or provide evidence for the author's points.

- Have students answer the second question in the **Write-In Reader.** Circulate to offer assistance and to make sure that they are taking notes about evidence from the text.

- Have students write their responses.

💬 **Classroom Collaboration**

Have pairs of "reading detectives" compare their responses and the clues they found in the text.

EXTRA PRACTICE

Independent Reading Have students read from a book of their choice and describe what they read in their reading logs.

SHARE OBJECTIVES

- Identify simple or compound direct objects.
- Discuss the realities and challenges of farm life.
- Read to build meaning for Target Vocabulary words.

MATERIALS

Write-In Reader pages 62–63

TERMS ABOUT READING/ LANGUAGE ARTS

simple direct object   compound direct object

ENGLISH LANGUAGE SUPPORT

Day 1

Vocabulary Help students build a word bank to use during the Talk About It activity. Use questions such as these to help students build the bank. *What might you hear on a farm? What might you see on a farm?*

Sentence Frames Review the term *direct object* with students. Then have students provide words to complete a frame like *As the cat ran away, it spilled _____.* Next, have students add an object to create a compound direct object. *As the cat ran away, it spilled _____ and _____.*
ELD ELD.PII.5.6

Oral Language Read the definition of a Target Vocabulary word to students. Then invite students to make up a sentence using the word and share it with the class. Continue until you have reviewed each of the Target Vocabulary words. **ELD** ELD.PI.5.1

Warm Up

Oral Grammar

Identifying Direct Objects

- Remind students that to determine the direct object of a sentence, they can repeat the subject and action verb and ask who or what, as in: *Rob kicked the ball.* Ask: *What did Rob kick?* (the ball) *So the ball is the direct object. It receives the action of the verb.*

- Explain that some sentences have compound direct objects. Say: *Rob kicked the ball and the bat.* More than one object receives the action of the verb.

Teacher says, then asks, *Direct object? Simple or Compound?*	Students respond
*Many people eat **oranges, apples, and grapes.***	compound
*My dad liked **history** the most.*	simple
*My parents read **graphic novels and the newspaper.***	compound
*The ball rammed **the table.***	simple

Talk About It

Help focus students' attention on what it might be like to move to a farm from the big city. Ask: *What might a city kid find exciting about farm life?*

Discuss the question, emphasizing these points:

- all of the different kinds of farm animals
- the peace and quiet
- the open spaces
- the fields of crops and the woods
- the beautiful scenery
- the awesome night sky

Target Vocabulary

Write-In Reader pages 62–63

- Read and discuss the poem. Then discuss the meaning of each Target Vocabulary word. Suggest that students underline words or phrases, if possible, that provide clues to meaning. **ELA** RF.5.4c, L.5.4a, L.5.5c, L.5.6 **ELD** ELD.PIII.5

- Allow time for students to write their responses. Then ask students to choose an answer that they would like to read aloud.

  Responses:

  1. lunging

  2. romp

  3. frantic

  4. Possible responses include basketball, football, and tennis.

  5. Possible responses might include favorite outdoor spots such as a local beach or public park.

Quick Check | Target Vocabulary

Ask each student to use one of the Target Vocabulary words in a sentence.
ELA W.5.2d

☑ TARGET VOCABULARY

Bounding is leaping at a fast pace.

Someone who is **frantic** is wild with excitement or worry.

Lunging is making a sudden forward movement.

Picturing something is forming a mental image of it.

A **romp** is energetic playing.

EXTRA PRACTICE

Build Fluency Have students read **Write-In Reader** pages 62–63 with a partner or a family member.

DAY 2

SHARE OBJECTIVES

- Read words with open syllables.
- Understand characters.
- Read on-level text to apply skills and strategies.

MATERIALS

Write-In Reader pages 64–67

TERMS ABOUT READING/ LANGUAGE ARTS

character

ENGLISH LANGUAGE SUPPORT

Day 2

Vocabulary Review the word *traits.* Then help students build a word bank of verbs to use during the Quick Check activity. Use questions such as these to help students build the bank. *What words could you use to describe how a character speaks? What words describe how a character moves?* Use gestures and pictures to help students understand any unfamiliar words.

Sentence Frames Prepare students to respond to the comprehension questions by using frames such as these to compare the way the narrator and Kwan feel about the country. *At first, the narrator thinks the country is ___ . In contrast, Kwan ____.*
ELD ELD.PI.5.6a

Oral Language As students answer the comprehension questions, challenge them to find sentences in the story that support their answers and read them aloud.
ELD ELD.PIII.5

Warm Up

Multisyllable Words

Focus: Open Syllables

Write these words on the board or on a pad.

1	decent	token	humid
2	rodent	virus	cubic
3	open	totem	bonus

Row 1: Say: *These words have a vowel-consonant-vowel letter pattern.* Demonstrate the letter pattern as shown. Then divide the word after the first vowel.

d e / c e n t	t o / k e n	h u / m i d
V C V	V C V	V C V

Read the first word, emphasizing each syllable. Ask: *What do we call the first syllable?* (open syllable) *How does this syllable end?* (with a vowel) *What is the vowel sound?* (long e) Point out the second syllable, *cent.* Ask: *Is this an open syllable, too?* (no) *Why not?* (It ends in consonants.) *What is the vowel sound?* (short e vowel sound). Then blend the syllables to read the whole word.

Row 2: Have volunteers identify the VCV pattern and divide the word after the first vowel. Choral-read the words.

Row 3: Listen to each student read the words. Make corrections as needed. Record your findings. **ELA** RF.5.3a **ELD** ELD.PIII.5

RETEACH

Understanding Characters

- Display a book that students have recently read. Have students name one of the main characters. Ask: *What do you know about this character? What details from the story support your thinking?*

- Remind students that authors give their characters realistic **traits,** or ways of speaking and acting. These traits help the reader infer what the character might do or say.

Quick Check | **Comprehension**

Ask students to describe the traits of a favorite character.

READ

"Nothing Ever Happens in the Country"

Write-In Reader pages 64–67

- Preview the selection with students using the **Think Aloud**.

Think Aloud *I see a boy wearing a sports shirt and holding a baseball mitt. He seems unhappy. This picture and the title make me think this story is about a boy who lives in the country. What clues do you see that make you think this story is about life in the country?*

- Together, review the steps to the Visualize strategy, **Write-In Reader** page 305. As needed, guide students in applying the strategy as they read.

READ

Ask students to read to confirm their predictions. Then choral-read page by page with students. Discuss, confirm, and revise student predictions based upon text details.
ELA RL.5.10, RF.5.4a **ELD** ELD.PIII.5

REREAD

Call on individuals to read aloud while others follow along. Stop to discuss each question. Allow time for students to write their responses before proceeding. Sample answers are provided.

Page 64: How would life on a farm be different from the family's <u>frantic</u> city life? (Life would feel slower. There would be more peace and quiet.)
ELA RF.5.4c, L.5.4a, L.5.5c, L.5.6 **ELD** ELD.PIII.5

Help unpack meaning, if needed, by asking: *What does the word* frantic *mean?* (to be wild with excitement or worry)

Unpack Meaning: For questions on pages 65–67, you may want to use the notes in the right-hand column.

Turn and Talk **Page 65:** Why does the narrator shrug his shoulders? (Possible response: He's not sure he wants to make new friends.) Have partners discuss the question and then share their answers with the group. **ELA** RL.5.6, RL.5.10, RF.5.4a **ELD** ELD.PIII.5

Page 66: What can you tell about the narrator from his thoughts about going outside? (He doesn't enjoy life in the country.) **ELA** RL.5.3, RL.5.6, RL.5.10, RF.5.4a **ELD** ELD.PI.5.6a, ELD.PIII.5

Page 67: What do Kwan's reactions to the country tell you about him? (Kwan is excited about his new experience. He's never been to a farm before.)
ELA RL.5.3, RL.5.10, RF.5.4a **ELD** ELD.PI.5.6a, ELD.PIII.5

UNPACK MEANING

Use prompts such as these if students have difficulty with a **Stop•Think•Write** question:

Page 65 *What did the narrator's mom say to him right before he shrugged his shoulders?* (She said he'll make new friends when school starts.) *What does it show when people shrug their shoulders?* (They are doubtful or unexcited.) **ELA** RL.5.1

Page 66 *What does the narrator say about the goat?* (He doesn't want to share his meals with the goat.) *About the chickens?* (He didn't need to have a romp with them.) *What does the narrator say about life in the city?* (He says he misses the noises of the city.)
ELA RL.5.1

Page 67 *What does the narrator notice about Kwan on the way home?* (Kwan could not hide his enthusiasm.) *What does Kwan point out on the drive home?* (a wild turkey, a groundhog, and a herd of cows)
ELA RL.5.3, RL.5.10, RF.5.4a **ELD** ELD.PI.5.6a, ELD.PIII.5

EXTRA PRACTICE

Build Fluency Have students read **Write-In Reader** pages 64–67 with a partner or a family member.

DAY 3

SHARE OBJECTIVES

- Distinguish between direct objects and indirect objects.
- Read aloud fluently to improve intonation.
- Read on-level text to apply skills and strategies.

MATERIALS

Write-In Reader pages 68–70

TERMS ABOUT READING/ LANGUAGE ARTS

intonation

ENGLISH LANGUAGE SUPPORT

Day 3

Vocabulary Teach the term *intonation*. Help students build a bank of words and phrases to use in the Fluency activity. Sample words: *rising, falling, dramatic.*

Sentence Frames Guide students to use sentence frames such as these as they participate in the Turn and Talk activity. *Before the hike, the narrator feels _____. His feelings change when _____.*
ELD ELD.PI.5.1, ELD.PI.5.6a

Oral Language Guide students to write a summary of the rest of "Nothing Ever Happens in the Country" as a class. Use this summary frame and write their responses on the board. *The morning after the boys arrive at the farm, _____. Next, _____. In the end, the narrator learned_____.* Guide students to choral-read the finished summary several times. Then have partners take turns summarizing the second part of this story to each other. **ELD** ELD.PI.5.2, ELD.PI.5.10b

Warm Up

Oral Grammar

Identifying Direct and Indirect Objects

- Read this sentence: *Sandy handed me the ball.* Ask: *What did Sandy hand me?* (the ball) So the ball *is the direct object. It receives the action of the verb.*

- Explain that some sentences (such as this one) have more than one kind of object. An indirect object can be a noun or a pronoun. It tells to whom or for whom/what the action of the verb is done. Repeat the sentence. Ask: *To whom did Sandy hand the ball?* (to me) So me *is the indirect object of this sentence.*

Teacher says, then asks, *Direct object? Indirect object?*	Students respond	
	Direct Object	**Indirect Object**
I bought my mom some fruit.	some fruit	my mom
Rita gave me rice and beans.	rice and beans	me
Ms. Feliciano taught us the history lesson.	history lesson	us
My sister reads my brother his stories.	his stories	my brother

RETEACH

Fluency: Intonation
Write-In Reader page 68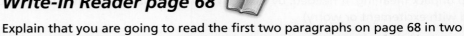

Explain that you are going to read the first two paragraphs on page 68 in two different ways and that you want students to evaluate your reading.

- First, read the paragraph without varying the tone of your voice as you read. Then, reread the text, letting the tone of your voice rise and fall to show proper intonation.

- Ask: *What did you think of my first reading? Explain. Was my second reading better? Explain.* Be sure students recognize that proper intonation makes stories easier to understand and more entertaining, and help listeners recognize important information and feelings. Point out that people use dramatic intonation when they speak to each other.

- Have students practice reading aloud the third paragraph on page 68, concentrating on intonation as they read. **ELA** RF.5.4a, RF.5.4b **ELD** ELD.PIII.5

READ

"Nothing Ever Happens in the Country"

Write-In Reader pages 68–70

Review the first part of the story with students. Ask: *What have we learned about life in the country so far?* Then preview today's reading. Have students look for clues to help them predict how this story will end.

READ

Ask students to read to confirm their predictions. Have students choral-read page by page with you. Discuss, confirm, and revise predictions based upon text details. Ask if there was anything about the way the story ended that surprised them. **ELA** RL.5.10, RF.5.4a **ELD** ELD.PIII.5

REREAD

Call on individuals to read aloud while others follow along. Stop to discuss each question. Allow time for students to write their responses before proceeding. Sample answers are provided.

Page 68: Why do you think Kwan was <u>bounding</u> over to the chicken coop? (He was excited.) **ELA** RL.5.10, RF.5.4a, RF.5.4c, L.5.6 **ELD** ELD.PIII.5

Help unpack meaning, if needed, by asking: *What does the word* bounding *mean?* (leaping at a fast pace) *How did Kwan feel when he found eggs in the chicken coop?* (He was thrilled.) **ELA** RL.5.10, RF.5.4a **ELD** ELD.PIII.5

Unpack Meaning: For questions on pages 69–70, you may want to use the notes in the right-hand column.

Turn and Talk **Page 69:** What changes the narrator's feelings about the hike? (Kwan shows him the amazing hawks.) Have partners discuss this question and then share their answers with the group. **ELA** RL.5.10, RF.5.4a **ELD** ELD.PIII.5

Page 70: Why don't Kwan and the narrator get too close to the skunks? (They don't want the skunks to spray them.) **ELA** RL.5.10, RF.5.4a **ELD** ELD.PIII.5

Quick Check **Retelling**

Have students retell the end of the story. Support the retelling by asking: *What did the narrator and his friend Kwan do the morning after he arrived? What amazed and excited Kwan? What did the narrator learn from his friend?* **ELA** RL.5.2, RL.5.3, RL.5.6 **ELD** ELD.PI.5.6a

---

UNPACK MEANING

Use prompts such as these if students have difficulty with a **Stop•Think•Write** question:

Page 69 *What did the boy's mother insist the boys take with them?* (binoculars) *What did the boys watch through their binoculars?* (hawks circling and a hawk catching a mouse)

Page 70 *What do wild animals do when they are frightened or threatened?* (defend themselves) *What do skunks do when they are frightened?* (They spray their scent.)

EXTRA PRACTICE

Build Fluency Have students read **Write-In Reader** pages 68–70 with a partner or a family member.

SHARE OBJECTIVES

- Read words with open syllables.
- Identify direct and indirect objects.
- Support answers to questions with evidence from the text.

MATERIALS

Write-In Reader pages 64–71

TERMS ABOUT READING/ LANGUAGE ARTS

direct object   indirect object

ENGLISH LANGUAGE SUPPORT

Day 4

Vocabulary Warm Up words such as *comet, locust,* and *bonus* may be unfamiliar to students. Use visuals, examples, and simple explanations to support understanding.

Sentence Frames Give students a frame they can use to complete the Quick Check activity, such as *My friend gave _____ a _____.* Tell them to fill in the first blank with the name of a person and the second blank with the name of a thing.

Oral Language Guide students to find direct objects in sample sentences from **Write-In Reader** pages 64–71. Write a few of the sentences on the board and prompt students to identify the direct object(s) and state whether they are simple or compound. **ELD** ELD.PI.5.1

Warm Up

Multisyllable Words

Focus: Open Syllables

Write these words on the board or on a pad.

1	hotel	habit	basic
2	cabin	exit	comet
3	locust	bonus	music

Row 1: Ask: *How are these words alike?* (They have a vowel-consonant-vowel letter pattern.) First, demonstrate how to divide *hotel* into parts. Then, read it.

h o / t e l   h a / b i t ⟹ h a b / i t

Point to *habit.* Say: *Let's divide the second word the same way.* Then pronounce the first vowel with a long *a* sound. Say: *That doesn't sound right, so I'll adjust by dividing the word after the* b. Say: *Now we have a closed syllable. How is the vowel pronounced in a closed syllable?* (short) Then blend each syllable to read *habit.*

Rows 2–3: Have volunteers identify the VCV pattern and divide after the first vowel, pronouncing the first syllable with a long vowel sound. Have them adjust by dividing after the consonant in the words *cabin* (cab / in), *exit* (ex / it), and *comet* (com / et). **ELA** RF.5.3a **ELD** ELD.PIII.5

RETEACH

Direct and Indirect Objects

- Remind students that a direct object identifies who or what receives the action of the verb. An indirect object tells to whom or for whom or what the action of the verb was done. Ask: *My friend gave Rosa a book. What did my friend give?* (a book) *To whom did my friend give the book?* (Rosa)

Turn and Talk Write: *The writer sent the paper an article.* Ask students to discuss how to identify direct and indirect objects.

Quick Check | Grammar

Ask students to write a sentence using a direct and an indirect object. Have students identify the direct and indirect object.

Look Back and Respond

Write-In Reader pages 64–71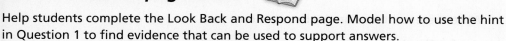

Help students complete the Look Back and Respond page. Model how to use the hint in Question 1 to find evidence that can be used to support answers.

- Explain that evidence is proof, clues, or information.

- Remind students that they can circle or underline the specific words in the selection that they used as evidence for their answers.

1. Why is it important that the boys take binoculars on their hike? (The binoculars help them see the hawks.) **ELA** RL.5.10, RF.5.4a **ELD** ELD.PIII.5

Help unpack meaning, if needed, by asking: *What do binoculars do?* (They make things look closer than they really are.) *What do the boys see through the binoculars?* (hawks)

Guide students as they answer Questions 2–4.

Unpack Meaning: For Questions 2–4, you may want to use the notes in the right-hand column to guide the discussion about student responses.

2. What animals are there on the farm? (a goat and chickens)
ELA RL.5.10, RF.5.4a **ELD** ELD.PIII.5

3. What can you tell about Kwan's character? (Kwan likes new experiences.)
ELA RL.5.3, RL.5.10, RF.5.4a **ELD** ELD.PI.5.6a, ELD.PIII.5

Turn and Talk Have students work independently on Question 4. When students have completed the page, have partners discuss their responses and then share them with the group. Sample responses are provided. Accept reasonable responses.

4. How do the narrator and Kwan differ? (The narrator thinks farm life is boring, and Kwan finds it exciting.) **ELA** RL.5.3, RL.5.10, RF.5.4a **ELD** ELD.PI.5.6a, ELD.PIII.5

UNPACK MEANING

Use prompts such as these if students have difficulty with a question:

2. *Turn to page 65. Who tries to steal the narrator's birthday cake?* (a goat) *Turn to page 66. What doesn't the narrator want to have a romp with?* (chickens)

3. *Turn to page 67. Has Kwan ever been on a farm?* (no) *Turn to page 69. What is Kwan's reaction to what he sees on the hike?* (Kwan was amazed.)

4. *Turn to page 65. How does the narrator describe his birthday on the farm?* (He says it is boring.) *Turn to page 68. What kind of mood is Kwan in when he wakes up on the farm?* (He is in a good mood.)

EXTRA PRACTICE

Retell Have students retell "Nothing Ever Happens in the Country" to a partner or a family member. **ELA** RL.5.2

DAY 5

SHARE OBJECTIVES

- Read words with open syllables or closed syllables.
- Demonstrate understanding of Target Vocabulary words.
- Preview Author's Purpose and the Analyze/Evaluate strategy.

MATERIALS

Context Cards: *bounding, checking, frantic, lunging, picturing, romp, shouldered, strained, stride, wheeled*

Write-In Reader pages 64–70

Leveled Reader: *Young Eagle and His Horse*

TERMS ABOUT READING/ LANGUAGE ARTS

| author's purpose | analyze | evaluate |

☑ TARGET VOCABULARY

Someone who is **checking** a person or thing is limiting or controlling the person or thing.

To have **shouldered** something is to have placed a weight on one's shoulders or to have accepted a burden or responsibility.

Someone who **strained** worked as hard as possible, either physically or mentally.

Stride is the rhythm of one's walking or the length of one's steps.

To have **wheeled** something is to have moved it on wheels.

ENGLISH LANGUAGE SUPPORT

Day 5

Vocabulary Help students build a word bank of descriptive words to use during the Write About It activity. Clarify the meaning of any unfamiliar words.

Multisyllable Words
Cumulative Review

Write these sentences on the board or on a pad.

1. The dog has good habits and is seldom lazy. (hab / its)
2. He ran to the cabin when he heard music. (cab / in; mu / sic)
3. He is a very decent and open man. (de / cent; o / pen)

Have student volunteers circle the words with a VCV letter pattern and then divide the words using the strategies they learned. Assign students to work with a partner to practice reading the sentences. Then listen to each student read one sentence. Record your findings. **ELA** RF.5.3a **ELD** ELD.PIII.5

REVIEW
Target Vocabulary

Context Cards

- Display the **Context Cards** for *bounding, frantic, lunging, picturing,* and *romp*. Review the meanings of these words. Then have students use the words in oral sentences about life in the country.

- Add the **Context Cards** for *checking, shouldered, strained, stride,* and *wheeled*. Distribute a card to each student. Have students act out their words for other students to identify.

WRITE ABOUT IT

- Ask students to think about what it might be like to move to the country. Or if students live in the country, have them imagine what it would be like to move to a large city. Ask students to describe the first day in their new home, using the word *romp* in their descriptions. **ELA** W.5.2d

PRETEACH

Author's Purpose; Analyze/Evaluate

Write-In Reader pages 64–70

- Introduce the skill and strategy. Say: *In the next lesson, we are going to focus on author's purpose. We'll also work on ways to analyze and evaluate passages.*

- Explain: *Authors have a purpose, or reason, for writing. Their purpose might be to persuade or convince the reader to believe or act in a certain way, or it might be to entertain the reader. Authors may also write to inform the reader or to describe an experience.*

- Explain that the story "Nothing Ever Happens in the Country" was written to entertain the reader. The author is telling a story that has an interesting plot and characters.

- Ask: *What details in the text help you know that the author wrote the story to entertain the reader?* (The story is about a boy who moves to the country. It tells the story from the boy's perspective, including funny scenes, such as the goat eating the boy's cake.)

- Point out that knowing an author's purpose for writing can help readers understand the text and evaluate what they are reading.

- Turn to and review the Analyze/Evaluate strategy found on page 303 in the **Write-In Reader**. Tell students that when they analyze, they carefully consider the details of a text. When they evaluate, they make judgments about the text. Have students analyze the text and use their ideas to form an opinion about the story.

APPLY READING SKILLS

- Introduce *Young Eagle and His Horse*. Choral-read the first few pages with students. Depending on their abilities, have students continue reading with partners or as a group.

● **Leveled Reader**

Quick Check | **Fluency**

Listen to individual students as they read the **Write-In Reader** selection. Make specific notes about words that presented difficulty to them.

RETURN TO THE ANCHOR TEXT

"Be a Reading Detective!"

Student Book pages 209–219
Write-In Reader pages 71A–71B

- Page through "Old Yeller" with students, and review the main characters and events.

- Remind students about the target skill: **understanding characters.** Point out that a character's actions and words let the reader know just what the character is like.

- Have students answer the first question in the **Write-In Reader.** Remind them that a reading detective looks for clues.

- Circulate to offer assistance and to make sure that students are taking notes about evidence from the text.

- Have students write their responses.

SPIRAL REVIEW

- Review the skill **compare and contrast** with students. Remind them that comparing characters or events means finding similarities and that contrasting means finding differences.

- Have students answer the second question in the **Write-In Reader.** Circulate to offer assistance and to make sure that they are taking notes about evidence from the text.

- Have students write their responses.

💬 Classroom Collaboration

Have pairs of "reading detectives" compare their responses and the clues they found in the text.

EXTRA PRACTICE

Independent Reading Have students read from a book of their choice and describe what they read in their reading logs.

DAY 1

SHARE OBJECTIVES

- Use conjunctions to combine sentences.
- Discuss the dangers of oil spills.
- Read to build meaning for Target Vocabulary words.

MATERIALS

Write-In Reader pages 72–73

TERMS ABOUT READING/ LANGUAGE ARTS

conjunction

ENGLISH LANGUAGE SUPPORT

Day 1

Vocabulary Help students build a word bank to use during the Quick Check activity. Sample words: *spills, resource, polluting*.

Sentence Frames Guide students to use conjunctions as they participate in the Quick Check activity, using frames such as these: *Examples of endangered animals are _____ and _____. The _____ is damaged, but we can restore it.* **ELD** ELD.PII.5.6

Oral Language Point out to students that the conjunction *and* is used to join ideas that are alike. The conjunction *but* is used to connect ideas that are different. Tell them to use the sentences in the right-hand column of the table in the Warm Up activity as a model work with a partner to make up sentences using *and* to connect similar ideas and *but* to show contrast. **ELD** ELD.PII.5.6

Warm Up

Oral Grammar

Coordinating Conjunctions

- Write the following conjunctions on the board.

and	but	or	nor	for	yet

- Explain to students that these words are conjunctions. They *join* words or groups of words in a sentence. Remind students that we can use conjunctions to combine our sentences.

- Prompt by reading two sentences. Students will combine them, using a conjunction that makes sense. **ELA** L.5.1a **ELD** ELD.PII.5.6

Teacher prompts	Students respond
My parents get up early every day. I get up early every day.	My parents **and** I get up early every day.
Michael plays the guitar. Michael does not play the piano.	Michael plays the guitar **but** not the piano.
My sister is a good student. My brother is a good student.	My sister **and** my brother are good students.
Those students are noisy. Those students are very serious.	Those students are noisy **yet** very serious.
I don't like onions. I don't like garlic.	I don't like onions **or** garlic.

Talk About It

Help focus students' attention on the dangers of oil spills. Ask: *What problems do you think oil spills create?*

Discuss the question, emphasizing these points:

- Oil spills harm the environment by polluting the water.

- People have to clean up the oil, which takes a long time.

- Oil is a valuable resource that we can't afford to waste.

- The oil covers vegetation on the coast.

- The oil harms or kills animals. Some of these animals may be endangered.

Target Vocabulary

Write-In Reader pages 72–73

- Read and discuss each paragraph. Then discuss the meaning of each Target Vocabulary word. Suggest that students underline words or phrases—when possible—that provide clues to meaning. Also point out the following:

  The word *endangered* can be used to describe both animals or things that are in danger of disappearing from existence. For example, *Eagles were once an endangered species. Many coastal communities are endangered because of rising tides.*

  In this instance, *restore* means "to return to an original state." The word can also mean "to return something to its proper owner," as in *The detective will restore the stolen goods to their owners. Restore* can also mean "to give something new strength" as in *A long vacation will restore your health.* **ELA** RF.5.4c, L.5.4a, L.5.6 **ELD** ELD.PIII.5

- Allow time for students to write their responses. Then ask students to choose an answer they would like to read aloud.

  Possible responses:

  1. limit, restrict
  2. algae, grass, shrubs, bushes
  3. Responses may include: at home—taking out the garbage; in school—erasing the board.
  4. The animal may disappear from Earth.
  5. a local marsh or riverfront

Quick Check | Target Vocabulary

Ask each student to use one of the Target Vocabulary words in a sentence.

✓ TARGET VOCABULARY

A group of animals or plants that is **endangered** is in danger of dying out.

To **regulate** is to control or direct according to rules.

A **responsibility** is a duty or job.

To **restore** is to return to an original state.

Vegetation is the plant life in an area.

EXTRA PRACTICE

Build Fluency Have students read **Write-In Reader** pages 72–73 with a partner or a family member.

DAY 2

SHARE OBJECTIVES

- Read words with open first syllables.
- Understand author's purpose.
- Read on-level text to apply skills and strategies.

MATERIALS

Write-In Reader pages 74–77

TERMS ABOUT READING/ LANGUAGE ARTS

persuade	analyze
evaluate	

ENGLISH LANGUAGE SUPPORT

Day 2

Vocabulary Help students build a word bank of subjects and action words to use during the Quick Check activity. Use questions such as these to help students build the bank. *What is a synonym for author's purpose? What is another way to say that an author is writing to* entertain? *to* inform? Use gestures and pictures to help students understand any unfamiliar words.

Sentence Frames Guide students to use text evidence when responding to the comprehension questions. Use frames such as the following: *I predicted that ___ because _____. I know my prediction is right/wrong because _____.* **ELD** ELD.PI.5.6a

Oral Language After students respond to the Turn and Talk question, guide them to express their own opinion, using frames such as the following: *I agree with the students because _____. I have a different opinion than the students do because _____.* **ELD** ELD.PI.5.3

Multisyllable Words

Focus: Open First Syllables

Write these words on the board or on a pad.

1	debug	recap	premix
2	recut	remix	preplan
3	rehang	resell	retag

Row 1: Ask: *How are these words alike?* (They all have a vowel-consonant-vowel letter pattern.) Point out also that these words all begin with a prefix, either *de, re,* or *pre.* Ask: *What kind of syllables are these prefixes?* (open) Ask students to look at the second syllables in this row. Ask: *What do you know about these syllables?* (They end in a consonant, so the vowels are short.) Remind students that we can divide longer words after the prefix to read them more easily: de / bug   re / cap   pre / mix

Row 2: Have volunteers circle the prefix and divide after it. Then have them blend the syllables to form a word.

Row 3: Listen to each student read the words. Make corrections as needed. Record your findings. **ELA** RF.5.3a **ELD** ELD.PIII.5

RETEACH

Author's Purpose

- Hold up a science or social studies textbook. Read the book title and some of the chapter titles. Ask: *Why do you think the author wrote this book?*

- Point out that the author's purpose is the reason he or she writes a book. Explain that authors may write to inform, to persuade, or to entertain. Remind students that an author can have more than one purpose for writing.

- Explain that knowing an author's purpose for writing can help readers evaluate, or judge, what the author is saying. Ask: *Would you read a nonfiction book the same way you would read a fiction book? Why? How might you read a book that tried to persuade you to do something?*

Quick Check   Comprehension

Ask students to name a book they have read that was meant to entertain, as well as a book that was meant to inform.

READ

"Oil Spill in Alaska"
Write-In Reader pages 74–77

- Preview the selection with students using the **Think Aloud** to set a purpose for reading. Guide students to use headings and photos to set their purpose. Record their ideas.

> **Think Aloud**   *The title of this story is "Oil Spill in Alaska." I'm going to read to find out exactly what happened as a result of the oil spill.*

- Together, review the steps to the Analyze/Evaluate strategy, **Write-In Reader** page 303. As needed, guide students in applying the strategy as they read.

READ

Ask students to read to confirm their predictions. Then choral-read page by page with students. Discuss, confirm, and revise student predictions based upon text details. **ELA** RF.5.4a **ELD** ELD.PIII.5

REREAD

Call on individuals to read aloud while others follow along. Stop to discuss each question. Allow time for students to write their responses before proceeding. Sample answers are provided.

Page 74: What do you predict this story will tell you about Kim's dad and the Alaska oil spill? (It will tell how the spill affected Kim's dad's job and how it hurt the environment.) **ELA** RF.5.4a **ELD** ELD.PIII.5

Help unpack meaning, if needed, by asking: *What does Kim's dad do for a living?* (He is a fisherman.) *How might a fisherman be affected by an oil spill on the ocean?* (It would be dangerous to fish in the ocean because the spill would make conditions bad and would probably kill the fish.) **ELA** RF.5.4a **ELD** ELD.PIII.5

Unpack Meaning: For questions on pages 75–77, you may want to use the notes in the right-hand column.

Page 75: What forms of <u>vegetation</u> might be affected by the oil spill? (Responses will vary, but students may say algae, grasses, and shrubs.) **ELA** RL.5.10, RF.5.4a, RF.5.4c, L.5.6 **ELD** ELD.PIII.5

Page 76: Why did the author include details about the town's citizens and mayor? (to show how ordinary citizens care about the environment and wanted to do something to clean up the oil spill) **ELA** RF.5.3a **ELD** ELD.PIII.5

> **Turn and Talk**   **Page 77:** Why do the students believe that everyone should help the animals? (The students believe they have a responsibility to help the animals because humans created the spill.) Have partners discuss this question and then share with the group.

UNPACK MEANING

Use prompts such as these if students have difficulty with a **Stop•Think•Write** question:

Page 75 *Can you think of a kind of plant that grows in the ocean?* (algae or seaweed) *Can you think of kinds of plants that might grow on the coast?* (grasses and shrubs)

Page 76 *What does Kim's mother say about the spill?* (She says it's their duty to help clean up the spill.) *How does the mayor respond to Kim's mother?* (He agrees.) *What does this make you think about the townspeople?* (It makes me think they are responsible and concerned.) **ELA** RL.5.1

Page 77 *What do the students want to do?* (help) *How do the students feel about statements made by Kim's mother and the mayor?* (They agree.) *Who do the students say caused the spill?* (humans)

EXTRA PRACTICE

Build Fluency Have students reread **Write-In Reader** pages 74–77 with a partner or a family member.

DAY 3

SHARE OBJECTIVES

- Use commas to separate nouns in a series.
- Read aloud fluently to improve rate.
- Read on-level text to apply skills and strategies.

MATERIALS

Write-In Reader pages 78–80

TERMS ABOUT READING/ LANGUAGE ARTS

noun   comma   rate

ENGLISH LANGUAGE SUPPORT

Day 3

Vocabulary Help students build a word bank of feeling words to use during the Fluency activity. Use gestures, expressions, and pictures to show the meanings of the words. Sample words: *pace, rate, emphasis.*

Sentence Frames Review the meaning of the words *argument* and *regulating* before students begin the Turn and Talk activity. Give a sentence frame to help students participate in the Turn and Talk activity. Then guide students to use sentence frames such as these to respond to the question: *One argument the author uses is _____. Another argument is _____. To me, the author's arguments are convincing/not convincing because _____.*
ELD ELD.PI.5.3, ELD.PI.5.6a, ELD.PI.5.11a

Oral Language Guide students to write a summary of the rest of "Oil Spill in Alaska" as a class. Use this summary frame and write their responses on the board. *The problem in the story is _____. The lesson Kim wants the oil companies to learn is _____. Kim herself learns _____.* Guide students to choral-read the finished summary several times. Then have partners take turns summarizing the second part of this story to each other. **ELD** ELD.PI.5.2, ELD.PI.5.10b

Oral Grammar

Nouns in a Series

- Tell students that you are going to read from something you wrote. First, you are going to read it quickly, and then, you will reread it. Explain that you are going to need students' help in deciding where to put the commas.

- First, read each of the following sentences without pausing. Then, tell students you want them to give you a *thumbs-up* to signal that you need to pause when you speak and to add a comma when you write. Model using the first sentence. (Commas are needed after the words in boldface.)
ELA L.5.2a

1. I don't like **apples oranges peaches** or plums.

2. My **cousins uncles aunts sisters** and brothers will be there.

3. I like animals including **dogs cats horses goats** and sheep.

4. I like to shop for **games dishes books music** and art.

RETEACH

Fluency: Adjust Rate to Purpose

Write-In Reader page 78

Explain that you are going to read from page 78 in two different ways and that you want students to evaluate your readings.

- First, read at a pace appropriate to informational text, pausing between words, reading key pieces of information more slowly for emphasis, and acknowledging punctuation. Then, reread the page more quickly, running words together.

- Ask: *What did you think of my first reading? Explain. Was my second reading better? Explain.* Tell students that the purpose of this story is to inform. Explain that reading informational text as you did in the first reading enables readers to think about, understand, and remember what they are learning about. Be sure they recognize how difficult it is to understand important ideas and the details that support them when someone reads too quickly.

- Have students practice reading aloud paragraphs from pages 74–77, concentrating on reading at a rate appropriate to informational text.
ELA RF.5.4b **ELD** ELD.PIII.5

READ

"Oil Spill in Alaska"
Write-In Reader pages 78–80

Review the first part of the story with students. Ask: *What have we learned about the oil spill so far?* Then preview today's reading. Have students adjust their purpose for reading the remainder of the story.

READ

Ask students to read to confirm their predictions. Have students choral-read page by page with you. Ask if there was anything about the way the story ended that surprised them. **ELA** RL.5.10, RF.5.4a **ELD** ELD.PIII.5

REREAD

Call on individuals to read aloud while others follow along. Stop to discuss each question. Allow time for students to write their responses before proceeding. Sample answers are provided.

Page 78: How might animals become <u>endangered</u>? (Animals become endangered when there are so few left that they might die out completely.) **ELA** RF.5.4c, L.5.4a, L.5.6 **ELD** ELD.PIII.5

Help unpack meaning, if needed, by asking: *What is the meaning of* endangered? (in danger of dying out) *Why might a type of animal be in danger of dying out?* (the climate changes, destroyed habitats)

Unpack Meaning: For questions on pages 79–80, you may want to use the notes in the right-hand column.

Page 79: How do you think the people of the town felt after hearing that the cleanup was ending? (relieved and happy) **ELA** RL.5.10, RF.5.4a **ELD** ELD.PIII.5

Turn and Talk **Page 80:** What arguments does the author give to persuade the reader about regulating oil shipping? (Regulating shipping will prevent oil spills and protect our environment.) Have partners discuss this question and then share with the group. **ELA** RL.5.10, RF.5.4a **ELD** ELD.PIII.5

Quick Check | Retelling

Have students retell the end of the story. Support the retelling by asking: *What valuable lesson does Kim hope the oil companies learned? What lessons has Kim learned?* **ELA** RL.5.2 **ELD** ELD.PI.5.6a

---

UNPACK MEANING

Use prompts such as these if students have difficulty with a **Stop•Think•Write** question:

Page 79 *What can Kim's father do again?* (fish) *How does Kim's father earn a living?* (fishing) *What can Kim do now that the cleanup is over?* (play on the beach)

Page 80 *How does Kim think the oil companies should change their shipping rules?* (They should regulate shipping more carefully.) *How will regulation help?* (It will prevent oil spills.)

EXTRA PRACTICE

Build Fluency Have students reread **Write-In Reader** pages 78–80 with a partner or a family member.

SHARE OBJECTIVES

- Read words with open syllables.
- Identify and understand coordinating conjunctions.
- Support answers to questions with evidence from the text.

MATERIALS

Write-In Reader pages 74–81

TERMS ABOUT READING/ LANGUAGE ARTS

coordinating conjunction

ENGLISH LANGUAGE SUPPORT

Day 4

Vocabulary Warm Up words such as *robot, menu, shady,* and *slimy* may be unfamiliar to students. Use visuals, examples, and simple explanations to support understanding.

Sentence Frames Guide students to use text evidence when participating in the Turn and Talk activity. Use frames such as the following: *The author makes the point that _____. I can find evidence to show this is true on page _____. The evidence is _____.* **ELD** ELD.PI.5.1, ELD.PI.5.6a, ELD.PI.5.11a

Oral Language Guide students to find coordinating conjunctions in sample sentences from **Write-In Reader** pages 74–81. Write a few of the sentences on the board and prompt students to explain the relationship created by each coordinating conjunction. For example, *and* connects ideas of equal importance, *but* shows a difference, and *so* sets up a cause-effect relationship. After working through several examples as a group, have students turn to a partner and talk about additional examples. **ELD** ELD.PII.5.6

Warm Up

Multisyllable Words

Focus: Open Syllables

Write these words on the board or on a pad.

1	robot	crazy	study
2	foxy	menu	slimy
3	nosy	shady	novel

Row 1: Identify the VCV letter pattern and divide the words before the consonant: ro/bot, cra/zy, stu/dy.

Say: *The first syllables are open syllables. What vowel sound should they have?* (long) Blend the syllables to read *robot* and *crazy*. Read *study* with a long vowel sound.

Say: *That doesn't sound right. Sometimes we have to divide words with a VCV letter pattern after the consonant. That syllable will have a short vowel sound.* Demonstrate dividing *study* before the *y*. Then read it correctly.

Row 2: Have volunteers identify the VCV letter patterns to divide and read the words.

Row 3: Listen to each student read the words. Make corrections as needed. Record your findings. **ELA** RF.5.3a **ELD** ELD.PIII.5

RETEACH

Coordinating Conjunctions

- Review that coordinating conjunctions are words such as *and, but, or, yet, for, and, nor,* and *so*. These words can be used to connect two complete thoughts.

- Ask students what conjunction they could use to connect these two complete thoughts: *Humans caused the oil spill. People worked together to clean it up.* (*so, and*)

Turn and Talk Have students reread the story to find examples of other complete thoughts that could be connected with a coordinating conjunction. (Responses will vary.) **ELA** L.5.1a **ELD** ELD.PII.5.6

Quick Check | Grammar

Have students write a sentence for each coordinating conjunction listed above.

Look Back and Respond

Write-In Reader pages 74–81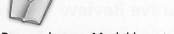

Help students complete the Look Back and Respond page. Model how to use the hint in Question 1 to find evidence that can be used to support answers.

- Explain that evidence is proof, clues, or information.

- Remind students that they can circle or underline the specific words in the selection that they used as evidence for their answers.

1. What effects does the oil spill have on the environment? (It harms the water, wildlife, and vegetation.) **ELA** RL.5.10, RF.5.4a **ELD** ELD.PIII.5

Help unpack meaning, if needed, by asking: *What problems does the oil cause on page 75?* (It covers the birds, sea animals, and vegetation.) *On page 79, why was Kim not allowed near the water?* (It was dirty.)

Unpack Meaning: For Questions 2–4, you may want to use the notes in the right-hand column to guide the discussion about student responses.

2. How does the oil spill affect the people of the town? (They learned that the consequences of human behavior can be bad and good.) **ELA** RL.5.10, RF.5.4a **ELD** ELD.PIII.5

3. Do you think the people succeeded in cleaning up the oil spill? (Possible response: The cleanup was good, but the long-term effects of the spill are still being felt.) **ELA** RL.5.10, RF.5.4a **ELD** ELD.PIII.5

Turn and Talk Have students work independently on Question 4. When students have completed the page, have partners discuss their responses and then share them with the group. Sample responses are provided. Accept reasonable responses. **ELA** SL.5.1b, SL.5.1d **ELD** ELD.PI.5.1

4. What point does the author make about taking responsibility? (The author makes the point that citizens have a responsibility to the environment and to wild animals, whether they caused the problems or not, and that companies have a responsibility to be more careful in doing things that could harm the environment in the first place.) **ELA** RL.5.2, RL.5.10, RF.5.4a **ELD** ELD.PI.5.6a, ELD.PIII.5

UNPACK MEANING

Use prompts such as these if students have difficulty with a question:

2. *On page 80, what does Kim say caused the oil spill?* (humans) *What does she say helped clean it up?* (people working together) **ELA** RL.5.1

3. *On page 79, what does the woman who works for the government say about the oil?* (She says that most of the oil has been removed.) *What else does she say about the town?* (She says that things will be much better in a year or two.) **ELA** RL.5.1

4. *On page 76, what do the citizens and mayor say about the cleanup effort?* (They say it is their duty as citizens to help clean the oil spill.) *On page 77, what responsibility do the students believe humans have?* (a responsibility to help wild animals) *On page 80, what lesson does the author say the oil companies may have learned?* (to regulate their shipping more carefully to prevent oil spills) **ELA** RL.5.1

EXTRA PRACTICE

Retell Have students retell "Oil Spill in Alaska" to a partner or family member. **ELA** RL.5.2

SHARE OBJECTIVES

- Read words with open syllables.
- Demonstrate understanding of Target Vocabulary words.
- Preview Conclusions/Generalizations and the Infer/Predict strategy.

MATERIALS

Context Cards: *adapted, attracted, conserving, endangered, guardians, regulate, responsibility, restore, unique, vegetation*

Write-In Reader pages 74–80

Leveled Reader: *Guardian of the Everglades*

TERMS ABOUT READING/ LANGUAGE ARTS

conclusion	generalization
infer	predict

☑ TARGET VOCABULARY

Something that is **adapted** for a certain purpose is especially designed for it.

To be **attracted** to something is to have your attention and interest drawn to it.

Conserving something is using it carefully so as not to waste it, use it all, or harm it.

Guardians are people who protect or take care of others.

Something that is **unique** is the only one of its kind.

ENGLISH LANGUAGE SUPPORT

Day 5

Oral Language Before students complete the Write About It activity, have them discuss with a partner how they plan to persuade people to help clean up the spill. **ELD** ELD.PI.5.1

Multisyllable Words

Cumulative Review

- Write these sentences on the board or on a pad.

  1. We can do some *basic* things to clean up.

  2. The pipes are *rusty* and *slimy*.

  3. They want to *resell* the swampland.

- Have student volunteers circle the multisyllable words with open syllables. Assign students to work with a partner to practice reading the sentences. Then listen to each student read one sentence. Record your findings.

  ELA RF.5.3a **ELD** ELD.PIII.5

Target Vocabulary

Context Cards

- Display the **Context Cards** for *adapted, attracted, conserving, guardians,* and *unique*. Review the meanings of these words. Then have students use the words in oral sentences about preventing oil spills.

- Add the **Context Cards** for *endangered, regulate, responsibility, restore,* and *vegetation*. Give one card to each student. Have students use their word to write a heading for a news article about the oil spill in Kim's town. Ask students to share their headlines. **ELA** L.5.6

WRITE ABOUT IT

- Ask students to think about what it may have been like to live in Kim's town during the oil spill. Have them write a one- or two-paragraph radio announcement to convince people of the community to come out and help clean up the spill. Ask students to use the word *responsibility* in their descriptions. **ELA** W.5.2b, W.5.2d

PRETEACH

Conclusions/Generalizations Infer/Predict

Write-In Reader pages 74–80

- Introduce skill and strategy. Say: *In the next lesson, we are going to focus on conclusions and generalizations. We'll also work on ways to infer and predict.*

- Explain: *Writers often use generalizations and conclusions to make larger points. Generalizations are broad statements about large groups of people or things. Conclusions are final thoughts on a topic, based on information.*

- Ask: *What was Kim's conclusion about the oil spill?* (Kim concludes that the oil companies need to regulate shipping to prevent more oil spills.) *What points did the writer of "Oil Spill in Alaska" use to make the conclusion convincing?* List the points on the board. **ELA** RL.5.2, RL.5.10, RF.5.4a **ELD** ELD.PI.5.6a, ELD.PIII.5

    Page 75: Waves carried the oil ashore. Oil covered plants and animals.

    Page 77: A student points out that humans made the mess, so they owe it to the animals to clean it up.

    Page 78: People worked for weeks.

    Page 79: Even after the cleanup ends, it takes a year or two for things to really get better.

    Page 80: Kim learns that people can have both bad and good effects on their environment.

- Turn to and review the Infer/Predict strategy found on page 304 in the **Write-In Reader**. Have students use the strategy to speculate on what the future holds for Kim's town and the surrounding coast. Ask: *Do you think there could ever be another oil spill? What clues from the text did you base your answer on?* **ELA** RL.5.1, RL.5.10, RF.5.4a **ELD** ELD.PI.5.11a, ELD.PIII.5

APPLY READING SKILLS

Introduce *Guardian of the Everglades*. Choral-read the first few pages with students. Depending on their abilities, students continue reading with partners or as a group.

Quick Check | Fluency

Listen to individual students as they read the **Write-In Reader** selection. Make specific notes about words that presented difficulty to them.

Leveled Reader

RETURN TO THE ANCHOR TEXT

"Be a Reading Detective!"

Student Book pages 239–249
Write-In Reader pages 81A–81B

- Page through "Everglades Forever" with students, and review the important ideas.

- Remind students about the target skill: **author's purpose.** Point out that an author provides details, reasons, and evidence to support particular points in the text.

- Have students answer the first question in the **Write-In Reader.** Remind them that a reading detective looks for clues.

- Circulate to offer assistance and to make sure that students are taking notes about evidence from the text.

- Have students write their responses.

SPIRAL REVIEW

- Review the skill **fact and opinion** with students. Remind them that a fact is a statement that can be proven true. An opinion is a person's thoughts, feelings, or beliefs, and it often includes adjectives or judgment words.

- Have students answer the second question in the **Write-In Reader.** Circulate to offer assistance and to make sure that they are taking notes about evidence from the text.

- Have students write their responses.

💬 **Classroom Collaboration**

Have pairs of "reading detectives" compare their responses and the clues they found in the text.

EXTRA PRACTICE

Independent Reading Have students read from a book of their choice and describe what they read in their reading logs.

DAY 1

SHARE OBJECTIVES

- Use subordinating conjunctions to make complex sentences.
- Discuss different types of emergencies and how they are handled.
- Read to build meaning for Target Vocabulary words.

MATERIALS

Write-In Reader pages 82–83

TERMS ABOUT READING/ LANGUAGE ARTS

conjunction   complex sentence

ENGLISH LANGUAGE SUPPORT

Day 1

Vocabulary When students complete the Quick Check activity, work with them to create a sentence for each of the multiple meanings of *critical* and *bundle*.

Sentence Frames Before leading the Warm Up, review the terms *compound sentence* and *complex sentence*. Guide students to use frames such as the following during the review: *To make a compound sentence, I use _____ conjunctions. In a compound sentence the ideas are of _____ importance. To make a complex sentence, I use _____ conjunctions. In a complex sentence, one idea is more _____ than the other.* **ELD** ELD.PII.5.6

Oral Language Read the teacher prompts in the Warm Up for students. Then have students choral-read the responses. After students read each example, ask: *What subordinating conjunction is used in this sentence? Which idea in this sentence is most important? How do you know?*
ELD ELD.PI.5.5

Oral Grammar

Complex Sentences

- Write the following subordinating conjunctions on the board.

after	if	unless	where	because	when
while	before	although	since	though	until

- Model by combining the first pair of sentences below to form one example of a complex sentence. Have students suggest an alternative.

- Then call on volunteers to combine subsequent sentences. **ELA** L.5.1a, L.5.3a **ELD** ELD.PII.5.6

Teacher Prompts	Student responds
First, I eat breakfast. Then, I get dressed.	After eating breakfast, I get dressed. Before I get dressed, I eat breakfast.
I always get up early. I love to watch the sunrise.	I always get up early because I love to watch the sunrise.
My sister plays the drums. My brother covers his ears.	When my sister plays the drums, my brother covers his ears. My brother covers his ears when my sister plays drums.

Talk About It

Help students share what they know about search and rescue workers. Ask: *What are some of the things that rescue workers face on the job?*

Discuss the questions, emphasizing these points:

- They fly in bad weather during storms and high winds.
- They rescue people from stormy seas.
- Sometimes they have to land in difficult places, such as hospital roofs and along roadways.
- They must be careful when helping injured people.
- They rush from one emergency site to another.

Target Vocabulary

Write-In Reader pages 82–83

• Read and discuss the passage. Then discuss the meaning of each Target Vocabulary word. Suggest that students underline words or phrases that provide clues to meaning. Also point out the following:

> Something that is *critical* is of great importance. *Critical* can also mean "tending to find fault with someone or something," as in *My friend is very critical of the way I wear my hair. Critical* can also be used to describe a patient who is in great medical danger, as in *He was in critical condition after the accident.*

> In this instance, *bundle* means "to dress or wrap someone warmly." *Bundle* can also mean "a number of things tied or held together," as in *We collected twigs and wrapped them into a bundle to use at our campsite.* **ELA** L.5.4a, L.5.6

• Ask students to choose an answer they would like to read aloud.

Responses:

1. critical

2. clammy

3. demolished

4. bundle

5. commotion

Quick Check | **Target Vocabulary**

Ask each student to use one of the Target Vocabulary words in a sentence.

DAY 2

SHARE OBJECTIVES

- Read words with open syllables.
- Make conclusions as you read.
- Read on-level text to apply skills and strategies.

MATERIALS

Write-In Reader pages 84–87

TERMS ABOUT READING/ LANGUAGE ARTS

conclusion	generalization
infer	predict

ENGLISH LANGUAGE SUPPORT

Day 2

Vocabulary Help students build a word bank of synonyms for *infer* to use during the Quick Check activity. Sample words and phrases: *conclude, generalize, read between the lines.*

Sentence Frames Guide students sentence frames such as the following when responding to the Quick Check activity. *If the audience is crying, I can conclude that the scene is ___ because _____ .* **ELD** ELD.PI.5.11a

Oral Language Before students read, invite them to share their predictions with a partner. After finishing the page-by-page choral reading, have partners point out the text evidence that proves their prediction was right or wrong to each other. **ELD** ELD.PI.5.1, ELD.PI.5.11a

Warm Up

Multisyllable Words

Focus: Open Syllables

Write these words on the board or on a pad.

1	selfishly	cunningly	bashfully
2	sluggishly	haplessly	commonly
3	splendidly	absently	abstractly

Row 1: Ask: *How are these words alike?* (They all have an *-ly* ending.) Divide the words using the vowel-consonant-consonant-vowel letter pattern and *-ly* ending. Blend syllables to read each word.

sel / f ish/ ly	cun/ning/ly	bash/ful/ly
V C C V	V C C V	V C C V

Rows 2–3: Have volunteers identify the VCCV letter patterns to divide and read the words. **ELA** RF.5.3a **ELD** ELD.PIII.3

RETEACH

Conclusions/Generalizations

- Pick up a letter or memo and role-play reading it silently. Then look very happy. Ask: *What can you guess about my letter?* Draw a chart to show the relationship.

Clues		Conclusion
I read a letter. I looked happy.	→	The letter had good news.

- Remind students that sometimes a reader needs to draw a conclusion about what the author means.

- Ask students to name a story that they have read. Ask them to draw a conclusion about the story's theme or one of the characters. Ask: *What clues led you to reach this conclusion?*

- Remind students that a generalization is a broad statement that is true most of the time. Ask: *What generalization can you make about rescue workers?* (They want to help people.)

Quick Check **Comprehension**

Have students respond to the following: *What can you conclude about a scene in a movie if the audience is crying?*

READ

"The Rescue Helicopter Team"

Write-In Reader pages 84–87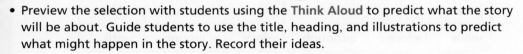

- Preview the selection with students using the **Think Aloud** to predict what the story will be about. Guide students to use the title, heading, and illustrations to predict what might happen in the story. Record their ideas.

> **Think Aloud** *On the first page, I see pictures of rescue workers and a life jacket. I think this story must have something to do with a water rescue. What other clues help you predict the story?*

- Together, review the steps to the Infer/Predict strategy, **Write-In Reader** page 304. As needed, guide students in applying the strategy as they read.

READ

Ask students to read to confirm their predictions. Then choral-read page by page with students. Discuss, confirm, and revise student predictions based upon text details.
ELA RL.5.10, RF.5.4a **ELD** ELD.PIII.5

REREAD

Call on individuals to read aloud while others follow along. Stop to discuss each question. Allow time for students to write their responses before proceeding. Sample answers are provided.

Page 84: Why does the helicopter rescue team do most of its work in bad weather? (That is when most people need help.) **ELA** RL.5.1, RL.5.10, RF.5.4a **ELD** ELD.PIII.5

Help unpack meaning, if needed, by asking: *Why did the helicopter team think they would not be busy?* (It was a perfect day.) *Why did the sky color and wind speed change?* (A storm was blowing in.)

Unpack Meaning: For questions on pages 85–87, you may want to use the notes in the right-hand column.

Page 85: What happens to something that is <u>demolished</u>? (It is destroyed.)
ELA RL.5.4, RF.5.4c, L.5.4a **ELD** ELD.PIII.5

Page 86: Why is it going to be a busy day after all? (There is an emergency that the rescue team must attend to.) **ELA** RL.5.1, RL.5.10, RF.5.4a **ELD** ELD.PIII.5

Turn and Talk **Page 87:** What causes the <u>commotion</u> at the scene of the rescue? (the noise of the storm and the helicopter) Have partners discuss their answers and then share with the group. **ELA** RL.5.1, RL.5.10, RF.5.4a **ELD** ELD.PIII.5

UNPACK MEANING

Use prompts such as these if students have difficulty with a **Stop•Think•Write** question:

Page 85 *What happened to the boat's sails?* (They were ripped by the strength of the storm.) *Why did Elena send a distress call?* (The damage to the boat was severe.)

Page 86 *Why did the controller talk with Elena?* (to find out what Elena's situation was) *What did the controller do next?* (alerted the team, gave them details)

Page 87 *What sounds did the blowing rain, wind, and waves make?* (Responses will vary but may include a howling roar or a crashing sound.) *Have you ever seen a helicopter in person, in a movie, or on a television show? Describe the experience.* (Responses will vary.)

EXTRA PRACTICE

Build Fluency Have students read **Write-In Reader** pages 84–87 with a partner or a family member.

DAY 3

SHARE OBJECTIVES

- Use subordinating conjunctions to make complex sentences.
- Read aloud fluently, using punctuation to help with phrasing.
- Read on-level text to apply skills and strategies.

MATERIALS

Write-In Reader pages 88–90

TERMS ABOUT READING/ LANGUAGE ARTS

subordinate conjunction   **complex sentence**

phrasing   **expression**

punctuation

ENGLISH LANGUAGE SUPPORT

Day 3

Vocabulary Help students build a word bank to use during the Turn and Talk activity. Use gestures, expressions, and pictures to show the meanings of the words. Sample words and phrases: *crew, rescue, emergency, hospital, medical treatment, landing pad.*

Sentence Frames Guide students to use frames similar to these as they complete the Quick Check: *After the storm hit, _____. Rescue crews responded by _____. The ending shows that rescue helicopter teams are _____.* **ELD** ELD.PII.5.2b

Oral Language As you read page 88 aloud, ask students to listen to what happens to your voice when you come to the end of a sentence. Guide them to notice that your pitch drops when you come to a period and rises when you ask a question.

Oral Grammar

Complex Sentences

- Write the following subordinating conjunctions on the board.

after	if	unless	where	because	when
while	before	although	since	though	until

- Have students use a subordinating conjunction to combine two sentences to make a complex sentence. Then encourage other students to provide additional examples. **ELA** L.5.1a, L.5.3a **ELD** ELD.PII.5.6

Teacher prompts	Student responds
On Saturday, I play soccer. I do not play soccer if it rains.	Unless it rains, I play soccer on Saturdays. I play soccer on Saturdays when it isn't raining. I play soccer on Saturdays, although (or though) not when it is raining.
We like to go to the park. The park we like has lots of trees.	We like to go to the park where there are lots of trees. The park where we like to go has a lot of trees.

RETEACH

Fluency: Phrasing

Write-In Reader page 88

Explain that you are going to read page 88 and that you want students to evaluate your reading. Ask students to follow along as you read aloud.

- Read the text, rushing over punctuation and pausing inappropriately. Ask: *What did you think of my reading? Explain.* Be sure students recognize that your reading was flawed. Point out that punctuation helps readers form phrases and add expression to their reading.

- Have students follow along as you read the passage correctly. After reading, discuss how responding to punctuation correctly helps listeners better understand a reading. Then have students practice reading the page aloud, using appropriate phrasing as they read. **ELA** RF.5.4b **ELD** ELD.PIII.5

READ

"The Rescue Helicopter Team"

Write-In Reader pages 88–90

Review the first part of the story with students. Ask: *What has happened in the rescue team's day so far?* Then preview today's reading. Have students look at headings, photographs, and illustrations for clues to help them predict what will happen next in the story. **ELA** RL.5.2, RF.5.4a **ELD** ELD.PIII.5

READ

Ask students to read to confirm their predictions. Then have students choral-read page by page with you. Discuss, confirm, and revise predictions based upon text details. Ask if there was anything about the way the story ended that surprised them. **ELA** RL.5.10, RF.5.4a **ELD** ELD.PIII.5

REREAD

Call on individuals to read aloud while others follow along. Stop to discuss each question. Allow time for students to write their responses before proceeding. Sample answers are provided.

Page 88: Why do you think a rescue crew needs to stay calm? (In an emergency situation, people needing help can be fearful, hurt, in shock, or out of control. Rescue crew members must stay calm and in control to properly do their job.)

Help unpack meaning, if needed, by asking: *What does a boat do in a crashing sea?* (It rocks violently up and down and from side to side.) *What would the helicopter pilot have to do to keep the helicopter over the boat?* (The pilot would have to concentrate.)

Unpack Meaning: For questions on pages 89–90, you may want to use the notes in the right-hand column.

Page 89: Why can't the ambulance rescue the hurt driver? (Trees and other objects blown by the storm are probably blocking the roads. These would block an ambulance's way to the wreck.) **ELA** RL.5.1, RL.5.10, RF.5.4a **ELD** ELD.PIII.5

Turn and Talk **Page 90:** What do you think happens after the helicopter lands on the hospital roof? (The patient is brought to the hospital's medical team.) Have partners discuss this question and then share with the group. **ELA** SL.5.1b, SL.5.1d **ELD** ELD.PI.5.1

Quick Check | Retelling

Have students retell the end of the story. Support the retelling by asking: *What happens to Manny? How does the storm affect people on land?*

UNPACK MEANING

Use prompts such as these if students have difficulty with a **Stop•Think•Write** question:

Page 89 *What does the text "the storm had hit hard on land" mean?* (The destruction must have been bad there, too.) *What do you see in the photograph?* (an overturned car, roofing material, downed trees) **ELA** RL.5.4, RL.5.7

Page 90 *Who are the people in white coats in the illustration?* (doctors and nurses) *Who is the bed in the illustration for?* (the injured driver) **ELA** RL.5.7

EXTRA PRACTICE

Build Fluency Have students read **Write-In Reader** pages 88–90 with a partner or a family member.

DAY 4

SHARE OBJECTIVES

- Read words with open and closed syllables.
- Identify conjunctions and dependent and independent clauses.
- Support answers to questions with evidence from the text.

MATERIALS

Write-In Reader pages 84–91

TERMS ABOUT READING/ LANGUAGE ARTS

complex sentence   conjunction

dependent clause   independent clause

ENGLISH LANGUAGE SUPPORT

Day 4

Vocabulary Warm Up root words such as *candid, tempt,* and *handy* may be unfamiliar to students. Use visuals, examples, and simple explanations to support understanding.

Sentence Frames Guide students to use text evidence when participating in the Turn and Talk activity. Use frames such as the following: *An example from the text that shows why working on a rescue helicopter team can be dangerous is _____. An example that shows why rescue helicopters are needed is _____ because _____.* **ELD** ELD.PI.5.1, ELD.PI.5.6a

Oral Language Before students complete the Complex Sentences Turn and Talk, review the terms *complex sentence, conjunction, dependent clause,* and *independent clause.* Then think aloud as you model how to follow the Turn and Talk directions. Finally, ask students to work with a partner to find complex sentences in the first two paragraphs on page 84. **ELD** ELD.PII.5.6

Multisyllable Words

Focus: Open and closed Syllables

Write these words on the board or on a pad.

1	candidly	unlucky	thrillingly
2	unjustly	temptingly	splendidly
3	trustingly	unhandy	selfishly

Row 1: Ask: *What endings do these words have?* (They have a letter *-y* or *-ly* ending.) Identify the VCCV or VCV pattern and divide the words. Then divide before the *-y* or *-ly* ending. Remind students that the letters *ck* act as one letter sound.

  c a n / d i d / l y   u n / l u c k / y   t h r i l / l i n g / l y

    V C C V   V C V   V C C V

Rows 2–3: Have volunteers identify the letter patterns and divide before the *-y* or *-ly* ending. Have them blend the syllables to read the words. **ELA** RF.5.3a **ELD** ELD.PIII.5

RETEACH

Complex Sentences

- Review that complex sentences can be made up of an independent clause and a dependent clause. A dependent clause does not express a complete thought and cannot stand alone as a sentence.

- Remind students that dependent clauses begin with a subordinating conjunction, such as *because, after, although, as, before, if, since, while, when,* and *until.* **ELA** L.5.1a, L.5.3a **ELD** ELD.PII.5.6

Turn and Talk Have students reread the first paragraph on page 84 to find the complex sentence. Have them identify whether the sentence has two independent clauses or an independent and dependent clause.

Quick Check   **Grammar**

Have students continue the exercise for the remaining two paragraphs.

Look Back and Respond

Write-In Reader pages 84–91

Help students complete the Look Back and Respond page. Model how to use the hint in Question 1 to find evidence that can be used to support answers. **ELA** W.5.1b **ELD** ELD.PI.5.6a

• Explain that evidence is proof, clues, or information.

• Remind students that they can circle or underline the specific words in the selection that they used as evidence for their answers.

1. Would working on a rescue helicopter team be dangerous? Explain. (Yes, because weather conditions and locations can be challenging.)

Help unpack meaning, if needed, by asking: *How would you describe the scene on page 87?* (dangerous, frightening) *How would you describe the scene on page 88?* (difficult, challenging, life-threatening) **ELA** RL.5.3, RL.5.10, RF.5.4a **ELD** ELD.PIII.5

Turn and Talk Have students work independently on Questions 2–4. When students have completed the page, have partners discuss their responses and then share them with the group. Sample responses are provided. Accept all reasonable responses. **ELA** SL.5.1b, SL.5.1d **ELD** ELD.PI.5.1

Unpack Meaning: For Questions 2–4, you may want to use the notes in the right-hand column to guide the discussion about student responses.

2. Why are rescue helicopters needed? (They can reach places quickly that automobiles and boats cannot.) **ELA** RL.5.10, RF.5.4a **ELD** ELD.PIII.5

3. Why might a hospital have a helicopter pad on the roof instead of on the ground? (It might be easier for the helicopter to land on the roof, away from trees and telephone wires. Also, patients might be transferred more directly into the hospital's care.)

4. In what ways can bad weather cause disasters? (A bad storm can cause many dangerous situations and many kinds of damage on land and water.) **ELA** RL.5.1

UNPACK MEANING

Use prompts such as these if students have difficulty with a question:

2. *Look at the illustration on page 87. What might have happened if a rescue boat had been sent out?* (It might have been overturned or damaged by the stormy seas, too.) *Why is the helicopter rescue team always on call?* (They are trained to react at a moment's notice.) **ELA** RL.5.7

3. *Have you ever seen a helicopter land? Describe what you saw.* (Responses will vary, but students may have noticed that people are careful of the helicopter's rotating blades and the wind they create.) *Have you ever been to a hospital complex? What did it look like?* (Responses will vary but may include that students saw many buildings close together, surrounded by busy roads, trees, and telephone wires.)

4. *What is the weather like in the picture on page 85?* (very stormy) *What can happen in stormy seas?* (Boats can capsize; people can drown.) *What do you see in the picture on page 89?* (a car wreck with injured people) *What caused the accident?* (bad weather) **ELA** RL.5.7

EXTRA PRACTICE

Retell Have students retell "The Rescue Helicopter Team" to a partner or a family member. **ELA** RL.5.2

DAY 5

SHARE OBJECTIVES

- Read words with open syllables.
- Demonstrate understanding of Target Vocabulary words.
- Preview Main Idea and Details and Monitor/Clarify strategy.

MATERIALS

Context Cards: *annoyance, bundle, critical, clammy, commotion, demolished, elite, realization, secured, squalling*

Write-In Reader pages 84–90

Leveled Reader: *Sugaring Weather*

TERMS ABOUT READING/ LANGUAGE ARTS

main idea   detail

TARGET VOCABULARY

An **annoyance** is something that is irritating.

A small group of individuals who are the best at what they do is **elite**.

A **realization** is a sudden awareness.

An object is **secured** when it is held down tightly.

Squalling is loud crying.

ENGLISH LANGUAGE SUPPORT

Day 5

Vocabulary Help students build a word bank of description and action words to use during the Write About It activity. Use gestures, expressions, and pictures to show the meanings of any unfamiliar words.

Oral Language Have students work with a partner to write a brief summary of the main idea of "The Rescue Helicopter Team." Invite them to read their summaries aloud. **ELD** ELD.PI.5.10b

Multisyllable Words
Cumulative Review

- Write these sentences on the board or on a pad.

    1. The storm watchers were unlucky that day.

    2. He said candidly that this storm could be bad.

    3. The sky was splendidly bright and hazy.

- Have student volunteers circle the multisyllable words with open syllables. Assign students to work with a partner to practice reading the sentences. Then listen to each student read one sentence. Record your findings.
ELA RF.5.3a **ELD** ELD.PIII.5

REVIEW

Target Vocabulary
Context Cards

- Display the **Context Cards** for *bundle, critical, clammy, commotion,* and *demolished.* Review the meanings of these words. Then have students use the words in oral sentences about the aftermath of an emergency.

- Show the **Context Cards** for *annoyance, elite, realization, secured,* and *squalling.* Assign one card to each student. Have students make up a riddle for their word. Then have them take turns reading aloud their riddles. The other students should identify the vocabulary word that correctly solves the riddle.

WRITE ABOUT IT

- Ask students to write a report from the point of view of the helicopter rescue team controller. Have them describe the two rescue events in the story, using the word *squalling* in their reports. **ELA** W.5.2d, W.5.4 **ELD** ELD.PI.5.10b

PRETEACH

Main Ideas and Details
Monitor/Clarify

Write-In Reader pages 84–90

- Introduce skill and strategy. Say: *In the next lesson, we are going to focus on the main ideas and details in a story. We'll also work on ways to monitor/clarify our understanding of the story.*

- Explain: *Most paragraphs have a main idea. The main idea is the most important idea. The main idea may be stated directly. Other times the reader may have to infer the main idea. Supporting details tell more about the main idea.*

- Say: *Read page 90 of "The Rescue Helicopter Team."* Ask: *Is the main idea stated directly?* (No)

- Ask: *How can we determine the main idea?* (Examine supporting details.) Invite students to offer supporting details. (The rescue helicopter team does most of their work in bad weather. The team responds to emergencies on land and sea. They sometimes respond to several emergencies in a day.) **ELA** RL.5.2, RL.5.5, RL.5.10, RF.5.4a **ELD** ELD.PII.5.1, ELD.PIII.5

- Ask: *What is the main idea?* (Rescue helicopter teams often perform heroic rescues in many different situations.) **ELA** RL.5.2, RL.5.10, RF.5.4a **ELD** ELD.PIII.5

APPLY READING SKILLS

Introduce *Sugaring Weather*. Choral-read the first few pages with students. Depending on their abilities, have students continue reading with partners or as a group.

Leveled Reader

Quick Check | Fluency

Listen to individual students as they read the **Write-In Reader** selection. Make specific notes about words or punctuation that presented difficulty to them.

RETURN TO THE ANCHOR TEXT

"Be a Reading Detective!"
Student Book pages 267–277
Write-In Reader pages 91A–91B

- Page through "Storm Warriors" with students, and review the main characters and events.

- Remind students about the target skill: **conclusions and generalizations.** Point out that conclusions are decisions based on information not stated directly in the text. A generalization is a broad statement that is true most of the time.

- Have students answer the first question in the **Write-In Reader**. Remind them that a reading detective looks for clues.

- Circulate to offer assistance and to make sure that students are taking notes about evidence from the text.

- Have students write their responses.

SPIRAL REVIEW

- Review the skill **understanding characters** with students. Remind them that a character's actions and words let the reader know just what the character is like.

- Have students answer the second question in the **Write-In Reader**. Circulate to offer assistance and to make sure that they are taking notes about evidence from the text.

- Have students write their responses.

💬 Classroom Collaboration

Have pairs of "reading detectives" compare their responses and the clues they found in the text.

EXTRA PRACTICE

Independent Reading Have students read from a book of their choice and describe what they read in their reading logs.

DAY 1

SHARE OBJECTIVES

- Use punctuation correctly in quotations.
- Discuss why some species of animals are endangered.
- Read to build meaning for Target Vocabulary words.

MATERIALS

Write-In Reader pages 92–93

TERMS ABOUT READING/LANGUAGE ARTS

quotation mark   punctuation

ENGLISH LANGUAGE SUPPORT

Day 1

Vocabulary Help students build a word bank to use during the Talk About It activity. Use questions such as these to help students build the bank. *What are bison? Where did they live? How did they help the Plains American Indians survive?*

Sentence Frames Discuss the target vocabulary word *unobserved* with students. Then work with them to make a list of other words beginning with *un-*, such as *unheard, unfed,* or *unspoken.* Guide students to explore the meaning of these words by using this frame: *When I add un- to the word _____, the word means "_____."* **ELD** ELD.PI.5.12b, ELD.PIII.5

Oral Language Help students practice punctuating quotations by asking volunteers to respond to questions such as *What is your favorite food?* Then write the response on the board in an unpunctuated sentence like the one in the first bullet of the Warm Up activity; for example, *Tan said pad thai is his favorite food.* Guide students to apply the four steps in punctuating a quotation to each sentence. **ELD** ELD.PI.5.1

Warm Up

Oral Grammar

Quotations

- Write this sentence on the board with no punctuation: *Maria asked do dogs make good pets.*
- Model four steps for punctuating a quotation.

  1. Look for the exact quotation and insert quotation marks around it.
  2. Punctuate the quotation.
  3. Capitalize the first word of the quotation.
  4. Insert a comma before the quotation if the speaker's name and the verb (*asked, said*) appear before the quotation.

Example: *Maria asked, "Do dogs make good pets?"*

- Provide a topic for students (e.g., soccer). Call on a student to say a declarative or interrogative sentence about the topic. Write the sentence on the board with the quotation. Do not punctuate it or address capitalization rules.
- Call on students to perform each of the steps to punctuate the sentence.
- Continue calling on students to provide sentences and to follow the steps for punctuating the sentence.

Talk About It

Help focus students' attention on bison. Ask: *What do you know about bison?*

Discuss the question, emphasizing these points:

- Bison are very large and powerful animals.
- They populated the Great Plains in large numbers.
- Herds moved great distances throughout the year in search of grasslands.
- Plains American Indians depended on the bison for food, clothing, and shelter.
- European settlers almost wiped out the bison population as they moved west.
- The government finally stepped in and protected the bison.

Target Vocabulary

Write-In Reader pages 92–93

- Read and discuss each paragraph. Then discuss the meaning of each Target Vocabulary word. Suggest that students underline words or phrases that provide clues to meaning. Also point out the following:

    In this instance, *ferocious* means "fierce and savage." The word can also mean "very intense," as in *The candidates had a ferocious debate*.

    The word *unobserved* begins with the prefix *un-*, which means "the opposite of; not." The word *observed* means "to watch or see." When adding *un-* to *observed*, the meaning becomes the opposite, "unseen." **ELA** RI.5.4, RF.5.4c, L.5.4a, L.5.6 **ELD** ELD.PIII.5

- Allow students time to respond. Then ask students to choose an answer they would like to read aloud.

    Possible answers:

    1. Many students will list common groceries.

    2. birds flying overhead; bugs crawling through the grass; squirrels sitting in tree branches

    3. sight, hearing

    4. Grizzly bears, lions, tigers, and sharks; they will attack people if they feel threatened.

    5. intense or strong

Quick Check Target Vocabulary

Ask each student to use one of the Target Vocabulary words in a sentence.

✅ TARGET VOCABULARY

Something that is **available** is ready to be used or taken.

Detecting something means discovering that it exists or is present.

A person or animal that is **ferocious** is fierce and savage.

Something that is **keen** is very quick, sharp, or sensitive.

Something that is **unobserved** is unseen.

EXTRA PRACTICE

Build Fluency Have students read **Write-In Reader** pages 92–93 with a partner or a family member.

DAY 2

SHARE OBJECTIVES

- Read words with open syllables.
- Determine main ideas and details.
- Read on-level text to apply skills and strategies.

MATERIALS

Write-In Reader pages 94–97

TERMS ABOUT READING/ LANGUAGE ARTS

main idea	detail
monitor	clarify

ENGLISH LANGUAGE SUPPORT

Day 2

Vocabulary Ask students to explain the relationship between the main idea and details in their own words. Then review the terms *monitor* and *clarify*.

Sentence Frames Guide students to use this frame when responding to the Turn and Talk activity: *The author compares bison to ___ to show _____.* **ELD** ELD.PI.5.6a

Oral Language Before students complete the Quick Check, work with them to list ideas from the paragraph they read on the board. Then guide them to summarize the paragraph, using this frame: *The main idea of this paragraph is _____. Details that support main ideas are _____ and _____.* **ELD** ELD.PI.5.10b

Warm Up

Multisyllable Words
Cumulative Review

- Write these sentences on the board or on a pad.
  1. The photo shows a baby bison.
  2. The kitten cunningly followed the rodent.
  3. It likes to be lazy in the morning.
- Have student volunteers circle the multisyllable words with open syllables. Assign students to work with a partner to practice reading the sentences. Then listen to each student read one sentence. Record your findings.
  ELA RF.5.3a **ELD** ELD.PIII.5

RETEACH

Main Ideas and Details

- Hold up a newspaper and read a short paragraph from an article of interest to students. Write the topic of the article on the board. Then ask: *What is the most important idea in this paragraph? What facts and examples does the author give to tell about this idea?*
- Remind students that an author may organize material around a main idea. The supporting details tell more about the main idea.
- Use an Idea-Support Map to show the main idea and details in the paragraph.
- Explain that when an author uses a main idea-support details structure, the paragraphs give main ideas about a topic. The supporting details give more information about the main idea in each paragraph. **ELA** RI.5.2, RI.5.3 **ELD** ELD.PI.5.6a

Quick Check   Comprehension

Ask students to find and read a paragraph in a magazine or newspaper. Have them state the main idea and the supporting details.

READ

"Bison Come Back to the Plains"
Write-In Reader pages 94–97

- Preview the selection with students using the **Think Aloud** to predict what the story is about. Record their ideas.

> **Think Aloud** *The title is "Bison Come Back to the Plains." I think this story will be about the history of the bison population in the United States. What other clues can help you make predictions?*

- Together, review the steps to the Monitor/Clarify Strategy, **Write-In Reader** page 304. As needed, guide students in applying the strategy as they read.

READ

Ask students to read to confirm their predictions. Then choral-read page by page with students. Discuss, confirm, and revise student predictions based upon text details.
ELA RI.5.10, RF.5.4a **ELD** ELD.PIII.5

REREAD

Call on individuals to read aloud while others follow along. Stop to discuss each question. Allow time for students to write their responses before proceeding. Sample answers are provided.

Page 94: Why did people say the Great Plains looked like "oceans of grass"? (The tall grass swaying in the wind looks like waves.) **ELA** RI.5.4

Help unpack meaning, if needed, by asking: *What is the land like in the Great Plains?* (The land is flat, with few trees to block the wind.) *What happens to the ocean's surface in the wind?* (The wind creates waves.)

Unpack Meaning: For questions on pages 95–97, you may want to use the notes in the right-hand column.

Page 95: Why would bison have to travel to find <u>available</u> fresh grass? (The bison traveled south during winter to warmer areas where they could find more grass growing.) **ELA** RI.5.4, RF.5.4c, L.5.6 **ELD** ELD.PIII.5

> **Turn and Talk** **Page 96:** What animal does the author compare to bison to show how fast the bison were? (horses) **ELA** RI.5.10, RF.5.4a **ELD** ELD.PIII.5

Page 97: How did the Plains Indians' hunting methods change after they began using horses? (They could hunt on horseback using bows and arrows, making hunting much easier.) Have partners discuss this question and then share with the group.

Use prompts such as these if students have difficulty with a **Stop•Think•Write** question:

Page 95 *What does the word* available *mean?* (ready to be used or taken) *In what seasons does grass grow?* (mostly in spring and summer) *What would bison have to do if there were not enough grass?* (migrate to places where there was more grass growing)

Page 96 *Underline the information in the text that helps you respond to the question.* (They could run as fast as horses.)

Page 97 *Before settlers arrived, how did Plains Indians kill bison?* (They drove the bison off a cliff.) *Why was this hunting method inefficient?* (They could not control how many bison fell over the cliff.)

EXTRA PRACTICE

Build Fluency Have students reread **Write-In Reader** pages 94–97 with a partner or a family member.

SHARE OBJECTIVES

- Use punctuation correctly for quotations and interjections.
- Read aloud fluently to improve stress.
- Read on-level text to apply skills and strategies.

MATERIALS

Write-In Reader pages 96, 98–100

TERMS ABOUT READING/ LANGUAGE ARTS

stress   emphasis

ENGLISH LANGUAGE SUPPORT

Day 3

Vocabulary Help students build a word bank of feeling words to use during the Turn and Talk activity. Use gestures, expressions, and pictures to show the meanings of the words. Sample words: *keen, sharp, sense, hearing, predator.*

Sentence Frames Teach terms and give a sentence frame to help students participate in the Turn and Talk activity. Review the term *explain.* Say that to explain something is to tell why you think the way you do. Point out that the word *because* can be used in an explanation. Guide students to use this frame. *I think Jen's feelings change because _____.* **ELD** ELD.PI.5.1, ELD.PI.5.11a, ELD.PII.5.6

Oral Language Guide students to write a summary of the rest of "Bison Come Back to the Plains" as a class. Use this summary frame and write their responses on the board. *The Plains American Indians depended on the bison for _____. After European settlers arrived, _____. Today, the bison population is _____ because _____.* Guide students to choral-read the finished summary several times. Then have partners take turns summarizing the second part of this story to each other. **ELD** ELD.PI.5.2, ELD.PI.5.10b, ELD.PII.5.2b

Oral Grammar

Quotations and Interjections

- Write: *hey look out for the snake yelled Sandy*
- Model these steps to punctuating a quotation.
  1. Insert quotation marks around the exact words spoken.
  2. Punctuate the quotation. If it begins with an interjection, insert a comma or an exclamation point after the interjection.
  3. Capitalize the first word of the quotation.
  4. Insert a comma before the quotation if the speaker's name and the verb (*yelled*) appear before the quotation. If the quotation occurs first, the punctuation precedes the verb and the name of the speaker.

Examples:

"Hey, look out for the snake!" yelled Sandy.
Sandy yelled, "Hey, look out for the snake!"

- Provide students with a topic. Call on a student to provide a sentence with an interjection. Work with the class to write the student's quotation with correct punctuation and capitalization. **ELA** L.5.1a **ELD** ELD.PII.5.6

RETEACH

Fluency: Stress

Write-In Reader page 96

Explain that you are going to read from page 96 and that you want students to evaluate your reading.

- First, read the first paragraph in a monotone voice. Then, read the same paragraph with feeling, using natural stress and intonation to emphasize key words and ideas, such as *very important, depended on, food, clothing,* and *shelter.*

- Ask: *What did you think of my first reading? Explain. Was my second reading better? Explain.* Be sure students recognize that appropriate expression helps listeners understand.

- Have partners take turns reading aloud the second paragraph on the page. Tell them to concentrate on emphasizing words and phrases that tell the most important and interesting pieces of information. **ELA** RF.5.4a **ELD** ELD.PIII.5

READ

"Bison Come Back to the Plains"

Write-In Reader pages 98–100

Review the first part of the story with students. Ask: *What have we learned about bison so far?* Then preview today's reading. Have students look for clues to help them predict what else they might learn about bison. **ELA** RI.5.2

READ

Ask students to read to confirm their predictions. Have students choral-read with you. Discuss, confirm, and revise predictions based upon text details. Ask if there was anything about the way the story ended that surprised them. **ELA** RI.5.10, RF.5.4a **ELD** ELD.PIII.5

REREAD

Call on individuals to read aloud while others follow along. Stop to discuss each question. Allow time for students to write their responses before proceeding. Sample answers are provided.

Page 98: Write three details that tell how American Indians used different parts of the bison. (They used bison skins to make teepees and clothes, bones to make tools, and dried bison meat for food.) **ELA** RI.5.2, RI.5.10, RF.5.4a **ELD** ELD.PIII.5

Help unpack meaning, if needed, by asking: *Were the Plains Indians wasteful?* (No, they used every part of the animals they hunted.) *What did the Plains Indians use to stay warm?* (fur coats, blankets, snug shelters)

Unpack Meaning: For questions on pages 99–100, you may want to use the notes in the right-hand column.

Page 99: Write two details that describe people's efforts to save bison. (Laws protecting bison have been passed; national parks provide a safe place for bison to roam free.) **ELA** RI.5.2, RI.5.10, RF.5.4a **ELD** ELD.PIII.5

Turn and Talk **Page 100:** How would a <u>keen</u> sense of hearing protect an animal? (It would enable the animal to hear an approaching predator.) Have partners discuss this question and then share their answers with the group. **ELA** RI.5.4, RI.5.10, RF.5.4a, L.5.6 **ELD** ELD.PIII.5

Quick Check | Retelling

Have students retell the last part of the story. Support the retelling by asking: *In what ways were bison important to American Indians? What happened to the bison after settlers from Europe arrived?* **ELA** RI.5.2

UNPACK MEANING

Use prompts such as these if students have difficulty with a **Stop•Think•Write** question:

Page 99 *Underline the details from the text that answer the question.* (Some men and women saved a group of bison that were left. The government passed laws protecting bison. National parks were created where bison would be cared for and protected.)

Page 100 *What does the word* keen *mean?* (sharp or sensitive) *What does it mean if someone has a keen sense of hearing?* (He or she hears very well.)

EXTRA PRACTICE

Build Fluency Have students reread **Write-In Reader** pages 98–100 with a partner or a family member.

SHARE OBJECTIVES

- Read words with open or closed syllables.
- Identify correct punctuation for quotations and interjections.
- Support answers to questions with evidence from the text.

MATERIALS

Write-In Reader pages 94–101

TERMS ABOUT READING/ LANGUAGE ARTS

punctuation   comma

quotation mark   interjection

ENGLISH LANGUAGE SUPPORT

Day 4

Vocabulary Work with students to make up or find examples of interjection. Examples: *Look out! Wow! Oh, my!*

Sentence Frames Guide students to use text evidence when participating in the Turn and Talk activity. Use frames such as the following to support the discussion: *The bison almost disappeared because _____. In the future, I predict that the bison population will _____ because _____.* **ELD** ELD.PI.5.3, ELD.PI.5.11a

Oral Language Work with students to create a brief dialogue. Write students' suggestions of what the characters in the dialogue might say on the board. Then ask students to tell you how to punctuate each line of dialogue. After the dialogue is finished, designate some students to read one character's lines and another group to read the second character's lines. Have students choral-read the dialogue until they can do it fluently. **ELD** ELD.PI.5.2

Warm Up

Multisyllable Words
Cumulative Review

- Write these sentences on the board or on a pad.

  1. They selfishly ruin our wild places.

  2. The deer looks temptingly tasty to the big cat.

  3. The bison was unjustly seen as a threat.

- Have student volunteers circle the multisyllable words with open syllables. Assign students to work with a partner to practice reading the sentences. Then listen to each student read one sentence. Make corrections as needed. Record your findings. **ELA** RF.5.3a **ELD** ELD.PIII.5

RETEACH

Quotations; Interjections

- Review that a quotation is a person's exact words, either spoken or in print. Remind students that they must use appropriate punctuation when quoting a person. Write the following sentence on the board: *Bison were once "the kings of the plains."*

- Ask: *What part of this sentence is a quotation from the text?* ("the kings of the plains") *How do you know these are the author's exact words?* (The words are written inside quotation marks.) Direct students to page 94 and have them find the quotation.

Turn and Talk Ask students to name another instance when writers use quotation marks. (dialogue) Then have students discuss punctuation used to indicate direct quotations.

Possible answer: We use quotation marks and a comma when we write dialogue. (Myra said, "I am going to Peru in March.")

- Remind students that dialogue may include interjections—words or phrases that show emotion, such as *hey* and *wow*. Ask: *What punctuation mark may follow an interjection?* (a comma or an exclamation point) **ELA** L.5.1b

Quick Check   Grammar

Have students write two or three examples of quotations, using the appropriate punctuation. Encourage them to use an interjection in one of their quotations.

Look Back and Respond

Write-In Reader pages 94–101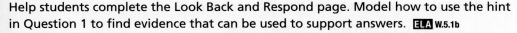

Help students complete the Look Back and Respond page. Model how to use the hint in Question 1 to find evidence that can be used to support answers. **ELA** W.5.1b

• Explain that evidence is proof, clues, or information.

• Remind students that they can circle or underline the specific words in the selection that they used as evidence for their answers.

1. What is this text mainly about? How can you tell? (The text is mainly about the bison population before and after the arrival of European settlers.)
ELA RI.5.2, RI.5.10, RF.5.4a **ELD** ELD.PIII.5

Help unpack meaning, if needed, by asking: *How did bison live a long time ago?* (They roamed freely in the Great Plains region.) *Where do most bison live today?* (in national parks set aside specifically for their protection)

Turn and Talk Have students work independently on Questions 2, 3, and 4. When students have completed the page, have partners discuss their responses and then share them with the group. Sample responses are provided. Accept reasonable responses. **ELA** SL.5.1b, SL.5.1d **ELD** ELD.PI.5.1

Unpack Meaning: For Questions 2–4, you may want to use the notes in the right-hand column to guide the discussion about student responses.

2. Why were bison paths three feet lower than the ground on either side? (The bison often walked along the same paths. Over time, their steps wore down the soil.)
ELA RI.5.3, RI.5.10, RF.5.4a **ELD** ELD.PIII.5

3. Why did bison almost disappear from Earth? (European settlers killed many bison for sport and to clear a path for the railroad.) **ELA** RI.5.2, RI.5.10, RF.5.4a **ELD** ELD.PIII.5

4. Predict what will happen to bison in the future. Use details from the text to support your answer. (Responses will vary, but students may say that with continued protection, the bison population will continue to grow.)
ELA RI.5.1, RI.5.10, RF.5.4a **ELD** ELD.PIII.5

UNPACK MEANING

Use prompts such as these if students have difficulty with a question:

2. *What did the bison do during the winter?* (They walked hundreds of miles south in search of grass.) *How did a bison herd travel these long distances?* (They often walked in a single line.) *What happens to a patch of ground when someone walks across it over and over again, year after year?* (The ground wears away.)

3. *What clues can you find on page 99 to help you answer the question?* (The settlers killed bison for sport and to clear paths for the railways. By the 1880s, fewer than 1,000 bison were left in North America.)

4. *Are there more or less bison today than in the 1880s?* (more) *Why did the bison population increase?* (because laws were passed to protect the animal) *What does the author say about the future of bison in the United States?* (With our help, bison will always have an open place to eat grass and roam free.) **ELA** RI.5.1

EXTRA PRACTICE

Retell Have students retell "Bison Come Back to the Plains" to a partner or a family member. **ELA** RI.5.2

DAY 5

SHARE OBJECTIVES

- Read words with open syllables.
- Demonstrate understanding of Target Vocabulary words.
- Preview Cause and Effect and the Visualize strategy.

MATERIALS

Context Cards: *available, contentment, detecting, ferocious, keen, mature, particular, resemble, unobserved, vary*

Write-In Reader pages 94–100

Leveled Reader: *Sharks*

TERMS ABOUT READING/ LANGUAGE ARTS

cause   effect   visualize

☑ TARGET VOCABULARY

Contentment is a feeling of satisfaction.

To **mature** is to grow and develop.

Something that is **particular** is specific or distinct from others.

To **resemble** is to look like someone or something.

To **vary** is to change.

ENGLISH LANGUAGE SUPPORT

Day 5

Vocabulary Help students build a word bank of description and action words to use during the Write About It activity. Use gestures, expressions, and pictures to show the meanings of any unfamiliar words.

Sentence Frames Teach sequence words and phrases, such as *at first, next, then, during,* and *after.* Guide students to use frames such as these to respond to the Write About It activity. *At first I felt _____. During ____, I felt _____.* **ELD** ELD.PII.5.2b

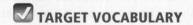

Warm Up

Multisyllable Words

Cumulative Review

- Write these sentences on the board or on a pad.

  1. They will catch and retag the big cat.

  2. Open land is a basic need.

  3. The unlucky cat cannot find an exit.

- Have student volunteers circle the multisyllable words with open syllables. Assign students to work with a partner to practice reading the sentences. Then listen to each student read one sentence. Make corrections as needed. Record your findings. **ELA** RF.5.3a **ELD** ELD.PIII.5

REVIEW

Target Vocabulary

Context Cards

- Display the **Context Cards** for *contentment, mature, particular, resemble,* and *vary.* Review the meanings of these words. Then have students use the words in oral sentences about animals that live in the wild.

- Add the **Context Cards** for *available, detecting, ferocious, keen,* and *unobserved.* Give one card to each student. Have the class try to guess each student's word by asking that student questions to reveal the word. For example: *Is the word a noun? Does the word name an action? Can the word be used to describe an animal?* **ELA** RI.5.4, L.5.6

WRITE ABOUT IT

- Ask students to write about an animal they would like to observe in the wild. Have them describe what they might see or hear, using the word *ferocious* in their descriptions. **ELA** W.5.2b, W.5.2d

PRETEACH

Cause and Effect; Visualize

Write-In Reader pages 94–100

- Introduce skill and strategy. Say: *In the next lesson, we are going to focus on cause and effect. We'll also work on ways to visualize what we read.*

- Remind students that a *cause* is an event that takes place; an *effect* is an event that takes place as a result of that cause.

- List on the board with students causes and effects from the story.

  Page 97: Cause: Horses were brought to America. Effect: Hunting bison became easier for the Plains Indians.

  Page 98: Cause: Bison meat was dried. Effect: It lasted for many weeks without spoiling.

  Page 99: Cause: Settlers hunted the bison for sport in large numbers. Effect: The bison population shrunk. **ELA** RI.5.3 **ELD** ELD.PI.5.6a, ELD.PIII.5

- Turn to and review the Visualize strategy found on page 305 in the **Write-In Reader**. Tell students that when reading a selection, they should picture in their mind what is happening in the text. Visualizing helps them better understand what they are reading. Have students identify descriptive words and phrases from the story that enabled them to visualize bison, their habitat, and their plight.

APPLY READING SKILLS

Introduce *Sharks*. Choral read the first few pages with students. Depending on their abilities, have students continue reading with partners or as a group.

Quick Check **Fluency**

Listen to individual students as they read the **Write-In Reader** selection. Make specific notes about words that presented difficulty to them.

 Leveled Reader

RETURN TO THE ANCHOR TEXT

"Be a Reading Detective!"

Student Book pages 295–305
Write-In Reader pages 101A–101B

- Page through "Cougars" with students, and review the important ideas.

- Remind students about the target skill: **main ideas and details**. Point out that an informational text presents many main ideas. The ideas are supported by details that give examples or provide evidence for the author's points.

- Have students answer the first question in the **Write-In Reader**. Remind them that a reading detective looks for clues.

- Circulate to offer assistance and to make sure that students are taking notes about evidence from the text.

- Have students write their responses.

SPIRAL REVIEW

- Review the skill **sequence of events** with students. Remind them that authors sometimes use a sequence of events, or a specific order in which things happen, to organize their writing.

- Have students answer the second question in the **Write-In Reader**. Circulate to offer assistance and to make sure that they are taking notes about evidence from the text.

- Have students write their responses.

Classroom Collaboration

Have pairs of "reading detectives" compare their responses and the clues they found in the text.

EXTRA PRACTICE

Independent Reading Have students read from a book of their choice and describe what they read in their reading logs.

Teacher Notes

Resources

Contents

- Use a book index and glossary.

MATERIALS

- **Student Book**
- science or social studies textbook

Parts of a Book

1 Teach/Model

Discuss the purpose of a **book index** and **glossary**. Then demonstrate how to use them.

- Explain that the *index* lists each topic from the book in alphabetical order. It also gives the pages where information on a topic can be found. Some topics include a cross-reference, or another index entry, to check.

- Name a topic in students' social studies or science textbooks. Demonstrate finding the index entry and the page(s) where information on that topic is given.

- Explain that the *glossary* is like a small dictionary. It gives pronunciations and definitions of words used in the book. A glossary's *pronunciation key* shows how to use the phonetic spellings to pronounce the sounds in a word.

- Review how to find and use an entry in the glossary of the students' social studies or science textbook or in the **Student Book.**

2 Guided Practice/Apply

- List selected topics from students' content-area textbooks. Have partners find the index entries and note the book pages where relevant information is given. Review their findings.

- List selected glossary words from the **Student Book**. Have partners find and share glossary pronunciations and definitions. **ELA** L.5.4c **ELD** ELD.PI.5.6b

- Choose the appropriate reference source.

MATERIALS

- dictionary, encyclopedia, and thesaurus

Appropriate Reference Sources

1 Teach/Model

Explain that students can use different reference sources to gather information. Students should let the type of information they are seeking determine which is the most appropriate type of source to use in a given instance. Display and discuss the purposes of a dictionary, an encyclopedia, and a thesaurus.

- A *dictionary* helps with words. It tells a word's pronunciation, syllabication, parts of speech, and meanings and often uses the word in a sentence.

- An *encyclopedia* is a set of books giving information about a variety of subjects.

- A *thesaurus* is used to find a word's synonyms and antonyms.

- Model how to decide which source to use to find the meaning of a word, a word's antonym, and facts about a famous person.

- Point out that many references sources are available in digital form—online and as computer software.

2 Guided Practice/Apply

- Divide students into groups and give each group a reference source. Ask questions such as

  What is the meaning of the word strained?
  In what year was the Everglades created?

  What is a synonym for frantic?

- Have students choose the appropriate source to use to answer each question. **ELA** RI.5.7, L.5.4c

- Identify and use text features of a magazine.

MATERIALS

- assorted magazines that are appropriate for students

Use Magazines

1 Teach/Model

Point out that a **magazine** is a collection of stories, articles, and other features. Compare and contrast magazines to other kinds of publications.

- Like newspapers, magazines are published regularly, often weekly or monthly.

- Magazines may be about one topic, such as dogs, cars, science, or events of interest. Magazines may also cover many interests.

- Like books, magazines have covers and tables of contents. The articles may be grouped into sections or categories, but page numbers tell where to find each article.

- Help students find and describe different sections and features in different magazines.

- Point out that many magazines make their content available on the Internet. Have students compare and contrast information provided online and in print form.

- Note that many libraries make magazines available to the public.

2 Guided Practice/Apply

- Have small groups look at several magazines. Then have them look up an article in the table of contents of one of the magazines, go to that page, and read the article. Have them list the name of the magazine and the title of the article. Then have them write a short summary of the article. **ELA** RI.5.2

▶ SHARE OBJECTIVE
- Know the parts of a library.

MATERIALS

- **Student Book**

Library Research

1 Teach/Model

Explain that a **library** is a place that has books, encyclopedias, magazines, newspapers, and many other resources. People are allowed to borrow or use public library materials.

- Point out that a library is organized to help people find materials easily. Adult and children's books are often in their own sections or rooms. Fiction and nonfiction books are shelved in separate sections and may be organized differently.

- Magazines and newspapers are usually grouped together in the same area as are dictionaries, encyclopedias, and other reference materials.

- A librarian or media specialist is often available to answer questions about using library resources.

- A print or electronic card catalog tells whether the library has a given book and where it is located. The catalog lists books in alphabetical order by author, title, and subject.

2 Guided Practice/Apply

- Have students draw maps of the school or local public library floor plan.

- Have them identify typical features, including the librarian's desk, card catalogs, magazine sections, and shelves housing fiction and nonfictional books of interest to them.

Library Card Catalog

1 Teach/Model

Explain that all books, CDs, and other library materials are listed in a **library card catalog**. Print and electronic catalogs provide ways to search for a book by title, by subject, or by author. Point out that author cards are filed alphabetically by the first letter of the author's last name. The title and subject cards are filed alphabetically by the first word, not including the words *a*, *an*, or *the*.

- Demonstrate how to find a book using an electronic or print card catalog. Choose a favorite author and find the author card.

- Choose a book from the list of titles on the card or search list. On the computer, type the title number or highlight the title.

- Point out the call number next to the title or at the top of the card. Explain that it matches a number on the book's spine and is used to find the book on the library shelves.

- Explain that a card catalog may suggest related titles and topics. An electronic catalog often shows details about the number of copies at the library and if the book is checked out.

- Discuss how students could search, by subject, for the same book used in the model.

2 Guided Practice/Apply

- Have partners select a book from the classroom library and specifically describe how they would search for this book in a public library by title, by author, and by subject.
  ELD ELD.PI.5.6b

How to Read a Diagram

1 Teach/Model

Point out the following features of a **diagram** of the International Space Station on **Student Book p. 62** or another text. Discuss these concepts:

- A diagram is a drawing or plan that shows parts of an object and/or how it works.

- An identifier, such as a title or caption, usually is included to tell what the diagram shows.

- Important parts or steps are usually identified. Sometimes labels and lines point to particular features. Alternatively, letters and a key may describe or explain parts in the drawing.

- Ask students questions about features in the diagram.

- Emphasize that a diagram often illustrates ideas too complicated to explain in words. The diagram may clarify what is being described in text.

2 Guided Practice/Apply

- Have partners follow the procedure to analyze and present a diagram in a social studies or science textbook. Have students write a summary of each diagram, telling what it shows and describing some of its features.

Problem Solving

Problem Solving

▶ SHARE OBJECTIVE

• Identify problems, gather information, and choose a solution.

MATERIALS

• **Student Book**
• science or social studies textbook

1 Teach/Model

Explain to students that there is a process they can follow to solve **problems**. Discuss the following steps of the process with them:

• Identify the problem.

• Research and gather information related to the problem. Be sure to draw on multiple sources.

• List and consider options for a solution based on the information you have gathered.

• Choose and implement a solution.

• Evaluate the effectiveness of the solution.

2 Guided Practice/Apply

• Guide students to identify one or more environmental problems in their neighborhood (such as trash in parks or dogs or cats needing to be adopted) or a problem discussed in the **Student Book** or a science or social studies textbook.

• Have students gather information about the problem, drawing on multiple print and digital sources.

• Students should list some possible solutions for the problem. A possible solution for local problems may be talking to local government officials.

• Have students choose a solution and write a paragraph explaining how it could be implemented and why it would be successful. **ELA** RI.5.7, W.5.8

▶ SHARE OBJECTIVE

• Analyze supported inferences to recognize faulty thinking.

MATERIALS

• ads from magazines
• computers with Internet access

Analyze Supported Inferences

1 Teach/Model

Explain to students that they may encounter faulty reasoning or misleading or exaggerated statements in many forms of persuasion. Discuss with students the following examples:

• *Testimonials:* "I ate this snack before every game. It helped me win the championship!"

• *Bandwagon:* "He is the best singer to come to our area. His concert will be a sellout. Get your tickets now."

• *Name Calling:* "The other candidate is foolish. If she's elected, our class won't get anything it needs."

• *Faulty Cause and Effect:* "My dad didn't buy me new sneakers. I didn't make the team. I would have done better in tryouts with new sneakers."

• *Generalization:* "Seven out of ten people chose our brand over Brand X. Our brand is the best."

• *Exaggeration:* "He's always complaining. He never has anything positive to say."

2 Guided Practice/Apply

• Have students reread **Student Book pp. 79, 87, 88, 189, 190** and identify any exaggerated or misleading statements.

• Have students study ads in magazines and on the Internet and analyze the wording of the ads to identify instances of faulty reasoning.

• Have students share examples of faulty reasoning and discuss their impact on the advertisements. Then have students use information from the discussion to draw a conclusion about persuasive techniques in advertising. **ELA** SL.5.1d **ELD** ELD.PI.5.6a

▶ **SHARE OBJECTIVE**
- Identify persuasive techniques in text.

▶ **SHARE OBJECTIVE**
- Identify persuasive techniques in text.

MATERIALS
- **Student Book**

Persuasion

1 Teach/Model

Authors often use **persuasive techniques** in texts to convince readers to think or act in a certain way. Identifying an author's viewpoint or position is an important skill when reading persuasive text.

- Have students reread "What Makes It Good?" on **Student Book pp. 188–190.** Point out a sentence spoken by Kay Nyne that demonstrates her viewpoint about "Old Yeller."

- Work with students to identify reasons and evidence used to support Kay Nyne's points.

2 Guided Practice/Apply

- Have partners read the words of Lester Year on **Student Book p. 190.**

- Have students identify his viewpoint about "Old Yeller."

- Then have them identify and explain the reasons and evidence Lester Year uses to support his points. *The accurate portrayal of animals makes "Old Yeller" good.*
  ELA RI.5.8 **ELD** ELD.PI.5.6a

▶ **SHARE OBJECTIVE**
- Identify the purpose and some design qualities of posters.

MATERIALS
- **Student Book**

Poster

1 Teach/Model

Tell students that the purpose of a **poster** is to announce an event, promote a service, sell a product, or spread an attitude.

Explain that a poster must capture an audience's attention and get the message across in a matter of seconds. To accomplish this, the person making a poster can use the following design techniques:

- *Color:* Color attracts and can be used to emphasize the most important points in a poster. Have students identify which colors are most eye-catching for them.

- *Lettering:* Lettering for posters should be simple, easy to read, and attractive.

- *Emphasis:* Some ways to achieve emphasis of the main points of the poster are to make one part larger and to use strong, contrasting colors, graphics, or bullets.

2 Guided Practice/Apply

- Have students look at the posters on **Student Book pp. 87–88.** Have them comment on the purpose, color, lettering, and emphasis of each poster.

- Have students choose the candidate from the Lesson 3 selection "Off and Running" that they would be most likely to vote for and create a campaign poster supporting him or her.

SHARE OBJECTIVE

- Use website features to judge usefulness and locate information.

MATERIALS

- computers with Internet access

Internet Strategy, Step 3

1 Teach/Model

Review Steps 1 and 2 of the Internet Strategy on page R7 of Unit 1 and then introduce **Step 3: Navigate**. Display an educational website. Discuss the importance of figuring out how it is organized and the usefulness of features such as

—menus, links, and a site map.

—a general statement of purpose.

—a list of contents or categories,

—diagrams, charts, and other graphics.

- Identify a question you want to answer. Demonstrate how to decide whether the site will provide the necessary information. Model how to skim a page or section to get an overall sense of the kind of information available on the site. Does the site still seem useful?

- Next, model how to identify and scan sections that appear to have relevant information. Read to find facts and important ideas.

- Model how to determine which information is useful and how to read more carefully. Take notes about main ideas and supporting details.

- Help students analyze the usefulness of a different website on the same topic.

2 Guided Practice/Apply

Have partners visit two websites on the same topic. Have them identify a question they want answered. Ask students to decide which site will probably provide more useful information about their topic and to explain why.

ELA RI.5.7 **ELD** ELD.PI.5.6b

SHARE OBJECTIVE

- Judge usefulness, quality, and reliability of website information.

MATERIALS

- computers with Internet access

Internet Strategy, Step 4

1 Teach/Model

Review Steps 1–3 of the Internet Strategy. Introduce **Step 4: Analyze and Evaluate**. Display a website and demonstrate how to apply Analyze/Evaluate to Internet reading. Discuss these considerations:

- Decide a website's usefulness. Does it provide details that support, explain, or expand upon ideas about the search topic?

- Determine the quality of information on the website by considering the following:

—the trustworthiness, purpose, and motives of the site host

—the qualifications of the site host or information source (What is the writer's background and experience?)

—how current the information is

—the completeness and objectivity of the materials (Are sides of an issue presented fairly, or is there bias? Are ideas wrong or misleading?)

—prior knowledge, such as personal experiences, research from different sites, and expert opinions

Stress that once students have determined that a website meets their needs, they can begin taking notes or seeking other useful sites.

2 Guided Practice/Apply

- Have partners analyze and evaluate several websites based on the considerations discussed earlier and their own Internet experiences.

- Have students share the results. **ELD** ELD.PI.5.6b

Word Lists

	☑ TARGET VOCABULARY	DOMAIN-SPECIFIC VOCABULARY	SPELLING WORDS	TERMS ABOUT READING/LANGUAGE ARTS
Lesson 1	disturbing staggered interrupted wobbled squashing collapsed specialty numb struggled shifted	acceleration momentum inertia physical property	breath numb comic wobble hymn bundle blister shovel solid crush gravity weather direct frantic energy promise swift stingy grasp feather	story simple subject conflict simple predicate resolution fragment point of view narrative irony details context plot text evidence sentence
Lesson 2	discomfort immersed primitive bungled interior contagious honored brandishing secretive imprinted	alternative mood medium performance dimension technique	awake display sheepish feast braces release stray thief remain greet ashamed sway praise sleeve training disease waist niece repeat beneath	theme interrogative scenes sentence characterization imperative prefix sentence affix exclamatory base word sentence declarative attitude sentence sensory words setting
Lesson 3	debate hesitated inflated scanned shaken stalled decorated beckoned gradually prodded	ballot election campaign slogan debate	sign compose odor groan dough spider reply height control thrown excite silent strike apply brighten mighty slight approach stroll define	compare and compound contrast sentence idioms complete subject formal language complete informal predicate language dialogue multiple- point of view meaning words cause and effect context
Lesson 4	unison element uniform routine mastered intimidated competition recite identical qualifying	athletics physical exam cardiovascular sportsmanship	glue lose route flute view cartoon youth confuse avenue accuse cruise include bruise jewel assume stew execute souvenir choose loose	sequence proper noun inference initials pacing acronym rhythm abbreviation suffix fictional narrative common noun plot dialogue
Lesson 5	officially typically preliminary gorgeous opponents supposedly brutal sweeping embarrassed obvious	cultural identity non-verbal language barrier communication perspective translation	ounce moist poison sprawl haunt August launch scowl auction loyal naughty royal avoid destroy coward basketball saucer awkward pounce encounter	theme singular noun dialogue plural noun sequence collective noun suffix sensory details affix (language) base word voice point of view

Word Lists

	TARGET VOCABULARY	DOMAIN-SPECIFIC VOCABULARY	SPELLING WORDS	TERMS ABOUT READING/LANGUAGE ARTS
Lesson 6	dwarfed · calculate presence · snug procedure · perch outfitted · enthusiastic transferred · beaming	adaptive · preservation endangered · satellite species · tracking habitat	glory · pardon · beware aware · warn · absorb carton · vary · armor adore · barely · stairway aboard · torch · perform dairy · barge · former ordeal · soar	cause-and- effect · synonyms relationship · linking verb quotation · action verb description · main verb domain-specific · helping verb words · verb tense antonyms · procedural composition
Lesson 7	frantic · bounding lunging · shouldered stride · strained checking · romp wheeled · picturing	decisiveness · obligation devotion · self-sacrificing maturity	earth · worthwhile · one-third peer · nerve · reverse twirl · pier · worship burnt · squirm · career smear · weary · research further · alert · volunteer appear · murmur	main character · compound sensory · direct object language · indirect object dialect · compare adage · contrast proverb · direct direct object · quotation
Lesson 8	endangered · restore unique · guardians adapted · attracted vegetation · regulate conserving · responsibility	carbon · natural footprint · resource ecosystem · wilderness	steel · lessen · berry steal · who's · bury aloud · whose · hanger allowed · manor · hangar ring · manner · overdo wring · pedal · overdue lesson · peddle	author's · word root purpose · coordinating domain-specific · conjunction words · subordinating affix · conjunction prefix · cause base word
Lesson 9	critical · clammy secured · squalling realization · commotion annoyance · demolished bundle · elite	bold · purpose competent · unflappable humility	wildlife · well-known · post office uproar · throughout · outspoken home run · life preserver · up-to-date headache · barefoot · awestruck top-secret · part-time · newscast teammate · warehouse wheelchair · overboard light bulb	conclusions · complex generalization · sentence inferences · subordinating first-person · conjunction point of view · correlative third-person · conjunction limited point · source of view · source list characterization · summarize root · paraphrase
Lesson 10	unobserved · resemble available · particular detecting · vary mature · contentment ferocious · keen	adaptation · observation development · trait instinctive	cellar · passenger · calendar flavor · major · quarter cougar · popular · lunar chapter · tractor · proper mayor · thunder · elevator anger · pillar · bitter senator · border	main ideas · direct supporting · quotation details · quotation marks scientific ideas · interjection domain-specific · source words · source list synonym · summarize context · paraphrase thesaurus

Extended Reading | See pp. T383–T428 for the Target Vocabulary that appears in *Hound Dog True*.

Word Lists

	☑ TARGET VOCABULARY		DOMAIN-SPECIFIC VOCABULARY		SPELLING WORDS			TERMS ABOUT READING/LANGUAGE ARTS	

Lesson 11	cramped
	distracted
	viewpoint
	shattered
	surveyed
		pressing
		representatives
		embark
		bracing
		conduct
			checks and
			balances
			congress
			declaration
				individual
				rights
				representation
					bargain
					journey
					pattern
					arrive
					object
					suppose
					shoulder
						permit
						sorrow
						tunnel
						subject
						custom
						suggest
						perhaps
							lawyer
							timber
							common
							publish
							burden
							scissors
								cause
								effect
								tone
								primary sources
								reference
								  materials
								dictionary
								glossary
									thesaurus
									pronoun
									subject pronoun
									object pronoun
									antecedent
									topic sentence
									concluding
									  sentence
									voice

Lesson 12	benefit repeal advantages temporary contrary	prohibit previously midst objected rebellious	colonies freedom protest	patriots revolution	human exact award behave credit basic vivid	evil modern nation robot panic select cousin	item police prefer menu novel deserve	facts opinions tone similes figurative language context	present tense past tense future tense position evidence
Lesson 13	legendary formal gushed strategy retreat	foes shimmering magnificent revolution plunged	commendation duty general	officer regiment	conflict orphan instant complex simply burglar laundry	laughter employ anchor merchant improve arctic mischief	childhood purchase dolphin partner complain tremble	conclusions generalizations domain-specific words text structure thesaurus synonyms	antonyms regular verb irregular verb persuade opinion reasons

Lesson 14	persuade
	apprentice
	contributions
	influential
	aspects
		authorities
		bondage
		provisions
		dexterity
		tentative
			abolitionist
			emancipate
			ethics
				humanity
				slavery
					actual
					cruel
					influence
					diet
					museum
					casual
					ruin
						pioneer
						trial
						visual
						realize
						create
						riot
						genuine
							area
							annual
							audio
							dial
							theater
							patriot
								sequence of
								  events
								historical
								  events
								main idea
								detail
								word root
								context
									semicolon
									comma
									persuade
									opinion
									logical order

Lesson 15	mimic mocking efficient personally lacked	rural tedious organize summons peal	defense democracy nationalism	pride union	formal whistle label puzzle legal angle normal	needle angel pupil struggle level local bicycle	channel global stumble quarrel article fossil	compare contrast text and graphic features text structure	prefix transition opinion paraphrasing reason

Word Lists

	☑ TARGET VOCABULARY		DOMAIN-SPECIFIC VOCABULARY		SPELLING WORDS			TERMS ABOUT READING/LANGUAGE ARTS	

Lesson 16	record
	mental
	launch
	assuming
	episodes
		developed
		feature
		incredibly
		villains
		thumbed
			continuity
			frame
				movement
				storyline
					scrubbed
					listening
					stunned
					knitting
					carpeting
					wandered
					gathering
						beginning
						skimmed
						chatting
						shrugged
						bothering
						whipped
						quizzed
							suffering
							scanned
							ordered
							totaled
							answered
							upsetting
								author's
								  purpose
								voice
								visual elements
								word origin
								adjective
									descriptive
									  adjective
									friendly
									heading
									salutation
									closing

Lesson 17	impressed
	admitted
	produced
	destination
	original
		concentrate
		collected
		rumor
		suspense
		compliment
			experimentation
			futuristic
			ingenuity
				patent
				revolutionize
					tiring
					borrowed
					freezing
					delivered
					whispered
					losing
					decided
						amazing
						performing
						resulting
						related
						attending
						damaged
						remarked
							practicing
							supported
							united
							expected
							amusing
							repeated
								story structure
								onomatopoeia
								point of view
								digital
								  dictionary
								pronunciation
								part of speech
								origin
									adverb
									frequency
									intensity
									character
									concrete
									  words
									dialogue

Lesson 18	career publication household edition required	formula background insights uneventful destruction	brainstorm creative license manuscript	publication target audience	duties earlier loveliest denied ferries sunnier terrified	abilities dirtier scariest trophies cozier enemies iciest	greediest drowsier victories horrified memories strategies	facts opinion main idea details pacing homophones	homographs preposition prepositional phrase autobiography sensory detail

Lesson 19	issue
	deteriorating
	dependent
	exception
	granted
		effective
		urge
		violations
		ordinance
		minimum
			charity
			coalition
			generosity
				neighborhood
				volunteer
					lately
					settlement
					watchful
					countless
					steadily
					closeness
					calmly
						government
						agreement
						cloudiness
						delightful
						noisily
						tardiness
						forgetful
							forgiveness
							harmless
							enjoyment
							appointment
							effortless
							plentiful
								purpose
								theme
								dialogue
								characterization
								suffix
								indefinite
								  pronoun
									possessive
									  pronoun
									interrogative
									  pronoun
									personal
									  narrative
									body
									main idea

Lesson 20	piercing descended quivered savage delicacy	fitful heave diminishing rhythmic marveling	behaviors cooperation patience	relationship training	salsa mattress tycoon burrito bandanna tomato poncho	dungarees lasso patio siesta cargo vanilla tsunami	iguana plaza caravan hammock pajamas gallant	story structure characters setting conflict resolution characterization theme simile	metaphor idiom title italic underline dialogue descriptive details voice
Extended Reading	See pp. T383-T420 for the Target Vocabulary that appears in *About Time*.								

Word Lists

	TARGET VOCABULARY	DOMAIN-SPECIFIC VOCABULARY	SPELLING WORDS	TERMS ABOUT READING/LANGUAGE ARTS
Lesson 21	undoubtedly pace salvation seep shuffled vain stunted mirages evident factor	atmosphere drought barometer thunderstorm climate	nature captain gesture certain departure fountain future surgeon furniture villain texture measure mountain curtain feature mixture creature adventure pleasure treasure	sequence of helping verb events irregular verb flashback subject-verb metaphor agreement vivid words editorial context transition synonym voice main idea

Lesson 22	reasoned spared
	margins nerve
	envy banish
	upright astonished
	bared deserted
		customs mythology
		indigenous values
		language
			storage passage detective
			olive voyage postage
			service knowledge cowardice
			relative image adjective
			cabbage creative village
			courage average language
			native justice
				theme past perfect tense
				visual elements present perfect
				dictionary entry tense
				glossary entry future perfect
				thesaurus entry tense
				perfect tense structure
				  opinion
				  reasons

Lesson 23	extending prospered
	dominated hostile
	residents acknowledged
	flourished sprawling
	acquainted decline
		gold rush rancher
		pioneer westward
		prospector expansion
			entry impress pirate
			limit respond spinach
			talent fortress adopt
			disturb neglect frighten
			entire patrol surround
			wisdom kitchen challenge
			dozen forbid
				text features proverb
				graphic features irregular verb
				main idea helping verb
				supporting opinion
				  details persuasive
				adage argument
				  claim

Lesson 24	rustling beacon
	balked mishap
	lectured surged
	disadvantage torment
	quaking fared
		frontier settlement
		trailblazers wagon train
		prairie
			mislead dishonest disagree
			dismiss insecure informal
			insincere unknown discover
			unable incomplete unwise
			indirect unequal mislaid
			mistreat unstable disgrace
			disaster misspell
				cause context
				effect comparative
				figurative adjective
				  language superlative
				hyperbole adjective
				simile comparative
				metaphor adverb
				point of view superlative adverb
				  response writing
				  journal format

Lesson 25	expedition techniques barrier resumed despite edible fulfilled tributaries range trek	discovery supplies expedition traveler route	elect confession imitate election decorate imitation tense decoration connect tension contribute connection react contribution admire reaction express admiration confess expression	main idea apostrophe supporting negative details conclusion implied opinion primary source topic sentence analogy contraction

Word Lists

	TARGET VOCABULARY		DOMAIN-SPECIFIC VOCABULARY		SPELLING WORDS			TERMS ABOUT READING/LANGUAGE ARTS	
Lesson 26	disturbing struggled primitive brandishing gradually	scanned identical routine gorgeous sweeping	echolocation infrasound fry	instinct navigate	produce company protect preview contain combat prejudge	commotion contest prefix progress computer confide convince	prospect confirm preflight provide propose promotion	text features graphic features visuals caption diagram chart graph map	multiple- meaning words singular possessive noun plural possessive noun definition
Lesson 27	dwarfed procedure transferred enthusiastic adapted	conserving critical realization available resemble	adventure tourist site	trek itinerary	vacant insistent reversible patriotism finalist honorable contestant	observant urgent pessimist comfortable absorbent optimism journalism	novelist terrible frequent laughable radiant collectible	characters analyze behavior traits motivation conflict	theme suffix abbreviations imagery sensory details
Lesson 28	viewpoint surveyed advantages previously legendary	retreat persuade aspects rural organize	carbon dating bitumen remains	extinct paleontologist terrestrial	telephone autograph microscope photograph televise biology microphone	paragraph symphony telegraph megaphone microwave photocopy biography	saxophone telescope calligraphy xylophone homophone homograph	fact opinion question idiom adage common saying	summarize main idea supporting details
Lesson 29	record incredibly destination suspense required	insights dependent effective diminishing marveling	adapt examination natural	observation scent	inspect export erupt predict respect bankrupt dictate	porter report spectacle deport interrupt dictator import	disrupt portable transport spectator verdict dictionary	conclusion generalization infer predict Greek root Latin root	appositive series opening statement body conclusion
Lesson 30	undoubtedly pace reasoned nerve underestimated	extending residents balked techniques barrier	labyrinth maze multicursal unicursal	grotto compass Minotaur	ballet echo bouquet cassette coupon safari portrait	barrette depot courtesy petite denim brunette buffet	garage khaki crochet chorus essay alphabet	main idea supporting detail summarize topic implied word origin	genre informational essay
Extended Reading	See pp. T349-T390 for the Target Vocabulary that appears in *Mysteries of the Mummy Kids*.								

Using Rubrics

A **rubric** *is a tool a teacher can use to score a student's work.*

A **rubric** *lists the criteria for evaluating the work and it describes different levels of success in meeting those criteria.*

Rubrics *are useful assessment tools for teachers but they can be just as useful for students. In fact, rubrics can be powerful teaching tools.*

Rubric for Collaborative Conversations

- Before students engage in a discussion, walk them through the criteria listed on the rubric, making sure they understand the discussion rules and their individual roles in the discussion.
- Have students focus on the criteria for excellence listed on the rubric so that they can aim for specific goals.

Rubrics for Presentations

- Before students make a presentation, discuss the criteria listed on the rubric. Have students focus on the criteria for excellence listed on the rubric so that they can aim for specific goals.
- Discuss the criteria for listening with students who will be in the audience. Point out the criteria for excellence listed on the rubric so that they can target specific goals.
- As students develop their projects in the Extended Reading lessons, they can measure and evaluate their progress against a student-friendly version of the rubric that appears on the Teacher's Edition page.
- Be sure that students understand the criteria by which their project work, both individually and as part of a team, will be assessed. Point out that these criteria include measures for collaboration, research, and presentation skills.

Rubrics for Performance Tasks and Writing

- As students face the prospect of high-stakes writing assessments, multiple practice opportunities with clear success criteria are vital to success.
- When you introduce students to analytical writing and performance tasks in a variety of writing modes, discuss the criteria listed on the rubric and discuss with students how their own writing can meet each criterion.
- Before students attempt a writing task of any kind, have them focus on the criteria for excellence listed on the specific rubrics so that they can set and keep clear goals.
- During both the drafting and revising stages, remind students to check their writing against the rubric to keep their focus and to determine if there are any aspects of their writing that they can improve.
- Students can use the rubrics to score their own writing. They can keep the marked rubric in their portfolios with the corresponding piece of writing. The marked rubrics will help students see their progress through the school year. In conferences with students and family members, you can refer to the rubrics to point out both strengths and weaknesses in students' writing.
- *See Grab-and-Go™ Resources for a student rubric.*

Analytic Writing RUBRIC

Score of 2	• The response is logical, is easy to understand, and has an identifiable pattern/sequence. • The response provides adequate evidence of student's ability to interpret information and/or make inferences and conclusions about the passage. • The response references clear evidence from the text that supports student's response. • The response includes specific examples and/or details that relate to the text.
Score of 1	• The response is logical and connected to the stimuli but may lack an identifiable pattern/sequence and be difficult to understand. • The response provides limited evidence of student's ability to interpret information and/or make inferences and conclusions. • The response references little evidence from the text that supports student's response. • The response includes some examples and/or details that relate to the text.
Score of 0	• The response provides no evidence of student's ability to interpret information and/or make inferences and conclusions. • The response includes no relevant information, evidence, or examples from the text.

Collaborative Conversations RUBRIC

Score of 2	• The student engages effectively in collaborative discussions, building on others' ideas and expressing her or his own clearly. • The student comes to discussions prepared, having read or studied required material. The student explicitly draws on that preparation and other information known about the topic to explore ideas under discussion. • The student follows agreed-upon rules for discussions and carries out assigned roles. • The student asks and answers questions to check understanding and makes comments that contribute to the discussion and link to the remarks of others. • The student reviews the key ideas expressed and explains her or his own ideas and understanding in light of the discussion.
Score of 1	• The student somewhat engages in collaborative discussions, sometimes building on others' ideas and expressing her or his own. • The student comes to some discussions prepared, having read or studied required material. The student draws on that preparation and other information known about the topic to explore ideas under discussion. • The student mostly follows agreed-upon rules for discussions and carries out assigned roles with some prompting. • The student asks and answers some questions and may make comments that contribute to the discussion. • The student reviews the ideas expressed and sometimes explains her or his own ideas and understanding in light of the discussion.
Score of 0	• The student does not engage in discussions and does not build on others' ideas or express her or his own. • The student does not come to discussions prepared. • The student does not follow agreed-upon rules for discussions or carry out assigned roles. • The student does not pose or respond to questions to follow up on information or make comments that contribute to the conversation.

Performance Task: Narrative Writing — RUBRIC

PURPOSE/ORGANIZATION

Score of 4
- The narrative is clear, focused, and well organized throughout.
- Contains an effective and complete plot
- Develops strong setting, narrator/characters
- Includes a variety of transitions to connect ideas
- Contains a logical sequence of events
- Includes an effective introduction and conclusion

Score of 3
- The narrative's organization is adequately maintained, and the focus is generally clear.
- Plot is mostly effective/may contain small flaws
- Develops setting, narrator/characters
- Adequate use of transitions to connect ideas
- Contains an adequate sequence of events
- Includes adequate introduction and conclusion

Score of 2
- The narrative is somewhat organized and may be unclear in some parts. Plot may be inconsistent.
- Minimal development of setting, narrator/characters
- Contains inconsistent use of transitions to connect ideas
- Sequence of events is weak or unclear
- Introduction and conclusion need improvement

Score of 1
- The narrative's focus and organization are not clear.
- Little or no plot
- Little or no development of setting, narrator/characters
- Contains few or inappropriate transitions and weak connections among ideas
- Sequence of events is not organized
- Introduction and/or conclusion may be missing

NS
- not intelligible
- not written in English
- not on topic
- contains text copied from source
- does not address the purpose for writing

DEVELOPMENT/ELABORATION

Score of 4
The narrative includes effective elaboration using details, dialogue, and description.
- Characters, setting, experiences, and events are well developed
- Links to sources may enrich the narrative
- Writer uses a variety of narrative techniques that strengthen the story or illustrate the experience
- Contains effective sensory, concrete, and figurative language
- Style is appropriate and effective

Score of 3
The narrative includes adequate elaboration using details, dialogue, and description.
- Characters, setting, experiences, and events are adequately developed
- Links to sources may contribute to the narrative
- Writer uses a variety of narrative techniques that generally move the story forward and illustrate the experience
- Contains adequate sensory, concrete, and figurative language
- Style is mostly appropriate

Score of 2
The narrative includes partial or ineffective elaboration using unclear or inconsistent details, dialogue, and description.
- Characters, setting, experiences, and events lack consistent development
- Links to sources may be unsuccessful but do not detract from the narrative
- Writer uses inconsistent or weak narrative techniques
- Contains weak sensory, concrete, and figurative language
- Style is inconsistent or inappropriate

Score of 1
The narrative includes little or no elaboration using few or no details, dialogue, and description.
- Very little development of characters, setting, experiences, and events
- Links to sources, if present, may interfere with the narrative
- Writer's use of narrative techniques are minimal and may be incorrect
- Little or no sensory, concrete, and figurative language
- Little or no evidence of style

NS
- not intelligible
- not written in English
- not on topic
- contains text copied from source
- does not address the purpose for writing

CONVENTIONS

Score of 2
The narrative demonstrates adequate command of conventions.
- Consistent use of correct sentence structures, punctuation, capitalization, grammar, and spelling

Score of 1
The narrative demonstrates partial command of conventions.
- Limited use of correct sentence structures, punctuation, capitalization, grammar, and spelling

Score of 0
The narrative demonstrates little or no command of conventions.
- Rare use of correct sentence structures, punctuation, capitalization, grammar, and spelling

NS
- not intelligible
- not written in English
- not on topic
- contains text copied from source

Performance Task: Informative/Explanatory Writing — RUBRIC

PURPOSE/ORGANIZATION

Score of 4	Score of 3	Score of 2	Score of 1	NS
The narrative is clear, focused, and well organized throughout.	The response's organization is adequately maintained, and the focus is generally clear.	The response is somewhat focused but may be unclear in parts. Organization may be inconsistent.	The response's focus and organization are not clear.	• not intelligible
• Main or central idea is clear, focused, and effective for task, audience, and purpose	• Main or central idea is clear, mostly focused, and mostly effective for task, audience, and purpose	• Main or central idea may be somewhat unclear, lack focus, or be ineffective for task, audience, and purpose	• Main or central idea may be confusing; response may be inappropriate for task, audience, and purpose	• not written in English
• Includes a variety of transitions to relate ideas	• Includes some variety of transitions to relate ideas	• Includes little variety of transitions to relate ideas	• Includes few or no transitions to relate ideas	• not on topic
• Contains a logical sequence of ideas with strong relationships between them	• Contains an adequate sequence of ideas with adequate relationships between them	• Sequence of ideas may be weak or unclear	• Sequence of ideas is unorganized; may include off-topic ideas	• contains text copied from source
• Includes an effective introduction and conclusion	• Includes an adequate introduction and conclusion	• Introduction and conclusion need improvement	• Introduction and/or conclusion may be missing	• does not address the purpose for writing

EVIDENCE/ELABORATION

Score of 4	Score of 3	Score of 2	Score of 1	NS
The response presents strong support for the main and supporting ideas with effective use of evidence from sources, facts, and details, elaborating with specific and effective language.	The response presents adequate support for the main and supporting ideas with evidence from sources, facts, and details, adequately elaborating with a mix of specific and general language.	The response presents inconsistent support for the main and supporting ideas with limited evidence from sources, facts, and details. Elaboration is inconsistent with simple language.	The response presents little support for the main and supporting ideas with little or no evidence from sources, facts, or details. Elaboration is inadequate or absent.	• not intelligible
• Evidence from sources is integrated, relevant, and supports key ideas	• Evidence from sources is integrated, relevant, and adequately supports key ideas	• Evidence from sources may be poorly integrated or irrelevant or only loosely supports key ideas	• Evidence from sources, if present, may be irrelevant with little support for key ideas	• not written in English
• Writer uses a variety of elaborative techniques	• Writer uses some elaborative techniques	• Writer uses few elaborative techniques	• Writer uses few or no elaborative techniques	• not on topic
• Vocabulary is clear and appropriate for task, audience, and purpose	• Vocabulary is mostly appropriate for task, audience, and purpose	• Vocabulary is somewhat inappropriate for task, audience, and purpose	• Vocabulary is inappropriate for task, audience, and purpose	• contains text copied from source
• Style is appropriate and effective	• Style is generally appropriate and effective	• Style is largely ineffective	• Style is weak or absent	• does not address the purpose for writing

CONVENTIONS

Score of 2	Score of 1	Score of 0	NS
The response demonstrates adequate command of conventions.	The response demonstrates partial command of conventions.	The response demonstrates little or no command of conventions.	• not intelligible
• Consistent use of correct sentence structures, punctuation, capitalization, grammar, and spelling	• Limited use of correct sentence structures, punctuation, capitalization, grammar, and spelling	• Rare use of correct sentence structures, punctuation, capitalization, grammar, and spelling	• not written in English
			• not on topic
			• contains text copied from source

PURPOSE/ORGANIZATION

Score of 4
- The response is clear, focused, and well organized throughout.
- Opinion is presented, clear, focused, and effective for task, audience, and purpose
- Includes a variety of transitions to relate ideas
- Contains a logical sequence of ideas with strong relationships between them
- Includes an effective introduction and conclusion

Score of 3
- The response's organization is adequately maintained, and the focus is generally clear.
- Opinion is clear, mostly focused, and mostly effective for task, audience, and purpose
- Includes some variety of transitions to relate ideas
- Contains an adequate sequence of ideas with adequate relationships between them
- Includes an adequate introduction and conclusion

Score of 2
- The response is somewhat focused but may be unclear in parts. Organization may be inconsistent.
- Opinion may be somewhat unclear, lack focus, or be ineffective for task, audience, and purpose
- Includes little variety of transitions to relate ideas
- Sequence of ideas may be weak or unclear
- Introduction and conclusion need improvement

Score of 1
- The response's focus and organization are not clear.
- Opinion may be confusing; response may be inappropriate for task, audience, and purpose
- Includes few or no transitions to relate ideas
- Sequence of ideas is unorganized; may include off-topic ideas
- Introduction and/or conclusion may be missing

NS
- not intelligible
- not written in English
- not on topic
- contains text copied from source
- does not address the purpose for writing

EVIDENCE/ELABORATION

Score of 4
- The response presents strong support for the opinion with effective use of evidence from sources, facts, and details, elaborating with specific and effective language.
- Evidence from sources is integrated, relevant, and supports key ideas
- Writer uses a variety of elaborative techniques
- Vocabulary is clear and appropriate for task, audience, and purpose
- Style is appropriate and effective

Score of 3
- The response presents adequate support for the opinion with evidence from sources, facts, and details, adequately elaborating with a mix of specific and general language.
- Evidence from sources is integrated, relevant, and adequately supports key ideas
- Writer uses some elaborative techniques
- Vocabulary is mostly appropriate for task, audience, and purpose
- Style is generally appropriate and effective

Score of 2
- The response presents inconsistent support for the opinion with limited evidence from sources, facts, and details. Elaboration is inconsistent with simple language.
- Evidence from sources may be poorly integrated or irrelevant or only loosely supports key ideas
- Writer uses few elaborative techniques
- Vocabulary is somewhat inappropriate for task, audience, and purpose
- Style is largely ineffective

Score of 1
- The response presents little support for the opinion with little or no evidence from sources, facts, or details. Elaboration is inadequate or absent.
- Evidence from sources, if present, may be irrelevant, with little support for key ideas
- Writer uses few or no elaborative techniques
- Vocabulary is inappropriate for task, audience, and purpose
- Style is weak or absent

NS
- not intelligible
- not written in English
- not on topic
- contains text copied from source

CONVENTIONS

Score of 2
- The response demonstrates adequate command of conventions.
- Consistent use of correct sentence structures, punctuation, capitalization, grammar, and spelling

Score of 1
- The response demonstrates partial command of conventions.
- Limited use of correct sentence structures, punctuation, capitalization, grammar, and spelling

Score of 0
- The response demonstrates little or no command of conventions.
- Rare use of correct sentence structures, punctuation, capitalization, grammar, and spelling

NS
- not intelligible
- not written in English
- not on topic
- contains text copied from source

Multipurpose Writing RUBRIC

Score	• FOCUS • SUPPORT	ORGANIZATION	• WORD CHOICE • VOICE	• CONVENTIONS • SENTENCE FLUENCY
6	The writer supports viewpoint with relevant facts or details.	The writer introduces topic or text clearly, organizes reasons and facts to support viewpoint, has relevant conclusion.	The writer links opinions and reasons with words, phrases. Uses specific language. Connects with reader in unique way.	The writer demonstrates exemplary command of conventions of standard written English. Includes variety of complete sentences that flow smoothly, naturally.
5	The writer mostly supports viewpoint with relevant facts or details.	The writer introduces topic or text, mostly organizes reasons and facts to support viewpoint, has mostly relevant conclusion.	The writer links most opinions and reasons with words, phrases. Uses specific language. Connects with reader.	The writer demonstrates good command of conventions of standard written English. Includes some variety of complete sentences that flow smoothly, naturally.
4	The writer adequately supports viewpoint with relevant facts or details.	The writer introduces topic or text, adequately organizes reasons and facts to support viewpoint, has adequate conclusion.	The writer links some opinions and reasons with words, phrases. Uses specific language. Connects with reader.	The writer demonstrates adequate command of conventions of standard written English. Includes some variety of complete sentences. Some flow smoothly, naturally.
3	The writer supports viewpoint with some relevant facts or details.	The writer introduces topic or text, organizes some reasons and facts to support viewpoint, has somewhat relevant conclusion.	The writer links some opinions and reasons with words, phrases. May use some specific language. May connect with reader.	The writer demonstrates command of some conventions of standard written English. Includes little variety of complete sentences. Few flow smoothly, naturally.
2	The writer supports viewpoint with few relevant facts or details.	The writer may introduce topic or text, organizes few reasons and facts to support viewpoint, may have somewhat relevant conclusion.	The writer attempts to link opinions and reasons with words. Rarely uses specific language. May not connect with reader.	The writer demonstrates growing attempted command of conventions of standard written English. Includes little sentence variety. Incomplete sentences hinder meaning.
1	The writer may not support viewpoint with relevant facts or details.	The writer may attempt to introduce topic or text, may not organize reasons and facts to support viewpoint, may not have relevant conclusion.	The writer may not link opinions and reasons with words. Does not use specific language or connect with reader.	The writer demonstrates little or no command of conventions of standard written English. Sentences do not vary. Incomplete sentences hinder meaning.

RUBRIC for Giving Presentations

	Score of 4	Score of 3	Score of 2	Score of 1
HANDWRITING	The slant of the letters is the same throughout the whole paper. The letters are clearly formed and the spacing between words is equal, which makes the text very easy to read.	The slant of the letters is usually the same. The letters are clearly formed most of the time. The spacing between words is usually equal.	The handwriting is readable. There are some differences in letter shape and form, slant, and spacing that make some words easier to read than others.	The letters are not formed correctly. The slant spacing is not the same throughout the paper, or there is no regular space between words. The paper is very difficult to read.
TECHNOLOGY	Fonts and sizes are used very well, which helps the reader enjoy reading the text. Multimedia components are very effective.	Fonts and sizes are used fairly well but could be improved upon. Multimedia components are effective.	Fonts and sizes are used well in some places but make the paper look cluttered in others. Multimedia components are somewhat effective.	The writer has used too many different fonts and sizes. It is very distracting to the reader. Multimedia components are not effective.
MARKERS	The title, subheads, page numbers, and bullets are used very well. They make it easy for the reader to find information in the text. These markers clearly show organized information.	The title, subheads, page numbers, and bullets are used fairly well. They usually help the reader find information.	The writer uses some markers, such as a title, page numbers, or bullets. However, the use of markers could be improved upon to help the reader get more meaning from the text.	There are no markers, such as title, page numbers, bullets, or subheads.
VISUALS	The writer uses visuals, such as illustrations, charts, graphs, maps, and tables very well. The text and visuals clearly relate to each other.	The writer uses visuals fairly well.	The writer uses visuals with the text, but the reader may not understand how they are related.	The visuals do not make sense with the text.
SPEAKING	The speaker uses very effective pace, volume, intonation, and expression.	The speaker uses effective pace, volume, intonation, and expression.	The speaker uses somewhat effective pace, volume, intonation, and expression.	The speaker's techniques are unclear or distracting to the listener.

Student Project RUBRIC

	PRESENTATION	CONTENT	RESEARCH AND TEXT EVIDENCE	COLLABORATION
Score of 4	• The presentation is exciting and keeps people's attention. • Information is shared in a useful way. • The presentation is well organized. • My group is able to give thoughtful answers to audience questions.	• Content stays on-topic through the whole project. • Written parts of the project are thought-out and answer the project question. • Visuals or multimedia make the project better. • The project has no errors.	• Information is organized in a way that makes sense. • My group used a mix of print and digital sources for our research. The sources are trustworthy. • My group kept a record of where we found our information. • My group used text evidence in our project.	• I made a valuable contribution to each task within the project. • I provided constructive feedback and input during preparation steps and check-ins. • I was polite and productive during discussions. • I fulfilled my role and collaborated toward project success.
Score of 3	• The presentation is exciting. • Information is shared in a useful way. • Parts of the presentation can be better organized. • My group is able to answer audience questions.	• Content stays on-topic through most of the project. • Written parts of the project are thought-out and answer the project question. • Visuals or multimedia make the project somewhat better. • The project has almost no errors.	• Information is mostly organized in a way that makes sense. • My group used a mix of print and digital sources for our research. The sources are mostly trustworthy. • My group kept a record of where we found our information, but it could be better organized. • My group used text evidence in some parts of our project.	• I made a contribution to each task within the project. • I provided some useful feedback and input during preparation steps and check-ins. • I was polite during discussions, but sometimes I got off-track. • I basically fulfilled my role and collaborated toward project success
Score of 2	• The presentation is helpful but could be more interesting. • Information is shared but sometimes confusing. • The presentation is poorly organized. • My group cannot answer all audience questions.	• Content stays on-topic for some of the project. • Written parts of the project give some information. • Visuals or multimedia do not make the project better. • The project has some errors.	• Information is somewhat organized. • My group used only print or only digital sources for our research. The sources are not always trustworthy. • My group did not keep records of where we found our information. • My group used little text evidence in our project.	• I made a partial contribution to tasks within the project. • I had trouble providing feedback and input during preparation steps and check-ins. • Sometimes I was disagreeable or got off-topic during discussions. • I made little effort to collaborate toward project success.
Score of 1	• The presentation is not on topic or not taken seriously. • Information is off-topic or confusing. • The presentation is not organized. • My group cannot answer any audience questions.	• Content goes off-topic for much of the project. • Written parts of the project do not address the project question. • There are no visuals or multimedia. • The project has major errors.	• Information is not organized. • My group may not have used trustworthy sources. • My group did very little research. • My group used no text evidence in our project	• I made few or no contributions to tasks within the project. • I did not provide much feedback or input during preparation steps and check-ins. • I did not participate much during discussions. • I had trouble working with a team.

Handwriting

Individual students have various levels of handwriting skills, but they all have the desire to communicate effectively. To write correctly, they must be familiar with concepts of

- size (tall, short)
- open and closed
- capital and lowercase letters
- manuscript vs. cursive letters
- letter and word spacing
- punctuation

Explain Stroke and Letter Formation

Tell students that most manuscript letters are formed with a continuous stroke, so students will not often pick up their pencils when writing a single letter. Explain that when they begin to use cursive handwriting, students will have to lift their pencils from the paper less frequently and will be able to write more fluently. Provide students with a copy of the manuscript and cursive handwriting models on pages R24–R27 for future reference.

Teach Writing Position

Establishing the correct posture, pen or pencil grip, and paper position for writing will help prevent handwriting problems.

Posture Tell students to sit with both feet on the floor and with hips to the back of the chair. They can lean forward slightly but should not slouch. Ask them to make sure their writing surface is smooth and flat. It should be at a height that allows their upper arms to be perpendicular to the surface and the elbows to be under the shoulders.

Writing Instrument Have students use an adult-sized number-two lead pencil for their writing assignments. Explain that as they become proficient in the use of cursive handwriting, they can use pens to write final drafts.

Paper Position and Pencil Grip Explain to students that as they write in cursive, the position of the paper plays an important role. The paper should be slanted along the line of the student's writing arm, and the student should use his or her nonwriting hand to hold the paper in place. Tell them to hold their pencils or pens slightly above the paint line—about one inch from the lead tip.

Then ask students to assume their writing position. Check each student's position, providing adjustments as necessary.

Develop Handwriting

The best instruction builds on what students already know and can do. Given the wide range in students' handwriting abilities, a variety of approaches may be needed. Use the following activities as you choose to provide regular handwriting practice to students of all proficiency levels.

Write in Cursive Duplicate for each student the appropriate model of the cursive alphabet on page R24 or R26. Have students trace each lowercase and uppercase letter. Then have students write each letter in both lowercase and uppercase on a separate sheet of lined paper.

Slant Letters Correctly Tell students that most cursive letters slant very slightly to the right. Have them practice writing the lowercase alphabet. Tell them to check that they have slanted their letters correctly by drawing a faint vertical line through the middle of each letter. If they have correctly slanted each letter, the lines will all be parallel to each other.

Letter Spacing Explain to students that when writing in cursive, they should leave an equal amount of space between each letter in a word. Tell students that if they leave too little or too much space between letters, their writing will be difficult to read. Write the following words on the board and have students write them on a sheet of lined paper: *batch, reject, vanish, sloppy, rhythm*.

Word Spacing Tell students that it is important to leave the correct amount of space between each word in a sentence. Tell students to leave a space about the width of a pencil between words. Demonstrate how to do this. Then have students practice letter and word spacing by writing phrases that describe the weather, such as hot and dry.

Join Uppercase and Lowercase Letters Tell students that when writing most proper nouns in cursive, they must join an uppercase and a lowercase letter. Have students practice joining uppercase and lowercase letters by writing the following state names: Alabama, California, Florida, New York. Then explain that some uppercase letters, such as D, P, T, V, and W, do not join with a lowercase letter. Have students practice writing the following proper nouns, making sure not to join the first and second letter: Dallas, Phoenix, Tennessee, Virginia, Washington.

Answer Questions Have students practice writing sentences by answering "how" questions about things they see and do on a daily basis. For example, you might ask, How do you get to school? Tell students to write their answers in complete sentences and using their best cursive writing.

Write Sentences Have students write five original sentences about their daily routines. Remind them to slant their letters correctly and to leave the correct amount of space between the letters in each word and between each word in a sentence. Have them trade papers with a classmate and give feedback on the legibility of their partner's cursive writing.

Write a Paragraph Have student write an original paragraph about a favorite book, sport, or other activity. Remind them to use the correct posture for writing, paying special attention to leaving spacing between letters in a word and between words in a sentence.

Assess Handwriting

To assess students' handwriting skills, review samples of their written work. Note whether they use correct letter formation and appropriate size and spacing. Note whether students follow the conventions of print, such as correct capitalization and punctuation. When writing messages, notes, and letters, or when publishing their writing, students should leave adequate spacing between letters and words to make the work readable for their audience.

$A \ B \ C \ D \ E \ F \ G \ H$

$I \ J \ K \ L \ M \ N \ O \ P$

$Q \ R \ S \ T \ U \ V \ W$

$X \ Y \ Z$

$a \ b \ c \ d \ e \ f \ g \ h$

$i \ j \ k \ l \ m \ n \ o \ p$

$q \ r \ s \ t \ u \ v \ w$

$x \ y \ z$

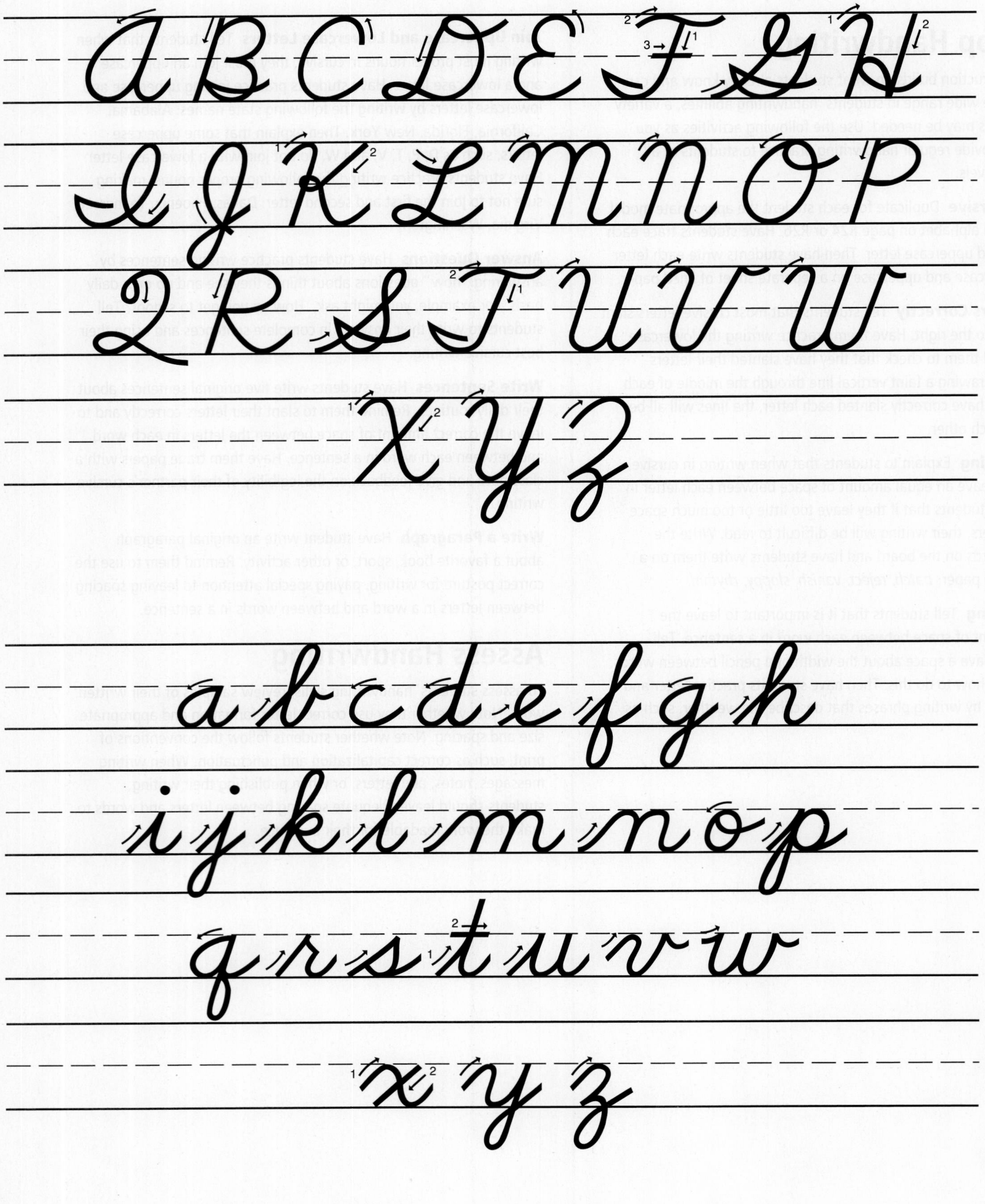

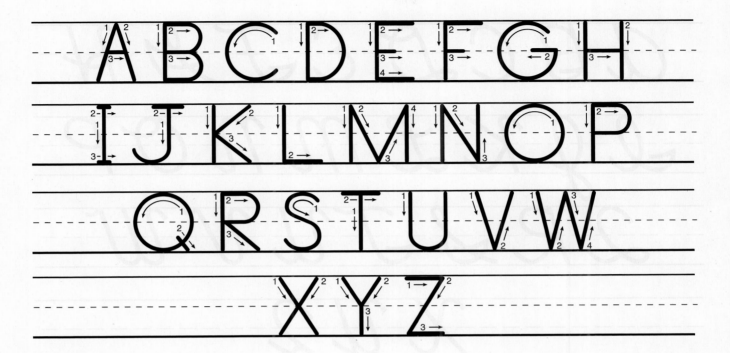

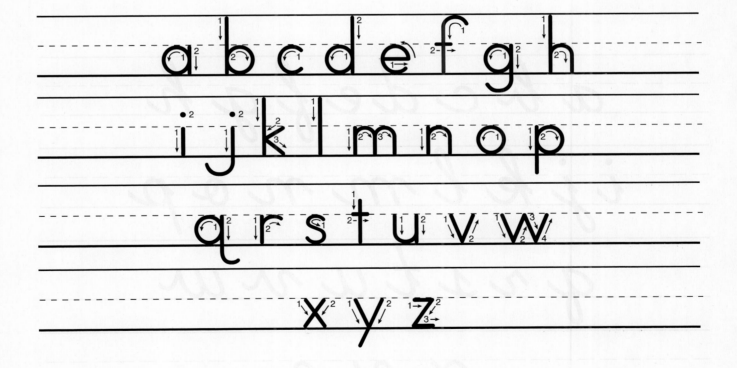

A B C D E F G H

I J K L M N O P

Q R S T U V W

X Y Z

a b c d e f g h

i j k l m n o p

q r s t u v w

x y z

D'Nealian Handwriting Manuscript Alphabet

A B C D E F G H

I J K L M N O P

Q R S T U V W

X Y Z

a b c d e f g h

i j k l m n o p

q r s t u v w

x y z

Keyboarding Lessons

Use these lessons to teach and practice good keyboarding technique. Becoming fluent keyboarders will help students become more effective writers, enabling them to devote more of their mental energy to *what* they are keyboarding—their ideas, supporting details, sentence structures, and writing conventions.

Lesson 1: Posture

Help students develop good keyboarding habits by modeling good posture, adjusting as needed for students with specific physical requirements:

- Place both feet flat on the floor, aligned with your shoulders.
- Relax your shoulders and hold your head and spine straight.
- Place your hands on the home row—[ASDF] and [JKL;]—with your wrists straight and fingers curved.
- If using a mouse, it should be positioned next to the keyboard.

Explain to students that proper posture will help them keep from getting tired and can even prevent overuse injuries. Encourage students to stand and gently stretch at regular intervals for good health, and model doing the same.

Tell students that anyone using a computer should take his or her eyes off the screen once every 15 minutes or so and look at an object across the room. In addition, you can encourage students to pause periodically and close their eyes to rest them. Explain that resting their eyes and stretching their bodies will help students avoid problems that can result from too much uninterrupted screen time.

Lesson 2: Home Row

Tell students to begin keyboarding by placing their hands on the home row: [ASDF] and [JKL;]. Explain that when practicing keyboarding, they will match each finger to a key on the home row. Have students position the fingers of their left hand over the keys [A] [S] [D] [F] and their right hand over the keys [J] [K] [L] [;]. Then have students practice correct technique for the home row keys as well as [ENTER/RETURN] and [SPACE] bar:

- Start from the home row.
- Use your thumb to tap the [SPACE] bar.
- Use your [;] finger to tap the [ENTER/RETURN] key.

Have students find each key and practice tapping it and then returning to the home row. Remind students to keep their eyes on the monitor, not on the keys. Then have students practice typing the keys in the home row:

- Tap each key quickly as I say it: **aa [SPACE], ss [SPACE], dd [SPACE], ff [SPACE], jj [SPACE], kk [SPACE], ll [SPACE], ;; [ENTER/RETURN]**

Lesson 3: Home Row Review and Backspacing

Remind students that they should always start from the home row when keyboarding. Explain that they should try to keep their eyes on the screen, not on the keyboard, as they type, and that using the home row will help them do that. Then have students practice correct technique for the home row keys plus [ENTER/RETURN] and [SPACE] bar:

- Start from the home row.

Display these words and combinations (without the commas between them) or read them aloud by spelling out the words letter by letter.

- Practice typing these words: **ask** [SPACE], **add** [SPACE], **all** [SPACE], **dad** [SPACE], **fall** [SPACE], **lad** [SPACE], **sad** [SPACE], **salad** [ENTER/RETURN].

If necessary, teach students how to use the [BACKSPACE] or [DELETE] key to back up and fix errors. Have students practice by typing each word above and then deleting it to type the next word.

Lesson 4: Home Row Plus Keys E, H

Remind students to start from the home row. Practice proper technique for keyboarding [e] and [h]:

- Start from the home row.
- Use your [d] finger to type [e].
- Use your [j] finger to type [h].

Have students find each key and practice typing it before returning to the home row. Then display these words and combinations, and have students practice typing them: **she sells sheds, he flees fleas, she held a bee, ask a seal, a lass leads, he shakes a leaf.**

Have students retype the phrases with three spaces after each one and then with a return after each one, to reinforce using [ENTER/RETURN] and the [SPACE] bar.

Lesson 5: Keys G, I

Remind students to start from the home row. Practice proper technique for keyboarding [g] and [i]:

- Start from the home row.
- Use your [f] finger to type [g].
- Use your [k] finger to type [i].

Have students find each key and practice typing it before returning to the home row. Then display these words or read them aloud letter by letter, and have students practice typing them: **kid, disk, glad, lid, slid, gas, sigh, glide, gill, hike, hide, kiss, hail, sail.**

Lesson 6: Keys R, O

Remind students to start from the home row. Practice proper technique for keyboarding [r] and [o]:

- Start from the home row.
- Use your [f] finger to type [r].
- Use your [l] finger to type [o].

Have students find each key and practice typing it and then returning to the home row.

Display these words and phrases, and have students practice typing them: **rash, ride, rode, free, grill, frill, rage, ear, oil, foil, old, fold, ore, roles, goal, rose, ride a seal, free a hog, reel a fish, drill a hole, kiss a kid, roll a log.**

Lesson 7: Shift, Period Keys

Remind students to start from the home row. Practice proper technique for the [SHIFT] and [PERIOD] keys:

- Start from the home row.
- Use your [a] finger to type the left-hand [SHIFT].
- Use your [;] finger to type the right-hand [SHIFT].
- Use your [l] finger to type a [PERIOD].

Have students find each key and practice typing it and then returning to the home row.

Read aloud each set of capital letters, and have students key them. Remind them to use the right-hand [SHIFT] key for these capitals: **AA, SS, DD, FF, GG, EE, RR**. Remind students to use the left-hand [SHIFT] key for these capitals: **JJ, KK, LL, HH, II, OO**.

Have students practice the [PERIOD] key with these abbreviations and names: **Dr., Jr., Sr., Dr. Jill D. Mali, Dr. R. J. Lee, Dr. Sal Dill.**

Lesson 8: Keys T, U

Remind students to start from the home row. Practice proper technique for keyboarding [t] and [u]:

- Start from the home row.
- Use your [f] finger to type [t].
- Use your [j] finger to type [u].

Have students find each key and practice typing it and then returning to the home row.

Display the following words, and have students practice typing them. Remind students to try to keep their eyes on the monitor. **tile, toe, the, that, those, toast, tree, treat, feet, lost, roast, at, use, turf, rush, rude, rough, dust, rug, huge, sulk, hulk, tough, soul.**

Lesson 9: Keys W, ?

Remind students to start from the home row. Practice proper technique for keyboarding [w] and [?]:

- Start from the home row.
- Use your [s] finger to type [w].

Have students find the key and practice typing it before returning to the home row.

- Say: Notice that the [?] symbol is on the upper part of the key. That means you have to hold down the [SHIFT] key when you type a question mark.

Have students practice using the [a] finger to hold [SHIFT] while typing the [?].

Display the following and remind students to try to keep their eyes on the monitor as they practice typing these words and sentences: **was, wash, were, war, wool, with, wig, wiggle, What? Where? How? Will we? Where is the gold kite? Did Wade ask for a kite? Do kids like kites? Do adults like kites? Did Julio get a kite?**

Lesson 10: Keys C, N

Remind students to start from the home row. Practice proper technique for keyboarding [c] and [n]:

- Start from the home row.
- Use your [d] finger to type [c].
- Use your [j] finger to type [n].

Have students find each key and practice typing it and then returning to the home row.

Display the following and remind students to sit up straight with their feet flat on the floor as they practice typing these words: **cat, car, cart, chill, court, chat, cost, cleat, click, code, sack, noon, note, none, note, nose, north, sing, song, nothing, neck, cane.**

Lesson 11: Keys P, B

Remind students to start from the home row. Practice proper technique for keyboarding [p] and [b]:

- Start from the home row.
- Use your [;] finger to type [p].
- Use your [f] finger to type [b].

Have students find each key and practice typing it and then returning to the home row.

Display the following, including the semicolons, and remind students to sit up straight with their feet flat on the floor as they practice typing. **;;;, ;p;, pool;, pack;, pile;, pale;, spot;, peek;, spike;, spool;, phone;, photo;, spoons, ball, base, bike, base, boot, bats, bees, basket, beard, beach, building.**

Keyboarding Lessons

Lesson 12: Keys M, !

Remind students to start from the home row. Practice proper technique for keyboarding [m] and [!]:

- Start from the home row.
- Use your [j] finger to type [m].

Have students find the key and practice typing it and then returning to the home row.

- Say: Notice that the [!] symbol is on the upper part of the key. That means you have to hold down the [SHIFT] key when you type an exclamation point.

Have students practice using the [;] finger to hold [SHIFT] while typing the [!] with the [a] finger.

Display the following and remind students to try to keep their eyes on the monitor as they practice typing these words and sentences: **moon, month, mess, lamp, come, melting, mother, much, mile. Jump! She won the race! What luck! What a great trick! How nice!**

Lesson 13: Keys Q, Y

Remind students to start from the home row. Practice proper technique for keyboarding [q] and [y]:

- Start from the home row.
- Use your [a] finger to type [q].
- Use your [j] finger to type [y].

Have students find each key and practice typing it before returning to the home row.

Display the following and remind students to keep their eyes on the monitor as they practice typing these words and sentences: **year, yellow, young, your, youth, yield, yesterday, lightly, quickly, slowly. Please be quiet! Run quickly! Go home! Try this quick trick.**

Lesson 14: Keys V, Z

Remind students to start from the home row. Practice proper technique for keyboarding [v] and [z]:

- Start from the home row.
- Use your [f] finger to type [v].
- Use your [a] finger to type [z].

Have students find each key and practice typing it before returning to the home row.

Display the following and remind students to keep their eyes on the monitor as they practice typing the following: **vote, visit, vary, vine, view, every, vane, oven, zoo, zero, zany, zebra, zoom, hazel, zone, zither. Zoe**

had a golf lesson. Devon was the teacher. Victor lost five golf balls. Victor and Zoe plan to practice very soon.

Have students practice using the [ENTER/RETURN] key by retyping each sentence on a separate line.

Lesson 15: Keys X, Comma

Remind students to start from the home row, to keep their feet flat on the floor, and to try to watch the monitor as they type. Practice proper technique for keyboarding [x] and the [COMMA]:

- Start from the home row.
- Use your [s] finger to type [x].
- Use your [k] finger to type a [COMMA].

Have students find each key and practice typing it before returning to the home row.

Display the following (including commas) and remind students to keep their eyes on the screen as they practice typing the following: **extra, exams, exit, lax, tax, relax, fox, box, excellent, boxes, expert, six, sixteen.**

Check that students have included a space after each comma.

Lesson 16: Keys ', :

Explain that the apostrophe (') is used in contractions to show where a letter or letters are missing and in possessives to show ownership. The colon (:) is used in many ways, including introducing a list and separating the hour from the minutes when showing the time. Practice proper technique for keyboarding these symbols.

- Start from the home row.
- The apostrophe is to the right of the semicolon, so you will use your [;] finger to type ['].
- The colon is on the same key as the semicolon, so you will use the same finger, but you will need to press left-hand [SHIFT] at the same time.

Have students find each key and practice typing it before returning to the home row.

Display the following and remind students to keep their eyes on the screen as they practice typing the following: **Tanya's book, Ramsey's pen, Carmen's markers, Juan's paper, Sara's pencil. When: [ENTER/RETURN] Where: [ENTER/RETURN] Follow these steps: [ENTER/RETURN] The game will start at 4:15 p.m.**

Lesson 17: Special Marks Used In Spanish

Explain that it can be very helpful to know how to type special marks that are often used in Spanish and in people's names. Some of these are accent marks, which are often used over the *e, i, a,* and *o,* and "upside-down" question marks and exclamation points that come at the beginning of Spanish questions and exclamations. Explain how to insert these symbols:

- Symbols and special characters can often be found in a special menu under the "Insert" menu.

- You can also use shortcuts. Practice these shortcuts:

  - for é, í, or another letter with an acute accent: Press [OPTION] [e] and then the letter.

  - for ñ: Press [OPTION] [n] and then [n].

  - for ¡: Press [OPTION] [!].

  - for ¿: Press [OPTION] [?].

Display the following, and have students type it with the proper symbols. Students may need to look at the keyboard. **Juan de Oñate was born in New Spain. His father was Cristóbal de Oñate. Juan took a journey to Nueva México. He crossed the Río del Norte. [ENTER/RETURN] ¿Dónde están los estudiantes? ¡Están aquí! ¿Pueden escribir en español? ¡Sí!**

Lesson 18: Alphabet Review, Caps Lock

Tell students that they have now learned to type all the letters of the alphabet as well as many symbols. Ask how they would type all the letters in their uppercase, or capital form, if they wanted to do so quickly; if necessary, point out the [CAPS LOCK] key and explain its use and the need to strike it again after use to turn it off.

Point out to students that they should not overdo capitalizing words for emphasis; for example, typing an e-mail in all capital letters can make the reader feel as if he or she is being shouted at.

Then have students practice the full alphabet, first in lowercase and then in capital letters: **abcdefghijklmnopqrstuvwxyz [ENTER/RETURN] ABCDEFGHIJKLMNOPQRSTUVWXYZ.**

If desired, have students also practice typing accent marks, tildes, and opening questions marks and exclamation points for Spanish: **é, í, ñ, ¡, ¿.**

Lesson 19: Fonts, Italics, Boldface

In a word processing program, allow students to explore the various menus at the top of the screen. Then have them open a working document on their screens, such as an essay from an earlier lesson. (If necessary, guide students to save a copy of the original document.)

Practice using fonts and type treatments as follows. (Note that features and menus vary by operating systems and word processing programs.) What follows will apply to many situations, but not all:

- In your document, select a sentence or group of words. (Show students how to use the cursor, via touchpad or mouse, to select.)

- Pull down the "Format" menu and click on "Font." Explain that a *font* is style of type or printed text. Some fonts have *serifs,* or small lines, attached to the ends of the strokes in letters or symbols, and some do not. Have students find one serif font and one that is *sans serif* (without serifs).

Point out that when students are writing for school, or any time they want their writing to be clear, they should use fonts and sizes that are easy to read. User-friendly fonts are often listed at the top of a font menu. In general, user-friendly fonts look like the fonts in students' textbooks and in newspapers.

Tell students the following:

- The numbers used to indicate the sizes of fonts are called *point sizes.* For most purposes, 12-point type is appropriate. For emphasis on a poster or title page, or in texts written for small children, students can use larger font sizes.

- Italic type can be used in place of underlining for book titles, words as words, and names of paintings and films as well as for emphasis.

- Boldface can sometimes be used for emphasis, especially for headings in nonfiction reports and on posters.

As time permits, allow students to experiment with fonts, point sizes, boldface, and italics. You may wish to extend this lesson into another session by having students create mini-posters on their computers, varying type styles and sizes for emphasis.

You might want to have students create posters listing classroom computer rules or keyboarding tips.

Keyboarding Lessons

Lesson 20: Numbers 2, 7, 1, 9

Have students find the numbers at the top of the keyboard. If students' keyboards also have a number pad to the right, explain that they can use either the pad or the numbers along the top.

Practice proper technique for keyboarding [2] and [7]:

- Start from the home row.
- Use your [s] finger to type [2].
- Use your [j] finger to type [7].

Have students find each key and practice typing it before returning to the home row.

Display the following and remind students to keep their eyes on the monitor as they practice typing these sentences: **There are 27 students in Room 272. [ENTER/RETURN] On August 27, school starts at 7 a.m. Keesha lives at 2227 Ridgewood Street.**

Next, practice proper technique for keyboarding [1] and [9]:

- Start from the home row.
- Use your [l] finger to type [9].
- Use your [a] finger to type [1].

Have students find each key and practice typing it before returning to the home row.

Display the following and remind students to keep their eyes on the monitor as they practice typing these numbers and sentences: **11; 99; 1999. There are 19 members on the gymnastics team. The 19 members won 7 blue ribbons, 9 red ribbons, and 2 white ribbons on June 1. They will compete again on July 11. Go team!**

Lesson 21: Numbers 4, 0, 3, 6

Remind students that the numbers appear along the top of the keyboard and sometimes also in a number pad on the right side of the keyboard.

Practice proper technique for keyboarding [4] and [0]:

- Start from the home row.
- Use your [f] finger to type [4].
- Use your [;] finger to type [0].

Have students find each key and practice typing it before returning to the home row.

Display the following and remind students to keep their eyes on the monitor as they practice typing these numbers and sentences: **400; 1940; 40 years; Kaya has 40 dollars. Lana has 400 quarters. A crowd of 100 people watched the game. The score was 4 to 0.**

Next, practice proper technique for keyboarding [3] and [6]:

- Start from the home row.
- Use your [d] finger to type [3].
- Use your [j] finger to type [6].

Have students find each key and practice typing it before returning to the home row.

Display the following and remind students to keep their eyes on the monitor as they practice typing the following: **336, 160 meters, 360 degrees, 6 centimeters, 67 soccer players, 16 years. 3:16 p.m.**

Lesson 22: Numbers 5, 8 Plus Number Review

Remind students that the numbers appear along the top of the keyboard and sometimes also in a number pad on the right side of the keyboard.

Practice proper technique for keyboarding [5] and [8]:

- Start from the home row.
- Use your [f] finger to type [5].
- Use your [k] finger to type [8].

Have students find each key and practice typing it before returning to the home row. Display the following and remind students to keep their eyes on the screen:

- Practice typing numbers and words: **85 yards, 58 degrees, Grade 5, Grade 8, Route 88. There are 58 students at the camp. They need 15 backpacks and 58 whistles. They will be hiking 8 miles. The hike starts at 8:15 a.m.**

- Practice the number keys: **0 tigers, 11 lions, 22 bears, 33 wolves, 44 seals, 55 deer, 66 camels, 77 walruses, 88 monkeys, 99 alligators, 100 elephants.**

Lesson 23: Quotation Marks

Remind students to start from the home row. Practice proper technique for keyboarding quotation marks and hyphens:

- Start from the home row.

- Notice that the quotation mark key is just to the left of the semicolon/colon key. Use your [;] finger to type ["].

Have students find each key and practice typing it before returning to the home row. Explain to students the following:

- When typing quotations, commas and periods should be placed inside the ending quotation mark. For example: **She said, "I am leaving now," and then she left.**

- With exclamation points and question marks, if the punctuation is part of the quotation, it goes inside the marks. If it is part of the larger sentence, it goes outside. For example: **He yelled, "Watch out!"** and **Did you hear that little boy say "please"?**

Display the following with line breaks, and have students type it:

"I have the house keys," Ricardo said.

"Please open the door," said Marissa.

"Why?" asked Stephan.

Did you hear the teacher say "stop"?

Hannah said, "Hurry!"

Lesson 24: Tab/Words Per Minute

Point out the [TAB] key to the left of the [Q] key. Have students practice using their [a] finger to press [TAB], which is used to indent a line of text, such as the start of a new paragraph. Remind students to use a paragraph indent each time they begin a new paragraph.

Wrap up the lessons with a timed practice.

- Say: Keyboard as much as you can of the text I will read to you. You will have one minute. I will tell you when to stop.

  Congratulations! You have learned many keyboarding skills. Now, be sure to practice. The key to building your speed and skill is practice. If you practice, your skills will improve. You will be able to type quickly. You will make fewer mistakes. This will save you a lot of time.

  In addition, good keyboarding skills can help you become a better writer. When you have good keyboarding skills, you do not have to think about keyboarding. It is quick and easy. Instead, you can think about your ideas and your sentences. So, keep practicing!

After one minute, have students count the number of words they have typed; have them exchange with a classmate to double-check. This is their WPM (words per minute) score. If possible, have students continue practicing during Center time until they become fairly fluent, typing 15–30 words correctly per minute.

Glossary

This glossary contains meanings and pronunciations for some of the words in this book. The Full Pronunciation Key shows how to pronounce each consonant and vowel in a special spelling. At the bottom of the glossary pages is a shortened form of the full key.

Full Pronunciation Key

Consonant Sounds

b	**bib, cabbage**	l	**lid, needle, tall**	th	**bath, thin**
ch	**church, stitch**	m	**am, man, dumb**	*th*	**bathe, this**
d	**deed, mailed, puddle**	n	**no, sudden**	v	**cave, valve, vine**
f	**fast, fife, off, phrase, rough**	ng	**thing, ink**	w	**with, wolf**
		p	**pop, happy**	y	**yes, yolk, onion**
g	**gag, get, finger**	r	**roar, rhyme**	z	**rose, size, xylophone, zebra**
h	**hat, who**	s	**miss, sauce, scene, see**		
hw	**which, where**			zh	**garage, pleasure, vision**
j	**judge, gem**	sh	**dish, ship, sugar, tissue**		
k	**cat, kick, school**				
kw	**choir, quick**	t	**tight, stopped**		

Vowel Sounds

ă	pat, laugh	ŏ	horrible, pot	ŭ	cut, flood, rough, some
ā	ape, aid, pay	ō	go, row, toe, though	û	circle, fur, heard, term, turn, urge, word
â	air, care, wear	ô	all, caught, for, paw		
ä	father, koala, yard	oi	boy, noise, oil		
ĕ	pet, pleasure, any	ou	cow, out	yōō	cure
ē	be, bee, easy, piano	oŏ	full, book, wolf	yōō	abuse, use
ĭ	if, pit, busy	ōō	boot, rude, fruit, flew	ə	ago, silent, pencil, lemon, circus
ī	ride, by, pie, high				
î	dear, deer, fierce, mere				

Stress Marks

Primary Stress ´: bi·ol·o·gy [bī **ŏl** ´ə jē]
Secondary Stress ´: bi·o·log·i·cal [bī ´ ə **lŏj** ´ ĭ kəl]

Pronunciation key and definitions copyright © 2007 by Houghton Mifflin Harcourt Publishing Company. Reproduced by permission from *The American Heritage Children's Dictionary* and *The American Heritage Student Dictionary.*

G1

---

acknowledge · balk

aspect
Aspect comes from the Latin prefix *ad-* ("at") and the Latin word root *specere,* which means "to look." A *spectator,* which comes from the same word root, is a watcher. A *prospect,* which is something that is looked forward to, comes from the prefix *pro-,* "in front of" or "before," and *specere.*

A

ac·knowl·edge (ăk nŏl´ ĭj) v. To recognize: *They were **acknowledged** as experts in science.*

ac·quaint·ed (ə kwānt´ ĭd) *adj.* Familiar or informed: *People **acquainted** through mutual friends develop meaningful relationships.*

a·dapt·ed (ə dăp´ tĭd) *adj.* Fitted or suitable, especially for a specific purpose: *A dog's claws are **adapted** for digging.*

ad·mit (ăd mĭt´) *v.* To acknowledge or confess to be true or real: *He **admitted** that I was right.*

attract
Attract comes from the Latin prefix *ad-* ("toward") and the Latin word root *trahere,* "to pull or to draw." The English word *tractor,* a vehicle that pulls another vehicle or object, also comes from *trahere. Contract,* an agreement between two or more parties, comes from the Latin prefix *com-* ("together") and *trahere,* which means "to take back," comes from the Latin prefix *re-* ("again") and *trahere.*

ad·van·tage (ăd văn´ tĭj) *n.* A beneficial factor or feature: *Museums and libraries are some of the **advantages** of city life.*

an·noy·ance (ə noi´ əns) *n.*
1. Something causing trouble or irritation; a nuisance: *His tummy ache was a minor **annoyance.***
2. Irritation or displeasure: *He swatted at the mosquito in **annoyance.***

ap·pren·tice (ə prĕn´ tĭs) *n.* A person who works for another without pay in return for instruction in a craft or trade: *The blacksmith's **apprentice** was trained to make horseshoes.*

as·pect (ăs´ pĕkt) *n.* A way in which something can be viewed by the mind; an element or facet: *The doctor reviewed all **aspects** of the patient's history.*

as·sum·ing (ə sōō´ mĭng) *conj.* If; supposing: ***Assuming** our guests arrive on time, we'll have dinner at 6:00.*

as·ton·ish (ə stŏn´ ĭsh) *v.* To surprise greatly; amaze: *It **astonished** me that we finished our project on time.*

at·tract (ə trăkt´) *v.* To cause to draw near; direct to oneself or itself by some quality or action: *Crowds were **attracted** to the beautiful beach.*

au·thor·i·ty (ə thôr´ ĭ tē) *n.* A person or an organization having power to enforce laws, command obedience, determine, or judge: *City **authorities** closed the street for repairs.*

a·vail·a·ble (ə vā´ lə bəl) *adj.* Capable of being obtained: *Tickets are **available** at the box office.*

B

back·ground (băk´ grōund´) *n.* A person's experience, training, and education: *Math knowledge is a perfect **background** for jobs in science.*

balk (bôk) *v.* To stop short and refuse to go on: *My pony **balked** at the gate and would not jump.*

---

banish · collapse

ban·ish (băn´ ĭsh) *v.* To drive out or away; expel: ***Banish** such thoughts from your mind.*

bare (bâr) *v.* To open up to view; uncover: *The bear opened its mouth and **bared** its teeth at the wolf.*

bar·ri·er (băr´ ē ər) *n.* Something that blocks movement or passage: *Cows crossing the road are a **barrier** to traffic.*

bea·con (bē´ kən) *n.* A light or fire used as a warning or guide: *The flashing **beacon** on the lighthouse warned the ship that it was nearing the coast.*

beam (bēm) *v.* To smile broadly: *The baseball player was **beaming** after he made the game-winning play.*

beck·on (bĕk´ ən) *v.* To signal (a person), as by nodding or waving: *The principal **beckoned** us to her office.*

ben·e·fit (bĕn´ ə fĭt) *n.* Something that is of help; an advantage: *The field trip was of great **benefit** to the students.*

bon·dage (bŏn´ dĭj) *n.* The condition of being held as a slave or serf; slavery or servitude: *The slaves were held in **bondage.***

bound (bound) *v.* To leap, jump, or spring: *The deer was **bounding** into the woods.*

brace (brās) *v.* To give support to; make firm; strengthen: *The camper is **bracing** a tent with poles.*

banish · collapse

bran·dish (brăn´ dĭsh) *v.* To wave triumphantly or threateningly: *She came home, **brandishing** the award she received at school.*

beacon

bru·tal (brōōt´ l) *adj.* Cruel; ruthless: *The enemy launched a **brutal** attack.*

bun·dle (bŭn´ dl) *v.* To dress (a person) warmly: *She made sure to **bundle** up before heading out in the snow.*

bun·gle (bŭng´ gəl) *v.* To manage, do, or handle badly: *He **bungled** dinner when he didn't follow a recipe.*

C

cal·cu·late (kăl´ kyə lāt´) *v.* To find by using addition, subtraction, multiplication, or division: *They **calculate** the number of supplies needed before starting the project.*

ca·reer (kə rîr´) *n.* A profession or occupation: *She is considering a **career** in medicine.*

check (chĕk) *v.* To stop or hold back: *The defenders were in charge of **checking** the opposing offense during the soccer match.*

clam·my (klăm´ ē) *adj.* Unpleasantly damp, sticky, and usually cold: *My feet feel **clammy** in wet boots.*

col·lapse (kə lăps´) *v.* To fall down or inward suddenly; cave in: *Part of the roof **collapsed** after the fire.*

ă rat / ā pay / â care / ä father / ĕ pet / ē be / ĭ pit / ī pie / î fierce / ŏ pot / ō go / ô paw, for / oi oil / ōō book

G2

ōō boot / ou out / ŭ cut / û fur / hw which / th thin / *th* this / zh vision / ə ago, silent, pencil, lemon, circus

G3

col·lect·ed (kə lĕk′ tĭd) *adj.* In full control of oneself; composed; calm: *He did his best to stay cool and **collected** when making his speech.*

com·mo·tion (kə mō′ shən) *n.* A disturbance or tumult: *The argument created a **commotion** in the hall.*

competition

com·pe·ti·tion (kŏm pĭ tĭsh′ ən) *n.* A test of skill or ability; a contest: *The soccer match was a **competition** between two talented teams.*

com·pli·ment (kŏm′ plə mənt) *n.* An expression of praise, admiration, or congratulation: *She gave me a **compliment**.*

con·cen·trate (kŏn′ sən trāt′) *v.* To keep or direct one's thoughts, attention, or efforts: *It's hard to **concentrate** on my homework when the television is on.*

con·duct (kŏn′ dŭkt) *n.* The act of directing; management: *The coach was responsible for the team's **conduct**.*

con·serve (kən sûrv′) *v.* To protect from loss or harm; preserve: ***Conserving** energy is important.*

con·ta·gious (kən tā′ jəs) *adj.* Spreading by direct or indirect contact: *Her desire to win the team relay was **contagious**.*

con·tent·ment (kən tĕnt′ mənt) *n.* The condition of being content; satisfaction: *Cats purr with **contentment** when they are satisfied.*

con·trar·y (kŏn′ trĕr′ ē) *adj.* Stubbornly opposed to others; willful: *Little children often become **contrary** when they need a nap.*

con·tri·bu·tion (kŏn′ trĭ byōō′ shən) *n.* Something that is given: *We made **contributions** of food to the poor.*

cramped (krămpt) *adj.* Confined and limited in space: *A family of four lived in a **cramped** little apartment.*

crit·i·cal (krĭt′ ĭ kal) *adj.* Extremely important or decisive: *The surgeon performed a **critical** surgery.*

D

de·bate (dĭ bāt′) *n.* A discussion or consideration of the arguments for and against something: *The class held a **debate** to discuss the fairness of the school dress code.*

de·cline (dĭ klīn′) *n.* The process or result of going down in number or quality: *Some people think the neighborhood is in **decline**.*

ā rat / ā pay / â care / ä father / ĕ pet / ē be / ĭ pit / ī pie / î fierce / ŏ pot / ō go / ô paw, for / oi oil / ōō book

G4

---

dec·o·rate (dĕk′ ər āt′) *v.* To furnish with something attractive, beautiful, or striking; adorn: *The students **decorated** the auditorium with flowers for graduation.*

del·i·ca·cy (dĕl′ ĭ kə sē) *n.* A choice food considered with regard to its rarity, costliness, or the like: *When my family travels, we always taste the local **delicacy**.*

de·mol·ish (dĭ mŏl′ ĭsh) *v.* To tear down completely; level: *They **demolished** the old building.*

de·pend·ent (dĭ pĕn′ dənt) *adj.* Relying on or needing the help of another for support: *Plants are **dependent** upon sunlight.*

de·scend (dĭ sĕnd′) *v.* To move from a higher to a lower place or position; go or come down: *The hikers **descended** from the top of the mountain.*

de·sert·ed (dĕ zûrt′ ĭd) *adj.* Left alone; abandoned: *The girl felt **deserted** when her friends walked away from her.*

de·spite (dĭ spīt′) *prep.* In spite of: *Lewis and Clark traveled to the Pacific **despite** the unknown land.*

des·ti·na·tion (dĕs′ tə nā′ shən) *n.* The place to which a person or thing is going or is sent: *The **destination** of that package is written on the label.*

de·struc·tion (dĭ strŭk′ shən) *n.* The condition of having been destroyed: *The tornado caused great **destruction**.*

de·tect (dĭ tĕkt′) *v.* To discover or determine the existence, presence, or fact of: ***Detecting** the smell of smoke could save your life.*

de·te·ri·o·rate (dĭ tîr′ ē ə rāt′) *v.* To make or become inferior in quality, character, or value; worsen: *The moisture is **deteriorating** the cover of the old book.*

de·vel·op (dĭ vĕl′ əp) *v.* To bring into being: *The author **developed** the book's plot gradually.*

dex·ter·i·ty (dĕks tĕr′ ĭ tē) *n.* Skill or grace in using the hands, body, or mind: *A silversmith with **dexterity** can make beautiful pots.*

di·min·ish (dĭ mĭn′ ĭsh) *v.* To make or become smaller or less: *The store's supply of clothing is **diminishing** because of the clearance sale.*

dis·ad·van·tage (dĭs′ əd văn′ tĭj) *n.* A circumstance or condition that makes it harder to do something or to be successful: *A **disadvantage** of river transportation is its slowness.*

dis·com·fort (dĭs kŭm′ fərt) *n.* A lack of comfort or ease: *The **discomfort** caused by her tight shoes made it difficult to run.*

destruction
Destruction comes from the Latin prefix *de-* ("off" or "down") and the Latin word root *struere*, which means "to construct." Related words are *structure*, "something that is constructed," and *instruct*, "to teach," which come from the same Latin word root.

---

dis·tract (dĭs trăkt′) *v.* To draw (the attention, for example) away from something: *The noise **distracted** the students in the library.*

dis·turb (dĭs tûrb′) *v.* To intrude upon; bother: *The visitors were **disturbing** the musician's practice.*

dom·i·nate (dŏm′ ə nāt′) *v.* To have controlling power or occupy a commanding position over: *The mayor **dominated** the town hall meeting.*

dwarf (dwôrf) *v.* To cause to look or seem smaller: *The cruise ship **dwarfed** the fishing boat.*

E

ed·i·ble (ĕd′ ə bal) *adj.* Safe to eat: *James was surprised to learn that some flowers are **edible**.*

e·di·tion (ĭ dĭsh′ ən) *n.* The entire number of copies of a book or newspaper printed at one time and having the same content: *Today's **edition** of the paper is sold out.*

ef·fec·tive (ĭ fĕk′ tĭv) *adj.* Having an intended or expected effect: *The vaccine is **effective** against the flu.*

ef·fi·cient (ĭ fĭsh′ ənt) *adj.* Acting or producing effectively with a minimum of waste, expense, or unnecessary effort: *High gas mileage makes this car an **efficient** vehicle.*

el·e·ment (ĕl′ ə mənt) *n.* A part of a whole, especially a fundamental or essential part: *The novel is a detective story with one **element** of a science fiction story.*

e·lite (ĭ lēt′) or (ā lēt′) *adj.* Relating to a small and privileged group: *The athletes were the **elite** stars of the sports world.*

em·bark (ĕm bärk′) *v.* To set out on an adventure; begin: *The sailors **embark** on an ocean voyage.*

em·bar·rass (ĕm băr′ əs) *v.* To cause to feel self-conscious or ill at ease; disconcert: *Not knowing the answer to the question **embarrassed** me.*

en·dan·gered (ĕn dān′ jərd) *adj.* Nearly extinct: *The **endangered** animals were put in a preserve.*

en·thu·si·as·tic (ĭn thōō′zē as′tĭk) *adj.* Full of or showing a strong interest, excitement, or admiration: *She is **enthusiastic** about going to summer camp with her friends.*

en·vy (ĕn′ vē) *n.* A feeling of discontent at the advantages or successes enjoyed by another, together with a strong desire to have them for oneself: *I was filled with **envy** when I saw their new car.*

ep·i·sode (ĕp′ ĭ sōd) *n.* An incident that forms a distinct part of a story: *The story was divided into six **episodes** for television.*

ā rat / ā pay / â care / ä father / ĕ pet / ē be / ĭ pit / ī pie / î fierce / ŏ pot / ō go / ô paw, for / oi oil / ōō book

G6

---

ev·i·dent (ĕv′ ĭ dənt) *adj.* Easy to see or notice; obvious: *From the dark clouds, it was **evident** that it would soon rain.*

ex·cep·tion (ĭk sĕp′ shən) *n.* The act of leaving out or the condition of being left out: *All of our guests have arrived, with the **exception** of two.*

ex·pe·di·tion (ĕk′ spĭ dĭsh′ ən) *n.* A group making a journey for a specific purpose: *The **expedition** cheered when they reached the top of Mt. Everest.*

ex·tend (ĭk stĕnd′) *v.* To stretch out; reach: *We saw a clothesline **extending** from the tree to the house.*

F

fac·tor (făk′ tar) *n.* Something that brings about a result: *A willingness to work hard is an important **factor** in achieving successes.*

fare (fâr) *v.* To get along; progress: *How are you **faring** with your project?*

fea·ture (fē′ chər) *v.* To give special attention to; offer prominently: *The exhibit will **feature** Native American pottery.*

fe·ro·cious (fə rō′ shəs) *adj.* Extremely savage; fierce: *The tiger's **ferocious** roar frightened the deer.*

fit·ful (fĭt′ fəl) *adj.* Starting and stopping: *During the storm, the wind blew in **fitful** gusts.*

flour·ish (flûr′ ĭsh) *v.* To do well; prosper: *Their business **flourished** and they became rich.*

foe (fō) *n.* An enemy, opponent, or adversary: ***Foes** of the new city dump met to fight the plan.*

for·mal (fôr′ məl) *adj.* Structured according to forms or conventions: *The board of directors met in a **formal** meeting.*

for·mu·la (fôr′ mya lə) *n.* A method of doing something; procedure: *The teacher gave us the **formula** for writing a good research paper.*

fran·tic (frăn′ tĭk) *adj.* Very excited with fear or anxiety; desperate; frenzied: *She was **frantic** with worry.*

ful·fill (fōōl fĭl′) *v.* To carry out: *Sharon **fulfilled** her responsibility when she finished cleaning her room.*

G

gor·geous (gôr′ jəs) *adj.* Dazzlingly beautiful or magnificent: *The snowcapped mountains were **gorgeous** in the sunset.*

ferocious

Glossary

household
Household is made up of *house*, meaning "a building made for people to live in," and *hold*, meaning "possession."

identical
Identical comes from a Latin word meaning "identity," the physical and personality characteristics that make up who a person is. Other English words relating to someone's identity come from the same Latin word root: *identity*, of course, *identify*, and *identification*.

inflate

grad·u·al·ly (grăj´ ōō əl lē) *adv.* Occurring in small stages or degrees, or by even, continuous change: *The water level in the lake changed gradually.*

grant (grănt) *v.* To give or allow (something asked for): *The teacher granted us permission to leave early.*

guar·di·an (gär´ dē ən) *n.* A person or thing that guards, protects, or watches over: *Courts act as guardians of the law.*

gush (gŭsh) *v.* To flow forth suddenly in great volume: *Water gushed from the broken pipe.*

H

heave (hēv) *v.* To lift with effort or force: *We had to heave the furniture onto the moving truck.*

hes·i·tate (hĕz´ i tāt´) *v.* To be slow to act, speak, or decide: *We hesitated about whether to go over the rickety bridge.*

hon·ored (ŏn´ ərd) *adj.* Proud to be given special respect or a special opportunity: *I felt honored to represent our class in the school talent show.*

hos·tile (hŏs´ təl) *adj.* Not friendly: *Don't give me such a hostile look.*

house·hold (hous´ hōld´) *n.* The members of a family and others living together in a single unit: *Every household has its own rules.*

I

i·den·ti·cal (ī dĕn´ tĭ kəl) *adj.* Exactly equal and alike: *We're riding identical bicycles.*

im·merse (ĭ mûrs´) *v.* To involve deeply; absorb: *She immersed herself in her character for the school play.*

im·press (ĭm prĕs´) *v.* To have a strong, often favorable effect on the mind or feelings of: *The worker impressed his manager and was promoted.*

im·print (ĭm prĭnt´) *v.* To make a mark or pattern on a surface by pressing or stamping: *The company's logo was imprinted on its products.*

in·cred·i·bly (ĭn krĕd´ ə blē) *adv.* In a way that is hard to believe: *The winner of the race ran incredibly fast.*

in·flate (ĭn flāt´) *v.* To cause to expand with air or gas: *She inflated the tires on her bicycle.*

in·flu·en·tial (ĭn´ flōō ĕn´ shəl) *adj.* Having or exercising influence: *Our city has an influential newspaper.*

in·sight (ĭn´ sīt) *n.* The perception of the true nature of something: *The movie critic's review had brilliant insights about the meaning of the movie.*

in·te·ri·or (ĭn tîr´ē ər) *n.* An inner part; inside: *The carvings appear on the interior walls of the cave.*

å rat / ā pay / â care / ä father / ĕ pet / ē be / ĭ pit / ī pie / î fierce / ŏ pot / ō go / ô paw, for / oi oil / ōō book

G8

in·ter·rupt (ĭn tər ŭpt´) *v.* To do something that hinders or stops the action or conversation of; break in on: *I was about to finish my joke when my brother interrupted me.*

in·tim·i·date (ĭn tĭm´ ĭ dāt) *v.* To fill with fear; to frighten, or discourage: *The rough water intimidated us in our light canoe.*

is·sue (ĭsh´ ōō) *n.* A subject being discussed or disputed; a question under debate: *The senator spoke about the issue of reforming campaign laws.*

K

keen (kēn) *adj.* Acute; sensitive: *The keen eyes of the owl help him to see at night.*

L

lack (lăk) *v.* To be without: *The neighborhood lacked streetlights.*

launch (lônch) ŏr (länch) *n.* The act of starting or setting into action: *The company was ready for the launch of its new research program.*

lec·ture (lĕk´ chər) *v.* To give an explanation or a scolding: *My father lectured me about going out after dark.*

leg·en·dar·y (lĕj´ ən dĕr´ ē) *adj.* Very well-known; famous: *Paul Revere's ride is legendary.*

lunge (lŭnj) *v.* To make a sudden forward movement: *She was lunging for the ball.*

M

mag·nif·i·cent (măg nĭf´ ĭ sənt) *adj.* Outstanding of its kind; excellent: *Jackie Robinson was a magnificent athlete.*

mar·gin (mär´ jĭn) *n.* An edge or border: *Weeds grew around the margins of the pond.*

mar·vel (mär´vəl) *v.* To be filled with surprise, astonishment, or wonder: *He stared at the ocean, marveling at its vastness.*

mas·ter (măs´ tər) *v.* To become the master of; bring under control: *He mastered a foreign language.*

ma·ture (mə tyŏŏr´) or (mə tŏŏr´) or (mə chŏŏr´) *v.* To grow older: *Most puppies mature into full-grown dogs in a year or two. adj.* Having reached full growth or development: *A mature redwood can be hundreds of feet tall.*

men·tal (mĕn´ tl) *adj.* Occurring in or done in the mind: *Good writing creates a mental image for the reader.*

midst (mĭdst) *n.* The middle position or part; the center: *They planted a tree in the midst of the garden.*

ōō boot / ou out / ŭ cut / û fur / hw which / th thin / th this / zh vision / ə ago, silent, pencil, lemon, circus

G9

numb
Numb comes from the Old English word *niman*, which literally means "to take." When you are numb, you cannot feel or move normally; feeling has been taken from you.

mim·ic (mĭm´ ĭk) *adj.* Acting as an imitation: *A snowman is a mimic person. v.* To resemble closely; simulate: *Children often mimic the mannerisms of their parents.*

min·i·mum (mĭn´ ə mam) *n.* The smallest amount or degree possible: *We need a minimum of an hour to make dinner.*

mi·rage (mĭ räzh´) *n.* An optical illusion in which something that is not really there appears to be seen in the distance: *In the desert we saw mirages that looked like lakes.*

mis·hap (mĭs´ hăp´) *n.* An unfortunate accident: *The trip ended without a mishap.*

mock (mŏk) *v.* To treat with scorn or contempt; deride: *I felt bad for Tom while his brother was mocking him.*

N

nerve (nûrv) *n.* Courage or daring: *It took all my nerve to talk to the new student in our class.*

numb (nŭm) *adj.* Deprived of the power to feel or move normally: *The boy's toes were numb with cold.*

O

ob·ject (əb´ jĕkt´) *v.* To be opposed; express disapproval: *We objected to the loud noises downstairs.*

ob·vi·ous (ŏb´ vē əs) *adj.* Easily perceived or understood; evident: *Large football players have an obvious advantage.*

of·fi·cial·ly (ə fĭsh´ əl lē) *adv.* By or in a way relating to an office or post of authority: *The winner was officially declared.*

op·po·nent (ə pō´ nənt) *n.* A person or group that opposes another in a battle, contest, controversy, or debate: *The two runners were opponents in the race.*

or·di·nance (ôr´ dn əns) *n.* A statute or regulation, especially one enacted by a city government: *The ordinance requires that every dog be on a leash.*

or·gan·ize (ôr´ gən īz´) *v.* To put together or arrange in an orderly, systematic way: *She was told to organize her messy room.*

o·rig·i·nal (ə rĭj´ ĭ nal) *adj.* Existing before all others; first: *Virginia is one of the original thirteen colonies.*

out·fit (out´fĭt´) *v.* To equip: *The campsite was outfitted with a tent and a grill.*

å rat / ā pay / â care / ä father / ĕ pet / ē be / ĭ pit / ī pie / î fierce / ŏ pot / ō go / ô paw, for / oi oil / ōō book

G10

primitive

P

pace (pās) *n.* Speed of motion or progress: *I love the fast pace of city life.*

par·tic·u·lar (par tĭk´ yə lər) *adj.* Separate and different from others of the same group or category: *The painter wanted the walls a particular shade of blue.*

peal (pēl) *n.* A loud burst of noise: *A peal of thunder frightened the baby.*

perch (pûrch) *n.* A branch or rod on which an animal can sit: *The cat climbed to the highest perch to avoid the dog.*

per·son·al·ly (pûr´ sən əl lē) *adv.* In person or by oneself; without the help of another: *I thanked her personally.*

per·suade (par swād´) *v.* To cause (someone) to do or believe something by arguing, pleading, or reasoning; convince: *He tried to persuade them to come with us.*

pic·ture (pĭk´ char) *v.* To form a mental image of; visualize; imagine: *He pictured himself winning the bike race.*

pierc·ing (pîr´ sĭng) *adj.* Loud and shrill: *The piercing sound of the alarm woke me up.*

plunge (plŭnj) *v.* To thrust, throw, or place forcefully or suddenly into something: *The farmer plunged the pitchfork into the hay.*

pre·lim·i·nar·y (prĭ lĭm´ ə nĕr´ē) *adj.* Prior to or preparing for the main matter, action, or business; introductory: *The architect showed preliminary sketches for a building.*

pres·ence (prĕz´əns) *n.* The fact or condition of being present or near: *The crying child was comforted by his mother's presence.*

press·ing (prĕs´ ĭng) *adj.* Demanding immediate attention; urgent: *Hunger is one of the world's most pressing problems.*

pre·vi·ous·ly (prē´ vē əs lē) *adv.* Before something else in time or order: *Previously, the girls lived in New Orleans.*

prim·i·tive (prĭm´ ĭ tĭv) *adj.* Simple or crude: *A log cabin is a primitive type of house.*

pro·ce·dure (prə sē´ jər) *n.* A way of doing something or getting something done, often by a series of steps: *To conduct a science experiment, he had to follow a procedure.*

prod (prŏd) *v.* To stir to action; urge: *She continually prodded him to do his homework.*

pro·duce (prə dōōs´) *v.* To create by mental or physical effort: *It takes time to produce a painting.*

ōō boot / ou out / ŭ cut / û fur / hw which / th thin / th this / zh vision / ə ago, silent, pencil, lemon, circus

G11

pro·hib·it (prō hĭb´ĭt) v. To forbid by law or authority: *The pool rules prohibit diving in the shallow end.*

pros·per (prŏs´pər) v. To be fortunate or successful; thrive: *The man prospered after graduating from college.*

provisions

pro·vi·sions (prə vĭzh´ənz) n. Stocks of foods and other necessary supplies: *Soldiers at war are given provisions.*

pub·li·ca·tion (pŭb´lĭ kā´shən) n. An issue of printed or electronic matter, such as a magazine, offered for sale or distribution: *The school's monthly publication is very informative.*

Q

quake (kwāk) v. To shiver or tremble, as from fear or cold: *I was so frightened that my legs were quaking.*

qual·i·fy (kwŏl´ə fī´) v. To make eligible or qualified, as for a position or task: *She received high grades, qualifying her for the Honor Society.*

quiv·er (kwĭv´ər) v. To shake with a slight vibrating motion; tremble: *Her voice quivered with excitement when she talked about her birthday party.*

R

range (rānj) n. An extended group or series, especially a row or chain of mountains: *The Rocky Mountain range is in the western United States.*

re·al·i·za·tion (rē al´ĭ zā´shən) n. The act of realizing or the condition of being realized: *The realization that he lost his wallet panicked him.*

rea·son (rē´zən) v. To use the ability to think clearly and sensibly: *I reasoned that I should stay inside because it was raining outside.*

re·bel·lious (rĭ bĕl´yəs) adj. Prone to or participating in a rebellion: *The rebellious farmer fought in the Revolutionary War.*

re·cite (rĭ sīt´) v. To repeat or say aloud (something prepared or memorized), especially before an audience: *The players recite the Pledge of Allegiance before each game.*

re·cord (rĕk´ərd) n. The highest or lowest measurement known, as in sports events or weather readings: *Death Valley holds the record for least rainfall in a year in the United States.*

reg·u·late (rĕg´yə lāt) v. To control or direct according to a rule or a law: *Rangers regulate park activities.*

re·peal (rĭ pēl´) v. To withdraw or cancel officially; revoke: *The Senate voted to repeal the law.*

ă rat / ā pay / â care / ä father / ĕ pet / ē be / ĭ pit / ī pie / î fierce / ŏ pot / ō go / ô paw, for / oi oil / ŏŏ book

G12

---

rep·re·sen·ta·tive (rĕp´rĭ zĕn´tə tĭv) n. A person who acts for one or more others: *Rob and Peter were elected as class representatives.*

re·quire (rĭ kwīr´) v. To be in need of; need: *Practice is required for a person to become better at a sport.*

re·sem·ble (rĭ zĕm´bəl) v. To have similarity or likeness to; be like: *Some house cats resemble cougars.*

res·i·dent (rĕz´ĭ dənt) n. A person who lives in a particular place: *Residents of the building had to leave because the power was out.*

re·spon·si·bil·i·ty (rĭ spŏn´sə bĭl´ĭ tē) n. Something that one is responsible for; a duty or obligation: *The two cats are my responsibility.*

re·store (rĭ stôr´) v. To bring back to an original condition: *The carpenter wanted to restore the old building.*

re·sume (rĭ zōōm´) v. To continue: *Classes resumed after school vacation.*

re·treat (rĭ trēt´) v. The act or process of withdrawing, especially from something dangerous or unpleasant: *Patriots forced the Hessians to retreat from battle.*

rev·o·lu·tion (rĕv´ə lōō´shən) n. The overthrow of one government and its replacement with another: *The goal of the American Patriots during their revolution was to overthrow British rule.*

rhyth·mic (rĭth´mĭk) adj. Of or having a movement, action, or condition that repeats in regular sequence: *The rhythmic sound of the drums had a calming effect.*

romp (rŏmp) n. Lively or spirited play: *The girls took their dogs for a romp in the park.*

rural

rou·tine (rōō tēn´) n. A series of activities performed or meant to be performed regularly; a standard or usual procedure: *They were delayed by the guards' routine of checking their passports.*

ru·mor (rōō´mər) n. A story or report, usually spread by word of mouth, that has not been established as true: *I heard a rumor that Peter is moving to China.*

rur·al (rŏŏr´əl) adj. Of, relating to, or characteristic of the country: *Farms are found in rural areas.*

rus·tle (rŭs´əl) v. To make a soft fluttering sound: *A rustling in the woods scared me away.*

S

sal·va·tion (săl vā´shən) n. Someone or something that saves or rescues: *The spring was the salvation of the thirsty traveler.*

sav·age (săv´ĭj) adj. Ferocious; fierce: *The savage tigers hunted their prey.*

scan (skăn) v. To examine (something) closely: *She scanned the report card.*

se·cre·tive (sē´krə tĭv) adj. Inclined to secrecy; tending to keep secrets: *We had to be secretive while we planned the surprise party.*

shattered

se·cure (sĭ kyŏŏr´) v. To cause to remain firmly in position or place; fasten: *We secured the ship's hatches.*

seep (sēp) v. To pass slowly through small openings; ooze: *Cold air could seep in through the cracks.*

shake (shāk) v. To make uneasy; disturb; agitate: *She was shaken by the bad news.*

shat·ter (shăt´ər) v. To break into pieces by force; smash: *The shattered glass was unfixable.*

shift (shĭft) v. To move or transfer from one place or position to another: *She shifted the heavy basket in her arms.*

shim·mer (shĭm´ər) v. To shine with a subdued, flickering light: *The shimmering candle could be seen in the darkness.*

shoul·der (shōl´dər) v. To place on the shoulder or shoulders for carrying: *The dad shouldered the boy so he could see over the crowd.*

shuf·fle (shŭf´əl) v. To walk slowly, while dragging the feet: *I shuffled my feet because I was so tired.*

snug (snŭg) adj. Fitting closely: *A bicycle helmet should be snug, so it doesn't fall off.*

spare (spâr) v. To show mercy or consideration to: *I spared your feelings by not telling you about the problems.*

spe·cial·ty (spĕsh´əl tē) n. A special pursuit, occupation, talent, or skill: *His specialty is portrait painting.*

sprawl·ing (sprôl´ĭng) adj. Spreading out in different directions: *I looked over the sprawling meadow.*

squall·ing (skwôl´ĭng) n. Loud crying: *The mother stopped her baby's squalling by singing him to sleep.* adj. Crying loudly: *They found the squalling kitten under a bush.*

squash (skwŏsh) v. To beat or flatten into a pulp; crush: *He was squashing the peach on the pavement.*

ă rat / ā pay / â care / ä father / ĕ pet / ē be / ĭ pit / ī pie / î fierce / ŏ pot / ō go / ô paw, for / oi oil / ŏŏ book

G14

---

stag·ger (stăg´ər) v. To move or stand unsteadily, as if carrying a great weight; totter: *Carrying the large boxes, she staggered clumsily.*

stall (stôl) v. To slow down or stop the process of; bring to a standstill: *The traffic stalled because of the accident ahead.*

strain (strān) v. To work as hard as possible; strive hard: *The boy strained to lift the heavy bag.*

strat·e·gy (străt´ə jē) n. The planning and directing of a series of actions that will be useful in gaining a goal: *General George Washington came up with a strategy for the battle.*

stride (strīd) n. A single, long step: *The giraffe took long strides.*

strug·gle (strŭg´əl) v. To make strenuous efforts; strive: *She struggled to stay awake.*

stunt·ed (stŭn´tĭd) adj. Slowed or stopped abnormally in growth or development: *The stunted tree did not grow because there was no water.*

sum·mon (sŭm´ən) v. To call forth; muster: *The smell of turkey summons memories of past Thanksgiving dinners.*

sup·pos·ed·ly (sə pō´zĭd lē) adv. Seemingly: *Until she lied, she was supposedly my friend.*

surge (sûrj) v. To move with gathering force, as rolling waves do: *The crowd surged forward.*

sur·vey (sər vā´) or (sûr´vā) v. To look over the parts or features of; view broadly: *We surveyed the neighborhood from a hilltop.*

sus·pense (sə spĕns´) n. The state or quality of being undecided or uncertain: *The movie left us in suspense.*

sweep·ing (swēp´ĭng) adj. Moving in, or as if in, a long curve: *The castaways waved to the rescue plane with sweeping gestures.*

T

tech·nique (tĕk nēk´) n. A procedure or method for carrying out a specific task: *Jason learned techniques for carving wooden toys.*

te·di·ous (tē´dē əs) adj. Tiresome because of slowness, dullness, or length; boring: *He didn't like math, so he thought the lecture was tedious.*

tem·po·rar·y (tĕm´pə rĕr´ē) adj. Lasting, used, serving, or enjoyed for a limited time; not permanent: *The man was given a temporary license until he could get a permanent one.*

ten·ta·tive (tĕn´tə tĭv) adj. Not fully worked out, concluded, or agreed on: *The publisher created a tentative production schedule.*

suspense
The word *suspense* comes from the Latin prefix *sub-*, meaning "from below," and the Latin word root *pendere*, "to hang." A *suspension* bridge is a bridge on which the roadway hangs from cables. The related word *depend*, which means "to rely on" or "be determined by," comes from the Latin prefix *de-*, "down from," and *pendere*.

Acknowledgments

thumb (thŭm) *v.* To scan written matter by turning the pages with the thumb: *She **thumbed** through the magazine.*

tor·ment (tôr′ mĕnt′) *n.* Great physical or mental pain: *I was in a state of **torment** listening to the teacher explain the homework assignment.*

trans·fer (trăns fûr′ *or* trăns′fər) *v.* To cause to move from one place to another: *She **transferred** money into her savings account.*

trek (trĕk) *n.* A long, hard journey, especially on foot: *Settlers made the **trek** to the West.*

trib·u·tar·y (trĭb′ yə tĕr′ ē) *n.* A river or stream that flows into a larger river or stream: *People enjoy boating on **tributaries** of the Mississippi River.*

typ·i·cal·ly (tĭp′ ĭ kəl lē) *adv.* In a way that is usual for a kind, group, or category: ***Typically**, school begins early in the morning.*

uni-
The basic meaning of the prefix *uni-* is "one." It comes from the Latin prefix *uni-*, which in turn comes from the Latin word root *unus*, "one." The word *unicorn*, a mythological one-horned horse, comes from *uni-* and the Latin word root *cornu*, "horn." *Uniform, unique, unison,* and *unicycle* all have "one" in their definitions.

U

un·doubt·ed·ly (ŭn dou′ tĭd lē) *adv.* Beyond question; undisputedly: *He was **undoubtedly** glad he made it to the meeting on time.*

un·e·vent·ful (ŭn′ ĭ vĕnt′ fəl) *adj.* Having no significant events: *The trip was **uneventful**.*

u·ni·form (yo͞o′ nə fôrm′) *adj.* Being the same as another or others: *He built the porch out of planks of **uniform** length.*

u·nique (yo͞o nēk′) *adj.* Being the only one of its kind: *The puppy had a **unique** mark on his back.*

u·ni·son (yo͞o′ nĭ sən) or (yo͞o′ nĭ zən) *n.* At the same time; at once: *The rowers must work in **unison** to win.*

un·ob·served (ŭn′ əb zûrvd′) *adj.* Not seen or noticed: *We crept up the walkway **unobserved**.*

up·right (ŭp′ rīt′) *adv.* Straight up: *I taught my dog to sit **upright** and beg for a biscuit.*

urge (ûrj) *v.* To entreat earnestly and repeatedly; exhort: *The coach continues to **urge us** to stay in shape over summer vacation.*

vegetation

V

vain (vān) *adj.* Having no success: *Firefighters made a **vain** attempt to save the burning building.*

var·y (vâr′ ē) *v.* To be different or diverse: *His diet will **vary** from day to day.*

veg·e·ta·tion (vĕj′ ĭ tā′ shən) *n.* The plants in an area or region; plant life: *There is little **vegetation** at the North Pole.*

ă rat / ā pay / â care / ä father / ĕ pet / ē be / ĭ pit / ī pie / î fierce / ŏ pot / ō go / ô paw, for / oi oil / o͝o book

view·point (vyo͞o′ point′) *n.* A position from which something is observed or considered; a point of view: *From the **viewpoint** of the British, their navy was the best.*

vil·lain (vĭl′ ən) *n.* A wicked or very bad person; a scoundrel: *The evil brothers were the **villains** of the movie.*

vi·o·la·tion (vī ə lā′ shən) *n.* The act or an instance of breaking or ignoring or the condition of (a law or rule) being broken or ignored: *She was fined for traffic **violations**.*

W

wheel (hwēl) *v.* To turn or whirl around in place: *She **wheeled** to see what had made the loud sound behind her.*

wob·ble (wŏb′ əl) *v.* To move unsteadily from side to side: *The old table **wobbled**.*

villain
The meaning of *villain* has changed over the centuries. The word comes from the Latin word root *villa*, which means "country house." It originally meant a peasant or serf who lived in the country. It gradually changed to mean a person with coarse feelings or a foolish person, and then a wicked person.

o͞o boot / ou out / ŭ cut / û fur / hw which / th thin / *th* this / zh vision / ə ago, silent, pencil, lemon, circus

Acknowledgments

The Birchbark House written and illustrated by Louise Erdrich. Copyright © 1999 by Louise Erdrich. Reprinted by permission of Hyperion Books. All rights reserved.

Can't You Make Them Behave, King George? by Jean Fritz, illustrated by Tomie dePaola. Text copyright © 1977 by Jean Fritz. Illustrations copyright © 1977 by Tomie dePaola. Reprinted by permission of Coward-McCann, a division of Penguin's Young Readers Group, a member of Penguin Group (USA). Inc., and Gina Maccoby Literary Agency.

Cougars by Patricia Corrigan, illustrated by John F. McGee. Copyright © 2001 by Northword Press. Reprinted by permission of T & N Children's Publishing.

Dangerous Crossing by Stephen Krensky, illustrated by Greg Harlin. Text copyright © 2005 by Stephen Krensky. Illustrations copyright © 2005 by Greg Harlin. All rights reserved including the right of reproduction in whole or in any form. Reprinted by permission of Dutton Children's Books, a member of Penguin's Young Readers Group, a division of Penguin Group (USA) Inc., and The Gersh Agency.

Darnell Rock Reporting by Walter Dean Myers. Copyright © 1994 by Walter Dean Myers. Reprinted by permission of Random House Children's Books, a division of Random House, Inc.

"Deanie McLeanie" by Walter Dean Myers. Copyright © 1994 by Walter Dean Myers. Reprinted by permission of Miriam Altshuler Literary Agency.

"Disturbed, the cat" from *The Penguin Book of Japanese Verse* (1967). Translated by Geoffrey Bownas and Anthony Thwaite. Reprinted by permission of Geoffrey Bownas.

"The Dog Newspaper" from *Five Pages a Day: A Writer's Journey* by Peg Kehret. Text copyright © 2005 by Peg Kehret. Reprinted by permission of Albert Whitman & Company and Curtis Brown, Ltd.

El Diario de Elisa by Doris Luisa Oronoz. Text copyright © by Doris Luisa Oronoz. Reprinted by permission of the author.

Everglades Forever: Restoring America's Great Wetlands by Trish Marx, photographs by Cindy Karp. Text copyright © 2004 by Trish Marx. Photographs copyright © 2004 by Cindy Karp. Reprinted by permission of Lee & Low Books, Inc., NY, NY 10016.

Excerpt from *The Black Stallion* by Walter Farley. Text copyright © 1941 by Walter Farley. Text copyright renewed © 1969 by Walter Farley. Reprinted by permission of Random House, Inc. and the Walter Farley Family Trust.

Excerpt from "Man Na Meri" from *Quest for the Tree Kangaroo: An Expedition to the Cloud Forest of New Guinea* by Sy Montgomery, photographs by Nic Bishop. Text copyright © 2006 by Sy Montgomery. Photographs copyright © 2006 by Nic Bishop. Reprinted by permission of Houghton Mifflin Harcourt Publishing Company.

"Genius" from *A Dime a Dozen* by Nikki Grimes. Copyright © 1998 by Nikki Grimes. Reprinted by permission of Dial Books for Young Readers, a division of Penguin Young Readers Group, a member of Penguin Group (USA) Inc. All rights reserved.

"Good Sportsmanship" from *All in Sport* by Richard Armour. Copyright © 1972 by Richard Armour. Reprinted by permission of Geoffrey Armour.

"James Forten" from *Now Is Your Time! The African-American Struggle for Freedom* by Walter Dean Myers. Copyright © 1991 by Walter Dean Myers. Reprinted by permission of HarperCollins Publishers.

"Karate Kid" by Jane Yolen from *Opening Day: Sports Poems*, published by Harcourt Brace & Co. Copyright © 1996 by Jane Yolen. Reprinted by permission of Curtis Brown, Ltd.

"LAFFF" by Lensey Namioka from *Within Reach: Ten Stories* edited by Donald P. Gallo. Copyright © 1983 by Lensey Namioka. Reprinted by permission of Lensey Namioka. All rights reserved by the author.

Lewis and Clark by R. Conrad Stein. Copyright © 1997 by Children's Press®, a division of Grolier Publishing Co., Inc. All rights reserved. Reprinted by permission of Scholastic Library Publishing.

Lunch Money by Andrew Clements. Text copyright © 2005 by Andrew Clements. Reprinted by permission of Simon & Schuster's Books for Young Readers, a division of Simon & Schuster's Children's Publishing Division, and Writers House, LLC, acting as agent for the author.

"A Package for Mrs. Jewls" from *Wayside School is Falling Down* by Louis Sachar, illustrated by Adam McCauley. Text copyright © 1989 by Louis Sachar. Illustrations copyright © 2003 by Adam McCauley. Reprinted by permission of HarperCollins Publishers.

Off and Running by Gary Soto. Text copyright © 1996 by Gary Soto. Reprinted by permission of the author and BookStop Literary Agency. All rights reserved. Jacket cover reprinted by permission of Random House Children's Books, a division of Random House, Inc.

Old Yeller by Fred Gipson. Copyright © 1956 by Fred Gipson. Reprinted by permission of HarperCollins Publishers and McIntosh & Otis, Inc.

"The Princess and the Pea" from *The Starlight Princess and Other Princess Stories* by Annie Dalton, illustrated by Belinda Downes. Text copyright © 1999 Dorling Kindersley Limited. Illustrations copyright © 1999 by Belinda Downes. Reprinted by permission of DK Publishing, Inc.

Rachel's Journal written and illustrated by Marissa Moss. Copyright © 1998 by Marissa Moss. All rights reserved. Reprinted by permission of Houghton Mifflin Harcourt Publishing Company and the Barbara S. Kouts Agency.

"Rockett Girls" from *Double Dutch: A Celebration of Jump Rope, Rhyme and Sisterhood* by Veronica Chambers. Copyright © 2002 by Veronica Chambers. Reprinted by permission of Hyperion Books for Children and the Sandra Dijkstra Literary Agency. All rights reserved.

"A Seeing Poem" from *Seeing Things* by Robert Froman, published by Thomas Y. Crowell, 1974. Copyright © 1974 by Robert Froman. Reprinted by permission of Katherine Froman.

Storm Warriors by Elisa Carbone. Copyright © 2001 by Elisa Carbone. Cover illustration copyright © 2001 by Don Demers. Reprinted by permission of Alfred A. Knopf, an imprint of Random House Children's Books, a division of Random House, Inc.

They Called Her Molly Pitcher by Anne Rockwell, illustrated by Cynthia von Buhler. Text copyright © 2002 by Anne Rockwell. Illustrations copyright © 2002 by Cynthia von Buhler. Reprinted by permission of Alfred A. Knopf, a division of Random House Children's Books, a division of Random House, Inc.

"Tiger" from *All the Small Poems and Fourteen More* by Valerie Worth. Copyright © 1987, 1994 by Valerie Worth. Reprinted by permission of Farrar, Straus and Giroux, LLC.

"A Tomcat Is" by J. Patrick Lewis from *Cat Poems*, published by Holiday House. Copyright © 1987 by J. Patrick Lewis. Reprinted by permission of Curtis Brown, Ltd.

"To Write Poetry/ Para escribir peosia" from *Iguanas in the Snow and Other Winter Poems/Iguanas en la nieve y otras poemas de invierno* by Francisco X. Alarcón. Copyright © 2001 by Francisco X. Alarcón. Reprinted by permission of Children's Book Press, San Francisco, CA, www.childrensbookpress.org

"Tucket's Travels" from *Tucket's Gold* by Gary Paulsen. Copyright © 1999 by Gary Paulsen. Reprinted by permission of Flannery Literary.

We Were There, Too! by Phillip Hoose. Text copyright © 2001 by Phillip Hoose. All rights reserved. Maps by Debra Ziss. Reprinted by permission of Farrar, Straus and Giroux, LLC.

"Words Free as *Confetti" from Confetti: Poems for Children* by Pat Mora. Copyright ©1996 by Pat Mora. Reprinted by permission of Lee and Low Books.

Credits

Photo Credits

Placement Key: (r) right, (l) left, (c) center, (t) top, (b) bottom, (bg) background

5 (t) ©George Shelley/Corbis; **5** (cl) ©Tom Carter/PhotoEdit; **6** (bl) ©Mark A Johnson/Corbis; **7** (tl) ©USCG Image Library; **10** (bl) ©Penguin Young Readers Group; **10** (cl) ©NASA; **11** (cl) ©Charlie Cantrell/Reuters/Landov; **12** (bl) ©Masterfile; **13** (cr) ©David David Gallery/Superstock; **14** (tl) ©Kar/Shutterstock; (tcl) ©Login/Shutterstock; (tcr) ©Alhovik/Shutterstock; (tr) ©file404/Shutterstock; **15** ©iStockPhoto.com; **16** (tl) ©Jim West/Alamy Images; **16** (tr) Blend Images/Alamy Images; **16** (bl) ©Patrick Giardino/Getty Images; **16** (br) Inspirestock/Jupiter Images; **17** (tc) ©Tom Morrison/Getty Images; **17** (tr) ©Blend Images/Alamy; **17** (bl) Ableimages/Getty Images; **17** (bc) ©Rick Gayle/Corbis; **17** (tl) ©Charles Gupton/Corbis; **17** (br) Digital Vision Ltd/Superstock; **18** ©Photodisc/Getty Images; **20** (t) Handout/Newscom; **33** (t) ©Photodisc/Getty Images; **33** (b) ©Jupiterimages/Getty Images; **35** (c) ©Jupiterimages/Getty Images; **39** (cr) ©Ron Levine/Getty Images; **44** (br) Photodisc/Getty Images; **44** (bl) ©Goodshoot/Jupiterimages/Getty Images; **44** (tl) Jupiterimages/Getty Images; **45** (tl) ©Jupiterimages/Alamy Images; **45** (tr) ©Corbis; **45** (tc) ©Corbis; **45** (bl) Brand X Pictures/Getty Images; **45** (bc) Brand X Pictures/Jupiterimages/Getty Images; **47** Creatas/Jupiterimages/Getty Images; **63** (b) Photodisc/Getty Images; **63** (t) ©Getty Images; **64** (b) ©Stockbyte/Getty Images; **65** ©stanislav rishnyak/Alamy Images; **75** (t) Brand X Pictures/Getty Images; **76** (cl) ©Corbis; **80** (tl) ©Tony Freeman/PhotoEdit; **80** (tr) ©Image Source/Alamy Images; **80** (bl) Corbis; **80** (br) ©Superstock; **80** (bl) Beard & Howell/Getty Images; **80** (tl) PhotoDisc/Getty Images; **81** (tr) ©Stockbyte/Getty Images; **81** (tl) ©Shutterstock; **81** (tc) ©Paul Conklin/PhotoEdit; **81** (bl) ©Mary Kate Denny/PhotoEdit; **81** (bc) ©Adam Taylor/Getty Images; **81** (br) ©Dann Tardiff/Corbis; **82** (b) ©Getty Images; **94** (tr) ©Marc Vaughn/Masterfile; **100** (b) © Ariel Skelley/Getty Images; **100** (t) ©Digital Vision/Getty Images; **102** (t) PhotoDisc/Getty Images; **102** (tl) PhotoDisc/Getty Images; **104** Age fotostock/Superstock; **105** (br) Getty Images/Digital Vision; **105** (tl) PhotoDisc/Getty Images; **110** ©George Shelley/Corbis; **110** (br) ©BananaStock/Superstock; **110** (bl) ©PNC/Getty Images; **110** (br) ©Tom Rosenthal/Superstock; **110** (tc) ©Tom Carter/PhotoEdit; **110** (br) ©Tom Rosenthal/Superstock; **111** (tl) ©WireImage/Masterfile; **111** (tc) ©David Sanger Photography/Alamy Images; **111** (tr) ©rudi von briel/PhotoEdit; **111** (bl) ©Tim Pannell/Corbis; **111** (bc) ©David Madison/Getty Images; **111** ©Dann Tardif/Corbis; **114** ©USA Jump Rope; **116** ©USA Jump Rope; **116** (tc) ©Lawrence Manning/Corbis; **120** (t) ©Bob Jacobson/Corbis; **124** (t) ©Bob Jacobson/Corbis; **127** (b) © Getty Images; **128** (t) Digital Vision/Alamy; **130** (tl) ©Tom Carter/PhotoEdit; **130** ©George Shelley/Corbis; **130** (tl) ©Tom Carter/PhotoEdit; **130** (cl) ©George Shelley/Corbis; **132** ©Warren Morgan/Corbis; **133** (tl) ©George Shelley/Corbis; **133** (cr) ©D. Hurst/Alamy Images; **133** (tc) ©Tom Carter/PhotoEdit; **138** (tc) ImageState/Alamy; **138** (tr) ©Mike Powell/Allsport Concepts/Getty Images; **138** (bc) ©SW Productions/Getty Images; **138** (br) ©Arco Images GmbH/Alamy Images; **139** (tr) ©Digital Vision/Getty Images; **139** (tl) ©JAMAL A. Wilson/Stringer/AFP/Getty Images; **139** (tc) ©Alistair Berg/Taxi/Getty Images; **139** (bc) ©Digital Vision/Alamy Images; **139** (br) ©Peter Beck/Corbis; **155** (t) ©Corbis Flirt/Alamy Images; **155** (b) ©Blend Images/Alamy Images; **156** (t) ©Getty Images; **161** (t) Jupiterimages/Getty Images; **161** (c) OJO Images/Getty Images; **161** (b) Comstock/Getty Images; [**169**] (l) ©David Mckee/Shutterstock; **170** (bl) Comstock/Getty Images; **170** (tl) Jupiter Images; **170** (tr) © Don Paulson Photography/SuperStock; **170** (br) ©Corbis; **171** (bc) © John Giustina/ Getty Images; **171** (tl) Georgia Department of Economic Development; **171** (bl) Corbis; **171** (tc) Getty Images/Photodisc; **171** (br) Don Mason/Blend Images/Getty Images; **173** Tom Brakefield/Getty Images; **191** (t) ©Leandro Gabrieli/Getty Images; **191** (b) Digital Vision/Getty Images; **192** (t) Corbis; **192** (b) Photodisc/Getty Images; **193** (c) ©Mary H Swift/Alamy Images; **199** (tl) ©Getty Images; **199** (tr) Photodisc/Getty Images; **204** (tc) ©The Granger Collection, New York; **204** (tr) ©The Granger Collection, New York; **204** (bc) ©The Granger Collection, New York; **204** (br) ©The Granger Collection, New York; **205** (tr) ©Nancy Beijersbergen/Alamy Images; **205** (tl) ©Catherine Karnow/Corbis; **205** (tc) ©Layne Kennedy/Corbis; **205** (bl) ©Adam Woolfitt/Corbis; **205** (bc) ©The Granger Collection, New York; **205** (br) ©Juniors Bildarchiv/Alamy Images; **208** (tr) ©Thomas D McAvoy/Stringer/Time & Life Pictures/Getty Images; **221** (t) ©Grambo Photography/All Canada Photos/Getty Images; **221** (b) Corbis; **222** (t) ©Corbis; **222** (br) Corbis; **223** (c) ©Corbis; **232** (tc) ©Daryl Benson/Masterfile; **232** (tr) ©David R. Frazier/PhotoEdit; **232** (tr) ©Mary H Swift/Alamy Images; **232** (bc) ©Peter Arnold, Inc./Alamy Images; **232** ©Mark A Johnson/Corbis; **233** (bc) ©Digital Vision/Getty Images; **233** (br) ©Image Source/Getty Images; **233** (tl) ©Paul Glendell/Alamy Images; **233** (tc)

©David R. Frazier/PhotoEdit; **233** (tr) ©Michael DeFreitas Wildlife/Alamy Images; **233** (bl) ©PhotoDisc/Superstock; **235** ©Getty Images; **251** (t) Pixel Shack/Alamy; **251** (b) ©Mark Downey/Photodisc/Getty Images; **252** (cl) ©Corel Corporation; **253** (c) ©Digital Vision/Getty Images; **254** ©Layne Kennedy/Digital Vision/Corbis; **254** ©Mark A Johnson/Corbis; **255** (br) ©Rob Howard/Corbis; **256** (tr) ©Jeff Vanuga/Corbis; **256** (bg) ©Courtesy of Scenics of America/Photolink Image & Design; **257** (tc) ©Mark A Johnson/Corbis; **257** (tr) © George McCarthy/Corbis; **257** (b) © Tom Algire/SuperStock; **262** (tc) ©Reuters/Corbis; **262** (tr) ©Joe Raedle/Getty Images; **262** (bc) ©John Kershaw/Alamy Images; **262** (br) ©Barbara Davidson/Dallas Morning News/Corbis; **262** (tl) ©USCG Image Library; **263** (bl) ©JGI/Blend Images/Corbis; **263** (tr) ©Jeff Curtes/Corbis; **263** (tc) ©Tony Freeman/PhotoEdit; **263** (tr) ©Jean-Bernard Vernier/Corbis Sygma; **263** (bc) ©Michael Ventura/PhotoEdit; **263** (br) ©Rubberball/Superstock; **265** © Jupiterimages/Getty Images; **267** (t) ©USCG Image Library; **280** (t) ©Photodisc/Getty Images; **281** (c) ©Glowimages/Getty Images; **282** (tl) ©USCG Image Library; **282** ©USCG Image Library; **284** (bg) ©USCG Image Library; **284** (inset) ©Chicamacomico Life-Saving Station Historic Site; **285** (tl) ©USCG Image Library; **290** (tc) ©Juniors Bildarchiv/Alamy Images; **290** (tr) ©Mark C Ross/Getty Images; **290** (bc) ©Richard Hamilton Smith/Corbis; **290** (br) ©Corbis RF/Getty Images; **291** (tc) ©Janice Lichtenberger/Alamy Images; **291** (bl) ©Houghton Mifflin Harcourt; **291** (tr) ©Chad Johnston/Masterfile; **291** (bc) ©Advance Images/Alamy Images; **291** (br) ©Ian O'Leary/Stone/Getty Images; **291** (tl) ©E. A. Janes/Photo Researchers, Inc.; **293** ©First Light/Alamy Images; **300** (bl) ©Radius Images/Alamy Images; **305** ©DLILLC/Corbis; **307** (t) PhotoDisc/Getty Images; **308** (t) ©Corbis; **308** (b) ©Image Source/Getty Images; **309** (c) ©Jupiterimages/Getty Images; **313** (b) ©Jeff Maloney/Getty Images; **313** (cr) ©DK Limited/Corbis; **321** (l) ©Tetra Images/Corbis; **322** (tc) ©North Wind Picture Archives; **322** (tr) ©The Granger Collection, New York; **322** (bc) ©Look and Learn/Bridgeman Art Library (New York); **322** (br) ©Science Museum, London, UK/Bridgeman Art Library (New York); **323** (tl) ©National Geographic/Getty Images; **323** (tc) ©North Wind Picture Archives; **323** (tr) ©Paul A. Souders/Corbis; **323** (bl) ©The Granger Collection, New York; **323** (bc) ©The Granger Collection, New York; **323** (br) ©Bates Littlehales/National Geographic Society/Image Collection; **324** ©Bates Littlehales/National Geographic Society/Image Collection; **326** (c) ©Image Farm Inc.; **341** (fg) Jupiterimages/Getty Images; **341** (br) © Artville/Getty Images; **342** (b) Jupiterimages/Brand X Pictures/ Getty Images; **344** (inset) ©North Wind Picture Archives/Alamy Images; **344** (border) Getty Images/Photodisc; **345** (inset) ©Edward Gooch/Getty Images; **345** (border) ©Houghton Mifflin Harcourt; **346** (tr) ©Corbis; **346** (border) ©Getty Images; **347** (b) ©Superstock/Getty Images; **348** (t) ©Photri Images/Alamy Images; **349** (t) Jupiterimages/Getty Images; **349** (c) Photodisc/Getty Images; **354** (tr) ©The Granger Collection, New York; **354** (bc) ©North Wind/North Wind Picture Archives; **354** (br) A View of the House of Commons, engraved by B. Cole (fl.1748-75) (engraving), English School, (18th century) /©Stapleton Collection, UK,/The Bridgeman Art Library; **355** (tl) ©The Granger Collection, New York; **355** (tc) ©Granger Collection; **355** (tr) ©The Granger Collection, New York; **355** (bl) ©The Granger Collection, New York; **355** (bc) ©Kevin Fleming/Corbis; **355** (br) ©Joseph Sohm; Visions of America/Corbis; **358** (br) ©Courtesy of Penguin Young Readers Group/Penguin Group (USA) Inc.; **371** (t) ©Aleksandr Ugorenkov/Alamy Images; **371** (b) ©Corbis; **372** (t) ©Tanya Constantine/Getty Images; **373** (br) ©Comstock/Getty Images; **376** (bg) North Wind Picture Archives/Alamy; **377** (tr) C Squared Studios/Photodisc/Getty Images; **377** (tr) Collection of the New-York Historical Society, USA/The Bridgeman Art Library International; **379** (t) American School, (19th century)/Private Collection/Peter Newark American Pictures/The Bridgeman Art Library International; **381** (c) ©Hulton Archive/Getty Images; **381** (tr) Allan Ramsay; **381** (tr) C Squared Studios/Photodisc/Getty Images; **382** (b) Franz Xaver Habermann/Corbis; **383** (t) ©Corbis; **383** (c) ©Hulton Archive/Getty Images; **383** (b) D. Hurst/Alamy; **388** (tc) ©Bettmann/Corbis; **388** (tr) ©The Granger Collection, New York; **388** (bc) ©Bettmann/Corbis; **388** (br) ©Granger Collection; **389** (tl) ©Bettmann/Corbis; **389** (tc) ©The Granger Collection, New York; **389** (tr) ©Granger Collection; **389** (bl) ©Bettmann/Corbis; **389** (bc) ©Granger Collection; **389** (br) ©North Wind Picture Archives/Alamy Images; **391** ©Library of Congress Prints & Photographs Division; **406** (t) ©Jupiterimages/Getty Images; **406** (b) ©Digital Vision/Getty Images; **416** (tc) ©North Wind/North Wind Picture Archives; **416** (tr) ©Colonial Williamsburg Foundation; **416** (bc) ©Kelly-Mooney Photography/Corbis; **416** (br) ©Bettmann/Corbis; **417** (tl) ©The Granger Collection, New York; **417** (tc) ©Colonial Williamsburg Foundation; **417** (bl) ©North Wind/North Wind Picture Archives; **417** (bc) ©Colonial Williamsburg Foundation; **417** (br) ©The Granger Collection, New York; **419** (b) ©Dave G. Houser/Corbis; **420** (c) ©HUGH GRANNUM/NewsCom; **426** ©The Granger Collection, New York; **428** (t) ©North Winds/North Wind Picture Archives; **430** (br) ©Leon Gardiner Collection/Historical Society of Pennsylvania; **433** (b) ©Ablestock.com/Jupiterimages/Getty Images; **433** (t) ©The Architect of the Capitol; **435** (c) Corel Stock Photo Library - royalty free; **438** (tl) ©Ross Warner/Alamy Images; **444** (tc) ©The Granger Collection, New York; **444** (tr) ©Colonial Williamsburg Foundation; **444** (bc) ©North Wind/North Wind Picture Archives; **444** (br) ©The Corcoran Gallery of Art/Corbis; **445** (tc) ©The Granger Collection, New York; **445** (tl) ©Colonial Williamsburg Foundation; **445** (tr) ©Colonial Williamsburg Foundation; **445** (bl) ©Colonial Williamsburg Foundation; **445** (bc) ©Colonial Williamsburg Foundation; **445** (br) ©Leif Skoogfors/Corbis; **447** ©Nancy Carter/Alamy Images; **448** ©Alan Crostwaite/Acclaim Images; **450** (l) ©Museum of Fine Arts, Boston; **450** (bg) ©Saniphoto/Shutterstock; **451** (c) ©The Granger Collection, New York; **451** (b) ©Ocean/Corbis; **452** (l) ©Jupiterimages/Brand X Pictures/Alamy Images; **452** (bg) ©Saniphoto/Shutterstock; **453** (t) ©The Granger Collection, New York; **454** (t) ©Don Farrall/PhotoDisc/Getty Images; **454** (bg) ©Saniphoto/Shutterstock; **455** (b) ©Ocean/Corbis; **456** (bg) ©Saniphoto/Shutterstock; **456** (tr) ©Michael Freeman/Corbis; **457** (t) ©The Granger Collection, New York; **457** (b) ©Ocean/Corbis; **458** (l) ©Colonial Williamsburg Foundation; **458** (bg) ©Saniphoto/Shutterstock; **459** (br) ©Darlene Bordwell Photography; **460** (tc) ©Rush Research/James O'Donnell/Smithsonian Images - National Postal Museum/U.S. Postal Service Licensing Group; **460** (bg) ©Saniphoto/Shutterstock; **461** ©Comstock Images/

G20

Getty Images; **464** (t) Getty Images; **465** (br) ©Joe Sohm/Visions of America/Getty Images; **477** ©Chris Clor/Blend Images/Corbis; **478** (bc) ©Corbis; **478** (tr) ©Lindsey Parnaby/EPA/Corbis; **478** (br) ©Masterfile; **479** (tl) ©Seth Wenig/Reuters/Corbis; **479** (tc) ©Lenora Gim/Getty Images; **479** (bl) ©Paul Harris/Dorling Kindersley LTD Picture Library; **479** (br) ©Everett Collection, Inc.; **495** (t) ©Photodisc/Getty Images; **496** (b) © Getty Images; **497** (c) ©Photodisc/Getty Images; **498** (cr) ©Library of Congress Prints & Photographs Division; **499** (bl) ©Hulton Archive/Getty Images; **506** (tc) ©Bob Daemmrich/PhotoEdit; **506** (tr) ©Stephen Bonk/Shutterstock; **506** (bc) ©Stockbyte/Superstock; **506** (br) ©Paul Gilham/Getty Images; **506** (tl) ©NASA; **507** (tl) ©Jon Arnold Images Ltd./Superstock; **507** (tc) ©Clive Brunskill/Getty Images; **507** (tr) ©Chris Whitehead/Digital Vision/Getty Images; **507** (bl) ©Mathew Gavanaugh/Stringer/Getty Images; **507** (bc) ©Timothy A. Clary/Staff/AFP/Getty Images; **507** (br) ©David Young-Wolff/Getty Images; **509** ©Fstop/Alamy Images; **527** (br) ©Steve Allen/Brand X Pictures/Getty Images; **528** (b) Comstock Images/Age Fotostock; **528** (c) ©Getty Images; **529** (c) ©Brand X Pictures/Alamy Images; **530** (br) ©The Granger Collection, New York; **530** ©NASA; **530** (tl) ©NASA; **532** (bl) ©BBC/Corbis; **532** ©Masterfile; **533** (tc) ©NASA; **538** (tl) ©Penguin Young Readers Group; **538** (tc) ©Bob Daemmrich/PhotoEdit; **538** (tr) ©Steve Hamblin/Alamy Images; **538** (bc) ©Danita Delimont/Alamy Images; **538** (br) ©Patrik Giardino/Corbis; **539** (tr) ©Dennis MacDonald/Alamy Images; **539** (tc) ©Shaun Botterill/Getty Images Sport/Getty Images; **539** (tr) Getty Images; **539** (bl) ©NASA Johnson Space Center; **539** (bc) ©John Neubauer/PhotoEdit; **539** (br) ©Steve Nudson/Alamy Images; **540** (fg) ©Getty Images; **553** (b) ©Brand X Pictures/Jupiterimages/Getty Images; **554** (t) ©Brand X Pictures/Getty Images; **554** (br) ©Artville/Getty Images; **556** (tl) ©Penguin Young Readers Group; **557** (br) ©Penguin Young Readers Group; **558** (br) ©ImageSource/Age Fotostock America, Inc.; **559** (c) ©Cocoon/Getty Images; **559** (tc) ©Penguin Young Readers Group; **563** (br) ©Peter Griffith/Masterfile; **564** (tc) ©Masterfile; **564** (tr) ©PhotoEdit; **564** (bc) ©Jim West/Alamy Images; **564** (br) ©Larry Lee/Larry Lee Photography/Corbis; **565** (tr) ©Blend Images/Alamy Images; **565** (tc) ©Corbis; **565** (tr) ©Myrleen Ferguson Cate/PhotoEdit; **565** (bl) ©David Young-Wolff/PhotoEdit; **565** (bc) ©Kayte M. Deioma/PhotoEdit; **565** (br) ©Rhoda Sidney/PhotoEdit; **567** Getty Images/Brand X Pictures; **583** (t) ©Image Source/Getty Images; **583** (b) ©Yellow Dog Productions/Getty Images; **584** (t) Christian Kargl/Getty Images; **585** (c) Photodisc/Getty Images; **586** (b) ©Ariel Skelley/Getty Images; **587** (t) ©jf/Getty Images; **587** (b) ©Getty Images; **588** (bl) ©Catchlight Visual Services/Alamy Images; **589** (c) Blend Images/Alamy; **594** (tl) National Oceanic and Atmospheric Association (NOAA); **594** (bl) ©Corbis; **594** (br) Corbis; **594** (tr) ©Greg Ewing/Getty Images; **594** (tl) ©Charlie Cantrell/Reuters/Landov; **595** (br) ©Corbis; **595** (bc) Corbis; **595** (bl) Photodisc/Getty Images; **595** (tc) Photodisc/Getty Images; **595** (tr) © Stephen Frink/Photographer's Choice RF/Getty Images; **597** Image Source/Alamy; **615** (t) ©keith taylor/Alamy Images; **615** (b) ©Mark Barrett/Alamy Images; **616** (t) ©nycshooter/Getty Images; **616** (b) ©WILDLIFE GmbH/Alamy Images; **617** (c) Comstock/Jupiterimages/Getty Images; **618** (bg) ©Charlie Cantrell/Reuters/Landov; **618** (tl) ©Charlie Cantrell/Reuters/Landov; **619** (t) ©Mira Oberman/AFP/Getty Images/NewsCom; **619** (b) ©AFP/Getty Images/NewsCom; **620** (t) ©David Grossman/Alamy Images; **620** (b) ©Aurora Photos/Alamy Images; **621** (c) Photodisc/Getty Images; **621** (b) ©Ariel Skelley/Blend Images/Getty Images; **621** (tl) ©Charlie Cantrell/Reuters/Landov; **629** ©iStockPhoto.com; **630** (tr) ©Library of Congress Prints & Photographs Division; **630** (tc) ©Granger Collection; **630** (bc) ©Nick Vedros & Assoc/Getty Images; **630** (br) ©LMR Media/Alamy Images; **631** (tl) ©North Wind Picture Archives/Alamy Images; **631** (tc) ©North Wind Picture Archives; **631** (tr) ©Vera Bogaerts/ShutterStock.com; **631** (bl) ©North Wind Picture Archives; **631** (bc) ©Bettmann/Corbis; **631** (br) ©Scott T. Smith/Corbis; **633** ©Adam Jones/Digital Vision/Getty Images; **634** (tc) ©AL GRILLO/AP Images; **651** (t) ©Corbis; **651** (b) ©Radius Images/Getty Images; **652** (t) ©Radius Images/Alamy Images; **653** ©Design Pics Inc./Alamy Images; **659** (t) ©PhotoAlto/Odilon Dimier/Getty Images; **659** (c) ©Ellen McKnight/Alamy Images; **664** (tc) ©Richard T. Nowitz/Corbis; **664** (tr) ©Rodolfo Arpia/Alamy Images; **664** (bc) ©Joel Sartore/Getty Images; **664** (br) ©Jim and Jamie Dutcher/Getty Images; **664** (tl) North Wind Picture Archives; **665** (tl) ©Alamy Images; **665** (bc) ©Chuck Eckert/Alamy Images; **665** (tc) ©franco pizzochero/Age Fotostock America, Inc.; **665** (tr) ©age fotostock/Superstock; **665** (bl) ©Doug Dreyer/Getty Images; **665** (br) ©age fotostock/Superstock; **668** (tc) ©Eric Miller/AP Images; **681** (t) PhotoDisc/Getty Images; **682** (tl) Photodisc/Getty Images; **684** North Wind Picture Archives; **684** (tl) North Wind Picture Archives; **685** (cr) ©Monroe P. Killy/Minnesota Historical Society; **685** (tr) ©Kenneth M. Wright Studos/Minnesota Historical Society; **686** ©Frances Densmore/Minnesota Historical Society; **687** (t) ©Only Horses Tbk/Alamy Images; **687** (b) Corbis; **687** (b) ©Bettmann/Corbis; **687** (tl) North Wind Picture Archives; **692** (tl) ©Masterfile; **692** (bl) ©Time & Life Pictures/Getty Images; **692** (tr) ©Richard Heinzen/Superstock; **692** (bc) ©William A. Allard/Getty Images; **692** (br) ©Barbara Rich/Getty Images; **693** (tl) ©Bob Daemmrich/PhotoEdit; **693** (tc) ©American Stock Contributor Collection/Getty Images; **693** (tr) ©Hind Sight Media/Alamy Images; **693** (bl) ©Jeff R. Clow/ShutterStock.com; **693** (bc) ©Michael Rutherford/Superstock; **693** (br) ©WireImageStock/Masterfile; **695** ©Emma Lee/Life File/Getty Images; **696** ©Craig Aurness/Corbis; **698** (b) ©The Granger Collection, New York; **699** (t) ©The Granger Collection, New York; **704** (b) ©Gilcrease Museum; **705** (r) ©The Everett Collection; **709** (t) ©Comstock Images/Getty Images; **709** (b) ©Thomas Northcut/Lifesize/Getty Images; **710** (br) Jack Hollingsworth/Corbis; **711** (c) Corbis; **712** (tl) ©Masterfile; **712** ©Masterfile; **714** ©Nancy Greifenhagen/Alamy Images; **715** (tl) ©Masterfile; **715** (cr) ©John and Lisa Merrill/Corbis; **720** (tr) ©Lee Jones/Alamy Images; **720** (tc) ©Yellow Dog Productions/Getty Images; **720** (bc) ©Layne Kennedy/Corbis; **720** (br) ©Kevin Foy/Alamy Images; **720** (tl) ©Underwood & Underwood/Corbis; **721** (tl) ©Jaume Gual/Age Fotostock America, Inc.; **721** (tc) ©Time & Life Pictures/Getty Images; **721** (tr) ©Kelvin Murray/Getty Images; **721** (bl) ©Livia Corona/Getty Images; **721** (br) ©Masterfile; **723** ©Design Pics/Carson Ganci/Getty Images; **737** (b) ©Brand X Pictures/Jupiterimages/Getty Images; **737** (t) ©Photodisc/Getty Images; **738** (c) Corbis; **739** (cr) © Comstock; **740** (bc) Art Resource, NY; **740** (bc) ©Snark/Art Resource; **740** (tl) ©Underwood & Underwood/Corbis; **741** (cr) ©Peter

G21

Newark American Pictures/Bridgeman Art Library (London); **741** (br) ©The Reliable Contraband (engraving) (b/w photo), Forbes, Edwin (1839-95)/Private Collection/The Bridgeman Art Library International; **742** ©Underwood & Underwood/Corbis; **742** (tr) ©The Granger Collection, New York; **742** (cl) ©Western History/Geneology Dept./Denver Public Library; **743** (cr) ©The Granger Collection, New York; **743** (br) ©James L. Amos/CORBIS; **743** (tl) ©Underwood & Underwood/Corbis; **748** (tl) ©Popperfoto/Getty Images; **748** (inset) ©David David Gallery/Superstock; **748** (tr) ©Alfaf Qadri/epa/Corbis; **748** (bl) ©Anne Ackermann/Taxi/Getty Images; **748** (br) ©STEPHEN ALVAREZ/National Geographic Society/Image Collection; **749** (tl) ©James L. Amos/Corbis; **749** (tc) ©Corbis; **749** (bl) ©Harald Eisenberger/Getty Images; **749** (br) ©Karin Dreyer/Blend Images/Getty Images; **749** (tr) ©Jim Bridger (1804-81) (b/w photo), American Photographer, (19th century)/© Private Collection, Peter Newark American Pictures/The Bridgeman Art Library (London); **750** (tl) ©David David Gallery/Superstock; **750** (b) © David David Gallery/SuperStock; **752** (tL0 (tl) ©David David Gallery/Superstock; **753** (cl) ©Richard Cummins/Superstock; **753** (cr) ©Richard Cummins/Superstock; **754** (b) ©Comstock Images/Getty Images; **756** (t) The Granger Collection, New York; **757** (b) ©SuperStock; **758** (br) ©Blue Lantern Studio/Corbis; **764** (tl) ©David David Gallery/Superstock; **765** (t) ©North Wind Picture Archives/Alamy Images; **767** (tr) ©David David Gallery/Superstock; **767** (c) ©HMH; **771** (tl) ©David David Gallery/Superstock; **771** (cr) The Granger Collection, New York; **G11** (br) ©Alamy Images

Illustration

158–160 Alessandra Cimatoribus; **194–198** Micha Archer; **589–612** Robert Barrett;

All other photos: Houghton Mifflin Harcourt Photo Libraries and Photographers.

G22

Research Bibliography

Achieve, Inc. (2007). *Closing the expectations gap 2007: An annual 50-state progress report on the alignment of high school policies with the demands of college and work.* Washington, DC: Author. http://www.achieve.org/files/50-state-07-Final.pdf.

Achugar, M., Schleppegrell, M., & Oteíza, T. (2007). Engaging teachers in language analysis: A functional linguistics approach to reflective literacy. *English Teaching: Practice and Critique,* 6 (2), 8–24.

ACT, Inc. (2006). *Reading between the lines: What the ACT reveals about college readiness in reading.* Iowa City, IA: Author.

ACT, Inc. (2009). *ACT National Curriculum Survey 2009.* Iowa City, IA: Author.

ACT, Inc. (2009). *The condition of college readiness 2009.* Iowa City, IA: Author.

Adams, M. J. (2009). The challenge of advanced texts: The interdependence of reading and learning. In E. H. Hiebert (Ed.), *Reading more, reading better: Are American students reading enough of the right stuff?* (pp. 163–189). New York, NY: Guilford.

Adams, M. J. (2000). *Beginning to Read: Thinking and Learning About Print.* Cambridge: MIT Press.

Afflerbach, P., Pearson, P. D., & Paris, S. G. (2008). Clarifying differences between reading skills and reading strategies. *The Reading Teacher,* 61, 364–373.

Anderson, Jeff. (2005). *Mechanically Inclined: Building Grammar, Usage, and Style into Writer's Workshop.* Portsmouth, NH: Heinemann.

Angelillo, Janet. (2002). *A Fresh Approach to Teaching Punctuation.* New York: Scholastic.

Armbruster, B., Anderson, T. H., & Ostertag, J. (1987). Does text structure/summarization instruction facilitate learning from expository text? *Reading Research Quarterly,* 22 (3), 331–346.

Armbruster, B., Lehr, F., & Osborn, J. (2001). *Put Reading First: The Research Building Blocks for Teaching Children to Read* (pp. 21–31). Washington, D.C.: National Institute for Literacy.

Askew, B. J. & Fountas, I. C. (1998). Building an early reading process: Active from the start! *The Reading Teacher,* 52 (2), 126–134.

August, D., Carlo, M., Dressler, C., & Snow, C. (2005). The Critical Role of Vocabulary Development for English Language Learners. Learning Disabilities Research and Practice 20 (1), 50–57.

August, D., & Shanahan, T. (2006). Developing literacy in second-language learners; Report of the National Literacy Panel on Language-Minority Children and Youth. Mahwah, NJ: Lawrence Erlbaum.

Baker, S. K., Chard, D. J., Ketterlin-Geller, L. R., Apichatabutra, C., & Doabler, C. (in press). The basis of evidence for Self-Regulated Strategy Development for students with or at risk for learning disabilities. *Exceptional Children.*

Ball, E., & Blachman, B. (1991). Does phoneme awareness training in kindergarten make a difference in early word recognition and developmental spelling? *Reading Research Quarterly,* 26 (1), 49–66.

Balmuth, M. (1992). *The roots of phonics: A historical introduction.* Baltimore, MD: York Press.

Bardovi-Harlig, K. (2000). *Tense and aspect in second language acquisition: Form, meaning, and use.* Language Learning Monograph Series. Malden, MA: Blackwell.

Bartholomae, D. (1980). The study of error. *College Composition and Communication,* 31 (3), 253–269.

Baumann, J. F. & Bergeron, B. S. (1993). Story map instruction using children's literature: Effects on first graders' comprehension of central narrative elements. *Journal of Reading Behavior,* 25 (4), 407–437.

Baumann, J. F., & Kame'enui, E. J. (1991). Research on vocabulary instruction: Ode to Voltaire. In J. Flood, J. M. Jensen, D. Lapp, & J. R. Squire (Eds.), *Handbook of research on teaching the English language arts* (pp. 604–632). New York, NY: Macmillan.

Baumann, J. F. & Kame'enui, E. J. (Eds.). (2004). *Vocabulary Instruction: Research to Practice.* New York: Guilford Press.

Baumann, J. F., Seifert-Kessell, N., & Jones, L. A. (1992). Effect of think-aloud instruction on elementary students' comprehension monitoring abilities. *Journal of Reading Behavior,* 24 (2), 143–172.

Bear, D. R. & Templeton, S. (1998). Explorations in developmental spelling: Foundations for learning and teaching phonics, spelling, and vocabulary. *The Reading Teacher,* 52 (3), 222–242.

Beck, I. L. (2006). *Making Sense of Phonics: The Hows and Whys.* New York: Guilford Press.

Beck, I. L. & McKeown, M. (2006). *Improving Comprehension with Questioning the Author: A Fresh and Expanded View of a Powerful Approach (Theory and Practice).* New York, NY: Scholastic.

Beck, I. L., & McKeown, M. G., (2001). Text talk: Capturing the benefits of read-aloud experiences for young children. *The Reading Teacher,* 55 (1), 10–20.

Beck, I. L., McKeown, M., Hamilton, R., & Kucan, L. (1997). *Questioning the Author: An Approach for Enhancing Student Engagement with Text.* Newark, DE: International Reading Association.

Beck, I. L., McKeown, M., Hamilton, R., & Kucan, L. (1998). Getting at the meaning. *American Educator,* Summer, 66–71.

Beck, I. L., McKeown, M. G., & Kucan, L. (2002). *Bringing Words to Life: Robust Vocabulary Instruction.* New York: Guilford Press.

Beck, I. L., McKeown, M. G., & Kucan, L. (2008). *Creating robust vocabulary: Frequently asked questions and extended examples.* New York, NY: Guilford.

Beck, I. L., Perfetti, C. A., & McKeown, M. G. (1982). Effects of long-term vocabulary instruction on lexical access and reading comprehension. *Journal of Educational Psychology,* 74 (4), 506–521.

Becker, W. C. (1977). Teaching reading and language to the disadvantaged—What we have learned from field research. *Harvard Educational Review,* 47, 518–543.

Bereiter, C. & Bird, M. (1985). Use of thinking aloud in identification and teaching of reading comprehension strategies. *Cognition and Instruction,* 2, 131–156.

Bettinger, E., & Long, B. T. (2009). Addressing the needs of underprepared students in higher education: Does college remediation work? *Journal of Human Resources,* 44, 736–771.

Betts, E. A. (1946). *Foundations of reading instruction, with emphasis on differentiated guidance.* New York, NY: American Book Company.

Biber, D. (1991). *Variation across speech and writing.* Cambridge, England: Cambridge University Press.

Biemiller, A. (2001). Teaching vocabulary: Early, direct, and sequential. *American Educator,* 25 (1), 24–28, 47.

Biemiller, A. (2001). Vocabulary development and instruction: A prerequisite for school learning. In D. Dickinson & S. Neuman (Eds.), *Handbook of Early Literacy Research,* (Vol. 2), New York: Guilford Press.

Biemiller, A. (2005). Size and sequence in vocabulary development: Implications for choosing words for primary grade vocabulary. In E. H. Hiebert & M. L. Kamil (Eds.), *Teaching and Learning Vocabulary* (pp. 223–242). Mahwah, NJ: Lawrence Erlbaum.

Biemiller, A. & Slonim, N. (2001). Estimating root word vocabulary growth in normative and advantaged populations: Evidence for a common sequence of vocabulary acquisition. *Journal of Educational Psychology,* 93 (3), 498–520.

Blachman, B. (2000). Phonological awareness. In M. Kamil, P. Mosenthal, P. D. Pearson, & R. Barr (Eds.), *Handbook of Reading Research,* (Vol. 3). Mahwah, NJ: Lawrence Erlbaum.

Blachman, B., Ball, E. W., Black, R. S., & Tangel, D. M. (1994). Kindergarten teachers develop phoneme awareness in low-income, inner-city classrooms: Does it make a difference? *Reading and Writing: An Interdisciplinary Journal,* 6 (1), 1–18.

Bowen, G. M., & Roth, W.-M. (1999, March). "Do-able" questions, covariation, and graphical representation: Do we adequately prepare preservice science teachers to teach inquiry? Paper presented at the annual conference of the National Association for Research in Science Teaching, Boston, MA.

Bowen, G. M., Roth, W.-M., & McGinn, M. K. (1999). Interpretations of graphs by university biology students and practicing scientists: Towards a social practice view of scientific re-presentation practices. *Journal of Research in Science Teaching,* 36, 1020–1043.

Bowen, G. M., Roth, W.-M., & McGinn, M. K. (2002). Why students may not learn to interpret scientific inscriptions. *Research in Science Education,* 32, 303–327.

Brown, I. S. & Felton, R. H. (1990). Effects of instruction on beginning reading skills in children at risk for reading disability. *Reading and Writing: An Interdisciplinary Journal,* 2 (3), 223–241.

Bryson, B. (1990). *The mother tongue: English and how it got that way.* New York, NY: Avon Books.

Buck Institute for Education (2011). *PBL in the Elementary Grades.* Novato, CA: Buck Institute for Education.

Bus, A. G., Van Ijzendoorn, M. H., & Pellegrini, A. D. (1995). *Joint book reading makes for success in reading: A meta-analysis on intergenerational transmission of literacy.* Review of Educational Research, 65 (5), 1–21.

Calderón, M., August, D., Slavin, R., Duran, D., Madden, N., & Cheung, A. (2005). Bring Words to Life in Classrooms with English Language Learners. In E. H. Hiebert & M. L. Kamil (Eds.), Teaching and Learning Vocabulary: Bringing Research to Practice. Mahwah, NJ: Lawrence Erlbaum.

Carlo, M. (2004). Closing the gap: Addressing the vocabulary needs of English-language learners in bilingual and mainstream classrooms. *Reading Research Quarterly,* 39 (2), 188–215.

Carver, R. P. (1994). Percentage of unknown vocabulary words in text as a function of the relative difficulty of the text: Implications for instruction. *Journal of Reading Behavior,* 26, 413–437.

Catts, H., Adolf, S. M., & Weismer, S. E. (2006). Language deficits in poor comprehenders: A case for the simple view of reading. *Journal of Speech, Language, and Hearing Research,* 49, 278–293.

Chall, J. (1996). *Learning to Read: The Great Debate (revised, with a new foreword).* New York: McGraw-Hill.

Chall, J. S., Conard, S., & Harris, S. (1977). *An analysis of textbooks in relation to declining SAT scores.* Princeton, NJ: College Entrance Examination Board.

Chard, D. J., Ketterlin-Geller, L. R., Baker, S. K., Doabler, C., & Apichatabutra, C. (2009). Repeated reading interventions for students with learning disabilities: Status of the evidence. *Exceptional Children,* 75 (3), 263–281.

Chard, D. J., Stoolmiller, M., Harn, B., Vaughn, S., Wanzek, J., Linan-Thompson, S., & Kame'enui, E. J. (2008). Predicting reading success in a multi-level school-wide reading model: A retrospective analysis. *Journal of Learning Disabilities,* 41 (2), 174–188.

Charity, A. H., Scarborough, H. E., & Griffin, D. M. (2004). Familiarity with school English in African American children and its relation to early reading achievement. *Child Development,* 75 (5), 1340–1356.

Chiappe, P. & Siegel, L. S. (2006). A longitudinal study of reading development of Canadian children from diverse linguistic backgrounds. *Elementary School Journal,* 107 (2), 135–152.

Coyne, M. D., Kame'enui, E. J., & Simmons, D. C. (2004). Improving beginning reading instruction and intervention for students with LD: Reconciling "all" with "each." *Journal of Learning Disabilities,* 37 (3), 231–239.

Coyne, M. D., Kame'enui, E. J., Simmons, D. C., & Harn, B. A. (2004). Beginning reading intervention as inoculation or insulin: First-grade reading performance of strong responders to kindergarten intervention. *Journal of Learning Disabilities,* 37 (2), 90–104.

Coyne, M. D., Zipoli Jr., R. P., Chard, D. J., Faggella-Luby, M., Ruby, M., Santoro, L. E., & Baker, S. (2009). Direct instruction of comprehension: Instructional examples from intervention research on listening and reading comprehension. *Reading & Writing Quarterly,* 25 (2), 221–245.

Coyne, M. D., Zipoli Jr., R. P., & Ruby, M. (2006). Beginning reading instruction for students at risk for reading disabilities: What, how, and when. *Intervention in School and Clinic,* 41 (3), 161–168.

Craig, H. K. & Washington, J. A. (2001). Recent research on the language and literacy skills of African American students in early years. In D. Dickinson & S. Neuman (Eds.), *Handbook of Early Literacy Research,* (Vol. 2), New York: Guilford Press.

Craig, H. K. & Washington, J. A. (2006). *Malik Goes to School: Examining the Language Skills of African American Students From Preschool-5th Grade.* Mahwah, NJ: Lawrence Erlbaum Associates.

Daneman, M., & Green, I. (1986). Individual differences in comprehending and producing words in context. *Journal of Memory and Language,* 25 (1), 1–18.

DeVilliers, J., & DeVilliers, P. (1973). A cross-sectional study of the acquisition of grammatical morphemes in child speech. *Journal of Psycholinguistic Research,* 2, 267–278.

Dickinson, D. K., & Smith, M. W. (1994). Long-term effects of preschool teachers' book readings on low-income children's vocabulary and story comprehension. *Reading Research Quarterly,* 29, 104–123.

Dixon, R. C., Isaacson, S., & Stein, M. (2002). Effective strategies for teaching writing. In E. J. Kame'enui, D. W. Carnine, R. C. Dixon, D. C. Simmons, & M. D. Coyne (Eds.), *Effective Teaching Strategies That Accommodate Diverse Learners* (2nd ed., pp. 93–119). Upper Saddle River, NJ: Merrill Prentice Hall.

Dowhower, S. L. (1987). Effects of repeated reading on second-grade transitional readers' fluency and comprehension. *Reading Research Quarterly,* 22 (4), 389–406.

Duke, N. K. (2000). 3.6 minutes a day: The scarcity of informational text in first grade. *Reading Research Quarterly,* 35 (2), 202–224.

Research Bibliography

Duke, N. K. & Pearson, P. D. (2002). Effective practices for developing reading comprehension. In A. E. Farstrup & S. J. Samuels (Eds.), *What Research Has to Say About Reading Instruction* (3rd ed., pp. 205–242). Newark, DE: International Reading Association.

Durán, E., Shefelbine, J., Carnine, L., Maldonado-Colón, E., & Gunn, B. (2003). *Systematic Instruction in Reading for Spanish-Speaking Students*. Springfield, IL: Charles C. Thomas.

Durkin, D. (1978). What classroom observations reveal about comprehension instruction. *Reading Research Quarterly,* 14, 481–533.

Edwards Santoro, L., Chard, D. J., Howard, L., & Baker, S. K. (2008). Making the VERY most of classroom read alouds: How to promote comprehension and vocabulary in K-2 classrooms. *The Reading Teacher,* 61 (5), 396–408.

Ehri, L. C. (1998). Grapheme-phoneme knowledge is essential for learning to read words in English. In J. Metsala & L. Ehri (Eds.), *Word Recognition in Beginning Literacy* (pp. 3–40). Hillsdale, NJ: Lawrence Erlbaum Associates.

Ehri, L. & Nunes, S. R. (2002). The role of phonemic awareness in learning to read. In A. E. Farstrup & S. J. Samuels (Eds.), *What Research Has to Say About Reading Instruction* (3rd ed., pp. 110–139). Newark, DE: International Reading Association.

Ehri, L. & Wilce, L. (1987). Does learning to spell help beginners learn to read words? *Reading Research Quarterly,* 22 (1), 48–65.

Erickson, B. L., & Strommer, D. W. (1991). *Teaching college freshmen.* San Francisco, CA: Jossey-Bass.

Farr, R. (1990). Reading. *Educational Leadership,* 47 (5), 82–83.

Farr, R., Lewis, M., Faszholz, J., Pinsky, E., Towle, S., Lipschutz, J. & Faulds, B. P. (1990). Writing in response to reading. *Educational Leadership,* 47 (6), 66–69.

Feitelson, D., Goldstein, Z., Iraqui, J., & Share, D. I. (1993). Effects of listening to story reading on aspects of literacy acquisition in a diglossic situation. *Reading Research Quarterly,* 28, 70–79.

Feitelson, D., Kita, B., & Goldstein, Z. (1986). Effects of listening to series stories on first graders' comprehension and use of language. *Research in the Teaching of English,* 20, 339–356.

Fletcher, J. M. & Lyon, G. R. (1998). Reading: A research-based approach. In Evers, W. M. (Ed.), *What's Gone Wrong in America's Classroom?* Palo Alto, CA: Hoover Institution Press, Stanford University.

Fogel, H., & Ehri, L. C. (2000). Teaching elementary students who speak Black English Vernacular to write in Standard English: Effects of dialect transformation practice. *Contemporary Educational Psychology,* 25, 212–235.

Foorman, B. (Ed.). (2003). *Preventing and Remediating Reading Difficulties.* Baltimore, MD: York Press.

Foorman, B. R., Francis, D. J., Fletcher, J., Schatschneider, C., & Mehta, P. (1998). The role of instruction in learning to read: Preventing reading failure in at-risk children. *Journal of Educational Psychology,* 90 (1), 37–55.

Fountas, Irene & Pinnell, Gay Su. (2001). *Guiding Readers and Writers: Grades 3-6.* Portsmouth, NH: Heinemann.

Francis D. J., Rivera, M., Lesaux, N., Kieffer, M., & Rivera, H. (2006). Practical Guidelines for the Education of English Language Learners: Research-based recommendations for instruction and academic interventions (Book 1). Texas Institute for Measurement, Evaluation, and Statistics. University of Houston for the Center on Instruction.

Francis D. J., Rivera, M., Lesaux, N., Kieffer, M., & Rivera, H. (2006). Practical Guidelines for the Education of English Language Learners: Research-based recommendations for serving adolescent newcomers (Book 2). Texas Institute for Measurement, Evaluation, and Statistics. University of Houston for the Center on Instruction.

Fromkin, V., Rodman, R., & Hyams, N. (2006). *An introduction to language* (8th ed.). Florence, KY: Wadsworth.

Fuchs, L., Fuchs, D., & Hosp, M. (2001). Oral reading fluency as an indicator of reading competence: A theoretical, empirical, and historical analysis. *Scientific Studies of Reading,* 5 (3), 239–256.

Fukkink, R. G. & de Glopper, K. (1998). Effects of instruction in deriving word meaning from context: A meta-analysis. *Review of Educational Research,* 68 (4), 450–469.

Fulkerson, R. (1996). *Teaching the argument in writing.* Urbana, IL: National Council of Teachers of English.

Gambrell, L. B., Morrow, L. M., & Pennington, C. (2002). Early childhood and elementary literature-based instruction: Current perspectives… *Reading Online,* 5 (6), 26–39.

Ganske, K. (2000). *Word journeys.* New York, NY: Guilford.

García, G. G., & Beltrám, D. (2003). Revisioning the blueprint: Building for the academic success of English learners. In G. G. García (Ed.), *English Learners* (pp. 197–226). Newark, DE: International Reading Association.

Gargani, J. (2006). *UC Davis/SCUSD Teaching American History Grant technical memo: Years 1 & 2 essay and CST analysis results.* Unpublished report.

Gebhard, M., Willett, J., Jiménez, J., & Piedra, A. (2011). Systemic Functional Linguistics, Teachers' Professional Development, and ELLs' Academic Literacy Practices. In T. Lucas (Ed.), Teacher Preparation for Linguistically Diverse Classrooms: A Resource for Teacher Educators (pp. 91–110). New York: Routledge/Taylor and Francis.

Genesee, F., Lindholm-Leary, K., Saunders, B., & Christian, D. (2006). Educating English Language Learners: A Synthesis of Research Evidence. New York: Cambridge University Press.

Gersten, R. (2005). Behind the scenes of an intervention research study. *Learning Disabilities Research & Practice,* 20 (4), 200–212.

Gersten, R. & Baker, S. (2000). What we know about effective instructional practices for English learners. *Exceptional Children,* 66 (4), 454–470.

Gersten, R., Baker, S. K., Haager, D., & Graves, A. W. (2005). Exploring the role of teacher quality in predicting reading outcomes for first-grade English learners: An observational study. *Remedial and Special Education,* 26 (4), 197–206.

Gersten, R. & Geva, E. (2003). Teaching reading to early language learners. *Educational Leadership,* 60 (7), 44–49.

Gersten, R. & Jiménez, R. (2002). Modulating instruction for English-language learners. In E. J. Kame'enui, D. W. Carnine, R. C. Dixon, D. C. Simmons, & M. D. Coyne (Eds.), *Effective Teaching Strategies That Accommodate Diverse Learners.* Upper Saddle River, NJ: Merrill Prentice Hall.

Gibbons, P. (2009). English Learners, Academic Literacy, and Thinking: Learning in the Challenge Zone. Portsmouth, NH: Heinemann.

Gipe, J. P. & Arnold, R. D. (1979). Teaching vocabulary through familiar associations and contexts. *Journal of Reading Behavior,* 11 (3), 281–285.

Goldenberg, C. (2008). Teaching English language learners: What the research does—and does not—say. American Educator, 32 (2), 8–23, 42–44.

Graff, G. (2003). *Clueless in academe*. New Haven, CT: Yale University Press.

Graham, S. & Hebert, M. (2010). *Writing to Read: Evidence for How Writing Can Improve Reading. A Carnegie Corporation Time to Act Report*. Washington, DC: Alliance for Excellent Education.

Graves, M. F. (2009). Teaching individual words: One size does not fit all. New York, NY: Teachers College Press and International Reading Association.

Griffith, P. L., Klesius, J. P., & Kromrey, J. D. (1992). The effect of phonemic awareness on the literacy development of first grade children in a traditional or a whole language classroom. *Journal of Research in Childhood Education*, 6 (2), 85–92.

Guthrie, J. & Wigfield, A. (2000). Engagement and motivation in reading. In M. Kamil, P. Mosenthal, P. Pearson, & R. Barr, (Eds.), *Handbook of Reading Research, Vol. III*, 403–422.

Guthrie, J. T., Wigfield, A., Barbosa, P., Perencevich, K. C., Taboada, A., Davis, M. H., et al. (2004). Increasing reading comprehension and engagement through concept-oriented reading instruction. *Journal of Educational Psychology,* 96 (3), 403–423.

Hale, E. (2008). *Crafting Writers: K-6*. Portsmouth, NH: Heinemann.

Hall, S. L. & Moats, L. C. (1999). *Straight Talk About Reading*. Chicago, IL: Contemporary Books.

Halliday, M. (1993). Toward a Language-Based Theory of Education. Linguistics and Education 5, 93–116.

Hammond, J., & Gibbons, P. (2005). Putting Scaffolding to Work: The Contribution of Scaffolding in Articulating ESL Education. Prospect Special Issue 20 (1), 6–30.

Hanna, P. R., Hanna, S., Hodges, R. E., & Rudorf, E. H. (1966). *Phoneme-grapheme correspondences as cues to spelling improvement*. Washington, DC: Department of Health, Education, and Welfare.

Harm, M. W., McCandliss, B. D. & Seidenberg, M. S. (2003). Modeling the successes and failures of interventions for disabled readers. *Scientific Studies of Reading*, 7 (2), 155–182.

Harn, B. A., Stoolmiller, M., & Chard, D. (2008). Identifying the dimensions of alphabetic principle on the reading development of first graders: The role of automaticity and unitization. *Journal of Learning disabilities,* 41 (2), 143–157.

Hart, B., & Risley, T. R. (1995). *Meaningful differences in the everyday experience of young American children*. Baltimore, MD: Brookes.

Hasbrouck, J. & Tindal, G. A. (2006). Oral reading fluency norms: A valuable assessment tool for reading teachers. *The Reading Teacher,* 59 (7), 636–644.

Hayes, D., & Ahrens, M. (1988). Vocabulary simplification for children: A special case of "motherese"? *Journal of Child Language,* 15, 395–410.

Hayes, D. P., & Ward, M. (1992, December). *Learning from texts: Effects of similar and dissimilar features of analogies in study guides*. Paper presented at the 42nd Annual Meeting of the National Reading Conference, San Antonio, TX.

Hayes, D. P., Wolfer, L. T., & Wolfe, M. F. (1996). Sourcebook simplification and its relation to the decline in SAT-Verbal scores. *American Educational Research Journal,* 33, 489–508.

Heller, R., & Greenleaf, C. (2007). *Literacy instruction in the content areas: Getting to the core of middle and high school improvement*. Washington, DC: Alliance for Excellent Education.

Henry, M. (2003). *Unlocking literacy: Effective decoding and spelling instruction*. Baltimore, MD: Brookes.

Herman, P. A., Anderson, R. C., Pearson, P. D., & Nagy, W. E. (1987). Incidental acquisition of word meaning from expositions with varied text features. *Reading Research Quarterly*, 22, 263–284.

Hiebert, E. H. & Kamil, M. L. (Eds.). (2005). *Teaching and Learning Vocabulary: Bringing Research to Practice*. Mahwah, NJ: Lawrence Erlbaum Associates.

Hoffman, J., Sabo, D., Bliss, J., & Hoy, W. (1994). Building a culture of trust. *Journal of School Leadership,* 4, 484–501.

Hoover, W. A., & Gough, P. B. (1990). The simple view of reading. *Reading and Writing,* 2, 127–160.

Horn, M., & Giacobbe, M. E. (2007). *Talking, Drawing, Writing: Lessons for Our Youngest Writers*. Portland, ME: Stenhouse.

Hseuh-chao, M. H., & Nation, P. (2000). Unknown vocabulary density and reading comprehension. *Reading in a Foreign Language,* 13 (1), 403–430.

Hudson, R., (2006). Using Repeated Reading and Readers Theater to Increase Fluency. Reading First National Conference. http://www3.ksde.org/sfp/rdgfirst/natl_rdgfirst_conf_2006/hudson_using_repeated_reading_to_increase_fluency.pdf.

Hudson, R., Lane, H., & Pullen, P. (2005). Reading fluency assessment and instruction: What, why, and how? *The Reading Teacher,* 58 (8), 702–714.

Hulit, L. M., Howard, M. R., & Fahey, K. R. (2010). Born to talk: An introduction to speech and language development. Boston, MA: Allyn & Bacon.

Intersegmental Committee of the Academic Senates of the California Community Colleges, the California State University, and the University of California (ICAS). (2002). *Academic literacy: A statement of competencies expected of students entering California's public colleges and universities*. Sacramento, CA: Author.

Juel, C. (1988). Learning to read and write: A longitudinal study of fifty-four children from first through fourth grades. *Journal of Educational Psychology,* 80 (4), 437–447.

Juel, C., & Minden-Cupp, C. (2000). Learning to read words: Linguistic units and instructional strategies. *Reading Research Quarterly,* 35 (4), 458–492.

Kamil, M. L., Mosenthal, P. B., Pearson, P. D., & Barr, R. (2000). *Handbook of Reading Research*. Vol. III. Mahwah, NJ: Lawrence Erlbaum Associates.

Kieffer, M., & Lesaux, N. (2008). The Role of Derivational Morphology in the Reading Comprehension of Spanish Speaking English Language Learners. Reading and Writing: An Interdisciplinary Journal 21 (8), 783–804.

Kintsch, W. (1998). *Comprehension: A paradigm for cognition*. New York, NY: Cambridge University Press.

Kintsch, W. (2009). Learning and constructivism. In S. Tobias & M. Duffy (Eds.), *Constructivist instruction: Success or failure?* (pp. 223–241). New York, NY: Routledge.

Krauthamer, H. S. (1999). *Spoken language interference patterns in written English*. New York, NY: Peter Lang.

Kutner, M., Greenberg, E., Jin, Y., Boyle, B., Hsu, Y., & Dunleavy, E. (2007). *Literacy in everyday life: Results from the 2003 National Assessment of Adult Literacy* (NCES 2007–480). U.S. Department of Education. Washington, DC: National Center for Education Statistics.

Landauer, T. K., & Dumais, S. T. (1997). A solution to Plato's problem: The latent semantic analysis theory of acquisition, induction, and representation of knowledge. *Psychological Review,* 104, 211–240.

Landauer, T. K., McNamara, D. S., Dennis, S., & Kintsch, W. (Eds.) (2007). *Handbook of latent semantic analysis*. London, England: Psychology Press.

Research Bibliography

Laufer, B. (1988). What percentage of text-lexis is essential for comprehension? In C. Laurén & M. Nordman (Eds.), *Special language: From humans to thinking machines* (pp. 316–323). Clevedon, England: Multilingual Matters.

Lefstein, A. (2009). Rhetorical grammar and the grammar of schooling: Teaching "powerful verbs" in the English National Literacy Strategy. *Linguistics and Education,* 20, 378–400.

Lehr, F. & Osborn, J. (2005). A Focus on Comprehension. Pacific Resources for Education and Learning (PREL) Monograph. U.S. Department of Education. www.prel.org/programs/rel/rel.asp.

Lehr, F., Osborn, J., & Hiebert, E. H. (2004). A Focus on Vocabulary. Pacific Resources for Education and Learning (PREL) Monograph. U.S. Department of Education. www.prel.org/programs/rel/rel.asp.

Lesaux, N. K., Kieffer, M. J., Faller, S. E., & Kelley, J. G. (2010). The effectiveness and ease of implementation of an academic English vocabulary intervention for linguistically diverse students in urban middle schools. *Reading Research Quarterly,* 45, 196–228.

Lesaux, N. K. & Siegel, L. S. (2003). The development of reading in children who speak English as a second language. *Developmental Psychology,* 39 (6), 1005–1019.

Lipson, M. Y., Mosenthal, J. H., Mekkelsen, J., & Russ, B. (2004). Building knowledge and fashioning success one school at a time. *The Reading Teacher,* 57 (6), 534–542.

Lipson, M. Y. & Wixson, K. K. (2008). New IRA commission will address RTI issues. *Reading Today,* 26 (1), 1, 5.

Lonigan, C. J., Burgess, S. R., & Anthony, J. L. (2000). Development of emergent literacy and early reading skills in preschool children: Evidence from a latent-variable longitudinal study. *Developmental Psychology,* 36 (5), 596–613.

Lundberg, I., Frost, J., & Petersen O. (1988). Effects of an extensive program for stimulating phonological awareness in preschool children. *Reading Research Quarterly,* 23 (3), 263–284.

McCardle, P. & Chhabra, V. (Eds.). (2004). *The Voice of Evidence in Reading Research*. Baltimore: Brooks.

McIntosh, A. S., Graves, A., & Gersten, R. (2007). The effects of response to intervention on literacy development in multiple-language settings. *Learning Disability Quarterly,* 30 (3), 197–212.

McIntosh, K., Chard, D. J., Boland, J. B., & Horner, R. H. (2006). Demonstration of combined efforts in school-wide academic and behavioral systems and incidence of reading and behavior challenges in early elementary grades. *Journal of Positive Behavior Interventions,* 8 (3), 146–154.

McIntosh, K., Horner, R. H., Chard, D. J., Boland, J. B., Good, R. H. (2006). The use of reading and behavior screening measures to predict non-response to school-wide positive behavior support: A longitudinal analysis. *School Psychology Review,* 35 (2), 275–291.

McIntosh, K., Horner, R. H., Chard, D. J., Dickey, C. R., & Braun, D. H. (2008). Reading skills and function of problem behavior in typical school settings. *The Journal of Special Education,* 42 (3), 131–147.

McKenna, M. C. & Stahl, S. A. (2003). *Assessment for Reading Instruction,* New York: Guilford Press.

McKeown, M. G. & Beck, I. L. (2001). Encouraging young children's language interactions with stories. In D. Dickinson & S. Neuman (Eds.), *Handbook of Early Literacy Research* (Vol. 2). New York: Guilford Press.

McKeown, M. G., Beck, I. L., Omanson, R. C., & Pople, M. T. (1985). Some effects of the nature and frequency of vocabulary instruction on the knowledge and use of words. *Reading Research Quarterly,* 20 (5), 522–535.

McNamara, D. S., Graesser, A. C., & Louwerse, M. M. (in press). Sources of text difficulty: Across the ages and genres. In J. P. Sabatini & E. Albro (Eds.), *Assessing reading in the 21st century: Aligning and applying advances in the reading and measurement sciences*. Lanham, MD: R&L Education.

Merino, B. & Scarcella, R. (2005). Teaching science to English learners. *University of California Linguistic Minority Research Institute Newsletter,* 14 (4).

Mesmer, H. A. E. (2008). *Tools for matching readers to texts: Research-based practices*. New York, NY: Guilford.

Milewski, G. B., Johnson, D., Glazer, N., & Kubota, M. (2005). *A survey to evaluate the alignment of the new SAT Writing and Critical Reading sections to curricula and instructional practices* (College Board Research Report No. 2005-1 / ETS RR-05-07). New York, NY: College Entrance Examination Board.

Miller, G. A. (1999). On knowing a word. *Annual Review of Psychology,* 50, 1–19.

Moats, L. (2001). When older students can't read. *Educational Leadership,* 58 (6), 36–46.

Moats, L. (2004). Efficacy of a structured, systematic language curriculum for adolescent poor readers. *Reading & Writing Quarterly,* 20 (2), 145–159.

Moats, L. C. (1998). Teaching decoding. *American Educator,* 22 (1 & 2), 42–49, 95–96.

Moats, L. C. (1999). *Teaching Reading Is Rocket Science*. Washington, DC: American Federation of Teachers.

Moats, L. C. (2000). *Speech to Print: Language Essentials for Teachers*. Baltimore, MD: Paul H. Brookes Publishing Co., Inc.

Moats, L. C. (2008). *Spellography for teachers: How English spelling works*. (LETRS Module 3). Longmont, CO: Sopris West.

Morrow, L. M. (2004). Developmentally appropriate practice in early literacy instruction. *The Reading Teacher,* 58 (1), 88–89.

Morrow, L. M., Kuhn, M. R., & Schwanenflugel, P. J. (2006/2007). The family fluency program. *The Reading Teacher,* 60 (4), 322–333.

Morrow, L. M. & Tracey, D. H. (1997). Strategies used for phonics instruction in early childhood classrooms. *The Reading Teacher,* 50 (8), 644–651.

Morrow, L. M., Tracey, D. H., Woo, D. G., & Pressley, M. (1999). Characteristics of exemplary first-grade literacy instruction. *The Reading Teacher,* 52 (5), 462–476.

Mosenthal, J. H., Lipson, M. Y., Torncello, S., Russ, B., & Mekkelsen, J. (2004). Contexts and practices of six schools successful in obtaining reading achievement. *Elementary School Journal,* 104 (5), 343–367. ABSTRACT ONLY.

Moss, B., & Newton, E. (2002). An examination of the informational text genre in basal readers. *Reading Psychology,* 23 (1), 1–13.

Nagy, W. E., Anderson, R. C., & Herman, P. A. (1987). Learning word meanings from context during normal reading. *American Educational Research Journal,* 24, 237–270.

Nagy, W. E., Herman, P., & Anderson, R. C. (1985). Learning words from context. *Reading Research Quarterly,* 20, 233–253.

Nagy, W. E. & Scott, J. A. (2000). Vocabulary processes. In M. L. Kamil, P. B. Mosenthal, P. D. Pearson, & R. Barr (Eds.), *Handbook of Reading Research,* (Vol. 3, 269–284). Mahwah, NJ: Erlbaum.

Nagy, W., & Townsend, D. (2012). Words as tools: Learning academic vocabulary as language acquisition. Reading Research Quarterly 47 (1), 91–108.

National Assessment Governing Board. (2006). *Writing framework and specifications for the 2007 National Assessment of Educational Progress*. Washington, DC: U.S. Government Printing Office.

National Assessment Governing Board. (2007). *Writing framework for the 2011 National Assessment of Educational Progress*, pre-publication edition. Iowa City, IA: ACT, Inc.

National Center to Improve Tools of Educators. NCITE: http://idea.uoregon.edu/~ncite/.

National Commission on Writing. (2004). *Writing: A Ticket to Work…or a Ticket Out*. New York: The College Board.

National Endowment for the Arts. (2004). *Reading at risk: A survey of literary reading in America*. Washington, DC: Author.

National Institute of Child Health and Human Development. (2000). *Report of the National Reading Panel. Teaching children to read: An evidence-based assessment of the scientific research literature on reading and its implications for reading instruction* (NIH Publication No. 00-4769). Washington, DC: U.S. Government Printing Office.

National Reading Panel (2000). *Teaching children to read: An evidence-based assessment of the scientific research literature on reading and its implications for reading instruction*. (NIH Publication No. 00-4754). Washington, DC: National Institute of Child Health and Human Development.

Neuman, S. B., & Dickinson, D. K., (Eds.). (2002). *Handbook of Early Literacy Research*. New York: Guilford Press.

O'Connor, R., Jenkins, J. R., & Slocum, T. A. (1995). Transfer among phonological tasks in kindergarten: Essential instructional content. *Journal of Educational Psychology*, 87 (2), 202–217.

Orkwis, R. & McLane, K. (1998, Fall). *A Curriculum Every Student Can Use: Design Principles for Student Access*. ERIC/OSEP Special Project, ERIC Clearinghouse on Disabilities and Gifted Education, Council for Exceptional Children.

Osborn, J. & Lehr, F. (2003). *A Focus on Fluency: Research-Based Practices in Early Reading Series*. Honolulu, HI: Pacific Resources for Education and Learning.

O'Shea, L. J., Sindelar, P. T., & O'Shea, D. J. (1985). The effects of repeated readings and attentional cues on reading fluency and comprehension. *Journal of Reading Behavior*, 17 (2), 129–142.

Paris, S. G., Cross, D. R., & Lipson, M. Y. (1984). Informed strategies for learning: A program to improve children's reading awareness and comprehension. *Journal of Educational Psychology*, 76 (6), 1239–1252.

The Partnership for Reading. (2003). *Put Reading First: The Research Building Blocks for Teaching Children to Read*. (2nd ed.). MD: National Institute for Literacy.

Patton, Alec (2012). Work that matters: The teacher's guide to project-based learning. Paul Hamlyn Foundation.

Payne, B. D., & Manning, B. H. (1992). Basal reader instruction: Effects of comprehension monitoring training on reading comprehension, strategy use and attitude. *Reading Research and Instruction*, 32 (1), 29–38.

Pence, K. L., & Justice, L. M. (2007). *Language development from theory to practice*. Upper Saddle River, NJ: Prentice-Hall.

Perfetti, C. A., Landi, N., & Oakhill, J. (2005). The acquisition of reading comprehension skill. In M. J. Snowling & C. Hulme (Eds.), *The science of reading: A handbook* (pp. 227–247). Oxford, England: Blackwell.

Phillips, B. M. & Torgesen, J. K. (2001). Phonemic awareness and reading: Beyond growth of initial reading accuracy. In D. Dickinson & S. Neuman (Eds.), *Handbook of Early Literacy Research* (Vol. 2). New York: Guilford Press.

Pikulski, J. J., (1998). Business we should finish. *Reading Today*, 15 (5), 30.

Pikulski, J. J., & Chard, D. J. (2005). Fluency: Bridge between decoding and reading comprehension. *The Reading Teacher*, 58 (6), 510–519.

Postman, N. (1997). *The end of education*. New York, NY: Knopf.

Pressley, M. (1998). *Reading Instruction That Works: The Case for Balanced Teaching*. New York: The Guilford Press.

Pritchard, M. E., Wilson, G. S., & Yamnitz, B. (2007). What predicts adjustment among college students? A longitudinal panel study. *Journal of American College Health*, 56 (1), 15–22.

Quinn, H., Lee, O., & Valdés, G. (2012). Language demands and opportunities in relation to next generation science standards for English language learners: What teachers need to know. Paper for the Understanding Language Initiative, Stanford University. Retrieved from http://ell.stanford.edu/publication/language-demands-and-opportunities-relation-next-generation-science-standards-ells.

RAND Reading Study Group. (2002). *Reading for understanding: Toward an R & D program in reading comprehension*. Santa Monica, CA: RAND.

Rasinski, T. (2003). *The Fluent Reader: Oral Reading Strategies for Building Word Recognition, Fluency and Comprehension*. New York: Scholastic.

Rasinski, T. V., Padak, N., Linek, W., & Sturtevant, E. (1994). Effects of fluency development on urban second-grade readers. *Journal of Educational Research*, 87 (3), 158–165.

Rayner, K., Foorman, B. R., Perfetti, C. A., Pesetsky, D., & Seidenberg, M. S. (2001). How psychological science informs the teaching of reading. *Psychological Science in the Public Interest*, 2 (2), 31–74.

Rayner, K., Foorman, B. R., Perfetti, C. A., Pesetsky, D., & Seidenberg, M. S. (2002) How should reading be taught? *Scientific American*, pp. 85–91.

Report from the National Reading Panel. (2000). *Teaching Children to Read: An Evidence-Based Assessment of the Scientific Research Literature on Reading and its Implications for Reading Instruction*. Bethesda, MD: National Institute of Child Health and Human Development. http://www.nationalreadingpanel.org/Publications/summary.htm.

Rinehart, S. D., Stahl, S. A., & Erickson, L. G. (1986). Some effects of summarization training on reading and studying. *Reading Research Quarterly*, 21 (4), 422–438.

Robbins, C. & Ehri, L. C. (1994). Reading storybooks to kindergartners helps them learn new vocabulary words. *Journal of Educational Psychology*, 86 (1), 54–64.

Rosenshine, B., & Meister, C. (1994). Reciprocal teaching: A review of research. *Review of Educational Research*, 64 (4), 479–530.

Rosenshine, B., Meister, C., & Chapman, S. (1996). Teaching students to generate questions: A review of the intervention studies. *Review of Educational Research*, 66 (2), 181–221.

Routman, R. (2000). *Conversations: Strategies for Teaching, Learning, and Evaluating*. Portsmouth, NH: Heinemann.

Samuels, S., Schermer, N., & Reinking, D. (1992). Reading fluency: Techniques for making decoding automatic. In S. J. Samuels, J. Samuels, & A. E. Farstrup (Eds.), *What Research Has to Say About Reading Instruction* (pp. 124–143). Newark, DE: International Reading Association.

Research Bibliography

Samuels, S. J. & Farstrup, A. E. (2006). *What Research Has to Say About Fluency Instruction*. Newark, DE: International Reading Association.

Saunders, W., & O'Brien, G. (2006). Oral Language. In F. Genesee, K. Lindholm-Leary, W. Saunders & D. Christian (Eds.) Educating English Language Learners: A Synthesis of Research Evidence. New York: Cambridge University Press.

Scarcella, R. (2003) Academic English: A conceptual framework. *The University of California Linguistic Minority Research Institute, Technical Report* 2003-1.

Scarcella, R. English learners and writing: Responding to linguistic diversity. http://wps.ablongman.com/wps/media/objects/133/136243/english.pdf.

Scarcella, R. (1990). *Teaching Language Minority Students in the Multicultural Classroom*. Englewood Cliffs, NJ: Prentice Hall Regents.

Scharer, P. L., Pinnell, G. S., Lyons, C., & Fountas, I. (2005). Becoming an engaged reader. *Educational Leadership,* 63 (2), 24–29.

Schleppegrell, M. (2001). Linguistic features of the language of schooling. *Linguistics and Education,* 12, 431–459.

Schleppegrell, M. (2004). *Teaching Academic Writing to English Learners,* 13 (2). Grant Report: University of California Linguistic Minority Research Institute.

Scott, J., & Nagy, W. E. (1997). Understanding the definitions of unfamiliar verbs. *Reading Research Quarterly,* 32, 184–200.

Sénéchal, M. (1997). The differential effect of storybook reading on preschoolers' acquisition of expressive and receptive vocabulary. *Journal of Child Language,* 24 (1), 123–138.

Shanahan, T. (2005). FAQs about Fluency. http://www.springfield.k12.il.us/resources/languagearts/readingwriting/readfluency.html.

Shanahan, T., & Shanahan, C. (2008). Teaching disciplinary literacy to adolescents: Rethinking content-area literacy. *Harvard Educational Review,* 78 (1), 40–59.

Shany, M. T. & Biemiller, A. (1995). Assisted reading practice: Effects on performance for poor readers in grades 3 and 4. *Reading Research Quarterly,* 30 (3), 382–395.

Shaughnessy, M. P. (1979). *Errors and expectations: A guide for the teacher of basic writing.* New York, NY: Oxford University Press.

Shaywitz, S. (2003). *Overcoming Dyslexia.* New York: Alfred A Knopf.

Short, D. J., & Fitzsimmons, S. (2007). *Double the work: Challenges and solutions to acquiring language and academic literacy for adolescent English language learners*. New York, NY: Alliance for Excellent Education.

Simmons, D. C., Kame'enui, E. J., Coyne, M. D. & Chard, D. J. (2002). Effective strategies for teaching beginning reading. In E. J. Kame'enui, D. W. Carnine, R. C. Dixon, D. C. Simmons, & M. D. Coyne (Eds.), *Effective Teaching Strategies That Accommodate Diverse Learners*. Upper Saddle River, NJ: Merrill Prentice Hall.

Sindelar, P. T., Monda, L. E., & O'Shea, L. J. (1990). Effects of repeated readings on instructional- and mastery-level readers. *Journal of Educational Research,* 83 (4), 220–226.

Snow, C., Burns, M., & Griffin, P. (Eds.). (1998). *Preventing Reading Difficulties in Young Children*. Washington, D.C.: National Academy Press.

Stahl, S. A. & Fairbanks, M. M. (1986). The effects of vocabulary instruction: A model-based meta-analysis. *Review of Educational Research,* 56 (1), 72–110.

Stanovich, K. E. (1986). Matthew effects in reading: Some consequences of individual differences in the acquisition of literacy. *Reading Research Quarterly,* 21, 360–407.

Stanovich, K. E. & Stanovich, P. J. (2003). Using research and reason in education: How teachers can use scientifically based research to make curricular & instructional decisions. Jessup, MD: National Institute for Literacy. Retrieved January, 26, 2006, http://www.nifl.gov/partnershipforreading/publications/pdf/Stanovich_Color.pdf.

Stenner, A. J., Koons, H., & Swartz, C. W. (in press). *Text complexity and developing expertise in reading.* Chapel Hill, NC: MetaMetrics, Inc.

Sternberg, R. J., & Powell, J. S. (1983). Comprehending verbal comprehension. *American Psychologist,* 38, 878–893.

Sticht, T. G., & James, J. H. (1984). Listening and reading. In P. D. Pearson, R. Barr, M. L. Kamil, & P. Mosenthal (Eds.), *Handbook of reading research* (Vol. 1) (pp. 293–317). White Plains, NY: Longman.

Strickland, D. S. (2002). The importance of effective early intervention. In A. E. Farstrup & S. J. Samuels (Eds.), *What Research Has to Say About Reading Instruction* (3rd ed., pp. 69–86). Newark, DE: International Reading Association.

Strickland, D. S. & Morrow, L. M. (2000). *Beginning Reading and Writing.* Newark, DE: International Reading Association.

Strickland, D. S., Snow, C., Griffin, P., Burns, S. M. & McNamara, P. (2002). *Preparing Our Teachers: Opportunities for Better Reading Instruction*. Washington, D.C.: Joseph Henry Press.

Stuart, L., Wright, F., Grigor, S., & Howey, A. (2002). *Spoken language difficulties: Practical strategies and activities for teachers and other professionals*. London, England: Fulton.

Tabors, P. O. & Snow, C. E. (2002). Young bilingual children and early literacy development. In S. Neuman & D. K. Dickinson (Eds.), *Handbook of Early Literacy Research* (pp. 159–178). New York: Guilford Press.

Templeton, S. (1986). Synthesis of research on the learning and teaching of spelling. *Educational Leadership,* 43 (6), 73–78.

Templeton, S., Cain, C. T., & Miller, J. O. (1981). Reconceptualizing readability: The relationship between surface and underlying structure analyses in predicting the difficulty of basal reader stories. *Journal of Educational Research,* 74 (6), 382–387.

Torgesen, J., Morgan, S., & Davis, C. (1992). Effects of two types of phonological awareness training on word learning in kindergarten children. *Journal of Educational Psychology,* 84 (3), 364–370.

Torgesen, J., Wagner, R., Rashotte, C., Rose, E., Lindamood, P., Conway, T., & Garvan, C. (1999). Preventing reading failure in young children with phonological processing disabilities: Group and individual responses to instruction. *Journal of Educational Psychology,* 91 (4), 579–593.

Torgesen, J. K. & Hudson, R. (2006). Reading fluency: Critical issues for struggling readers. In S. J. Samuels & A. Farstrup (Eds.), *What Research Has to Say About Fluency Instruction*. Newark, DE: International Reading Association.

Torgesen, J. K., & Mathes, P. (2000). *A Basic Guide to Understanding, Assessing, and Teaching Phonological Awareness*. Austin, TX: PRO-ED.

Torgesen, J. K., Rashotte, C. A., & Alexander, A. (2001). Principles of fluency instruction in reading: Relationships with established empirical outcomes. In M. Wolf (Ed.), *Dyslexia, Fluency, and the Brain*. Parkton, MD: York Press.

Valdés, G. (2014). Second language acquisition, learner differences and teacher knowledge in an age of mass migration. Paper presented at the Workshop on Immigration, Cultural Sustainability and Social Cohesion, National Academy of Education, Washington DC.

Valencia, S. W., Au, K. H., Scheu, J. A., & Kawakami, A. J. (1990). Assessment of students' ownership of literacy. *The Reading Teacher,* 44 (2), 154–156.

Valencia, S. W. & Buly, M. R. (2004). Behind test scores: What struggling readers *really* need. *The Reading Teacher,* 57 (6), 520–531.

Valencia, S. W. & Sulzby, E. (1991). Assessment of emergent literacy: Storybook reading. *The Reading Teacher,* 44 (7), 498–500.

van den Broek, P., Lorch, Jr., R. F., Linderholm, T., & Gustafson, M. (2001). The effects of readers' goals on inference generation and memory for texts. *Memory and Cognition,* 29, 1081–1087.

van den Broek, P., Risden, K., & Husebye-Hartmann, E. (1995). The role of readers' standards for coherence in the generation of inferences during reading. In R. F. Lorch & E. J. O'Brien (Eds.), *Sources of coherence in reading* (pp. 353–373). Hillsdale, NJ: Erlbaum.

Vaughn, S. & Linan-Thompson, S. (2004). *Research-Based Methods of Reading Instruction: Grades K-3.* Alexandria, VA: ASCD.

Vaughn, S., Linan-Thompson, S., Pollard-Durodola, S. D., Mathes, P. G. & Hagan, E. C. (2001). Effective interventions for English language learners (Spanish-English) at risk for reading difficulties. In D. Dickinson & S. Neuman (Eds.), *Handbook of Early Literacy Research* (Vol. 2, pp. 185–197). New York: Guilford Press.

Vaughn, S., Moody, S. W., & Shuman, J. S. (1998). Broken promises: Reading instruction in the resource room. *Exceptional Children,* 64 (2), 211–225.

Vellutino, F. R., & Scanlon, D. M. (1987). Phonological coding, phonological awareness, and reading ability: Evidence from a longitudinal and experimental study. *Merrill-Palmer Quarterly,* 33 (3), 321–363.

Venezky, R. (2001). *The American way of spelling.* New York, NY: Guilford.

Vogt, M. (2004/2005). Fitful nights. *Reading Today,* 22 (3), 6.

Vogt, M. & Nagano, P. (2003). Turn it on with light bulb reading!: Sound-switching strategies for struggling readers. *The Reading Teacher,* 57 (3), 214–221.

Vygotsky, L. S. (1978). Mind In Society: The Development of Higher Psychological Processes. Cambridge: Cambridge University Press.

Walqui, A., & van Lier, L. (2010). Scaffolding the Academic Success of Adolescent English Language Learners: A Pedagogy of Promise. San Francisco: WestEd.

Washington, J. A. (2001). Early literacy skills in African-American children: Research considerations. *Learning Disabilities Research and Practice,* 16 (4), 213–221.

Weaver, Constance. (2007). *The Grammar Plan Book: A Guide to Smart Teaching.* Portsmouth, NH: Heinemann.

Wheeler, R., & Swords, R. (2004). Code-switching: Tools of language and culture transform the dialectally diverse classroom. *Language Arts,* 81, 470–480.

Whipple, G. (Ed.) (1925). The Twenty-fourth Yearbook of the National Society for the Study of Education: Report of the National Committee on Reading. Bloomington, IL: Public School Publishing Company.

White, T. G., Graves, M. F., & Slater, W. H. (1990). Growth of reading vocabulary in diverse elementary schools: Decoding and word meaning. *Journal of Educational Psychology,* 82 (2), 281–290.

Whitehurst, G. J., Falco, F. L., Lonigan, C. J., Fischel, J. E., DeBaryshe, B. D., Valdez-Menchaca, M. C., & Caufield, M. (1988). Accelerating language development through picture book reading. *Developmental Psychology,* 24, 552–558.

Williams, G. (2000). Children's literature, children and uses of language description. In L. Unsworth (Ed.), *Researching Language in Schools and Communities: Functional Linguistic Perspectives* (pp. 111–129). London, England: Cassell.

Williams, G. (2005). Grammatics in schools. In R. Hasan, C. M. I. M. Matthiessen, & J. Webster (Eds.), *Continuing discourse on language* (pp. 281–310). London, England: Equinox.

Williams, J. M., & McEnerney, L. (n.d.). *Writing in college: A short guide to college writing.* http://writing-program.uchicago.edu/resources/collegewriting/index.htm.

Williamson, G. L. (2006). *Aligning the journey with a destination: A model for K–16 reading standards.* Durham, NC: MetaMetrics, Inc.

Wirt, J., Choy, S., Rooney, P., Provasnik, S., Sen, A., & Tobin, R. (2004). The condition of education 2004 (NCES 2004-077). U.S. Department of Education, National Center for Education Statistics. Washington, DC: U.S. Government Printing Office. http://nces.ed.gov/pubs2004/2004077.pdf.

Wixson, K. K. (1986). Vocabulary instruction and children's comprehension of basal stories. *Reading Research Quarterly,* 21 (3), 317–329.

Wong Fillmore, L., & Fillmore, C. (2012). What Does Text Complexity Mean for English Learners and Language Minority Students? Paper for the Understanding Language Initiative, Stanford University. Retrieved from http://ell.stanford.edu/publication/what-does-text-complexity-mean-english-learners-and-language-minority-students.

Yopp, H. K., & Yopp, R. H. (2006). Primary students and informational texts. *Science and Children,* 44 (3), 22–25.

Index

Index

Index

Index

evaluating writing. *See* rubrics

exclamatory sentences. *See* sentences

expression. *See* fluency, expression

extended reading trade book lessons

fact and opinion. *See* comprehension skills

fantasy. *See* Student Book, genre

fiction. *See* Student Book, genre

flexible grouping. *See* literacy centers

fluency

accuracy, **5-1**: T23, T27, T86, T95, T117, T126, T148, T149, T150, T151, S16; **5-2**: T388, T406; **5-3**: T12, T21, T41, T48, T70, T71, T72, T73, S6; **5-4**: T312, T329, T341, T348, T374, T375, T376, T377, T402, S46; **5-5**: T240, T249, T265, T272, T294, T295, T296, T297, S36; **5-6**: T198, T207, T213, T215, T224, T291, T347, T372, S46

adjusting rate, **5-2**: T166, T179, T193, T200, T222, T223, T224, T225, S26; **5-6**: T58, T67, T73, T75, T84, T261, T317, S16

expression, **5-1**: T12, T34, T37, T44, T66, T67, T68, T69, T110, T192, T266, T340, S6; **5-2**: T12, T21, T43, T50, T72, T73, T74, T75, S6; **5-3**: T244, T257, T269, T276, T298, T299, T300, T301, S36; **5-4**: T388; **5-5**: T166, T179, T191, T198, T220, T221, T222, T223, S26; **5-6**: T106, T115, T119, T121, T130, T271, T327, S26

intonation, **5-1**: T168, T185, T195, T202, T224, T225, T226, T227, S26; **5-2**: T92, T103, T117, T124, T146, T147, T148, T149, S16; **5-3**: T148, T149, T150, T318, T327, T345, T352, S46; **5-4**: T86, T99, T115, T122, T144, T145, T146, T147, S16

partner read, **5-2**: T38, T114, T190, T264, T338; **5-3**: T36, T112, T192, T266, T342; **5-4**: T34, T112, T184, T260, T338; **5-5**: T38, T114, T188, T262, T336

phrasing, **5-1**: T244, T253, T269, T276, T298, T299, T300, T301, S36; **5-2**: T242, T251, T267, T274, T296, T297, T298, T299, S36; **5-3**: T170, T185, T195, T202, T224, T225, T226, T227, S26; **5-4**: T164, T173, T187, T194, T216, T217, T218, T219, S26; **5-5**: T12, T21, T43, T50, T72, T73, T74, T75, T314, T329, T339, T346, T372, T373, T374, T375, S6, S46; **5-6**: T10, T19, T25, T27, T36, T240, T251, T296, T307, T354, S6

rate, **5-3**: T90, T99, T115, T128, T150, T151, T152, T153, S16; **5-4**: T12, T25, T37, T44, T66, T67,

---

T68, T69, S6; **5-5**: T92, T103, T117, T124, T146, T147, T148, T149, S16

self-correction, **5-2**: T388, T406; **5-3**: T12, T21, T41, T48, T70, T71, T72, T73, S6; **5-5**: T240, T249, T265, T272, T294, T295, T296, T297, S36

stress, **5-1**: T318, T327, T343, T350, T376, T377, T378, T379, S46; **5-2**: T316, T329, T341, T348, T374, T375, T376, T377, S46; **5-4**: T236, T245, T263, T270, T292, T293, T294, T295, S36; **5-6**: T152, T159, T165, T167, T176, T281, T337, S36

fluency tests. *See* assessment, *Assess It Online!*; Cold Reads; Grab-and-Go!™ fluency tests

focus wall, **5-1**: T1, T75, T157, T233, T307; **5-2**: T1, T81, T155, T231, T305; **5-3**: T1, T79, T159, T233, T307; **5-4**: T1, T75, T153, T225, T301; **5-5**: T1, T81, T155, T229, T303; **5-6**: T1, T49, T97, T143, T189

formal and informal language. *See* English Language Support, formal and informal language

Formative Assessment. *See* assessment, Formative Assessment; Response to Intervention, Formative Assessment

generating ideas. *See* writing process; writing traits

generating questions. *See* comprehension strategies

genre. *See* Student Book, genre; Student Magazine, genre

gifted and talented students. *See* differentiated instruction, advanced

glossary, Student Book, **5-1**: R34–R38; **5-2**: R34–R38; **5-3**: R34–R38; **5-4**: R34–R38; **5-5**: R34–R38

Grab-and-Go!™

chant, **5-6**: T60, T200

dialogue, **5-6**: T12, T108, T154

Dig Deeper, **5-2**: T395, T403, T411, T415, T419; **5-4**: T395, T400, T408, T411; **5-6**: T249, T259, T269, T305, T361, T365, T369, T377, T382

English learners, **5-1**: T15, T16, T89, T90, T171, T172, T247, T248, T321, T322; **5-2**: T15, T16, T95, T96, T169, T170, T245, T246, T319, T320; **5-3**: T15, T16, T93, T94, T173, T174, T247, T248, T321, T322; **5-4**: T15, T16, T89, T90, T167, T168, T239, T240, T315, T316; **5-5**: T15, T16, T95, T96, T169, T170, T243, T244, T317, T318; **5-6**: T12, T13, T60, T61, T108, T109, T154, T155, T200, T201

fluency tests, **5-1**: T57, T139, T215, T289, T363; **5-2**: T63, T137, T213, T287, T361; **5-3**: T61,

---

T141, T215, T289, T365; **5-4**: T57, T135, T207, T283, T361; **5-5**: T63, T137, T211, T285, T359; **5-6**: T47, T95, T141, T187, T235

grammar, **5-1**: T48, T49, T50, T130, T131, T132, T206, T207, T208, T280, T281, T282, T354, T355, T356; **5-2**: T54, T55, T56, T128, T129, T130, T204, T205, T206, T278, T279, T280, T352, T353, T354; **5-3**: T52, T53, T54, T132, T133, T134, T206, T207, T208, T280, T281, T282, T356, T357, T358; **5-4**: T48, T49, T50, T126, T127, T128, T198, T199, T200, T274, T275, T276, T352, T353, T354; **5-5**: T54, T55, T56, T128, T129, T130, T202, T203, T204, T276, T277, T278, T350, T351, T352; **5-6**: T40, T88, T134, T180, T228

leveled practice, **5-1**: T41, T123, T199, T273, T347; **5-2**: T47, T121, T197, T271, T345; **5-3**: T45, T125, T199, T273, T349; **5-4**: T41, T119, T191, T267, T345; **5-5**: T47, T121, T195, T269, T343

leveled reader, **5-1**: T62–T63, T66, T67, T68, T69, T144–T145, T148, T149, T150, T151, T220–T221, T224, T225, T226, T227, T294–T295, T298, T299, T300, T301, T372–T373, T376, T377, T378, T379; **5-2**: T68–T69, T72, T73, T74, T75, T142–T143, T146, T147, T148, T149, T218–T219, T222, T223, T224, T225, T292–T293, T296, T297, T298, T299, T370–T371, T374, T375, T376, T377; **5-3**: T66–T67, T70, T71, T72, T73, T146–T147, T148, T149, T150, T151, T152, T153, T220–T221, T224, T225, T226, T227, T294–T295, T298, T299, T300, T301, T374–T375; **5-4**: T62–T63, T66, T67, T68, T69, T140–T141, T144, T145, T146, T147, T212–T213, T216, T217, T218, T219, T288–T289, T292, T293, T294, T295, T370–T371, T374, T375, T376, T377; **5-5**: T68–T69, T72, T73, T74, T75, T142–T143, T146, T147, T148, T149, T216–T217, T220, T221, T222, T223, T290–T291, T294, T295, T296, T297, T368–T369, T372, T373, T374, T375

read and comprehend, **5-1**: T16, T90, T91, T172, T173, T248, T249, T322, T323; **5-2**: T96, T97, T170, T171, T246, T247, T320, T321; **5-3**: T16, T17, T94, T95, T174, T175, T248, T249, T322, T323; **5-4**: T16, T17, T90, T91, T168, T169, T240, T241, T316, T317; **5-5**: T16, T17, T96, T97, T170, T171, T244, T245, T318, T319

reading chapters, **5-6**: T242, T252, T262, T272, T282, T298, T308, T318, T328, T338

Reading Logs, **5-1**: T34, T110, T192, T266, T340; **5-2**: T38, T114, T190, T264, T338; **5-3**: T36, T112, T192, T266, T342; **5-4**: T34, T112, T184, T260, T338; **5-5**: T38, T114, T188, T262, T336

small group resources, **5-1**: T4–T5, T78–T79, T160–T161, T236–T237, T310–T311; **5-2**: T4–T5,

Index

Venn diagram, **5-1**: T172; **5-3**: T322; **5-4**: T364; **5-6**: T371

web, **5-2**: T320, T364; **5-5**: T318; **5-6**: T379

guided practice, **5-1**: T16, T31, T41, T44, T46, T47, T51, T90, T107, T123, T126, T128, T129, T133, T172, T189, T199, T202, T204, T205, T209, T248, T263, T273, T276, T278, T279, T283, T322, T337, T347, T350, T352, T353, T357, R2, R3, R4, R5, R6, R7; **5-2**: T16, T35, T47, T50, T52, T53, T57, T96, T111, T121, T124, T126, T127, T131, T170, T187, T197, T200, T202, T203, T207, T246, T261, T271, T274, T276, T277, T281, T320, T335, T345, T348, T350, T351, T355, R2, R3, R4, R5, R6, R7; **5-3**: T16, T33, T45, T48, T50, T51, T55, T94, T109, T125, T128, T130, T131, T135, T174, T189, T199, T202, T204, T205, T209, T248, T263, T273, T276, T278, T279, T283, T322, T339, T349, T352, T354, T355, T359, R2, R3, R4, R5, R6, R7; **5-4**: T16, T31, T41, T44, T46, T47, T51, T90, T109, T119, T122, T124, T125, T129, T168, T181, T191, T194, T196, T197, T201, T240, T257, T267, T270, T272, T273, T277, T316, T335, T345, T348, T350, T351, T355, R2, R3, R4, R5, R6, R7; **5-5**: T16, T35, T47, T50, T52, T53, T57, T96, T111, T121, T124, T126, T127, T131, T170, T185, T195, T198, T200, T201, T205, T244, T259, T269, T272, T274, T275, T279, T318, T333, T343, T346, T348, T349, T353, R2, R3, R4, R5, R6, R7; **5-6**: T13, T23, T33, T38, T39, T61, T71, T81, T86, T87, T109, T117, T127, T132, T133, T155, T163, T173, T178, T179, T201, T211, T221, T226, T227, R2, R3, R4, R5

H

handwriting, **5-1**: R22–R27; **5-2**: R22–R27; **5-3**: R22–R27; **5-4**: R22–R27; **5-5**: R22–R27; **5-6**: R20–R25

handwriting tip, **5-1**: T54, T136, T212, T286, T360; **5-2**: T60, T134, T210, T284, T358; **5-3**: T58, T138, T212, T286, T362; **5-4**: T54, T132, T204, T280, T358; **5-5**: T60, T134, T208, T282, T356; **5-6**: T44, T92, T138, T184, T232

historical fiction. *See* Student Book, genre

homographs. *See* vocabulary strategies

homophones. *See* vocabulary strategies

humorous fiction. *See* Student Book, genre

I

illustrations, analyze. *See* comprehension skills

independent activities. *See* digital resources; independent reading; literacy centers

independent reading, **5-1**: T7, T18, T34–T35,

T83, T92, T110–T111, T163, T174, T192–T193, T239, T250, T266–T267, T313, T324, T340–T341, S11, S21, S31, S41, S51; **5-2**: T7, T18, T38–T39, T87, T98, T114–T115, T161, T172, T190–T191, T237, T248, T264–T265, T311, T322, T338–T339, T391, T395, T403, T406, T411, T415, T419, T424, S11, S21, S31, S41, S51; **5-3**: T7, T18, T36–T37, T85, T96, T112–T113, T165, T176, T192–T193, T239, T250, T266–T267, T313, T324, T342–T343, S11, S21, S31, S41, S51; **5-4**: T9, T18, T34–T35, T83, T112–T113, T161, T170, T184–T185, T233, T242, T260–T261, T309, T318, T338–T339, T391, T395, T400, T402, T408, T411, T416, S11, S21, S31, S41, S51; **5-5**: T7, T18, T38–T39, T87, T98, T114–T115, T161, T172, T188–T189, T235, T246, T262–T263, T309, T320, T336–T337, S11, S21, S31, S41, S51; **5-6**: T14, T62, T110, T156, T202, T357, T361, T365, T369, T372, T377, T382, T386, S11, S21, S31, S41, S51

informational text. *See* Student Book, genre; Student Magazine, genre; writing forms, research report

information books. *See* Student Book, genre

integrated language arts review, **5-2**: T393, T397, T401, T405, T409, T413, T417, T421, T425; **5-4**: T393, T397, T405, T413, T417; **5-6**: T359, T363, T367, T371, T375, T379, T387

interrogative sentences. *See* sentences, kinds of sentences

intervention. *See* response to intervention

intonation. *See* fluency

J

journal entry. *See* Student Magazine, genre

K

keyboarding lessons, **5-1**: R28–R33; **5-2**: R28–R33; **5-3**: R28–R33; **5-4**: R28–R33; **5-5**: R28–R33; **5-6**: R26–R31

key ideas, **5-1**: T9, T81, T165, T241, T315; **5-2**: T9, T83, T163, T239, T313, T385, T427; **5-3**: T9, T87, T167, T241, T315; **5-4**: T7, T81, T159, T231, T307, T385, T419, T420; **5-5**: T9, T89, T163, T237, T311; **5-6**: T5, T53, T99, T145, T193, T351, T389, T390

L

language arts. *See* grammar; integrated language arts review; spelling; writing

Language Detective, **5-1**: T14, T21, T30, T88, T97, T106, T170, T179, T188, T246, T261, T262, T320, T331, T336; **5-2**: T14, T31, T34, T94, T109, T110, T168, T181, T186, T244, T259, T260, T318, T333, T334; **5-3**: T14, T29, T32, T92, T106, T108, T172, T181, T188, T246, T253, T262, T320, T335, T338; **5-4**: T14, T23, T30, T88, T105, T108, T166, T173, T180, T238, T249, T256, T314, T331, T334; **5-5**: T14, T31, T34, T94, T101, T110, T168, T175, T184, T242, T257, T258, T316, T323, T332; **5-6**: T22, T70, T116, T162, T210

language development. *See* differentiated instruction, English learners

Language Support Cards, **5-1**: T17, T91, T173, T249, T323; **5-2**: T97, T171, T247, T258, T321; **5-3**: T17, T30, T95, T102, T106, T175, T180, T186, T249, T256, T260, T323, T330, T336; **5-4**: T17, T91, T106, T169, T241, T254, T317, T332; **5-5**: T17, T32, T97, T108, T171, T245, T319, T330; **5-6**: T12, T108, T200

Language Workshop, **5-1**: xxi; **5-2**: xxi; **5-3**: xxi; **5-4**: xxi; **5-5**: xxi; **5-6**: xxi

Language Workshop Assessment Handbook, **5-1**: T58, T140, T216, T290, T364; **5-2**: T64, T138, T214, T288, T362; **5-3**: T62, T142, T216, T290, T366; **5-4**: T58, T136, T208, T284, T362; **5-5**: T64, T138, T212, T286, T360; **5-6**: T48, T96, T142, T188, T236

Language Workshop Teacher's Guide, **5-1**: T58, T140, T216, T290, T364; **5-2**: T64, T138, T214, T288, T362; **5-3**: T62, T142, T216, T290, T366; **5-4**: T58, T136, T208, T284, T362; **5-5**: T64, T138, T212, T286, T360; **5-6**: T48, T96, T142, T188, T236

legend. *See* Student Book, genre

lesson planners. *See* small group instruction; weekly planner

lesson topic

adaptations and instincts, **5-6**: T1, T13, T17, T19, T24, T26, T27, T28, T30, T34–T35

African American history, **5-3**: T233, T249, T253, T255, T268, T269, T274–T275

animal behaviors, **5-2**: T305, T321, T327, T329, T340, T341, T346–T347

archaeology, **5-6**: T97, T109, T113, T118, T119, T120, T121, T122, T124, T128–T129

arts, performance and visual, **5-1**: T75, T91, T95, T97, T103, T112, T113, T115, T119, T124–T125

arts, visual, **5-4**: T1, T17, T23, T25, T27, T36, T37, T42–T43

community involvement, **5-4**: T225, T241, T247, T249, T253, T262, T263, T268–T269

conservation, **5-2**: T155, T171, T175, T179, T181, T185, T192, T193, T198–T199

courage, **5-2**: T231, T247, T251, T253, T266, T267, T272–T273 creative inventions, **5-4**: T75, T91, T95, T97, T105, T114, T115, T120–T121

creative writing, **5-4**: T153, T169, T173, T175, T179, T186, T187, T192–T193

curiosity, **5-6**: T189, T201, T205, T212, T213, T214, T215, T216, T218, T222–T223

early American government, **5-3**: T1, T17, T21, T25, T29, T38, T39, T46–T47

encounters with nature, **5-6**: T143, T155, T161, T164, T165, T166, T167, T168, T170, T174–T175

experiments, **5-1**: T1, T17, T27, T29, T36, T37, T42–T43

exploration, **5-5**: T42–T43, T303, T319, T323, T329, T338, T339

extreme environments, **5-5**: T1, T17, T21, T25, T27, T31, T40, T41, T48–T49

friendship, **5-2**: T383, T390, T407

human-animal interaction, **5-4**: T301, T317, T321, T325, T327, T331, T340, T341, T346–T347

independence, **5-3**: T79, T95, T101, T105, T114, T115, T117, T119, T121, T126–T127

language and expression, **5-1**: T307, T323, T329, T331, T335, T342, T343, T348–T349

life on the battlefield, **5-3**: T159, T175, T181, T185, T194, T195, T200–T201

mummies, **5-6**: T349, T356, T373

patriotism, **5-3**: T307, T323, T327, T331, T335, T344, T345, T350–T351

physical fitness, **5-1**: T233, T249, T255, T257, T261, T269, T274–T275

pioneers, **5-5**: T229, T245, T249, T253, T264, T265, T270–T271

politics, **5-1**: T157, T173, T177, T179, T183, T187, T194, T195, T200–T201

responsibility, **5-2**: T81, T97, T101, T116, T117, T122–T123

time measurement, **5-4**: T383, T390, T403

traditions, **5-5**: T81, T97, T103, T105, T116, T117, T122–T123

West, the, **5-5**: T155, T171, T175, T177, T181, T190, T191, T196–T197

wild animals, **5-2**: T1, T17, T21, T25, T27, T31, T40, T41, T48–T49

world travel, **5-6**: T49, T61, T65, T67, T72, T73, T74, T75, T76, T78, T82–T83

See also preview the topic

leveled practice. See Grab-and-Go!™, leveled reader

Leveled Readers

advanced

Abigail Adams, **5-3**: T150

Another View, **5-4**: T294

Artist for the Revolution, An, **5-3**: T72

Day of the Coyotes, **5-4**: T376

Dear Cousin, **5-5**: T296

Decision at Fort Laramie, **5-5**: T74

Far From Home, **5-1**: T378

Friends Along the Way, **5-5**: T374

Geography Bee, The, **5-1**: T226

George Washington's Invisible Enemy, **5-3**: T226

Home at Mount Vernon, A, **5-3**: T152

How Barbed Wire Changed the West, **5-5**: T222

Isabel Allende, **5-4**: T218

Jack and the Mean Beans, **5-1**: T150

Mad for Marsupials!, **5-2**: T74

Night of the Killer Waves, **5-2**: T298

Noble French Patriot, A, **5-3**: T300

Old Bark's Cure, **5-5**: T148

Pancakes, **5-4**: T146

Project Bug, **5-1**: T68

Riding with the Camel Corps, **5-2**: T148

Salton Sea, The, **5-2**: T224

Saving the Mexican Wolves, **5-2**: T376

Three R's, The, **5-4**: T68

Title IX, **5-1**: T300

English learners

American Fur Trade, The, **5-5**: T375

America's City Parks, **5-2**: T225

Animals in the Rain Forest, **5-2**: T75

Baseball Memories, **5-1**: T379

Better Plan, A, **5-1**: T227

Big Hunt, The, **5-5**: T149

Blazing a Cattle Trail, **5-5**: T223

Chan Li's Pot of Gold, **5-5**: T297

In the City, In the Country, **5-1**: T151

Dinner for Two Hundred, **5-1**: T69

Grizzly Bears Return to Yellowstone, **5-2**: T377

Joseph Warren: An American Hero, **5-3**: T227

Kendria's Watch, **5-4**: T147

Life of B.B. King, The, **5-4**: T219

Life of Phillis Wheatley, The, **5-3**: T151

Long Cattle Drive, The, **5-2**: T149

Lost Comic Book, The, **5-4**: T69

Lost in a Canyon, **5-4**: T377

Ned Rides for the Pony Express, **5-5**: T75

Old Tree, The, **5-4**: T295

Patsy Mink and Title IX, **5-1**: T301

Printed Words of the Revolution, **5-3**: T153

Rising River, The, **5-2**: T299

Special Night, A, **5-3**: T73

Thomas Peters: A Remarkable Man, **5-3**: T301

genre

adventure, **5-4**: T374, T375, T376, T377

biography, **5-4**: T216, T217, T218, T219

historical fiction, **5-2**: T146, T147, T148, T149, T296, T297, T298, T299; **5-3**: T70, T71, T72, T73; **5-5**: T72, T73, T74, T75, T146, T147, T148, T149, T294, T295, T296, T297

informational text, **5-1**: T298, T299, T300, T301; **5-2**: T72, T73, T74, T75, T222, T223, T224, T225, T374, T375, T376, T377; **5-5**: T220, T221, T222, T223, T372, T373, T374, T375

narrative nonfiction, **5-3**: T148, T149, T150, T151, T152, T153, T224, T225, T226, T227, T298, T299, T300, T301

play, **5-1**: T148, T149, T150, T151

realistic fiction, **5-1**: T66, T67, T68, T69, T224, T225, T226, T227, T376, T377, T378, T379; **5-4**: T66, T67, T68, T69, T292, T293, T294, T295

science fiction, **5-4**: T144, T145, T146, T147

on level

America's Urban Parks, **5-2**: T223

Baseball Blues, **5-1**: T377

B.B. King, **5-4**: T217

Buffalo Hunt, **5-5**: T147

City Cousin, Country Cousin, **5-1**: T149

Extraordinary Life of Thomas Peters, The, **5-3**: T299

Gold for Chan Li, **5-5**: T295

Goodnight–Loving Trail, The, **5-5**: T221

History of the Fur Trade, **5-5**: T373

Incognito, **5-4**: T67

On the Long Drive, **5-2**: T147

Night to Remember, A, **5-3**: T71

Pamphleteers of the Revolution, **5-3**: T151

Patsy Mink, **5-1**: T299

Phillis Wheatley, **5-3**: T149

Presentation, The, **5-1**: T225

Return of the Yellowstone Grizzly, The, **5-2**: T375

Riding with the Pony Express, **5-5**: T73

River Kept Rising, The, **5-2**: T297

Saving the General, **5-4**: T293

Serves Two Hundred, **5-1**: T67

On the Trail of Rain Forest Wildlife, **5-2**: T73

Unsung American Hero, An, **5-3**: T225

Watch Girl, The, **5-4**: T145

Wilderness Rangers, **5-4**: T375

struggling readers

Benedict Arnold, **5-3**: T148, S51

Big Interview, The, **5-4**: T292, S41

Cafeteria Contest, The, **5-1**: T66, S11

City in the Cliffs, **5-5**: T146, S21

Corps of Discovery, The, **5-5**: T372, S51

Deer, The, **5-4**: T374, S51

Dog Walker, Inc., **5-4**: T66, S11

Down the Columbia, **5-5**: T294, S41

Ella's Big Night, **5-1**: T148, S21

Emily Geiger's Dangerous Mission, **5-3**: T224, S31

Fife and Drum Boys, **5-3**: T70, S11

Games We Play, **5-1**: T298, S41

Index

Index

Index

Index

Index

figurative language, **5-3:** T124–T125, T154–T155, T156; **5-4:** T344–T345, T378–T379, T380

Greek and Latin roots, **5-2:** T270–T271, T300–T301, T302; **5-3:** T272–T273, T302–T303, T304; **5-6:** T172–T173, T274, T275, T330, T331

Greek and Latin suffixes, **5-4:** T296–T297

Greek and Latin suffixes *-ism, -ist, -able, -ible,* **5-4:** T266–T267, T298

homophones and homographs, **5-4:** T190–T191, T220–T221, T222

idioms, **5-6:** T126–T127, T264, T265, T320, T321

multiple-meaning words, **5-6:** T32–T33, T244, T245, T300, T301

prefixes *en-, re-, pre-, pro-,* **5-2:** T196–T197, T226–T227, T228

prefixes *in-, im-, il-, ir-,* **5-3:** T348–T349, T382–T383, T384

prefixes *non-, un-, dis-, mis-,* **5-1:** T122–T123, T152–T153, T154

reference materials, **5-3:** T44–T45, T74–T75, T76, T198–T199, T228–T229, T230; **5-4:** T118–T119, T148–T149, T150; **5-5:** T120–T121, T150–T151, T152

review, **5-6:** T244, T254, T264, T274, T284, T300, T310, T320, T330, T340

shades of meaning, **5-2:** T344–T345, T378–T379, T380; **5-5:** T46–T47, T76–T77, T78

suffixes *-ion, -tion,* **5-1:** T272–T273, T302–T303, T304

suffixes *-ly, -ful,* **5-1:** T346–T347, T380–T381, T382

suffixes *-ness, -less, -ment,* **5-6:** T80–T81, T254, T255, T310, T311

synonyms, **5-2:** T46–T47, T76–T77, T78

using context, **5-5:** T268–T269, T298–T299, T300

word origins, **5-4:** T40–T41, T70–T71, T72; **5-6:** T220–T221, T284, T285, T340, T341

weekly planner, 5-1: xxxiv–xxxv, T10–T11, T84–T85, T166–T167, T242–T243, T316–T317; **5-2:** viii–ix, T10–T11, T90–T91, T164–T165, T240–T241, T314–T315, T386–T387; **5-3:** viii–ix, T10–T11, T88–T89, T168–T169, T242–T243, T316–T317; **5-4:** viii–ix, T10–T11, T84–T85, T162–T163, T234–T235, T310–T311, T386–T387; **5-5:** viii–ix, T10–T11, T90–T91, T164–T165, T238–T239, T312–T313; **5-6:** viii–ix, T6–T7, T54–T55, T102–T103, T148–T149, T194–T195, T352–T353

whole group resources. *See* Analyze the Text; comprehension; grammar; spelling; Teacher Read Aloud; vocabulary; vocabulary strategies; writing

word lists, 5-1: R8–R13; **5-2:** R8–R13; **5-3:** R8–R13; **5-4:** R8–R13; **5-5:** R8–R13; **5-6:** R6–R11

See also vocabulary strategies

word study. *See* vocabulary strategies

Write About Independent Reading, 5-4: T405

Write About Media, 5-2: T393; **5-4:** T393; **5-6:** T359

Write About Reading, 5-2: T397, T401, T405, T409, T413, T417, T421, T422, T425; **5-4:** T397, T400, T408, T413, T414, T417; **5-6:** T363, T367, T371, T375, T379, T382, T384, T387

Write-In Reader, 5-1: S1, S3, S5, S6, S7, S9, S11, S13, S15, S16, S17, S19, S21, S23, S25, S26, S27, S29, S31, S33, S35, S36, S37, S39, S41, S43, S45, S46, S47, S49, S51; **5-2:** S1, S3, S5, S6, S7, S9, S11, S13, S15, S16, S17, S19, S21, S23, S25, S26, S27, S29, S31, S33, S35, S36, S37, S39, S41, S43, S45, S46, S47, S49, S51; **5-3:** S1, S3, S5, S6, S7, S8, S9, S11, S13, S15, S16, S17, S19, S21, S23, S25, S26, S27, S29, S31, S33, S35, S36, S37, S39, S41, S43, S45, S46, S47, S49, S51; **5-4:** S1, S3, S5, S6, S7, S8, S9, S11, S13, S15, S16, S17, S19, S21, S23, S25, S26, S27, S29, S31, S33, S35, S36, S37, S39, S41, S43, S45, S47, S49, S51; **5-5:** S1, S3, S5, S6, S7, S9, S11, S13, S15, S16, S17, S19, S21, S23, S25, S26, S27, S29, S31, S33, S35, S36, S37, S39, S41, S43, S45, S47, S49, S51; **5-6:** S1, S3, S5, S6, S7, S9, S11, S13, S15, S16, S17, S19, S21, S23, S25, S26, S27, S29, S31, S33, S35, S36, S37, S39, S41, S43, S45, S47, S49, S51

writer's craft. *See* comprehension skills, author's craft

writing

collaborative, **5-1:** T33, T52, T109, T134, T191, T210, T265, T284, T339, T358; **5-2:** T37, T58, T113, T132, T189, T208, T263, T282, T337, T356; **5-3:** T35, T56, T111, T136, T191, T210, T265, T284, T341, T360; **5-4:** T33, T52, T111, T130, T183, T202, T259, T278, T337, T356; **5-5:** T37, T58, T113, T132, T187, T206, T261, T280, T335, T354; **5-6:** T136

interactive, **5-2:** T32, T108, T258, T332; **5-3:** T30, T106, T186, T260, T336; **5-4:** T106, T254; **5-5:** T32, T182

predictive, **5-1:** T19, T93, T175, T251, T325; **5-2:** T19, T99, T173, T249, T323, T391; **5-3:** T19, T97, T177, T251, T325; **5-4:** T19, T171, T243, T319, T391; **5-5:** T19, T99, T173, T247, T321; **5-6:** T15, T63, T111, T157, T203, T357

prewrite

cause-and-effect chart, **5-2:** T209

column chart, **5-4:** T131

flow chart, **5-1:** T53, T211; **5-2:** T59; **5-4:** T203, T280; **5-5:** T59

idea-support map, **5-3:** T57, T137, T211, T286; **5-4:** T53; **5-5:** T133

story map, **5-1:** T286

T-map, **5-5:** T282; **5-6:** T184

Venn diagram, **5-2:** T133

web, **5-1:** T135; **5-6:** T137

quick write, **5-1:** T35, T111, T193, T267, T341; **5-2:** T39, T115, T191, T265, T339; **5-3:** T37, T113, T193, T267, T343; **5-4:** T35, T113, T185, T261, T339; **5-5:** T39, T115, T189, T263, T337

writing forms

autobiography, **5-4:** T202, T203

book report, **5-6:** T375

cause-and-effect essay, **5-2:** T208, T209

character description, **5-4:** T130, T131; **5-6:** T367

compare-and-contrast essay, **5-2:** T132, T133, T401; **5-4:** T417; **5-6:** T371

description, **5-1:** T134, T135; **5-6:** T42, T43

dialogue, **5-1:** T210, T211; **5-2:** T409; **5-6:** T363

diary entry, **5-2:** T393

editorial, **5-5:** T58, T59

e-mail, **5-4:** T397

exploring a topic, **5-1:** T285

fictional narrative, **5-1:** T284, T358

friendly letter, **5-4:** T52, T53

informational essay, **5-2:** T364, T365, T366; **5-6:** T182, T183, T230, T231

journal entry, **5-6:** T90, T91, T387

lecture, **5-4:** T405

letter, **5-2:** T413; **5-4:** T393; **5-6:** T359

literary analysis essay, **5-4:** T364, T365, T366

narrative short story, **5-2:** T397

opinion essay, **5-3:** T56, T57, T368, T369, T370

personal narrative, **5-4:** T278, T279, T356, T357

persuasive argument, **5-5:** T206, T207

persuasive essay, **5-3:** T284, T285, T360, T361

persuasive letter, **5-3:** T210, T211; **5-6:** T379

point of view, **5-1:** T359

problem-solution composition, **5-3:** T136, T137

procedural composition, **5-2:** T58, T59, T405, T425

research report, **5-2:** T282, T284, T356, T357

response essay, **5-5:** T280, T281, T354, T355

response to literature, **5-5:** T132, T133, T362, T363, T364

script, **5-4:** T413

sensory language, **5-1:** T359

short story, **5-1:** T52, T53; **5-2:** T421

story, **5-1:** T366, T367, T368

summary, **5-2:** T417; **5-6:** T136, T137

writing mode

analytic writing, **5-2:** T397, T401, T405, T409, T413, T417, T421, T422, T425; **5-4:** T397, T400, T408, T413, T414, T417; **5-6:** T363, T367, T371, T375, T379, T382, T384, T387

informative writing, **5-2:** T53, T58–T61, T79, T127, T132–T135, T153, T203, T208–T211, T229, T277, T282–T285, T303, T351, T356–T359, T381; **5-6:** T39, T42–T45, T87, T90–T93, T133, T136–T139, T179, T182–T185, T227, T230–T233

Index

Acknowledgments

T21 ©Johner Images/Alamy Images; **T25** ©Louise Heusinkveld/Alamy Images; **T27** Comstock/Jupiterimages/Getty Images; **T40** ©DLILLC/Corbis; **T48** (bl) ©Getty Images; **T49** (br) ©Getty Images; **T101** ©Blend Images/Alamy Images; **T116** ©Getty Images; **T122** (bl) ©Getty Images; **T175** © Corbis; **T179** © Steven Trainoff, Ph.D./Flickr/Getty Images; **T185** John Pitcher/iStock; **T192** Getty Images/PhotoDisc; **T198** (bl) ©Corbis; **T199** (br) ©Getty Images; **T251** ©Corbis; **T272** (bl) ©Getty Images; **T273** (br) ©Photodisc/Getty Images; **T325** ©Liquidlibrary/Jupiterimages/Getty Images; **T327** © Gerry Ellis/Getty Images; **T340** ©Digital Vision/Getty Images; **T346** (bl) ©LMR Group/Alamy Images; **T347** (br) ©Getty Images